COLONIAL COPYRIGHT

Colonial Copyright

Intellectual Property in Mandate Palestine

By
MICHAEL D. BIRNHACK

OXFORD
UNIVERSITY PRESS

Great Clarendon Street, Oxford, OX2 6DP,
United Kingdom

Oxford University Press is a department of the University of Oxford.
It furthers the University's objective of excellence in research, scholarship,
and education by publishing worldwide. Oxford is a registered trade mark of
Oxford University Press in the UK and in certain other countries

© M. Birnhack 2012

The moral rights of the author have been asserted

First Edition published in 2012

Impression: 1

All rights reserved. No part of this publication may be reproduced, stored in
a retrieval system, or transmitted, in any form or by any means, without the
prior permission in writing of Oxford University Press, or as expressly permitted
by law, by licence or under terms agreed with the appropriate reprographics
rights organization. Enquiries concerning reproduction outside the scope of the
above should be sent to the Rights Department, Oxford University Press, at the
address above

You must not circulate this work in any other form
and you must impose this same condition on any acquirer

Crown copyright material is reproduced under Class License
Number C01P0000148 with the permission of OPSI
and the Queen's Printer for Scotland

British Library Cataloguing in Publication Data

Data available

ISBN 978–0–19–966113–8

Printed and bound in Great Britain by
CPI Group (UK) Ltd, Croydon, CR0 4YY

Links to third party websites are provided by Oxford in good faith and
for information only. Oxford disclaims any responsibility for the materials
contained in any third party website referenced in this work.

For my mother, Juliette, a child of the Empire, and my father, Gideon, a child of the Mandate.

Preface

Copyright history is a developing and promising research field. Scholars search for the origins of contemporary copyright law, exploring the legal, social, political, and technological events that shaped the law. Copyright historians seek also to expose the intellectual history of intellectual property law: the ideas and social processes that resulted in the law being as it was. Many of the lessons of history are relevant for today's legal and political trends, such as the ongoing globalization of copyright law. British copyright law has thus far been told almost entirely from the British point of view. The British perspective was applied also in the discussion of colonial copyright, a term used in the mid-nineteenth century to denote British interests in the colonies. This book turns this term upside down, and tells the story of Colonial Copyright from the other side, that of the colonized. The leading case study is that of Mandate Palestine (1917–48).

The story unfolded here is a legal history research, but one which is located in at least two other frameworks. One is *law and society*, which means that it pays close attention to the interaction between the social realm and the legal one. The law is always part of society and should not be treated as an autonomous entity. The second framework applied here, where relevant, is that of *law and technology*, which pays close attention to the complex relationship between the two fields, searching for their mutual influences (rather than opting for just one view, such as that the law lags behind technology). The result is a critical cultural legal historical analysis.

The book wishes to supplement a gap in the research as to the history of copyright law in Mandate Palestine, but it wishes to do more: it offers a systematic view of the process of legal transplants, and it tells this story from the peripheral, colonized point of view rather than from the centre. The book thus aims at several circles of readers: legal historians in general and particularly copyright historians, colonial and postcolonial studies scholars, historians of Mandate Palestine, scholars of media and technology will find several of the chapters that tell the battles of old technologies and new ones, translated into legal battles of copyright law. Finally, Israeli and hopefully also Palestinian copyright lawyers will find here some answers to contemporary questions.

Acknowledgements

Since I started teaching copyright law to Israeli students, I wondered about its origins, and found no answers in the literature. After several years, my colleague at Tel-Aviv University Assaf Likhovski urged me to go to the archives. His book, *Law and Identity in Mandate Palestine*, inspired the current project. Numerous friends and colleagues were of great help in commenting on drafts and presentations, suggesting avenues to explore, making connections which I did not see, and pointing to new directions. I am indebted to all: Iris Agmon, Michal Alberstein, Eytan Almog, Danya Amichay-Michlin, Stuart Banner, Lionel Bently, Binyamin Blum, Maurizio Borghi, Nathan Brun, Diren Çakmak, Michael Crystal, David De Vries, Owen Dean, Zohar Efroni, Niva Elkin-Koren, Orit Fishman Afori, Paul Geller, Shubha Ghosh, Ron Harris, Adam Hofri-Winogradow, Eyal Katvan, Ariel Katz, Friedemann Kawohl, Nir Kedar, Sandy Kedar, Martin Kretschmer, Assaf Likhovski, Michael Lobban, Tal Morse, Neil Netanel, David Nimmer, Gadi Oron, Omri Paz, Oren Perez, Guy Pessach, Ariel Porat, Amihai Radzyner, Anthony Reese, Anat Rosenberg, Orit Rozin, Avi Rubin, Rona Sela, Yoram Shachar, Robert Spoo, Ehud Toledano, Elimelech Westreich, Matthias Wiessner, Martha Woodmansee, Tal Zarsky, and Diane Zimmerman.

Participants in the following conferences provided illuminating comments: The Construction of Immateriality, International Society for the History and Theory of Intellectual Property (ISHTIP, Bocconi University, Milan, June 2009); The Annual Conference of the Law and History Association (Van Leer Institute, Jerusalem, September 2009); Copyright Culture, Copyright History (Faculty of Law, Tel-Aviv University, January 2010); American Society of Legal History, Annual Conference (Philadelphia, November 2010). I thank participants in faculty seminars at Tel-Aviv University and the Hebrew University of Jerusalem; workshops at the Centre for International and Public Law, Brunel University Law School; UCLA Law School, Entertainment, Media and IP Colloquium; Faculty of Law, Bar-Ilan University; Faculty of Law, Haifa University; Institute of Advanced Legal Studies, University of London, and at the Centre for Innovation Law and Policy, University of Toronto.

Along the way relatives of some of the people mentioned in the book provided helpful information or access to privately held material: Israel Agranat, Hanan Benayahu, Rachel Edelman Schocken, Miriam Falk, and Nitzan Zeira. I thank them all for their kind assistance.

Librarians and archivists were of immense assistance: Professor Gila Ballas and Vered Drori (Ziffer House); John Entwisle (Thomson-Reuters, Reuters archive); Ray Lukar (PRS); Oren Mass (Mass Press); Louise North (BBC Written Archives); Tamar Salomon (JNF); Dvora Stavi (Hebrew Authors Association) and the staff at the Israel State Archive, Central Zionist Archive (Jerusalem), National Archives

(London), Tel-Aviv Municipality Archive and Jerusalem Municipality Archive. Tel-Aviv University libraries, the National Library in Jerusalem, the British Library in London, and libraries at IALS and LSE in London provided endless resources.

The Cegla Center for Interdisciplinary Research of Law at the Faculty of Law, Tel-Aviv University, my home institution, provided financial assistance. The Sabbatical I spent at the Institute of Advanced Legal Studies (IALS) at the University of London enabled me a wonderful working environment and I wish to thank its director Professor Avrom Sherr.

This book could not be possible without devoted research assistants: first and foremost, Ricki Newman who accompanied this project from her very first day at the Tel-Aviv University Law faculty, and Yael Levi Shahaf, Lior Siew, and Salameh Abu Rabyiaa, to whom I all thank.

My thanks are due also to the staff at Oxford University Press, and especially to Natasha Flemming. Tal Morse came up with the idea for the cover, which was designed by OUP.

Finally, my mother, Juliette, a pioneer in audio-visual librarianship, was my English teacher and to this day, has been the first editor of my English texts. My father, Gideon, has always tinkered with technological devices with endless curiosity and has always been happy to tell stories about his childhood in Tel-Aviv in Mandate times. It is to my parents that I dedicate this book, with much love.

Contents

List of Abbreviations	xv
Note to Reader	xvi
Introduction	1
A. Premises: Copyright, Culture, Technology	3
(1) Copyright–culture	4
(2) Copyright–technology	6
B. Frameworks	9
(1) Colonial copyright	9
(2) Authorship	12
(3) Mandate Palestine	14
C. Structure and Outline	16
D. Methodology and Scope	20
1. Colonial Transplants	22
A. Introduction	22
B. Legal Transplants	23
C. Legal Colonialism	26
(1) Rule of law	27
(2) Imperial typology	28
(3) Law-making	30
(4) The colonial meets the local	32
D. Colonial Transplants	34
E. Method	36
F. Conclusion	39
2. Colonial Copyright	40
A. Introduction	40
B. Progress	41
C. Creativity	45
(1) Uncovering hidden assumptions	45
(2) The authorship project	46
(3) Eurocentric copyright	48
D. Intangibility	50
(1) The challenge	50
(2) Cultural balances	51
E. Colonial Copyright	54
F. Conclusion	57

3. The Making of British Colonial Copyright	60
A. Introduction	60
B. Intra-Imperial Copyright until 1886	62
C. International Copyright: 1886–1911	68
D. A New Imperial Order: 1886–1911–1917	71
(1) Towards an imperial Act	72
(2) Applying the 1911 Act in the Empire	73
(3) Assuring uniformity	75
E. Conclusion	77
4. Legislating Copyright in Palestine	79
A. Introduction	79
B. The Ottoman Authors' Rights Act	81
(1) The Ottoman Empire: law and reform	81
(2) The Authors' Rights Act 1910	83
(3) The Act in practice?	86
C. British Legislation	92
(1) The legislative process	93
(2) First British steps: the 1920 Copyright Ordinance	96
(3) The man behind the law	98
(4) The 1924 copyright legislations	100
(5) Subsequent legislation	102
(6) Copyright relationship with the United States	103
(7) Publication and translation of the law	105
D. Conclusion	107
5. Constructing Culture and the Image of the Hebrew Author	109
A. Introduction	109
B. The Emerging Hebrew Cultural Field	110
(1) The cultural timeline	111
(2) Jewish culture, Arab culture	120
(3) Internal divisions within the Jewish community	121
(4) Hebrew	124
(5) The British point of view	125
(6) What about the law?	127
C. The Hebrew Author	128
(1) The image of the author	128
(2) The irrelevance of the law	134
D. Conclusion	137
6. Copyright Law and Social Norms	139
A. Introduction	139
B. The Legal Field	139
(1) Judicial systems	140
(2) Lawyers	141
(3) Legal education	142

(4) Libraries	143
(5) Legal literature	143
(6) Popular and professional press	144
(7) Interim summary	145
C. Needs and Solutions	145
(1) The authors: originality	146
(2) Publishers, translations, and commercial norms	147
(3) Theatre, authors, translators, and social norms	150
(4) Authors and publishers: contractual and social norms	152
(5) Authors' attribution and integrity of works	154
(6) International transactions	157
(7) Private ordering: evaluation	158
D. Conclusion	161

7. Setting the Law in Motion — 163
A. Introduction — 163
B. Law, Sound, Action! — 164
   (1) Performing rights — 165
   (2) New tunes — 167
   (3) Enter Meir Kovalsky — 168
C. Mendelsohn, Beethoven, and Schumann in Zion — 170
   (1) The lawyer's strategy — 171
   (2) The judgment — 173
   (3) The aftermath of the case — 174
D. Enforcing Copyright — 175
   (1) A business plan — 175
   (2) Litigating copyright — 179
   (3) Hebrew music: ACUM — 184
E. Copyright Glocalization — 186
F. Conclusion — 188

8. Copyright on the Air — 190
A. Introduction — 190
B. The Road to the Radio — 191
   (1) Initial thoughts and a growing demand (August 1930–May 1933) — 192
   (2) Decision and planning (June 1933–April 1934) — 197
   (3) Executing the plan (May 1934–March 1936) — 200
C. Copyright Issues — 203
   (1) Copyright in broadcasting — 204
   (2) The community listening project — 208
D. Conclusion — 210

9. Telegraphic News — 212
A. Introduction — 212
B. News in Palestine — 213
  (1) Local press — 213
  (2) Telegraph and news agencies — 217
  (3) The market of telegraphic news — 218
C. News in the Courts — 225
  (1) Owning news — 225
  (2) Litigation strategy — 228
  (3) Judgments — 229
D. The Impact of the Case — 234
  (1) Statutory protection for telegraphic news — 235
  (2) Broadcast vs telegraph — 236
E. Conclusion — 237

10. Arab Copyright — 239
A. Introduction — 239
B. The Arab Cultural and Legal Fields — 241
  (1) The cultural field — 242
  (2) The legal field — 245
C. The British Attitude — 247
  (1) The Copyright Act — 247
  (2) The radio — 248
D. First Steps towards Active Usage of Copyright — 250
E. El-Amiri v Katul — 252
F. Conclusion — 254

11. At a Crossroad — 256
A. Introduction — 256
B. Herzl, Ahad Ha'am, and the Biblical Concordance — 257
  (1) Herzl's writings — 257
  (2) Ahad Ha'am — 260
  (3) The concordance — 263
C. Jewish Copyright Law and Old Texts — 267
  (1) Jewish copyright law — 269
  (2) Old texts — 272
D. Copyright becomes Routine — 276
E. Conclusion — 279

Conclusion — 280

Bibliography — 289
Index — 307

List of Abbreviations

ACUM	*Agudat Compositorim u'Mehabrim* (Israeli performing rights society)
A-G	Attorney General
AP	Associated Press
BoT	Board of Trade
CA	Civil Appeal
CC	Civil Case
CO	Colonial Office
CS	Chief Secretary of the Government of Mandate Palestine
CZA	Central Zionist Archive
EIT	Eretz-Israel Theatre
Gnazim	HAA Archive
HAA	Hebrew Authors Association
HC	High Commissioner of Palestine
IDCPA	Israeli Documentation Centre for the Performing Arts
IP	intellectual property
ISA	Israel State Archive
JCA	Jerusalem City Archive
JNF or KKL	Jewish National Fund (*Keren Kayemeth LeIsrael*)
JTA	Jewish Telegraphic Agency
JV	Jüdischer Verlag
LP	Lira Palestine (equivalent to £)
LSI	Law Statutes of Israel
NA	National Archives
OG	Official Gazette
PBS	Palestine Broadcasting Service
PD	*Piskey Din* (Official publication of Israel's Supreme Court cases)
PLR	Palestine Law Reports
PMG	Postmaster General
PRS	Performing Rights Society
PTA	Palestine Telegraphic Agency
TAU	Tel-Aviv University
TCA	Tel-Aviv City Archive
TRIPs	Agreement on Trade Related Aspects of Intellectual Property Rights
WIPO	World Intellectual Property Organization

Note to Reader

Translations from Hebrew are by the author; translation from Ottoman Turkish is by Omri Paz, and translations from Arabic are by Lior Siew, Salameh Abu-Rabyiaa, and Uri Bitan. Whenever the sources cited are in a language other than English, the title provided is as it appears in the original book, or if it has not so appeared, the title was translated. Dates cited in original documents according to the Jewish calendar were converted to the Gregorian calendar.

Introduction

> This work covers, briefly but with sufficient thoroughness, the whole field indicated by the title, with the single exception that the chapter on Colonial Copyright does not attempt to deal with the local legislation of the colonies, but merely with 'the rights of a work published in one part of the British Dominions to receive protection in any other part of the British Dominions'.
>
> Harvard Law Review Board, reviewing E J Macgillivray,
> *A Treatise Upon the Law of Copyright*, 1903.[1]

More than a century ago, when the British discussed *colonial copyright*, they meant their own interests in the colonies. They hardly referred to the local cultural and legal interests. Until recently, scholarly engagement with colonial copyright still followed the imperial path of the nineteenth century, and was told almost exclusively from a British, imperial point of view. This book reverses the perspective and provides an account as seen and understood from the colonized side.

This book explores the legal history of copyright law in the British Empire, during the first decades of the twentieth century by focusing on Mandate Palestine (1917–48) as a leading case study. It is a story about the use of law as a tool to secure British interests throughout the Empire, but also as a tool applied to promote progress and culture, at least according to the imperial vision of culture. Colonial copyright is the widespread imposition of copyright law throughout the British Empire. It occurred when a foreign power exported its own legal toolkit from home and applied it to territories and its peoples, previously unfamiliar with the idea of legal protection for creative works, at least not in the form today known as copyright. Accordingly, Colonial Copyright is a legal and cultural category about the diffusion and transplanting of the legal field that regulates some of the main institutional aspects of culture, under conditions of an imperial rule.

In recent years, new voices have emerged in the history of copyright law. First studies that took a similar path to that taken here, focused on the English speaking, self-governing dominions, namely Canada, Australia, New Zealand, and South Africa. This book provides the yet-untold story of copyright law in additional

---

[1] HLB, 'A Treatise Upon the Law of Copyright in the United Kingdom and the Dominions of the Crown and in the United States of America, Containing a Full Appendix of All Acts of Parliament, International Conventions, Orders in Council, Treasury Minutes, and Acts of Congress Now in Force' (1903) 16 Harv L Rev 234.

British territories thus filling the gap in the developing academic discipline of copyright history. Moreover, much of contemporary scholarship on copyright history ends the discussion with the enactment of the 1911 Imperial Copyright Act. Indeed, the 1911 Act consolidated the law, ending many of the long nineteenth century debates. But as it set closure to some debates, it opened up new issues. The book takes the end point of previous research as its starting point.

The legal history of copyright law in Mandate Palestine illustrates how we can better understand what happens when a foreign law meets a local culture: why it began in the first place, what exactly occurred at the meeting point(s), and how does it play out. Though Palestine was not a crown colony, it exemplifies the basic tension between a foreign entity that brought with it its legal, political, and cultural agenda, and the local communities that might have had a different set of values. The absence of direct British interests in the form of protecting British settlers (there were only administrative and military personnel stationed in Palestine, occasionally with their families but on a temporary basis) crystallizes the questions and sharpens the initial tension between the transplanting party and the recipient, between the foreign and the local. These lessons from almost a century ago are highly relevant today for the debate about globalization.

Archival findings indicate that colonial copyright in Palestine was not a smooth one-way imposition of foreign law onto a local community, but rather a process of gradual reception of the law over time, a process which rolled out in different ways in the different local communities. There were hurdles, but no upfront resistance. Copyright law was implemented in Palestine (first in 1920, by modifying a little-known Ottoman Authors' Rights Act, and then again in 1924) due to a mix of British imperial interests that were informed by the special characteristics of the subject matter of copyright law; the law was first ignored by the local communities who either used alternative mechanisms of social norms (in the late 1920s) or none at all; the law was set in motion by foreign players who entered the Palestinian field and successfully protected their interests (1930 onwards); only then did the Jewish community begin to use the law (in the mid 1930s), with the Arab community joining in towards the end of the Mandate (in the mid 1940s). The British government exercised the law in its own operations (especially in the mid 1930s), but in a manner that reveals its differential treatment of the local communities.

This yet-untold history is framed within several overlapping frameworks. First, as to the colonial process, I develop an explanatory model of Colonial Copyright, building on literature of legal transplants and of legal postcolonial studies. This dual model is supplemented by a third framework that looks closely at the regulated subject matter at stake, copyright in this case. Second, as to the operation of the law, I apply insights from socio-legal studies, especially as to the use of social norms as an alternative to formal law. The entire discussion is located within a socio-legal understanding that rejects attempts to isolate the law and study it as if it were autonomous. The law is intertwined all along with social norms, social behaviour, and social change. Third, in explaining the different stages of the law's reception, I examine the image of the local authors (the non-copyright reader should note that in copyright law discourse, *authors* is used as a generic term, to denote all kinds of creative people producing *works of authorship*, namely music, film, paintings, sculpture, architecture etc). The discussion is informed by the *authorship project*, which as of the 1980s engages in deciphering copyright law's hidden assumptions as to the image of the author and the creative process. Fourth, I apply a *law & technology* prism in studying some of the developments along the way. The law was developed also as a response to technological developments, especially new modes of music production and dissemination (gramophone and radio), the emergence of cinema, and the rise—and then fall—of the telegraph as a means to transfer news. The entire discussion is contextualized within the time and place of Mandate Palestine.

The discussion is one of legal history, based on primary research of original documents as to the operation of the law in Mandate Palestine and on secondary materials as to the political and cultural setting of the time and place, along theoretical scholarship. The research focuses on the Mandate period (1917–48), but extends in both directions: It also covers the state of copyright law in the pre-Mandate time, both on the imperial level and the Palestinian level, where I discuss the last years of the Ottoman Empire. The conclusion glances at the fate of British law in the State of Israel, established in 1948, which first addressed copyright law in 1953 by amending British law. The basic colonial structure of copyright law served as the skeleton for Israeli copyright law until at least 2008.[2]

This Introduction presents the premises of the analysis, focusing on the relationship between copyright law, culture, society, and technology. I then provide an overview of the main frameworks of the discussion, especially colonial copyright and the authorship project. These are all discussed in-depth in Chapters 1 and 2, and the overview here is included for those who are less interested in the general theoretical frameworks that inform and guide the project, and enables them to delve directly into the case study. This Introduction then proceeds with a broad-brush sketch of Palestine under the Mandate, for those unfamiliar with the history of the region at the time. The Introduction then outlines the contents of the book, concluding with a short note on the methodology of the research and its periodization, and commenting on the developing discipline of copyright history.

A. Premises: Copyright, Culture, Technology

There are many ways to study copyright law and indeed there is an abundance of studies available. Some of these studies are within the formalistic approach and focus on the law itself, searching for its internal logic, maintaining its consistency in application, identifying gaps, and responding to new challenges. While this is a

---

[2] Copyright Act 2007, s 78 instructs that infringements that took place before the entry of the Act into force will be decided according to the prior law. Given the statute of limitations, this will apply until 2015. However, as for ownership of works made before the entry into force, the prior law applies. For an English translation see http://www.tau.ac.il/law/members/birnhack/IsraeliCopyrightAct2007.pdf.

valid and important form of study, it treats the law as autonomous and isolates it, copyright law in this case, from its social contexts. These are political, economic, cultural, social, and technological contexts. At this point in the progress of legal scholarship there is no longer a need to justify the non-formalistic engagement with law. The following paragraphs outline the particular premises on which the current book builds: the underlying assumptions about the relationship between several crucial elements that join together to compose a rich and dynamic field. It is the field of cultural production, to borrow Pierre Bourdieu's phrase, but with an emphasis on the law as an important factor in this field.[3]

The historical account of colonial copyright unfolded in this book will teach us that theory was almost entirely absent from the imperial legal discourse. The theoretical discussions of copyright law are a twentieth century phenomenon.[4] What mattered were practical challenges along commercial and political interests. Most of the rhetoric in the context of colonial copyright took it for granted that there are rights to be protected, but these were the rights of the British authors most of the time. Occasionally, rhetoric of public interest found its way into the law, especially in the few cases where the colonies expressed their own views.[5]

(1) Copyright–culture

Whether one adheres to one theory of copyright law or another, whether we believe that the law protects something that already 'is' or that the law creates the right, all should agree that the law has practical implications: it regulates the cultural field and provides players in this field with initial tools. The law recognizes/creates legal protection in works of authorship and delineates the scope of the protection, its power and limits. These rules constitute the *copyright regime*. By determining which works are protected and which are not, within each work, what is protected (original expression, but not ideas or facts), the content of the legal protection, its duration, and no less important, the exceptions which allow users to use the work in ways that would otherwise be infringing, by determining ownership and allowing transfer of works and rights, and by providing means of enforcement— all these shape the behaviour of the parties. They enable the formation of cultural and legal categories of 'author', 'work', 'content industry', 'user', and much more. The law determines who can do what with the work and who cannot; who the owner is and who is a user. Thus, *copyright law is a legal field that regulates basic elements of our culture*. The law constructs the institutional aspects of our culture and affects the content of our culture. For example, by allowing users to use protected works in certain ways, the law determines the available raw materials

---

[3] Pierre Bourdieu, *The Field of Cultural Production: Essays on Art and Literature* (Cambridge University Press, 1993).

[4] For comprehensive discussions of theories of copyright law see Justin Hughes, 'The Philosophy of Intellectual Property' (1988) 77 Geo L J 287; Edwin C Hettinger, 'Justifying Intellectual Property' (1989) 18 Phil & Pub Aff 31.

[5] See Isabella Alexander, *Copyright Law and the Public Interest in the Nineteenth Century* (Hart, 2010).

that can serve subsequent authors. The fair use (the American term) or fair dealing (the English term) defence allows the use of original expressions. Thus, one important element of the copyright–culture relationship is that the former participates in shaping the latter.

The relationship between copyright and culture has additional layers. It is not only a one-way relationship where copyright law shapes the cultural field. The relationship is a dialectic one, with an ongoing negotiation between law and culture. Thus, a second layer that lies beneath the previous one is that copyright law embeds, in a concise and condensed form, a society's views about creativity, about the production of information and knowledge, and about culture. The rules that compose the *copyright regime* within a jurisdiction reflect (and also construct) the social values about the creative process. For example, when the law chooses to protect expressions but not ideas, it announces a principle, that ideas should be 'free as the air to common use', in the powerful words of Justice Louis Brandeis.[6] By setting the duration of protection to a certain level and not another, the law states a preference. By allowing users a certain leeway in using works, the law declares its views about access to knowledge, the creative process, and distribution of power. For example, when the law permits parodies but not music sampling, it determines which works can be produced freely and which not at all, but it also reflects a view, that parodies are important enough whereas samplings are not. Each detail separately, and all together reflect a set of cultural preferences.

In composing the particular copyright regime many decisions are made, reflecting numerous hidden assumptions about the creative process. For example, when the law requires that the work of authorship is fixed in a tangible form (as is the law in the United States,) it denies protection of oral works. This choice reflects a prior underestimation of such works (or, at best, it provides an incentive to codify oral practices). When the law insists on calculating the duration of the legal protection according to the life of a single author, as does, for example, the law in Israel, it reflects an assumption that creative works are made by one or few known individuals. Other modes of production are de facto excluded: works created over time by a community, often called traditional knowledge or works created by thousands of people, such as Wikipedia, need to find creative ways to represent themselves so as to fit in with the legal categories.

Thus, copyright law is a socially constructed space that reflects a society's decisions about power, access to knowledge, distribution of cultural resources, perhaps fairness, and much more. This premise, that copyright law reflects a set of views, social preferences and values, is not unique to copyright law. It is also not the only legal instrument that regulates our culture. Laws and regulations about public funding, regulation of the telecommunications sector, or limits on freedom of expression—a non-exhaustive list—play an important role in constructing the creative process and the cultural field.

---

[6] *International News Service v Associated Press* 248 US 215, 250 (1918) (Brandeis, J, dissenting).

Copyright law is, however, the main legal machinery that *directly* attempts to regulate all these processes. Hence, it is also a mirror of a society's values and beliefs towards its culture. If you wish, we can address a jurisdiction: show me your copyright law and I will tell you who you are. Thus, the second layer of the copyright–culture relationship is that societal views about creativity and culture are concentrated, condensed, and translated into a set of legal principles and applicable rules.

Accepting that the legal space is loaded with social meaning rather than a technical set of arbitrary, supposedly neutral set of rules, a wide array of questions immediately arises: who are the players involved in making the law? What are their motivations and interests? How is the law made? What are the underlying assumptions as to the creative process, knowledge etc? Why were some value choices made rather than others? How does the legal reflect the social? How does the legal affect and construct the cultural?

Focusing on the cultural field and copyright law, we would expect a close match between a community's social views about the creative process and the set of beliefs and views of those who make the law. This match is sometimes disturbed. In non-democratic societies, no such match is even attempted. Within democratic societies, there might be various gaps between the community and those who make and operate the law, for example a technological gap between members of Parliament and a younger generation, or a preference for high culture at the expense of popular culture. There might be other distortions in the process, such as hindrance of interested commercial parties who leverage their power and manage to dominate the outcomes.

Colonial copyright, I shall argue, was yet another major cause of distortion of the match between a community's values on the one hand and the law and its makers' values on the other hand. The mismatch seems obvious: the law was foreign and reflected the values of the country of origin, whereas the regulated culture was local—the colony to which the law was applied. Note that this is not a dichotomy. Surely, there was some overlap between the origin's values and those of the recipients, and surely the local culture was not entirely isolated from other cultures (though not necessarily the British culture). From the colonizer's perspective it was part of a civilizing mission,[7] which carried with it the set of Western values about literature, culture, and much more. From the recipients' perspective it was something else.

(2) Copyright–technology

Copyright law has had a long relationship with technology. New devices are on both sides of the copyright equation—production and use.[8] On the one hand, new

---

[7] Sally Engle Merry, 'Law and Colonialism' (1991) 25 L & Soc Rev 869, 890 (discussing the centrality of law in the British 'civilizing mission').

[8] The users' side has deserved rather little attention until the path-breaking work of L Ray Patterson and Stanley W Lindberg, *The Nature of Copyright: A Law of Users' Rights* (University of Georgia Press,

technologies enable new modes of production and distribution of works. The printing press enabled wider and cheaper distribution of books and texts in general, the telegraph enabled transmitting information that was input for the news industry, gramophones enabled the public performance of musical works, the advancement of silent and then talking movies and radio—all carved new means to create new kinds of works. Later, television and digital technologies once again reshuffled the cultural field, enabling additional works, new modes of production and new ways for dissemination and use. On the other hand, new technologies such as photocopy machines, tape recorders, video cassette recorders, and various digital technologies, enabled easier, faster, and cheaper ways of copying works. Some of these technologies enable both functions—production and reproduction, and all enable both legitimate uses and infringing ones. The dual use nature of these technologies has indeed raised many hard legal questions.[9]

While today we are rightfully excited about the new opportunities and are anxious about the perils of digital technologies, its impact on the content industries, creativity, and our public sphere, this is by no means a new concern. With the advancement of each new technology it became apparent that copyright law's fundamental concepts and their applicable rules were based on a previous technology. When movies emerged in the early twentieth century, copyright law needed adjustments. Technological changes dramatically affected the modes of production and consumption of music. The emergence of the radio in the 1920s raised a bewildering set of questions: when the radio plays a record, is it 'public performance'? When a private or public premise enables guests to listen to the radio, is that considered a performance of the musical works broadcasted? What about foreign works? The interaction between different technologies stirred some businesses. For example, the emergence of the telegraph in the mid-nineteenth century as a means to convey information required newspapers to reinvent their way of gathering news. When radio started to broadcast news, the field once again needed adjustment, and when the telephone came into use as a means to gather the news, it sent a clear signal to the telegraph that its days are limited. These technological changes, their internal battles are all reflected in copyright law, then, as they are today.

Technology should not be treated as a given fact. The relationship between law and technology is more complex than a one-way 'technology triggers the law' interaction. As contemporary events and discussions regarding the digital environment illustrate, the law affects the technology in numerous ways. When the law is silent about a specific or a generic technology, it by default allows it. When the law finds that some technologies facilitate infringement and do not have 'substantial

---

1991). The digital environment renewed the interest in users. It is framed as access to knowledge (A2K): see Gaëlle Krikorian and Amy Kapczynski (eds), *Access to Knowledge in the Intellectual Property Age* (Zone Books, 2010), or as rights: Julie E Cohen, 'The Place of the User in Copyright Law' (2005) 74 Fordham L Rev 347. The production side deserved a critical analysis. See Yochai Benkler, *The Wealth of Networks: How Social Production Transforms Markets and Freedom* (Yale University Press, 2006).

[9] See the ultimate victory of the video cassette recorder (VCR) in *Sony Corp of America v Universal City Studios, Inc* 464 US 417 (1984).

non-infringing uses', in the words of the 1984 US Supreme Court case in its *Sony* decision, the law declares them illegal.[10] In some cases the law prohibits *ex ante* the making of technologies that will enable circumventing technological devices that protect works (Digital Rights Management—DRM). These are blunt interventions in the development of technology, and much criticized they are.[11]

Technology often responds to the law. Thus, a by-now famous case is that of the development of file-sharing programs over the first decade of the current century. The law (American federal courts) found that Napster, a file-sharing program that had a central search engine that enabled users to connect to each other, contributed to infringement of copyright and hence was illegal. Technology replied, by creating distributed file-sharing programs that have no central point. Some of the companies operating such programs were found liable for contributory infringement or for inducing the infringement.[12]

Another kind of relationship is that the technology and the law join hands and both strive to achieve the same goals. Joel Reidenberg termed this situation *Lex Informatica*, and Lawrence Lessig famously coined it as 'code is law', meaning that code—technology—shapes our behaviour no less than the law.[13]

The different facets of the copyright–technology relationship reveal yet another feature of technology: it is not void of values. Technologies are not developed out of thin air.[14] Rather, they are developed by people and corporations who are situated in their society, bound by the law. Designing a technology in one way or another reflects the values of the designer, whether in an explicit or an implicit manner. A technology that enables mass distribution of works promotes values of access, dissemination of works etc, and at the same time it might also enable mass infringements. Thus, the values embedded in a technology are not of one cloth. They might be supportive of copyright goals or disruptive thereof. This is an important premise of the discussion that follows: it rejects technological determinism.[15]

While the value-embedded-technology view and the rejection of technological determinism are not the topic of the current book, it provides an important background frame. Mandate Palestine saw the introduction of several important new

---

[10] *Sony*, ibid.

[11] WIPO Copyright Treaty, 20 December 1996, 36 ILM 65 (1997), Art 11; Digital Millennium Copyright Act 1998, 17 USC §§ 1201–5; for criticism, see eg *The Law & Technology of Digital Rights Managements: Symposium Issue* (2003) 18(2) Berkeley Tech L J.

[12] *A&M Records, Inc v Napster, Inc* 284 F 3d 1091 (9th Cir 2002); *Metro-Goldwyn-Mayer Studios, Inc v Grokster Ltd* 545 US 913 (2005); *In Re Aimster Copyright Litigation* 334 F 3d 643 (7th Cir 2003).

[13] Joel R Reidenberg, 'Lex Informatica: The Formulation of Information Policy Rules through Technology' (1997–8) 76 Texas L Rev 553; Lawrence Lessig, *Code: Version 2.0* (Basic Books, 2006) 122–4.

[14] For a contrary view, arguing that technology is autonomous, see Kevin Kelly, *What Technology Wants* (Vicking, 2010).

[15] See Batya Friedman (ed), *Human Values and the Design of Computer Technology* (Cambridge University Press, 1997). Once we acknowledge that technologies embed values, we can attempt to design technologies accordingly. For example, the notion of privacy by design, advocates the technological design of various systems to protect privacy. See Ann Cavoukian, *Privacy by Design* (Information and Privacy Commissioner, Ontario, 2009).

technologies, especially means of playing recorded music, cinema, the radio, and the telegraph. Each of these new technologies raised new copyright questions. Thus, it falls within the first of the copyright–technology interactions listed here ('technology triggers the law'), but when delving into the details and the copyright law stories, we should place a metaphoric memory note, that technology in itself is not neutral. Understanding the normative element of technologies will enable us to appreciate the power and social meaning of the new technologies. This will be especially relevant in the case of telegraph, which is a story about the complex interaction of two kinds of technology (print and telegraph), and their related business models.

B. Frameworks

The history of copyright law is not only a coincidence of events. To better understand the meaning of the different events, this book applies several conceptual frameworks. Their purpose is to organize the discussion, direct us to question otherwise unnoticeable elements, and provide a basis for the study and analysis of other jurisdictions or periods with sufficiently similar experiences, thus also enabling comparisons. The main, overarching framework is that of Colonial Copyright, which I present now in brief and expand in Chapters 1 and 2. A second framework which will assist in discussing some of copyright events is the authorship project, to which I shall return in Chapter 2. A related framework that guides the discussion is the importance of identity in figuring out the law under a colonial setting in general, and in the case of Palestine in particular. Other frameworks which will be utilized in the discussion of specific cases derive from the premises just discussed, of the copyright–culture and copyright–technology relationships: they will direct us to look beneath the legal surface, and explore its cultural and technological subtexts.

(1) Colonial copyright

Building on the premises discussed above, we can ask about the players, their motivations, the choices they made, and the roads they chose not to take. This book closely examines a widespread mismatch between the set of values and choices about the creative process that formed a copyright regime and the actual beliefs, views and needs of the community (or communities) to which the law applied. This is the case of colonial copyright law. When a foreign ruler picked up a legal field that evolved and developed in its own social, cultural, and legal setting and imposed it onto another setting, there was an inherent initial friction. The proposition I made earlier, that copyright law regulates *our* culture, collapses. Under a colonial paradigm, foreign concepts regulate another society's culture.

This book attempts to decipher this friction that lies between foreign copyright law and the local culture, between the colonizer's copyright law, and the culture of those colonized. The friction can develop into an outright conflict or it can be diffused, and the conflict is dissolved. It might be a case of two separate ingredients that remain distinct, or of two elements that blend to form a new compound.

Applying a biological metaphor that has gained power in legal discourse over the past few decades, the donor's legal transplant can be either rejected or assimilated within the recipient body. Chapter 1 will present a general model that explains the case of colonial transplants as the intersection of legal transplants and legal colonialism, and Chapter 2 will then apply it to copyright law.

The case of Mandate Palestine, like any other case study, has its peculiarities and unique features, but it tells a broader story in at least two more dimensions. One is the ubiquity of colonial copyright as a paradigm of spreading copyright law in large parts of the world in the late nineteenth and early twentieth centuries. The history of intellectual property in general and copyright law in particular as it developed in its homeland country, has deserved close attention,[16] and so has one of its most important offspring, copyright law in the United States.[17] However, these discussions, important as they are, are told from the centre's point of view, namely from the British (or American) perspective. An illustration is the very term of *colonial copyright*, which I apply here. It was first used in the title of the British Colonial Copyright Act 1847, better known as the Foreign Reprint Act.[18] The Act set a general structure for the colonies, as to a narrow (but pressing at the time) issue. It allowed the importation of unauthorized British reprints into the colonies, subject to a duty which was intended to reach the British authors and publishers. It was a law about British interests rather than about local copyright in the colonies. The Act had another side to it, in that it enabled easier colonial access to British knowledge, or at least an easier *legal* access, as de facto there were many unauthorized reprints available for lower prices.[19]

Subsequently, the term colonial copyright was used in legal commentary to refer to British interests. We find such uses of the term at least as of 1870 and well into the twentieth century.[20] It took an American review of an English copyright book

---

[16] Mark Rose, *Authors and Owners: The Invention of Copyright* (Harvard University Press, 1993); Brad Sherman and Lionel Bently, *The Making of Modern Intellectual Property Law: The British Experience, 1760–1911* (Cambridge University Press, 1999); Catherine Seville, *Literary Copyright Reform in Early Victorian England: The Framing of The 1842 Copyright Act* (Cambridge University Press, 1999); Ronan Deazley, *On the Origin of the Right to Copy: Charting the Movement of Copyright Law in Eighteenth-Century Britain (1695–1775)* (Hart Publishing, 2004); Ronan Deazley, *Rethinking Copyright: History, Theory, Language* (Edward Elgar, 2006); Alexander, *Copyright*, above n 5.

[17] Bruce W Bugbee, *Genesis of American Patent and Copyright Law* (Public Affairs Press, 1967); Lyman Ray Patterson, *Copyright in Historical Perspective* (Vanderbilt University Press, 1968); Edward C Walterscheid, *The Nature of the Intellectual Property Clause: A Study in Historical Perspective* (W S Hein & Co, 2002).

[18] An Act to amend the Law relating to the Protection in the Colonies of Works entitled to Copyright in the United Kingdom, 10 & 11 Vict c 95. See Ch 3 for a detailed discussion.

[19] Seville examines the tension between Britain, the United States, and Canada. Her discussion begins with the British interests overseas, but takes into account also the colonial (Canadian) interests regarding its local readership and industries. See Catherine Seville, *The Internationalisation of Copyright Law: Books, Buccaneers and the Black Flag in the Nineteenth Century* (Cambridge University Press, 2006) 78 et seq.

[20] The first substantial discussion is found in the first edition of Copinger's influential treatise. See Walter Arthur Copinger, *The Law of Copyright in Works of Literature and Art* (Stevens and Haynes, 1870) 234. Thereafter, almost all books on copyright devoted some space to the matter. See eg Augustine Birrell, *Seven Lectures on The Law and History of Copyright in Books* (Cassell and Co Ltd, 1899) 211 ('The Subject of Colonial Copyright would probably not have excited the interest it has but

to note this peculiar use of the term, to refer only to the British interests in the colonies rather than to the colonies' interests. The 1903 Harvard Law Review's comment on a then-new English book, quoted above, illustrates this critique.[21] The view taken in the current book is that of the other side; I ask not only about the British interest, but also about the reception of the law. Colonial copyright is used here in a much broader way than its nineteenth century uses and in fact, turns it inside out.

In recent years we have noticed the emergence of important and revealing scholarship on copyright history in other parts of the world, usually focusing on particular issues, such as Lionel Bently's work on statutory protection of telegraphic news in Australia or the modifications to British law inserted by the government of India.[22] Another important thread in copyright history looks at the development of copyright law in a particular area and tells its unique story, such as work about Australia, Canada, or South Africa. Most of these works end with the implementation of the Imperial Copyright Act in the colony discussed. Catherine Seville offers a broader view, discussing the internationalization of copyright law. She argues that several dimensions should be studied together: the Anglo-American, colonial, imperial, and international laws. She focuses on Canada and ends her discussion with the certification of the Canadian Copyright Act 1921.[23]

This book engages in both threads: the specific and the general, and takes the discussion beyond the immediate implementation of the 1911 Imperial Copyright Act. The British Empire carried copyright law in its legal kitbag to its colonies (mandates included). Many countries can trace their copyright laws to the colonial era. Some have diverged, such as American copyright law (which was inspired by earlier British laws, in the eighteenth century), but the roots of copyright law in many other countries, such as Australia, Canada, Cyprus, India, Malta, Nigeria, Singapore, Tanzania (then Tanganyika), and Israel are found in British times. Thus, the case study of Mandate Palestine extends beyond its specificities. By marking many dots, an overall picture emerges, one of colonial copyright. Other jurisdictions have their own unique dots and lines, but some of the patterns are similar. The convergence and divergence is of course a vast area that requires further

---

for the proximity of Canada to the United States of America.'); William Briggs, *The Law of International Copyright* (Stevens and Haynes, 1906) 475 (Part IV, entitled 'International Copyright in British Dominions'). The term was still used in Copinger's later editions in 1927 (6th edn), 1936 (7th edn), and 1948 (8th edn). The 9th edition published in 1958, provided the discussion under the heading 'Copyright in the British Commonwealth'.

[21] See above n 1.

[22] Lionel Bently, 'Copyright and the Victorian Internet: Telegraphic Property Laws in Colonial Australia' (2004) 38 Loy LA L Rev 71; Lionel Bently, 'Copyright, Translations, and Relations between Britain and India in the Nineteenth and Early Twentieth Centuries' (2007) 82 Chi Kent L Rev 1181. See also Shubha Ghosh, 'A Roadmap for TRIPS: Copyright and Film in Colonial and Independent India' (2011) 1(2) Queen Mary J IP 146.

[23] Seville, *The Internationalisation*, above n 19, at 10 (the intertwined dimensions), and at 78–145 (British–Canadian copyright relationship).

scholarly attention. I attempt some of it in Chapter 3, regarding the first years of the 1911 Imperial Copyright Act.[24]

The story of colonial copyright law has yet a second dimension, a contemporary one. Globalization is a buzzword applied to many fields and contexts. In the field of intellectual property it has gained a rather negative meaning. As of the mid 1990s we witness a rapid process aimed towards a *global copyright*. Powerful international political instruments were put in place, such as the Agreement on Trade Related Aspects of Intellectual Property Rights (TRIPs) of 1995, which is part of the World Trade Organization scheme, or the World Intellectual Property Organization (WIPO) Copyright Treaty 1996. Combined with a dense network of free trade agreements and unilateral, rather aggressive inspections of the United States, the result is that copyright law transformed from its local incarnations to a new global level, by and large one of trade rather than culture. Over the last fifteen years, more countries in the world enacted copyright laws or refined their existing laws.[25] These processes have not gone unnoticed and met academic critique and actual resistance, political and popular. The various patterns of the contemporary phase of globalization has been extensively documented and studied. In its abstract form, contemporary global copyright is a case of a foreign law imposed onto local cultures. Framed in this way, the earlier paradigm of colonial copyright becomes an immediate relevant historical experience. To be sure, early twentieth century colonial processes differ greatly from late twentieth century globalization processes. But there are many similar dots on the early and contemporary maps. Lessons from history might be relevant to our own times.

(2) Authorship

The study is informed by an ongoing academic project that closely scrutinizes copyright law, aiming to expose its underlying assumptions about the creative process. This project began with a focus on the author and his or her role in copyright law. The trigger was Michel Foucault's question, *What is an Author?*[26] A first response searched for the image of the author and found it in Germany's Romantic Movement in the eighteenth century, as a deliberate construct of interested authors. Similar researchers found that the author was a social or political construct in other places as well, during the eighteenth and nineteenth centuries.[27]

---

[24] 1 & 2 Geo 5 c 46.
[25] For the globalization of copyright law from a critical view, see Pamela Samuelson, 'The Copyright Grab' (1996) Wired 4.01; Peter Drahos with John Braithwaite, *Information Feudalism: Who Owns the Knowledge Economy?* (New Press, 2002) 114–20; Laurence R Helfer, 'Regime Shifting: The TRIPS Agreement and New Dynamics of International Intellectual Property Lawmaking' (2004) 29 Yale J Int'l L 1; Peter K Yu, 'The First Ten Years of the TRIPS Agreement: TRIPS and Its Discontents' (2006) 10 Marq IP L Rev 369.
[26] Michel Foucault, 'What Is an Author?' in Paul Rabinow (ed), *The Foucault Reader* (Pantheon, 1979) 101.
[27] Martha Woodmansee, 'The Genius and the Copyright: Economic and Legal Conditions of the Emergence of the Author' (1984) 17 Eighteenth-Century Studies 425; Carla Hesse, 'Enlightenment Epistemology and the Laws of Authorship in Revolutionary France, 1777–1793' (1990) 30

A second phase in the academic project followed, querying whether the image of the romantic author had an impact on the law, and if so how.[28] A third phase of the authorship project was critical: what are the implications of copyright law's obsession with the romantic author? One main thread pointed to other kinds of authors that do not fully fit within the rubric of the romantic author and hence might be excluded.[29] Traditional knowledge, for example, might be set aside: when a story is created by a community, passed orally from one generation to another, each participant in each time perhaps added or changed the story a bit so that no one can pinpoint the authors and the work might not enjoy copyright law at all. In other words, the critique is that copyright law is a Eurocentric concept that doesn't encompass non-European modes of cultural production. A current critique is that copyright law does not deal well with works created by multiple authors, especially in a global digital environment.[30]

Framing the discussion of colonial copyright within the authorship project directs us to look at the modes of cultural production applied by the different communities in the colonized region. In the case of Mandate Palestine, these groups were mainly the Jews (Zionist-Hebrew and orthodox), and Arabs (Muslim and Christian). The authorship project frame, combined with the colonial copyright paradigm, further directs us to query the image of the author within each community, and then to compare it with the image reflected in the British, foreign law. Thus, the research continuously searches for the social perceptions within the various local communities as to the creative process and juxtaposes these with British law. For example, the Hebrew authors had a strong national and collectivist ethos, a blend of socialism and Zionism. What did this mean in terms of the creative process at the time and place examined? How did these views interact with British law?

Another result of framing the discussion within its social context is that it draws our attention to the complexity of the picture. This exercise might carry a further lesson, a contribution to the authorship project: thus far, the romantic author was described as an individual figure, driven by an egoistic and selfish muse. A yet-understudied element is the role of nationality: other than a country's national interests in promoting its culture and other interests,[31] has the national identity

---

Representations 109; Martha Woodmansee and Peter Jaszi (eds), *The Construction of Authorship: Textual Appropriation in Law and Literature* (Duke University Press Books, 1994).

[28] Peter Jaszi, 'Toward a Theory of Copyright: The Metamorphosis of "Authorship"' (1991) 41 Duke L J 455.

[29] James Boyle, *Shamans, Software, and Spleens: Law and the Construction of the Information Society* (Harvard University Press, 1996) 114. cf a critique of the romantic view of the public domain, Anupam Chander and Madhavi Sunder, 'The Romance of the Public Domain' (2004) 92 Cal L Rev 1331.

[30] Benkler, *The Wealth of Networks*, above n 8.

[31] Sherman and Bently argue that nationality indeed played a role in this level. In discussing the lobby efforts for an international copyright treaty in the nineteenth century, they conclude that: 'More specifically, the reason why the option of a multilateral treaty was rejected as the means of establishing international copyright protection can be traced to the belief that just as literature was said to reflect national character, copyright laws reflected the national character of the country in which they operated.' See Sherman and Bently, *The Making*, above n 16, at 113–14. Catherine Seville agrees,

of an author played a role in the construction of copyright law as we know it? Was the English romantic author different from the German romantic author in a way that required different copyright regimes? Perhaps religion plays a role: does a Christian romantic author behave differently than a Jewish or Muslim romantic author? Nationality and group affiliations have not yet deserved sufficient attention in the authorship project.

Once we do not focus on the law alone as if it were an autonomous entity, but situate it within the social and cultural contexts, the issue of identity surfaces. In the case of Palestine, instead of a single foreign–local friction, we should discuss multiple frictions between the British law and the various communities and also between the local communities themselves. As Assaf Likhovski commented, 'British, Jewish and Arab legal thought in Palestine was defined by an obsession with identity'.[32] This argument applies to the copyright field as well.

(3) Mandate Palestine

The story of copyright law in Mandate Palestine is also a story about Palestine. Mandate Palestine is the territory that was under British rule between 1917–18 and 1948, in the area that today composes Israel (excluding the Golan Heights), the West Bank, and Gaza Strip. The east bank of the Jordan River, then known as Trans-Jordan (today's Jordan), was initially part of the same administrative unit, but was politically separated from Palestine in 1923. The historical timeline of the current research begins at the end of World War I, when the British ended four centuries of Ottoman rule in the region. Initially, the British ran a military administration, replaced in July 1920 by a civil administration. Two years later, the League of Nations, the predecessor of the United Nations, entrusted his Majesty King George V, with the Mandate of Palestine. The goal was for Britain to advance the territory of which it was a custodian, so to achieve the political goal of establishing a national home for the Jewish people in Palestine.

The first half of the twentieth century was a time of dramatic changes in the region. The Jewish nationalist movement, Zionism, was no longer an intellectual idea. As of the late nineteenth century, several waves of immigration (*aliyah*, Hebrew for immigration to the Land of Israel: *Eretz Israel*) took place. The first two waves took place under Ottoman rule (1881, 1904). These were rather small in numbers, but, of crucial significance. The leading group was composed of Zionist immigrants who positioned an alternative to the Old Jew: they were younger, independent rather than dependent on foreign donations (though the first wave of immigration heavily relied on the Rothschild family), nationalist rather than

---

and writes that: 'Copyright was thus seen to affect national identity, national education, national literature, national integrity and national autonomy... Every system of copyright law must determine which works are protected, for how long and from what encroachment. These questions are contentious even in a national context, but become more so when the international dimension is added.' See Seville, *The Internationalisation*, above n 19, at 10–11.

[32] Assaf Likhovski, *Law and Identity in Mandate Palestine* (University of North Carolina Press, 2006) 214.

religious; they built new settlements in rural areas rather than dwell in the crowded old cities. The dominant (though small) group among these immigrants, especially of the second wave, were collectively known as *Halutzim* (pioneers). They came mostly from Eastern Europe. At the time, the country was mostly populated with Arabs: there are heated debates about the demographics, but estimates for 1914 range between 60,000 Jews (based on Ottoman census) to 85,000 (based on Jewish estimations at the time), and about 683,000 Arabs (Muslims and Christians).[33] First violent clashes took place in the 1880s.[34] World War I left the region in ruins, deteriorated health conditions, hunger, and general disorder.[35] The number of Jews in Palestine is estimated to be less than 60,000,[36] and to climb so that by 1922 (based on British census) there were 84,000 Jews, with the Arab population reaching 668,000.[37]

The British restored order. Subsequent waves of Jewish immigration followed. The third wave (1919–23) was similar to the second in many instances, with an influential group of young enthusiastic *Halutzim*. The Balfour declaration of 1917 promising to establish a national home for the Jewish people in Palestine and the massive waves of immigration did not go unnoticed by the Arab population. The Jews were building settlements and with the assistance of Jewish organizations purchased land wherever they could. Tensions grew, and several violent clashes occurred. The 1921 events in Jaffa left dozens of dead Jews and Arabs. A prominent Hebrew author who was a central pillar of the emerging Hebrew culture, Yosef Haim Brenner, was killed in these events. The 1920s saw yet another wave of immigration, the fourth wave. This time, the immigrants came mostly from Poland. They were Zionists that fled their original home countries due to growing oppression. Many of the new immigrants settled in the cities, especially Tel-Aviv, the young Hebrew neighbourhood of Jaffa that earned a status of an independent town, and the Northern port city of Haifa. The economic structure of the city dwellers changed. They were bourgeois, made a living from the money they brought with them from Europe and urban sources of income: shop owners, land owners. Authors and artists were mostly members of the third and fourth waves of immigration, and lived in the cities, especially Tel-Aviv. The 1920s were times of economic and cultural changes. Towns grew, industries built new plants, and infrastructure was put in place. The Jewish–Arab tensions intensified.

---

[33] For the lower figures of the Jewish population, see Justin McCarthy, *The Population of Palestine: Population History and Statistics of the Late Ottoman Period and the Mandate* (Columbia University Press, 1990). For the higher figures, see D Gurevich (supervision), A Gertz (ed), A Zankar (assistant), *Statistical Handbook of Jewish Palestine* (Department of Statistics, The Jewish Agency for Palestine, Jerusalem, 1947) 37; *Statistical Abstract for Palestine* (Office of Statistics, Jerusalem, 1936).
[34] Alan Palmer, *The Decline and Fall of the Ottoman Empire* (J Murray, 1992) 194–5.
[35] Donna Robinson Divine, *Politics and Society in Ottoman Palestine: The Arab Struggle for Survival and Power* (Lynne Rienner Pub, 1993) 169 (describing the region during the war as turmoil and destruction).
[36] Thus, according to the higher data for 1914, there was a substantial decrease in the number of Jews, while according to the lower figure for 1914 there was a minimal change.
[37] *Statistical Handbook*, above n 33, at 45.

The late 1920s witnessed the violent events known as the Wailing Wall riots. Hundreds were killed. The British government was struggling with its policies as to Jewish immigration and land purchases. In the meantime, Arab nationalism developed in the region, as well as in Palestine. As of the early 1930s, a new, younger Arab generation emphasized the national identity of Palestinians as part of Greater Syria. The opponents were no longer the Jews alone. Criticism was now directed also at the British. This was the background of the Arab revolt of 1936–9. It started as a general strike and turned into a long period of escalating violence between the British, Arabs, and Jews.

The local events were not isolated from events elsewhere. Nearby Egypt was politically unstable; the Italian engagement in Ethiopia—the Abyssinian war of 1935–6 affected British foreign policies, and dramatic political changes took place in Europe: the rise of Hitler and the Nazi government in Germany in 1933, and Mussolini's Fascist regime in Italy. These events had direct effect on Palestine: Jews fled from Germany, external instability radiated internal political mood. Later, World War II had a dramatic impact on the entire region. Though it suffered few direct attacks (an Italian air raid in 1940), Palestine was part of the War. Jews in Palestine joined the British army against the German and Italian forces in Europe, but at the same time, continued to resist the British policies that limited Jewish immigration from Europe. As the news about the terrible fate of Jews under Nazi occupation started to reach Palestine, the dual approach—support the British in the war against Germany but actively resist the British immigration policy—intensified. The post-War years saw active Jewish resistance, including the assassination of a British Minister, Lord Moyne (1944), and the explosion of the King David Hotel in Jerusalem (1946).

Copyright law was obviously a peripheral issue at times of such dramatic events. But it provides a good sample of the broader events. The building of the Jewish National Home, the emergence of Arab nationalism, the inevitable tensions and clashes between the two populations—left traces in the story of copyright law. Copyright law provides us with a means to see the more subtle cultural developments: amidst tensions, clashes, and two world wars people lived their lives, struggling as they did, but also trying to engage in daily social and cultural activities. These were often part of the nationalist agenda (of all sectors).

C. Structure and Outline

A history can be (re)told in many ways. A chronological order is an obvious template. However, making sense of the events sometimes requires a non-linear story that can provide a thicker story. This is especially so, when several developments in different fields take place simultaneously. This book is organized first along the paradigm of colonial copyright: the imperial widespread use of a legal transplant of a unique subject matter that was already partially regulated at the time by international instruments. This framework dictates an order that roughly corresponds to the chronological timeline and to technological developments as well as cultural fields, but the overlap is not complete. The purpose is to make sense of the history and to present it so that each chapter can stand alone. The first two chapters establish the conceptual frameworks; the following five chapters (3–7) ask about the British motivation in the copyright field, on a British imperial level and a Palestinian level, about its initial indifferent reception, and then its activation by foreign players. The latter chapters are also roughly chronological and address a specific technology and a specific cultural field: literature and print in the 1920s, music and the music industry in the 1930s. The subsequent chapters (8–11) each tells a story of either a particular technology or legal cases, and the organizing lines are identity, technology, and the cultural field: the British (radio, music), Jews and Arabs (telegraph, gathering and disseminating news), the Arab community, and the Jewish community (literature once again, covering both the new, Hebrew community, known as the Yishuv, and the old, Orthodox community).

Chapter 1 begins with laying some foundations about legal transplants and legal colonialism. The combination of the two provides a general model for studying colonial law and provides the concrete guideline for the sequence of the discussion throughout the book, along the timeline of the legal transplant. I also explain the methodology used, of a back-and-forth examination of the colonial and the imperial, ie studying both the central authority (the London Colonial Office policies, in this case), and the local activities, within each colony.

Chapter 2 adds the particular regulated subject matter of copyright law. I highlight copyright's ideological affiliation with the idea of progress, its hidden assumptions as to the figure of the author. The creative process and its characteristic as an intangible asset that easily crosses political borders are also examined. The latter raises enforcement challenges and provides motivation to achieve extraterritorial protection on imperial and international levels. Adding the subject matter onto the previous frameworks produces colonial copyright as a legal and cultural paradigm.

Chapter 3 examines the making of colonial copyright in the British Empire at the end of the nineteenth and the beginning of the twentieth centuries. The purpose is to lay the background for the discussion of Mandatory Palestine, and to trace imperial patterns of colonial copyright. Most of the research done thus far on this topic has been told from a British perspective. Exceptions are Seville's work, which focuses on the international dimension, but intertwines it with colonial and imperial views, and Bently's work. Bently pointed to two stages of the British policy: first, the absence of an imperial strategy and secondly, a trend towards uniformity. This chapter nuances these observations and further adds the phase immediately after the enactment of the 1911 Imperial Copyright Act, when the interest in uniformity turned to a well-coordinated strategy to assure that uniformity is achieved.

Chapter 4 delves into the case of Mandate Palestine. I begin with a discussion of the first copyright law in the region, the little known—then as today—Ottoman Authors' Rights Act 1910. There are no indications that the law was known or applied in any way during its short lived life in Palestine.

When the British replaced the Ottomans, one of their first enactments was the Copyright Ordinance 1920. This chapter explores the first steps of the legal transplantation process and queries the British motivation in enacting copyright law in Mandate Palestine at such an early day. I provide several answers: that copyright law was a British imperial interest, intertwined with the international agenda of copyright law; that it fit the British mission of developing the country according to the Mandate, and lastly, a personal motivation of those involved. This list does not include local demand: none existed in the first place, at least no demand for the British form of copyright law. Jumping ahead in time, this chapter also discusses subsequent statutory events: the late official publication and rather poor translation to Hebrew and Arabic, later statutory amendments, and the establishment of copyright relationship with the United States. These subsequent statutory events reveal a growing absorption and familiarity of the law within the local communities, especially in the Jewish population.

Chapter 5 turns to the next link in the chain of colonial copyright—its initial reception. I argue that it took a while for copyright law to resonate with the local communities. This and the following chapter attempt to explain this slow reception. This chapter provides one answer, by looking closely at the Hebrew, Jewish Zionist community (the Yishuv). I discuss the emergence of the Hebrew cultural field in the late nineteenth and early twentieth centuries. Everything in the Jewish Zionist community was Hebrew and had to be Hebrew, in its enthusiastic, national, and mostly secular meaning. The Image of the Hebrew author was a mixture of individuality and collectivism, romanticism and Zionism. This image had only little in common with the image of the author as imagined by the colonial copyright.

Chapter 6 provides a second, socio-legal explanation for the slow reception of colonial copyright within the Hebrew community. I discuss the state of the legal field, and conclude that until circa 1930, it was unable to handle copyright cases. However, despite the cultural gap discussed in the previous chapter and the state of the legal field, the local cultural field did face some legal difficulties and challenges. The participants in the local field developed an alternative set of norms, adding to an overall scheme of private ordering. It included literary norms, contractual norms, business and industry practices, and social norms. The latter were mostly of public shaming.

Chapter 7 discusses the process of setting the law in motion. The law was finally activated in the 1930s. The context was of music rather than the book industry. The new technologies that enabled public performance of music, the development of local culture(s), and emergence of a cafe/entertainment culture, placed copyright in the spotlight of the relevant industries. The players that activated the law and brought the first copyright cases to the Mandate courts were foreign: European performing rights societies, first the German society (GEMA) and then, the English Performing Rights Society (PRS). This fits a general pattern of colonial copyright, that foreign players are the first to use the colonial law.

The discussion is one of micro-history and provides a close anatomy of the process. I trace the first steps of copyright law in courts and the issues addressed. We will observe the challenges, litigation strategies, and the judicial response.

The pattern of a foreign interested party who is the first to put the law in operation, feeds the discussion in previous chapters, regarding the British motivations in enacting the law and the alternative avenue of social norms. The foreign players also inspired local entrepreneurs to establish a local, Hebrew performing rights society, ACUM, in the mid 1930s.

Chapter 8 tells the institutional history that led to the establishment of the governmental radio station, the Palestine Broadcasting Service (PBS), which started broadcasting in late March 1936. The British designed and executed the establishment of the PBS with great care and attention to details. Copyright law was one ingredient in this matter. The PBS was a governmental station, thus, once again, it was the foreign player who implemented copyright law, mostly to the benefit of other foreign players, namely the PRS. An important player in this story was the BBC that advised the Colonial Office in all its decisions. By the mid 1930s the BBC was already established as a world leader in broadcasting. It was the voice of the Empire. Copyright issues were raised as to the broadcasting itself which included the public performance of recorded or live music and also as to subsequent public performances. The British deployed a rural broadcasting scheme, in which the government provided radio sets to (mostly Arab) villages. The differential treatment of Hebrew and Arabic music and the rural scheme added the identity issue to the copyright mix.

Chapter 9 goes back a few years earlier, to the first major copyright case in Palestine. This was the case of the *Palestine Telegraphic Agency (PTA) v Adel Jaber*. The PTA was a Jewish-owned news agency, a subsidiary of the Jewish Telegraphic Agency. Jaber was the owner of a new (and short lived) Arab newspaper. The PTA claimed that the newspaper copied its telegraphic news. This case, other than being first to be decided in the Supreme Court and setting some important copyright law principles, is part of at least two other broader stories. One is that of technological developments which resulted in competition between old (print) and new (telegraph) means of communication and media. Similar cases took place around the globe. The 1918 US Supreme Court case of *International News Service v Associated Press* is the best known of all, all composing attempts to achieve legal protection for news. A second broader story is, once again, the Palestinian identity puzzle. It was no accident that a Jewish corporation sued an Arab one in a colonial court, reflecting national divisions of power and political tensions. More so, defendant newspaper was affiliated with the emerging national movement in the Arab community, a movement that culminated a few years later with the Arab Revolt (1936–9).

Chapter 10 looks closely at the reception (or lack thereof) of copyright law in the Arab community. By then, we will have encountered Arabs in the course of the publication of the Copyright Act (Chapter 4), the establishment of the radio (Chapter 8), and the PTA case (Chapter 9). This chapter joins the dots and tells the story of the only all-Arab copyright case litigated in the Mandatory courts, as late as 1945. Other 'copyright incidents' are gathered, accompanied with an examination of the use of copyright notices in Arabic books published in Palestine. The overall picture reveals the British indifference to the Arab cultural needs, at least as far as copyright law was concerned. It reinforces the discussion of the British motivation in enacting copyright law in Palestine to begin with, and illustrates the Eurocentric nature of copyright law and its irrelevance to the local culture at the time: it was a more oral culture than a written one, and it applied social norms instead of the formal foreign law.

Chapter 11 returns to the Jewish community towards the end of the Mandate. As the local legal and cultural fields matured, courts and lawyers grew familiarized with the concept of copyright law. The first all-Jewish copyright cases reached litigation in the mid 1930s. Few cases illustrate the complexities of issues which the local Hebrew community had to face, especially, difficult issues of choice of law. The first of these cases addressed the works of no other than the most important Zionist figure, Theodor Herzl. Interestingly, the case was discussed in a private arbitration. A second case was of another prominent Zionist figure, Asher Ginzberg, known by his penname *Ahad Ha'am* (Hebrew: one of the people). A third case addressed a new version of the leading Bible concordance.

We will then look at another segment of the Jewish population, the non-Zionist, orthodox Jewish community. Jewish law developed a body of copyright law. But, it was absent from the legal scene in Palestine. No indications were found that it was applied at the time. Two attempts to activate it failed, due to lack of cooperation of one of the parties. One case provides a window to observe the internal norms and relationship within a small group of scholars who studied old Jewish texts.

Finally, the Conclusion ties the threads together and provides a broad outline of the fate of colonial copyright in its Israeli reincarnation. In 1948, Israeli law adopted the then-existing British Mandatory law across the board, with minor changes that reflected the new state. In the course of the following decades, Israel occasionally amended copyright law, reflecting new international commitments, technological changes, and other developments. Courts, in the meantime, interpreted the law, initially and for about forty years, mostly along the lines of British law. In the 1990s we notice a gradual interpretive shift towards American copyright law. Only in 2007 did the Knesset replace the British laws, with a new Act.

D. Methodology and Scope

The research presented here is based on archival work, conducted in public and private archives in Israel and in the United Kingdom, supplemented with legal research of materials from other jurisdictions to the extent of relevance and availability. Many of these archives contain material published here for the first time, including legislation, case law, official correspondence, internal memoranda of governmental officials and of those in the private sectors involved, as well as other private documents. As for case law, importantly, only a handful of copyright judgments were published during the Mandate in any official publications. The research found many other cases as well as the rediscovery of the Ottoman Authors' Rights Act 1910. The original materials were gathered and analysed, supplemented by searching newspapers of the time (Palestinian and English, in

Hebrew, English, and Arabic), with secondary sources regarding the people, events, and general background: historical, legal, and cultural. In some cases, short interviews or correspondence with descendants of those involved were conducted to complete the picture. On occasion, comparative material was advised. As the discussion addresses also pre-Mandatory copyright law and imperial policies in the nineteenth and early twentieth centuries, the current study builds on primary materials (legislation, British correspondence from the early twentieth century, and legal scholarship of the time), and contemporary research of legal historians.

The research covers the period of the Mandate, which was officially entrusted to Britain in 1922 and ended with the establishment of the State of Israel in May 1948. But, like most other historical analyses, the beginning and finishing lines are not taken as strict borders. Accordingly, I begin in 1910 with the Ottoman Act and end with the Israeli 1953 amendment, with a glimpse at the subsequent fifty-five years under Israeli law.

This book is located within a growing interest in copyright history. As Ronan Deazley writes: 'In the last 30 years, the history of copyright has been transformed from a subject of interest to a few book historians into a field of study engaging the interest and attention of scholars drawn from across the breadth of the humanities.'[38] There is a sound warning about the use of history for the purposes of current, much heated debates about copyright. Kathy Bowrey and Natalie Fowell point to an obsession to use history to settle contemporary disputes and call for a more critical and nuanced view of copyright history.[39] Deazley replied: 'There can be no such thing as *the* history of copyright, just as there can be no definitive understanding or reading of the Statute of Anne. To claim otherwise is to deceive—either oneself, or one's audience, or both.'[40] The current book takes the warning seriously, but at the same time is also aware of the limits of retelling history.

---

[38] Ronan Deazley, 'What's New about the Statute of Anne? Or Six Observations in Search of an Act' in Lionel Bently, Uma Suthersanen and Paul Torremans (eds), *Global Copyright: Three Hundred Years since the Statute of Anne, from 1709 to Cyberspace* (Edward Elgar, 2010) 26, 52.

[39] They write: 'We need to abandon, for a time, the preoccupation with the global policy stage and look at what has gone on at the local level—the contours of the local politics, the nuances, compromises and the boundaries. In doing so, our histories will become more reflective, more inclined to question our own judgments, and likely to embed our personal convictions with the nuances still intact.' See Kathy Bowrey and Natalie Fowell, 'Digging Up Fragments and Building IP Franchises' (2009) 31 Sydney L Rev 185, 210.

[40] Deazley, 'What's New', above n 38, at 52.

1
Colonial Transplants

[C]olonialism takes its power in the name of history, yet it repeatedly exercises its authority through the drama of the law.

Diane Kirkby and Catherine Coleborne, 2001.[1]

A. Introduction

The British Empire was an engine for disseminating its law around the world. Copyright law is one piece of a multidimensional picture which included constitutional, administrative criminal, and commercial law. Under the *imperial typology*, there were many colonies, protectorates, mandates, and other forms of British rule in many parts of the Empire. Each area had a unique mix of features: different degrees of British involvement, different degrees of legal fusion with the local, precolonial laws and legal systems, different local cultural field(s), particular cultural needs, and a wide variety of unique economic, political, ethnic, religious, and social attributes. The uniqueness draws the observer to examine each territory on its own terms. However, alongside the diverging routes, there are several points of convergence.

We need to construct a general model that will enable us to better examine specific case studies and yet see the larger picture. Such a model should guide us to ask leading questions, assist in noticing some elements that otherwise might escape our attention and overall, should help in making sense of the many different points that compose each case. Here, I am interested in legal diffusion processes, where a law from one place found its way—to use a neutral term if such is possible—to another place, and especially in the context of legal colonialism.

This book offers the model of *colonial copyright*. The term deliberately appropriates and reverses the nineteenth century meaning of the same term, which referred to British interests in the colonies. Colonial copyright as used here, is a mode of legal transplantation, of imposing copyright law from above and outside, by a foreign imperial power onto a governed territory and its people(s), in a way that serves first, the colonizer's interests, second, an overall imperial agenda, and third, it supports an emerging international agenda regarding copyright law. Colonial

---

[1] Diane Kirkby and Catherine Coleborne, 'Introduction' in Diane Kirkby and Catherine Coleborne (eds), *Law, History, Colonialism: The Reach of the Empire* (Manchester University Press, 2001) 2.

copyright took little care, if any, of local cultural needs. As far as copyright law is concerned, the meeting place of the imperial and the local was usually not one of resistance, but simply of indifference, resulting in a gap between the law in the books and the law in its inaction. This is a gap of irrelevance.

This chapter discusses two of the building blocks of this model: legal transplants and legal colonialism. A third framework, discussed in Chapter 2, is that of the particular subject matter at stake: copyright law.

B. Legal Transplants

There is a growing body of literature on the topic of legal transplants, referring to a law originating from one jurisdiction that is installed in another jurisdiction.[2] Framing the discussion of colonial copyright in the paradigm of legal transplants is helpful in noting its general features, those that tie the colonial experience to contemporary globalization. Alan Watson, perhaps the pioneer of the legal transplants discourse, pointed to this pervasive phenomenon in the course of his discussion of the importance of comparative law. He defined the legal transplants as 'the moving of a rule or a system of law from one country to another, or from one people to another'.[3] Note his choice of verb: moving. The subject matter of a transplant varies: it might be the entire legal system, a specific field of law or a particular piece of legislation, as Watson wrote: 'Actually, receptions and transplants come in all shapes and sizes. One might think also of an imposed reception, solicited imposition, penetration, infiltration, crypto-reception, inoculation and so on.'[4]

The language used in the transplant discourse is intriguing. The very metaphor of transplants is telling. Like all metaphors, it is one that reflects a series of hidden assumptions and conveys a certain message. Scholars offered alternatives. David Nelken explored the meaning of the transplant metaphor: 'On this approach, legal transfers, when they succeed, blossom, are fertile and set root, fail when the body recognises them as "incompatible."'[5] Thus, the transplant metaphor draws our attention to the relationship between the new part and the existing body, or, in Nelken's words: 'The legal transplant metaphor does suggest that any given transfer involves moving only a part of a wider legal and general culture. It rightly signals the need to consider the relationship between the part and the whole—on the side of both the giver and receiver.'[6] Nelken further pointed to alternative metaphors: some have a mechanical character: export,

---

[2] See (2009) 10(2) Theoretical Inq L; Michele Graziadei, 'Comparative Law as the Study of Transplants and Receptions' in Mathias Reimann, Reinhard Zimmerman (eds), *The Oxford Handbook of Comparative Law* (Oxford University Press, 2006) 441.

[3] Alan Watson, *Legal Transplants: An Approach to Comparative Law* (2nd edn, University of Georgia Press, 1993 (1974)) 21.

[4] Ibid, at 30.

[5] David Nelken, 'Towards a Sociology of Legal Adaptation' in David Nelken and Johannes Fees (eds), *Adapting Legal Cultures* (Hart Publishing, 2001) 16.

[6] Ibid, at 19.

import, circulation, diffusion, imposition,[7] or a discursive character: translation, and within the organic metaphors he notes grafts, viruses, contamination, and of course, transplants. William Twining listed a series of labels which include 'reception, transplants, spread, expansion, transfer, exports and imports, imposition, circulation, transmigration, transposition, and transfrontier mobility of law'.[8] He himself opted for the broader term of diffusion. Gunther Teubner rejected the dichotomous spirit of the transplant metaphor and suggested an alternative of 'legal irritants'.[9] Esin Örücü suggested a musical metaphor, of transposition and tuning.[10]

The alternative metaphors challenge the hidden assumptions of the transplants language. Indeed, Watson's general acceptance of the phenomenon has been much criticized for being agnostic of power relations involved in transplanting. The alternative metaphors enable us to replace many of the rather naïve, somewhat generic and occasionally simplistic structure of a legal transplant with a richer and a more nuanced diversity of situations. For example, 'transplant' implies a binary result: either the transplant is rejected by the receiving body or it becomes part of the new body. Instead of this outcome-oriented dichotomy, the alternative metaphors and views offer a process-based continuum. This aspect is crucial to understanding legal transplants. A legal transplant does not end when the authoritative body enacts a law which had originated in another jurisdiction. The new (borrowed) law needs to be assimilated within existing legal and cultural systems that include other laws, the structure of the legal system (the relationship between legislature and judiciary, for example) and many other social and political factors.[11] The borrowing and absorption is thus a process.

Moreover, borrowing cannot happen 'as is'. Pierre Legrand made this point clearly: 'No rule in the borrowing jurisdiction can have any significance as regards the rule in the jurisdiction from which it was borrowed. As it crosses boundaries, the original rule necessarily undergoes a change that affects it *qua* rule.'[12] In fact, Watson also acknowledged the change: 'Transplanting frequently, perhaps always, involves legal transformation. Even where the transplanted rule remains unchanged, its impact in the new social setting may be different.'[13] Accordingly, focusing on the *process* of borrowing of legal rules from one system and implementing them in another system, draws our attention to the fate of the transplant, both independently and in relation to its origin. It is possible that the two—the source and the transplant—will diverge and develop separately in different directions.

---

[7] Ibid, at 16.
[8] William Twining, 'Diffusion of Law: A Global Perspective' (2004) 49 J Legal Pluralism 1, 5.
[9] Gunther Teubner, 'Legal Irritants: Good Faith in British Law or How Unifying Law Ends Up in New Divergences' (1998) 61 MLR 11.
[10] Esin Örücü, 'Law as Transposition' (2002) 51 ICLQ 205.
[11] Margit Cohn points also to the temporal dimension and the multiplicity of players. See Margit Cohn, 'Legal Transplant Chronicles: The Evolution of Unreasonableness and Proportionality Review of the Administration in the United Kingdom' (2010) 58 AJCL 583. She encapsulates this observation in writing that 'no transplant is an island' (at 584, 599).
[12] Pierre Legrand, 'What "Legal Transplant"?' in *Adapting Legal Cultures*, above n 5, at 55, 63.
[13] Watson, *Legal Transplants,* above n 3, at 116.

Again, in Watson's words: 'A successful legal transplant—like that of a human organ—will grow in its new body and become part of that body just as the rule or institution would have continued to develop in its parent system. Subsequent development in the host system should not be confused with rejection.'[14] But the variety of options is broader than the Watsonian optimistic vision. The transplanted law can change in some aspects and not in others, it can rely on the donor for interpretation, it can respond and converse with the original, perhaps even affecting it.

What are the conditions that enable better reception of the transplant? According to Watson, in a comment that easily fits a colonizer's view of the colonized, '[r]eception is possible and still easy when the receiving society is much less advanced materially and culturally'.[15] But Watson believed that the entry barriers into the new legal regime are not too high in any case: '[t]he transplanting of legal rules is socially easy. Whatever opposition there might be from the bar or legislature, it remains true that legal rules move easily and are accepted into the system without too great difficulty'.[16] Legal transplants are indeed easier, in the technical meaning, when the two parties are of unequal power, but the easier they are in this sense the more troublesome they are from many other points of view. Scholars showed that a legal transplant succeeds and is effective when there is a local demand for the law and intermediaries respond to the demand.[17] The local demand can result in the transplant being adapted to the local needs. The same effect can be achieved when the local population is familiar with the underlying principles of the transplant.[18] Others emphasized the role of individuals, acting as agents of change.[19] In other words, measuring the success of a transplant depends on the criteria that we use. Applying a technical criterion (was a law enacted?) or a political one (was it effective? How did it play in the long run?), yields different conclusions.[20]

Indeed, others, notably Otto Kahn-Freund, warned against brute transplants.[21] A pre-designed transplant, he instructed, should study the transplant's background—the social, economic, and political power relations in which it is embedded, as these conditions might be different from those in the source country. He eloquently concluded that: '[W]e cannot take for granted that rules or institutions are transplantable ... [a]ny attempt to use a pattern of law outside the consciousness of its origin continues to entail the risk of rejection ... [comparative law's] use

---

[14] Ibid, at 27.   [15] Ibid, at 99.   [16] Ibid, at 95–6.
[17] Daniel Berkowitz, Katharina Pistor, Jean-Francois Richard, 'The Transplant Effect' (2003) 51 AJCL 163.
[18] Ibid.
[19] Michele Graziadei, 'Legal Transplants and the Frontiers of Legal Knowledge' (2009) 10 Theoretical Inq L 723, 730, 738.
[20] An interesting thread in the literature searches for the factors that yielded better transplantation results, using a contemporary measure of the rule of law. One approach looked at the legal system (common law, civil law etc). Another pointed to the degree of local representation in the legislative bodies in a colony and the integration of the local courts with the foreign ones. See Ronald J Daniels, Michael J Trebilcock, Lindsey D Carson, 'The Legacy of Empire: The Common Law Inheritance and Commitments to Legality in Former British Colonies' (2011) 59 AJCL 111.
[21] Otto Kahn-Freund, 'On Uses and Misuses of Comparative Law' (1974) 37 MLR 1.

requires a knowledge not only of foreign law, but also of its social, and above all its political, context.'[22]

This is not the place to solve the many debates within the legal transplant discourse. For our purposes, an interim summary teaches us that placing a body of law within a prism of legal transplants, and more so, within such a critical prism, immediately raises interesting questions that can conveniently be framed along the timeline of the transplanting process: What is the origin of the transplant? Who initiated the transplant? Why?[23] When? What kind of a transplant is at stake?[24] What was transplanted and perhaps what was omitted in the process, and if so, why? What was the manner of transplantation (borrowing or imposition)? How was the transplant received? Did it change during the process of its reception?[25] How do we measure its success?[26]

Thus, the framework of legal transplants is rather generic. This is also its main problem: the generality of the framework risks the removal of the political, cultural, and social from the legal; it might neutralize the relations and naturalize the process of legal transplants. Put differently, the Watsonian framing is embedded within legal formalism that views the law as autonomous. The critique of his theory is embedded within the paradigm of law and society.[27] However, legal transplants are rarely benign. They are infused all over with power and politics. Colonialism is such a brute form of power. Hence its interaction with legal transplants is important.

C. Legal Colonialism

The study of colonialism is an extraordinarily broad topic covering a vast literature, discussing many facets of colonialism, either from within the colonial perspective or from a postcolonial perspective. The scope of the discussion that follows is necessarily narrower and instrumental. I am interested in the *legal* aspects of British colonialism, rather than political, economic, or other aspects. Within *legal*

---

[22] Ibid, at 27.

[23] In discussing pre-designed international projects of transplants Jonathan Miller offered a typology of legal transplants, classified into four types, according to the motivation: (1) cost-saving transplant, ie borrowing a ready-made law from another country; (2) externally dictated transplant, where a foreign business entity or government requires another jurisdiction to change its laws, as a prerequisite for doing business in that country; (3) entrepreneurial transplant, where a local entrepreneur initiates a transplant; and (4) the legitimacy-generating transplant that generates prestige for the adopting country. Miller observes that many transplants are a mix of the four motivations. See Jonathan M Miller, 'A Typology of Legal Transplants: Using Sociology, Legal History and Argentine Examples to Explain the Transplant Process' (2003) 51 AJCL 839. These motivations fit modern transplants more than colonial ones, as they focus on the motivations of the recipient, rather than the origin country.

[24] Graziadei commented that '[t]he literature on legal transplants abounds with terminological distinctions'. See Graziadei, 'Legal Transplants', above n 19, at 731.

[25] Joshua Getzler, 'Transplantation and Mutation in Anglo-American Trust Law' (2009) 10 Theoretical Inq L 355 (discussing the changes made to English trust law when transplanted in America).

[26] For Nelken's set of questions, see above n 5, at 21–2.

[27] Cohn, 'Legal Transplant Chronicles', above n 11, at 587.

colonialism, the current interest is the *content* of the colonial law and within this subset, a particular instance of colonial law-making, in the form of legal transplants, where a colonial donor transplanted its law onto a recipient colonized territory and its peoples. This is the intersection of legal transplants and legal colonialism. I begin with analysing the elements of colonial law and then intersect with it with the framework of legal transplants. In order to appreciate the complexity of law to the imperial project, I break it down into its overall ideology (rule of law), and then characterize the process of law-making for the colonies.

(1) Rule of law

Empires often carried their laws with them to their colonies, either tailored laws or the Empire's very own laws. The Ottoman Empire, for example, enacted one legal system for the entire Empire, though it left some leeway for local laws, especially in issues of personal status. In the case of the British Empire, law played a central tool of imperial governing. As a senior British officer described it in the late 1940s, the British saw the basis of their government in the colonies as a rule of law.[28]

Such a statement sounds progressive and benevolent, and is in line with other colonial statements of the time about the enlightened modernizing force of the Empire and its civilizing mission.[29] Indeed, the law was seen as part of a mission to achieve progress. British law abolished slavery and provided other values that today we take for granted. When the British allowed local law to maintain its power, it was always subject to a British veto. The veto enabled the British to block what they viewed as uncivilized or non-modern. Olawale Elias, in a work written at the end of the Empire, wrote that English colonial law realized that 'there are many roads that lead to justice. Laws as diverse as those of the Greeks and the Hindus or of the French and the African are allowed to flourish within it and to govern men's lives today as ever they did in former days, without any attempt to treat them as unworthy except where they have been found to be barbarous or contrary to natural justice and good conscience'.[30] This is an admiring view of the British mission.

But, as postcolonial scholars have argued, the imperial rule of law was less benevolent than it might seem. The almost technical and orderly term of the *rule of law* might disguise the values and ideologies embedded within the laws and the

---

[28] Charles Joseph Jeffries, *The Colonial Office* (Allen and Unwin, 1956) 167. Jeffries was a deputy Under-Secretary of State for the colonies. Marouf Hasian quotes Ramsey Muir, who in the context of India commented in 1917 that the rule of law was one of the few 'priceless gifts' of colonialism to the colonized. Marouf A Hasian, *Colonial Legacies in Postcolonial Contexts: A Critical Rhetorical Examination of Legal Histories* (Peter Lang publishing, 2002) 5.

[29] Frederick D Lugard, first Governor General of Nigeria (1914–19), and later Lord Lugard, evaluated the British colonial role in Africa as a dual mandate: 'Let it be admitted...that Europe is in Africa for the mutual benefit of her own industrial classes, and of the native races in their progress to a higher plane...'—Lord Lugard, *The Dual Mandate in British Tropical Africa* (5th edn, Frank Cass, 1965) 617. As for Britain, Lugard wrote: '[we British are] bringing to the dark places of the earth, the abode of barbarism and cruelty, the torch of culture and progress, while ministering to the material needs of our own civilisation' (at 618).

[30] T Olawale Elias, *British Colonial Law: A Comparative Study of the Interaction between English and Local Laws in British Dependencies* (Stevens & Sons, 1962) 17.

very notion of rule of law, thus naturalizing them.[31] When the law abolishes slavery, the ideology is upfront. But all elements of the rule of law were always political. They were normative all over. Progress itself, is also less neutral than it might sound. As Thomas Skouteris argues in regard to contemporary international law, the very use of the language of progress is an ideological strategy.[32] The concept of the rule of law itself is a contested term.[33] Contemporary scholars acknowledge the central place of the rule of law in the ideology of the British Empire, but challenge its meaning. Kirkby and Coleborne write that: 'Law, the rule of law, was at the heart of the English colonial enterprise.'[34] Peter Fitzpatrick writes that '[t]o the imperial eye law was preeminent among the "gifts" of an expansive civilization, one which could extend in its abounding generosity to the entire globe'. But he argues that it was a 'grim present'.[35]

Imposing the rule of law was a deliberate scheme: it served the colonizers. The rule of law is indeed progressive and today, for democracies, it is obvious. But the colonial version had its other side as well. The British, Eurocentric, often capitalist choices did not always fit the choices of the colonized. We shall return to this postcolonial critique later on. For the time being, it is important that we remember the power relations behind seemingly neutral facades and that we query these relations. Later on, the application of this postcolonial critical view to the case of Mandate Palestine will reveal that the British rule of law resonated better with some governed populations than others.

(2) Imperial typology

Focusing on the British Empire, and in order to appreciate the wide variety of lawmaking options, which are outlined shortly, we need to recall the British imperial typology as to the territories under Empire rule, namely crown colonies, self-governing dominions, protectorates, mandates, and condominium territories.[36] Some were settler colonies; a territory could have several colonial modes at once (as in the case of India), or shift between such modes over time.

---

[31] Hasian writes: 'While the colonial rationalizations that were used to justify imperialism manifested themselves in many ways, there is little doubt that legal texts and other judicial artifacts were an important means of transmitting many of the relational messages that were needed in colonial policymaking.' Hasian, *Colonial Legacies*, above n 28, at 4. For a strong critique of the rule of law in colonial and contemporary times, see Ugo Mattei and Laura Nader, *Plunder: When the Rule of Law is Illegal* (Blackwell, 2008).

[32] Thomas Skouteris, *The Notion of Progress in International Law Discourse* (TMC Asser Press, 2010) 21.

[33] For discussion of this concept in another region of the British Empire, see John McLaren, 'Reflections on the Rule of Law: The Georgian Colonies of New South Wales and Upper Canada, 1788–1837' in *Law, History, Colonialism*, above n 1, at 46.

[34] Kirkby and Coleborne, 'Introduction', above n 1, at 3.

[35] Peter Fitzpatrick, 'Terminal Legality: Imperialism and the (de)composition of Law' in *Law, History, Colonialism*, above n 1, at 9, 19.

[36] See Charles O H Parkinson, *Bills of Rights and Decolonization: The Emergence of Domestic Human Rights Instruments in Britain's Overseas Territories* (Oxford University Press, 2008) 15–16; Jeffries, *The Colonial Office*, above n 28, at 29–31.

Crown colonies were various territories that came under British rule by way of conquest, settlement, cession of another country, or annexation by Britain. To these, British law applied directly as of a point in time of legal 'reception'. A repeat pattern was that at the start point of British rule, the principles of common law and equity and British statutes of general application applied to the new territory. At a later date it was followed by specific statutes that were tailored to the colony and required special enactments, either of the local legislature or from London.[37]

Self-governing dominions enjoyed a much greater autonomy and independence, but were still tied to London. These were Canada, Australia, New Zealand, the Union of South Africa, and Newfoundland (then separate from Canada), and later on the Irish Free State. In these, the local, governed peoples had the greatest voice.

Protectorates were territories that came under British rule as a result of an agreement or treaty with a local ruler. Some territories were under British rule as a result of informal agreements.

Mandates were an outcome of World War I, in the form of a League of Nations' entrustment of the mandatory powers with the responsibility over a territory, previously governed by an enemy.[38] The mandates themselves were classified into three classes, according to the prior ruler and the level of development of the area.[39] Class A was composed of ex-Ottoman territories in the Middle East: Iraq, Palestine, and Syria (the latter under French Mandate). Class B covered former German territories in central Africa, such as Tanganyika. Class C was composed of territories in South-West Africa and the Pacific. The degree of independence of each mandate differed according to its class. The authorizing document, the Covenant of the League of Nations was quite explicit about the progressive mission of the mandatory powers over their mandates: 'the tutelage of such peoples should be entrusted to advanced nations, who by reason of their resources, their experience, or their geographical position, can best undertake this responsibility . . .' and 'The character of the Mandate must differ according to the stage of development of the people . . .'. As for class A, which included Palestine, the Covenant stated:

Certain communities formally belonging to the Turkish Empire have reached a stage of development where their existence as independent nations can be provisionally recognised subject to the rendering of administrative advice and assistance by a Mandatory, until such time as they are able to stand alone. The wishes of these communities must be a principal consideration in the selection of the Mandatory.

Condominium territories were territories administered with another power. Britain and Egypt together ruled the Sudan, for example.

---

[37] For a succinct description see the introductory comments of a compilation of sources on the Empire's laws: Jerry Dupont, *The Common Law Abroad: Constitutional and Legal Legacy of the British Empire* (Fred B Rothman Publications, 2001) xvii-xviii. I use 'London' as a metonymy for purposes of style rather than substance. There were many British colonial officers, judges and others who were Scottish, Irish, Welsh, or non-Londoners.

[38] Covenant of the League of Nations, Art 22.

[39] For a discussion, see Lugard, above n 29, at 50–1.

(3) Law-making

Different methods of law-making processes were applied in the various colonies, according to their type under the imperial typology. The legislative process was part of the complex management of the Empire.[40] It was composed of two elements: the imperial, either stemming from London or from the local colonial government, and from the local, governed people(s) in each territory. Motivation and inspiration came from both directions and from external sources. The different structures of law-making in the different types of colonies can be measured along two criteria. One is the division of labour between the Empire and the colony, a specific imperial–local mix, as the amount of the two ingredients varied in quantity and in form. The second criterion is the level of control that the British maintained.[41]

As for the first criterion, we can draw a hypothetical spectrum. At the one end, there may be a situation of full imperial law-making for the colony and no local law-making. At the opposite end, the situation could be one of full local law-making and no imperial law-making. This end, arguably, is no longer a colonial situation. In between the two ends, there are numerous points. Chapter 3 will provide some examples regarding copyright law of all these options, and the case of Mandate Palestine provides a detailed example. In addition to the imperial typology, a further complication is that the law-making mix was not static. A territory could move up or down on this spectrum over time, having at any point in time different kinds of legislation from different sources. Again, we shall see a recurrent example of this regarding copyright law.

As for the second criterion, of the level of British control, we will encounter different legislative strategies: some strategies allowed local legislation, subject only to a later British vetoing power. This form was applied especially in the case of the self-governing dominions, but not only.[42] Another strategy required *ex ante* British authorization for local legislation. In other cases, London suggested that the colonies enact local laws but did not demand it, and in yet other cases, it demanded legislation but allowed the colonies to opt out or modify some elements. There are numerous variations and examples for the many options, and we shall see some of them in Chapters 3 and 4. Borrowing from the international law discourse, we can rephrase the imperial legislative strategies along lines of *hard imperial law* and *soft imperial law*. The former leaves little room for local initiatives and is closer to a dictation, whereas the latter, soft imperial law, allows more leeway.

The combination of the two criteria suggested here, the division of labour and the hard/soft imperial law-making was adjusted according to the kind of the colony,

---

[40] Peter Burroughs, 'Imperial Institutions and the Government of Empire' in Andrew Porter (ed), 3 *The Oxford History of The British Empire: The Nineteenth Century* (Oxford University Press, 1999) 170.

[41] Daniels et al argue that the degree of local representation has had an effect in the long term, over current levels of the rule of law. See above n 20.

[42] See eg the Foreign Reprints Act 1847, discussed in Ch 3.

to the topic at stake, and might have changed over time. We can locate either colonies in general or a specific kind of legislation. It illustrates the wide variety of legislative options.

Placed on the imperial–local legislative powers spectrum, the crown colonies had the least local legislative powers and the self-governing dominions had the greatest local legislative leeway. The British laws in the former applied automatically, subject to London-inserted modifications whereas in the latter, locally enacted laws were subject only to an *ex post* London review, which inquired whether the law at stake was repugnant to British law in some way. We can assume that the mere existence of the possibility of such an imperial check might have had an effect on the local legislative process, but the process was often one of a dialogue and mutual influence, rather than a one way dictate from London.[43] The level of British involvement was thus anywhere between direct and exclusive legislation to an indirect later check. Jeffries, a colonial officer, described the legislative process: 'The enactment of the laws is the business of the local Legislature, however constituted. But the Crown has to be advised whether the laws so enacted are or are not repugnant to an Act of Parliament, or to an Order in Council or other instrument issued under an Act of Parliament, since any legislation so repugnant is void.'[44]

Alongside this *ex post* examining mechanism, the Crown maintained the general power to legislate for the territories by an Order in Council.[45] Thus, not only the legislative process varied from one kind of territory to another, within each, there could be a mix of locally enacted laws and British enacted laws.

On the hard–soft law axis, we can expect to find crown colonies more often at the hard law end and the self-governing dominions closer to the soft law end. However, we should be careful about such generalizations, as it depended on the subject matter at stake.

Of course, legislation is only one part of the law. In the common law system, the judiciary makes law no less than the legislation. Due to the principle of separation of powers, to the extent that it was maintained and respected, it is more difficult to treat colonial adjudication in a unified form. Judges in each colony acted differently, applying the local colonial law, which was usually a mixture of British colonial and pre-colonial local law(s). Colonial courts' decisions were subject to appeals to the Privy Council in London, but it is fair to say that each colony developed its own jurisprudence, some closer to English law than others. There are many more factors at stake here, like the professional and educational background

---

[43] Egerton discusses the complex relationship of the centre and the colonies regarding issues of preferential trade treatment of Britain, tariffs and defence policies. Each colony had its set of issues with Britain. With Australia, for example, the issues of conflict were also the 'White Australia' policy, the fate of the 'New Hebrides' islands, and defence. See Hugh Edward Egerton, *British Colonial Policy in the XXth Century* (Methuen, 1922). See also Robert Burrell, 'Copyright Reform in the Early Twentieth Century: the View from Australia' (2006) 27 J Leg Hist 239, 259–60.
[44] Jeffries, *The Colonial Office*, above n 28, at 170.
[45] Ibid, at 171.

of the judges, and their previous—or next—position, as many had careers in the imperial system, moving from one colony to another.[46]

(4) The colonial meets the local

The legal-colonial picture is further complicated: The colonizer–colonized interaction was in itself a dynamic, rich surface. The overall relationship might have changed over time. There might have been areas of cooperation and at the same time areas of struggle. The colonized were in many cases not a unified native people but composed of several ethnic or religious groups. Likhovski warns against a simplistic colonizer–native dichotomy in the case of Palestine, and this is indeed an important lesson for the study of many if not all colonies.[47] These colonial situations are not reducible to a single statement. This complexity of the colonial–local interface is reflected in the law, which is an important meeting point, especially under a 'rule of law' Empire.

In most cases, British law did not fill a legal vacuum. In many, if not all colonized territories, there was some sort of prior law: either local or the law of a prior colonizer/empire, formal or customary, single or plural. Some territories were somewhat (if not all the way through) artificially composed (or amalgamated, a term often used in the case of Nigeria) of several, previously separate geopolitical regions. Indeed, colonialism imposed a new political form for many areas.[48] The pre-colonial law did not always cover all aspects that were covered by the British legal system, but core issues were often regulated in some way. Thus, legal colonialism intersected with local laws and legal systems, accepting, modifying, or rejecting them and replacing them altogether. In other words, it was a process of simultaneous legal continuity and discontinuity.[49] This meeting point of the foreign and the local legal systems deserved much attention in the literature, under the heading of legal pluralism. This literature examined the interaction, subsequent changes in either legal system or both (or more than two in some cases), and in their dynamics towards each other.[50]

It was often the case that the colonizer's law and the pre-colonial law did not fully replace each other in some horizontal way, but rather the intersection played out differently in different legal areas, in a vertical division. For example, in the case of

---

[46] For discussion of the law in Mandate Palestine along these lines, see Assaf Likhovski, *Law and Identity in Mandate Palestine* (North Carolina University Press, 2006).

[47] Ibid, at 5–7.

[48] See Jackton Ojwang, 'Legal Transplantations: Rethinking the Role and Significance of Western Law in Africa' in Peter Sack and Elizabeth Minchin (eds), *Legal Pluralism* (Proceeding of the Canberra Law Workshop VII, 1986) 99, 101: 'Each colonial state created was necessarily a negation of the very basis of African law—the ethnic group as an autonomous, self-regulating entity with its own laws affecting behaviour in society...The colonial state, in its structure an organisation, was essentially a new phenomenon in political life in Africa.'

[49] For a critical discussion see Peter Fitzpatrick, 'Custom, Law and Resistance' in *Legal Pluralism*, ibid, at 63.

[50] For an early descriptive overview of the interactions of British laws with local laws, often called customary law, see Elias, *British Colonial Law*, above n 30. For a critical analysis, see Sally Engle Merry, 'Law and Colonialism' (1991) 25 L Soc Rev 869.

Palestine, the British accepted as a general matter the pre-colonial, Ottoman law, subject to a series of modifications and British enactments over the years.[51] Some legal areas were left untouched, such as personal status (as in many other colonies).[52] In matrimonial and other religious issues the British adhered to the Ottoman principle and left the jurisdiction in the hands of religious courts of listed congregations, each adjudicating according to its religious law (a principle still largely maintained in Israel). In some cases, the British colonizer tried to codify local practices, sometimes more successfully than in other cases. This was, for example the case of customary law codified by the British in Nigeria.[53] The meeting point of the colonial and the local laws had the potential of friction and resistance, a risk that materialized in some cases, though in the case of copyright law, to anticipate the discussion, resistance was quite rare.[54]

In practice, at the time, the complexity of legal colonialism meant that the Empire required a large bureaucracy to handle all. The task was with the Colonial Office and its head, the Secretary of State for the Colonies alongside the India Office. In 1925, the Dominions Office took over the management of the self-governing dominions as well as the Free Irish State, and the Imperial Conferences.[55] Within this scheme, each territory deserved special attention, but it was obviously easier to handle some issues from London's central management and apply one policy to as many territories as possible.[56] However, the different degrees of autonomy of the territories, the internal divisions of the Colonial Office, and the complexity of the colonial machinery meant that internal imperial coordination was not always easily achieved.

Thus, we should appreciate the rich arsenal of law-making processes that served the colonial power, in legislation, in adjudication, and in practice. A full picture

---

[51] See Palestine Order in Council 1922, s 46:

> The jurisdiction of the civil courts shall be exercised in conformity with the Ottoman law in force in Palestine on November 1st, 1914, and such later Ottoman laws as have been or may be declared to be in force by Public Notice, and such Orders in Council, Ordinances and regulations as are in force in Palestine at the date of the commencement of this Order, or may be hereafter be applied or enacted; and subject thereto and so far as the same shall not extend or apply, shall be exercised in conformity with the substance of the common law, and the doctrines of equity in force in England, and with the powers vested in and according to the procedure and practice observed by or before Courts of Justice and Justices of the Peace in England, according to their respective jurisdictions and authorities at that date, save in so far as the said powers, procedure and practice may have been or may hereafter be modified, amended or replaced by any other provisions. Provided always that the said common law and doctrines of equity shall be in force in Palestine so far only as the circumstances of Palestine and its inhabitants and the limits of His Majesty's jurisdiction permits and subject to such qualification as local circumstances render necessary.

[52] Palestine Order in Council 1922, ss 51–7.
[53] Musa Yakubu, 'Origins and Practice of Legal Pluralism in Nigeria' in *Legal Pluralism*, above n 48, at 83.
[54] The most resistant colony was Canada. See Catherine Seville, *The Internationalisation of Copyright Law: Books, Buccaneers and the Black Flag in the Nineteenth Century* (Cambridge University Press, 2006) 78–145.
[55] Jeffries, *The Colonial Office*, above n 28, at 25.
[56] Egerton, *British Colonial Policy*, above n 43, at 135.

should draw on all aspects of law-making and law practicing, including an inquiry of the interaction of the colonial law with the local pre-colonial law(s). The case of Mandate Palestine illustrates all these dynamics: There was a slow process of anglicization of the local law, taking place both in the legislative and the judicial spheres, a process which was accelerated or slowed down according to the judges' legal and general attitudes and beliefs. In the 1930s anglicization accelerated.[57]

D. Colonial Transplants

It is time to place the first framework discussed above, that of legal transplants alongside the framework of legal colonialism. The relationship between the two provides a productive conceptual juncture, assisting us in figuring out each of their mechanisms respectively. Many of the legal colonial studies can be situated at this intersection, though most were not explicitly reflective about it. Lawrence Friedman helpfully distinguished between at least two forms of transplants, one is voluntary borrowing for various internal reasons of the borrowing jurisdiction, and the other is external imposition.[58] He then explained the latter, providing an example: 'A lot of "transplanting" has occurred throughout history by way of conquest and colonisation. The common law, for example, is a worldwide system because the British had a worldwide empire.'[59] Similarly other scholars who write within the paradigm of legal transplants take it for granted that: '[A]n early wave of large-scale legal transplants was driven by colonialism. Legal transplants could be viewed as a tool for colonists to control their new settlements.'[60] James Whitman, however, argues that instead of the view that the law spread as a result of colonialism, (Western) law has an internal driving force to spread, or put more generally, the law itself is colonial.[61] Whitman does not go so far as to argue that the law's driving colonial force caused colonialism.

The interaction of legal transplants and legal colonialism can be schematically described as two partially overlapping circles, as shown in Figure 1.1.

Colonial transplants is the subset of legal transplants, covering the imposed installation of a foreign law onto a colonized territory and its people(s). But the imperial–local mix renders the interaction between the two frameworks more

---

[57] Likhovski, *Law and Identity*, above n 46. See also Ron Harris, Alexandre (Sandy) Kedar, Pnina Lahav, Assaf Likhovski, 'Israeli Legal History: Past and Present' in Ron Harris, Alexandre (Sandy) Kedar, Pnina Lahav, Assaf Likhovski (eds), *The History of Law in a Multi-Cultural Society: Israel: 1917–1967* (Ashgate Publishing, 2002) 1, 6.
[58] Lawrence Friedman, 'Some Comments on Cotterrell and Legal Transplants' in *Adapting Legal Cultures*, above n 5, at 93.
[59] Ibid, at 94.
[60] Li-Wen Lin, 'Legal Transplants through Private Contracting: Codes of Vendor Conduct in Global Supply Chains as an Example' (2009) 57 AJCL 711. See also Graziadei, 'Comparative Law', above n 2, at 456.
[61] James Q Whitman, 'Western Legal Imperialism: Thinking about the Deep Historical Roots' (2009) 10 Theoretical Inq L 308.

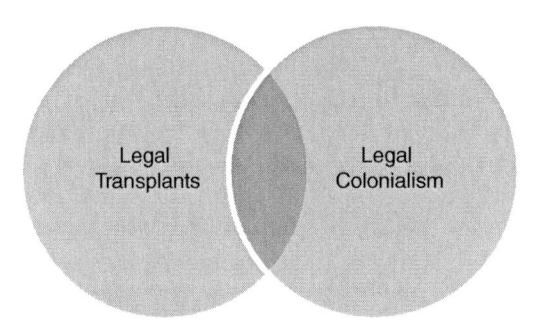

Fig. 1.1 Colonial transplants

complex. The intersection can guide us in studying the development of a specific legal field, such as copyright law, in several ways.

First, a premise for the entire discussion is that we should not treat the law in isolation. Its imperial and local contexts are crucial to understand the law at stake. Legal transplants are not neutral, especially not those that are the result of colonialism. Rather, a colonial transplant is one that is situated in a context. This is a lesson from the law and society movement in general and from a critical view of legal transplants.

Second, the (critical) transplants framework guides us not to settle for the mere observation that a transplant occurred, but to ask about the donor and its motivations, about the transplant itself, about the timing and the process, and about the process of reception. None of these should be taken for granted.

Third, the legal colonialism framework instructs us to conduct careful comparisons with other colonized territories, so to see a larger picture. In comparisons one should be aware of the imperial typology, of the intersections of the imperial and local laws, and of the colonial machinery: the horizontal replacement of local law in its entirety and the vertical replacement of some laws but not others. We might realize, for instance, that a legal transplant was not necessarily tailored for one territory, but part of a general imperial scheme. The legal colonialism framework instructs us to conduct an ongoing zoom-in and zoom-out process, in which we search both for converging practices and general patterns, and at the same time search for diverging practices and particular instances. I shall expand this methodology in the next section.

Fourth, the postcolonial mode of analysis guides us first to search for, and then to question, hidden ideologies carried within the seemingly neutral legal concepts, each on their own and all together under the heading of the rule of law. An ideology so carried does not necessarily root itself in the new soil without change.

Fifth and last, another dimension that the legal colonialism framework adds to that of legal transplants is the temporal one. The transplants framework might narrow one's examination to a specific point in time, that of enactment or legal reception. The interest in the reception *process* replaces this fixed point of view. Colonialism was not limited to one moment. It was an ongoing legal transplantation project. Perhaps the transplant metaphor should be replaced with one of intravenous infusion.

Indeed, legal historians that study colonial settings do offer nuanced accounts. Likhovski broadly characterizes the study of law in colonial societies as falling into one of two perceptions: one emphasizes the civilizing force of colonialism and the other views the 'law as an instrument of colonial power'.[62] Within the latter he points to three variants, the first is that the law served the colonizer to oppress the native population; the second is that law was used to achieve cultural hegemony by proving the advantages of colonial law, and the third variant is the inverted use of colonial law by the natives, as a tool to resist foreign power. He argues that the two perceptions reinforce the colonizer/colonized dichotomy.

The case of copyright law is complex in this manner. Framed within this taxonomy, the story of colonial copyright is mostly within the second perspective, in that it is unwilling to take for granted that colonial copyright law was only about modernization and enlightened progress. It is also a story about colonial power, although it was not brute power and the divisions of power were not always clear. This subtlety needs to be deciphered. In the case of copyright, the law often reflects a set of social beliefs about creativity, about creative people, and about the importance of certain kinds of culture, and by omission it excludes other modes of cultural production. In this sense, copyright law served to advance a British cultural hegemony *as to culture itself*. The identity of the players in this legal cultural field, the British and the 'natives' is crucial for understanding the issues.

We are now equipped with a set of questions, but the picture is still more complicated. Other than the who, why, when, and how questions, we should also ask *what* was transplanted? We can offer many classifications along different criteria. The next chapter will focus on one aspect of the transplanted subject matter: what does the specific topic teach us? But, before we continue, we should also reflect on the methodological lessons of the above discussion. How should we connect the evidence, the factual separate dots together, to form a sensible story?

E. Method

Given the spread of the British Empire, studying each jurisdiction on its own is highly desirable, as it will draw the researcher's attention to the special features of the time and place under examination. Case-specific studies enable close scrutiny of local processes and acknowledge the importance of the bits and pieces that join to tell the story of the peoples and territory under study. In many cases, colonial law was the basis of contemporary law. At the same time, too close a focus might result in losing sight of a general picture. Like the popular figure of a painter, we need to go back and forth in order to better understand how the parts fit the whole. This is an ongoing process of an intellectual zoom-in and zoom-out. Of course, the overall

---

[62] Likhovski, *Law and Identity*, above n 46, at 7–9.

picture has its own benefits, especially when the subject matter is the behaviour of one empire which engaged in many different territories. Adding the different stories of all the places together will enable us to have a broader perspective, and then observe or deduce a general structure that is shared by the components or is repeated in some way within each of them.

The methodology this book suggests is composed of three stages: gathering data from separate cases, deducing general patterns, and then applying them to each component separately. The first stage requires extensive research in as many relevant jurisdictions as possible. The second stage requires adding the different stories and components together and deducing a general model. It is a process in which parts of the larger picture are stacked as in the process of making an (analogue) cartoon, composed of sketches that are drawn on transparent plates. When we place one transparent plate on top of the other, eventually the steady elements that are dominant in each, will provide us with the skeleton or underlying template of the cartoon as a whole. The minor details of each of the separate sketches will disappear. In this manner, recurrent themes become visible and the specific features that do not have parallels in other plates, fade. To be sure, this process applied to colonial copyright is only an intellectual exercise. It is not meant to eliminate the special story of each component, to the contrary. Accordingly, the third stage of the methodology takes the general model and compares it to each of its separate components. Thus, we will be able to see where the local story behaved exactly like the general pattern and where it diverged from it.

An example for the importance of the back-and-forth methodology is the motivation of the British in enacting copyright law in the first place, a matter taken up in Chapters 3 and 4. Focusing on one jurisdiction might take us forward to some extent, but only that far. We might or might not find a 'smoking gun' that explains the legislative motivation in a specific region, such as a local demand or political lobbying by an interested party. New Zealand's 1842 Copyright Ordinance provides such an example, as it was the result of a demand by a local clergyman who published a book on Maori grammar and wanted it to be protected.[63] But, compiling British copyright legislative practices from around the Empire clearly indicates that there was an imperial copyright agenda.

Another interesting finding that emerges is that in many colonies, the copyright law remained in the books for quite some time and it was usually foreign players who first applied it, be it British publishers, performing rights societies, or prominent individuals. In South Africa, for example, the first copyright case was brought to a local court by no other than Charles Dickens.[64]

Of course, one might respond, that those who study the centre, namely the Colonial Office's, policies, would easily reach similar conclusions. This is indeed a valid research avenue. But it risks telling a partial story, one that omits the

---

[63] Geoff McLay, 'New Zealand and the Imperial Copyright Tradition' in Ysolde Gendreau and Uma Suthersanen (eds), *A Shifting Empire: 100 Years of the Copyright Act 1911* (Edward Elgar, forthcoming 2012).

[64] See discussion in Ch 3.

periphery. In fact, most copyright history on colonial copyright was thus far told from the British perspective with only few notable exceptions. The back-and-forth process suggested here emphasizes that both sides of the colonial process are important and more so, the interaction between them might be revealing.

Such exercises are sometimes undertaken by comparative lawyers. For example, the excellent research of Charles Parkinson, who studied the emergence of bills of rights in several British territories in the late 1950s to the early 1960s, applies a similar methodology.[65] Parkinson examined several territories' decision to adopt a bill of rights on the background of each of these territories' individual circumstances: geopolitical situation, economy, local politics etc. He was then able to draw general conclusions and compare the separate cases.[66] The result is an illuminating account of both the separate territories and the internal dynamics of London's central government and its relations with each territory. In the copyright field, there are few such attempts, though more specific. An important example is Lionel Bently's study of the *sui generis* legal protection for telegraphic news, that began with the Australian experience and spread to other places,[67] and another is an anthology of articles about the fate of the 1911 Imperial Copyright Act in several territories.[68]

Thus, figuring out the general pattern in the area of colonial copyright law would require gathering different parts of the picture and adding them together. I undertake such a task directly in the context of the making of British imperial copyright law following the enactment of the 1911 Imperial Copyright Act in Chapter 3 and build on important—but too little—research coming from former colonies, supplemented with newer research. More specific topics to be discussed in later chapters will also inspect other colonial cases.

By now we can see the first indications of general patterns that emerge from separate studies. Legal history studies of copyright law in several colonies are already available, though most of them relate to self-governing colonies,[69] alongside short

---

[65] Parkinson, *Bills of Rights*, above n 36.
[66] Ibid, at 10–11 (explaining the methodology).
[67] Lionel Bently, 'Copyright and the Victorian Internet: Telegraphic Property Laws in Colonial Australia' (2004) 38 Loy LA L Rev 71.
[68] Gendreau and Suthersanen, *A Shifting Empire*, above n 63.
[69] See the following important sources:

Australia: Jeremy Finn, 'Particularism versus Uniformity: Factors Shaping the Development of Australasian Intellectual Property Law in the Nineteenth Century' (2000) 6 Aust J Legal Hist 113; Burrell, 'Copyright Reform', above n 43; Benedict Atkinson, *True History of Copyright: The Australian Experience 1905–2005* (Sydney University Press, 2007).

Canada: Seville, *The Internationalisation*, above n 54; Pierre-Emanuel Moyse, 'Canadian Colonial Copyright: The Colony Strikes Back' in Ysolde Gendreau (ed), *An Emerging Intellectual Property Paradigm* (Edward Elgar, 2008) 107; Pierre-Emanuel Moyse, 'Colonial Copyright Redux: 1709 v. 1832' in Lionel Bently, Uma Suthersanen, and Paul Torremans (eds), *Global Copyright: Three Hundred Years since the Statute of Anne, from 1709 to Cyberspace* (Edward Elgar, 2010) 144; Myra J Tawfik, 'History in Balance: Copyright and Access to Knowledge' in Michael Geist (ed), *From Radical Extremism to Balanced Copyright* (Irwin Law, 2010) 69.

New Zealand: McLay, above n 63.

comments about other former colonies' law, usually appearing in the introductory sections of books on contemporary copyright, as well as work on Latin America, under a different colonial regime.[70] Specific examples are found in primary sources where available and occasional cross-references which were gathered at the time, either by the Colonial Office or in the legal commentary. The pieces join together, thus enabling us to point to at least some general patterns.

F. Conclusion

This chapter began the construction of a conceptual model to assist us in figuring out the diffusion of law under the colonial situation. The overlapping of two frameworks will enable us to approach the spread of copyright law with a rich toolkit. These are a critical view of legal transplants and legal colonialism.

The intersection of these two conceptual frameworks guides us to ask certain questions. It provides us with a general and generic prism to query the different players, their motivations, and the process chosen for implementation. It guides us to question the nature of the transplant and to acknowledge that its reception is one of a process rather than a singular event and that the process might fail, backlash, or feedback into the donor. Moreover, the critical prism of the transplants discourse guides us to search for inequalities of power, to be instrumentally suspicious about motivations and interests and to appreciate the many facets of the process.

Applying a postcolonial prism draws our attention to yet further complexities of the map. The multiplicity of kinds of colonies (the imperial typology), the various channels of legislative law-making for the colonies, and the many possible interactions of the colonial law with pre-existing laws in the colony are all intertwined. The legal colonialism prism requires us to be attentive to power relationships, to question the seemingly neutral rule of law, and search for the underlying hidden assumptions and ideologies that are embedded within the colonial law.

We cannot settle for either the imperial point of view or for a specific colony's point of view. As in many other fields, we should try and see both the individual trees and the forest all at once and query their relationship and how the forest came into being. This methodology fits the lessons of the critical legal transplants' discourse and the postcolonial perspective.

We now have a general conceptual model. It structures the discussion that follows. One crucial piece should be added to the picture and this is where the general model becomes concrete. We should look at the regulated subject matter and study it carefully, to see if and how it affects the general and abstract discussion. This is the task of the following chapter.

South Africa: Owen H Dean, *The Application of the Copyright Act 1978 to Works Made Prior to 1979* (Doctoral Dissertation, University of Stellenbosch, 1988).

[70] Jose Bellido, 'Latin American and Spanish Copyright Relations (1880–1904)' (2009) 17 J World IP 1.

2
Colonial Copyright

Our Colonies have hitherto not troubled themselves much about new books. Nobody need sneer at them for that. If you are going to live up country you will hardly care to take with you all Balzac's novels or even all Miss Braddon's. A few well-thumbed volumes must be your companions. The Bible, Shakespeare, and Macaulay's Essays were said to be the books most frequently taken with them by our early colonists, and could one be convinced that these books were not only taken but read, we should be supplied with a reason succinct and conclusive why we have so greatly succeeded as a colonizing nation.

Augustine Birrell, 1899.[1]

The discovery of the English book establishes both a measure of mimesis and a mode of civil authority and order . . . As a signifier of authority, the English book acquires its meaning after the traumatic scenario of colonial difference, cultural or racial, returns the eye of power to some prior, archaic image or identity.

Homi Bhabha, 1994.[2]

A. Introduction

The imperial and international spread of copyright law in the early twentieth century was a pre-designed scheme, a major project of legal transplants, channelled through the colonial machinery. It was *colonial copyright*: a law meant to protect the *English book* that Birrell mentioned in the heyday of colonial times, the book which was a signifier of authority, according to Bhabha's observation. This is the idea of a book being the sign of progress and authority, like the law itself, but one that represents also the control of those colonized.

This chapter continues the construction of the conceptual model of colonial copyright. In discussing a specific legal field that lies at the intersection of the frameworks of legal transplants and legal colonialism, we should pay special

---

[1] Augustine Birrell, *Seven Lectures on The Law and History of Copyright in Books* (Cassell and Co Ltd, 1899) 212. cf R E N Twopeny, *Town Life in Australia* (Elliot Stock, 1883) 221, who wrote about Australia in the nineteenth century that: 'This is essentially the land of newspapers. The colonist is by nature an inquisitive animal, who likes to know what is going on around him. The young colonial has inherited this proclivity. Excepting the Bible, Shakespeare, and Macaulay's "Essays," the only literature within the bushman's reach are newspapers.'

[2] Homi Bhabha, *The Location of Culture* (Routledge, 1994, 2010) 152–3.

attention to the regulated subject matter. At this point the general discussion becomes more concrete. The focus on the regulated subject matter is instrumental. I am searching for those attributes of the legal transplant that are most salient and relevant to the transplantation process: the features that might shed light on the motivation to colonialize copyright law: making it an item on the imperial agenda, or the attributes that explain the reception of the law. Seeking for such relevant attributes of the subject matter contextualizes the discussion.

In the case of copyright law, I identify three relevant attributes: (1) The almost explicit ideology of copyright law as a means to promote progress, which also fits the declared colonial mission of advancing colonized peoples. (2) The implicit ideology of copyright law as a reflection (and construction) of a particular creative process. This ideology exposes the Eurocentric characteristics of colonial copyright and the gap between the colonizer and the colonized. (3) The intangibility of the subject matter of legal protection, which raised (and still does) practical challenges, which were an important catalyst in imperializing and internationalizing copyright law.

I first discuss the attributes separately, then join them to form a third framework, and map it onto the two frameworks discussed in Chapter 1 (legal transplants and legal colonialism). The discussion takes us to appreciate the cultural balance between the colonizer and the colonies. The interest is thus in the area where all three frameworks intersect and overlap. The overlapping area is that of colonial copyright: the imposed legal transplant of copyright law through colonial mechanisms, onto colonized people(s), which might not have been interested in the regulation of their own literary and artistic fields at the time, at least not within the European form of copyright law.

B. Progress

What was the (British) theoretical justification for copyright law during the nineteenth century? What was its underlying rationale? What were the goals it was meant to achieve? Which messages did copyright law carry with it? Put differently, what was the ideology of copyright law? This section points to an almost explicit ideology, which is one of progress.

Historians of English copyright law identified several phases in the development of copyright law.[3] Initially, and mostly prior to the 1709 Statute of Anne, copyright

---

[3] See (listed chronologically): Birrell, *Seven Lectures*, above n 1; Harry Ransom, *The First Copyright Statute: An Essay on an Act for the Encouragement of Learning, 1710* (University of Texas, 1956); Cyprian Blagden, *The Stationers' Company: A History 1403–1959* (Stanford University Press, 1960); Brad Sherman and Lionel Bently, *The Making of Modern Intellectual Property Law: The British Experience, 1760–1911* (Cambridge University Press, 1999); Catherine Seville, *Literary Copyright Reform in Early Victorian England: The Framing of The 1842 Copyright Act* (Cambridge University Press, 1999); Ronan Deazley, *On the Origin of the Right to Copy: Charting the Movement of Copyright Law in Eighteenth-Century Britain (1695–1775)* (Hart Publishing, 2004); Ronan Deazley, *Rethinking Copyright: History, Theory, Language* (Edward Elgar, 2006); Catherine Seville, *The Internationalisation of Copyright Law: Books, Buccaneers and the Black Flag in the Nineteenth Century* (Cambridge University Press, 2006).

law served the dual purposes of governmental control over the content of books, an indirect tool of censorship, as well as a statutory monopoly in the hands of the publishers and booksellers. Theory, philosophical justifications, and rationales appeared only later.

A second stage began with the enactment of the statute in 1709. Although today the Act is considered to be the first modern copyright law, Brad Sherman and Lionel Bently showed that this understanding was a later, mid-nineteenth century construction of the statute.[4] For over sixty years, the statute was more a matter of trade regulation of the book industry, namely printers and publishers.[5] But, the Act carried the seeds of a new understanding. Its opening words, which until the late eighteenth century were rather void of real meaning, declared that it was an Act for 'the encouragement of learning'. In other words, the statute had a purpose and it was a political one, rather than just an economic one. The meaning of copyright law was debated in English courts during the eighteenth century, as documented by scholars under the heading of the 'battle of the booksellers'.[6]

The third phase of copyright law started when the battle of the booksellers was decided in *Donaldson v Becket*,[7] with the House of Lords clarifying, or perhaps determining, that the copyright in published works was a statutory matter rather than a natural right. Once this choice was made, a new question prominently surfaced: why did the legislature create such legal protection? Many answers are offered, but here I wish to point to the close kinship of copyright law and the idea of progress, especially in the late eighteenth century.

The idea of progress is today obvious and perhaps mundane. In the eighteenth century, it was revolutionary, almost subversive.[8] The idea held that humanity is on a linear course of inevitable development and betterment. That's all, and at the time, it was a lot. The idea was optimistic yet required humans to assume control of their own lives. It replaced cyclical views in the form of 'rise and fall' with a linear promise of continuous advancement. Historians of the idea of progress offer definitions. Here is Robert Nisbet's, inspired by St. Augustine:

---

[4] Sherman and Bently, *The Making*, ibid.
[5] Lyman Ray Patterson, *Copyright in Historical Perspective* (Vanderbilt University Press, 1968) 14, 143, 150.
[6] Birrell, *Seven Lectures*, above n 1, at 99–138; Mark Rose, *Authors and Owners: The Invention of Copyright* (Harvard University Press, 1993). See also Deazley, *On the Origin*, above n 3, at xxvi, who criticizes the traditional history of English copyright. His analysis of the eighteenth century developments is that copyright law was concerned with the public interest rather than with the author or the publishers. See also his discussion of the 'history of the history of copyright', in Deazley, *Rethinking Copyright*, above n 3.
[7] *Donaldson v Becket*, [1774] 4 Burr 2408, 98 ER 257.
[8] There is vast literature on the idea of progress in the eighteenth century. See eg Edwin Thomas Martin, *Thomas Jefferson and the Idea of Progress* (PhD dissertation, University of Wisconsin, 1941); Rutherford E Delmage, 'The American Idea of Progress, 1750–1800' (1947) 91 Proceedings of American Philosophical Society 307; Sidney Pollard, *The Idea of Progress: History and Society* (Penguin, 1968); Margarita Mathiopoulos, *History and Progress: In Search of the European and American Mind* (Praeger Publishers, 1989); Robert A Nisbet, *The History of The Idea of Progress* (Transaction Publishers, 1994).

[t]he vision of an unfolding cumulative advancement of the human race in time... the conception of time as a linear, single flow, the use of evolving stages and epochs in the history of humanity, belief in the necessary, as well as sacred character of mankind's history as set forth in the Old Testament, and finally, the envisagement of a future, distinctly utopian end of history when the saved would go to eternal heaven.[9]

David Spadafora offers a secular definition: '[t]he belief in the movement over time of some aspect or aspects of human existence, within a social setting, towards a better condition'.[10] The roots of the idea of progress can be found in the Renaissance, with its celebration of humanity and creativity, and later on, in the Enlightenment, with its emphasis on reason, scientific method, and a constant and relentless strive to learn and know more. Progress had a close affinity with knowledge. Knowledge was conceived as a key to progress. Today this is probably an obvious truism.

The idea of progress occupied a central place in the minds and actions of many thinkers and policymakers at the time. It had a prescriptive element, in that it allocated humans an active role in promoting their own good. Once humans were at the centre, in charge of their own fate, they had a role and a responsibility to advance their lives. Literacy and education are obvious scenes of progress, alongside the development of culture and arts. The law could serve as a tool to promote progress.

Copyright law emerged simultaneously with the idea of progress in the eighteenth century, and matured alongside it, in the nineteenth century. Spadafora concludes his study of the idea in Britain with observing that 'the idea reached its high-water mark in Britain during the Victorian era'.[11] Copyright law is almost an obvious legal site to achieve progress.[12] This is apparent in the United States. The Constitution, which sets its goal 'to form a more perfect union', empowers Congress to act on various issues, including copyright law. The language is telling. It states that 'Congress shall have Power... To *promote the Progress* of Science and useful Arts, by securing for limited Times to Authors and Inventors, the exclusive Right to their respective Writings and Discoveries'.[13] Thus, the idea of progress literally and explicitly found its way into the heart of copyright law.

American copyright law stemmed from English roots, though this legal transplant had undergone some transformations in its local reception process.[14] The conceptual roots are the instrumental view of the law as a means to achieve the goal of the advancement of learning. The conception of copyright law as a means to an

---

[9] Nisbet, *The History*, ibid, at xiii.
[10] David Spadafora, *The Idea of Progress in Eighteenth Century Britain* (Yale University Press, 1990) 6.
[11] Ibid, at 385.
[12] However, only few have tied the idea of progress to copyright law. See Margaret Chon, 'Postmodern "Progress:" Reconsidering the Copyright and Patent Power' (1993) 43 DePaul L Rev 97; Michael D Birnhack, 'The Idea of Progress in Copyright Law' (2001) 1 Buff IP L J 3; Malla Pollack, 'What is Congress Supposed to Promote?: Defining "Progress" in Article I, Section 8, Clause 8 of the United States Constitution, or Introducing The Progress Clause' (2002) 80 Neb L Rev 754.
[13] US Const art I, s 8, cl 8. Emphasis added.
[14] Patterson, *Copyright*, above n 5.

end, rather than an end in itself, and portraying the end as a public goal rather than an individualistic one, are important elements of progress.

Copyright law reflects the idea of progress in many of its doctrines. The structure of the law offers authors with incentives to make new works, in that it provides them with tools to fight those who copy their works without permission and thus diminish the author's financial motivation to make works in the first place. Bedrock principles such as the requirement of originality, the idea/expression dichotomy, and the fair dealing (or fair use) defence can all be explained as a concretization of the idea of progress.[15] Prevalent metaphors in copyright law also reflect the cumulative, linear advancement of human knowledge, such as the notion of building knowledge step by step and the metaphor of dwarfs who stand on giants' shoulders, and hence can see farther than the giants.[16]

The idea of progress today has lost its vogue. For some, this is because it was proved to be wrong: pointing to the terrible mass killings of the twentieth century and other injustices. For others, progress is so obvious that it requires no special emphasis. I am not here to settle this debate, but rather, limit it to the realm of human knowledge, culture, science, and technology. At least as to the process of enhancing knowledge, there seems to be an agreement that the human race has progressed and is progressing. To be sure, there are many challenges to address; the digital environment amplifies this point.

Once we view copyright law on the background of the idea of progress and recall the stated imperial views about the role of colonialism cited in the previous chapter, the connection between copyright law and colonialism becomes clear. Colonialism was portrayed by its supporters as carrying a progressive and civilizing mission. In the aftermath of World War I, the League of Nations entrusted Britain (and other countries) with a Mandate over the territories of the defeated side, so to advance the peoples in those territories. The Covenant of the League speaks aloud, in both language and music, of the idea of progress.[17] Copyright law, which served as a tool of progress in its country of origin, was designated the same role in less developed territories.

In his important discussion of colonialism, Homi Bhabha points to the importance of the English book as a sign of order and civil authority in the colonies. In many of the colonies, the British were the first to introduce books (usually the

---

[15] See Birnhack, 'The Idea', above n 12, at 41–56.

[16] The metaphor is usually attributed to Isaac Newton, but Robert Merton traced its origins back to Bernard of Chartres in the early twelfth century. See Robert K Merton, *On the Shoulders of Giants: A Shandean Postscript* (University of Chicago Press, 1993). Another early formulation of the metaphor by an Italian Jewish thinker in the early thirteenth century: Abrham Y M Vertheimer (ed), *Rabbi Yisha'ya DeTrani, The Responsa of Hary"d* (Rubin Mass, 1975) 75 (Hebrew). Today, the slogan has been partially appropriated by Google, in its scholar search application, stating: 'Stand on the Shoulders of Giants'.

[17] See Covenant of the League of Nations, Art 22: 'Certain communities formally belonging to the Turkish Empire have reached a stage of development where their existence as independent nations can be provisionally recognised subject to the rendering of administrative advice and assistance by a Mandatory, until such time as they are able to stand alone.'

Bible).[18] The book symbolized enlightenment and progress. With the book came the language, and more so, writing itself. As Ashcroft, Griffiths, and Tiffin write: 'Writing does not merely introduce a communicative instrument, but also involves an entirely different and intrusive (invasive) orientation to knowledge and interpretation. In many postcolonial societies, it was not the English language which had the greatest effect, but writing itself.'[19] Thus, it is only natural for the law to follow and protect the book and the practice of writing. The legal protection elevates the book to a higher standard, adding to its sanctity.

Thus, this short discussion of the idea of progress as applied to the subject matter of the colonial legal transplant, explains the imperial (explicit) ideological motivation to enact copyright law in the colonies. Under this view, both copyright and colonialism share the goal of promoting progress. They are both engines to promote the betterment of humankind. Viewed through this prism, colonialism and copyright law mutually support each other.

However, the colonialism-as-progress view reinforces the gaps between the colonizer and the colonized and places them on a hierarchical ladder. On this ladder of progress, it is clear which people and culture are superior, and which are inferior. This is where the colonialism reveals its judgmental and subordinating face. Thus, we should critically question this progressive ideology and ask about other ideologies and motivations, perhaps less explicit ones. We should ask whose progress is advanced, at what cost, and whether there are alternatives.[20] The hidden assumptions about creativity and the creative process are such ideologies and they add complexity to the seemingly benign picture.

C. Creativity

(1) Uncovering hidden assumptions

Copyright law also carried with it implicit ideologies. The law, in determining which works are worthy of its protection and which are not, in determining the conditions for such legal protection, in drawing the contours of protection in terms of subject matter, in composing a particular bundle of rights, in subjecting them to specific kinds of exceptions, and in providing a series of remedies and tools to enforce the rights—in all of these, the law says something about its subject matter. If the law purports to regulate some aspects of the cultural field, it necessarily has some vision as to how intellectual works come into being in the first place. Otherwise, the law would be just an arbitrary and senseless collection of incoherent rules. Just as contract law should have an underlying vision about how contracts are

---

[18] Bhabha, *The Location*, above n 2. Ania Loomba writes that '"the English book" (the Western text, whether religious like the Bible, or literary like Shakespeare) is made to symbolise English authority itself'. See Ania Loomba, *Colonialism/Postcolonialism* (2nd edn, Routledge, 2005) 78.
[19] Bill Ashcroft, Gareth Griffiths, Helen Tiffin, *The Empire Writes Back: Theory and Practice in Post-Colonial Literatures* (2nd edn, Routledge, 2002) 81.
[20] Replace 'colonialism' in the text with 'globalization' and the argument is as valid today.

made and criminal law contains underlying views about how people behave and how they should not behave, any legal field carries—or should carry—with it assumptions as to its subject matter.

The hidden assumptions are not always clear, coherent, or valid. Indeed, this is why the law is a scene of debate and why laws are amended and interpreted to fit newer social beliefs and values. Some laws rely on empirical evidence and are relatively straightforward. In other cases, we need to decipher the laws and expose the hidden assumptions. These are not necessarily deliberate attempts to disguise the real purpose. Rather, I am interested in the legislature's mindset, which is projected onto the law and is reflected in the law's text and subtext.

Importantly, this is a two-way process. The law reflects social and cultural assumptions about creativity, but at the same time, it constructs social views. If the law protects one kind of works and not others, arguably at least some potential authors or their employers will restructure their work so that it does fall within the law's ambit.

Uncovering hidden assumptions can better explain the reception process of a law which is based on one ideology, when it is carried to a place which does not necessarily share the same ideology. In other words, by searching for the underlying ideologies of a legal transplant we might better understand the meeting point of the donor–receiver of the legal transplant, or in the colonial case, of the imperial–local, or for this matter, today, of the global–local transplant. This is the case of colonial copyright law.

(2) The authorship project

We have today a rich body of literature which undertook exactly this task, of uncovering hidden assumptions that are carried along within copyright law. Beginning in the 1980s scholars searched for the authorial figure which copyright law presupposes. This is the *Authorship Project*. Following Michel Foucault's question, 'What is an Author?',[21] scholars searched for this author and found a social construction, deeply embedded in the European romantic movement. Martha Woodmansee was first to recognize this, in her research of Germany. She showed how the image of the author was constructed in the eighteenth century by a new class of authors who wanted to make a living from their new profession.[22] Others undertook similar historical endeavours in other jurisdictions and found that the romantic author was born—or created—during the eighteenth and nineteenth centuries.[23] In England, the author first came to occupy the stage in the Statute

---

[21] Michel Foucault, 'What is an Author?' in Paul Rabinow (ed), *The Foucault Reader* (Pantheon, 1979) 101.
[22] Martha Woodmansee, 'The Genius and the Copyright: Economic and Legal Conditions of the Emergence of the Author' (1984) 17 Eighteenth Century Studies 425.
[23] In France, see Carla Hesse, 'Enlightenment Epistemology and the Laws of Authorship in Revolutionary France, 1777–1793' (1990) 30 Representations 109. Hesse concluded that it was a deliberate construct of the state, which tried to diminish the power of publishers. The French Revolution gave the concept a new meaning, celebrating the author's persona. Ginsburg, on the

of Anne, but historical research found that it was the booksellers' plan and an instrumental invocation of authorship. Once the author became a player in the cultural field, it was only a short step to form its reflection in a legal mirror.

The next stage of the authorship project was to search the traces of the image of the romantic author in the law. Peter Jaszi was first to engage in such a project. He found the romantic author all over copyright law,[24] though the 'author' affected the law in different, not always coherent, ways. Jaszi also argued that the construct of authorship was a destabilizing force in the erection of the legal doctrines.[25] At least in the American context, the argument about the extensive role of the author in copyright law has been challenged.[26] In this context, a striking absence from the Anglo-American copyright law scene until the twentieth century is that of moral rights. Rights of attribution of the integrity of the work deposit powerful tools in the hands of the author to control the work, its meaning, and the relationship between the author and his or her work, even after the physical object or the legal rights have found their way into other hands.[27]

For the current purposes, we should look at the 1911 Copyright Act, the main vehicle of colonial copyright in the twentieth century. The Act assumes that there is an owner of the original work, who has the sole right to engage in the work in the ways listed there, and hence to allow others to use it (section 2(1)). The owner was usually the author (section 5(1)), unless the work was made in the context of a commissioned work or employment (sections 5(1)(a), (b)). A special provision allowed the author to reproduce his own work even if he was no longer the owner of the copyright (section 2(1)(ii)). The Act recognized that works could be authored by more than one person, under the category of 'joint authorship' (section 16), but the language suggests that the Act assumed a small group of collaborators, usually two authors. The Act further assumes that the intellectual work has a physical embodiment. This is encapsulated in the notion of 'work',[28] and is explicitly required in the case of some works, which are usually oral, such as dramatic

---

other hand, found that the post-revolutionary copyright law of 1793 saw a shift towards the author, but far less than is usually attributed to it. See Jane C Ginsburg, 'A Tale of Two Copyrights: Literary Property in Revolutionary France and America' in Brad Sherman and Alain Strowel (eds), *Of Authors and Origins: Essays on Copyright Law* (Oxford University Press, 1994) 131, 144.

The first phase of the Authorship Project was consolidated in Martha Woodmansee and Peter Jaszi (eds), *The Construction of Authorship: Textual Appropriation in Law and Literature* (Duke University Press Books, 1993) and in Sherman and Strowel, *Of Authors*, ibid.

[24] Peter Jaszi and Martha Woodmansee, 'Introduction' in *The Construction*, ibid, at 7. Peter Jaszi, 'Toward a Theory of Copyright: The Metamorphosis of "Authorship"' (1991) Duke L J 455.

[25] See also his subsequent research, Peter Jaszi, 'On the Author Effect: Contemporary Copyright and Collective Creativity' in *The Construction*, above n 23, at 29.

[26] Oren Bracha, 'The Ideology of Authorship Revisited: Authors, Markets and Liberal Virtues in Early American Copyright' (2008) 118 Yale L J 186. In the English context, the author has recently been acquitted from being solely responsible for copyright law's expansion. See Lionel Bently, 'R v The Author: From Death Penalty to Community Service' (2008) 32 Colum J L & The Arts 1.

[27] For the influence of the image of the author on French law, see Laurent Pfister, 'Author and Work in the French Print Privileges System: Some Milestones' in Ronan Deazley, Martin Kretschmer, Lionel Bently (eds), *Privilege and Property: Essays on the History of Copyright* (Open Book Publishers, 2010) 115.

[28] See Brad Sherman, 'What is a Copyright Work?' (2011) 12 Theoretical Inq L 99.

works (section 35(1), definition of 'dramatic work'). The history of copyright law leaves little doubt that the law developed and was shaped along the technology of print, which is fixed in a tangible object, rather than an oral form of creativity.

A third stage in the authorship project was a critical one. One objection comes from literary criticism, about the role of the author in the making, delivering, and fixing the meaning of a text.[29] For our purposes, a second kind of critique looks at the negation of the romantic author: the authors that are excluded by default. If the law assumes a particular creative process, how does it treat other modes of cultural production? More specifically, the first wave of critique examined traditional, non-European modes of creativity. This is the critique relevant to the current discussion.[30] To complete the picture, we should note that the rise of digital technologies resulted in another wave of critique, this time pointing to the shortcomings of the romantic figure to encompass collective modes of cultural production, such as Wikipedia, or other kinds of user generated content produced over networks.[31]

With this in mind, we can better approach the meeting point of the imperial and the local.

(3) Eurocentric copyright

Once copyright law is structured on the basis of the assumption of a particular kind of an author—as a singular, passion-motivated persona who makes creative works in an individual setting, detached from other works or other people, then creativity is narrowed and confined to a rather limited set of creative modes. The requirement of fixation of the work in a tangible form further limits the coverage of the law. Works created by different kinds of authors, such as collaborative works, communal works and/or in a different manner (orally rather than fixed) do not fit into the law's definitions.

This was the case in many of the British colonies, especially those that we too often refer to as 'less developed', judged according to a Western (now Northern) scale. There was a lot of cultural production in all the colonies, but it was local in nature and did not necessarily fit the Western patterns of creativity, as the latter were reflected and embedded in the law. For example, cultural production in Nigeria was largely oral: stories, music, performing arts.[32] But these were not fixed in a tangible form and often created by a community over time rather than

---

[29] See eg Roland Barthes' declaration about the death of the author in Roland Barthes, *Image, Music, Text* (Hill and Wang, 1978) 142.

[30] See eg James Boyle, *Shamans, Software, and Spleens: Law and the Construction of the Information Society* (Harvard University Press, 1996); Bruce H Ziff and Pratima V Rao (eds), *Borrowed Power: Essays on Cultural Appropriation* (Rutgers University Press, 1997); Marie Battiste and James Youngblood Henderson, *Protecting Indigenous Knowledge and Heritage: A Global Challenge* (Purich Pub, 2000); Anupam Chander and Madhavi Sunder, 'The Romance of the Public Domain' (2004) 92 Cal L Rev 1331.

[31] See Yochai Benkler, *The Wealth of Networks: How Social Production Transforms Markets and Freedom* (Yale University Press, 2006).

[32] Peter Ocheme, *The Law and Practice of Copyright in Nigeria* (Ahmadu Bello University Press, 2000) 6–7.

by an identifiable individual. In other cases, where there was one recognized author, the property was held by the community, rather than the individual. Marisella Ouma writes about Africa, that: 'In most cases, there were no permanent records as the works were transient and dynamic in nature. The individual was often seen as an extension of the community. Ownership of corporal property was normally at a collective community level.'[33] A similar example comes from The Malay colonies (today's Malaysia). A contemporary commentator writes about colonial times that: 'Malay literary works were more often heard than read and were handed down from one generation to the next by oral tradition. Where written versions of these works were made, there was often no reference to the authorship of the works.'[34]

These examples show how, in at least some colonies, local cultural works did not fit into British copyright law. The oral, unfixed works with no identified author did not meet the European criteria of copyright protection. At the time, with this necessarily being a gross generalization, the colonizers were simply uninterested in the local colonial cultures, at least not in a way that required them to recognize copyright in these works. Importantly, this does not mean that local cultures did not regulate cultural production. Many did, though not in a formal, positivist set of legal rules. Social norms and practices offered various rules, acting on a local communal level, rather than general and universal.[35]

Thus, exposing the hidden assumptions on which the imperial copyright law was built as to the author's figure at the centre of stage and the creative process, exposes the gap between the Western, European law, and the local cultures. This being the case, it is further understood why the interest in spreading copyright was an imperial interest rather than local. This cultural–legal gap further explains the absence of resistance to copyright law when it was first applied to the colonies: in at least some cases, it was simply irrelevant to the local authors. The single and salient exception is Canada, which continuously resisted the British copyright demands. However, the cultural gaps between Britain and Canada were narrower than other gaps.[36]

This theme will come up again in several points along the book: in the discussion of British motivation to enact he law in the first place (Chapter 4), social norms of Hebrew authors (Chapter 6), Arab music on the Palestine Broadcasting Service (Chapter 8), and copyright in the Arab community (Chapter 10). The discussion also carries practical guidelines for the student of colonial copyright: we should study not only the imperial image of the author (a task already undertaken by the authorship project), but also the local image of the authors: how did the authors within a colony conceive themselves? Was there a gap between the imperial British image and the local, colonized one?

---

[33] Marisella Ouma, 'Copyright and the Music Industry in Africa' (2004) 7 J World IP 919, 921.
[34] Khaw Lake Tee, *Copyright Law in Malaysia* (Lexis Law Pub, 1994) 2, n 4.
[35] For a similar point focusing on Chinese intellectual property social norms, see Seung-Hwan Mun, *Culture-Related Aspects of Intellectual Property Rights: A Cross-Cultural Analysis of Copyright* (PhD dissertation, University of Texas, Austin, 2008) 53–6.
[36] See Seville, *The Internationalisation*, above n 3, at 78.

D. Intangibility

(1) The challenge

A third important attribute of the subject matter of copyright law is its intangibility. A fundamental principle in copyright law is that the law protects the intellectual, original work rather than the physical object in which it is embedded. This means that the owner of a book can do with the physical bound pages whatever she wishes, as she is the owner thereof, but she is not the owner of the content, and should not reproduce it without the copyright owner's permission in the absence of some defence. The protection of an abstract asset was not always easy to grasp, and we see some indications of that in the law. For example, the 1911 Copyright Act recognized copyright in photographs only if they were fixed in a negative; the protection started from the day the negative was produced (section 21). Ownership of the copyright in the photograph was also determined according to the ownership of the tangible object. Today, in a digital era, it is probably much easier to grasp the separation of the intellectual from the tangible, of the digital bits from the analogue atoms.[37]

But intangibility means also difficulties in enforcing the right. It is easier to track tangible boxes rather than their intangible content or tracing ephemeral public performances. Customs authorities are gatekeepers in the very literal sense and can inspect the content of luggage or other deliverables, but they lack tools to inspect the minds of people who carry with them ideas and memories of works they read, heard or saw, which they then reduce to a tangible (unauthorized) reproduction. Or, a legitimate copy of a book might later be used to reproduce infringing copies. Thus, the challenge then as today, was how to control cross-border transfers of intangible intellectual works.

The cross-border challenge is also a result of the law's territorial character: with few exceptions, each country's law applies only within its sovereign borders. Taken to the imperial level, the challenge is enhanced. How could the Empire deal with the intra-imperial cross-border transfer of intangible works? Some laws might have been relevant for only one colony; other laws had general application (eg criminal law). Other areas of law addressed international aspects: navigation in the high seas, for example, which was obviously important for the functioning of the Empire. Later on, the regulation of international means of communication, such as the telegraph required legal arrangements that exceeded the borders of one territory. Commerce was also on the imperial legislative table, especially when the articles of commerce were deemed illegal: arms and ammunition, drugs, and the human 'articles' of commerce, namely the slave trade, which the British later abolished.

For intellectual property, the challenge was a different one. Unlike drugs and ammunition, the laws of intellectual property, namely copyright law, patent law, and trademark law regulated then (as today) a positive subject matter: one that

---

[37] Nicholas Negroponte, *Being Digital* (Vintage, 1996).

enhances culture and intellectual development (copyright), science and technology (patents), and fair commercial activity (trademarks). The challenge was thus not to ban cross-border transfers of intellectual products, but rather to foster such commerce, albeit in ways that do not undermine it. The goal was to make sure that when works of authorship crossed borders, as they did within the Empire and outside it, they were legal copies with the copyright owners' permission. A related challenge was to assure that there was no 'copyright haven'.

During the nineteenth century it became clearer that the special subject matter required legal regulation addressing cross-border flows of protected works in two dimensions: within the Empire, and on an international level—between the Empire and foreign countries. As Catherine Seville argues, these two dimensions should be evaluated against each other.[38] This was especially the case regarding literary works. The age of mechanical reproduction had already reached the book industry, but was yet to arrive in the artistic and musical fields.[39] Books easily crossed borders. One copy could be reproduced in another colony or a foreign country if it had sufficient printing capabilities.

(2) Cultural balances

From an imperial point of view, the cross-border challenge had several aspects. The first challenge was Britain's interest as an *exporter* of cultural goods to other colonies within the Empire (and to other countries), to protect British copyright owners also outside the shores of the United Kingdom. This was important especially in relation to the self-governing dominions (Australia, Canada, Newfoundland, New Zealand, and South Africa), where there were English reading audiences and local publishers, and in relation to places where translations to local languages were practised, such as in India. The (real) concern was that British works were reprinted and republished across the Atlantic and the Pacific, to the dismay of the copyright owners in Britain.

The second challenge—second in time and in importance—was Britain's interests as an *importer* of cultural goods. The challenge was to protect works first written and published in the colonies, not only in their respective colonies, but throughout the Empire. The authors could be British officers on a mission in a colony, or local residents, authoring *colonial works*. However, once we recall the discussion in the previous section, about the difficulty of many colonial cultural works to fit into the Eurocentric British copyright law, it becomes clear that only some works were protected by the law: those that fell within the paradigm of a Western work. A book written by a colonial officer posted in a colony could be protected, but an original dramatic play that was not fixed in a tangible form, created by a local author in the same colony did not deserve the law's protection.

---

[38] Seville, *The Internationalisation*, above n 3, at 10.
[39] Walter Benjamin, *The Work of Art in the Age of its Technological Reproducibility and other Writings on Media* (Harvard University Press, 2008 (1936)).

The British challenge at the time was thus narrowed to deal only with works that were deemed worthy of legal protection in the eyes of British law.

The interest in the cross-border flow of works of authorship could become relevant only on the background of several factors. A first factor was the emergence of similar, reading audience in the country of origin and in the overseas territories. This is a matter of language and literacy. A book in English was not of much worth in a place where no one could read English. Once English translations of works into other languages commenced, as in the case of India, the British interest did not shy away from prying into the Indian legislative process, though not always with full success.[40] If Britain was the only place on earth to speak English at the time, perhaps copyright law would have developed differently, but English followed British colonialism. A second factor for the emergence of unauthorized cross-border flow of authorial works was the existence of a book trade, or in a broader term, a viable economy. For this trade to emerge, the prerequisite was that a stable market existed. During the nineteenth century these conditions of language, literacy, and economy matured in many places, though surely not all over the Empire. The interests in adopting cross-border protection depended very much on the status of a territory as an exporter or an importer of cultural works, namely, the net-cultural balance. Britain was a net-exporter of cultural works.

From the point of view of the colonized, however, the balance of interests was somewhat different, with a wide variety among the colonies. The English-speaking self governing dominions were both importers of English culture and at least potentially, exporters. But many of the colonies were on one side of this cultural balance, being only importers of foreign culture rather than exporters. Language, content, markets, and technology created barriers to such exporting. As for language, not many English people spoke African languages, Hindi, or other local languages spoken in the many colonies. Local cultural content was not of much interest to the English, at least not to sufficiently large segments to provide incentives to export the books to Britain. Sufficiently developed markets that could engage in exporting cultural goods were also quite rare in most of the colonies in the nineteenth century. Printing facilities were also not as developed or pervasive as in Europe.

The unique local conditions directly affected the flow of cultural works into a colony and within it. A commentator on copyright law in Ghana writes, referring to the local conditions until at least the late 1940s: 'Books circulating in Ghana were non-Ghanaian in origin, authorship was confined to schools and missionary organizations. Even here, people were not publishing novels, plays or history books. Most of the texts were translations or stories retold in English or in the various Ghanaian languages.'[41] Thus, in the late nineteenth century and well into the twentieth century, the British copyright law was simply irrelevant to local Ghanaian culture, as it was mostly oral, and hence unprotected. The law

---

[40] See Lionel Bently, 'Copyright, Translations, and Relations between Britain and India in the Nineteenth and Early Twentieth Centuries' (2007) 82 Chi Kent L Rev 1181.

[41] Andrew Ofoe Amegatcher, *Ghanaian Law of Copyright* (Omega, 1993) 3.

could protect the foreign British owners, but in the absence of local infrastructure (printers, distribution channels, consumers), there was no threat and they could distribute their books without any concern.

Central elements of a copyright system were absent in the colonies, namely industries (literary publishers, music publishers, theatres, and the like), and authors' associations. The differences, however, did not disturb an imperial agenda from going ahead and implementing copyright law.

A third challenge was the flow of works between colonies. It depended on similar considerations on a relative scale. If Australian authors, for example, produced literary works which were of interest in another colony, despite language, culture, and other barriers, it was in the exporter's interest to assure that the work was protected both at home and in the destination territory. The exporting colony, however, lacked the power to enact imperial-wide arrangements and had to rely on its own laws and on the imperial law, to the extent that it covered such cross-colonial commerce.

Similar considerations applied to foreign countries. Countries which had similar language, levels of literacy and close enough cultures, a similar level of technological advancement and a functioning market, were a threat to British authors and publishers, as the entry barriers into the foreign market were low. Indeed, this was the case of the United States for many years: American publishers copied British works and often distributed them not only in the United States, but also to other colonies, especially to nearby Canada.[42] Only in 1891 did the United States protect works of foreign origin,[43] and only ninety-eight years thereafter, did it join the Berne Convention.[44] As to other countries, once translations became available, the barriers of entry were also lower. This was the case of English works translated to French or German, for example. Of course, the response to the challenge needed to be on an international level. As for other countries with greater cultural, technological, and economic differences, the concern was milder. The cultural balance of the United Kingdom vis-à-vis other countries determined the level of British interest in arranging a copyright relationship in one way or another.

The fourth challenge was the internal flow of copyrighted works within a colony. It left each colony to decide for itself whether to enact local copyright law and of what sort, at least during the nineteenth century and until the enactment of the

---

[42] See Seville, *The Internationalisation*, above n 3, at 78. British publishers often charged higher prices for first editions, which enhanced the Americans' incentive to produce cheaper editions. See Jeremy Finn, 'Particularism versus Uniformity: Factors Shaping the Development of Australasian Intellectual Property Law in the Nineteenth Century' (2000) 6 Aust J Legal Hist 113, 116. The American reprinting of British books triggered the enactment of the 1847 Foreign Reprints Act. See discussion in Ch 3.

[43] See International Copyright Act 1891 (Chace Act); Steven Wilf, 'Copyright and Social Movements in Late Nineteenth-Century America' (2011) 12 Theoretical Inq L 123; Oren Bracha, 'The Statute of Anne: An American Mythology' (2010) 47 Hous L Rev 877, 902–5 (discussing the impact of the Statute on Anne on the American approach to international copyright law).

[44] See Jane C Ginsburg and John M Kernochan, 'One Hundred and Two Years Later: The United States Joins the Berne Convention' (1988) 13 Colum VLA J L & the Arts 1.

Imperial Copyright Act in 1911. Some colonies did enact such laws, not surprisingly, the self-governing dominions were first to do so, as well as India.

Thus, the interests were spread unevenly between the colonial centre and the colonized periphery. It was not for the colonized to determine the new international copyright order, but for rather narrow local windows that the imperial order enabled.[45]

E. Colonial Copyright

How does the particular framework of the regulated subject matter intersect with the frameworks of legal transplants and of legal colonialism, discussed in the previous chapter? The focus is on the overlapping area of all three, as shown in Figure 2.1.

On the eve of the coming into force of the TRIPs Agreement in 1995, Paul Edward Geller explored the then-new phase of globalization of intellectual property through a legal transplants lens. He pointed to technological advancements as a reason for growth of cross-border diffusion, which served as a pressure to harmonize the series of national laws, which in turn was achieved by legal transplants. Geller discussed the Berne Convention as an 'instrument for transplanting copyright',[46] and pointed to the practical difficulties of interpreting an international legal instrument in various countries, each with its language and legal culture. This is

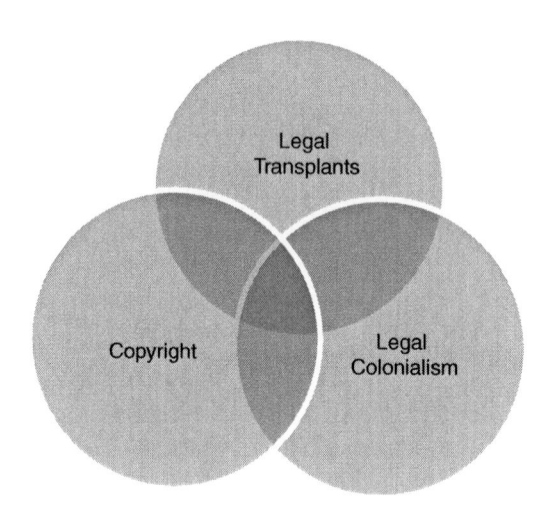

Fig. 2.1 Colonial copyright

---

[45] Before the enactment of the 1911 Copyright Act, few undertook this option. Section 27 allowed some local modifications as long as they had only local affects. This was a rarely used avenue. An example was India's different treatment of translations. See Bently, 'Copyright, Translations', above n 40.

[46] Paul Edward Geller, 'Legal Transplants in International Copyright: Some Problems with Method' (1994) 13 UCLA Pac Basin L J 199, 227.

indeed a useful and valid discussion that assists in exploring other patterns of legal transplants of copyright law, such as colonial copyright.[47]

Put in *legal transplants* language, the cultural exporters were the donors of the transplant and the cultural importers were the recipients of the law. The transplant was required to protect the authors of the donor country. Note that this is opposite to the medical transplant language, where the donor gives up an organ so that it saves the recipient. Using the legal transplants language on its own would thus be misleading.

Adding the legal colonialism framework onto that of legal transplants identifies the parties: the donor was the colonizer, the recipients were the colonized. The legal transplant was not structured according to the needs of the colonized people, but rather along the needs of the colonizer. Looking at the local cultural balance within many of the colonies, further explains this last proposition: there was not much of a chance that a colony would export cultural products in a way that would disrupt British authors.

Framing the discussion in terms of the legal subject matter at stake, draws our attention to three important features: first, the close ideological kinship of copyright law with the idea of progress, which in turn is also an important element of colonialism itself. This ideological affinity explains the colonizer's interests in enacting copyright law throughout the Empire. Second, it draws our attention to the hidden assumptions about authorship and the creative process that reflect a European (enlightened and progressive) image of creativity, excluding by default other forms. This feature exposes the uneven and asymmetric interests of the colonizer and the colonized. Third, the intangibility of intellectual works, explains the motivation in transplanting a similar (or even identical) law in as many territories as possible. If the legal transplant was to be effective throughout the Empire (and in fact, around the world), any major difference between the levels of protection had to be eliminated. Otherwise, it might have resulted in the creation of loopholes in the legal network. The subject matter required an international arrangement to be as unified as possible. Hence, we can expect to see a greater level of imperial coordination in areas which require such global coverage. Such protection was needed so as to protect the authors at home. It is also clear that the players in the field were not of equal power. Britain and perhaps some of the self-governing dominions were on the production and export end, while most other colonial territories were at most on the consuming and import end. The former were interested for their law to follow the works and protect their owners wherever they are, while the latter were either indifferent due to the inadequacy of the law to fit local culture, or, they were interested in (cheaper) access to knowledge and cultural content.[48]

---

[47] Geller mentions colonial copyright: 'The British Copyright Act of 1911 is another example: it was transplanted throughout the British Empire in the twentieth century, until such time as British colonies and dominions became independent and enacted their own copyright laws, more or less on the British model.' Ibid, at 200.

[48] The latter interest was made explicit by the Canadians. See Pierre-Emanuel Moyse, 'Colonial Copyright Redux: 1709 v. 1832' in Lionel Bently, Uma Suthersanen, and Paul Torremans (eds),

To realize the importance of the centralized imperial pattern of diffusion needed (in the colonizer's eyes) for copyright law, we can compare it to the diffusion of other fields of law.

One example is the diffusion of criminal law around the Empire. The need for criminal law is universal, meaning that all colonies and their motherland required such a field. In this sense, criminal law is one of general application. But in most aspects of criminal law in the nineteenth century, the laws were local, leaving international crimes, piracy in the high seas and the like to be regulated separately in a *sui generis* way. Criminal law can surely reflect and constitute local values: some acts might be considered criminal in one country but not in another. Hence, one could expect a general imperial framework that allows some local leeway. But, as Norman Abrams and Yoram Shachar showed, the pattern of diffusion of criminal law throughout the Empire took a somewhat strange route.[49] Instead of a unified criminal law imposed from above, or a series of local laws, they traced the route of the 1936 Criminal Code in Mandate Palestine back to the criminal law in Queensland, Australia, authored by its Chief Justice, Sir Samuel Walker Griffith (previously premier, and later Chief Justice of the High Court of Australia), and enacted there in 1899; the law was then copied and enacted in the Protectorate of Northern Nigeria in 1904, and upon the amalgamation of northern and southern Nigeria in 1914, it became the law there. In 1925, the now-Nigerian law served London as a model for criminal legislation for the East African colonies. This in turn served as the basis of the criminal law in Cyprus, from which it finally crossed the Mediterranean to become the Criminal law of Palestine. It is quite likely that other laws travelled in similar patterns around the Empire, in what we can today re-conceptualize, applying Anne-Marie Slaughter's terms, as an early case of an international network of the Empire's civil servants.[50] In Chapter 9 we will see a similar pattern of legal diffusion within the Empire, regarding the *sui generis* protection of news.[51]

Another example is the diffusion of company law. Ron Harris and Michael Crystal studied the enactment of Palestine's company law in 1929, and importantly, framed it in the legal transplant discourse.[52] The initial point of company law in the Empire, they observed, was a 'patchwork quilt of regimes',[53] that the British strived to harmonize. 'The subject matter of company law invited implementation from England and consistency across the Empire.'[54] They noted the importance of

---

Global Copyright: Three Hundred Years since the Statute of Anne, from 1709 to Cyberspace (Edward Elgar, 2010) 144. See also Seville, *The Internationalisation*, above n 3, at 16, who points to similar arguments by the Americans.

[49] Norman Abrams, 'Interpreting the Criminal Code Ordinance, 1936: The Untapped Well' (1972) 7 Isr L Rev 25; Yoram Shachar, 'The Sources of the Criminal Code Ordinance, 1936' (1979) 7 Tel-Aviv U L Rev 75 (Hebrew).

[50] Anne-Marie Slaughter, *A New World Order* (Princeton University Press, 2005).

[51] See also Lionel Bently, 'Copyright and the Victorian Internet: Telegraphic Property Laws in Colonial Australia' (2004) 38 Loy LA L Rev 71.

[52] Ron Harris and Michael Crystal, 'Some Reflections on the Transplantation of British Company Law in Post-Ottoman Palestine' (2009) 10 Theoretical Inq L 561.

[53] Ibid, at 569.   [54] Ibid, at 568.

the context: the legal commercial context, the relationship between the Colonial Office and the British staff in Jerusalem, and so on. Company law did reach a state of similarity of principle, but yet, it was not one law for all colonies.

Copyright law took a different path than criminal or company law, to a great extent due to its subject matter: as a legal field, it was rather independent (unlike company law that was to be studied together with partnership law, bankruptcy law, etc). Copyright law was not tied to land or territory like real property. Its reflection and constitution of values about creativity, culture, and knowledge were rather subtle, unlike the apparent connection of criminal law to social values. Moreover, it was in the Empire's interest to achieve greater coherence and uniformity, so to protect its own authors and copyright owners. Harmonization, like in the case of company law was not enough. A higher degree of uniformity was needed. In all of this, the local colonized people(s), were taken for granted.

We can now notice first buds of the framework of colonial copyright emerging in the literature. Pierre-Emmanuel Moyse used a similar (though not identical) framework to analyse the first copyright legislation of Lower Canada in 1832.[55] He applied Frederick Hayek's distinction of grown norms and made norms, and contrasted the English 1709 Statute of Anne with the Canadian 1832 Act using these terms,[56] as well as a distinction between a functionalist approach to legal transplants and a realist one.[57] Importantly, his approach is critical, and does not settle for the formal events. Moyse writes: '[C]olonial narratives are not always found in the positive manifestation of the law, in our case in the colonial copyright legislation, but rather in the subtext where the political and social tensions lie.'[58] This is a much needed approach, and the one undertaken here. Seville's study of the complicated copyright relationship between Britain and Canada during the nineteenth century provides yet another example. She discusses the ways in which the British tried to deal with the problem of cheap, unauthorized reprints of British works that were imported from the United States to Canada. She points to the political and commercial circumstances within Canada and how they played in the debate. The current work undertakes the further steps explicitly, and instead of examining colonial copyright from the donor's perspective, it looks at it from the recipient's side. The study goes beyond the self-governing dominions, and beyond 1911.

F. Conclusion

This chapter searched for the attributes of copyright law that bear most on our understanding the processes of the law's diffusion from one place to another. The discussion led to identify the ideological background of copyright law as it crystallized by the late nineteenth century. It was an ideology of the idea of progress. This feature corresponds to the enlightening version of colonialism.

---

[55] Moyse, 'Colonial Copyright Redux', above n 48.
[56] Ibid, at 155.   [57] Ibid, at 159.   [58] Ibid, at 146.

A second feature drew our attention to the hidden assumptions of copyright law, as to its main figure, that of the author and the creative process. Other kinds of authors and other modes of cultural production did not easily fit within the British colonial law, and by default, many indigenous forms of creativity were excluded from legal protection. This feature corresponds with the critical view of colonialism that emphasizes its overt and covert power relations.

A third feature was the physicality of the subject matter, or to be more precise, the absence of physicality. Intellectual works could easily cross political and physical borders within the Empire and beyond it. The challenge that faced the decision makers of the day was how to facilitate this imperial and international transfer, while protecting the copyright owners' rights and interests. The dual prism of legal transplants and of legal colonialism highlighted the unequal interests of the colonizers and the colonized. Each had a different cultural import–export balance, which was a result of language, cultural, and economic barriers that worked better for the colonizer than for the colonized.

For copyright scholars in the early twenty-first century, it is almost impossible not to notice the many contemporary parallels to the colonial and early international manifestations of copyright law, namely, globalization.[59] To be sure, there are many differences between colonial copyright and contemporary globalization. The earlier phase was voluntary for the countries that joined the new international conventions (but less so for the colonies); the contemporary phase of copyright globalization is rather aggressive for all those not in the leading loop.[60] The earlier phase went almost unnoticed and with little resistance, while the current phase meets much popular and political criticism.[61] The meeting point of the colonial and the local is now replaced with the meeting point of the global and the local, producing the 'glocal'.[62] There are more differences, but no doubt that current discussions of globalization can greatly benefit from the earlier experience.[63]

---

[59] Elsewhere I argued that Global Copyright should be evaluated on the background of a complex set of local factors: the legal system as a whole, the economy, cultural features, and unique political situation. See Michael Birnhack, 'Trading Copyright: Global Pressure on Local Culture' in Neil Weinstock Netanel (ed), *The Development Agenda: Global Intellectual Property and Developing Countries* (Oxford University Press, 2008) 365.

[60] The patterns of current IP globalization are many, ranging from rather blunt acts of power (see Pamela Samuelson, 'The Copyright Grab' (1996) Wired 4.01), to sophisticated diplomacy of widening circles of negotiations (see Peter Drahos and Ruth Mayne (eds), *Global Intellectual Property Rights: Knowledge, Access and Development* (Palgrave Macmillan, 2002)), forum shifting (see Laurence R Helfer, 'Regime Shifting: The TRIPS Agreement and New Dynamics of International Intellectual Property Lawmaking' (2004) 29 Yale J Int'l L 1), and bundling copyright law to other issues (see Peter K Yu, 'The First Ten Years of the TRIPS Agreement: TRIPS and Its Discontents' (2006) 10 Marq Intell Prop L Rev 369).

[61] For the political response, see *The Development Agenda*, above n 59.

[62] Michael D Birnhack, 'Global Copyright, Local Speech' (2006) 24 Cardozo Arts & Ent L J 491.

[63] The globalization discourse can further benefit from its discussion alongside the framework of legal transplants. David Nelken is somewhat sceptical about this option: 'it is doubtful whether everything that is currently going on in the way of legal transfer can be captured by the term "globalisation" without giving the term too expansive a meaning'. See David Nelken, 'Towards a Sociology of Legal Adaptation' in David Nelken and Johannes Fees (eds), *Adapting Legal Cultures* (Hart Publishing, 2001) 29. For a more optimistic view of the globalization–transplants discourse, see

We now have a conceptual model to assist us in explaining the legal developments. It focuses on the overlapping area of legal transplants, legal colonialism, and the regulated subject matter of copyright law. This overlapping area is the scene of *colonial copyright*. It is a legal and cultural category of its own. It is time to move on to greater detail and historical evidence. Once we have the dots and know how to connect them, it is time to fill the drawing with colours. The model guides us as to the order of the task. We begin with collecting data from many colonies and searching for patterns of colonial diffusion of the legal transplant. This is the task of the next chapter. Thereafter, we shall move on to see how the transplant was received in Mandate Palestine.

Ralf Michaels, 'Comparative Law by Numbers? Legal Origins Thesis, Doing Business Reports and the Silence of Traditional Comparative Law' (2009) 57 AJCL 765, 787–8.

3
The Making of British Colonial Copyright

A. Introduction

How did *colonial copyright* develop? What were the patterns of its transplanting and diffusion? Copyright historians have thus far documented important segments of this process, focusing mostly on internal British legislation that dealt with colonial and international copyright, on British relationship with the English speaking colonies (especially Canada), and on the Anglo–American relationship.[1] This is highly valuable research. However, it is mostly told from the centre, namely from a British point of view. Exceptions are specific discussions of Canada and Australia,[2] and Catherine Seville's discussion of the international dimension, tying it to the British, imperial and American dimensions.[3] Other colonies, especially those which were not self governing dominions, have not yet deserved sufficient attention. A second feature of the current literature on copyright history is that most of it ends with the enactment of the 1911 Imperial Copyright Act (or earlier).[4] From a copyright law perspective, the 'long nineteenth century' ended with the enactment of the 1911 Act, but while closing some debates, it opened new ones.

This chapter fills in the immediate gap as to the fate of the 1911 Act in the colonies and supplements the historical record with the story of colonial copyright in the second decade of the twentieth century. The entire project undertaken in this

---

[1] See eg Simon Nowell-Smith, *International Copyright Law and the Publisher in the Reign of Queen Victoria* (Oxford University Press, 1968); John Feather, *Publishing, Piracy and Politics: An Historical Study of Copyright in Britain* (Mansell, 1994) 149–72; Brad Sherman and Lionel Bently, *The Making of Modern Intellectual Property Law: The British Experience, 1760–1911* (Cambridge University Press, 1999) 136–7; Catherine Seville, *Literary Copyright Reform in Early Victorian England: The Framing of The 1842 Copyright Act* (Cambridge University Press, 1999); Ronan Deazley, *On the Origin of the Right to Copy: Charting the Movement of Copyright Law in Eighteenth-Century Britain (1695–1775)* (Hart Publishing, 2004); Ronan Deazley, *Rethinking Copyright: History, Theory, Language* (Edward Elgar, 2006); Catherine Seville, *The Internationalisation of Copyright Law: Books, Buccaneers and the Black Flag in the Nineteenth Century* (Cambridge University Press, 2006); Isabella Alexander, *Copyright Law and the Public Interest in the Nineteenth Century* (Hart, 2010) 10.

[2] See eg Pierre-Emanuel Moyse, 'Colonial Copyright Redux: 1709 v 1832' in Lionel Bently, Uma Suthersanen, and Paul Torremans (eds), *Global Copyright: Three Hundred Years since the Statute of Anne, from 1709 to Cyberspace* (Edward Elgar, 2010) 144; Jeremy Finn, 'Particularism versus Uniformity: Factors Shaping the Development of Australasian Intellectual Property Law in the Nineteenth Century' (2000) 6 Aust J Legal Hist 113.

[3] Seville, *The Internationalisation*, above n 1.

[4] See eg Sherman and Bently, *The Making*, above n 1; Alexander, *Copyright Law*, above n 1, at 11. The other sources cited above end their research even earlier.

book attempts to provide the view from the colonies alongside—and occasionally in contradiction—to the imperial point of view. Thus, this chapter contextualizes the historical developments as patterns of the diffusion of colonial copyright, providing not only a general description, but also explanations of additional configurations within the overall picture.

Lionel Bently provided an overview of colonial copyright in the nineteenth century (ending with the 1911 Act), concluding that initially, there was no imperial strategy as to colonial intellectual property law and only towards the end of that century there was a growing desire for uniformity.[5] The discussion here nuances these observations: I argue that the initial phase did have a colonial copyright strategy, though a very loose one: it was one that placed only British interests on the stage. The second phase was, as Bently argues, one of growing uniformity. In the third phase, post-1911, the desire for uniformity turned into a deliberate and coordinated imperial strategy. The change in policy was towards greater imperial involvement and harder forms of law.

The discussion is guided by the lessons of the previous chapters: We should not take it for granted that the law was transplanted as is out of thin air, but instead, ask why, how, and when this was done, and query the law's reception processes. We should study the patterns of legal diffusion on the background of understanding the importance of the rule of law in the project of the Empire's building, on the background of the imperial typology, while appreciating the wide spectrum of possible law-making procedures within the Empire, and finally, with bearing in mind that imperial law did not always fill a void and met (some) local laws. The picture presented here is based on the back-and-forth methodology discussed in Chapter 1, which instructs us to gather individual data from as many colonies as possible and then deduce general patterns.

We shall see that the imperial transplanting project was not confined to the Empire, large as it was. It both affected and was affected by a parallel discussion, within an emerging paradigm of international copyright law.[6] Many of the cross-border challenges within the Empire paralleled those outside it, between Britain and foreign countries. Accordingly, we can identify three developments in the process of British colonial copyright. On a temporal dimension, these developments partially overlap and indeed, mutually reinforce each other.

The first development took place within the Empire, until the enactment of the 1886 International Copyright Act.[7] This was when both the imperial and international challenges and the British interests became clearer, and first solutions were sought. The second and interrelated development was the international one, culminating with the 1886 Berne Convention for the Protection of Literary and Artistic Works. It converged with the first development. The Convention

---

[5] Lionel Bently, 'The "Extraordinary Multiplicity" of Intellectual Property Laws in the British Colonies in the Nineteenth Century' (2011) 12 Theoretical Inq L 161. See also Seville, *The Internationalisation*, above n 1, at 142.

[6] See also Seville, *The Internationalisation*, above n 1, at 10–11; Bently, 'The Extraordinary Multiplicity', ibid, at 192.

[7] International Copyright Act 1886, 49 & 50 Vict c 33 (1886).

established the international framework for copyright protection which lasted for over a century. It was amended along the years several times. Within the period discussed here, the Berlin revision of 1908 was crucial. The third development was again within the imperial sphere, in the aftermath of the 1908 Berlin revision of the Berne Convention. A first component of this phase refers to the attempts to reorganize imperial copyright law, culminating in the 1911 Imperial Copyright Act. A second component was the aftermath of the 1911 Act and the efforts to implement, harmonize, and unify it throughout the Empire. The chapter progresses along these developments. It builds on the existing literature as to the first two dimensions as well as on the relevant legislation,[8] commentaries of the nineteenth century, and as to the third phase, on primary sources.

B. Intra-Imperial Copyright until 1886

Copyright's feature as an intangible asset meant that creative works could easily cross political and physical borders in all directions. A series of factors determined whether the works actually did cross the borders, and in which direction. These were cultural factors (language, literacy rates, cultural proximity of the original author and the potential readers), economic factors (a viable market, availability of raw materials, active traders), and technological factors (printing facilities). Thus, and especially where these barriers of entry were low, there was a motivation to produce cheap copies and export them to the place of demand. There was an opposite British motivation, namely the interests of British authors and industries, to attach legal protection to the works. The law was designed so as to follow the flow of the intellectual works.

As the English language became more popular around the world, as literacy rates improved (to a large extent due to colonial emphasis on education), as printing technology became cheaper and more available, and markets developed, the barriers were lowered. John Feather points also to the jurisprudential changes, namely copyright legislation in the relevant markets for British works, especially the American and French markets.[9] Accordingly, there was a growing British economic interest in protecting British authors and content industries, such as printers and publishers. The commercial interests were accompanied with an ideological motivation to spread copyright law, as it served progress, just like the enlightened version of the imperial project at large. However, the ideology came only second, after the commercial interests.

By the late nineteenth century several copyright laws were in place around the world, most notably in Britain (as of 1709), in the United States (1790, with some predecessors in the individual colonies/states), and several other European

---

[8] British legislation mentioned here is available at Lionel Bently and Martin Kretschmer (eds), *Primary Sources on Copyright (1450–1900)*, available at http://www.copyrighthistory.org, alongside valuable commentaries by Ronan Deazley.

[9] Feather, *Publishing*, above n 1, at 150–1.

countries, such as Denmark (1741), and France (1791).[10] As the British Empire itself expanded, technology developed and authors established themselves as professionals, the copyright challenges surfaced. Was a work published by a British author protected in Grenada or in Canada? Were works first published in India or South Africa, protected in London? The initial British response to the challenges had several legal prongs, on the imperial level, discussed here, and on the international level, discussed in the next section.

The road to achieve an equal level of protection for all authors, British and colonial, for all their works, whether published or not and wherever first published, was a long one with several hurdles. The first response was internal, within the contours of the Empire, divided into two elements. The Copyright Act 1814 and then the Copyright Act 1842, protected authors of literary works first published in the United Kingdom (whether the authors were British, colonial, or foreign), throughout the Empire.[11] But the 1814 and 1842 Acts did not cover works of fine arts. They referred only to those works that were published, and as the 1842 Act was later interpreted, it referred only to works first published in the United Kingdom. These three conditions meant that many works were not protected. Non-textual works were protected in separate laws. Only twenty years later, the Fine Art Copyright Act 1862 (which addressed drawings, paintings, and photographs) provided artists with similar Empire-wide protection.[12] It was unclear whether unpublished works were protected by common law, or not protected at all. The House of Lords ruled in *Routledge v Low* (1868) that works first published in the colonies were not protected by the 1842 Act.[13] The result was that copyright

---

[10] For US copyright history, see Bruce W Bugbee, *Genesis of American Patent and Copyright Law* (Public Affairs Press, 1967); Lyman Ray Patterson, *Copyright in Historical Perspective* (Vanderbilt University Press, 1968); Dotan Oliar, 'The (Constitutional) Convention on IP: A New Reading' (2009) 57 UCLA L Rev 421.
For Denmark's law, see JAL Sterling, *World Copyright Law* (2nd edn, Thomson Professional Pub, 2003) paras 1.09, 80.05.
For the French copyright law, see Jane C Ginsburg, 'A Tale of Two Copyrights: Literary Property in Revolutionary France and America' in Brad Sherman and Alain Strowel (eds), *Of Authors and Origins* (Oxford University Press, 1994) 131, 143–51 and Christophe Geiger, 'The Influence (Past and Present) of the Statute of Anne in France' in Bently et al (eds), *Global Copyright*, above n 2, at 122.
[11] Copyright Act 1814, 54 Geo III, c 156; An Act to Amend the Law of Copyright, 5 & 6 Vict c 45 (1842) (known as the Copyright Amendment Act (1842)). For the background of the 1814 Act and its scope, see Bently, 'The Extraordinary Multiplicity', above n 5, at 172–3. For a thorough discussion of the 1842 Act, see Seville, *Literary Copyright Reform*, above n 1.
[12] Fine Art Copyright Act 25 & 26 Vict c 68 (1862). For discussion, see Ronan Deazley, 'Breaking the Mould? The Radical Nature of the Fine Arts Copyright Bill 1862' in Ronan Deazley, Martin Kretschmer, Lionel Bently (eds), *Privilege and Property: Essays on the History of Copyright* (Open Book Publishers, 2010) 289.
[13] (1868) LR 3 HL 100. An American author, Maria Cummins, published her book in London. During the London publication, she stayed for a few days in Canada, and assigned the copyright to Low. Routledge then reproduced the work for one-eighth of Low's price. Low sued in London, and won the case. The House of Lords affirmed the requirement of first publication in the UK as a condition for British copyright protection. See discussion in Augustine Birrell, *Seven Lectures on The Law and History of Copyright in Books* (Cassell & Co Ltd, 1899) 151–2; Walter Arthur Copinger and F E Skone James, *Copinger on the Law of Copyright in Works of Literature, Art, Agriculture, Photography, Music and the Drama* (6th edn, Sweet & Maxwell, 1927) 298; Seville, *The Internationalisation*, above n 1, at 92.

protection was partial (published works of certain kinds) and asymmetric (only for British works in the colonies, not vice versa). During the nineteenth century these problems became increasingly apparent.

How was a British copyright owner to enforce his rights, if infringed in a crown colony? More precisely, how was a copyright owner who first published the book in the United Kingdom able to sue elsewhere? Under the 1842 Copyright Act the copyright owner could sue in the territory where the infringement took place.[14] Indeed, such suits were brought in some colonies, such as the first copyright case in South Africa, brought by Charles Dickens, in 1861.[15] However, for such a suit to materialize, a sufficiently functioning legal system had to be in place in the colony. This was the case in the Cape, but not in many other parts of the Empire.

While the British protected British works, they were less concerned with protecting colonial works. The asymmetry is apparent in a series of colonial, mid-nineteenth century laws that installed a levy system in the colonies, regarding British works only. The Acts were the result of the Colonial Copyright Act 1847, better known as the Foreign Reprints Act.[16] It partially overruled the 1842 Act and allowed importation of unauthorized reprints of British works done outside the United Kingdom into the colonies, subject to 'reasonable protection' of the British books. This protection was applied in the form of imposing levies, to be paid to the copyright owners. The Act permitted the colonies to legislate on the matter, at their own will, but under London's scrutiny. In other words, it was an opt-in, soft legal scheme, rather than an opt-out or a hard form of law. Most of the colonies did not yet have a local copyright law, but nevertheless, they were encouraged to protect the British author (or publisher). This was not a hidden agenda. It was explicit and straightforward. Between 1848 and 1857, nineteen colonies enacted such laws, often under the title 'An Act to regulate the Importation of Books *and to protect the British Author*', as read the title of

---

[14] Section 15 of the 1842 Act instructed that 'such offender be liable to a special action on the case at the suit of the proprietor of such copyright, to be brought in any court of record in that part of the British Dominions in which the offence shall be committed'.

[15] Dickens sued for an alleged infringement of his *Great Expectations*, by a local newspaper, at the very time that he was lobbying for international copyright law. See *Dickens v Eastern Province Herald* (1861) 4 Searle 33, and discussion in Graham Glover, 'Maybe the Courts are not Such a "Bleak House" After All? Or "Please, Sir, I Want Some More Copyright"' (2002) 119 S African L J 63. As Glover discusses, Dickens brought many copyright cases in various places and was active in lobbying for international copyright protection. Owen Dean, who studied the history of copyright law in South Africa, found that there were only eight copyright cases between 1861 and 1917, when the Imperial Act came into force. Six of these dealt with British performing rights. See Owen H Dean, *The Application of the Copyright Act, 1978 to Works Made Prior to 1979* (Doctorate Dissertation, University of Stellenbosch, 1988) 224 (number of cases), 234 (identity of plaintiffs).

[16] An Act to amend the Law relating to the Protection in the Colonies of Works entitled to Copyright in the United Kingdom, 10 & 11 Vict c 95. In the nineteenth century treaties the Act was often referred to as the Colonial Copyright Act. See eg William Briggs, *The Law of International Copyright* (Stevens and Haynes, 1906).

the first of these laws stated, in New Brunswick's 1848 Act.[17] Canada was the only known colony to resist.[18]

The levies were to reach the author, after reducing a collecting fee. The colonial reprint Acts varied from one colony to another and were applied inconsistently. On the one hand, British authors (and publishers) were dissatisfied. In 1889 the English Copyright Association published a compilation of colonial acts then in force. The laws varied so much, that the Association's Secretary wrote in the introduction that 'it is practically impossible for the injured Author to learn the extent to which he has been wronged'.[19] He further complained that '[t]he amount of duties actually collected seldom find its ways to the rightful owner', and that some colonies (notably Canada) did not require stamping the legitimate copies.[20] His conclusion was that the colonial Acts 'are practically useless in most instances, and illusory in all, because no one has sufficient interest in carrying them out to give them proper attention'.[21] Moreover, the higher the levies, the more expensive were the British books, resulting in a stronger incentive to 'pirate' them, especially in the United States, and then to channel the pirated copies into the colonies.

The House of Lords' ruling that the 1842 Act did not extend to colonial works that were first published in the colonies (or elsewhere, but in any case, not first published in the United Kingdom), meant that the colonies had to enact local laws, if interested, so to protect their own authors. The self-governing dominions were at the top of the list in this regard. Australia, Canada, Newfoundland, New Zealand, and South Africa, had English reading audiences and also local authors writing in English. Indeed, each of the dominions (and most of their provinces) enacted local copyright laws during the nineteenth century, as well as India.[22] In some cases the

---

[17] Emphasis added. See Frederic R Daldy, 'Introduction' in *The Colonial Copyright Acts* (Longmans & Co, 1889). The colonies that enacted these were: in 1848: New Brunswick, Nova Scotia, Prince Edward Island, Barbados, Bermuda, Bahamas; in 1849: Newfoundland, Saint Christopher, Antigua; between 1850 and 1856: St Lucia, Canada, British Guiana, St Vincent, Mauritius, Grenada, Cape of Good Hope, Nevis, Natal, Jamaica. In 1874 Trinidad became the twentieth colony to enact a similar law.

[18] Seville, *The Internationalisation*, above n 1, at 87; Moyse, 'Colonial Copyright Redux', above n 2, at 159–63.

[19] Daldy, *The Colonial Copyright Acts*, above n 17, at vii.

[20] Ibid, at viii.

[21] Ibid, at ix. Copinger made a similar observation, nineteen years earlier: 'These measures are next to inoperative, and the whole thing is little better than delusion.' See Walter Arthur Copinger, *The Law of Copyright in Works of Literature and Art* (Stevens & Haynes, 1870) 236. Nothing much had changed until at least 1889, when Birrell commented that the 'Act was a ludicrous failure'. Birrell, *Seven Lectures*, above n 13, at 216.

[22] Lower Canada's first copyright law dates to 1832, borrowing from the US law rather than the British, and to be enacted in the Province of Canada in 1841 and then adopted by the Dominion of Canada in 1868. See Moyse, 'Colonial Copyright Redux', above n 2; Myra J Tawfik, 'History in Balance: Copyright and Access to Knowledge' in Michael Geist (ed), *From 'Radical Extremism' to 'Balanced Copyright': Canadian Copyright and the Digital Agenda* (Irwin Law, 2010) 69, 79–83.

In New Zealand, a Copyright Ordinance was enacted quite early in the day, as the eighteenth law passed by the new colony, in 1842. See Geoff McLay, 'New Zealand and the Imperial Copyright Tradition' in Ysolde Gendreau and Uma Suthersanen (eds), *A Shifting Empire: 100 Years of the Copyright Act 1911* (Edward Elgar, forthcoming 2012); Finn, 'Particularism', above n 2, at 127.

India, not a self-governing dominion, was next, when it enacted Act No 20, 1847 ('An Act for the encouragement of learning in the territories subject to the Government of the East India Company, by defining and providing for the enforcement of the right called Copyright therein').

motivation was local, as in the case of New Zealand, where a local clergyman lobbied for legal protection for his book,[23] or a result of lobbying by interest groups, as in Australia.[24] Of the other colonies, only India enacted local copyright laws that protected local works.[25]

As for crown colonies, which had far less local legislative powers compared to the self-governing dominions, the question of whether British copyright law applied, remained somewhat unclear. The general pattern of legal colonialism in these colonies was to set a date of reception of British law for each colony. English law was applied in the receiving colony from the set date of reception, subject to limitations and other conditions,[26] either instead of, or alongside pre-colonial laws. The received body of law included statutes of general application, and common law and equity principles. Was copyright law included in any of these laws?

The formal answer is that different contemporary commentators who studied copyright law in some of these colonies dispute the status of copyright law in the respectively studied colonies prior to the 1911 Imperial Copyright Act. To the extent that unpublished works were protected by common law principles in the United Kingdom, one can argue that these works should have deserved the same level of protection in the colonies. As for published works, which were protected under statute, the question was whether copyright law was one of 'general application'. These doubts were made explicit by the government of India, in the preamble to its 1847 Act, stating that 'for the encouragement of learning, it is desirable that the existence of the said right should be placed beyond doubt, and that the said right should be made capable of easy enforcement in every part of the said Territories'.

The shorter and practical answer is that in most other colonies, it did not matter very much, since internal copyright law (as opposed to external law, to protect British authors) remained a virtual legal reality for quite a while during colonial times, and in some cases also for some time after colonialism ended.

In Australia, the date of reception of English law was 1828, but being a self-governing dominion, each of the colonies enacted its own copyright law, and some were slower than others (see Robert Burrell, 'Copyright Reform in the Early Twentieth Century: the View from Australia' (2006) 27 J of Leg Hist 239, 242–3). Victoria was the first, enacting its copyright Act in 1869. See Finn, 'Particularism', above n 2, at 127–8.

In the colonies that were to form the Union of South Africa in 1910, the British copyright law applied as of 1842. See Dean, *The Application*, above n 15, at 224, 233. Specific local legislation followed, first as to importation of copyrighted works to the Cape colony (1854), then the Copyright Act 1873 and subsequent amendments, followed by the other colonies. See Dean, ibid, at 237–55 (Cape), at 255–88 (Natal—an importation Act in 1856 and a copyright Act in 1896), at 288–304 (Transvaal, first Act in 1887). The Orange Free State did not enact a copyright Act. Ibid, at 304–5.

[23] McLay, 'New Zealand', ibid.
[24] Finn, 'Particularism', above n 2, at 127.
[25] For the development of copyright law in India, see Shubha Ghosh, 'A Roadmap for TRIPS: Copyright and Film in Colonial and Independent India' (2011) 1(2) Queen Mary J IP 146.
[26] Later on we will see such a limitation in Palestine, subjecting the received English law to 'the circumstances of Palestine and its inhabitants and the limits of His Majesty's jurisdiction permits'. Palestine Order in Council 1922, s 46.

The Making of British Colonial Copyright 67

For example, the date of reception for the Straits Settlements (composed of modern day Singapore and a few areas in Malaysia) was 1826, but commentators note that there are no reported cases from the Straits Settlements courts or from Singapore, until the late 1980s.[27] A similar report refers to Malay States (the federated and un-federated, as well as North Borneo and the Sarawak), about which a commentator wrote: 'There is, however, no evidence that these laws [the British copyright laws of the nineteenth century] were actually applied or that any copyright cases arose for adjudication in the Settlements.'[28] Moreover, 'At the time, it was felt that the need for a law of copyright did not arise, nor was there any public demand for it'.[29] As for Nigeria, there seems to be a debate, with one commentator arguing that during colonialism, the 1709 Statue of Anne applied there through the general reception mechanism until 1912, when the Imperial Act came into force,[30] whereas another commentator argues that common law did not include copyright and the British copyright acts were not considered 'of general application', hence no copyright law was in place until 1912.[31] In any case, the latter commentator states that '[i]t does not appear that much notice was taken of this statute', referring to the 1912 enactment.[32] Another example is that of Kenya, where the date of reception was 1897. According to one commentator, copyright law was considered to be of general application and applied as of that year.[33] Regarding Ghana we learn that 'literacy came rather late, therefore it took some time before copyright could make any headway', and that: 'The Imperial Copyright Act did not have any impact on the local situation, as can be seen for instance, from the absence of copyright cases in our own law reports until 1964.'[34] As for South Africa, a self-governing dominion, a legal historian comments that: 'There is nothing in the development of the South African law to suggest that British common law copyright was ever accepted or adopted in South African law.'[35]

Two intermediate conclusions can be drawn from these examples: the first is that until the enactment of the 1911 Imperial Act, there was uncertainty as to the

---

[27] Ng-Loy Wee Loon, *Law of Intellectual Property of Singapore* (Thomson Sweet & Maxwell Asia, 2008) 59. Loon reports the case of *Ng Sui Nam v Butterworth's & Co (Publishers) Ltd* [1987] SLR 66 (CA), which cites July 1912 as the date for the 1911 Imperial Copyright Act to come into force in Singapore. In 1914 the Act was modified, renamed, and supplemented with a Copyright Ordinance. See also George Wei, *The Law of Copyright in Singapore* (Singapore National Printers, 1989) 79.
[28] Khaw Lake Tee, *Copyright Law in Malaysia* (Butterworths Asia, 1994) 3.
[29] Ibid, at 4.
[30] Peter Ocheme, *The Law and Practice of Copyright in Nigeria* (Ahmadu Bello University Press, 2000) 9.
[31] Egerton Uvieghara, 'Copyright Protection in Nigeria: New Trends and Prospects' in Bankole Sodipo and Bunmi Fagbemi (eds), *Nigeria's Foreign Investment Laws and Intellectual Property Rights* (Centre of Commercial Law Studies, Queen Mary University, 1994) 158.
[32] Ibid.
[33] John Waruingi Chege, *Copyright Law and Publishing in Kenya* (Kenya Literature Bureau, 1978) 97.
[34] Andrew Ofoe Amegatcher, *Ghanaian Law of Copyright* (Omega, 1993) 3.
[35] Dean, *The Application*, above n 15, at 207–8. The British imperial law in South Africa met Dutch law, including copyright law, but Dean suggests that: 'It may well be that the 19th century South African lawyers were in a blissful ignorance of the availability of copyright protection under the Roman-Dutch common law.' Ibid, at 223.

application of copyright law in the colonies. The self-governing dominions and India enacted local laws to remove this doubt, but no other colonies followed suit. The second conclusion is that to the extent we know, it was not uncommon for the law to remain only in the books, before or after 1911.

Another pattern that emerges from the research conducted as to various former colonies (self-governing dominions included), is that in most cases the driving force to enact local laws and then the first to bring cases to local courts, were foreigners, namely, British copyright owners and associations.[36] Later on we will see a similar pattern in Mandate Palestine, though the activation of the law did not take as long as in the above mentioned examples.[37]

Thus, as Bently argues, there was no deliberate strategy as to colonial copyright, but there was a goal and there was a policy: to protect British authors throughout the Empire, disregarding local needs in the colonies. When the British spoke of colonial copyright in the nineteenth century, they meant their own copyright in the colonies, rather than the colonies' copyright laws. The Foreign Reprints Act 1847 was the focal point of this policy. As far as British authors were concerned, the law was centralized; under the 1842 Act they were to enjoy empire-wide protection for their works first published in the United Kingdom. Practice was a far cry from this policy. The 1847 Act made concessions to the colonies and the form of legislation was softer, enabling local legislation but not demanding it, and in any case, subject to British scrutiny and veto.

The solution to the imperial challenges was finally achieved with the enactment of the International Copyright Act 1886, which was to implement the Berne Convention. The 1886 Act equalized the level for all works: British and colonial works, whether published in the United Kingdom or in any of the colonies, and of all kinds were protected throughout the Empire. Registration of works was to be either local, within a colony, or in the United Kingdom. The imperial copyright level was thus tidied up to some extent, though in most of the colonies there was no local copyright law.

C. International Copyright: 1886–1911

The British response to the cross-border challenges, of protecting British authors throughout the colonies and spreading copyright law throughout the Empire, was

---

[36] In New Zealand, although the 1842 Ordinance was a result of the efforts a local lobbyist, McLay comments that 'the major driver for modern intellectual property in New Zealand was overseas influence'. See 'New Zealand', above n 22. In South Africa, the first copyright case was brought by Charles Dickens, and six of the first eight cases litigated prior to 1917 (when the Imperial Copyright Act became the law), dealt with rights of British dramatists. See Dean, *The Application*, above n 15, at 234. In the Straits Settlements, the British parties directed their not always successful efforts at local legislation in the 1930s, especially the Performing Rights Society (PRS). See Lake Tee, *Copyright Law in Malaysia*, above n 28, at 4–5.

[37] See Ch 7. This pattern reinforces the call to study the micro level of individual action, to better understand a legal transplant. See Michele Graziadei, 'Legal Transplants and the Frontiers of Legal Knowledge' (2009) 12 Theoretical Inq L 723.

only a first step. There were other jurisdictions outside the Empire, some read English, and chief among them was the United States. However, as in the Empire, not all countries had the same cultural import–export balance, and thus their interests varied. Those that did share similar concerns joined together. Once translations became available in non-English speaking jurisdictions, the costs of spreading intellectual works across borders were further lowered and new markets emerged. The legal response needed to face two interrelated challenges: first, how to protect foreign works in the United Kingdom and in the Empire. This challenge faced other countries too, especially France.[38] The second challenge was how to protect British (and colonial) works in foreign countries.[39]

As for the first challenge, protecting foreign works in the Empire, the response was a legal structure that included first, a general law authorizing the protection of foreign works. During the mid-nineteenth century, Parliament enacted several, rather clumsy, International Copyright Acts which provided protection for certain foreign works. Each of the laws required clarification, which resulted in amendments, in most cases further obscuring the legal situation.[40] Second, the response included a bilateral treaty with a foreign country, followed by an Order in Council effectuating the treaty.[41] The result was a series of bilateral agreements, each promulgated in the United Kingdom by an Order in Council. Similar strategy was applied in other European countries, resulting in Copinger's observation at the time that there were 'a large number' of such orders.[42] Ricketson documented seventy-one of these.[43] The treaties and subsequent legislation also answered the second challenge, of protecting British (and colonial) works in the foreign countries. But it became clear that the network of agreements was too complicated to handle. It was difficult to maintain and had large gaps. An international solution was needed, one that would go beyond the Empire's borders and would streamline the international protection.[44]

---

[38] Sherman and Bently, *The Making*, above n 1, at 111–12 (France was the main engine in promoting international copyright).

[39] Sherman and Bently, *The Making*, above n 1, at 112, argue: 'The primary motivation behind the calls for international copyright in the United Kingdom was the protection of British interests (which extended not only to the United Kingdom but also to its colonies and dominions.'

[40] An Act for Securing to Authors in certain Cases the Benefit of International Copyright 1838, 1 & 2 Vict c 59; An Act to Amend the Law relating to International Copyright 1844, 7 & 8 Vict c 12.

[41] See eg An Act to enable Her Majesty to carry into effect a Convention with France on the subject of Copyright 1852, 15 & 16 Vict c 12.

[42] *Copinger on the Law of Copyright*, above n 13, at 271.

[43] Sam Ricketson, *The Berne Convention for the Protection of Literary and Artistic Works: 1886–1986* (Kluwer, 1987) 37, where he provided a graphic network, showing the agreements. See also Seville, *The Internationalisation*, above n 1, at 54–6.

[44] Contemporary comparisons are inevitable. Despite the global harmonizing effect of the TRIPs Agreement, we witness another layer of copyright protection over the last decade, in the form of a series of bilateral Free Trade Agreements. The contents of these is usually regarded as TRIPs +, meaning that it adds further protections above those required by TRIPs. For discussion of this process, see Peter Drahos with John Braithwaite, *Information Feudalism: Who Owns the Knowledge Economy?* (New Press, 2002) 85; Michael D Birnhack, 'Global Copyright, Local Speech' (2006) 24 Cardozo Arts & Ent L J 491, 513–16.

Towards the end of the nineteenth century, a solution was finally achieved, in the formation of the Berne Convention for the Protection of Literary and Artistic Works of 1886.[45] The first signatories were the European powers of the time: Belgium, France, Germany, Italy, Spain,[46] Switzerland, and the United Kingdom, as well as Tunisia (all signed in 1887), later joined by Luxemburg (1888), Norway (1896), Monaco (1899), and Japan (1899).[47] Local British legislation was needed to facilitate the internationalization.[48] By the time of the 1911 Imperial Copyright Act (yet to be discussed), Denmark (1903), Sweden (1904), and Portugal (1911) joined the Berne Convention. The United States participated in the discussions, but was notably absent from the signatory list. This remained so for more than 100 years, until its cultural balance shifted and it was no longer a net importer of cultural works, but rather a net exporter of such works.[49] Importantly for the discussion later on of Mandate Palestine, the Austro-Hungarian Empire and the Ottoman Empire did not join the Berne Union. In order to achieve reciprocal copyright with countries that were not Berne Union members, the old legal scheme, of bilateral agreements was needed.[50]

The Berne Convention established the Union for the protection of the rights of authors and set the principle of international copyright for decades: it required minimal standards for legal protection: it set the floor and allowed each signatory to determine its own ceiling. The Convention protected unpublished and published works, subject to formalities in the originating country (Article 2). The protected works could be literary, dramatic, musical compositions, or works of fine art (Article 4). It regulated translations (Articles 5–6), and serial novels (Article 7). The Convention enabled each country to decide about exceptions (Article 8). The bundle of rights included reproduction, public performances (Article 9), and adaptations (Article 10).

But setting the same minimal level of protection was not enough. A stronger mechanism of reciprocal protection was needed. The principle of national treatment was to achieve this goal. Article 2 (in the 1886 text) required that the member states provide copyright protection for published or unpublished works of authors of all member states, with the same level of protection applied to its own nationals.

---

[45] For the history of the Convention, see Ricketson, *The Berne Convention*, above n 43, at 39–80; Feather, *Publishing*, above n 1, at 163–5. Victor Hugo was particularly instrumental in promoting the international solution, in his role as President of the *Association Littéraire et Artistique Internationale* (ALAI).

[46] For the Spanish interests, see Jose Bellido, 'Colonial Copyright Extensions: Spain at the Berne Convention (1883–1899)' (2011) 58 J Copyright Soc'y of the USA 243.

[47] For the current list of member states and the dates of their joining, see http://www.wipo.int/treaties/en/ShowResults.jsp?lang = en&treaty_id = 15.

[48] International Copyright Act 1886, 49 & 50 Vict c 33.

[49] Jane C Ginsburg and John M Kernochan, 'One Hundred and Two Years Later: The United States Joins the Berne Convention' (1988) 13 Colum VLA J L & Arts 1.

[50] eg the bilateral agreement between the United States and South Africa 1924, as discussed in A J C Copeling, *Copyright Law in South Africa* (Butterworths, 1969) 272–5.

Thus, the Convention required an equal protection of all member states' authors, in any of those states.[51]

Within two decades of its existence, it was clear that the Convention required some changes. An 1896 international conference in Paris added minor changes and set another conference several years later. This finally took place in Berlin, in 1908.[52] The discussions ended with a revised text: the Berlin Revision of 1908. The principle of national treatment was maintained,[53] but the revised text instructed that the enjoyment of copyright should not be subject to any formality. Thus, registration, deposit, or notice, the three typical formal conditions of copyright protection were no longer required. Protection of foreign works became much easier. The revised Convention protected literary works, fine arts, photography, dramatic works, musical compositions, as well as translations, adaptations, and cinematography. The required duration of the protection was for the life of the author and fifty years after death. The bundle of rights covered reproduction, adaptations, and public performances. The revised text also established the Office of the International Union for the Protection of Literary and Artistic Works, placed under the auspice of the Swiss government (later to be subsumed by WIPO). Article 26 allowed that 'contracting countries shall have the power to accede to the present Convention at any time for their colonies or foreign possessions'. The revised text came into force in 1910.

D. A New Imperial Order: 1886–1911–1917

The state of copyright law in Britain after Berne (and still so after the 1908 Berlin revision) was one of a mess, or 'glorious muddle', in the words of Lord Monkswell.[54] Copyright law consisted of many separate laws, not always consistent, and difficult to apply. There was still some legal uncertainty as to the fate of unpublished works. The developments in the international dimension, namely, the Berlin revision, required changes in the internal British copyright law. Local copyright Acts were by now already enacted by the self-governing dominions, and

---

[51] See Berne Convention (1886), Art 2: 'Authors of any one of the countries of the Union, or their lawful representatives, shall enjoy in the other countries for their works, whether published in one of those countries or unpublished, the rights which the respective laws do now or may hereafter grant to natives.'

[52] For a detailed report of the Berlin conference, see Library of Congress, Report of the Delegate of the United States to the International Conference for the Revision of the Berne Copyright Convention, Held at Berlin, Germany, 14 October to 14 November 1908, Copyright Office Bulletin, No 13 (Washington, 1908). For a later discussion, see Ricketson, above n 43, at 87–96, and for a recent discussion, see Daniel Gervais, 'The 1909 Copyright Act in International Context' (2010) 26 Santa Clara Comp & High-Tech L J 185.

[53] Berlin text (1908), Art 4: 'Authors within the jurisdiction of one of the countries of the Union enjoy for their works, whether unpublished or published for the first time in one of the countries of the Union, such rights, in the country other than the country of origin of the work, as the respective laws now accord or shall hereafter accord to natives, as well as the rights specially accorded by the present Convention.' This principle is found in Art 3 of the current text of the Convention.

[54] Quoted in Sherman and Bently, *The Making*, above n 1, at 135.

in India. Within the Empire, the 1886 International Copyright Act solved some problems, but also raised new ones. Some back and forth discussions were going on between these colonies and London: The Australian 1905 Copyright Act was more advanced than the British laws,[55] and Canadian objections were heard in London.[56] In the background, the United States had just adopted its 1909 Copyright Act (which was not Berne or Berlin compliant).[57] All these factors joined together. Copyright law gained importance and drew growing attention. London realized that it had to update its own laws and those of the Empire, and take careful care of the colonial dimension. The latter task was to be coordinated by the Colonial Office. The purpose was once again to protect British authors, but the progressive characteristic of copyright, suited the general colonial agenda.

(1) Towards an imperial Act

A first step in restoring order in the copyright regime throughout the Empire was an imperial conference that took place in 1910. Imperial conferences started in 1887 and lasted until the 1930s. Once every few years, the Colonial Office convened representatives of the self-governing dominions in London (and once in Ottawa).[58] The conferences discussed either general issues or concrete proposals such as naturalization within the Empire or double income tax.[59] Between the meetings of the formal conferences there were occasional subsidiary conferences. In 1910 such a subsidiary conference dealt with copyright law.[60]

Several important decisions were reached.[61] One, was that Britain will ratify the Berlin revision on behalf of the entire Empire. The self-governing dominions were not to be bound by this ratification and had the right to withdraw. Obviously, this imperial ratification was to give an impressive boost to the Berne Union. Second, London committed to enact a new unified Copyright Act, which would replace the long list of separate laws. The new Act would apply in the entire Empire; the self-governing dominions would have to declare the application of the law in their territory.[62]

The efforts of all vectors pushing in the same direction and having reached an agreement with the dominions, resulted in the enactment of the Imperial

---

[55] Burrell, 'Copyright Reform', above n 22.
[56] Sherman and Bently, *The Making*, above n 1, at 111–15, 136–7, argue that imperial copyright affected local British copyright law.
[57] For discussion of the US 1909 Copyright Act, see Gervais, 'The 1909 Copyright Act', above n 52.
[58] About the imperial conferences in general, see Hugh Edward Egerton, *British Colonial Policy in the XXth Century* (Methuen, 1922) 135; Arthur Berriedale Keith, *The Governments of the British Empire* (Macmillan & Co, 1935) 179–83.
[59] Egerton, *British Colonial Policy*, ibid, at 137–40.
[60] Keith, *The Governments*, above n 58, at 182; Alexander, *Copyright Law*, above n 1, at 267; Seville, *The Internationalisation*, above n 1, at 139–42.
[61] *Copinger on Copyright*, above n 13, at 297; Burrell, 'Copyright Reform', above n 22, at 255; Bently, 'The Extraordinary Multiplicity', above n 5, at 190.
[62] Other decisions were about Canada's copyright law. See Keith, *The Governments*, above n 58, at 182.

Copyright Act 1911 on 16 December 1911.[63] It came into force on 1 July 1912. The Act followed the Berlin revision of the Berne Convention. It unified all kinds of works (literary, fine arts etc) into one law. The Act was up to date with technological advancements and offered protection also for cinematographic works. The bundle of rights included the rights to produce and reproduce a work, publicly perform it, first publish it, as well as the right to translate the work, dramatize it or de-dramatize it, and record it (section 1(2)). The Act contained the defence of fair dealing (section 2(1)(i)). According to the requirements of the Berlin revision, no formalities were required. A work was protected as of its making, even if unpublished. The only substantial requirement was that it should be original (section 1(1)), a term left undefined in the law. As for fixation in a tangible form, the Act was explicit as far as dramatic works were at stake (section 35) and photographs, in which case the protection was tied to the making of the negative (section 21). The legal protection lasted for duration of fifty years posthumously (section 3). Further sections dealt with ownership (section 5), civil enforcement (sections 6–10), criminal proceedings (section 11), and customs (section 14). Importantly, moral rights were absent in the law.

(2) Applying the 1911 Act in the Empire

The Act was imperial as it was meant to be. It applied both in the United Kingdom and the British territories in one unified form, with minor exceptions. The imperial aspect was an inseparable and important element of the law. The first section instructed that 'copyright shall subsist throughout the parts of His Majesty's dominions to which this Act extends', thus setting a unified law for all. Wherever in the Empire a work was created, it should enjoy copyright law throughout the Empire. The exact form of the reception of the Act within each territory depended on its kind, according to the imperial typology. Sections 25–8 set out the rules.

Section 25(1) instructed that the Act applied automatically to all crown colonies, without some of its sections. Per section 13 of the Act, the sections that applied directly only in the United Kingdom were sections 11–12, entitled 'Summary Remedies', which dealt with criminal proceedings and appeals. Section 15 required deposit of copies with the British Museum and other British libraries. By its language this section was limited to the United Kingdom. All other sections applied to all colonies. Section 14, which empowered the Commissioners of Customs and Excise to prohibit importation of infringing copies into the United Kingdom, later raised some questions.

The reminder of section 25(1) addressed the self-governing dominions, defined in section 35(1) to include Canada, the Commonwealth of Australia, New Zealand, the Union of South Africa, and Newfoundland (the Irish Free State deserved a similar status in 1930). In these, the Act extended only upon a declaration of the legislature of that dominion, which could also modify the Act

---

[63] 1 & 2 Geo 5 Ch 46.

(subject to conditions). Thus, for the self-governing dominions, the Act was in the form of 'opt-in', whereas the crown colonies (and later also Mandates) did not even have an 'opt-out' choice. The Act provided yet another avenue for the self-governing dominions: the Secretary of State in London could certify that a dominion's existing copyright law was to be treated like a dominion to which the Act extended. The conditions for such certification were that the dominion's existing copyright law protected authors who were either British or residents of one of the British territories, and that the protection was 'substantially identical' to that conferred by the 1911 Act.

Section 27 allowed the legislatures of the colonies (of any kind) to modify the law regarding procedures, or other modifications but only in so far as the modifications applied to its own authors or works published there. India utilized this avenue regarding translation rights.[64]

Finally, section 28 empowered the King to extend the application of the law to 'any territories under his protection', by way of an Order in Council. Later on, the British determined that this language included the mandates. This provision was used to extend copyright law to the mandate territories, Palestine and Tanganyika.

This elaborate set of rules covered all kinds of territories. Its purpose was clear: it was meant to assure that copyright law throughout the Empire was unified. With the crown colonies, this was achieved immediately. Indeed, a long list of territories had statutory copyright law as of 1912.[65] Local changes were allowed only in respect of procedural issues or such modifications that had only a local effect within a colony. As for the self-governing dominions, the Act offered a carrot and stick: join—and your authors will enjoy the same protection as in the United Kingdom, or if you don't join—your authors will not enjoy the same rights. Each dominion had its own set of considerations, within the copyright context, and no doubt also external considerations, such as its general relationship with Britain. Australia enacted a Copyright Act in 1912 and declared the application of the Imperial Act with some minor modifications. South Africa did the same in 1916, including the Imperial Act in a schedule of its Act, again with minor modifications. New Zealand (1913) and Canada (1921) enacted their own copyright acts, which were certified (in 1914 and 1923, respectively) by the Secretary of State for the Colonies as providing adequate protection for British authors, pursuant to section 26(3) of the Imperial Act.[66]

---

[64] Lionel Bently, 'Copyright, Translations, and Relations between Britain and India in the Nineteenth and Early Twentieth Centuries' (2007) 82 Chi Kent L Rev 1181.

[65] See Colonial Office (CO) to Treasury, Treasury to CO (28 January 1913) NA T 1/11521, asking about the application of the 1911 Copyright Act in the colonies, and the CO's reply (12 February 1913), listing the following colonies as those in which the Act came into force in 1912: Newfoundland (a self-governing dominion), Antigua, Bahamas, Barbados, Bermuda, British Guiana, Grenada, Jamaica, Mauritius, St Lucia, St Christopher and Nevis, St Vincent, Trinidad. This is not a conclusive list, as other colonies also cite 1912 as the date of commencement of the Act, such as Singapore, Nigeria, and Kenya.

[66] The New Zealand certification was given on 20 April 1913, SR & O, No 1604, and was effective as of 20 April 1914. The certification for Canada was given on 6 December 1923, SR & O, No 1605, and was effective as of 1 January 1924.

Another circle of diffusions of the Act (sections 29–30) allowed its extension to protect foreign works. This was in-line with the Berne Convention and its Berlin revision, and provided the mechanism to execute Britain's Berne commitments. An Order in Council was needed to put it into effect. The protection of foreign works was conditioned on mutual protection so to make sure that the foreign works were not protected more than British works. Indeed, alongside the coming into force of the 1911 Act (in June 1912), an Order in Council regulated the copyright relations with the members of the Berne Union, and later on, additional orders regulated copyright relations with the new members of the Berne Union: an Order in Council regarding the Netherlands (1912); Denmark and Japan (1913); Sweden (1919) etc. The channel of Order in Council was also applied to establish copyright relationships with non-Berne Union members, first and foremost the United States.

Thus, by the late 1910s, a legal mechanism was in place to achieve the interests of protecting British and colonial authors and their works throughout the Empire, and complying with the international treaties. The imperial centralist scheme was set in place. From this point of convergence, each colony was on its own to modify the law—subject to British approval, or in the case of the self-governing dominions, subject to certification. Criminal regulation at the colonial level was allowed. Put in the terms offered in Chapter 1 about colonial law making, the form of legislation shifted from a rather loose, soft law pattern to a hard law, though with some local leeway as to crown colonies, and a larger leeway for self-governing dominions, accompanied with the imperial stick and carrot.

(3) Assuring uniformity

One problem became apparent within the first few years of the imperial spread of copyright, regarding customs. Section 14 of the 1911 Act empowered the UK customs to act so as to prevent the importation of infringing copies, but it was clear that this section could not apply as is to the colonies: it mentioned the Commissioner of Customs and Excise as the authority to enforce the prohibition on importing infringing works into the United Kingdom. Section 14(7) instructed that section 14 'shall, with the necessary modifications, apply to the importation into a British possession to which this Act extends of copies or works made out of that possession'. But many of the colonies did not have a local Customs Commissioner. Was a copyright owner, suspecting infringing copies are about to be imported into a colony, supposed to approach the Commissioner in Britain?

The result was that each colony acted differently: some enacted a local ordinance that copied section 14 of the 1911 Act, others enacted the section with modifications, and yet others did nothing at all in this regard.[67] The Colonial Office provided

---

[67] See the following examples:
Grenada: Governor to CO (21 May 1914) NA CO 321/276/39 (reporting the enactment of Ordinance (No 5 of 1914), entitled An Ordinance to facilitate the operation in this colony of the Imperial Copyright Act, 1911, in respect of infringing copies of works in which copyright subsists; CO

some instructions in 1913. A year later, the UK Customs had some reservations and was of the opinion that no local colonial re-enactments are required, except for clarifications: notices about infringing copies should be directed to the UK customs rather than the local customs representatives.[68]

The Colonial Office communicated with all crown colonies on the matter for several years. In the meantime, the Board of Trade changed its mind, now agreeing that local legislation is needed in the colonies, based on a model law.[69] The road was paved for a 'circular despatch', admitting 'considerable confusion' in the matter, circulated in November 1917, with instructions to enact the model law in each colony.[70] The colonies obeyed.[71]

The handling of the customs issue illustrates the central control London had over the legislative process: the initial law spread from the centre to the periphery, the colonies acted locally within a narrow leeway, but under the watchful eye of the centre. Once the centre realized that there was a recurring problem, it coordinated the amendment in a centralist way.

The practical result of this imperial scheme was that the territories (other than the self-governing) had two pieces of copyright legislation: one was the Imperial Copyright Act itself, as applied automatically (to colonies), or extended by an Order in Council (to other territories). The Act was the same for all colonies, with the exception of local matters, an option rarely utilized. A supplemental legislation, which was locally issued by the legislature of each territory, dealt with criminal aspects and customs, though the latter issue was imperially coordinated so as to achieve uniformity. By 1918, this dual pattern appeared in all crown colonies, later to be adopted also in the new Mandates of Palestine and Tanganyika. The content of the local legislations, usually titled Copyright Ordinance, followed the non-applicable sections of the 1911 Act (sections 11–12 as to criminal proceedings, and section 14 as to customs), and were similar to one other.

The law was transplanted as a set of rules. The underlying theories and philosophical justifications of copyright law were not necessarily transferred along with

---

to the Governor (30 November 1914) (replying that 'His Majesty will not be advised to exercise his power of disallowance with regard to this Act').

St Lucia: Governor to CO (3 July 1914) NA CO 321/279 (reporting the enactment of a local supplementary law, which included both the customs and the criminal proceedings aspect. The Governor's letter was accompanied by a report of the Chief Justice of the colony, explaining the Ordinance).

British Honduras: Governor to CO (1 April 1915) NA CO 123/281 (reporting the enactment of a local law, accompanied by a certification of the Attorney General).

Hong Kong: Governor to CO (22 June 1915) NA CO 323/655/54 (enclosing the lengthy bill for approval). Interestingly, the bill included a few paragraphs of 'Objects and Reasons', stating inter alia that the Act 'was one of those Imperial Statutes designed to be applicable throughout the British Empire'.

[68] Customs to CO (17 July 1914) NA CO 323/646/15.

[69] Customs to CO (12 November 1917) NA CO 323/764/22.

[70] Circular Despatch from the Secretary of State for the Colonies (29 November 1917) NA CO 323/692/7.

[71] eg reports of the Governors of the following colonies to the CO: Trinidad (18 April 1918) NA CO 295/516/55; Jamaica (8 June 1918) NA CO 137/726; Grenada (4 July 1918) NA CO 321/299/36.

the rules. But the progressive spirit was there. The task of finding out the rationales of the law was left to the judicial branch within each colony. For those colonies that had an open legal channel to English law, guidance could be found in the homeland of the law. But the structure of the law itself, its scope and coverage still carried the spirit of the Statute of Anne, as constructed some years after its enactment: Copyright was to achieve a public goal of advancing human knowledge. Its protection of the then-new technological developments made it a cutting-edge law, at the forefront of human progress.

The British central control of copyright law also continued after the initial implementation of the Imperial Act. The Dominions Office followed up the legislation in the self-governing dominions. Once the Act was implemented there in one form or another, the Dominions Office dealt with subsequent legal issues, the three most discussed issues being local amendments to the laws, adherence to the Berne Union, and copyright relationships with foreign, non-Berne Union members, such as the United States.[72] The Empire's interest in uniformity further continued in the new kind of its territories, the mandates.

E. Conclusion

The making of British colonial copyright law was accelerated in the late nineteenth century. A mix of factors converged so as to make copyright an important item on the imperial agenda: technological developments enabled the reproduction and then other uses (public performance) of works. Cultural conditions of the spread of English, rising literacy rates and first signs towards cultural homogeneity resulted in a growing demand for such works across political borders. Economic developments enabled the activity of intermediaries, willing to undertake the financial risks and engage in commerce. On the political side, authors and their organizations demanded stronger and better legal protection and lobbied for legislation on local and international levels. As the nineteenth century progressed, it became evident to the British that their interests should be protected both on the imperial and international levels. The muddled state of copyright law within Britain also required attention.

The result was a steady development towards a unified law within the Empire and one which was in harmony with foreign laws. To achieve these goals, the imperial making of copyright law could not be left to its own devices. In the case of copyright law, there was a deliberate centralized coordination.[73] Copyright law was

---

[72] See correspondence in NA CO 886/8/68, as to New Zealand, South Africa, and Newfoundland, during 1914–18; NA CO 886/8/71, as to all self-governing dominions, during 1919–21; and NA CO 886/9/86 as to all dominions, during 1922–4.

[73] To be sure, there were other legal fields that were unified across the Empire, at least to some extent. Assaf Likhovski discussed tax law, and concluded that while the Tax Ordinance was applied according to 'a one-size-fits-all colonial model', its application in practice adapted the law to local needs. See Assaf Likhovski, 'Is Tax Law Culturally Specific? Lessons from the History of Income Tax Law in Mandatory Palestine' (2010) 11 Theoretical Inq L 725.

diffused from above, through the 1911 Imperial Copyright Act and subsequent enforcement and coordination mechanisms. The pattern of diffusion of the legal transplant was from the centre to the periphery, utilizing colonial power to achieve the legislative goals all over the many colonies. Local needs were allowed only in the case of the self-governing dominions or on limited local matters. In all other cases, the local pre-colonial law on copyright, if there was any, was simply ignored. Thus, the mix of British interests in the homeland, the interest in protecting its authors offshores, and the rising importance of the international copyright treaties, fuelled the colonial legislative engine. With the Imperial Conference of 1910 and the enactment of the 1911 Copyright Act, copyright law was placed on the imperial agenda. The mechanism for legal colonialism was operated. Colonial copyright became a legal reality.

The reception of the imperial law in each territory was a different story. We have already noticed two important patterns that emerged from the discussion. One was that in many colonies there was no local demand for copyright law, as it was irrelevant to the local modes of cultural production. A second related pattern was that the first to use colonial copyright, were British, rather than local, copyright owners. As we move to inquire the case of Mandate Palestine, we should ask to which extent the local Palestinian story fitted this general pattern, where it diverged, why and how?

By the end of the period discussed here, the first few years after the enactment of the 1911 Imperial Copyright Act, many of the 'big' copyright questions were already settled. The protection of an intangible work was no longer questioned, the kinds of works to be protected, the scope of the bundle of rights, rules of ownership, and even exceptions were all set. These were all up for interpretation and application, but were no longer doubted. The imperial copyright scheme had been successful, at least *de jure*.

As the Colonial Office circulated its instructions about the issue of customs regarding copyright in November 1917, James Arthur Balfour, the foreign minister, has just issued the *Balfour Declaration*, committing Britain to assist the Jewish people in building its national home in Palestine. At the same time, General Edmund Allenby was beginning his military campaign in southern Palestine against the Ottoman soldiers.

4
Legislating Copyright in Palestine

> The subject of Copyright is of considerable importance and interest to many people in Palestine... It is hardly necessary to point out that with the large Jewish population in Palestine the position is somewhat different from that of other British Colonies.
>
> Palestine's Registrar of Patents and Designs, 1932.[1]
>
> The subject is not one with which the average member of the public is closely concerned and any local advocate who might be engaged in a suit arising under the Act would be in a position easily to discover its terms without recourse to an official publication of the Palestine Government.
>
> A G Wauchope, High Commissioner for Palestine to
> Sir Phillip Cunliffe-Lister, Secretary of State for the Colonies, 1932.[2]

A. Introduction

In 1932, the chief official intellectual property expert in Palestine recommended that the main copyright legislation in force, the 1911 Copyright Act, be published in the local Official Gazette. But the High Commissioner rejected his advice. The former provided a cultural reason, emphasizing the importance of copyright law to the local communities, but the latter provided a practical legal reason, that copyright was a highly specialized field. None of the two referred to the formal legal function of the publication of laws. The early 1930s were a turning point in the life of copyright law in Palestine. First cases reached the local courts, foreign performing rights societies began enforcing their rights, an important case about copyright in news was turning up in the courts, to reach the Supreme Court in that year. But for all this to happen, a copyright law had to be in place. This chapter unfolds the introduction of copyright law in Palestine.

The British kitbag,[3] which the Mandatory government carried along to Palestine, included the English concept of the rule of law and a host of laws and

---

[1] Director of the Department of Customs, Excises & Trade to Chief Secretary (CS) (21 June 1932) ISA M32/2 doc 57.
[2] High Commissioner (HC) to the Secretary of State for the Colonies (9 July 1932) ISA M32/2 doc 67.
[3] This is a small homage to a 1915 song, 'Pack Up Your Troubles in Your Old Kit Bag', written by George Asaf and composed by Felix Powell (Francis, Day & Hunter, 1915). The song was the subject of litigation in Palestine in 1937.

doctrines. Copyright law was one of the first items to be legislated. In fact, after establishing the British civil administration in Palestine in July 1920, copyright deserved high priority and was the fourth piece of legislation. It is safe to say that there were far more important issues at the time. World War I (1914–8) left the region in ruins. In late 1917 and during 1918, the British army, headed by General Edmund Allenby conquered the entire region, ending four centuries of the Ottoman Empire rule. Within two and a half years of military administration the British stabilized Palestine, started rebuilding the infrastructure, and changed the political map for decades to come. In 1920 a civil administration replaced the military one and two years later, the League of Nations entrusted His Majesty with the mandate over Palestine. Jewish immigration which halted at the outbreak of the War was renewed, creating anxiety among the Arab population and disturbances in the political scene.

By the time copyright was legislated in Palestine, the fundamental principles of the law were already settled. It was no longer disputed in English law that copyright was a statutory construct rather than a right of the common law, that the authorial work was protected separately from the tangible object in which it is fixed, that the protection extended posthumously, and, as per the Berne Convention (revised in Berlin in 1908) that protection applied to original works without any formal requirements of notice, deposit, or registration. Copyright law was regulated on an international level, leaving behind the debates of the nineteenth century. It also became an item on the imperial checklist, with a deliberate and clear strategy to spread it throughout the Empire, in as unified a form as possible. Thus, the subject matter of the legal transplantation by the colonial power to its new territory was consolidated. In the imperial typology, Palestine was not a crown colony: the Mandate system was a post-war international institution. Palestine was a Class A Mandate and its single most important particular characteristic was that it carried along the British political commitment towards establishing a national home for the Jewish people in Palestine.

This chapter argues that the Palestinian story of copyright law generally fits the imperial pattern of *colonial copyright*, as discussed in the previous chapters. The first enactment in 1920 was a rather local episode, soon amended by two enactments in 1924. The motivation to legislate copyright in 1924 came from London. It was an imperial interest, meant to serve first and foremost British interests, though there were no such concrete interests in Palestine at the time due to differences of language, culture, and literacy between the local peoples and the British. Local considerations were not taken into account, though the progressive spirit of copyright law fit the Mandatory mission of developing the country. As we shall see later on in Chapters 7 and 8, the first to use the law were indeed foreign copyright owners and the British government.

But the British were not the first to legislate copyright law in the region. The hardly noticed Ottoman Authors' Rights Act 1910 was first. The Ottoman episode of copyright law was short and did not leave its mark on the law. After a brief presentation of the Ottoman Act, I trace the British legislative steps in 1920 and 1924. We shall explore the legislative process, the motivation behind it, the delayed publication of the main Act, and subsequent events such as the impact of one local relentless lawyer on the copyright protection of many authors around the Empire.

The focus here is on the legislation—rather than its actual application. This separation reflects the gap between the law in the books and the law in action. The discussion thus follows the first steps of the legal transplant.

B. The Ottoman Authors' Rights Act

(1) The Ottoman Empire: law and reform

The legal system of the Ottoman Empire was one for the entire Empire, leaving some fields for other legal systems, such as religious law in matters of personal status. The law also allowed some leeway to local governance of the different districts.[4] But the general law in Istanbul, Damascus, or Jerusalem was by and large the same law. Initially, for several centuries, the law was based on religious, Islamic law (*sharia*), Sultanic law (*kanun*), and customary law (*örf*), but in the nineteenth century the Empire dramatically shifted towards secularization, modernization, and westernization, namely Europeanization, though with an original Ottoman flavour. Contemporary scholars of the Ottoman Empire have recently challenged the paradigms of westernization and secularization, replacing them with more nuanced and thicker descriptions of the European legal transplant (especially French), and the way they were received by the Ottomans. Avi Rubin, for example, in discussing the Nizamiye court system established in the late nineteenth century, which was based on the French system, argues that 'the Ottoman reception of Continental law, when examined from a sociolegal perspective, provides an effective illustration of modernity in non-Western contexts'.[5] In other words, the Ottoman reception of the French legal transplant included an adaptation to the local legal culture. The Authors' Rights Act 1910 fits this pattern as well.

The most intense reforms that took place in the Ottoman Empire are known as the *Tanzimat*. The reforms began in 1839, followed by a second wave in 1856, and ended in 1876.[6] The reforms shifted the basis of individual legal status from one based on affiliation to a religious group to that of citizenship, accompanied by a principle of equality: an Ottoman citizen was to be equal to others, no matter

---

[4] Especially in the outer parts of the Empire. See Kemal H Karpat with Robert W Zens (eds), *Ottoman Borderlands: Issues, Personalities and Political Changes* (University of Wisconsin Press, 2003).

[5] Avi Rubin, 'Legal Borrowing and its Impact on Ottoman Legal Culture in the Late Nineteenth Century' (2007) 22(2) Continuity and Change 279, 281. As for secularization, he argues that the secular–religious distinction is a later invention. See Avi Rubin, 'Ottoman Judicial Change in the Age of Modernity: A Reappraisal' (2009) 7(1) History Compass 119, 129; Avi Rubin, *Ottoman Nizamiye Courts: Law and Modernity* (Palgrave Macmillan, 2011).

[6] Roderic H Davison, *Reforms in the Ottoman Empire 1856–1876* (Gordian Press, 1973). Historians of the Ottoman Empire argue that the reforms originated earlier, in the late eighteenth century, and ended later, at the beginning of the twentieth century. This periodization fits 'the long nineteenth century', a term coined by Eric Hobsbawm, extending the nineteenth century till the outbreak of the World War in 1914.

if Muslim or not.⁷ The Tanzimat covered all fields of life: the underlying basis of the regime was transformed, with substantive economic,⁸ administrative, legal, educational,⁹ technological changes, with political and cultural ramifications.

In the cultural field, the Tanzimat resulted in the rise of the press (though still regulated), literature, and artistic activity. Şükrü Hanioğlu points to the term Alla Franca, which became a buzzword at the time, denoting the superiority of European culture, an idea which, as he notes, is closely linked to the notion of progress.¹⁰ The Western influence was especially apparent among the elite. Literature and theatre, foreign and local, thrived. The Western winds changed the style and content of literature and drama.¹¹ The cultural changes were evident also in educational reforms. Donald Quataert reports the dramatic increase in literacy during the nineteenth century and provides figures for books published as an example and evidence: before 1840 only eleven books were published in Istanbul per year; by 1908 the figure rose to 285.¹²

In the legal field, other than the shift from religion to citizenship as the fundamental political unit, the reforms meant a shift towards European, civil law and the adoption of civil codes,¹³ though often with additional original, Ottoman elements and an original mix, or in Rubin's words, a non-Western modernity. The jewel in the crown was the *Mejelle* (Mecelle, in modern Turkish), a sixteen chapter codification of mostly religious laws regarding civil matters. The project began in 1868 and was completed in 1876. It was a more secular law, and more individualistic than the prior Muslim law, and it was far more progressive in spirit.¹⁴

The beginning of the twentieth century was again a time of dramatic change. As the Sultan gained power towards an autocracy, opposition grew, culminating in the 1908 Young Turks Revolution. It was a political revolution more than a popular one, resulting in the restoration of the 1876 Constitution and of a parliamentary

---

⁷ Davison, ibid, at 8.
⁸ Reşat Kasaba, *The Ottoman Empire and the World Economy: The Nineteenth Century* (State University of New York Press, 1988) 50–4, who argues that the purpose of the Tanzimat was to improve the taxation system.
⁹ Literacy rates were up, further enhancing the processes of modernization. See Benjamin C Fortna, *Learning to Read in the Late Ottoman Empire and the Early Turkish Republic* (Palgrave Macmillan, 2011) 21. Similar to Rubin's argument regarding the legal field, Fortna also mitigates the argument about secularization, and argues that it was more religious than thus far acknowledged. Ibid, at 77.
¹⁰ M Şükrü Hanioğlu, *A Brief History of the Late Ottoman Empire* (Princeton University Press, 2008) 100.
¹¹ Hanioğlu, *A Brief History*, ibid, at 94–100.
¹² Donald Quataert, *The Ottoman Empire, 1700–1922* (2000) 167–8. See also Fortna, *Learning to Read*, above n 9.
¹³ Esin Örücü, 'Turkey: Change under Pressure' in Esin Örücü, Elspeth Attwooll, Sean Coyle (eds), *Studies in Legal Systems: Mixed and Mixing* (Kluwer Law International, 1996) 89, 90–2.
¹⁴ Rubin, above n 5, argues that describing the legal reforms as secular is misplaced, and a better description is of local law/foreign law. For the French influence on the legal aspects of the Tanzimat, see Davison, above n 6, at 97–8. The Mejelle did codify some Muslim rulings (sharia), although the changes in form meant also changes in content. See Iris Agmon, 'Late-Ottoman Legal Reforms and the Sharia Courts: A Few Comments on Women, Gender, and Family' in Eyal Katvan, Margalit Shilo, Ruth Halperin-Kadari (eds), *One Law for Man and Woman: Woman, Rights and Law in Mandatory Palestine* (Bar-Ilan University Press, 2010) 117, 122–3 (Hebrew).

government.[15] The revolution had cultural affects. One result was an increase in the circulation of newspapers and a reduction in censorship.[16] Another result was an increase of literary activity and theatre. The new winds reached also Palestine.[17]

The administrative structure of the Empire was such that it was controlled by the central government in Istanbul (Constantinople). As of 1864, there was an administrative division into *vilayets* (provinces), each further divided to *sanjaks* (districts), and these were further subdivided into *kaza* (sub-district). In the late nineteenth and early twentieth centuries, the area to become Palestine was part of the Beirut Vilayet, composed of two districts: the Acre (Akko) Sanjak and Nablus Sanjak. Jerusalem and the southern part of the country (including Jaffa) enjoyed the status of an independent sanjak, subject directly to Istanbul (called *mutasarriflik*). Geographically, these three districts later composed Mandatory Palestine, with the addition of part of the southern district of Ma'an. It covers today's Israel, inclusive of the occupied West Bank and the Gaza Strip and exclusive of the Golan Heights. Under this administrative structure, the area to become Palestine was just another region in the Empire, composed of several separate administrative units, and rather remote and of no particular importance.[18]

(2) The Authors' Rights Act 1910[19]

The Authors' Rights Act 1910 was little known at the time or even thereafter.[20] Contemporary Turkish literature on intellectual property mentions the Act in passing, providing little information, without much elaboration.[21] It seems that with the establishment of the Republic of Turkey in 1923, the Ottoman period was bracketed for some time, waiting for scholars to explore, though in recent years this

---

[15] Hanioğlu, *A Brief History*, above n 10, at 147–8; Quataret, *The Ottoman Empire*, above n 12, at 64; Alan Palmer, *The Decline and Fall of the Ottoman Empire* (J Murray, 1992) 203–20.
[16] Quataret, *The Ottoman Empire*, above n 12, at 168; Donna Robinson Divine, *Politics and Society in Ottoman Palestine: The Arab Struggle for Survival and Power* (Lynne Rienner Publishers, 1993) 145–6.
[17] Divine, *Politics*, ibid, at 162 (discussing the changes in the Arab literary and theatrical fields in Jerusalem).
[18] For Palestine under the Ottomans, see David Kushner (ed), *Palestine in the Late Ottoman Period: Political, Social and Economic Transformation* (Yad Ben-Zvi, 1986); Michelle U Campos, *Ottoman Brothers: Muslims, Christians and Jews in Early Twentieth Century Palestine* (Stanford University Press, 2011) (discussing citizenship and identity in Ottoman Palestine).
[19] Hakk-ı Telif Kanunu, 2 Düstur 273 (1910), 12 Jamad ul Awal 1328 (Muslim calendar), 22 May 1910 (Gregorian calendar). I am indebted to Omri Paz for the translation.
[20] There are two exceptions in the literature: Elad Lapidot, 'Damaging the Interests of Creators and Israeli Companies in the West Bank' (2000) 14 Law & Army 289, 292 (Hebrew); Ihab G Samaan, *A Historical View of Intellectual Property Rights in the Palestinian Territories* (LLM Thesis, University of Georgia, 2003). Both mention the Ottoman Act but did not have the text thereof. Lapidot mentioned the Ottoman Act and assumed it was replaced de facto by British law. Samaan corrected the record, by pointing to the British 1920 Copyright Ordinance which explicitly repealed the Ottoman Act.
[21] Diren Çakmak, 'Concerning the Ottoman Copyright Legislation' (2007) 21 Selçuk U Turcology Study J 191 (Turkish). Other than this article, current Turkish literature on copyright law at best mentions the 1910 Act in passing, without elaboration. Email from Prof Dr Ergun Özsunay, Faculty of Law, Istanbul University (27 August 2009).

has changed.²² Nevertheless, scholars of Ottoman law have yet to explore its copyright law. There are no positive indications that the Act was used in Palestine and there are good reasons to believe that it was hardly utilized at all. The British knew only a little about the Act.²³

The Tanzimat and then the 1908 Young Turks Revolution provided the background for the enactment of the Authors' Rights Act, as well as other legislation in land law, procedural and personal status.²⁴ The Authors' Rights Act was progressive—in the sense that it reflected the idea of progress, and it fitted the cultural and legal reforms and their progressive spirit. It was based on Western, European notions of authorship.

Copyright was not included in the Mejelle. In 1910, shortly after the 1908 Revolution, the Ottomans codified their prior acts of 1850, 1857, and 1872. It resulted in the forty two sections that constituted the 1910 Act. The general features and legal principles, which I will summarize immediately, were European in nature, though the Act does not seem like a translation of any particular European copyright act of the time. For example, the duration of the copyright in the 1910 Act was thirty years posthumously, which was the practice in the nineteenth century in many European countries, though the French had already extended the duration to fifty years posthumously in 1866.²⁵

The Act provided legal protection for literary and pictorial works, engravings, sculptures, maps, technical designs, musical works, and notes (section 2), as well as lectures (section 3), and news articles (section 4), the latter subject to a copyright notice. Legislation was excluded from protection (section 8). The bundle of rights included copying, distribution, translation, dramatization (sections 3, 6, 29), as well as public performance of theatre plays and opera (section 10), all subject to a right to publish political speeches and judicial proceedings (section 3), and to criticism (section 31). Interpretation or notes were also allowed (section 31).

The Ottoman Empire was not a member of the Berne Union, nor did it have any bilateral copyright relationships. Thus, it is not surprising to find that the 1910 Act required formalities: the notice requirement (section 4) instructed that a note of 'all rights reserved' should appear on articles and photographs published in daily

---

²² For a while, the Ottoman period was portrayed (not by its students) in a rather dim light. See André Raymond, *Arab Cities in the Ottoman Period* (Ashgate, 2002) 19, who points to the prejudice against the Ottoman Era. This bracketing and renewed interest is also true of Palestine. In 2002, the editors of a book on legal history in Israel wrote: 'In short, for legal historians, the Ottoman period remains almost terra incognita.' Ron Harris, Alexandre (Sandy) Kedar, Pnina Lahav, Assaf Likhovski, 'Israeli Legal History: Past and Present' in *The History of Law in a Multi-Cultural Society: Israel: 1917–1967* (2002) 1, 5–6. Since then, work by Agmon, Paz, Rubin, and others is filling the gap.

²³ For British comments on Ottoman copyright law prior to the 1910 codification, see William Morris Colles and Harold Hardy, *Playright and Copyright in All Countries* (Macmillan, 1906) 88–9. For post-1910 comments, see Walter Arthur Copinger, and J M Easton, *The Law of Copyright in works of Literature, Art, Architecture, Photography, Music and the Drama* (Stevens and Haynes 5th edn, 1915) 458–60.

²⁴ Robert Eisenman, 'The Young Turk Legislation, 1913–17 and its Application in Palestine/Israel' in *Palestine in the Late Ottoman Period*, above n 18, at 59.

²⁵ For the nineteenth century French and various Germanic copyright laws, see Lionel Bently and Martin Kretschmer (eds), Primary Sources on Copyright (1450–1900), available at http://www.copyrighthistory.org.

newspapers and other temporal publications. The language of the section makes it clear that the requirement was constitutive of the legal protection for such works: without it, copyright did not subsist. A second formality was registration (sections 21–4). Works could be registered, for a fee, with the Ministry of Public Instruction, providing data about the author, the title of the work, date and place of printing, number of pages, comments, and a serial number. However, the registration was not constitutive of copyright and was only a prerequisite to initiate a lawsuit (section 24). A last formal requirement was of deposit (section 20). Three copies of the works were to be handed to the Ministry. It remains unclear whether this was a constitutive requirement, as the section stated that the deposit was meant to secure the rights.

Subject to the formalities, the copyright commenced upon publication of the work (section 9) and lasted for the lifetime of the author and thirty years after death, to lie with the immediate family (section 6): evenly split between the children, the spouse, and the parents. As for charts, engravings, and maps, the duration of the copyright was only for eighteen years after death (section 7). Translators owned the copyright in the translations, a right that lasted for fifteen years after the translator's death (section 14). A special rule applied to orphan works whose authors had died and left no heirs (or if the heirs were no longer alive)—the work could be reprinted, published, and translated (section 17). The person who wanted to use an unpublished orphan work could apply to the Ministry for a privilege, which would then last for 10–15 years, on the condition that printing would commence within a year (section 18). The ministry also had the power to publish a work that could benefit the public, even if no printed copy was found, or in case no further publications were made due to poverty or even disagreements among heirs (section 19). The Ministry had further roles, such as registering transactions of copyrights (sections 25–6).

The Act prohibited a publisher to make changes to the work without the author's consent and if such changes were made, the publisher had to publish a notice in a newspaper, so to warn the public not to buy the work (section 28). In other words, the Act protected the integrity of the work, albeit this particular form of moral right was limited to the author–publisher relationship and did not extend to third parties.

Besides criminal penalties in the Authors' Rights Act itself (section 32), infringement constituted an external criminal offence as well, covering direct infringement and contributory infringement for commercial purpose and importation.[26]

As for its geographical coverage, the Ottoman Act applied throughout the Ottoman Empire of the time at once, without a need to re-legislate it in the specific regions. In Palestine the Act was modified by the British in 1920 and repealed in

---

[26] See Ottoman Penal Code 1858, s 241, in John A S Bucknill and Haig A S Utidjian, *The Imperial Ottoman Penal Code: A Translation from the Turkish Text* (Cyprus printed, 1913) 190. For a discussion of the 1858 Penal Code, locating it within the Tanzimat, see Omri Paz, *Crime, Criminals and the Ottoman State: Anatolia between the late 1830s and the late 1860s* (PhD Dissertation, Tel-Aviv University, 2010).

86   *Colonial Copyright*

1924. It remained the law in Transjordan, later Jordan, until 1992.[27] In Turkey itself, the first major Copyright Act was enacted in 1951.[28]

(3) The Act in practice?

There are no indications that the Ottoman Act reached a court in the region during its rather short de facto lifetime or that it was taken notice of in any other form. I discuss positive evidence and then circumstantial evidence that make the case for the irrelevance of the Ottoman Act: it did not leave any mark in Palestine's copyright law.

(a) Positive evidence

The Act came into force in 1910, but within a few years the region and the Ottoman Empire were in a war, with much disruption to daily lives. It is quite unlikely that anyone could engage in copyright at that time. During the British military administration (1917–20) a judicial system was re-established, but there are no reported cases dealing with copyright law, nor is there any indirect evidence about such cases (such as newspaper reports). In fact, the Ottoman Act survived in the books until 1924, though subject to important British modifications in 1920. But no cases were reported in this interim period (1920–4). In 1930 a British judge was reported to have written that the copyright case he adjudicated was the first.[29] Although such a statement does not appear in the judgment itself, it seems to be correct. We can rely on that comment as far as the British government is concerned, ie to refer to the period beginning in 1917. The general dismissive attitude of the British towards Ottoman law makes this reported judicial comment less reliable as far as the pre-British lifetime of the Act is concerned, but neither is there evidence to the contrary. Unfortunately, Nizamiye court records from late Ottoman Palestine are unavailable.

It might be that the law was used in private dealings such as contracts and transactions, without disputes arising, or at least not disputes that were brought into the courts. Perhaps disputes were negotiated or settled in other ways. One feature of the Act could be of some assistance in searching for its actual application and use: the Act required formalities for some kinds of works. Although not required for books, a sample of books published in Palestine indicates that the use of a notice started only in the 1920s in Hebrew books, and in Arabic books,

---

[27] Mohammed El Said, *The Development of Intellectual Property Protection in the Arab World* (Edwin Mellen Press, 2008) 225, 227, 231.
[28] Ergun Özsunay, 'Turkey' (2001) 7 *International Encyclopaedia of Laws: Intellectual Property* 32, 48.
[29] 'Protection of Authors Rights in the Country' (16 January 1930) *Haaretz*, at 4 (Hebrew). The case was File 1844/29 *The A-G (represented by Friedenberg) v Guth & Peretz* (9 January 1930) PRS Archive A209 Palestine 2 (PRS-2). It was a criminal case, brought by a local representative of the German performing rights society. I will discuss the case in Ch 7. In determining the fine imposed, the judge did take into consideration 'the practice prevalent in this country up till now in regard to intellectual creations in Palestine'.

later on.[30] Another place to find out about the use of copyright law in practice still awaits research—the archives of the Ottoman Ministry of Public Instruction and its regional offices, if these survived. However, under the Act, registration was for a fee and was required only for bringing a case to court, thus, such registries would provide only a partial picture.

Another indication that the Ottoman Act was not in fact used comes from a copyright case litigated in Palestine in 1937, during the British Mandate.[31] The plaintiffs were the Performing Rights Society (PRS) from London, acting through their local (Jewish) attorney, Shimon Agranat.[32] The case was about the unauthorized public performance of *Pack Up Your Troubles in Your Old Kit Bag*, which was composed in 1915, prior to the coming into force of the British copyright enactments. Agranat faced a problem: it was clear to him that the English law did not apply and hence he turned to the Ottoman Act—but he was unable to obtain it in Palestine.[33] The PRS sent him a summary of the Act in French, as well as the relevant pages in *Copinger on Copyright*, though it was clear to the PRS, too, that the Ottoman Act did not provide owners of musical works (other than operas) with the public performance right.[34] Nevertheless, Agranat argued in court that the work was protected directly under the British 1911 Imperial Copyright Act, as the works were first published in the United Kingdom. Agranat thought his own argument was unsound, as he confided to his client in London.[35] However, the judge construed a complex argument and found for the plaintiffs. He explained that the first British enactment in 1920 amended—but did not repeal—the Ottoman Act of 1910. Hence the latter applied. He then extended the criminal sections of the 1920 British Ordinance so as to cover public performances retroactively. Thus, the Ottoman Act finally deserved some attention, by awarding copyright protection to works made prior to the British enactments. The content of the Ottoman law was subjected to the British law.

(b) Circumstantial evidence: the cultural and legal fields

Circumstantial evidence about the cultural field at the time supports the conclusion that the Ottoman Act remained in the books. The cultural field was unstructured, rather dull in quantity, lacked a critical mass of activity, and lacked the kind of

---

[30] The sample included fifty books published in Hebrew, in Palestine between the years 1915 and 1947 and fifty-one books published in Arabic between the years 1922 and 1947. The first Hebrew copyright notices appeared in 1924 and their appearance increased in the course of the years. The first Arabic notice was found in a 1924 book published by a Franciscan Order, but only in the 1930s there was a slow increase in the number of notices, which in the 1940s became a common—though not absolute—practice. The books were examined in the Sourasky Central Library at Tel-Aviv University. Note that the British copyright law did not require notice.

[31] CC (Hi) 20/36 *Francis, Day & Hunter Ltd v Belozersky* (9 May 1937) PRS Archive A319, Agranat Files 1 (PRS-A1).

[32] Agranat, then a young lawyer working in Haifa, was later a Justice of the Israeli Supreme Court and its third Chief Justice (1965–76). We shall meet him again in Ch 7.

[33] See Agranat to PRS (24 March 1937) PRS-A1.

[34] PRS to Agranat (2 April 1937) PRS-A1.

[35] Agranat to PRS, above n 33.

transactions, interactions, and players that could use copyright law. In both the local communities, the Jewish (Zionist-Hebrew and Orthodox) and the Arab there was little cultural production, little consumption, and almost no content industries. In other words, while there was cultural activity, there was hardly a cultural field.

As for the Jewish community, during the Ottoman period most of it was part of the Old Yishuv, namely non-Zionist, Orthodox Jews who lived in the old cities of Jerusalem, Safed, Tiberias, and Hebron. Books circulating among this community were almost exclusively religious texts. The first Jewish printing houses in the region operated in Safed in 1576–87 and then again only in 1831–7, but each printed only six books.[36] A third publishing attempt was in 1840 in Jerusalem, when a printer received monopoly status from local rabbis. In 1862, an internal religious tribunal decided that the monopoly was not permanent, thus opening the printing market for competition.[37] New printers started up and the employees even unionized and declared a strike in 1902 and again in 1909.[38] Nevertheless, the texts were still mostly unoriginal reprints of religious texts.

As for the New Yishuv, the cultural field within the Hebrew, Zionist community during the Ottoman times was in its infancy. There were two main waves of Jewish immigration (in Hebrew: *aliyah*): the first, starting in the early 1880s until 1904 and the second from 1904 lasting until the outbreak of the World War in 1914. The number of Jews grew from 24,000 in 1882 to anywhere between 60,000 and 85,000 in 1914.[39] The immigrants that survived and remained in the region were busy establishing new settlements, not leaving much time for leisure, culture, or legal affairs.

Nevertheless, there were beginnings of Hebrew culture at the time. It was national in its motivation and saturated with the Hebrew language. Historians of the period provide a detailed account of the emerging Hebrew culture: pointing to its complex dialogue with Europe and to its national overtones.[40] But the field was not yet mature in a way that could produce any engagement with copyright law. In 1906, following a decision by the Seventh Zionist Congress, Professor Boris Schatz, a Jewish immigrant from Lithuania (who lived in Bulgaria), established a

---

[36] Shoshana HaLevy, *First Issues in the Yishuv's History* (Jerusalem, 1989) 48–50, 54 (Hebrew); Izhak Ben-Zvi, *Eretz-Israel under Ottoman Rule: Four Centuries of History* (Yad Ben-Zvi, 1969) 187, 368 (Hebrew).

[37] HaLevy, *First Issues*, ibid, at 142.

[38] See HaLevy, *First Issues*, ibid, at 143–8; Yehoshua Kaniel, *Continuation and Change: The Old Yishuv and the New Yishuv during the First and Second Aliyah* (Yad Ben-Zvi, 1982) 292 (Hebrew).

[39] The demographics are debated. Compare the higher figure in D Gurevich (supervision), A Gertz (ed), A Zankar (assistant), *Statistical Handbook of Jewish Palestine* (Department of Statistics, The Jewish Agency for Palestine, Jerusalem, 1947) 37; *Statistical Abstract for Palestine* (Office of Statistics, Jerusalem, 1936), to the lower figure, in Justin McCarthy, *The Population of Palestine: Population History and Statistics of the Late Ottoman Period and the Mandate* (Columbia University Press, 1990).

[40] Zohar Shavit (ed), *The Construction of Hebrew Culture in Eretz Yisrael* (Bialik Institute, 1989) (Hebrew); Arieh Bruce Saposnik, *Becoming Hebrew: The Creation of a Jewish National Culture in Ottoman Palestine* (Oxford University Press, 2008). For subsequent developments, see the survey in Haim Gamzu, *Painting and Sculpture in Israel: The Plastic Arts from Bezalel Period to the Present Day* (Eshkol, 1951).

first arts school in Jerusalem, the Bezalel School of Arts and Crafts.[41] First music bands were formed in the new *moshavot* (Hebrew: colonies), and first music classes were taught in the Hebrew schools in Jaffa;[42] first steps of local theatre emerged, though still amateur at that stage.[43] The Hebrew literary centre was still located in Europe. The few authors that immigrated, Haim Brenner and Shmuel Yosef (Shai) Agnon being the dominant figures, had most of their literary activities conducted with publishers in Europe, where most of their readership lived. Very few others wrote in Hebrew and they too were engaged in reinventing the Hebrew person.[44] Local newspapers in Hebrew emerged already in the 1860s, but did not yet run into any copyright issues.[45] Arieh Saposnik discusses also folk forms of culture, such as music and folk dance. However, these did not easily fit within the Western form of copyright law, as the music and dances were not fixed in a tangible form and it was impossible to identify their author, if there was ever such a singular author.[46]

As for the Arab community, the largest community in the region at the time, most of the cultural activity originated either from the North—from Beirut and Damascus or from the South—Cairo. There was little local cultural production in the form that was protected by copyright law. Ami Ayalon gathered data indicating a low number of Palestinian books in Arabic published throughout the British Mandate, with very few publications in the pre-British period: according to one of his sources, between 1847 and 1948 there were 962 books and pamphlets written in Arabic printed in Palestine. Of these, 119 were printed before 1910.[47] Literacy rates were very low. Printers appeared only later, with a relative boom after the 1908 Young Turks Revolution and the slackening of censorship.[48] Newspapers appeared at that time. The forms of culture that did take place were not of the kind protected by copyright law, such as oral culture. Few Christian printers were established by priests as of the nineteenth century, but they printed mostly non-original, translated religious texts, and only rarely did they print original material.[49] In other words, the Arab cultural field too was not ripe to deal with copyright law issues.

---

[41] Saposnik, *Becoming Hebrew*, ibid, at 105, 125, 129, 132. About Schatz, see Naomi Feuchtwanger, 'Barukh (Boris) Schatz' in Ze'ev Tzahor (ed), *The Second Aliyah: Biographies* (Yad Ben-Zvi, 1997) 392–8 (Hebrew).

[42] Yehoash Hirshberg, 'The Development of Music Performing Groups' in *The Construction*, above n 40, at 263–77 (Hebrew).

[43] Shimon Lev-Ari, 'The Development of the Theaters' in *The Construction*, above n 40, at 343–4 (Hebrew).

[44] See Yaffa Berlovitz, *Inventing a Land, Inventing a People* (HaKibbutz HaMeuchad, 1996) (Hebrew).

[45] Ouzi Elyada, in discussing the early Hebrew journalism in the period, mentions that one of the Hebrew papers, *HaZvi*, used information which it received from a Turkish news agency. See Ouzi Elyada, 'The Sensational Journalism in Eretz-Israel at the Early Twentieth Century' (1992) 11 Kesher 70 (Hebrew).

[46] Saposnik, *Becoming Hebrew*, above n 40, at 167–8.

[47] Ami Ayalon, *Reading Palestine: Printing and Literacy, 1900–1948* (University of Texas Press, 2004) 66–9. The source cited in the text is an unpublished list composed by Rasim Jbarah.

[48] Ayalon, *Reading Palestine*, ibid; Divine, *Politics*, above n 16.

[49] Ben-Zvi, *Eretz-Israel*, above n 36, at 65.

Furthermore, even if there were copyright-related issues, the legal field was too small to handle it. The same applied in British times, at least until the late 1920s. There were very few lawyers in the country;[50] there was a court system, but it was described as corrupt and dysfunctional, though these descriptions come mostly from Westerners.[51]

(c) Translations

One issue that could have raised questions of copyright law and thus trigger the application and use of the Ottoman Act was that of translations. Today, and as of the Berne Convention, translations immediately raise copyright issues, as they are derivative works. The law today protects the original author's right to translate the work and it protects the translation as an independent original work. In Ottoman Palestine, foreign books were translated into Arabic and Hebrew, but nevertheless, no copyright issues were reported.

The Eretz-Israel office of the Jewish Agency initiated a large scale translation project of classic literature, which engaged a group of Hebrew authors during the 1910s. The project came to a halt by the end of World War I. The idea was twofold: to promote Hebrew readership, and to provide work and income for local authors and publishers.[52] The project was the result of the strong kinship between nationalism and culture. The Hebrew language played an important role in the emerging Hebrew cultural field.[53] Zionism revived Hebrew, updated it, and within a generation managed to turn it into the dominant language spoken by the Jews in Palestine. The emphasis on Hebrew was a powerful incentive for writing; works in foreign languages were controversial. The importance of classic works was recognized, but they posed competition to the project of reviving Hebrew. The solution was translation, in the words of a Hebrew commentator later on: '[T]he variety of

---

[50] Assaf Likhovski, *Law and Identity in Mandate Palestine* (University of North Carolina Press, 2006) 25, who cites the figure of nearly 100 lawyers by the end of 1920, most of whom did not have formal legal education.

[51] See eg the report of a Jewish traveller in 1899–1901, who complained that: 'There is no government and no discipline in this country, but for the *bakshish* [bribe—M.B.], to which the justice, law, equity kneel, and there is no stronger force that can defeat it, but for a larger *bakshish*.'— A S Hirschberg, *The Way of the New Yishuv in Eretz Yisrael* (photocopy of the Vilna Edition), 1901 (Yad Ben-Zvi, 1979) 30 (Hebrew). For contemporary, unbiased descriptions, see eg Nathan Brun, *Judges and Lawyers in Eretz Yisrael* (Magnes, 2008) (Hebrew).

[52] A special translations committee was formed. The minutes of the committee's meetings do not expound on the rationale of the project. They do list the translators, among them important authors on their own behalf, such as Levin Kipnis, Yosef Haim Brenner, A D Gordon, and A Z Rabinovitch (Azar). The works translated were of, eg Alphonse Daudet (by Steinberg), Leo Tolstoy (by Brenner), Aleksander Kuprin (by Temkin). It was decided that the translators will be paid per-translation. See minutes of the Translations Committee CZA L2/91-5, L2/91-9, L2/91-17, L2/91-21, L2/91-43, L2/91-48 (the dates are listed according to the Jewish calendar and are not always clearly written. As far as I could decipher them, they refer to February 1916; March 1917, and January 1918). For discussion, see Zohar Shavit, 'The Development of the Hebrew Publishing in Eretz-Israel' in *The Construction*, above n 40, at 199, 206–10, 213–15 (Hebrew).

[53] See Rafael Nir, 'The Status of Hebrew Language in the Process of National Revival' in *The Construction*, above n 40, at 31 (Hebrew).

translations forces the reader to engage in Hebrew literature.'[54] Moreover, the immigrants spoke many different languages: Yiddish, Russian, Polish, German, Arabic, and more. Thus, Hebrew served as a common denominator.

There are no indications that permission from the original, European copyright owners was sought. In some cases, the works might already have been in the public domain (the duration of copyright law in many European countries was thirty years posthumously at the time). In other cases, the law in the original country did not protect the original author's right to translate the work, though the translator often enjoyed an independent protection of his translation. Thus, everyone who so wished could translate a work, but could not copy other translations. Thus, the discrepancy between the Ottoman law and European laws can explain why copyright law was not triggered.

A month after the death of Leo Tolstoy in November 1910, a Jewish publisher, Shlomo Sherbrek, wrote to Tolstoy's daughter asking permission to translate some of her father's writings published prior to 1881. The daughter promptly responded, refusing permission, but then, in an undated letter to the publisher, a different reply was provided on her behalf, ignoring the previous reply. Without regard to the date of publication of the original writings, explained the second reply, under the applicable law, no permission was required at all.[55] This probably referred to Russian law at the time,[56] and although Sherbrek operated in Europe rather than in Palestine, the incident indicates the practice as to translations. Indeed, other European copyright legislation of the nineteenth century protected the right to translate only under certain circumstances.[57]

As for the Ottoman Act, the legal protection it awarded the author explicitly included the right to translate the work (sections 3, 6); with the exception of an orphan work (section 17). The notice requirement, when applied, had to include the warning that no other translations are permitted (section 4)—though this might have referred to the translator's independent right. The translator enjoyed an independent right in the translation, which lasted for only fifteen years posthumously (section 14). However, none of these rules applied to foreign works, as the Ottoman Empire was not party to the Berne Convention and did not have any bilateral copyright relationships.

---

[54] Michael Assaf, 'On Translations' (7 June 1929) *Davar*, Saturday Supp, at 4.
[55] The exchange is reprinted in A A Akavia (ed), *The Memories of the Publisher Shlomo Sherbrek* (Sherbrek, 1955) 232 (Hebrew).
[56] Serge L Levitsky, *Introduction to Soviet Copyright Law* (Sythoff, 1962) 28, refers to pre-Soviet law, and notes that: 'Soviet legislation does not, as a rule, consider translation as infringement of copyright.'
[57] For example, the Prussian Copyright law 1837 stated that translation does not infringe the rights of the original author, unless the translation is from a classic language to German, or that the original author reserved the right of translation by announcing his intentions to translate his own work within a period of two years. The 1870 Copyright Act for the German Empire maintained similar rules, though in a different wording. In the UK, the International Copyright Act 1844 (An Act to Amend the Law relating to International Copyright, 7 & 8 Vict *c* 12) explicitly allowed translations (s 18). The Berne Convention included translations within the realm of the original author's control (Art 8), as did the 1911 Imperial Copyright Act (s 1(2)(a)).

Thus, the case of translations is neutral evidence: one can conclude that copyright law was simply ignored, as no copyright-related discussions took place, or, one can conclude the opposite: that since the law (either of the European country of origin of the work or the country of destination, namely the Ottoman Empire) did not prohibit translation of such (foreign) works, the law was permissive and enabled the translation.

*

The conclusion is that there is no positive evidence about the use of the Ottoman Authors' Rights Act during its legal life time and there are some indications and good reasons to conclude that it was not used. Thus, the Ottoman Act was the first in time but contributed little if anything at all to the development of either the law or the local culture. It was easy to replace it with a new law.

C. British Legislation

The British were quick to implement copyright law in Palestine. The urgency is somewhat peculiar: after all, there were far more urgent matters to deal with. The British occupied the region in 1917–18, faced the challenge of rebuilding the country in the aftermath of the World War, amidst renewed waves of Jewish immigration and growing tensions between Jews and Arabs over land ownership.[58] The military rule was replaced in July 1920 with a civil administration, headed by Sir Herbert Samuel, the first High Commissioner in Palestine. There was no local demand for copyright law. So why did the British act so promptly on this matter?

This part traces the copyright legislation in Mandatory Palestine. There were two stages of legislative developments, the first, a little-known 1920 Ordinance, issued by the High Commissioner, which left the Ottoman law in place but subjected it to substantial amendments that made it more compatible with the Berne Convention as revised in Berlin. The second stage was in 1924, with the extension of the 1911 Imperial Copyright Act to Palestine, accompanied by a local Ordinance that dealt with criminal sanctions and customs, thus bringing Palestinian copyright law in-line with the imperial structure, as was implemented throughout the Empire during the 1910s. The questions that guide this discussion are those of motivation and process: why did they British legislate copyright laws at the time and in the

---

[58] For the immigration and land challenges, see Nathaniel Katzburg, 'Introduction: Britain and the Question of Palestine, 1915–1925' in Rachela Makover, *Government and Administration of Palestine, 1917–1925* (Yad Ben-Zvi, 1988) 11 (Hebrew). The new administration itself had also to be constructed. See Makover, ibid. Other items on the High Commissioner's table were the pardon he gave to Arab leaders who were involved in the April 1920 Nabie Musa riots, press censorship, and the forthcoming visit of the Minister of the Colonies, Winston Churchill, a visit that took place in March 1921. See Bernard Wasserstein, *The British in Palestine: The Mandatory Government and the Arab-Jewish Conflict 1917–1929* (2nd edn, Blackwell, 1991) 91–9.

For discussion of the activities of the Mandate government in its first decade, see Gideon Biger, *Crown Colony or National Homeland? British Influence upon Palestine, 1917–1930, A Geo-Historical Analysis* (Yad Ben-Zvi, 1983) (Hebrew) (discussing mostly transportation, building, and planning systems).

way they did? The interest in the process—who initiated the legislation and how it proceeded—follows the line of legal transplants, querying the route of the law from the colonizer to the colonized.

(1) The legislative process

Once the British civil administration fell into place, the local government did not spare time. It was at the legislative desk at once. During the first few months of the civil administration, from July to October 1920, the High Commissioner issued fifteen local Ordinances on his own, assisted only by the Attorney General and his small office.[59] The list is impressive in its quantity and scope. It covered the burning issues of immigration and land, some necessary financial issues, and first regulations of specific markets.

The first was the Advertisements Ordinance (July 1920).[60] It prohibited the publishing of advertisements on public walls, trees, and fences, and authorized local municipalities to make and regulate public boards. It was based on an Official Notice proclaimed by Jerusalem's military governor, Ronald Storrs in 1918. Storrs was concerned with the unorderly planning and building of the holy city. His regulation was to preserve and protect Jerusalem 'by an aesthetic, as well as liturgical and political *Status Quo*'.[61] The Attorney General, Norman Bentwich explained the purpose of this regulation: 'Steps were taken to protect the historic scenes and the holy towns of Palestine from defacement by advertisements.'[62] Extending this local notice to the country level as the first official legislation acknowledged the importance the British saw in their mission and as custodians of the Holy Land.

The second legislation was the Immigration Ordinance (August 1920), a first attempt in regulating the major political issue of the day and by far not the last such regulation.[63] The third piece of legislation was the State Flags Ordinance (August 1920), prohibiting the use of state flags in partisan demonstrations, thus trying to depoliticize the country, protect the symbols of government, and reaffirm the British role as custodians of the country.[64]

But then came the Copyright Ordinance, as the fourth piece of legislation.[65] This high priority to an issue of no particular urgency, not directly related to the government's role as custodian of the country or to the functioning of its market, is quite puzzling. (Among intellectual property laws, copyright was first, with the Trade Marks Ordinance following in 1922, and the Patent and Design Ordinance in 1925.)[66] The remainder of this first group of legislation included several land

---

[59] For the full list, see *An Interim Report, Civil Administration of Palestine, During the Period 1st July 1920–30th June 1921*, Appendix I, at 23.
[60] Advertisements Ordinance, 157 OG 2 (16 August 1920).
[61] Ronald Storrs, *Orientations* (Nicholson & Watson, 1937) 363, 460.
[62] Norman Bentwich, 'Palestine' (1922) 4 J Comp Legis & Int'l L 177, 180.
[63] Immigration Ordinance, 27 OG 2 (16 September 1920).
[64] State Flags Ordinance, 171 OG 3 (1 October 1920).
[65] Copyright Ordinance, 172 OG 3 (1 October 1920).
[66] Trade Marks Ordinance, 2 Laws of Palestine 2269 (15 January 1922); Patent and Design Ordinance, 2 Laws of Palestine 1910 (1 January 1925).

laws and laws dealing with mortgages, fisheries, antiquities, cooperatives, forestry, and animal trade. Seen on the background of this list, the prominence given to copyright remains puzzling. It is helpful to locate these legislative acts within the overall legislative process in Palestine.

After this first intense legislative wave, an Advisory Council was established to assist the High Commissioner.[67] A second wave of ordinances dealt with town planning, police and criminal issues, and regulating the sale of medicines. This structure of the legislative process was meant to be intermediate, as in July 1922 the League of Nations deposited the Mandate of Palestine with Britain.[68] Importantly, article 19 of the Mandate instructed the Mandatory government, to adhere on behalf of the Administration of Palestine to international conventions in several fields. These included: slave traffic, traffic in arms and ammunition, traffic in drugs, conventions relating to commercial equality, freedom of transit and navigation, aerial navigation and postal, telegraphic, and wireless communication, and finally, literary, artistic, or industrial property. Indeed, the Mandate government adhered to such conventions within a few years, though the local implementing legislation was in some cases a bit slower.[69]

The Mandate was then followed by the King's Order in Council for Palestine 1922.[70] This was the Constitution of Palestine. The Order in Council outlined the executive, legislative, and judicial powers. As for the second of these, it ordered the establishment of an elected legislative council.[71] However, such a council never materialized, due to Arab opposition.[72] For the remainder of the Mandate, the High Commissioners issued Ordinances with the advice of the Advisory Council, without any local democratic process.[73]

Various accounts of the legislative process in Mandate Palestine emphasize the role of the local, Palestine government in initiating and legislating, while rendering the Colonial Office in London only the role of approving the legislation *ex post*.[74] The first influential Attorney General, Norman Bentwich, provided a first-hand account:

> The procedure of legislation was simple. Measures drafted in my office and approved in Executive Council were submitted to the Advisory Council and criticized in detail. But the authority was in the High Commissioner, subject to the unqualified veto and amending power of the Second Chamber in Downing Street.[75]

---

[67] Minutes of the Advisory Council Meetings 1920–3, NA CO 814/6.
[68] Initially, the Mandate covered also Transjordan, but according to Art 25 of the Mandate and a subsequent resolution of the League of Nations (16 September 1922) Transjordan was separated.
[69] For a list of treaties to which the British government adhered on behalf of Palestine, see Frederic M Goadby, *International and Inter-religious Private Law in Palestine* (Hamadpis Press, 1926) 14–16.
[70] The Palestine Order in Council 1922, 3 Laws of Palestine 2569.
[71] Part III of the Order in Council 1922, ss 17–34.
[72] For a summary, see Jerry Dupont, *The Common Law Abroad: Constitutional and Legal Legacy in the British Empire* (Fred B Rothman Publications, 2001) 864.
[73] For the legislative process, see Likhovski, *Law and Identity*, above n 50, at 24–5.
[74] See eg Likhovski, *Law and Identity*, above n 50, at 25; Elyakim Rubinshtein, 'The Jewish Institutes and the Yishuv's Institutions' in Binyamin Eliav (ed), *The Jewish National Home: From the Balfour Declaration to Independence* (Keter, 1976) 136, 210 (Hebrew).
[75] Norman Bentwich, *Wanderer between Two Worlds* (K Paul, Trench, Trübner, 1941) 111.

Jacob Reuveny explains that the Mandate government had relatively wide leeway to copy legislation from other colonies and British dominions, as well as the British laws. He further notes that the Colonial Office discouraged the enactment of original new laws which did not have a British colonial precedent.[76] The division of legislative labour was probably more complex than this description. Recent research into specific legal fields indicates that the initiative for the law came from London more often than thus far assumed. An example is Ron Harris and Michael Crystal's study of company law, showing that Westminster led and coordinated this legislative process.[77] Assaf Likhovski showed how the Income Tax Ordinance in Palestine—once legislated in 1941—was based on 'a one-size-fits-all colonial model'.[78] The case of copyright law supports this view, that London had a greater role in initiating the laws for Palestine than thus far assumed.

From a broader perspective, located on the general model offered in Chapter 1, the legislative power as to Palestine was shared between the local government and the Colonial Office, with some local leeway, but always subject to the approval of the latter. On occasion, London did interfere and assumed a more active role. Unlike self-governing dominions, the Jerusalem government was not elected. It had no elected members representing local communities (though the Advisory Council had representatives of several communities) and its legal department was composed of British civil servants. Thus, the imperial–local distinction is blurred and the legislative process can be treated in a unified manner as British.

As for the content of the legislation, several scholars pointed to a British project of gradually dismissing Ottoman legislation in favour of English law. This was the anglicization of the law. Importantly, the 1922 Order in Council did not repeal Ottoman law. Instead, it accepted all law that was in place until the outbreak of the War in 1914, but subjected it to new British legislation, and to a judicial filter: the Ottoman law was to be exercised in conformity with the substance of the common law and the doctrines of equity in force in England but, 'provided always that the said common law and doctrines of equity shall be in force in Palestine so far only as the circumstances of Palestine and its inhabitants and the limits of His Majesty's jurisdiction permits and subject to such qualification as local circumstances render necessary'.[79]

In the course of the Mandate period, British legislation did repeal much of the Ottoman law. The first Ottoman laws to be erased from the law books were those which the British identified as inspired by French legislation.[80] Likhovski analysed

---

[76] Jacob Reuveny, *The Administration of Palestine under the British Mandate 1920–1948: An Institutional Analysis* (Bar-Ilan University Press, 1993) 118, 123–4 (Hebrew).

[77] Ron Harris and Michael Crystal, 'Some Reflections on the Transplantation of British Company Law in Post-Ottoman Palestine' (2009) 10 Theoretical Inq L 561, 567–8, 571–3.

[78] Assaf Likhovski, 'Is Tax Law Culturally Specific? Lessons from the History of Income Tax Law in Mandatory Palestine' (2010) 11 Theoretical Inq L 725.

[79] Palestine Order-in-Council 1922, s 46. For discussion, see Uri Yadin, 'Reception and Rejection of English Law in Israel' (1962) 11 ICLQ 59, 61.

[80] Daniel Friedmann, 'Infusion of the Common Law into the Legal System of Israel' (1975) 10 Isr L Rev 324, 328; Robert H Eisenman, *Islamic Law in Mandate Palestine and Modern Israel: A Study of the Survival and Repeal of Ottoman Legislative Reform* (PhD, Columbia University, 1977) 36;

the Mandatory legislative project and the anglicization process and concluded that '[t]he British were not eager to replace local substantive law but were more willing to replace procedural law', and that '[t]he British began with procedural and public law and gradually moved on to more private/substantive areas of law'.[81]

The puzzle presented above, about the rush to enact copyright law is now contextualized within the general legislative process in Palestine, but not yet solved. The 1920 Copyright Ordinance did not repeal the Ottoman French-inspired law, but settled for modifying it. In 1920, before the Mandate was awarded to Britain, copyright law was not yet on a duty list of the sort included in the Mandate two years later. Moreover, copyright law does not quite fit the picture drawn by Likhovski, as it is more substantive and private rather than procedural and public (though it has some public features). So how can one explain the prominence of copyright law in the Mandatory's to-do list and its fast realization? I now turn to discuss the enactment of the 1920 Ordinance and then the 1924 legislation.

(2) First British steps: the 1920 Copyright Ordinance

No direct evidence was found as to the legislative process of the 1920 Copyright Ordinance, or who initiated it. But the general structure of legislation just described, the contents of the enactment and later documents imply that it was a local, Jerusalem-based initiative, and there are good reasons to believe that it was the Attorney General, Norman Bentwich who drafted it.

The Ordinance's first section clarified that the Ottoman Act be applied in Palestine and extended its application to all persons without regard to their nationality. This extension fitted the international dimension of copyright law and English law in particular, which were based on the place of first publication rather than on the author's nationality. Section 2 extended the Ottoman Act to cover the then-relatively new technologies of photography and perforated rolls, namely, mechanical means to record and play music. The section instructed that the copyright duration commenced upon the making of the negative or the making of the original plate. Ownership of copyright was to be determined based on the ownership of the tangible object. These rules were obviously based on section 21 (photographs) and section 19 (perforated rolls) of the 1911 Imperial Copyright Act. Section 3 of the 1920 Ordinance extended the duration from the thirty years posthumous period to fifty years and set the duration for the new protected subject matter of photographs and recordable instruments to fifty years from their making. Once again, the source of these amendments is easily traced to the 1911 Act. Section 4 nullified the Ottoman requirements of deposit and registration. This change was in line with the 1908 Berlin Revision of the Berne Convention and

---

Likhovski, *Law and Identity*, above n 50, at 58; Harris and Crystal comment that 'Hostility to Ottoman law was augmented in the field of commercial law by hostility to French law', above n 77, at 566.

[81] Likhovski, *Law and Identity*, above n 50, at 55, 57. The judicial process of anglicization was enhanced during the 1930s. See Likhovski, *Law and Identity*, at 67–74.

the 1911 Act. Finally, section 5 repealed the Ottoman criminal penalties and set criminal offences of making, selling, offering for sale, distributing, displaying, or importing infringing copies. The punishment was a fine for the first offence, and a fine and/or imprisonment of up to two months with or without hard labour for a second offence. These were clearly based on section 11 of the Imperial Act.

The content of the law was inspired by the Imperial Act, but it is quite unlikely that such an amalgamated law, a British construction imposed onto an Ottoman Act with French overtones, would emerge from the Colonial Office in London. In Chapter 3 we saw that in the 1910s, the Colonial Office made an active and deliberate effort to unify the copyright laws in the Empire as much as possible. A 1917 Circular Despatch instructed the colonies in detail as to supplementing the Imperial Act with local legislation regarding customs and criminal offences.[82] The 1920 Palestinian Ordinance did not deal with customs at all and left in place some elements of the Ottoman Act which had no parallels in the British Imperial Act or in the Berne Convention. For example, the Ottoman notice requirement was not repealed; the Ordinance did not explicitly provide for a general public performing right (the Ottoman Act referred only to opera and theatrical productions); the Ordinance did not provide a fair dealing defence and its international dimension was lacking. Although a foreign subject could enjoy copyright under the Ordinance, it seems that the work had to be first published in Palestine to trigger such protection.

A comment of the High Commissioner in his first annual report, for the years 1920–1 indicates that attention was indeed given in Jerusalem to the matter, thus strengthening the conclusion that the initiative to enact the 1920 Ordinance came from Jerusalem rather than from London. The High Commissioner's report commended the Ottoman copyright law to be more modern that its patent laws, but, nevertheless, his report stated, new international obligations required some amendments to the former.[83] At the same time, in his opening speech to the Advisory Council, the High Commissioner discussed some of the legislation that was enacted up to that point, but he ignored copyright law.[84]

Another indication as to the source of the legislative initiative and its reasoning appears in later correspondence between Jerusalem and the Colonial Office, during 1922–3, as to full scale copyright legislation in Palestine. Shortly after the Mandate and the enactment of the 1922 Order in Council, the Secretary for the Colonies, Winston Churchill, sent a despatch to Jerusalem, with some instructions.[85] The High Commissioner replied, explaining that: 'The Palestine Copyright Ordinance

---

[82] Circular despatch from the Secretary of State for the Colonies (29 November 1917) NA CO 323/692/7.
[83] *Report on the Administration of Palestine, July 1920–December 1921*, submitted by the HC to Winston Churchill, the Principal Secretary of State for the Colonies, 4 July 1922, at Pt VI, p 21, NA CO 733/22.
[84] Minutes of the Advisory Council, First Meeting (6 October 1920) NA CO 814/6.
[85] Secretary of State to HC, Despatch 1201 (12 October 1922). Unfortunately, the despatch was not found in the ISA. The NA in London does not hold outgoing despatches, other than a registration (see NA CO 794/1, 12 October 1922). However, the content of the despatch was referred to in subsequent correspondence.

of 1920 was intended only as a provisional measure pending the determination of the question as to whether Palestine was territory under His Majesty's protection.'[86] A subsequent letter from Jerusalem to London, which enclosed a draft of a proposed Ordinance (to become the Copyright Ordinance 1924), indicates that the 1917 Colonial Office's Circular Despatch reached Jerusalem only in 1922, with Churchill's despatch.[87]

The accumulated sources thus indicate that the 1920 Copyright Ordinance was Jerusalem's initiative, not based on the 1917 Circular Despatch or otherwise triggered by London. Since it was before the League of Nations' Mandate of 1922, there was no external requirement to do so. Why then, the question keeps begging, did copyright deserve such a prominent place?

(3) The man behind the law

The 1920 Ordinance was clearly drafted by someone familiar with the 1911 Imperial Copyright Act who appreciated copyright law. It seems there is only one suspect: Norman Bentwich. He was a powerful Attorney General, prolific, enthusiastic about his job and highly motivated. He was responsible for all legislation and was proud of his role.[88] Bentwich was a Jewish, English barrister, who arrived in Palestine after a colonial post in Cairo. He served as the legal advisor of the British military administration and then the Attorney General to the civil administration and the Mandate.[89]

Bentwich came from a Zionist family. His father was a Zionist leader in London. Likhovski points to Bentwich's Zionist ideology as a driving force and argues that '[a]s a Zionist, Bentwich concentrated his efforts on providing Palestine with a set of modern commercial laws that he believed would facilitate economic development and thus attract more Jewish immigration'.[90] Copyright law fits within this category: it was related to commerce, it was modern and progressive. Copyright law was considered a cutting-edge legal field at the time—as it is today—and one that was deeply rooted in the idea of progress. It perfectly fitted the British Mandate and it perfectly fit Bentwich.

---

[86] HC to Secretary of State, Despatch 18 (5 January 1923) ISA M575/12.
[87] HC to Secretary of State, Despatch 77 (19 January 1923) NA 733/41/702.
[88] Bentwich routinely reported the legislative developments in Palestine in the Journal of Comparative Legislation and International Law, which circulated among legal departments in the Empire. See 'Palestine' (1918) 2 J Comp Legis & Int'l L 168; 'Palestine' (1922) 4 J Comp Legis & Int'l L 177 (this report also mentions the 1920 Copyright Ordinance, at 180: 'The Ottoman Law of Copyright issued in 1910 was found to be defective, and in order to bring the law into accord with those of the later international conventions, it was amended...'); 'The Legislation of Palestine 1918–1925' (1926) 8 J Comp Legis & Int'l L 9; 'Palestine' (1926) 8 J Comp Legis & Int'l L 228 (this report included a brief mentioning of the 1924 enactments, at 231).
[89] Bentwich was also a prolific writer. See Norman Bentwich, *England in Palestine* (Kegan Paul, Trench, Trübner & Co, 1932); Norman Bentwich, *Fulfilment in the Promised Land, 1917–1937* (Soncino Press, 1938); Margery Bentwich and Norman Bentwich, *Herbert Bentwich: The Pilgrim Father* (Hotza'ah Ivrith, 1940); Bentwich, *Wanderer*, above n 75.
[90] Likhovski, *Law and Identity*, above n 50, at 57.

But there was more to it. Bentwich was intimately familiar with this body of law; his father, Herbert Bentwich (1856–1932), was a copyright lawyer and co-author of an important book on the law of designs (1908).[91] Herbert Bentwich counselled art publishers as a solicitor in continuous litigation, with cases reaching the House of Lords.[92] Interestingly, these cases dealt with foreign works. He even testified in the House of Lords when it debated an early bill, later to become the 1911 Act.[93] Herbert was an influential and dominant character in Norman's life and he followed his father's profession. Norman and one of his sisters, Margery, published a book about their father in 1940. One chapter, entitled 'The Lawyer',[94] discusses the copyright cases in which Herbert was involved in great detail and also mentions that he testified before the Committee of the House of Lords which took up copyright reform. Several of his father's recommendations, Norman (more likely than Margery) wrote, were adopted in the 1911 Copyright Act.[95] While there is no explicit mention in Norman and Margery's book or in any of Norman's other writings on Mandate law, linking the father's practice and scholarship to the son's legislative activity, the former, at the very least, familiarized Norman with this field of law, thus enabling its smooth introduction into Palestine.

Another detail of family background further explains Bentwich's interest in copyright law: one of his sisters, Thelma Yellin, was a successful and well-known cello player, Margery was a violinist. They followed their brother to Palestine, where Thelma founded the Jerusalem Music Society.[96] Bentwich himself later became the Chairman of the Society.[97] Other members of the family were also musicians, professional or amateur. The arts deserved special attention in the Bentwich family.

Bentwich's official role, his ideological and personal background, his personal interest in copyright and in music—all taken together, joined by the indications that the 1920 Ordinance originated in Jerusalem rather than in London, suggest that he was the drafter of the 1920 Ordinance.

---

[91] Lewis Edmunds and Herbert Bentwich, *The Law of Copyright in Designs* (2nd edn, Sweet & Maxwell, 1908).
[92] See eg *Tuck & Sons v Priester* [1887] 19 QBD 48; *Hanfstaengl Art Publishing Co v Holloway* [1893] 2 QB 1; *Hanfstaengl v Empire Palace* [1894] 3 Ch 109; *Hanfstaengl v American Tobacco Co* [1894] 1 QB 347; *Hanfstaengl v H R Baines & Co Ltd* [1895] AC 20.
[93] Report from the Selected Committee of the House of Lords on the Copyright Bill, 1899 Session, at 221.
[94] *Herbert Bentwich,* above n 89, at 132–41.
[95] Ibid, at 135.
[96] Jehoash Hirshberg, 'Western Music in Mandatory Jerusalem' in Yehoshua Ben-Arieh (ed), *Jerusalem and the British Mandate: Interaction and Legacy* (Yad Ben-Zvi, 2003) 433, 437–8 (Hebrew).
[97] In this capacity, in 1931, Bentwich called the PRS in London, asking for a reduction in the fairs the Jerusalem Music Society was asked to pay. The PRS wrote to its agent in Palestine at the time: 'In view of the important office which Mr Bentwich holds as Attorney General, we think it would be good policy to make some such concession to the Musical Society, and so to evince to him that the Society is willing to act in a reasonable manner.' See PRS to Friedenberg (1 June 1931) PRS-2.

(4) The 1924 copyright legislations

By late 1922, the conditions for a full scale, British copyright legislation for Palestine were ripe. *On the British side*, copyright law was consolidated more than a decade before. *On the international side*, the Berne Convention gained force. By then, twenty-three countries were members of the Berne Union, including all European colonial powers, so global coverage was extensive. *On the imperial side*, copyright law was added to the imperial checklist. The 1917 Circular Despatch assured uniformity throughout the Empire. In 1921 even Canada, which took the most resistant position among the colonies, finally enacted its copyright law. *On the Palestinian side*, after the official Mandate over Palestine was awarded to Britain, copyright law was now also on its Palestine agenda. The Mandate explicitly required Britain to adhere to intellectual property treaties on behalf of Palestine. The Mandate was to advance the country, and the ideology of copyright law as one of progress, easily fit this goal.

Given that the basis of copyright law in place in Palestine was the Ottoman Act, based on nineteenth century French ideas, non-Berne compliant, and given that it's 1920 modifications in the Copyright Ordinance were somewhat clumsy, it was almost an obvious step for London to enact full copyright laws for Palestine.

Indeed, the 1924 copyright legislation of Palestine was initiated in London, rather than in Jerusalem. A despatch from the Secretary of State for the Colonies, Churchill, instructed thus in late 1922.[98] The High Commissioner acknowledged that the road to a copyright law was paved and proposed to submit a draft of an Order to repeal the 1920 Ordinance and the Ottoman Act, and along the lines of the 1917 Circular Despatch.[99] Within two weeks the draft was sent to London, accompanied by a formal request to extend the 1911 Imperial Act to Palestine.[100] The Colonial Office then sent the draft to the Board of Trade, where the Department of Industrial Property was located.[101]

The back-office bureaucracy took a while, but the form of the legislation was determined. It was to be a two-prong legislation, similar in form to that applied in other colonies, though not identical. Once the Mandate was official, the legal question about the status of Palestine as a 'territory under his [Majesty's] protection' in terms of the 1911 Act, was answered positively. The route chosen for legislation was a Crown Order, extending the 1911 Imperial Act to Palestine. The authority to enact the Extension Order derived from the British Foreign Jurisdiction Act 1890 and from the Imperial Copyright Act itself, rather than the Palestine Order in Council 1922.[102] The Jerusalem government was already familiar with

---

[98] See above n 85.
[99] HC to Secretary of State, Despatch 18 (5 January 1923) ISA M575/12.
[100] HC to Secretary of State, Despatch 77 (19 January 1923) NA CO 733/41/702.
[101] Colonial Office (CO) to Comptroller of the Industrial Property Department, Board of Trade (BoT) 5062/23 (8 February 1923) NA CO 733/41/708.
[102] The author of a leading textbook on Palestine law provided copyright law as an example of this channel of legislative power. See 2 Charles A Hooper, *The Civil Law of Palestine and Trans-Jordan* (Sweet & Maxwell, 1936) 61.

the idea of copyright law. It supplemented the extension with local legislation according to the 1917 Circular Despatch, like many other colonies. The authority to enact the Ordinance derived from the Palestine Order in Council 1922. The enactment of the two pieces of legislation was coordinated. Per the Palestine Order in Council, drafts of local enactments were to be published in the Official Gazette, a requirement that did not apply to the King's Orders.

On 21 March 1924, the Privy Council issued an Order in Council, extending the 1911 Imperial Act to Palestine, with minor modifications as to the dates of its commencement.[103] The extending order—but not the extended Act— was published in the Official Gazette. On 23 April 1924, the High Commissioner published a Proclamation bringing the Imperial Act into force, retroactively, as of the date of the Extension Order.[104] On 1 May 1924, the draft of the Copyright Ordinance 1924 was officially published.[105] On 5 June 1924, the Copyright Ordinance was promulgated in the form of the draft.[106] The Ottoman Authors' Rights Act was repealed and British copyright law was instantiated. Similar copyright legislation that was extended to Tanganyika, another British Mandate (a Class B Mandate) at the same time, further indicates that the enactments were part of the British imperial agenda.[107]

The Imperial Act set out the general structure of copyright law: it defined the subject matter of copyright law (original literary, dramatic, musical, and artistic works), the scope of the legal protection (the sole right of the owner to produce, reproduce, or publish a translation of the work, to perform or deliver it in public), some defences (fair dealing, reuse by the author, publicly located sculptures, educational use, news reporting), the duration of copyright (life plus fifty years), rules of ownership, civil remedies, including injunction, summary remedies, importation of copies, and some special provisions for certain works (joint works, posthumous works, government publications, mechanical instruments, political speeches, photographs, foreign works). The Copyright Ordinance dealt with customs and criminal sanctions. The punishment of hard labour was omitted. The Act did not include moral rights (which were only incorporated in Israeli law in 1981). Thus, a full-scale copyright law was applied in Palestine, at least *de jure*.

Copyright law was imposed in a top-down manner, dictated in content and in form from London. The local interests, needs, or the state of the cultural fields

---

[103] Copyright Act 1911 (Extension to Palestine) Order 1924, 114 OG 643 (21 March 1924). The Order updated the dates regarding the application to mechanical rights and to then-existing works. See Imperial Copyright Act, ss 19(7), 19(8), 24(1)(b).

[104] Copyright Act 1911 (Extension to Palestine) Order 1924—Proclamation, 114 OG 643 (23 April 1924).

[105] 114 OG 623 (1 May 1924).

[106] Copyright Ordinance 1924, 117 OG 711 (5 June 1924).

[107] The Colonial Office (CO) asked the Board of Trade (BoT) about the desirability of the Tanganyika enactment, and the latter responded positively, suggesting that 'this might be effected as in the case of Palestine by an Order-in-Council under s 28 of the Copyright Act 1911'—BoT to CO (2 April 1924) NA CO 323/920/8. Enactments followed: See The Copyright Act 1911 (Extension to the Tanganyika Territory) Order 1924. Copyright law in Tanganyika is yet to deserve full attention. It has been listed in several publications, but not discussed. See eg J S R Cole and W N Denison, *Tanganyika: The Development of its Laws and Constitution* (Stevens, 1964) 236.

were not taken into consideration. Copyright was not inapposite to local needs, but it is fair to say that in 1924 most of it was premature, as the local state of technology was still lagging behind the British, the cultural fields were still in their early stages of formation, and the legal field was not yet equipped to handle such specialization. In this sense, the British copyright enactments were quite arbitrary: at the time, there were not even any direct British interests in having copyright in Palestine: the local population spoke (and only some read) various languages, but little English. Unlike the United States or the English speaking dominions of the nineteenth century, in the 1920s, Palestine did not pose any danger to British publishers and authors. Perhaps the British anticipated that in the course of time such interests would arise. If they acted on this assumption, they turned out to be correct, as we will see in Chapter 7. Hence, the British interests in implementing copyright in Palestine had at the time less to do with direct British interests and more with their general imperial copyright agenda. In a sense, the absence of such conditions enabled the implementation of the law: it was easier to apply a new legal field (dismissing the Ottoman predecessors), than to reform an active field. The British enactments also remained the law of the land when the British left and most of Palestine came under Israel's rule.[108]

(5) Subsequent legislation

To complete the legislative picture, we should take a quick glance at subsequent legislative amendments. Most were initiated from London (with one exception regarding the copyright relationship with the United States), and each has a relatively straightforward explanation.

In 1928 the provisional orders set by the Board of Trade in England were applied to Palestine, not without some confusion.[109] In 1929, the Director of Customs issued the Copyright Regulations.[110] Additionally, an official notice of the extension of the 1911 Copyright Act to several countries was published.[111] The extension meant that the works first published in foreign countries were

---

[108] In 1953 Israel amended copyright law for the first time. The dual structure (the Imperial Act and a local Ordinance) remained in force until 2007. As for the West Bank, in 1950 it was annexed to Jordan, but the copyright law remained the prior law. Gaza, under Egyptian control, also maintained the British copyright law. See Samaan, *A Historical View*, above n 20, at 11–12, 14, 36. Once occupied by Israel in 1967, copyright law again remained untouched. In 1993, the Palestinian Authority took power over parts of the West Bank, per the Oslo Agreement with Israel. It has not yet changed the copyright law, which remains the last territory where the 1911 Imperial Copyright Act is still the law in force. See Palestinian Legal and Judicial System Al-Muqtafi, Institute of Law, Bir-Zeit University, available at http://muqtafi.birzeit.edu/en/. The Jewish settlers in the West Bank are subject to personal jurisdiction of Israeli law.

[109] Internal correspondence in CO (18 March–17 April 1929) NA CO 733/170/1. The orders set new rates of royalties to be paid according to the compulsory licence scheme for mechanical rights: Copyright Mechanical Instruments (Royalties) Order 1928, 1929 OG 20.

[110] Copyright Regulations 1929, 163 OG 231. See also the internal discussions in the CO on this matter, NA CO 733/170/1.

[111] Notice under the Copyright Act 1911 (Extension to Palestine) Order 1924, 1929, 717 OG 1012.

protected under the Act 'in like manner as if they were first published in the parts of His Majesty's dominions to which this Act extends', and that the Act provided protection also for authors who were citizens of foreign countries, as if they were British subjects.[112] During the 1930s there was a series of extensions of the Imperial Act to additional jurisdictions.[113] In 1933 the Act was applied to works of citizens of countries who were parties to the Rome Convention of 1928, which amended the Berne Convention,[114] and thereafter it was extended to additional countries.[115] Thus, the British continued weaving the imperial and international networks of copyright law. It remained a high priority in their copyright policies at least since the 1911 Act.

World War II brought about some copyright changes, with the enactment of emergency measures that empowered the Registrar of Trade Marks, Patents and Designs to grant licences under the patents, trademarks, and copyright of enemy subjects.[116] The 1910s–1920s imperial top-down coordination of copyright law was once again applied.[117]

There were some additional specific legislative issues, such as an official Notice on the reproduction of the government's survey maps, which set the cost and other conditions for reproduction.[118] In 1932 the government enacted the Telegraphic Press Messages Ordinance, which will be discussed in Chapter 9. One important change addressed the copyright relationship with the United States, stirred by a few Passover illustrations.

(6) Copyright relationship with the United States

The United States was not a member of the Berne Convention at the time (nor did it become one until 1989), and hence the copyright relationship between Britain and the United States required a special arrangement. This was achieved by a proclamation of the American President and a British Order in Council in 1915,[119] but while the US–Britain copyright relationship extended to crown colonies, it did

---

[112] Copyright Act 1911, 1 & 2 Geo 5, *c* 46, s 29(1)(a), (b).
[113] Copyright (Federated Malay States) Order 1931, 3 Laws of Palestine 2499 (Drayton); Copyright (Sarawak) Order 1937, 1066 OG 78; Copyright (North Borneo) Order 1937, 740 OG 1179.
[114] Copyright (Rome Convention) Order 1933, 3 Laws of Palestine 2501 (Drayton) (containing a reference to the Convention's text in Palestine Gazette 491 (1935), supp 1).
[115] Copyright (Rome Convention) (Morocco (Spanish Zone)) Order 1935, 511 OG 423; Copyright (Rome Convention) (Vatican City) Order 1935, 598 OG 367; Copyright (Rome Convention) (Latvia) Order 1937, 721 OG 855.
[116] Patents, Designs, Copyright and Trade Marks (Emergency) Ordinance 1939, 973 Palestine Gazette, 1485 & supp 1 at 171; Rules Under Patents, Designs, Copyright and Trade Marks (Emergency) Ordinance 1939, 973 Palestine Gazette, supp 2; see also report in 'Special Powers Conferred in Registrar of Trade Marks' (29 December 1939) *Palestine Post*, at 2.
[117] See eg BoT to Secretary of State (28 May 1940) NA CO 323/1747/21 regarding the emergency acts in Palestine and Hong Kong.
[118] Government of Palestine, Copyright Ordinance—Notice (1937) CZA A192/618. The file includes also a permission to David Idelovitch (a teacher, one of the first to teach in Hebrew, who also wrote one of the first books for children, in Hebrew), to use such maps of Rishon LeZion.
[119] Order in Council, Under the Copyright Act 1911 (1 & 2 Geo 5 *c* 46), Regulating Copyright Relations with the United States of America 1915, 3 Laws of Palestine 2509 (Drayton).

not extend to either British protectorates or, later, to mandates (Tanganyika and Palestine). Thus, works published in the United States were not protected in Palestine and vice versa. The situation was noticed only in 1930 and remedied in August 1933 by extending the British–US Order in Council to Palestine,[120] accompanied by another American Presidential Proclamation.[121] But the initiative came not from London or Jerusalem, but from a Jewish author and his Palestinian lawyer. This was a deviation from the legislative pattern.

Nahum Liphshitz published the *Illustrated Hagada, First Jerusalem Edition* in 1930. The Hagada (usually spelled Haggadah) is the traditional religious book of prayers and songs read by Jews at the festive Passover dinner. Liphshitz's *Hagada* provided the traditional Hebrew text alongside an original English translation, musical arrangements, and illustrations.[122] His potential market was the Jewish community in the United States and so he sought copyright registration with the Library of Congress. However, to his surprise, the request was denied: the American registrar explained to Liphshitz's lawyer, Dr Ellie Cohen, that the authors were citizens of Palestine, and no copyright relationship had been established between the United States and Palestine. The Library of Congress returned the registration fee of $2, but retained the copy for the Library.[123]

Cohen was unwilling to accept this result and started pulling strings. He wrote to the Chief Secretary of the government of Palestine, complaining that the Americans were wrong and that under a 1929 Public Notice , the Copyright Act was extended to the United States. He asked the Chief Secretary to take steps for the protection of Palestinian works in the United States.[124] The government replied that it would 'cause steps to be taken' to establish such copyright relationship.[125] And so the Jerusalem government acted. It approached the Colonial Office, which then consulted the Board of Trade and then wrote to the Foreign Office, which turned to the British Representatives in Washington, who turned to the US government.[126] The process took time, as the British realized that the same

---

[120] Copyright (United States of America) Order 1915 (Extension to Palestine) Order 1933, 405 Palestine Gazette 1767.

[121] Proclamation by the President of the United States of America, Copyright—Palestine (Excluding Trans-Jordan) (28 November 1933), reprinted in 405 Palestine Gazette 1767.

[122] The translation was by Julian Meltzer; the music by Solomon Rosowsky, and the illustrations by Arieh Al-Hanani.

[123] Acting Registrar of Copyrights, Library of Congress, to Dr Elli Cohen (1 August 1930) CZA 525/5504. The current entry for the Hagada indicates that it was donated later on. See http://lccn.loc.gov/2008427456.

[124] Cohen to CS (25 August 1930) CZA 525/5504. The issue was not new to the government, as the 1929 Notice drew the attention of another Jewish lawyer, Kalman Friedenberg, who six months before Cohen had written to the government that the British 1915 Order in Council regarding the United States contained some limitations. See A-G to CS (28 February 1930) ISA M32/2 doc 11. We shall meet Friedenberg again later on, in Chs 7 and 9. A clarifying notice was published in March 1930. See ISA M32/2 doc 14.

[125] Acting CS to Cohen (5 September 1930) CZA 525/5504.

[126] Officer Administering the Government to the Secretary of State, Despatch 818 (12 September 1930) ISA M32/2 doc 23; Secretary of State to HC (25 August 1931) ISA M32/2 doc 48 (enclosing the letter of the CO to the Foreign Office); CO to the Industrial Property Department at the BoT (31 October 1930) NA CO 323/1098/20 doc 2; Industrial Property Department at the BoT to CO

legal gap applied to citizens of other protectorates and mandates: their works were not protected in the United States. The result was the establishment of a copyright relationship between the United States and *all* British protectorates and mandates. One illustrated Haggadah managed to drive the President of the United State to allow copyright to the works of citizens of British mandates and protectorates.

This was quite a remarkable achievement. It could occur only on the basis of several cumulative factors—an emerging local cultural field, emerging local legal expertise, British understanding of the importance of global copyright, and a willingness to assist. Of course, a bit of *chutzpa* was helpful as well. This episode also illuminates the neglect of the colonies until then: when the British enacted copyright laws for their colonies, they were concerned about British authors and publishers. The Imperial Act protected both the British and the colonized territories' authors, but with the probably inadvertent omission of the protectorates (the mandates came later on). The colonized authors were simply not on the British agenda.

The last to know about all of these developments was Liphshitz himself. In January 1934, sometime after the copyright relationship between Palestine and the United States was established, he called upon the American Economic Committee for Palestine and asked for their assistance. The society wrote to the Political Department of the Jewish Agency, asking it to pull strings, as well as to the government itself.[127] The reply was short, directing the Committee's attention to the 1933 establishment of such a copyright relationship.[128] The Committee apologized.[129]

(7) Publication and translation of the law

The comprehensive statutory scheme might convey the impression that there was a full and orderly legal copyright regime in Mandate Palestine. However, the Ottoman Authors' Rights Act was not formally published or easily accessible in Palestine, and some of the earlier British laws were inaccessible until the mid 1930s. Chief among them was the 1911 Imperial Copyright Act itself, the cornerstone of the copyright regime. While the Extension Order was published in the Official Gazette in 1924, the extended Act was not published there. It was published in 1926 in an unofficial compilation, which was not as widely circulated as the Gazette.[130] It took a decade for the Act to be officially published in English in

---

(7 November 1930) NA CO 323/1098/20 doc 3; Industrial Property Department at the BoT to CO (10 December 1930) NA CO 323/1098/20 doc 5.

[127] See American Economic Committee for Palestine to the Jewish Agency (26 January 1934, 8 February 1934, 21 November 1935) CZA 525/5504; American Economic Committee for Palestine to CS (25 November 1935) ISA M32/2 doc 122.

[128] CS to American Economic Committee for Palestine (5 December 1935) ISA M32/2 doc 124.

[129] American Economic Committee for Palestine to the Jewish Agency (9 December 1935) CZA 525/5504.

[130] Copyright Act 1911, Legislation of Palestine 412 (Bentwich 1918–25) (published 1926).

the collection edited by Robert Harry Drayton (1934),[131] and another two years before it was translated into Hebrew (1936)[132] and Arabic (1936).[133]

The lack of official publication caused some confusion. One of the first copyright cases, and the first to reach the Supreme Court, was *Palestine Telegraphic Agency v Jaber* (1931).[134] The Palestine Telegraphic Agency and the Palestine Bulletin sued Jaber, the editor and publisher of an Arab newspaper, *Al-Hayat*, for the unauthorized copying of news reports. The case has several layers that will be taken up in Chapter 9. For the time being, one argument made by the defendant requires attention. He argued that the Act 'although extended to Palestine by the Order-in-Council of 21st March 1924, has never been promulgated in Palestine, and therefore cannot be held to form part of the Law of Palestine'.[135] Kalman Friedenberg, attorney for the plaintiff, responded that the 1922 Order in Council required only the publication of *local* Ordinances, but did not apply to legislation issued by the Crown and the Privy Council. The magistrate and district courts agreed. The issue was not raised in the appeal to the Supreme Court. Nevertheless, Friedenberg himself voiced the concern that similar arguments would be made in the future and suggested that the Copyright Act be published.[136]

The petitions were taken seriously. The Director of Customs, who was the Registrar of Patents and Designs, advocated an exception for copyright law and urged ('I feel strongly') that it be published. His reasoning is telling:

[A]n exception should be made in the case of the Copyright Act 1911, since the subject of Copyright is of considerable importance and interest to many people in Palestine as correspondence on the subject filed at this Office shows... It is hardly possible to point out that with the large Jewish population in Palestine the position is somewhat different from that of other British Colonies.[137]

There were two arguments made here: that copyright was different, and that Palestine was different. The justification for publication was found in the

---

[131] Copyright Act 1911, 3 Laws of Palestine 2475 (Drayton). The publication of the Drayton collection was an important event in the development of the law in Palestine. See Eliezer Malchi, *The History of Law in Eretz Yisrael: A Historical Introduction to the Law in Israel* (2nd edn, Dinim, 1953) 122 (Hebrew).

[132] Copyright Act 1911, 3 Hukei Eretz Yisrael 2633 (1917–33) (Hebrew).

[133] Copyright Act 1911, Qawaneen Falasteen (1917–33) (Arabic).

[134] See the two Magistrate's decisions: *Palestine Telegraphic Agency v Jaber* (9 October 1931) (published 11 October 1931) Palestine Bulletin, and the final judgment of 7 November 1931 (published 9 November 1931) Palestine Bulletin; the District Court's decision: CA 236/31 *Palestine Telegraphic Agency v Jaber* (nd) CZA JAS/1; the Supreme Court's decision: CA 66/32 *Palestine Telegraphic Agency v Jaber* [1933] 1 PLR 780. For news reports, see 'Appeal in the Copyright Case' (20 January 1932) *Haaretz*, at 1 (Hebrew); 'PTA Appeal on Copyright Case' (5 January 1933) *Haaretz*, at 1 (Hebrew); 'In the Courts' (5 January 1933) *Palestine Post*, at 4.

[135] Quoted in PRS to Secretary of State (19 April 1932) ISA M32/2 doc 51a.

[136] Friedenberg to CS (1 September 1932) ISA M32/2 doc 66. Friedenberg, who served as an attorney for the PRS at the time, pulled that string as well and asked the PRS to approach the Colonial Office in London on the same matter. See Friedenberg to PRS (7 April 1932) PRS-2. The PRS followed his advice. See PRS to Secretary of State, ibid.

[137] Director of the Department of Customs, Excises & Trade to CS (21 June 1932) ISA M32/2 doc 57.

connection between the Jewish community and the law (copyright). No less interesting is the absence of the Arab population from this explanation. Recall that the publication issue was raised in court by an Arab defendant.[138] These themes as presented by the British officials at the time—the uniqueness of copyright law, the special cultural needs of the Jews, and the exclusion of Arabs—are part of the identity puzzle in Palestine.[139]

The internal discussion within the Mandate government ended temporarily with the High Commissioner's decision not to publish the Act. The reasons provided to the Secretary of the Colonies were that there was 'no practical necessity for doing so, and publication would involve translating the Act into Arabic and Hebrew', and that '[t]he subject is not one with which the average member of the public is closely concerned', whereas lawyers would be able to find the Act.[140] Copyright law was finally and officially published in September 1934, when the Mandate government issued three volumes of the Laws of Palestine edited by Drayton.

It took another two years until the Hebrew edition was published. The translation was made by Izhak Abbady, the Chief Hebrew translator of the Mandate government, or by one of his assistants. Abbady explained that most of the translations were based on the Hebrew versions of the Official Gazette, with some corrections and unification of terms. Interestingly, Abbady reflected on the methodology of translation, pointing to two options: literal translation and interpretive translation. The ideal way, he concluded, was to translate the original text in a literal manner and turn to the interpretive method only when necessary.[141] Unfortunately, the Hebrew translation of the 1911 Act was rather poor, earning it notoriety in the years to come.[142]

D. Conclusion

The Ottomans were first to introduce copyright law to the Middle East, but their nineteenth century European-inspired law remained in the Ottoman books, books which were hardly available in Palestine. The British were quick to apply their version of copyright law, a modern, comprehensive, and international legal regime. The first step was an initiative of the Jerusalem government of Palestine and quite

---

[138] The defendant had an Arab lawyer for the first two phases of the litigation, and his Jewish partner, David Goitein, for the Supreme Court. Goitein was later to become a Supreme Court Justice in Israel (1953–61). See Ch 9.

[139] Likhovski, *Law and Identity*, above n 50.

[140] HC to Secretary of State (9 July 1932) ISA M32/2 doc 67. The High Commissioner pointed to the reproduction of the Copyright Act in the 'Legislation of Palestine'. The reference is to a compilation edited by Bentwich. The Colonial Office followed suit and replied to the PRS along similar lines. See CO to PRS (28 July 1932) PRS-2.

[141] Izhak Abbady, 'Hebrew Introduction to Hukei Eretz Yisrael' (Robert Harry Drayton ed, 1936) 9 (Hebrew).

[142] Most regretful was the omission of the word 'original' from s 1(1), the single most important condition for copyright protection. Only in 1985 did the Israeli Supreme Court clarify that the original language of the 1911 Copyright Act is binding and originality has not been omitted from Israeli copyright law. CA 360/83 *Strosky Ltd v Vitman Ice-cream Ltd*, 40(3) PD 340, 346 (1985).

likely, that of the Attorney General, Norman Bentwich. The second step came at the direction of Westminster, who led the process from above and instructed what should be done. The rather prominent place that copyright law deserved under the British rule of Palestine poses a puzzle.

This chapter provided some explanations: by the early twentieth century, copyright law was consolidated, it was on the imperial agenda which intertwined with the international agenda. The colonial copyright project continued. It also fit the British agenda for Palestine, of developing the region, and it fit the personal and ideological agenda of the man behind the first enactment, Bentwich. The law was meant to serve first and foremost the British interests, though at the time there were no such specific British interests. One major player was absent from this discussion: the local population. This is a pattern which we saw in the previous chapter regarding other colonies: copyright law was imposed from the centre onto the periphery in a top-down process, without paying attention to the local culture. This lack of attention to the local, colonized peoples' needs is evident in the legislative process, detailed above, and in subsequent episodes such as the delayed publication and poor translation of the law. The next chapter asks about the first reception of the British law among one group, namely Hebrew authors in the late 1920s.

5
Constructing Culture and the Image of the Hebrew Author

> With the same devotion that our young pioneers demonstrated when they deserted all the good in the old homeland, with its halls of science and art and the beauty of its life, and took over the wasteland fields of Zion, to cultivate them and fertilise them with the sweat of their brow and the prime of their life, so did the people of this profession, the profession of theatre in Eretz-Israel, to place it on a new level, different from that of the Jewish theatre in the exile.
>
> Menachem Gnessin, Director of the Eretz-Israel Theatre, 1946.[1]

A. Introduction

As the curtains came up on the first plays of the Eretz-Israel Theatre (EIT) in Tel-Aviv in 1925, the Hebrew actor was at the centre of the stage. By then, a full *copyright regime* was in place in Palestine. Guided by the framework of *colonial copyright*, this chapter begins the exploration of the next links in the chain of the legal transplant: the first steps of the reception of British copyright law in Palestine. As far as the British were concerned, the transplantation ended in 1924 with the formal enactments of the Copyright Act and the Copyright Ordinance. As far as the colonized were concerned, the implementation only started.

The gap between the legislation of the legal transplant and the de facto reception guides this chapter. It discusses the Yishuv—the new, Zionist Hebrew community. We begin with outlining the cultural background for the legal story: the emergence of the local Hebrew culture in Palestine. During the 1920s the Hebrew community was undergoing dramatic changes (as it did at any point during the Mandate). Hundreds of thousands of Jewish immigrants settled in Palestine, mostly from Eastern and central Europe; new settlements and towns were built; the economy first boomed and then receded. The tensions with the local Arab community intensified, leading to violent clashes especially in 1921 and 1929, anticipating the much more violent decade that would follow. Amidst these dynamic events, the Hebrew community was forming its cultural life and constructing fields of cultural

---

[1] Menachem Gnessin, *My Way with the Hebrew Theatre* (HaKibbutz HaMeuchad, 1946) 12 (Hebrew).

production.² The building of the cultural field was deliberately national all over and was conceived as part of the project of national revival.

The players in the cultural fields could have turned to British copyright law and used its ready-made rules in the construction of the local culture, but they did not. The law could have regulated at least some aspects of the field: the scope of the bundle of rights associated with a copyrighted work, issues of ownership, transfer of rights, licensing, and enforcement. Instead, the players constructed their own rules. Only a decade later they turned to use formal law.

Why didn't the Hebrew authors and publishers use the available law until the mid 1930s? I offer two kinds of explanations. One, discussed in this chapter, is a legal–cultural explanation, and the second, discussed in Chapter 6, is socio-legal. The foreign, British law reflected British conceptions of the creative process and of the author, which did not fit the parallel Hebrew conceptions. Colonial copyright ignored local cultural needs. Importantly, the British law in the books and the Hebrew cultural needs did not directly conflict: they were simply on different tracks. Within the Zionist cultural field, the image of the author was of a romantic figure, though less individualistic than his (or her, in only a few cases) European counterparts, but with a collective spin: the author was expected to place the Hebrew community first, and himself only in second place. This local image was not reflected in the foreign law.

B. The Emerging Hebrew Cultural Field

The Hebrew community in Mandate Palestine was actively constructing its cultural life. It was viewed as a crucial element of Zionism. Arieh Saposnik aptly observed that 'to Zionism's activities in Palestine, generating culture... meant generating the nation itself'.³ The seeds were sowed earlier, with the first two waves (Hebrew: *aliyah*) of immigration to the region in the late nineteenth century and the beginning of the twentieth century. The third wave during the late 1910s and early 1920s, and more so the fourth wave during the 1920s, boosted the cultural developments. All cultural fields were infused all the way through with a national ideology. Fine arts, photography, theatre, film, music, literature, and journalism, were all to serve the national cause.

We begin with a broad-brush overview of the emerging cultural life, so to lay the background for the discussion of the image of the author, and to indicate where and when copyright law was operated. We shall see the main developments in several cultural fields;⁴ discuss the relationship of the Hebrew community with the Arab community, and the former's internal divisions. A special attention is given

---

² Pierre Bourdieu, *The Field of Cultural Production: Essays on Art and Literature* (Cambridge University Press, 1993).

³ Arieh Bruce Saposnik, *Becoming Hebrew: The Creation of a Jewish National Culture in Ottoman Palestine* (Oxford University Press, 2008) 18.

⁴ The discussion builds on detailed research conducted by other scholars as to each cultural field, supplemented with primary archival materials.

to the Hebrewness of the culture, and finally, to the role of the British government, which was mostly one of a bystander.

(1) The cultural timeline

The first steps of building the Zionist culture in Palestine were undertaken in the late nineteenth century, especially in theatre and literature, but these were mostly local—geographically limited to the single rural town, the *moshava* (Hebrew: colony, single form; plural form: *moshavot*). These attempts were amateur and not sustainable.[5] The first decade of the twentieth century met with more such attempts, with the addition of music and first deliberate attempts to create sustainable activities, especially in literature and the arts. The 1910s were times of political unrest, with World War I attracting attention, energy, and financial resources, and then the new British military administration. Nevertheless, some cultural advancement took place, notably the establishment of local movie theatres. The first Hebrew films were produced towards the end of the 1910s.

In the 1920s, especially during the second half of the decade, Palestine, now under British administration, witnessed substantial progress. Two universities provided higher education: the Hebrew University in Jerusalem and the Technion in Haifa. The cultural activity shifted from the local level to the national, from the rural areas to the cities (especially the fast growing Hebrew town, Tel-Aviv). It was better organized and became more professional. By the end of the decade the Hebrew cultural fields, especially literature, arts, and music, matured and became a fact.

The following is a broad summary of the main cultural fields in the Yishuv. The focus is on the mainstream rather than the fringes, with an eye to the fields that could, but did not, turn to copyright law to settle some of their issues.

(a) Fine arts

In the field of fine arts, the first important development took place in 1906, when Boris Schatz established the Bezalel School of Arts and Crafts in Jerusalem.[6] The school has operated almost continuously, with some suspension during World War I to the present day. It took some time to produce local artists, and the students often travelled to Europe, especially France, for advanced studies.[7] In 1910, art classes were also offered in Tel-Aviv. The field earned a substantial boost in the 1920s, with the establishment of a Hebrew Artists Society, and later a series of public exhibitions, known as the *Tower of David Art Exhibitions*.[8] The opening

---

[5] For the literature of the first wave of immigration, see Yaffa Berlovitz, *Inventing A Land, Inventing A People* (HaKibbutz HaMeuchad, 1996) 9, 199–200, 217–19.

[6] See Dalia Manor, *Art in Zion: The Genesis of Modern National Art in Jewish Palestine* (Routledge, 2005) 9–42 (discussing the history, ideology, and shortcomings of Bezalel).

[7] Graciela Trajtenberg, *Between Nationalism and Art* (Magnes, 2005) 21 (Hebrew).

[8] Ibid, at 2 (the 1910 classes), at 28–9, 34 (the Artists' Society, which in 1934 was renamed as the Association of Painters and Sculptures of Eretz-Israel).

112   *Colonial Copyright*

of Tel-Aviv Museum followed in 1932 and was an important stabilizing event.[9] Outside Tel-Aviv and Jerusalem there were some local painters, sculptures, and others engaging in fine arts.

By and large, copyright law was not part of the fine arts field. Interestingly, during the Mandate there was only one documented copyright case related to fine arts, much later in the day. It dealt with a specially commissioned tombstone that was copied by the constructor.[10]

Photography was also developing, though newspapers did not use photographs until the 1930s.[11] Photographers were usually freelancers who worked for Jewish institutions, such as the Jewish National Fund (JNF; Hebrew: *Keren Kayemeth LeIsrael*, KKL), and the United Israel Appeal (*Keren Hayesod*), either on a regular basis or on a per-item basis. This pattern of commissioned works, meant that the institutions closely watched and dictated the content.[12] The institutions insisted on receiving the negatives of the photographs, so that they are free to reuse them. Rona Sela argues that the institutions' purpose was to build a long-lasting Zionist archive, documenting Zionism.[13] We can add the legal reasoning behind this demand. According to the Copyright Act (section 21), the party that owned the negative owned the copyright in the photograph. The institutions could assure their ownership through contracts and the pattern of the work (as a work made for hire, either as employers or as commissioners of the work, according to section 5(1) of the Act), but the ownership of the negatives assured their control. Only much later on, professional photographers who were members of the fifth wave of immigration, many of whom were Jews fleeing Nazi Germany, objected to giving up their copyright, despite repeat demands. The Jewish Institutions remained the owners of the negatives—and of the copyright in the photographs.[14]

(b) Music

Musical activity developed in a bottom-up way, first with small local amateur concerts and later on with institutional components adding up. The first orchestras formed in the *moshavot* in the late nineteenth century. Notable among these was the Rishon LeZion orchestra, funded by its residents with the financial support of

---

[9] Ibid, at 37.
[10] See Ch 11.
[11] See Shlomo Shva, 'The Eretz-Israeli Photojournalism' (1989) 5 Kesher 110 (Hebrew).
[12] Rona Sela, *Photography in Palestine in the 1930s–1940s* (HaKibbutz Hameuchad, 2000) 45, 156–60 (Hebrew).
[13] Ibid, at 150.
[14] Ibid, at 151–6. Sela reports one lawsuit of a photographer, Walter Zadek, against the JNF, in 1945. The suit was submitted to the internal court of the Zionist Organization. The cause of action was copyright infringement and 'unfair and immoral' behaviour. *Zadek v JNF* (18 August 1945) CZA KKL5/14127. The JNF was surprised that anyone could sue it in that court, as it wrote to the chairman of the court. It is unclear whether the case was litigated at all. For the fifth wave of immigration, see Yoav Gelber, *New Homeland: Immigration and Absorption of Central European Jews 1933–1948* (Yad Ben-Zvi, 1990) (Hebrew).

Baron Rothschild.[15] Choirs were formed a bit later. A highly successful and influential music school was established by Shulamit Ruppin in Jaffa, in 1910, with a less successful Jerusalem branch in 1911.[16] Jehoash Hirshberg pointed out that Ruppin's model was based on European schools with which she was familiar and without interaction with Arab or Jewish-Sephardi music.[17] The music school staged concerts during the 1910s.

As in most other cultural fields, the boost to the musical life took place in the 1920s, with the growing number of immigrants, including musicians. In 1921 a Hebrew Music Society was formed in Tel-Aviv: it performed a first opera two years later.[18] The second half of the 1920s signalled a significant change, as the financial situation improved (with the fourth wave of immigration, though a recession followed as well).[19] Meir Kovalsky, who opened a first music shop in Tel-Aviv in 1914, now opened more shops in Jerusalem and Haifa. He was to become a central figure in the implementation of copyright law in Palestine, later on.[20]

For the first time, musicians found full-time employment in their profession. A popular job was to play music in cafes and in cinema theatres, alongside silent movies.[21] This development was important in copyright terms, as playing music in such public venues amounted to public performances. Indeed, the very first copyright case to be brought to a court of law, in 1929, was directed at the owners of a Jerusalem theatre.[22] Ironically, by the time copyright law caught up, this practice had faded, as talking movies—the talkies, as they were called—rapidly replaced the silent movie. Live music in movie theatres became obsolete at once.[23]

The British brought English music with them, with growing popularity. The 1930s signalled the entrance of foreign copyright owners into the local field. The foreign performing rights societies initiated local legal activities: they collected royalties and were the first to use the formal law to enforce their rights. This will be the subject of Chapter 7. The Hebrew musicians watched and followed suit: in the early 1930s they started their own performing rights society, ACUM. The next substantial development for the local musical life was the establishment of the radio station by the British government in 1936 (Chapter 8).

---

[15] Jehoash Hirshberg, *Music in the Jewish Community of Palestine 1880–1948: A Social History* (Oxford University Press, 1995) 25–8.

[16] Ibid, at 38–40.

[17] Yehoash Hirshberg, 'Setting the Framework of Musical Life' in Zohar Shavit (ed), *The Construction of Hebrew Culture in Eretz Yisrael* (Bialik Institute, 1989) 100–1 (Hebrew).

[18] Hirshberg, *Music*, above n 15, at 69.

[19] Dan Giladi, *The Yishuv during the Fourth Wave of Immigration (1924–1929): An Economic and Political Discussion* (Am Oved, 1973) (Hebrew).

[20] Hirshberg, *Music*, above n 15, at 113, 116. We will meet Kovalsky again in Ch 7.

[21] Ibid, at 61–3. The archives of the Zion Theatre in Jerusalem include what seems to be the first such contract between the theatre owners, Gut and Peretz, and Mrs Cohen, a pianist (22 November 1921). It stipulated that she should play the piano whenever a movie is screened. Her payment was ten Egyptian Pennies per play. Thereafter, there are no contracts filed, until 1928. See contracts between Gut & Peretz (as proprietors of Aviv Cinema) and Max Lampel, a pianist (29 June 1928); Yakov Ladislaouz, a violinist (29 June 1928); Issac Averbouch, a violinist (23 April 1929), and a contract with the Eretz-Israeli Opera (23 October 1929), JCA 472 File 80.

[22] See Ch 7.

[23] Hirshberg, *Music*, above n 15, at 63–4.

(c) Theatre

Theatre was a vibrant cultural field in the Yishuv.[24] The idea of theatre was foreign to the Old Yishuv, but the Zionist immigrants brought it from Europe. Theatre was a scene of both entertainment and politics, perhaps like all arts. As in the case of music, the first Hebrew theatrical events were local and amateur: productions were performed in front of small audiences for the participants' own pleasure. The first documented play in Hebrew was Moshe Leib Lilienblum's *Zerubbabel*, produced by a Jerusalem teacher, David Yellin in 1890.[25] Shimon Lev-Ari documented twenty-three performances of this kind until 1904.[26]

Professional theatre emerged during the second and third waves of immigration, in the late 1910s and early 1920s. The first professional theatre company was the *Hebrew Theatre*, which operated until 1927,[27] and the second was the EIT, established by the actress Miriam Bernstein-Cohen and the energetic director, Menachem Gnessin, in 1924 in Berlin. The EIT immigrated to Palestine a year later.[28] Both theatres were heavily inspired by Russian and German theatre. Gnessin, in the EIT, was especially keen to follow *HaBima* (Hebrew: The Stage), the Jewish Theatre established in Moscow in 1918 that had already won wide appreciation. *HaBima* toured Palestine in 1928–9 and settled in Tel-Aviv in 1931.[29] The EIT was absorbed into *HaBima*. By the late 1920s theatre was a well-established cultural form in Palestine, with a third commercial theatre established in 1925, *HaOhel* (Hebrew: The Tent) and two satirical theatres *HaKumkum* (Hebrew: The Kettle) in 1927, and *HaMatate* (Hebrew: The Broom), in 1928.[30]

In terms of organization, the theatre companies were in the form of collectives, meaning that the actors made decisions regarding the repertoire, local and international tours, and management decisions, even though each had its own dominant figures. This structure led, not surprisingly, to continuous debates about the language (Hebrew won over Yiddish), accent (the players undertook much effort to speak in the Sephardi rather than the Ashkenazi accent), and about the plays

---

[24] Mendel Kohansky, *The Hebrew Theatre: Its First Fifty Years* (Israel Universities Press, 1969) (Hebrew).

[25] Shlomo Haramati, 'Zerubbabel: The First Play in Eretz-Israel' (2002) 5 Hed HaHinuch 28 (Hebrew).

[26] Shimon Lev-Ari, 'Setting the Framework of Theater Life' in *The Construction of Hebrew Culture*, above n 17, at 93 (Hebrew).

[27] Shimon Lev-Ari, 'The Development of the Theaters' in *The Construction of Hebrew Culture*, above n 17, at 343, 345–50 (Hebrew).

[28] See Lev-Ari, 'The Development', ibid, at 350–3; Shelly Zer-Zion, 'The Eretz-Israel Theatre: Moving between Cultural Peripheries' (2007) 99 Zmanim 16 (Hebrew); Sara Leshem, *T.A.I.* (MA Thesis, Faculty of Fine Arts, Department of Theatre, TAU, 1990) (Hebrew).

[29] Shimon Lev-Ari, 'The "Habima" Theater: From Russia to Eretz-Israel' in *The Construction of Hebrew Culture*, above n 17, at 57–67 (Hebrew).

[30] Lev-Ari, 'The Development', above n 27, at 354–7; David Alexander, *HaKumkum: The First Satirical Theatre in Israel (1926–1929)* (MA Thesis, Faculty of Arts, Theatre Arts Department, Tel-Aviv University, 1975) (Hebrew). Alexander mentions several instances in which authors complained that Avigdor HaMeiri, the founder of HaKumkum, substantially edited their material, omitted their credit and inserted his own (at 136–7).

themselves. The latter was a persistent item on the theatre's agenda. There were insufficient original Hebrew plays, especially during the 1920s, hence the collectives chose plays that were written by Jews in Europe, either in Hebrew or translated from Yiddish.[31] The actors knew they were educating the Yishuv and they were highly aware of their role in the construction of social cohesion. On the stage and behind the scenes everything was as personal as it was political.

Perhaps it was the organizational structure, the constant concerns about finances and the political and personal issues that kept them occupied, but the result was that the theatres gave little attention to copyright issues. In fact, the theatres were recurrent players, on the accused side. Authors and translators kept complaining that the theatres produced their plays or used their translations without asking for permission, attributing it to them, or paying them. We shall see such examples in Chapter 6.

(d) Movies

Cinematography was the newest and most exciting form of entertainment during the first decades of the twentieth century in Palestine. It was popular culture and thus struggled to gain appreciation of the elite.[32] The Palestinian field lagged a bit behind other countries. The initial steps started in the late nineteenth century. We can observe a sustainable field only in the 1930s.[33]

Local and sporadic screenings started in 1908 in Jerusalem and Jaffa, by non-Jews,[34] and the first Hebrew cinema—*Eden*—opened its doors in Tel-Aviv in 1914, but only in 1919 it started showing movies on a regular basis. Its owners received a thirteen year monopoly for operating theatres from the town's council. The result was that another theatre was established in neighbouring Jaffa, and when *Eden*'s monopoly expired in 1927 several cinemas opened at once.[35] The first cinema in Jerusalem was the Zion Theatre, established in 1916.[36] As mentioned, theatre owners arranged for live music played alongside the silent films, which was a trigger for the entrance of copyright law in late 1929. The first talking movie, an Al Jolson film, went on show in 1929.

---

[31] See eg the memoirs of Miriam Bernstein-Cohen, *A Drop in the Sea* (Massada, 1971) 116, 144 (Hebrew).
[32] An art critic offered an interesting and sophisticated analysis of film as a cultural form. See Gabriel Talpir, 'The Film' (13 August 1926) *Ktuvim*, at 4 (Hebrew).
[33] See Moshe Zimmerman, 'The Development of Hebrew Cinema in the Jewish Settlement' in *The Construction*, above n 17, at 573 (Hebrew); Nathan and Jacob Gross, *The Hebrew Movie: Chapters in the History of the Silent and Talking Movie in Israel* (Nathan and Jacob Gross, 1991) (Hebrew); Moshe Zimmerman, *Signs of Cinema: the History of Israeli Cinema, 1896–1948* (Dionon, 2001) (Hebrew); Ariel L Feldstein, *Pioneer, Toil, Camera: Cinema in Service of the Zionist Ideology, 1917–1939* (Am Oved, 2009) (Hebrew).
[34] Shoshana HaLevy, *First Issues in the Yishuv's History* (Jerusalem, 1989) 105–6 (Hebrew).
[35] See L Be'eri, 'Movies and Silent Movie Cinemas' in A B Yaffe (ed), *Literature and Art in Small Tel-Aviv, 1909–1929* (HaKibbutz HaMeuchad, 1980) 272, 274–8 (Hebrew); David Shalit, *Projecting Power: The Cinema Houses, the Movies and the Israelis* (Resling Publishing, 2006) 19–26 (Hebrew).
[36] HaLevy, *First Issues*, above n 34, at 107. The Zion Theatre was the defendant in the first copyright case in Palestine. See Ch 7.

The first shootings were made by foreigners, the earliest known in 1895.[37] The first Zionist movie shot in Palestine was in 1911, for the purpose of screening it to the Zionist Congress in Basel. It was appropriately entitled: *The First Film of Palestine*.[38]

The first local Hebrew movies were produced in the late 1910s, with Jacob Ben-Dov being the first producer. His movies were short, silent, semi-documentary, and above all, overtly Zionist in their content and purpose.[39] Ben-Dov was offered employment with the JNF, but preferred to maintain his artistic freedom.[40] Thus, he funded his first movie (*Yehuda HaMeshuchreret—Liberated Judea*) himself and then tried to sell it to the JNF. In following years he produced more such movies and sold the rights to the Jewish institutions. One of these contracts was found, dating to 1923, just before the 1924 copyright enactments: Ben-Dov transferred all his rights to the JNF.[41] It is an early and rare case where there was an explicit reference to copyright. Perhaps the reason was that the JNF was incorporated as a British company, or due to its experience with still photographs.[42]

Liberated Judea resulted in a legal dispute, the first about movies. The movie was sold to Yechiel Weizmann (the brother of the influential Jewish statesman, Chaim Weizmann), who failed to market it in the United Kingdom. Weizmann then deposited the film with an employee of the Zionist Agency in London, who then sold it to a third party. A dispute as to the ownership of the film broke out. It was adjudicated in the Jerusalem Court of the Hebrew Law of Peace, which was an internal Hebrew court, operated by laymen. The judges found in favour of the plaintiff and ordered the agency's employee to return the movie or pay compensation.[43] For the purpose of our discussion, the dispute is intriguing, more for what is not in it: copyright law was not the issue. It was a property dispute about ownership of the tangible film. Today, an equivalent dispute would be exactly the opposite: about the copyright and not about the object. At the time, the party

---

[37] Feldstein, *Pioneer*, above n 33, at 19; Zimmerman, 'The Development', above n 33, at 573; Joseph Halachmi, *Fresh Wind: The First Zionist Film in Palestine 1899–1902* (Carmel, 2009) 68–73 (Hebrew).

[38] The producer/photographer was a British Jew, Murrey (Moshe) Rosenberg. See Feldstein, *Pioneer*, above n 33, at 20.

[39] For Ben-Dov's movie making, see Feldstein, *Pioneer*, above n 33, at 29–67; Zimmerman, *Signs*, above n 33, at 44–56.

[40] Feldstein, *Pioneer*, above n 33, at 32–4; Zimmerman, *Signs*, above n 33, at 45; Gross, *The Hebrew Movie*, above n 33, at 22.

[41] Covenant, 19 February 1923, CZA KKL2/236–32, 33 (Hebrew). Section 10 reads: 'Both regarding the film and the photographic pictures, KKL [the JNF] owns all rights (ownership rights, authors rights, etc), and Mr Ben-Dov does not have the right to use them in any manner.'

[42] The Fifth Zionist Congress decided in 1901 to establish the JNF; in 1907 it registered as a company in England, and in 1920 as a foreign company operating in Palestine.

[43] Case 17/684 (District Court, Hebrew Law of Peace, Jerusalem, 5 August 1924). The full transcript and the decision are reproduced in Gross, *The Hebrew Movie*, above n 33, at 57–62. For discussion, see Gross, at 22; Feldstein, *Pioneer*, above n 33, at 34; Zimmerman, *Signs*, above n 33, at 45–6. Later on, the employee informed the court that he managed to regain the movie from the buyer, but that the plaintiff was uninterested in it. Tish to Hebrew Court of the Peace, 23 December 1924, reproduced in Gross (at 62).

that held the object controlled its use. In today's digital world, the object and the work, the chattel and the content are separable.

The early 1930s saw the expansion of the field as well as first uses of copyright law in the local film market. The active party was the Performing Rights Society (PRS), through its local agent, Meir Kovalsky. We shall return to the PRS in Chapter 7. New cinemas opened their doors and the audience showed up enthusiastically. Most of the films were foreign and translated into Hebrew. Local distributors served as intermediaries between the foreign production companies and the local cinemas.[44] Their contracts reveal that payment was per movie; copyright law or references to distribution rights were not mentioned,[45] but for a few warnings: in 1936, a film distributor in Tel-Aviv notified the proprietors of the Zion Theatre in Jerusalem that it held the sole right for the exploitation of several movies. The distributor added that it had learned that 'there are people who made copies of the movies and offer them to the cinemas'.[46] Thus, by then, copyright law was used in the industry and enforced against first pirates. The industry norms have incorporated copyright law, in the sense that screening was understood to amount to a public performance. In 1937 the Polish-Palestine Chamber of Commerce inquired with the Tel-Aviv Municipality whether Polish movies had been screened in local cinemas, for purposes of collecting royalties. The city asked the information from the cinemas, without disclosing the purpose.[47]

The cinema owners competed fiercely but collaborated in negotiating with third parties such as equipment providers or newspapers, regarding the scope of advertising.[48] In 1933, they established a Cinema Proprietors' Association. Movie critics now routinely reviewed films (the first was Avigdor HaMeiri, in 1927).[49] More local filmmakers operated (in the form of a production company, though most did not last long), and more local movies were produced. Two of these are notable: one was *Oded HaNoded* (*Wandering Oded*), a silent movie produced in 1932, which drew much attention.[50] It also resulted in some legal by-products about credit to the studio,[51] and about unauthorized performance in a

---

[44] See the memoirs of a central player in the distribution and translation channels, Yerushalayim Segal, *Memoirs: Yerushalayim in Tel-Aviv* (Moledet, 1993) (Hebrew).
[45] See eg Correspondence between Zion Theatre in Jerusalem and MGM (1941–3) JCA 473.
[46] Aptekmann Pictures to Zion Theatre (28 May 1936) JCA 471. See also a similar complaint later on, by Marco Mesri (distributor of Paramount Films) to Gut & Peretz (10 June 1947) JCA 477.
[47] See Polish-Palestine Chamber of Commerce to Tel-Aviv Municipality (27 October 1937); internal memo of the Municipality, instructing to ask the cinema owners without explaining the reason (31 October 1937); Tel-Aviv Municipality to the Association of Cinema Proprietors (7 November 1937); Mugrabi Cinema to the Polish-Palestine Chamber of Commerce (7 November 1937); Tel-Aviv Municipality to Polish-Palestine Chamber of Commerce (18 February 1938) TCA 4/1023 File B-1913.
[48] Zion Theatre Archive, JCA 471 File 17 (January 1934).
[49] Be'eri, 'Movies', above n 35, at 287–9.
[50] For discussion of the movie, see Feldstein, *Pioneer*, above n 33, at 77–89.
[51] Yerushalayim Segal demanded that his studio (Moledet) should have been acknowledged. Interestingly, he published a notice in the newspaper about this, a pattern that we will meet later on. See Gross, *The Hebrew Movie*, above n 33, at 99; Zimmerman, *Signs*, above n 33, at 95–6, 101–3. Zimmerman reads this as an indication of the lack of clarity regarding copyright and the early sensitivity to attribution (at 95–6, 102). However, as for his first point, copyright law at the time

theatre.[52] The second was *Zot Hi Haaretz* (Hebrew: *This is the Land*), produced in 1935 by Baruch Agadati. It was the first talking Hebrew movie.[53] It too had some legal consequences, regarding unauthorized reproduction of another film.[54] In 1933 a new filmmaking company announced its intentions to produce talking movies in Hebrew, concluding that: 'This initiative is not the private business of the group, but a much more important national project.'[55] The company earned the blessing of Tel-Aviv's mayor, Meir Dizengoff: 'We shall build the Hebrew Hollywood here in our country.'[56]

Thus, the field of film was thriving, committed to the Zionist project, and triggering the operation of copyright law: the public performance of music alongside silent films (in 1929–30), the performance of the films themselves (in the 1930s), and the commercial relationships between the various players in the field (1923 as to the filmmaker and commissioner; in the 1930s as to the distributors).

(e) The literary field

Finally, in the 1920s, engagement with literature, newspaper, and other writings was the most active and advanced cultural field of all among the Hebrew community, perhaps because it was more easily transferrable to a new territory, or perhaps the reason is the individuality of writing, at least under a romantic perception. The literary field was the first cultural field to reach maturity in terms of a vibrant, steady activity, accompanied by various social and cultural institutions.

Zohar Shavit, a leading scholar of the literary field in Mandate Palestine, documented its emergence.[57] She identifies three stages of development: the first, in the 1910s, marked by the figure of Yosef Haim Brenner; the second was a time of crisis, in the early 1920s, following Brenner's murder, and the third stage, dated to 1924, marked by the beginning of the fourth wave of immigration. This wave brought with it many authors, chief among them was Haim Nahman Bialik, a well-established author long before he immigrated.[58]

The mid 1920s were a tipping point: authors and publishers relocated their activity to Palestine and the field stabilized: literary events took places, a Hebrew

---

was very clear: it simply did not include the moral right of attribution, let alone for a studio rather than an individual.

[52] A daily Hebrew newspaper reported that the Eretz-Israeli Film company sued *Gan Rina* (a cinema established in Tel-Aviv in 1929), for the unauthorized screening of the movie. The report further noted that the movie will not be screened there until the court hearing. There are no other indications about the case. See 'Without the Owners' Consent' (13 September 1935) *Davar*, at 20.

[53] See Feldstein, *Pioneer*, above n 33, at 108–27.

[54] Feldstein, *Pioneer*, above n 33, at 126; Gross, *The Hebrew Movie*, above n 33, at 141, 160; Zimmerman, *Signs*, above n 33, at 154–7. I shall return to this dispute in Ch 6.

[55] OFC, Orient Film Co (7 August 1933) TCA 4-1023 File A-1913.

[56] Dizengoff to OFK (11 August 1933); OFK to Dizengoff (17 August 1933) TCA 4-1023 File A-1913.

[57] Zohar Shavit, *The Literary Life in Eretz Yisrael 1910–1933* (HaKibbutz HaMeuchad, 1982) (Hebrew) and an edited volume: *The Construction of Hebrew Culture*, above n 17.

[58] Zohar Shavit, 'The Main Stages in the Development of the Center in Eretz-Israel and its Rise to Hegemony' in *The Construction*, above n 17, at 87 (Hebrew).

Authors Association (HAA) was first established in 1921 but did not carry on for long; a second attempt in 1926 was more successful. The size of the Hebrew reading audience continued to grow substantially. Literary journals were now published routinely: *Hedim* (Hebrew: Echoes), operated between 1922–8; *Ktuvim* (Hebrew: Writings), operated between 1926–33,[59] and after a major split of the HAA, the majority of its members led by Bialik published *Moznayim* (Hebrew: Scales) as of 1929.[60] The literary journals were a focal place for the literary activity. They served as platforms for publishing poems, short stories, scholarly essays, and op-eds on cultural matters. A second function of the journals was a billboard: announcements about literary events, new publications, forthcoming publications, immigration of authors, deaths and much more. *Ktuvim* in particular fulfilled this function.

Like in other fields, the literary one had its internal debates: Hebrew successfully competed with other languages spoken by the immigrants. Translations were considered secondary to original Hebrew literature, but there was not much choice but to use them, as there was an insufficient local supply of Hebrew materials. The debates were also personal: the younger, modernist generation rebelled against the older one. The split in the HAA, followed by the emergence of *Moznayim* alongside *Ktuvim*, symbolized the debates.

In terms of organization and financial aspects, despite the boom in its activity, the local market struggled. Publishers hardly covered the expenses—some were single-book publishers. The local community read enthusiastically, but it was too small to cover all costs. The larger publishers worked hard to subscribe readers in the United States and Europe, with partial success. Donations were another source of income. On the authors' side, making a living of writing was unlikely for the vast majority of authors. Many of the authors had additional writing-related jobs, such as translations, editing, and journalism. Some were also in the publishing business, such as Bialik himself.[61] Shavit writes that those who did earn some money from their literary work reinvested it in publishing their next work.[62] Few were lucky to be supported by affluent Jews. Shai Agnon, later a Nobel laureate, was thus supported by Salman Schocken, a prominent businessman and publisher (whom we shall meet again in Chapter 11). The financial difficulties implicated the daily transactions between authors and publishers. The HAA played an important role here, in setting industry standards for authors' rates, and later on, in the 1940s, for translators' rates.[63]

---

[59] *Ktuvim* is the third part of the Jewish *Tanac'h*, which includes the books of Psalms, Proverbs, Job, the five scrolls, the book of Daniel, Ezra ve'Nechemia, and Chronicles.

[60] For discussion of these journals, see Zohar Shavit, 'The Development of Newspapers and Periodicals' in *The Construction*, above n 17, at 123, 136–9 (*Hedim*), 139–42 (*Ktuvim*), and 149–54 (*Moznayim*) (Hebrew).

[61] The same applied to artists. See Trajtenberg, *Between Nationalism*, above n 7, at 27.

[62] Zohar Shavit, 'The Development of Hebrew Publishing in Eretz-Israel' in *The Construction*, above n 17, at 199, 226 (Hebrew).

[63] Zohar Shavit, 'The Writers' Union' in *The Construction*, above n 17, at 401–3 (Hebrew).

120   *Colonial Copyright*

The emergence of the literary field coincided with the 1924 copyright enactments, but the law played no role in this development. Despite the need, copyright law was not called upon to regulate the relationship amongst authors, translators, publishers, foreign and local.

(2) Jewish culture, Arab culture

A comment is in place about the relationship between the Hebrew community and the Arab community (the latter discussed in greater detail in Chapter 10). There is an ongoing debate among economic historians of Mandate Palestine, whether to treat it as one economy or as two separate ones, Jewish and Arab.[64] There are numerous discussions of the political situation and tensions among the two communities. But, as far as the cultural industries and cultural activity were concerned, the Arab and Jewish cultural economies mostly developed separately.

The national ideologies of each community, the different languages, and the European background of most of the members of the Yishuv provide the rather obvious explanations for this cultural separation. Hebrew authors and publishers published in Hebrew; Arab authors and publishers published in Arabic. The literacy rates among the Arab Palestinian community were substantially lower than the Jewish rates (this gap was narrowed only as the Mandate progressed). The cultural centres of the local Arab community were founded in Damascus and Cairo, more than in Jerusalem or Jaffa.

This is not to say that the two communities were completely isolated from each other. There were occasional mutual influences in the content of culture, especially in the arts. Hebrew painters depicted Arab characters so to represent the biblical Jew. Art historians argue that the Arabs were presented as the authentic natives of the land.[65] This representation did not last for long, and by the end of the 1920s was all but gone.[66]

But the usual state of affairs was one of separate cultural activity. As a result, there were few commercial or cultural meeting points of the two neighbouring cultural fields, and thus, less legal friction, with two important exceptions. One took place in the mid 1930s, mediated by the British government, when the British established and managed the radio service, and a second legal meeting point was the legal

---

[64] For the two economies argument, see Jacob Metzer, *The Divided Economy of Mandatory Palestine* (Cambridge University Press, 1998); Barbara J Smith, *The Roots of Separatism in Palestine: British Economic Policy, 1920–1929* (I N Tauris & Co, Ltd 1983); cf Deborah S Bernstein, *Constructing Boundaries: Jewish and Arab Workers in Mandatory Palestine* (State University of New York, 2000) (arguing that the two economies mutually affected each other and discussing the relationship between Jews and Arabs in Mandatory Haifa, in the construction sector).

[65] See Batia Donner, 'The Development of Applied Graphics in the Yishuv' in *The Construction*, above n 17, at 539 (Hebrew); Haim Gamzu, *Painting and Sculpture in Israel: The Plastic Arts from Bezalel Period to the Present Day* (Eshkol, 1951) 14; Saposnik, *Becoming Hebrew*, above n 3, at 49 (quoting Hemda Ben-Yehuda); Manor, *Art in Zion*, above n 6, at 135, 142–8.

[66] For the appearance and disappearance of the Arab from the Hebrew art, see Trajtenberg, *Between Nationalism and Art*, above n 7, at 202–9, 213.

battle over property in news in the early 1930s, where a Jewish copyright owner sued an Arab newspaper. These are discussed in Chapters 8 and 9 respectively.

(3) Internal divisions within the Jewish community

The Jewish community was not homogenous. There were several divisions and tensions that should be noted as so to better understand the features of the emerging culture: along Zionist and non-Zionist lines, between the urban centre and rural periphery, between members of the different waves of immigration, and along lines of ethnicity.

(a) Old and new

One internal Jewish cultural division was between the Hebrew, Zionist New Yishuv and the more religious Old Yishuv. When the Zionists turned to Eretz-Israel in the nineteenth century, several tens of thousands of Jews were already living in the region, mostly in the four holy cities of Jerusalem, Safed, Tiberias, and Hebron. They were mostly orthodox, non-Zionist, in the sense that they did not hold national ideas, though they did maintain strong religious affiliation with the land. They were not necessarily anti-Zionist as some factions of the ultra-orthodox Jews are today. For income, members of the Old Yishuv relied mostly on donations from Jewish communities abroad. The religious way of life of the Orthodox community meant that most of its members did not engage in fine arts, music, or theatre. Its main cultural production was religious, scholarly texts, in which they excelled.[67]

The New Yishuv stood in sharp contrast. There was little cultural interaction between the Old Yishuv and the new, Hebrew Yishuv. The latter constructed itself deliberately as a negation of the Jewish life in exile and the Old Yishuv was associated with exile in this sense. The immigrants were enthusiastic Zionists; they were determined to create a new image of a Jewish person, as an independent, productive, and national person.[68] They lived outside the walls of Jerusalem, physically and symbolically. They purchased land, established new settlements, passionately cultivated the land, assisted their fellow Zionists in Europe to immigrate to the Land of Israel, and actively engaged in constructing a new society. This contrast between the Old Jew and the New Jew was also reflected in the image of the author, as discussed in the following part.

---

[67] Jehoash Hirshberg reports that music was played in the old Yishuv during the first half of the nineteenth century, but then, in the Ashkenazi community, a prominent rabbi ordered that this practice is ceased. See Hirshberg, *Music*, above n 15, at 10–11. Chapter 11 will discuss one copyright case in this community.

[68] For the contrast between the Old Yishuv and the New Yishuv, see Yehoshua Kaniel, *Continuation and Change: The Old Yishuv and the New Yishuv During the First and Second Aliyah* (Yad Ben-Zvi, 1982) (Hebrew), especially at 46 (secularization of the New Yishuv), 153 (use of Hebrew), and 273 (ideology of the first wave).

(b) Centre and periphery

Another internal social–cultural division was between the urban centre and the rural periphery, namely between Tel-Aviv, Jerusalem (in this order), and all the rest. The rural towns and later the kibbutzim were simply too small at the time to draw sufficient audiences (reading, listening, or viewing) to enable an ongoing viable cultural activity. Thus, the cultural activity that did take place was either of the individual sort (writing, painting), or amateur.[69] Cultural activities that required an industrial and/or financial support were rare in the smaller towns, unless there was a specific source. This was the case, for example, with the Rishon LeZion orchestra, that in its first incarnation operated between 1895 and 1905.[70] But this too, was a rather short-lived experience and probably not of the highest quality.

In the 1920s, once Tel-Aviv became the cultural centre for almost all arts and activities, the periphery enjoyed it as well. Tel-Aviv was where the theatre and opera were located, where music concerts took place, where the cinemas were most active (though cinemas spread quickly), and where most of the publishers and newspapers were. Jerusalem had its share, mostly of musicians and a few authors (notably Agnon), as did other places, but it was clear that the centre was in Tel-Aviv.

In examining the cultural life of the evolving society, the divisions between centre and periphery roughly fit the differences between the first three waves of immigration and the fourth wave, or to be more precise, between the images of each of these waves. The first three waves turned to agricultural work in the rural areas, at least more so than the fourth wave. For those who were draining the swamps, paving roads and building new settlements, cultural activity deserved only a secondary place in the early stages of the Zionist project. Some of these, especially those living in the *moshavot* engaged in arts, music, literature, and theatre, with first steps taken in all fields. But as we saw earlier, these were only first steps, local and sporadic.

The fourth wave of immigration (1924–30), building on the previous three, provided a boost to the cultural life. It took place during the British rule, and it coincided with the 1924 copyright enactments. This was a period in which the cultural field was established, led by the city dwellers, many of whom were associated with the fourth wave.

The differences between the members of the different waves resulted in a subtle social tension. Members of the first three waves (especially the second and third) were epitomized by the image of the *Halutz* (Hebrew: the pioneer, single male form; *Halutza*—female form; *Halutzim*—plural form). The *Halutzim* were not the majority among the first three waves, but their image captured the imagination of all. The social hierarchy clearly preferred the *Halutzim* to the city dwellers.

---

[69] In a historical-fiction book, Assaf Inbari describes how members of Kibbutz Afikim referred to the musician among them as a parasite for not being productive. He replied that he stole the tunes from the streets of Kiev. See Assaf Inbari, *Home* (Yediot Ahronot/Hemed, 2009) 30 (Hebrew). This musician became a prominent composer—in Tel-Aviv.

[70] See above n 15.

These divides between the city dwellers and the pioneers in the country, between the typical member of the fourth wave of immigration and the members of the previous waves, played a crucial role in the construction of the image of the Hebrew author. The artists, authors, and others who were engaged in cultural activities had to bridge the gap between themselves and those working in the swamps and fields under the hot sun. They had to justify to themselves and to their fellow Zionists that they were as productive and as important to the Zionist cause. Later on we shall see one solution they found: constructing the image of the Hebrew author as equivalent of the *Halutz*, in the form of an intellectual *Halutz*.

(c) Ashkenazi and Sephardi

Yet another internal division was the one between Ashkenazi and Sephardi Jews. By the time the British took over the region, the vast majority of the Jewish immigrants and the population were of Ashkenazi origins, meaning eastern and central Europe. Only a minority were of Sephardi origin: members of the Old Yishuv and immigrants from neighbouring Arab countries. A significant group of Jewish immigrants came from Yemen, most of whom immigrated in 1881–2, roughly at the same time as the first wave of Zionist immigrants arrived from Russia.

The Yemenite immigration had its own unique culture and traditions. It provides us an example of the Eurocentric point of view of copyright law.[71] One of the arts in which Yemenite Jews excelled was dancing. Yemenite dancing had unique features and it has had a long-standing effect on Israeli folk dance. Giora Manor discusses these features: the dance is part of a coherent cultural–artistic tradition, tying text, tune, and dance together.[72] The dance movements were unique and easily distinguished from other dancing traditions, though they left substantial leeway for improvisation of the dancers. The dance steps were passed from one generation to another, without fixing it in a tangible form, to apply contemporary copyright language.[73] It was often unclear who the choreographer of each dance was. Thus, even if a Yemenite dancer/choreographer wished to enjoy copyright protection, the British law was unlikely to support it. At the time, there was no practical need for such legal protection, as there was no (commercial) market for dancing.[74]

Interestingly, some Yemenite dance movements were fixed in tangible forms, though not by the dancers, but rather by outsiders: in 1903 Thomas Edison's company filmed one of the first movies in Palestine, which included footage of

---

[71] See Ch 2. The Eurocentric view of copyright converged with what Dalia Manor describes as the Ashkenazi 'fascination with "exotic" Jews'. Manor, *Art in Zion*, above n 6, at 67.

[72] Giora Manor, 'The Development of Dance in the Jewish Settlement' in *The Construction*, above n 17, at 557, 566 (Hebrew).

[73] Ibid, at 567.

[74] A case about copyright infringement in folk dances reached an Israeli court in 2008. The parties were two competing folk dance companies that arranged dancing classes and events. CC 8303/06 (Jerusalem District Court) *Mehola, HaMerkaz leMahol v Cohen* (2008). Plaintiffs won the case regarding some of the dances they composed, as they videotaped their unique dance movements and were able to prove their original work.

a group of Yemenite Jewish dancers.[75] A second instance was of the (Ashkenazi) choreographer (and later filmmaker and artist) Baruch Agadati, who created a special dance (*Yemenite Ecstasy*), based inter alia on Yemenite elements.[76] As Dalia Manor writes, Agadati built also on Hasidic, Arab, and Sephardi folk dancing, with the aspiration of creating an original Hebrew dance.[77] As in other cases of cultural appropriation of folk art and traditional knowledge elsewhere, had Edison or Agadati sought copyright protection for their own work, they would probably have enjoyed it, while the underlying traditional material would not.

Sephardi music also had to struggle, and gained mainstream recognition only in the 1930s, with the famous singer Bracha Zefira, and then the radio broadcasts of Iraqi-born composer, Ezra Aharon.

(4) Hebrew

The emerging cultural life was saturated with nationality. Hebrew was not only a language. It was everything. It was all about Zionism and about creating a new, Hebrew community, and a new, Hebrew person.[78] Importantly, the community came before its members. The Hebrew culture provided a framework which included a complete set of social meanings, or, to apply Clifford Geertz's definition of culture, Hebrew was 'a system of inherited conceptions expressed in symbolic forms'.[79] Everything had to be Hebrew. The Hebrew culture offered a new way of life, suitable for the New Jew, negating the Old Jew who remained in European exile, or the Jews of the Old Yishuv. The Old Jew spoke Yiddish and read Russian or German; the New Jew spoke and read Hebrew. The Old Jew spent time studying the Talmud; the New Jew was to engage in physical labour and advance Zionist thought.[80] The Hebrew culture was an important component of Zionism, serving a tool for constructing a new society.[81]

As a language, Hebrew also had an instrumental role. Jews came to Palestine from various countries, Germany, Poland, Russia, the Austro-Hungarian Empire, and other places. Once in the region, they met Jews who came from the other European countries, as well as Jewish immigrants from Yemen, and the members of the Old Yishuv. A common language was needed for communication. Yiddish was such a language for some of the immigrants, but not for all, but it was associated

---

[75] As reported by Manor, 'The Development of Dance', above n 72, at 557.
[76] Ibid, at 559.
[77] Dalia Manor, *Art in Zion*, above n 6, at 139–41.
[78] See eg Itamar Even-Zohar, 'The Rise and Consolidation of a Local, Indigenous, Hebrew Culture in the Land of Israel, 1882–1948' (1980) 16 Katedra 165, 171–2 (Hebrew); Yaacov Shavit, 'The Status of Culture in the Process of Creating a National Society in Eretz Yisrael: Basic Attitudes and Concepts' in *The Construction*, above n 17, at 23 (Hebrew).
[79] Clifford Geertz, *The Interpretation of Cultures* (Basic Books, 1973) 89.
[80] For Hebrew as a culture, see Menachem Mautner, *Law and the Culture of Israel* (Oxford University Press, 2011) 21–4.
[81] See Saposnik, *Becoming Hebrew*, above n 3.

with the old world, deliberately left behind. Hebrew provided a solution.[82] For two millennia it was used only for reading the Bible and other religious texts but it was hardly spoken. The Enlightenment first and then Zionism revived it, refreshed and reinvented it where needed, a project often associated with Eliezer Ben-Yehuda (1858–1922), known as the reviver of the Hebrew language. Now Hebrew was to be spoken by the Hebrew people and it was the only language to be spoken.[83] This was not an easy task and the tendency to retreat to the familiar, richer languages was tempting. Thus, there was a strong social norm against speaking in foreign languages, especially Yiddish, now relegated to the status of a foreign language, referred to as the 'jargon'. In the 1910s, there was a fierce debate about the language to be used in the Technion, the technological university built in Haifa: Hebrew or German. When the Technion finally opened in 1925, Hebrew won.[84] During the 1920s and well into the 1930s, beginning in Tel-Aviv and spreading throughout the country, organized groups of high school students undertook the task of actively policing the use of the language ('The Battalion of Defenders of the Hebrew Language'). One of their activities was to eavesdrop on conversations in the streets and when hearing non-Hebrew languages, interfering and even publicly shaming the non-Hebrew speakers.[85] In the 1930s the effort was channelled especially to fight the use of German in public forums, such as cinemas.[86] The cultural scene usually took a calmer approach, but nevertheless insisted on Hebrew, especially in the theatre, movies, and in its literature. Hebrew thus served as a tool of social cohesion.

Accordingly, it was important that literature was written, published, sang, and played in Hebrew. The content and form were often inspired by European literature, but the language had to be the local one.[87] Translations from other languages to Hebrew played an important role in accustoming the people to the language: while original literature in Hebrew was still the top priority, translations provided a practical solution and an alternative to reading in foreign languages. It was not Hebrew literature, but at least it was in Hebrew.

(5) The British point of view

The Hebrew cultural fields in Palestine developed in an autonomous independent way, mostly without direct British involvement, either supportive or interfering.

---

[82] For the role of Hebrew as a tool of communication and its relationship with Yiddish, see Rafael Nir, 'The State of Hebrew Language in the Process of National Revival' in *The Construction*, above n 17, at 36–7 (Hebrew).

[83] For the revival of Hebrew, see Saposnik, *Becoming Hebrew*, above n 3, at 65–92.

[84] Rafael Nir, 'The Function of the Yishuv Institutes in the Hebrew Revival' in *The Construction*, above n 17, at 107, 111.

[85] Anat Helman, *Urban Culture in 1920s and 1930s Tel-Aviv* (Haifa University Press, 2007) 49–50 (Hebrew).

[86] Ibid, at 50–1. For example, the Zion Theatre in Jerusalem received in 1935 a letter from the Committee for the Boycott of German Products, requiring the Committee's pre-approval for any screening of German movies. See Notice, Committee for the Boycott of German Products (25 March 1935) JCA 471 File 5.

[87] Even-Zohar, 'The Rise', above n 78, at 185.

The Mandate government had only a general policy of advancing the country according to the League of Nations' Mandate, including its commitment to secure the establishment of the Jewish national home. This mission was also to support the development of self-governing institutions, and 'encourage local autonomy'.[88] Thus, the British did not have a deliberate cultural policy other than promoting education and raising literacy. The lack of official involvement is also explained in financial terms: the cultural industries did not yield much revenue. Various statistical reports that list the country's industries, do not include the cultural ones, but for the printing and paper industry, the smallest of the surveyed industries.

Some of the leading British officers were involved in specific cultural activities, which they assumed in their own personal interests rather than in their official capacity. Ronald Storrs, the Governor of Jerusalem, served as the President of the Jerusalem Musical Society, followed by two High Commissioners.[89] Storrs also served as the president of the Pro-Jerusalem Society, which held the first art exhibitions (*The Tower of David Art Exhibitions*).[90] This was part of his vision of the British as custodians of the holy city.[91] Norman Bentwich, the Attorney General, was also the Chair of the Jerusalem Musical Society, founded by his sister Thelma Yellin.[92] But at least until the mid 1930s there was no official regulatory cultural policy. In the mid 1930s, the government established the Palestine Broadcasting Service, which was to become an important cultural (and political) player. But by and large, the local communities were left to their own cultural devices.

This British approach fitted both the Jews and the British. Zohar Shavit notes that the Yishuv preferred a high level of autonomy and in any case, did not consider the English culture as a worthy source of inspiration.[93] The British were quite impressed with the Jewish cultural activity. During World War II, when more British soldiers were in the country, they found, perhaps to their surprise, a rather rich cultural life.[94] A 1945 British report, towards the end of the Mandate, noted the importance of culture to the building of the national home. The report lists the establishment of the Hebrew University in Jerusalem, daily newspapers, journals, orchestra, opera, choirs, theatre, literature, arts schools, and artistic and literary prizes.[95] Interestingly, the report's section dealing with the Arab sector did not

---

[88] The Mandate for Palestine 1922, Arts 2, 3.

[89] Hirshberg, *Music*, above n 15, at 103.

[90] See Ronald Storrs, *Orientations* (Nicholson & Watson, 1937) 370; and discussion in Gila Ballas, 'Israel Painters and Sculptures Association' in *The Construction*, above n 17, at 416, 418 (Hebrew).

[91] For the same reasons, Storrs prohibited bars, hotel dances, and cabarets in the Old City of Jerusalem. See *Orientations*, ibid, at 461. See also discussion in Trajtenberg, *Between Nationalism*, above n 7, at 35–7, and the Advertisement Ordinance 1920, which was based on Storrs vision of Jerusalem as an advertisement-free zone, discussed in Ch 4.

[92] For the Bentwich family's musical background, see Ch 4. David Yellin, whom we met earlier as the teacher who produced the first Hebrew play in the region, was Thelma's father-in-law.

[93] Zohar Shavit, 'The Decline of the European Centers' in *The Construction*, above n 17, at 43–4.

[94] A J Sherman, *Mandate Days: British Lives in Palestine, 1918–1948* (Thames and HudsonPress, 1997) 163–7.

[95] A Survey of Palestine, prepared in December 1945 and January 1946 for the information of the Anglo-American Committee of Inquiry, Vol II, at 676–8.

include discussion of cultural activities. This omission does not mean there was no Arab cultural activity. Rather, it is an indication of the orientalist British view, disregarding 'folk', or 'popular culture'.

(6) What about the law?

The law is absent from the story of the cultural development in the Hebrew Yishuv, at least in any direct way. Non-lawyers might be surprised at this comment, holding the view that art and the cultural field have nothing to do with the law and should not be affected by the law. But law does have a role in the construction of culture, for good or for bad. It need not be a direct involvement. The law can operate in the three distinct ways: protective background rules that facilitate the environment and enable the arts to develop, active background rules that enable a market, and active direct involvement.

First and foremost, freedom of artistic creativity and freedom of expression should be respected. Under conditions of censorial regulation, art and culture are impeded and chilled.

When the law secures a free environment, it supports the flourishing of creativity.[96] Beginning with modern Zionism in the region, there was a gradual liberation of the censorial rules. As the Ottoman regime turned more modern, especially after the 1908 Young Turks Revolution, it loosened its regulation. Once the War and the British military administration were over and replaced with the civil administration, there was even more breathing space, though far from today's (Western) norms of freedom of expression. Newspapers, plays, and movies were subject to censorship. In the 1930s, the radio was owned and run by the government, so it had direct control over its contents.

Secondly, to facilitate the emergence and well functioning of a free market (in a capitalist market), the law enables several building blocks: private property rights, enforcement of contracts, and regulation of companies. These were in place and with the 1924 Copyright enactments, the law in the books did as much as it could to enable a free commercial market without interfering in it. But, as we shall see in the subsequent chapter, these laws were not used for some time. The cultural fields developed without resort to external law. Instead, it applied contractual norms accompanied with social norms and an active organizational framework (though not always successful one).[97] More sophisticated indirect tools of promoting the market are consumer protection laws, and antitrust laws, but the local conditions were not mature enough for these.

A third layer of legal regulation, building on the previous layers, is an active governmental promotion of cultural activities. This can be in the form of

---

[96] In this sense, free speech is the engine of copyright law, thus reversing the famous statement by the United States Supreme Court that copyright is the engine of free speech. See *Harper & Row Publishers v The Nation Enterprise*, 471 US 539, 558 (1985).

[97] Thus for example, the HAA was successful in negotiating better terms for the authors in their commercial relationships with the publishers, but did not do much in the copyright field. See Shavit, 'The Writers' Union', above n 63, at 403.

governmental speech, or subsidies of various sorts. Democratic countries today apply such tools while striving to create protective buffers between the governmental finance and the artistic content. But no such active engagement was applied at the time in Palestine, other than education and the establishment of the radio.

Copyright law could have been part of the governmental scheme. But it remained in the books for some time.

C. The Hebrew Author

The formation of a cultural field requires, inter alia, establishing commercial and social relationships between the players: amongst authors (including translators), amongst publishers, and between these two groups. In the case of Palestine, there was also an international dimension, first with Jewish authors and publishers in Europe and then also in the United States. Users, much discussed today, were not yet active players, though of course readership was crucial. Copyright law could have provided important background rules for the field/market, but it was hardly consulted until the 1930s, with the exception of the contractual norms applied by the Jewish institutions regarding photography and film. This part provides one explanation for the initial indifference to the law among Hebrew authors and publishers. It is a legal–cultural explanation that builds on the authorship project. The subsequent chapter offers another explanation, which turns to the legal field and the local alternatives to it.

In a nutshell, the argument advanced here is that the self-image of the Hebrew author differed substantially from the authorial image that was imagined by and reflected in the colonial copyright. The Hebrew author was a bit romantic, but part of a collective, occasionally socialist, and always Zionist. The author had a special role in the construction of the Hebrew culture. These national and collectivist features were not part of the foreign law. The author imagined by the colonial copyright was more romantic, an individual, at least potentially capitalist, and void of any special national motivation.

The irrelevance of the foreign law to the local cultural field in its first phases was not unique to Palestine. In other British territories it also took a while until local authors and industries turned to use the colonial copyright law.[98] Each territory deserves its own legal–cultural analysis. The discussion here provides a prototype for such a discussion. I begin with the image of the Hebrew author and then turn to the irrelevance of the foreign law.

(1) The image of the author

In the past decades scholars approached copyright law not only from an internal, legal point of view that perceives the law as an autonomous field, but turned to

---

[98] See eg the Straits Settlements, Malay States, and Ghana, discussed in Ch 3.

explore it from the outside, beyond the traditional contours of the law. Interdisciplinary research followed and among its precious fruit was the authorship project, discussed in the Introduction and in Chapter 2. Following the work of Martha Woodmansee, Peter Jaszi, Carla Hesse, Mark Rose, and James Boyle, the figure of the author was placed under the spotlight.

During the past 300 years of modern copyright law in Britain and other European countries, the image of the author changed. Initially the author was considered a craftsman, one of several producers of the book. But gradually, the author moved to the front of the stage. At first, the author was sent there by others and was operated from behind the scenes by the industries, namely the publishers. This is a well-documented segment of copyright history, addressing mostly the eighteenth century developments of the 1710 Statute of Anne.[99] Later on, the author became more independent, deserving rights on his own rather than being a pawn controlled by other stakeholders. The romantic movement in German literature, the rise of a class of intellectuals in France, and other developments have emphasized the author as a romantic figure.[100]

Scholars showed how the image of the romantic author affected the development of copyright law, leaving its marks on several of its doctrines and often surfacing in judicial opinions. The critique that followed was that this image excludes by default less-romantic modes of cultural production, such as collaborative work, either that classified as traditional knowledge and folklore,[101] or the digital mass collaboration of Wikipedia and open source projects.

What, then, was the image of the Hebrew author? To the extent that we can generalize, the Hebrew author was a conflicted figure (under a romantic perspective, could it be otherwise?), with romantic undertones and a public collectivist commitment, and above all, with strong Zionist overtones. The dynamic decade of the 1920s exposed the complexity of the image of the author: a mixture of romanticism and nationalism, individuality and collectivism. The typical Hebrew author of the 1920s was a city dweller, a member of the fourth wave of immigration (or of earlier waves, but moved to the city), and searching for his unique Zionist voice. Most of the authors were men. These are broad statements and there were exceptions: there were few authors who were members of the previous waves of immigration (Brenner, who was murdered in 1921; Agnon, who first immigrated in 1909, left in 1912 and returned in 1924, to Jerusalem), there were few well-known female authors (some known by their first names—Rachel and Elisheva,[102]

---

[99] See references in Ch 2.
[100] Martha Woodmansee, 'The Genius and the Copyright: Economic and Legal Conditions of the Emergence of the Author' (1984) 17 Eighteenth-Century Studies 425; Carla Hesse, 'Enlightenment Epistemology and the Laws of Authorship in Revolutionary France, 1777–1793' (1990) 30 Representations 109.
[101] See eg James Boyle, *Shamans, Software, and Spleens: Law and the Construction of the Information Society* (Harvard University Press, 1996) 114.
[102] Elisheva was a non-Jewish Russian author who married a Jew and immigrated with him to Palestine.

as well as Nehama Pukhachewsky, and Esther Raab), and a few authors and artists who lived and worked in the rural areas.

In this and in many other cases, the *image* of the author was more important than the reality, though in our case, there was only a little gap between the image and reality. Let us look at each of the components of the image of the Hebrew author: romanticism, collectivism, socialism, and Zionism. Importantly, these were all combined in almost all authors, the separation here is instrumental.

Romanticism. The Hebrew author surely had the romantic edge, though it was not the dominant characteristic. This is not surprising. Some would say that this is the human nature, while others might search for the social perception. In the case of the Hebrew authors, it is easy to find: many of them were born or spent their authorial formative years in central Europe, especially in Berlin. They read the Russian, German, and French classics. They enjoyed high esteem as individuals and for their Zionist role. As for the artists—many of them spent a formative time in arts schools in Paris, Germany, and Italy. Graciela Trajtenberg argues that the European influence was a central element in the artists' social activity.[103]

The authors had their own, individual interests. The internal disputes within the HAA in the late 1920s were driven by a clash between different literary ideologies, but no doubt they were also about ego. Bialik, the great poet and author was famous long before he immigrated to Eretz-Israel in 1924. Upon his arrival, he instantly became the leader of the literary centre, but the 1927 split in the HAA indicated that not everybody was happy with his leadership. The group that continued publishing *Ktuvim* was thrown out.

Other than internal politics, a recurring issue that the authors raised was their miserable economic situation, perhaps a typical characteristic of the popular image of the romantic author. Complaints about the payments that they received and those they did not receive in due time, were cast in dramatic terms. The authors were quick to describe themselves as poor beggars, but money was positioned in a second place. A prominent journalist announced that: 'We the Hebrew journalists—not for the penny do we work, and not for the pennies we strive. We just want to be heard. Give us your sole, oh reader, and we would give up your pennies.'[104] The financial concerns lasted throughout the Mandate. The authors kept complaining, but gradually shifted their ways of conveying the message from individuals' public statements to organized and mediated action through the HAA and courts, but this happened only in the 1940s, and we are still in earlier times.

The romance appeared also in the internal debates about the essence of art. The modern view positioned the artists as a genius, a unique individual who creates from the blood of his or her heart.[105] This is the quintessential romantic author. The younger generation among the authors (the *Ktuvim* party, led by poet Avraham Shlonsky) and the artists were modernist, seeking to make art for the sake of art, reflecting their own personalities.

---

[103] Trajtenberg, *Between Nationalism*, above n 7, at 22.
[104] Quoted and criticized in (5 July 1928) *Ktuvim*, at 4 (Hebrew).
[105] Trajtenberg, *Between Nationalism*, above n 7, at 24–5, 72–4.

Another 'romantic' concern was with attribution and the integrity of the work. The concern for attribution should be placed in the time and place: the small (though growing) number of authors and the size of the reading audience, meant that everybody knew everyone else, in many cases, in person. Pseudonyms such as Ahad Ha'am (Hebrew: one of the people) were no disguise (nor did Asher Ginzberg attempt to hide his identity); using the first name only (Rachel, Elisheva) was enough, and signing by initials was also sufficient to identify the author. When the attributes were omitted, the authors were quick to claim it back. In the next chapter we will see a few cases in which authors insisted on attribution. All these concerns combined, indicate that the Hebrew authors held, regarding themselves, some, if not all of the traits, associated with the romantic author. Thus, the romantic author immigrated to Palestine; the author made an *aliyah*.

Collectivism. A stronger characteristic of the Hebrew authors was that they considered themselves as part of a community, mostly the national Hebrew collective and occasionally with a socialist spin. This should also be no surprise. The notion of total individuality reached the Hebrew community much later, thirty years into the State of Israel.[106] During the Mandate times, one's identity was defined based on his or her membership of a collective and community. The members of the Yishuv were well organized in their social lives. There were various political parties, civil associations, congregations, and other clear marks of affiliation.[107] One's identity would be constituted as religious or not, according to the ethnic origin (Ashkenazi or Sephardi), the country of origin, class membership (member of the *Histadrut*—the Labour Union) or another smaller union, occupation, economic status (eg being a homeowner or tenant), and much more. The affiliations were important. The multiple options enabled mixing and matching and constructing semi-individual identities, but there was no category of a free individual.

Moreover, the collective came first and the individual person came only second. Moshe Lissak describes a dominant self-image in the Yishuv as 'an open and mobile society, absorbing and non-discriminatory, that prefers individual talent with relentless commitment to the collective cause, over any other trait'.[108] While for the twenty-first century reader this statement might sound as an oxymoron, it was perfectly sound for the Hebrew person of the Mandate era, especially in its earlier days. People were expected to excel, but sacrifice their own good for that of the collective. The expectation to be a loyal member of the collective in all aspects of life was a strong one: it was a rigid social demand. At home, some people might have thought differently, but outside, the public persona had to be a collectivist one.

---

[106] For a discussion of the changes in Israeli society and Israeli law, and the shift from collectivism to individuality, see Mautner, *Law and the Culture*, above n 80.

[107] Moshe Lissak points out that the Yishuv discouraged differential organizations, while encouraging voluntary, ideological political affiliations. See Moshe Lissak, 'Images of Society and Status in the Yishuv and Israeli Society: Patterns of Change in the Ideology and Class Structure' in Eisenstadt, Adler, Bar-Yossef, Kahana (eds), *The Social Structure of Israel* (Academon, 1965) 203 (Hebrew).

[108] Ibid, at 205.

Socialism. For some (but surely not all) the commitment to the collective was not only the state of things: it was a deliberate ideology, a socialist one. The first kibbutz was established in 1910 (Degania), igniting the hearts of Jews in Eastern Europe and in Palestine for its unique form of life. More kibbutzim followed, in which means of production were jointly owned by all. Private property was non-existent within the kibbutzim. It was based on ideas of mutual support, total equality and principles of social and distributive justice, for example the principle that each member is expected to contribute to the community as much as he or she *can*, and that each member will receive as much as he or she *needs*. While this extreme form of socialist life was not the common rule throughout the Yishuv, it was part of the Hebrew scene, reinforcing the collectivist spirit. For those authors that were socialist, owning copyright was simply impossible.

Zionism. Finally, the most dominant and unique characteristic of the Hebrew author was that the author's image was closely tied to the national Zionist ideology.[109] The Hebrew author was a national person, Zionist, part of the Hebrew community in Palestine. Zionism was the overarching collective that unified all members of the Yishuv, despite their ethnic, religious, social, commercial, and political affiliations. Zionism had its internal divisions and politics, but the fundamental idea that the Land of Israel is the national home of the Jewish people and should be advanced as such, was shared by all members of the Yishuv. To better understand the author's image, it is helpful to look at its local reference point, that of the *Halutzim*.

The image of the *Halutz* was that of a productive, energetic Zionist who drained the swamps and constructed new settlements. The *Halutzim* were mostly members of the first three waves of immigration, especially the second and third. The *Halutz* was adventurous and rebellious (as compared to his or her parents' generation, who remained in Europe). This was the quintessential New Jew, constructed as the negation of the Old Jew.[110] The *Halutz* was part of a collective, with its socialist–communitarian emphasis. The image of the passionate *Halutz* captured the imagination of generations to come and served as the protagonist of a leading narrative in the Yishuv.[111]

By contrast, members of the fourth wave of immigration (1924–8) and many of the authors were mostly city dwellers. The dominant group among the fourth wave was middle class and urban. Their bourgeois image stood in sharp contrast to the image of the *Halutz* and was disliked by the previous immigrants.[112] This gap between the image of the *Halutz* and the typical Hebrew author required attention.

---

[109] See Yaacov Shavit, 'The Status', above n 78, at 9.

[110] Anita Shapira, *New Jews, Old Jews* (Am Oved, 1997) 168, 185, 194–6 (Hebrew).

[111] For the passion of the Halutzim, see Boaz Neumann, *Land and Desire in Early Zionism* (Am Oved, 2009) (Hebrew). The image played a crucial role, as most of the members of the second wave were far less motivated by ideology and many of them turned to non-agricultural works. For discussion of the second wave in a broader context of immigration, see Gur Alroey, *Immigrants: Jewish Immigration to Palestine in the Early Twentieth Century* (Yad Ben-Zvi, 2004) (Hebrew). Alroey found that the image of the Halutz carried its influence mostly later on, rather than in real time (at 231).

[112] Orit Rozin, *Duty and Love: Individualism and Collectivism in 1950s Israel* (Tel-Aviv University Press, 2008) 181–2 (Hebrew).

The authors solved it by assuming the role of mediators between the country and the city, between the practical and the intellectual Zionists. They achieved this by actively creating the image of the New Jew, the *Halutz* and assuming the role of narrators of the Hebrew narrative.[113] The image of the author was thus closely tied—by the authors themselves—to the national Zionist ideology.[114]

Authors considered themselves to be acting on behalf of the national collective. Individuality, a dominant characteristic of the image of the romantic author, was allowed only to the extent that it served the collective. The authors were passionate about their role in the Zionist project and proud of it. They had a strong sense of responsibility towards the collective. Authors engaged in the lively public discourse and in politics on all levels. Indeed, many of them considered themselves, or perhaps, presented themselves, as the parallels of the *Halutzim*: while the latter cultivated the land, they cultivated the spirit. Here are some examples.[115]

On the eve of the first HAA Convention in 1921, an op-ed in *Haaretz* voiced a preference for popular literature rather than 'high literature'. The writer was excited about the convening of authors in Eretz-Israel: 'Like the pioneers [*Halutzim*] of the people they [the authors] came from the corners of the Diaspora, and founded important literary projects.'[116] One of the Convention's resolutions was a plea to the Zionist organizations, to treat Hebrew literature as an inseparable part of the 'Zionist work', and support it alike.[117] A report about the 1926 HAA Convention described its purpose as uniting the forces of the intelligentsia in Eretz-Israel and the Diaspora to redeem the land.[118] Another comment published in the inaugural volume of *Ktuvim* (1926) discussed the state of Hebrew literature: 'We have forgotten that our literature is pioneer [*halutz*] literature, and its conquests and failures [are] the conquests of the Halutzim and their failures....'.[119] The editor of *Ktuvim*, in advocating a new mindset for the distribution of books ('we should take the bag of books off the donkey's back and start using the modern transport'), wrote 'we should realise that the Hebrew book, made in the Aretz [Hebrew: the Land], is the golden-apple in the intellectual orchard'.[120] The use of an agricultural metaphor was a clear reference to the *Halutzim*'s productive cultivation of the land. Bialik, in the closing speech of the second convention, was, of course, poetic:

My heart tells me that times of spring and flourishing among authors are to come, days of sunlight in our mutual relationships. Not a herd dancing to one flute. This is the goal of the Authors' Association. Each in his unique path, blessed by God, will play his tune so to join

---

[113] Shapira, *New Jews*, above n 110, at 174.
[114] See Yaacov Shavit, 'The Status', above n 78, at 9.
[115] Self-representation as a pioneer was not limited to authors. Later on we will meet a self-proclaimed copyright pioneer (Meir Kovalsky, in Ch 7), and a self-proclaimed radio pioneer (Mendel Abramowitz, in Ch 8).
[116] K S 'About the Authors Convention' (26 April 1921) *Haaretz*, at 1 (Hebrew). K S was probably Kadish Silman.
[117] (2 May 1921) *Haaretz*, at 2.
[118] 'The Day of the Author and Artist' (9 February 1926) *Haaretz*, at 3 (Hebrew).
[119] Ya'akov Rabinovich, 'About the Declining Will' (24 July 1926) *Ktuvim*, at 2 (Hebrew).
[120] A Shteinman, 'Lishkat HaSefer' (14 January 1927) *Ktuvim*, at 3 (Hebrew).

the upper and lower streams to one national symphony that will become first among the nations' life, an instructor for the daily lives of the people.[121]

Given the internal debates in the HAA, this statement should be read in that context, but for our purposes here, the interesting element is the possibility of individuality and a simultaneous commitment to the national collective, as well as the leading role of the authors in the national project. These views about the role of the authors were shared by the Zionist politicians. In the same convention, a message from the Zionist institutions was read aloud:

> An important and difficult national task is imposed on the Hebrew authors and journalists in Eretz-Israel, particularly in these times. In addition to the economic difficulties in our country today, there is a more severe crisis that spreads in our fields: a spiritual crisis. The most dangerous enemy—the weakening of the belief in our power—attacks our hearts despite the major success achieved in only few years. The role of the author and journalist is to be first among those fighting against this internal enemy, and light our way and clear the air, that so many try to poison.[122]

Once again, the authors were recruited to the national cause. The Zionist motivation was shared by all participants in the emerging Hebrew culture. Menachem Gnessin, the director of the EIT described the role of his fellow actors, in the quotation brought at the beginning of this chapter. All elements were there: the emphasis on the new, Hebrew culture, equating the artists to the *Haluztim*, the personal sacrifice for the sake of the collective, Zionist cause, and the negation of the Old Jew, to be left behind, in the exile. Thus, all participants in the field shared a common view: the Hebrew author was a national figure with a national task.

Thus, from within the evolving Hebrew culture, an image of the Hebrew author emerged. The Hebrew author could be romantic and individualistic but yet, was always to be part of a collective, more important than each of its components. The Hebrew author was a Zionist, New Jew, proud figure, conceiving himself an integral part of the Zionist project.

(2) The irrelevance of the law

After identifying the image of the author as a romantic figure, the authorship project turned to examine the impact that this image had over copyright law. But, thus far, this kind of research was undertaken in countries which developed their own copyright laws (Britain, France, Germany, and later on, the United States). Under a colonial condition, where the law was imposed from above and from the outside, and adjudicated by colonial courts, this prong of the authorship project is simply irrelevant. In the current case study, the Hebrew author was not reflected in copyright law in Palestine, as the law was British and foreign, imposed on a non-English culture. The national characteristic of the individual author could not leave

---

[121] Quoted in 'The Opening Meeting of the Author's Convention' (11 April 1927) *Davar* (Hebrew).
[122] 'In the Author's Convention' (12 April 1927) *Haaretz*, at 1 (Hebrew).

its mark on the development of copyright law. The national aspirations needed an alternative channel.

The author imagined by the foreign British copyright law was far more individualistic and commercially oriented than the image of the Hebrew author. The imagined British author was not a national character, let alone Zionist. Colonial copyright law assumed a different image: the author was conceived as part of a long, sustainable cultural tradition. The idea of progress, translated to the memorable statement about the ability of dwarfs standing on the shoulders of giants to see farther away, symbolizes this view. The author was to lay another brick in the wall, not build a new one. The image of the British author fitted this description. He or she had no particular role in constructing a new society. Perhaps maintaining and advancing it—but there was no need to create a new culture. Under the assumptions of British copyright law, the authors were committed first and foremost to themselves. The underlying ideology was one of private ownership, romanticism, and an instrumental view of copyright law.

British copyright law did care about national and collective goals. Anthony Trollope's famous statement reflects this mindset: 'Take away from English authors their copyrights, and you would very soon take away from England her authors.'[123] Under this formulation, the author was allowed and expected to be individualistic, to care only about his own good and nothing else, if he so wished. The uncoordinated cumulative effect of many individuals was to achieve the public good (the encouragement of learning, in the opening words of the Statute of Anne), by recognizing and protecting private property. It fitted Adam Smith's assumption that: 'It is not from the benevolence of the butcher, the brewer, or the baker, that we expect our dinner, but from their regard to their own interest.'[124] In other words, it was a capitalist, free market argument.

By contrast, until the early 1930s, the Hebrew author did not have the privilege of caring only about oneself. Writing had to serve the Hebrew cause, not the individual's selfish gain. Although the Hebrew author relied on Judaism, on European, and other sources, the work was conceived as new and novel: the authors thought of themselves as the giants rather than the dwarfs, not because they were superior, but because they assumed the role of being pioneers. Two hypothetical cases assist in explaining the irrelevance of British law to the Hebrew cultural fields.

First, let us imagine a Hebrew author at the time, for example the well-known poet Rachel Bluwstein, better known then and today by her first name, Rachel (1890–1931).[125] Born in Russia, Rachel first immigrated to Palestine in 1909 (the second wave of immigration) and lived in the new settlement of Rehovot, and then in an agricultural school near the Sea of Galilee. She returned to Europe in 1913 and immigrated once again in 1919 (third wave), and settled in the first kibbutz,

---

[123] *Autobiography of Anthony Trollope* (Serenity Publishers, 2009) 68 (originally published posthumously by his son, Henry Trollope in 1883).
[124] Adam Smith, *An Inquiry into the Nature and Causes of the Wealth of Nations* (Edwin Cannan (ed), Random House, Inc 1994) 15 (1776).
[125] For her biography, see Uri Milstein (ed), *Rachel* (Smoira-Bittan, 1985) (Hebrew).

Degania. She suffered from tuberculosis and had to leave—in fact, she was expelled. She then spent her time in Jerusalem and Tel-Aviv. She died at the age of 41. Thus, Rachel was a typical *Halutza*, member of the second and third waves of immigration, romantic in her poetry and her tragic life, but with a strong socialist, Zionist, national commitment. Even when forced to leave the collective community, she was part of the larger group. Her poetry, by the way, was romantic and mostly individualistic, with topics of loneliness, unfulfilled love, and an occasional poem about her yearning to the Sea of Galilee. Literary critic Michael Gluzman views her as a modernist, promoting minimalist modernist aesthetics.[126]

Had Rachel read the British copyright law in 1924, she would have likely felt that it did not relate to her. She might have found some of the rules interesting, such as those about initial ownership of a work made under a contract of service (section 5(1)(b) of the 1911 Copyright Act), the veto rights of authors of articles in periodicals regarding republication (ibid), the rules that allow assigning the work (section 5(2)), and might have had interest in other sections of the Act. But her overall impression was likely to be that this was a law for a British author, working in a British cultural field and a capitalist market rather than one that addressed her. Her colleagues in Tel-Aviv, members of the fourth wave of immigration, were more likely to find themselves between the lines of the British Act, but not fully so.

Note that the Act did not outright exclude non-British authors. The authorship project has thus far pointed to such cases of direct exclusion, for example by pointing to works made by a collective overtime in such a manner that it is difficult to identify any single person as the author, and hence they fail to gain copyright protection.[127] The cultural gap between the image of the British author and the Hebrew image was more subtle. It was not a matter of exclusion, but rather of estrangement.

A second hypothetical that illustrates the gap between the image of the law and the self-image of the authors, is to imagine what a local, Hebrew copyright law would look like, if the local authors were to legislate their own copyright law, so to reflect their own image, isolated from external influences. An extreme version would have included a content-based criterion: only works that promote the collectivist Zionist cause would be protected. The socialist faction would argue that the copyright should be owned by the collective. The more individualistic faction would advocate the regulation of the relationship between authors and publishers, as this matter was often the source of disputes. The hypothetical Hebrew copyright law would surely allow using protected works in a very liberal manner if they were to serve the common Zionist cause, such as promoting the use of Hebrew as a language, cultural activities, and Hebrew education. This could have been done either under a broad fair use exception, specific exceptions

---

[126] Michael Gluzman, *The Politics of Canonicity: Lines of Resistance in Modernist Hebrew Poetry* (Stanford University Press, 2003) 117–24.

[127] See eg Marie Battiste and James Youngblood Henderson, *Protecting Indigenous Knowledge and Heritage: A Global Challenge* (Purich Pub, 2000); Bruce H Ziff and Pratima V Rao (eds), *Borrowed Power: Essays on Cultural Appropriation* (Rutgers University Press, 1997); Anupam Chander and Madhavi Sunder, 'The Romance of the Public Domain' (2004) 92 Cal L Rev 1331.

(especially such that would allow the Jewish institutions to use works liberally), or under a scheme of compulsory licensing. Translations, at least from a foreign language to Hebrew, would probably be allowed, once again, to strengthen Hebrew. We could expect also more specific rules such as a requirement to deposit works with a national repository and perhaps powers to some public body to manage orphan works. Under such a hypothetical copyright regime, authors would have enjoyed moral rights, to answer the limited romanticism and individuality that was socially permitted.

Of course, such a copyright regime would run afoul of international standards on almost every point. The Berne Convention as revised in Berlin did not allow content-based protection, it required protection of translations, prohibited formalities, allowed only rather narrow exceptions and did not include compulsory licensing for literary and artistic works. The point here is to illustrate the irrelevance of the colonial copyright to the time and place. It reflected a strange set of ideas as to creativity, its role, the construction of culture, and the image of the author. It was a foreign law, in the deepest sense.

D. Conclusion

Copyright law was transplanted in the Middle East as early as 1910 and then again, in Mandate Palestine, in the 1920s. The foreign law imposed onto the region was set, all tidy and orderly, but for twenty years the transplant was just there, a strange element within the recipient's body. It was not resisted, nor was it rejected, it was simply unnoticed and unused. One might argue that from a historical perspective, a twenty year delay is not particularly long, but in Mandate Palestine, the pace was so intense, if you wish, every year counted as ten. This chapter offered one explanation for this gap: the underlying assumptions of the foreign, colonial copyright about authors and culture did not fit the self, local image of the Hebrew author.

Hebrew culture constructed, expected, and demanded a particular image of the author: an amalgam of individualistic romanticism and socialist Zionism. The foreign law did not have the capacity to respond to national authors. It was to wait for internal social changes before it could fit.

Viewed on the background of the image of the Hebrew author, a broader research question comes up: was the (mostly European) romantic author also a national character? If so, how did the authors' nationality shape, if at all, the law? The role of nationality in the development of copyright law has occasionally been mentioned in the literature, but these comments referred to the interests of states to promote copyright law rather than on the individual authors' nationality.[128] But

---

[128] See eg Brad Sherman and Lionel Bently, *The Making of Modern Intellectual Property Law: The British Experience, 1760–1911* (Cambridge University Press, 1999) 113–14; Catherine Seville, *The Internationalisation of Copyright Law: Books, Buccaneers and the Black Flag in the Nineteenth Century* (Cambridge University Press, 2006) 10–11.

the more subtle influence that the nationality of the individual authors might have had over the development of copyright law, still awaits further exploration.

The cultural–legal explanation offered here is not the only one. The legal field too was yet to develop so to be able to deal with copyright issues. In the meantime, the local community did not wait. It devised its own tools to address its local unique needs. This is the subject of the following chapter.

6
Copyright Law and Social Norms

> Hungry, bitter, you stroll to the publisher, like a poor person in the city park, and beg: give me something, at least for lunch! 'No, and tomorrow neither'
> D—Hebrew Author, 1928.[1]

A. Introduction

The Hebrew author could not find his image reflected in or between the lines of the British colonial copyright, but even if the author would be interested in pursuing a legal action in a Palestinian court, he would be unable to do so until *circa* 1930. The reason is that the legal field was not ripe for dealing with such sophisticated matters: the law in the books was ahead of the lawyers. This chapter offers another explanation for the irrelevance of colonial copyright: the status of the legal field.

The cultural gap and the legal deficiency meant that the authors had to devise their own mechanisms to deal with various issues that came up in the course of constructing the Hebrew cultural field. There were several recurring legal problems. We shall examine the commercial and personal needs and the answers given. One practical solution was private ordering in the form of contracts and industry standards formed in a bottom-up manner. Based on reports about some contracts and disputes, and a survey of dozens of contracts of the period, I redraw the contractual norms. A second solution was an enforcement mechanism: the authors turned to public shaming, in the form of public letters and announcements in the literary journals. Under the conditions of a small, close-knit community, composed of repeat players, the social norms were quite effective, at least for a while, during the late 1920s.

B. The Legal Field

In the 1920s, the local legal field was not yet ready for copyright law. Colonial courts were in place, but lawyers, artists, and the content industry knew little about copyright. Negative evidence is based on the study of the general legal field, which shows little circulation of information on copyright law. Positive evidence is based

---

[1] D, 'Some Happenings' (30 August 1928) *Ktuvim*, at 3.

on the few cases decided during the Mandate, which only began in the 1930s and the alternative practices, which will be discussed in the next part. Searching for copyright law footprints takes us to several locations within the legal field of the time: the judicial system, the lawyers, legal education, libraries, legal scholarship, and the general press.

(1) Judicial systems

The British had already established a court system during the military administration.[2] The colonial courts had jurisdiction for all civil and criminal matters, excluding matters of personal status, which were under the exclusive jurisdiction of religious courts. The judges were mostly British, but as the Mandate progressed, local Arab and Jewish judges were appointed.

Turning to copyright, one might argue that the absence of copyright cases in colonial courts until 1930 reflects hostility to the British courts. However, this was not the case. Jews did turn to the colonial courts to solve civil disputes. The Hebrew hostility towards the British grew only later, towards the late 1930s and during the 1940s. By then, there were the first copyright cases of Jewish plaintiffs suing Jewish defendants.

In the Yishuv there were two non-state judicial systems: the *Hebrew Law of Peace* (1909–49),[3] and the *Comrades' Law* (established 1923), operated by the *Histadrut*, the influential labour union.[4] The two systems were secular in nature, composed mostly of lay judges who applied common sense as a guiding principle, rather than the formal positivist state law.[5] Both adjudicated civil matters between individuals and between individuals and institutions. The motivation of both systems was the interest to operate non-state mechanisms as an alternative to the foreign (colonial) power.[6]

During the 1920s and early 1930s these internal, semi-judicial avenues were not approached to solve copyright disputes. The research found only two cases that indirectly bear upon copyright: one was the dispute over the ownership of a film

---

[2] Nathan Brun, *Judges and Lawyers in Eretz Yisrael* (Magnes, 2008) (Hebrew).

[3] See Paltiel Daykan (Dikshtein), *The History of the Hebrew Law of Peace: Trends, Activities and Achievements* (Yavne Press, 1964) (Hebrew); Eliahu Epstein-HaLevy, 'Hebrew Law of Peace, Its Direction and Needed Changes' (1927) 2 HaMishpat 120 (Hebrew). Its power diminished substantially by the end of the 1920s. See Daykan, at 35; Paltiel Dikshtein, 'On the Expansion of the Function of the Hebrew Law of Peace' (1927) 1 HaMishpat 154, 158 (Hebrew). For a contemporary analysis see Ronen Shamir, 'Lex Moriendi: On the Death of Israeli Law' in Menachem Mautner, Avi Sagi, Ronen Shamir (eds), *Multiculturalism in a Democratic and Jewish State: The Ariel Rosen-Zvi Memorial Book* (Ramot, 1998) 589 (Hebrew).

[4] Israel Bar-Shira, 'About the Substance of the Comrades' Law' (1930) 4 HaMishpat 103 (Hebrew). For a contemporary analysis, see David De Vries, 'The Making of Labour Zionism as a Moral Community-Workers' Tribunals in 1920s Palestine' (2000) 65 Lab Hist Rev 139.

[5] Shamir, 'Lex Moriendi', above n 3, at 593, 615. Shamir further observes a division of litigants between the two systems and no apparent competition: Ronen Shamir, 'The Comrades Law of Hebrew Workers in Palestine: A Study in Socialist Justice' (2002) 20 Law & Hist Rev 279, 285.

[6] Daykan, *The History*, above n 3, at 14; Shamir, 'The Comrades Law' ibid, at 284–5; Shamir, 'Lex Moriendi', above n 3, at 601.

(the physical object) in 1924, and the second was a dispute over payment for the translation of a book, in 1937.[7] There are no other indications that either tribunal adjudicated copyright issues, but there are several reports of other private arbitrations. A case about Theodor Herzl's writings was a first such case, decided by an arbitrator in 1936 (see Chapter 11). During the 1940s, the Hebrew Authors Association (HAA) arbitrated several disputes between authors and publishers.[8] It maintained the option to turn to colonial courts. In the 1940s, the HAA did exactly that, regarding translators' rights.[9] This signalled the maturation of the book industry and the regulation of the relationship between the different players in the market. In 1945 a photographer sued the Jewish National Fund which commissioned his photographs, for infringement. But all of these legal issues took place more than twenty years after the initial imposition of the British law.

(2) Lawyers

By the end of World War I, there were very few trained lawyers in Palestine; most were Arabs.[10] The few who had a European background did not practice law; a few others had studied law in Istanbul and were rehearsed in Ottoman law, but it is unclear whether they studied intellectual property law. The post-war waves of Jewish immigration, the third and even more so the fourth, brought Jewish lawyers trained in Europe, especially Germany.[11] Thus, during the 1920s, among the small Zionist population there were few lawyers (thirty-eight practicing Jewish lawyers as compared to eighty-five Arab lawyers in 1922).[12] Most of the graduates of the Jerusalem Law Classes were Arab.[13]

---

[7] See respectively: Case 17/684 (District Court, Hebrew Law of Peace, Jerusalem, 5 August 1924, discussed in Ch 5, and CC 8135 *Dweck v Kahana* (Tel-Aviv Hebrew Law of Peace, 6 June 1937).

[8] eg a dispute between Re'uveny and Masada-LeGvulam Press and a dispute between Teilhaber and Shapira over the Historical Atlas, both discussed in Minutes of the Board of HAA (4 January 1944) (Gnazim 84850); a dispute between Hermoni and Tversky Press (1948), see Minutes of the Board of HAA (1 November 1948) (Gnazim 84840) (after the establishment of Israel); Zohar Shavit, *The Literary Life in Eretz Yisrael 1910–1933* (HaKibbutz HaMeuchad, 1982) 403 (Hebrew).

[9] Two translators, Y H Yevin and Leib Hazan, sued Masada Press over royalties for new editions. Yevin translated a book by Guy de Maupassant and Hazan books by Ivan Sergeyevich Turgenev. The suit was settled, with the active involvement of the HAA. It resulted in a detailed agreement about the royalties for republications of translations into Hebrew, setting a market norm. See news reports of the trial: 'Case on Translator's Rights' (8 January 1946) *Davar*, at 4 (Hebrew); 'The Copyright Case Continued' (9 January 1946) *Davar*, at 4 (Hebrew). Both the HAA and the Publishers' Association closely followed the case, as indicated in numerous minutes of the HAA executive board's meetings. See Minutes of the Board of HAA (15, 22 October 1945; 19 November 1945; 31 December 1945; 6, 14, 21, 28 January 1946; 4 February 1946) (Gnazim 84850, 84851, 84852), in which the terms of the compromise were agreed upon. See also the discussion in Shavit, *The Literary Life*, ibid, at 401.

[10] Brun, *Judges*, above n 2, at 59; Gabriel Strassman, *Wearing the Robes: A History of the Legal Profession until 1962* (Israeli Bar Association Press, 1984) (Hebrew).

[11] Fania Oz-Salzberger and Eli M Salzberger, 'The Hidden German Sources of the Israeli Supreme Court' (2000) 15 Tel-Aviv U Stud L 79, 83; Rakefet Sela-Sheffy, 'The Jekes in the Legal Field and Bourgeois Culture in Pre-Israel British Palestine' (2003) 13 Iyunim BiTkumat Israel 295 (Hebrew).

[12] See Assaf Likhovski, *Law and Identity in Mandate Palestine* (University of North Carolina Press, 2006) 26.

[13] Brun, *Judges*, above n 2, at 64.

There was hardly any specialization, let alone in copyright law. The pioneer in the field was Kalman Friedenberg—whom we met in Chapter 4. He followed the 1929 Copyright notice about the British–US copyright relationship and brought the first copyright case to court in 1929. In the early 1930s he represented the Palestine Telegraphic Agency in its suit against an Arab newspaper. He earns the title of the first copyright lawyer in Palestine.[14]

A second lawyer who dealt with copyright law, in what seems to be a single—though dramatic involvement was Dr Ellie Cohen. He was the lawyer that represented the author of the *Illustrated Hagada*, which was refused registration in the Copyright Office. His efforts resulted in the establishment of Empire-wide copyright relationship between all British protectorates and mandates and the United States. His copyright engagement took place in 1930.[15]

A third lawyer engaged with copyright law, whom we have already met in Chapter 4 regarding the application of the Ottoman Authors' Rights Act, and will meet again later on, was Shimon Agranat. His seven year copyright practice representing the English Performing Rights Society (PRS) started only in the 1930s.

Other than these, there were only a few lawyers who dealt with copyright cases, and in any case, not before 1929.

(3) Legal education

In 1920, the Mandate government established the Law Classes in Jerusalem,[16] which operated until the establishment of the State of Israel in 1948. The Law Classes curriculum shows no indication of any intellectual property (IP) material. In 1935, the School of Law and Economics was established in Tel-Aviv.[17] Its curriculum had no specialized IP courses.[18] The syllabus of the course on public international law as taught by Professor Laserson in the summer of 1939 also included 'Protection of the Author's Rights'.[19] The listed reading material, however, did not include any IP-related material. By 1945 there were some indications of IP material being included in the curriculum. The course description of 'Law of Commerce' included, inter alia, the topic of 'patents, trademarks, industrial drawings, copy-right'.[20] Another course on criminal commercial law included the

---

[14] For the 1929 involvement, see Ch 4; for the PRS cases, see Ch 7, and for the PTA case, see Ch 9.
[15] See Ch 4.
[16] Likhovski, *Law and Identity*, above n 12, at 109–23.
[17] In 1959 the school became a branch of the Hebrew University of Jerusalem and in 1967 part of Tel-Aviv University. The school had a distinct legal (and cultural) ideology, that aimed to revive Jewish law in a secular form. See discussion in Menachem Mautner, *Law and the Culture of Israel* (Oxford University Press, 2011) 34, 36.
[18] Shmuel Eisenstadt, *The Law and Economics School: The History of the Institution and Its Development, 1939–1959* (nd) (unpublished manuscript, on file with TAU File 20:900.969).
[19] Material for Final Exams 7 (11 May 1939) TAU File 20:900.273.
[20] School of Law and Economics, Course Procedures and Contents for 1944/45, at 10, TAU File 19:900.275. The criminal law course included the topic of counterfeiting documents, stamps, coins and bills, but this seems to be a matter of fraud, rather than an IP issue.

topic of 'Trade Mark and Products Marks. Patents. Trespass (Author's Rights. Unfair Competition)'.[21] In 1941, Jerusalem's Law Classes reported that a new teacher had been added to the staff, 'who will lecture on Trade Mark and Patent Copyright'.[22] In other words, copyright deserved little attention in the legal education system, and not before 1939.

(4) Libraries

The two law schools did not have rich libraries. The reading materials for the classes consisted mostly of legislation (Ottoman, Mandatory, international, and Jewish law), Mandatory case law, and a few books. By the late 1920s, the library at the Hebrew University held a legal section, which held foreign legal books—mostly German, with English and French only second.[23] In many cases the professors issued their class notes to their students. As for copyright law, the leading book on English copyright law was *Copinger on Copyright*, the sixth (1927), and seventh editions (1936), but it was not held in the libraries. Some local lawyers did own a copy. Friedenberg and Agranat, the lawyers of the PRS, received it from London.[24] Other lawyers occasionally cited the book, though not always the latest edition.[25]

(5) Legal literature

Local academic literature on copyright law was rare. One book that was cited in the syllabi of some courses was originally published in Russia in 1917, translated into Hebrew and published in Jerusalem in 1923, by Professor Pokorovski.[26] The author devoted a chapter to the 'problem of immaterial interests', which discussed intellectual property alongside what we would call *in personam* rights, such as breach of contract and violation of privacy.[27] The author briefly described the evolution of the legal protection of intangibles and surveyed several legal systems, including Roman, French, German, Swiss, and Russian law, but none on English law.

---

[21] Ibid, at 12.
[22] '130 Enrolled in New Law Class' (23 November 1941) *Palestine Post*, at 2. The newspaper mentioned Dr H Kiewe as the lecturer. This is probably Dr Hans Kiewe (1890–1963), a Jewish lawyer from Berlin. He died in Chile. See a biographical note in Simone Ladwig-Winters, *Anwalt ohne Recht: das Schicksal jüdischer Rechtsanwälte in Berlin nach 1933* (Bebra, 2007) 195 (German).
[23] Strassman, *Wearing the Robes*, above n 10, at 47.
[24] Kovalsky to PRS (11 July 1933) PRS-3 (acknowledging the receipt of the book, and writing that it and an English decision that were sent 'have been of big interest to our lawyer in Haifa, Mr Agranat').
[25] Dr H Goldberg on behalf of ACUM to CS (4 March 1947) ISA M32/3 doc 1 (citing the 6th edition of *Copinger on Copyright*, 1927). At that time, the 7th edition had already been published.
[26] I A Pokorovski, *The Fundamental Problems of Civil Law* (A Litai trans, Y Yonovich ed, Poalim Press, 1923) (first published in 1917).
[27] Ibid, at 95.

A second scholarly publication was an article by Ze'ev Markon, who wrote from Moscow. His article, published in 1927, was an overview of copyright in Jewish law.[28] The British law in Palestine was not mentioned at all.

A third scholarly piece on copyright law was a brief comment on the 1944 case of the heirs of Ahad Ha'am.[29] Following an English precedent, the Supreme Court denied the heirs' motion but was clearly uncomfortable with the outcome. A 1945 comment by Dr Ludwig Bendix criticized the decision for its overly formalistic approach.[30] The criticism demonstrated a close familiarity with the subject. By 1945, copyright law was no longer a strange legal field.[31]

A final scholarly engagement with copyright law during the period of the British Mandate was an article by Ze'ev Falk, who later became a law professor.[32] The article was published in 1947, when Falk was a second-year student at the Law Classes.[33] He argued that intellectual property law is an example of the law addressing new needs. He cited the 1911 Imperial Copyright Act, but most of the article addressed Jewish copyright law.

General legal literature mentioned copyright law in passing, at best.[34] Thus, copyright scholarship was yet undeveloped.

(6) Popular and professional press

Another source of information about copyright law was the press. Reports on the activities of the HAA regularly appeared in the Hebrew press, but copyright law hardly featured in the HAA meetings during the 1920s.[35] During the 1930s and onwards, copyright issues were occasionally reported in the press, on general

---

[28] Ze'ev Markon, 'The People and the Book: Material on the History of Author's Rights' (1927) 2 HaMishpat 192 (Hebrew).

[29] CA 332/43 *Ossorguine v Hotza'ah Ivrit Ltd* [1944] 11 PLR 419. See Ch 11.

[30] L Bendix, 'Early Protection of the Author's Right' (1945) 2 HaPraklit 216 (Hebrew). Bendix was a Jewish lawyer who immigrated to Palestine from Germany, and in 1947 emigrated to the US. This was considered a loss to the local academic community at the time. See Editorial, 'Farewell' (1947) 4 HaPraklit 62 (Hebrew).

[31] See discussion in Ch 11 about the case and the critique.

[32] Ze'ev Falk, *The Intellectual Property in Israel Law: Sources and Inquiries on Authors' and Inventors' Rights* (1947) (Hebrew). 'Israel Law' refers to Jewish law.

[33] Falk researched jurisprudence, Talmudic law, comparative, and international law. See Michael Korinaldi, 'Comments to Ze'ev Falk's Biography' in Har, Silman, Horowitz, and Korinaldi (eds), *Memorial Book to Professor Ze'ev Falk: Articles in Jewish Sciences and Contemporary Issues* (Mesharim Press, 2005) 13 (Hebrew). Falk was also a poet, which might explain his interest in the field of copyright, which was not his usual research engagement. Telephone interview with Mrs Miriam Falk (18 May 2009).

[34] Frederic M Goadby, *Introduction to the Study of Law: a Handbook for the Use of Law Students in Egypt and Palestine* (3rd edn, Butterworth, 1921) 284, 340–1 (copyright as an example of proprietary rights); C A Hooper, 2 *The Civil Law of Palestine and Trans-Jordan* (Azriel Printing Works, 1936) 61 (copyright as an example for the legislative technique of conferring the Crown powers to legislate through the privy council).

[35] An exception was a comment made at the HAA Convention in December 1928 that the British government was planning to enact a Copyright Act. See 'Authors' Convention' (14 December 1928) *Haaretz*, at 3.

matters,[36] specific local cases,[37] or foreign cases of special interest, such as the copyright disputes in the United States over Hitler's book.[38] These reports were usually brief and assumed a certain familiarity with the idea of copyright law.

The literary journals, read mostly by the industry and the intellectuals, reported news about copyright cases in other countries. *Moznayim*, published by the HAA from 1930 onwards reported news about a French plagiarist who was banned from any literary activity; a Danish judicial decision that authors have lending rights; changes in US copyright law; printing rights of the Bible in England; a copyright dispute in New York; an authors' convention in London that discussed copyright law; an authors' convention in Paris about translators' rights; a publishers' convention; and the Rome Convention.[39] These short reports familiarized the local literary circles with the idea of copyright law.

(7) Interim summary

The overall picture of the legal field is clear. Like the literary field, the legal one was still under construction. It was small, growing quite fast, but until the 1930s it was lacking many elements that form a solid field. Familiarity with copyright law was rare and in fact, throughout the Mandate period there were only a handful of Jewish lawyers that dealt with it. As we saw in Chapter 4, the 1911 Copyright Act was only officially published in 1934, and its unsatisfying Hebrew translation only in 1936. To the extent the authors and publishers knew something about copyright law, it was their experience back in Europe, reflecting nineteenth century central and Eastern European law, rather than modern, Berne-compliant, colonial copyright.

C. Needs and Solutions

The fact that the colonial copyright was not applied or used by the Hebrew community until the latter part of the 1930s does not mean that there were no related legal issues. As the number of players in the cultural field increased, there were more transactions and more competition. Commercial needs surfaced and it became more apparent that the field needed a set of rules. Incentives to create

---

[36] See eg Yishayahu Pavzger, 'On the Legal System in Palestine' (9 February 1926) *Haaretz*, at 2 (Hebrew) (explaining the Mandatory legal system and positing copyright law as an example of copying British laws in their entirety).

[37] See the *Palestine Post's* reports: 'In the Courts' (5 January 1933) at 4 (re the PTA case, discussed in Ch 9); 'Grand Cafe Fined: Use of Copyright Music' (19 October 1933) at 2 (re a PRS case, discussed in Ch 7); 'Writer's Copyright Ruling' (26 May 1943) at 3 (re the case of Ahad Ha'am's heirs, discussed in Ch 11); 'Rights to Use of Ancient Letters' (30 June 1947) at 3 (re *Azuz v Benayahu*, discussed in Ch 11).

[38] '"*Kampf*" over "*Mein Kampf*"' (12 January 1939) *Palestine Post*, at 5; 'Hitler's Copyright in America' (25 June 1939) *Palestine Post*, at 4 (probably referring to Houghton *Mifflin Co v Stackpole Sons, Inc*, 104 F2d 306 (2d Cir 1939)).

[39] See respectively, 4 June 1930, at 15; 28 August 1930, at 16; 26 February 1931, at 22; 12 March 1931, at 15; 21 May 1931, at 16; 4 June 1931, at 16; 25 June 1931, at 16; 30 July 1931, at 16; 3 September 1931, at 15 (all in *Moznayim*, in Hebrew).

were plentiful: personal desire to express oneself and a drive to contribute to the national collective.

The needs and problems emerged hand in hand with the emerging of the new cultural fields. The solutions sought were a mix of a literary norm of originality, commercial norms (backed with contract law), and social norms. They joined together to form a scheme of private ordering. It was a partial and unstable scheme and indeed later on, as the cultural and legal fields matured, it gave way to formal copyright law. But for a few years during the late 1920s, these bottom-up local rules were a reasonable substitute for the top-down foreign law. I point to several relevant contexts in the field regarding the relationships between the players. For each context I explore how it was addressed, and conclude with evaluating the overall efficacy of the private ordering scheme.

(1) The authors: originality

Amongst the Hebrew authors no formal rules were needed. Typical allegations between authors today are of copying the original work, either by reproducing it or by making a derivate work, often without due credit. But among Hebrew authors throughout the Mandate, none of these issues came up. Only two incidents of an allegation of unauthorized copying were found: in 1941 a complaint was lodged with the Mandate government regarding the unauthorized reproduction of a geographical atlas, but this case was of an author against a publisher, rather than against another author.[40] The first case to reach the court with an explicit claim of copying was among two Arab authors, in 1945.[41] No complaints or even mentioning of copying amongst authors were raised in the discussions of the Hebrew Authors' Association over the years, nor was any incident mentioned in the literary journals or general newspapers.

Viewed on the background of the emerging Hebrew literary field, this is not surprising. The authors' community and its overall production were small enough to prevent copying. The authors read everything their colleagues wrote. They commented on and discussed each other's writings. Within such a close-knit community, any copying would have been spotted immediately. Thus, there was no need to articulate any explicit formal rule, social or legal. The governing norm was originality in the strongest sense.

This is not to say that there was no competition amongst the authors. Competition, envy, passionate love and hate relationships were there, with the occasional literary—and always personal—scandal. Hebrew authors did not dissolve themselves of ego.[42] The competition was about the reader's attention and about fame, but also about getting a literary job, namely editing and translations.

---

[40] Dr Braver to Department of Education (17 May 1944) ISA M698/13 doc 29a. See discussion in Ch 11.
[41] CA 320/45 *el-Amiri v Katul* [1946] PLR 189. The case is discussed in Ch 10.
[42] For the personal relationships of the authors on the background of the literary field, see Haim Be'er, *Their Love and Their Hate: H.N. Bialik, Y.H. Brenner, S.Y. Agnon Relations* (Am Oved, 1992) (Hebrew).

In any case, copying was not an issue in the cultural field, with the exception of one case regarding movies. In 1935, Baruch Agadati used about five minutes of footage from one movie (*LeHaim Hadashim*—To New Life) in his own movie (*Zot Hi HaAretz*—This is the Land). It was spotted immediately by the composers of a song played in that part and by *Keren HaYesod*, the copyright owners. The composer published an open letter in a daily newspaper,[43] and the *Keren* insisted that their part is edited out of the movie.[44]

(2) Publishers, translations, and commercial norms

Among the publishers the relationships were more commercial than in the authors' sphere, though the personal dimension was not absent in it either: the publishers knew each other well. Given the small number of authors writing in Hebrew, the emphasis on reading Hebrew and its cultural importance, a frequent publishing activity was translation. This was where publishers clashed the most.

A typical translation transaction raised three sets of relationships: (1) between the publisher and the copyright owner of the underlying work; (2) between competing publishers; and (3) between the publisher and the translator. In many cases, instead of figuring out the legal status of translations, the players formed their own commercial and social norms as they conducted business. In some cases they acted without regard to the law, in yet other cases they seem to have reinvented the law; occasionally, they ran afoul of the law, and in any case, their rules were a matter of private ordering: contracts and market norms.

(a) Author–publisher

It was not always clear who could authorize the translation of an original work. Under several European laws of the time, the right to translate a work either did not exist (as in the case of Russian law, at least until 1911), or was rather limited.[45] Interestingly, the Ottoman Authors' Rights Act 1910, by now no longer law in Palestine, provided some protection for translations,[46] as well as the British 1911 Copyright Act (section 1(2)). The interest in translations into Hebrew referred to a variety of European books (mostly Russian, German, and French), each subject to a different law. To add to the complexity, in some cases the law in the country of origin had changed over time. Palestine, as part of the British Empire, had copyright relationships with some countries that were members of the Berne

---

[43] See M T, 'Issues in Zot Hi HaAretz' (13 March 1935) *Haaretz*, at 2 (Hebrew); Ariel L Feldstein, *Pioneer, Toil, Camera: Cinema in Service of the Zionist Ideology, 1917–1939* (Am Oved, 2009) 126 (Hebrew).
[44] Moshe Zimmerman, *Signs of Cinema: the History of Israeli Cinema, 1896–1948* (Dionon, 2001) 154–7 (Hebrew).
[45] In 1910 the publisher Shlomo Sherbrek, still in Europe, approached Tolstoy's family asking for permission to translate his works (to Yiddish) and learned that no authorization was needed. See exchange of the letters is reprinted in A A Akavia (ed) *The Memories of the Publisher Shlomo Sherbrek* 232 (Sherbrek, 1955) (Hebrew), and discussion in Ch 4.
[46] See Ch 4.

Union, but not with other countries, notably Russia. Thus, the question of the applicable law was quite complicated.

In the absence of clear and unified rules, the publishers behaved in different ways. In some cases, especially earlier in the day, the original authors' rights were simply ignored. This seems to be the case with the organized translation project of the 1910s. Primary and secondary sources did not indicate any regard to the legal aspects of the project.[47] In the mid 1920s, the Hebrew Theatre and the Eretz-Israel Theatre (EIT) did not care much about the original author's rights. Later on, some publishers sometimes approached the copyright owners and bought the right to translate their works. For example, in the late 1920s Avraham Stybel bought the rights to translate Jack London's *Martin Eden*, and Mitzpe Press bought the rights to Upton Sinclair's *Oil!*. Both were quick to publicly announce their purchases.

(b) Among publishers

Often the publishers did not hold the exclusive right to translate the work. They knew that their competitors, just like themselves, did not always bother to seek the original author's consent. There was no public registration system that could have informed the publishers as to who held the translation rights to which work. Taken together, these practices gave rise to concerns: a publisher was concerned that he would invest in translation, only to find out that another publisher was ahead of him. To avoid this waste—or put less favourably, to pre-empt competition—the publishers turned to a different norm: they publicly asserted their rights to translate a work. The public notice was of course also an advertisement, but it served to inform and warn competitors. Here are some examples.

In 1926, Avraham Stybel, whose international press had also a Palestine branch, published a letter in *Ktuvim*, the main literary journal of the time. He wrote that he had learned that another publisher, the *Committee for Publishing Ansky's Writings*, intended to publish a book by Ansky on the destruction of Polish Jewry, in Hebrew. Ansky was the penname of Shloyme Zanvl Rappoport who died a few years earlier. Stybel announced that he had bought the Hebrew translation rights from the author for 10,000 rubles, back in 1916, presumably in Russia.[48] The book was eventually published by Stybel in 1929. Had there been a copyright case in court against another publisher, it would have been a complicated one: what was the applicable law? Was it Palestinian law that should have governed? If so, Russian works were not protected in Palestine at the time. Given that the transaction was made in 1916, was the local (at the time) Ottoman law to be applied? Did either law include translation rights at the time? In any event, copyright law

---

[47] See Minutes of the Translations Committee of the Eretz-Israel office of the Jewish Agency, CZA L2/91–5, L2/91–9, L2/91–11; Zohar Shavit, 'The Development of the Hebrew Publishing in Eretz-Israel' in Zohar Shavit (ed), *The Construction of Hebrew Culture in Eretz Yisrael* (Bialik Institute, 1989) 199, 206–10, 213–15 (Hebrew).

[48] Avraham Stybel, 'Letter' (3 December 1926) *Ktuvim*, at 5 (Hebrew).

was not mentioned and no case was ever initiated. The public assertion and perhaps the daunting complexity of the legal issues were sufficient to settle the debate.

In another incident, in 1929, the Mitzpe Press informed readers and other publishers of its recent purchase of the Hebrew translation rights of Upton Sinclair's *Oil!* The public notice explained that following the publication of the book in Poland, the press had the sole right to the book, which was soon to be published in Hebrew.[49] Shortly thereafter, *Ktuvim* reported that Mitzpe sued Moriya Press for publishing the book without the author's permission.[50] Such a suit would have raised complex legal issues, other than issues of applicable law. For example, we can question the standing of the licensee (Mitzpe) to sue on behalf of the copyright owner.[51] It is unclear whether a suit was indeed filed at all. No other indications of such a suit were found.

Thus, at least among some publishers, a commercial norm developed, of announcing their recent purchases.[52] In itself, the practice reveals that not all publishers bothered to seek the consent of the original author (or the heirs). Had they done so, they were likely to learn that the rights had already been transferred or licensed to another publisher.

Where did this practice of public notification emerge from? Its immediate sources are unclear. It might have been the publishers' own innovation: para-legal mechanisms are not uncommon in the commercial world.[53] Perhaps the source of the publishers' practice can be found in nineteenth century European practices. Copyright law in Prussia and Austria provided the author or publisher with one year of exclusivity as to the translation of the literary work if they explicitly reserved the right to do so in the title page of the original work.[54] It might be that this practice found its way to Palestine.

In 1930 the law finally entered the picture directly and the power and use of the commercial norms diminished. A short report in *Moznyim* informed that a judge in Tel-Aviv ordered that copies of Mitzpe Press's unauthorized translation of Jack

---

[49] The notice was published in both literary journals of the time, see 'News' (7 November 1929) *Ktuvim*, at 4; 'Letters to the Editor' (8 November 1929) *Moznayim*, at 15 (Hebrew). The reference to the publication in Poland probably refers to a Hebrew translation of the book, published in 1929 by Medura Press, in Warsaw.

[50] 'News' (28 November 1929) *Ktuvim*, at 4 (Hebrew).

[51] This question was raised again under Israeli law in 1965, in a composer's lawsuit against a theatre. See CA 240/65 *Zarai v HaTe'atron HaVarod*, 19(2) PD 442 (1965), and then in a few other cases, in which the courts usually avoided deciding it. It was finally settled in the positive only in the Copyright Act 2007, s 54.

[52] See eg Dania Amichay-Michlin, *The Love of AJ Stybel* (Bialik Institute, 2000) 142 (reporting an advertisement in *Haaretz*, about Styble's intentions to publish a translation of Knut Hamsun's *Growth of the Soil*); 'News' (3 November 1927) *Ktuvim*, at 4 (Hebrew) (Stybel announcing forthcoming books); 'News' (6 September 1928) *Ktuvim*, at 4 (Hebrew) (Mitzpe Press announcing forthcoming books).

[53] See eg the discussion of contractual commitments which are not legally enforceable, in David Charny, 'Nonlegal Sanctions in Commercial Relations' (1990) 104 Harv L Rev 373. Charny discusses the relationship of contractual parties, which does not apply to competing publishers.

[54] eg Austrian Copyright Act 1846, s 5(c), reprinted in Lionel Bently and Martin Kretschmer (eds), *Primary Sources on Copyright (1450–1900)* (2008), http://www.copyrighthistory.org. I am indebted to Friedmann Kawohl for drawing my attention to this point.

London's *Martin Eden* should be collected from shops. Stybel Press argued that it had received the exclusive rights from London's heirs.[55] No further details were found about this incident. If the report is accurate, it indicates a shift from the social commercial norms to a formal legal avenue.

(c) Publisher–translator

As for the third prong of the typical translation transaction, the publisher–translator relationship, the commercial and social norms were less clear. Most translators received a lump sum for their work and the contracts were usually silent as to subsequent editions or additional uses (such as a theatre production). Only in the 1940s, under the pressure of a pending lawsuit, was an industry norm formulated, awarding the translators a second payment in case of new editions.[56]

(3) Theatre, authors, translators, and social norms

The professional theatres ran into disputes with authors and translators more than once. Menachem Gnessin, the manager of the EIT, did not always bother to ask for permission to perform the plays, as he himself admitted in his memoirs,[57] although on occasion he had done so.[58] In the 1920s, the concept of performing rights was yet to be developed. The theatres' unfortunate relationship with several authors and translators produced a new kind of solution: social norms, in the form of public shaming. Here are a few examples.

Saul Tchernichovsky was a physician and one of the most esteemed poets and translators of the time. During the 1920s he spent most of the time in Berlin (until he finally immigrated in 1931). While there, Tchernichovsky translated *Le Malade Imaginaire* by Moliere into Hebrew, for publication in book form. But the translation found its way to the theatre stage without his permission and without him having been paid. Tchernichovsky published a letter in *Ktuvim* and described the events at length. The EIT's managers ignored his letters at first, and then they responded in vague terms. In *Ktuvim*, Tchernichovsky wrote bitterly:

I am sure that those who supervise the scenes, those who arrange the chairs, the cleaners of the hall, those who designed the advertisements, printed them and posted them—all

---

[55] 'People, Books and Events' (28 February 1930) *Moznayim*, at 16 (Hebrew).
[56] See above n 9.
[57] Menachem Gnessin, *My Way with the Hebrew Theatre* (HaKibbutz HaMeuchad, 1946) 32 (Hebrew) (reporting his meeting with author Shalom Ash, who learned that his play was produced by the EIT, and requested Gnessin no to do so again because of the low quality of the actors rather than for copyright reasons); at 35 (reporting how he accidently found a translation of a play in which he was interested, and edited it substantially).
[58] eg a contract between the EIT and the heirs of Jerzy Żuławski, permitting the EIT to produce the latter's play, *Shabtai Tsevi*, in return for 3 per cent of the returns. See Official Programme of the EIT, at 13 (1927) IDCPA doc 26.5.1. Gnessin reports in his memoirs other cases in which he sought permission from the authors, see Gnessin, *My Way*, ibid, at 36 (Gnessin's request to Brenner); at 39–40 (Gnessin's request to Shalom Aleichem).

received their payments. But the author? His work is ownerless. Anyone who wants it, gets it.[59]

Interestingly, and quite uniquely among his colleagues, Tchernichovsky referred to copyright law: 'I know that an English protection act for literary material applies in Palestine. But Mr Gnessin and the [theatre's] Board know, and the actors all know, that as long as I am in Berlin, I can do nothing to them.'[60] He then declared that he was prohibiting the use of his translation. The letter—or perhaps the hint about the option of a legal action—was effective in yielding a reply. Gnessin's reply was published within two weeks. He explained that he had received the material and could not have known that the translator had not given his consent. He then apologetically explained that he was no longer with the theatre, that while there he had been the artistic manager rather than the administrator, and, in any event, he promised to pay the sum that he had committed to pay himself, well, as soon as he could.[61] Perhaps surprisingly, the record indicates that Gnessin's personal excuses were correct.[62]

In another case, a translator of a play published a short note in *Ktuvim*, asserting his rights and complaining that the Association of Eretz-Israeli Players—quite likely the Hebrew Theatre—omitted his name from advertisements. This omission, he complained, amounted to deceiving the public, which might think that the play was originally written in Hebrew. Finally, he complained that he did not receive payment.[63]

Kadish Silman was upset when the Hebrew Theatre refused to provide him with more than two free tickets to a play he himself had translated (*God, Man and the Devil*, by Jacob Gordin).[64] Silman's public letter listed all the wrongs: that his permission to use his translation in the play had not been sought, that he had not been paid for the translation, and, finally, that he had not received the tickets ('not that I missed much', he added). But then he pulled out the joker: '[T]he educated public should know that the Theatre provides tickets only to those who write positive commentaries or none at all,' but not to those who criticize it. This public exposure was the author's revenge.

---

[59] Saul Tchernichovsky, 'Letter' (31 December 1926) *Ktuvim*, at 6 (Hebrew).
[60] Ibid.
[61] M Gnessin, 'Reply to Tchernichovsky' (14 January 1927) *Ktuvim*, at 4 (Hebrew).
[62] Due to internal arguments with his colleagues at the EIT, Gnessin left the EIT for a few weeks, during which Miriam Bernstein-Cohen decided to produce Moliere's play. Zer-Zion reports that once Gnessin returned to the theatre, the actors added his name as a director, even though he had nothing to do with it. See Shelly Zer-Zion, 'The Eretz-Israel Theatre: Moving between Cultural Peripheries' (2007) 99 Zmanim 16, 24 (Hebrew).
[63] A Ben-Shemer, 'Letter to the Editor' (29 June 1927) *Ktuvim*, at 4 (Hebrew). Shimon Lev-Ari provides a list of the plays produced by the Hebrew Theatre. It's very last production was *Yizkor*, the play about which Ben-Shemer complained. It was played for one month, in June 1927. See Shimon Lev-Ari, 'The Development of the Theatres' in *The Construction*, above n 47, at 350.
[64] K Silman, 'Critique' (25 September 1927) *Ktuvim*, at 5 (Hebrew). Silman too addressed his complaint against the Association of Eretz-Israeli Players. The play, performed in 1927, is listed by Lev-Ari, 'The Development', ibid, at 350.

Israeli author Haim Be'er reports an incident which allows us to appreciate the power of public shaming.[65] It involved prominent figures in the field. At stake was the EIT's production of a play by Richard Beer-Hofmann (1866–1945), *Jacob's Dream*. The author, who lived in Vienna, whose permission was not sought, had learned about the forthcoming production and quickly wrote to his friend, Shmuel Yossef (Shai) Agnon, who lived in Palestine, asking for his intervention. Beer-Hofmann authorized Agnon to publish his letter in *Hedim*, another literary journal. Be'er reports that Agnon was slow to react, and *Jacob's Dream* became a reality on the Hebrew stage. Agnon then met Gnessin and threatened that if the EIT does not reach an agreement with Beer-Hofmann, he would publish Beer-Hofmann's letter. Gnessin rushed to Haim Bialik asking for help, and Bialik persuaded Agnon to let go, which he eventually did.[66]

The threat of public shaming was used in this incident to enforce the author's rights, though in the end it gave way to personal relationships. We can only speculate whether the story would have unfolded in the same manner had Beer-Hofmann lived in Palestine: perhaps his permission would have been asked for in advance, or perhaps he would have managed to solve the matter in a different way. He was an outsider, one or two steps removed from the inner circle of Hebrew authors, and the power of the social norm was somewhat weaker. Agnon was not the most assertive representative. Eventually Agnon saw the play himself, and reported that it was 'bad and tiring'.[67] Beer-Hofmann himself did not let go so fast and asked again about publishing his complaint, but his query was left unanswered.

(4) Authors and publishers: contractual and social norms

The relationships between authors and publishers were a problematic axis of the cultural field and the one most prone for disputes. A repetitive issue was that of payment: the authors naturally expected payment for their work of writing, translating, or editing. A norm was needed, so as to address the event in which they were not paid on time or not paid at all. It was primarily a contract law matter, but copyright law offered some background rules that could have assisted, especially rules determining initial ownership. But none of these legal options were pursued.

Some archival records and other reports about author–publisher contracts enable us to reconstruct the commercial and legal norms at the time.[68] Phrased in contemporary copyright law terms, until the 1930s, most authors and publishers considered writing and translation as a work made for hire under a contract *for*

---

[65] Be'er, *Their Love*, above n 42, at 240–5. See also Agnon's letters to his wife, which mention the events briefly: Shmuel Yosef Agnon, *My Dear Esterline, Letters, 1924–1931* (Schocken, 1983) 108 (letter dated 8 July 1925, reporting Beer-Hofmann's permission to protest the events).

[66] Be'er, *Their Love*, ibid. Gnessin's memoirs does not mention the event.

[67] Be'er, *Their Love*, ibid; Agnon, *Esterline*, above n 65, at 114 (5 August 1925; his views on the play).

[68] See eg contract between Dvir Press and Mr Yeari-Polskin (21 August 1925), regarding the publication of a book about Tel-Aviv, TCA 3/566/B75.

service (rather than employees, under a contract *to* service). In the 1920s, the typical contract stipulated that the publisher owned the right to produce the book (which can be viewed as either transfer of rights or the determination about initial ownership), that the author received a lump sum rather than royalties, and was entitled to a few free copies.[69]

When the contracts were breached, the authors first demanded their payments in private (by sending a letter or confronting the publisher personally), and if this did not help, they turned to public shaming, by publishing a notice in *Ktuvim*. All players in the small market read *Ktuvim* at the time. No one could miss such notices. Anger and hunger produced sarcastic letters, perhaps proving that the romantic author was not a myth. An author who gave his signature only as D wrote in a public letter about a contract he had signed with a publisher and the subsequent breach of contract:

> In the three corners of our house we squashed together, the four of us; two made a living at the expense of the third who received support, and I and my brother drew on 'one poem a month.'... Today we have market relationships. The theatre, books and bread are bought for money. We have private capital—labour market; five degrees of economy. With us, the battle of the classes continues in a different form. And now, the author is hungry again. He again makes his living from a 'poem a month.' He writes poems, good poems, but the publishers are market institutions who surrender to the market forces.[70]

The romantic author, then, realized that he had to adjust to the new ideology of the free market. The understanding that a public notice might be more efficient than a lawsuit teaches us perhaps that the authors' economic intuitions were not so bad after all.

Following the increase in the volume of literary business, the commercial norms changed during the 1930s and onwards, and the transactions between authors and publishers were streamlined. The most visible change was a shift from a lump-sum payment to royalties, based on sales. Only few of the Hebrew publishing houses of those days still operate in one form or another, and unfortunately, most of the original contracts did not survive. The Rubin Mass Press is an exception. It was established in Berlin in 1927. Its owner immigrated to Palestine in 1933, and re-established his business there.[71] The Press made hundreds of contracts with authors in those days, of two kinds: distribution and publication. The contracts have a similar pattern, with some occasional interesting variations.[72] A typical contract stipulated that the sole right to publish the book—clearly copyright law inspired language—was with the publisher, and then went on to detail the number of copies to be printed and distributed (between 500 and 3000), with a simple royalties

---

[69] An unusual contract agreed between Stybel Press and the prestigious author Micha Yosef Berdyczewski in Germany, in 1919, serves as a benchmark. Berdyczewski was to receive royalties of 30 per cent from the sale price of each copy. He committed to publish only with Stybel. See Amichay-Michlin, *The Love*, above n 52, at 121. The terms of the contracts raised some brows at the time. See ibid.
[70] D, 'Some Happenings' (30 August 1928) *Ktuvim*, at 3 (Hebrew).
[71] See Rubin Mass Ltd at http://www.rubin-mass.com (Hebrew).
[72] I reviewed the contracts at the Press's Jerusalem offices, in May 2010.

scheme (typically 10 per cent) to be paid after a minimum sale of books (usually between 100 and 300). The author was entitled to receive a few copies free of charge (beginning in about thirty copies in the 1930s, and dropping to ten in the 1940s). Some of the contracts indicate a growing commercial sophistication and legal familiarity. For example, in several contracts the author explicitly retained the right to translate the work;[73] authors received the right to republish parts of the books in academic journals, subject to citing the first publication;[74] in some cases the publisher had the right of first refusal for additional books by the author;[75] in the 1940s there was an increase in the use of an arbitration clause.[76] In a few contracts the author or translator undertook responsibility for potential copyright suits by third parties.[77] Only one contract (1940) was found that explicitly mentioned copyright.[78]

Thus, only in the 1930s, routine business practices were based, at least implicitly, on copyright law. As the commercial norms stabilized, the use of social norms in the form of public shaming declined.

(5) Authors' attribution and integrity of works

Another issue that occurred more than once was the credit given—or not given—to the authors and translators, or, put in contemporary copyright law terminology, the moral right of attribution. The attribution was the authors' cultural capital, which they cashed in getting the next writing, translating, or editing job. We also find complaints about the integrity of the work: that it was edited or changed in a way that the author disapproved of. Publishers and the theatres were not always careful to respect these rights.

Dania Amichay-Michlin reports the scandal regarding the translation of Homer's *Iliad* that took place in Russia, in 1918. Saul Tchernichovsky translated it for a new literary magazine, to be published in Moscow. Frischman, the editor, made some changes that Tchernichovsky objected to, but his objection reached the editor and the publisher, Avraham Stybel, too late. Frischman omitted the former's credit and placed his own. Ultimately, the journal appeared with an explanatory

---

[73] eg contracts between Rubin Mass Press Ltd and Paltiel Dikstein and Moshe Wager (21 December 1939); Bat-Sheva Aharoni (16 May 1940); Martin Zeliger (September 1940); Itamar Ben-Hur (15 October 1941). In a couple of contracts the translation rights were reserved to the publisher: see eg contract with Peter Guardnoitz (26 July 1937); Fritz Lowenstein (21 September 1941).

[74] eg contracts between Rubin Mass Press Ltd and I Klugai (26 August 1936); A Z Eshkoli (4 December 1936); M. Zonsiger (6 February 1938); Y Izkovich (11 September 1938).

[75] eg contracts between Rubin Mass Press Ltd and Z Lachman (28 July 1941); Menachem Naor (28 July 1942); I Wasserstein (16 August 1943); Israel Harling (21 July 1941); Tuvia Ashkenazi (7 May 1945).

[76] The first arbitration clause appeared in the contract between the Mass Press and Paltiel Dikstein and Moshe Wager (21 December 1939). Dikstein, a prominent lawyer, was the dominant character behind the Hebrew Law of Peace. See above n 3.

[77] Contract between Rubin Mass Press Ltd and Jacob Levy (11 June 1937); Menachem Naor (28 July 1942); Sara Moshavitski (28 February 1947).

[78] Contract between Rubin Mass Press Ltd and Martin Zeliger (September 1940).

note.⁷⁹ The dispute demonstrates the importance of the integrity of the work and the attribution to the authors, perhaps emphasizing their romantic character.⁸⁰

Here are additional examples: Tchernichovsky and Ben-Shemer insisted on their credit vis-à-vis the theatre;⁸¹ later on in the day (1935), a composer complained about a film producer for omitting his credit.⁸² Avigdor HaMeiri, an author, poet, film critic, founder of the satirical theatre *HaKumkum*, and later one of the founders of *ACUM*, the Hebrew Performing Rights Association, published the following notice in *Ktuvim* in 1927:

Last week I...forbade anyone to use my song *Hi, Hi, Na'alayim* [*Shoes*] in front of an audience, with the music of Mr Weinberg, since the song has already been the public's domain with the music of the composer, Mr Engel.⁸³

Phrased in contemporary copyright terms, HaMeiri permitted the public performance of his work only in a particular way, as put to music by one composer and not another. His use of the term *public domain* means publication, rather than contemporary meaning of the term, referring to works which are not protected by copyright law. In contemporary terms this demand can be phrased either as a condition for a licence to publicly perform a work, or as a concern for the integrity of the work, in the eyes of the author. The former formulation builds on material rights and contractual norms; the latter builds on moral rights.

Another example is that of Nachum Gutman, a famous illustrator of the time (who was also a prolific artist, author, and costume designer). He publicly complained that publishers deleted his signature from the illustrations he had made and did not attribute them to him.⁸⁴

Although the practice of public shaming decreased in the early 1930s, we occasionally find some cases later on. In 1935 a composer complained about a film producer who used his work without authorization or attribution. Daniel Samborsky published a lengthy letter in *Haaretz*, reviewing the much discussed film, *Zot Hi Haaretz*, produced by Baruch Agadati. He detailed the omission, and added that: 'To the benefit of Aga-Film [Agadati's company] I have only one thing to say: it is not the only one. Many did and do the same.' He then lodged another complaint, addressed at an unnamed theatre, and concluded:

---

⁷⁹ See Amichay-Michlin, *The Love*, above n 52, at 52–3. While this incident took place earlier than the period discussed in this chapter, and in Russia, the players remained the same, as they immigrated to Palestine. The social norms evolved already there.
⁸⁰ Ibid.
⁸¹ Above nn 59 and 63.
⁸² Above n 43.
⁸³ Avigdor HaMeiri, 'Letter to the Editor' (20 August 1927) *Ktuvim*, at 6 (Hebrew). The song was a hit at the time. It was first published in a theatrical journal, *Theatre & Art*, alongside the composition of Engel. See the comments of the journal's editor: Miriam Bernstein-Cohen, *A Drop in the Sea* (Massada, 1971) 144 (Hebrew), and listen to the song at http://www.zemereshet.co.il/FlashPlayer/player.asp?version_id=2626 (performance: Renanim Group).
⁸⁴ Nachum Gutman, 'About Illustrations' (22 May 1928) *Ktuvim*, at 2 (Hebrew); see also Graciela Trajtenberg, *Between Nationalism and Art* (Magnes, 2005) 24 (Hebrew), who views this incident as an example of the romantic image of a modernist author.

I mention this example with one intention: that as of now, this habit will cease, that Aga-Film will rehabilitate and Alexander-Film will not sin to begin with; and that theatres will be more careful about the honour of the author. It is enough that central national institutions occasionally do so; they publish songs in special editions without asking for permission. Private institutions should not do the same.[85]

This complaint indicates the frustration on one hand, and the willingness to forgive the public institutions of the Zionist collective on the other hand.

The guardians of moral rights were not only the offended authors themselves. Authors at large kept an open eye and reported cases of omissions, thus establishing a social norm of attribution. Parnass wrote about a new educational book, *Language and Country*, praising it for its use of local content. But then he found that the book contained local songs and extracts from short novels, without providing any attributions. The students who use the book, he commented, were entitled to know who wrote what. He concluded that it was an abuse of authors' rights.[86] He also complained about the 'wonderful' amendments to the original material, to its detriment, in his opinion. Interestingly, the concern for the authors was entangled with a concern for education.[87] Once again, the public letter was effective. The editor of the book, Dr Fania Shergorodska, was quick to respond. She explained that due to her recent immigration to Palestine, the production of the book had met with some difficulties, the omission of names being one of them. She had prepared a list of the authors, but it had been lost.[88] She had managed to recall some, but not all the names, and mentioned in the book that the full list would follow. As for the accusation of tampering with the integrity of the material, the editor explained that 'the author's dignity lies where he published', and that given the attribution (which was missing), the reader could refer to the full text.[89] Parnass responded, dissatisfied, that there is a moral defect in the editor's behaviour, commenting that the material was the private property of the authors.[90]

There were other cases where the shaming was to set the record straight, and provide the credit to those who deserve it. In one such case, the complaint was about a Jewish publisher in Berlin who reproduced scholarship by an author (David Slutski), who died some fifty years earlier.[91] Attribution norms were also asserted in the reverse manner, when the true identity of an anonymous or pseudonymous author was exposed. In a short article, Z Fischman complained about several cases in which the identity of authors had been revealed. For example, the editor of a bibliographic list signed it with his initials 'Y R'. When another publisher

---

[85] Reported by M T, above n 43, at 7.
[86] B Parnass, 'Authors' Abuse' (2 January 1930) *Ktuvim*, at 4 (Hebrew).
[87] See also Braver's complaint to the Mandate government, later in the day, in 1941, which also expressed a concern with the quality of the allegedly infringing work. See above n 40.
[88] Shergorodska's publisher was Rubin Mass. The original contract survived. It was made in Berlin, in March 1928. It stipulates that the author transfers all her rights to the publisher; the contract explicitly refers to the preparation of the indexes and their translation—the author was responsible for all.
[89] F Shergorodska, 'Reply to 'Authors' Abuse'' (16 January 1930) *Ktuvim*, at 4 (Hebrew).
[90] B Parnass, 'Reply' (16 January 1930) *Ktuvim*, at 4 (Hebrew).
[91] Abrhama Kahana, 'Theft' (14 January 1927) *Ktuvim*, at 4 (Hebrew).

republished it, the initials were replaced with what was supposedly the full name: 'Y R (amon)'.[92]

Thus, the publishers, who were the main users of copyrighted material, were under a form of social policing, and when they failed to meet their obligations, the court of public opinion—rather than the court of law—was sought.

(6) International transactions

The Hebrew publishing market was not confined to Palestine. The gradual relocation of the literary centre from Europe to Palestine over the 1920s and 1930s meant that there were still Hebrew publishers in Europe, though as of 1933, those that operated in Germany, were under growing pressure from the Nazi regime and most moved out of just in time. Thus, international transactions were on occasion carried out, for example, a publisher in Germany contracting with an author in Palestine. The picture became far more complicated when a transaction was first carried out abroad, but by the time a second edition or translation was published, the parties were in Palestine. The issue of applicable law in such cases gave rise to the final acceptance of copyright law within the Hebrew community, but this would happen only in the mid 1930s: the cases concerned the writings of Herzl, Ahad Ha'am, and the biblical concordance. Chapter 11 will address these cases.

Another international aspect was the close cultural relationship with Hebrew centres elsewhere. These contacts produced some frictions. The Hebrew authors were famous enough for their articles to be republished in Europe and America. The problem was that permission was not always sought and compensation was not always paid. Even Bilaik, the national poet, was subjected to such unauthorized foreign republication. Upon learning that some of his poems were translated into English, and a collection was published in London, he wrote the publisher in London, Mr S G, emphasizing that the publication was unauthorized, demanding 10 per cent of the book's price and a copy of the book.[93] In other cases he was more successful in asserting his rights. For example, he agreed to a French translation and publication of one of his books, for 10 per cent of the market price, but insisted that the translator should have 'a poetic taste' and sufficient knowledge of both languages.[94]

Apparently, Yiddish authors based in Europe faced a similar problem with American journals, though after complaints the issue was solved. With the rise of the literary centre in Palestine and the rise of Hebrew, the same issues reappeared, this time affecting Hebrew authors. In the Lower East Side of Manhattan one could find several newspapers in Yiddish and later, with some Hebrew sections. The American publishers sought material in Hebrew and found it in Palestine.

[92] Z Fischman, 'About Revealing Pseudonym' (9 September 1926) *Ktuvim*, at 2 (Hebrew).
[93] P Lachover (ed), 3 *Letters of Haim Nachman Bialik*, letter 427 (6 March 1925), at 23, (Dvir, 1938). A month later Bialik wrote again, unsatisfied with the answer he received (which is unknown), and demanded that 50 per cent of the payment is made immediately and the rest within three months. See letter 435 (30 April 1925), at 28.
[94] Bialik to I H Kastel (20 July 1925), in *Letters*, ibid, at 49 (letter 461).

Some authors managed to guard their rights across the sea. For examples, Bialik wrote poems and short stories for *Eden*, a children's Hebrew newspaper published in New York. He kept emphasizing the importance of immediate payments.[95] Others, lacking Bialik's prestige and commercial power, let alone the resources to seek legal advice, could not do much more than complain, which they did, bitterly and sarcastically. Under the heading 'Theft' a frustrated author wrote in 1927 a short comment published in *Ktuvim*, targeting an American Yiddish journal, published in New York:

> The *Togblat*, for example, which has somewhat declined and even the Rabbis' wives stopped reading it, repented at its old age. Together with the pages in English, it now has a Hebrew page. Perhaps this is also divinity, perhaps a talisman for readership. But the page is all theft. Simple: cut with a scissors, an article from here, a feuilleton from there, and especially from the newspapers of Eretz-Israel. Of course, these have the custom of being published in Hebrew. It does not matter if the article is beheaded or its legs parted, hence more than a page cannot be done... And the name of the author appears earnestly, as if he sent the section, article or drawing... to begin with. Easy and convenient.[96]

Rephrased in contemporary terms, the complaint was both of copying and of violating the integrity of the work. In the light of attribution to the mutated work, perhaps we could add a claim of false attribution. Copyright law was not referred to in this debate, and for a reason. In 1927 the copyright relations between Palestine and the United States had not yet been established. Moreover, neither US law nor copyright law in Palestine provided protection for moral rights. In the absence of an applicable law on this point, the turn to public shaming was all the local authors could do. It was not likely to affect the New York journals, but at least it served as a venting opportunity. It also served as an internal political catalyst: the HAA decided to write to the Yiddish newspapers in the United States and to the Hebrew Federation of America, asking them to discontinue this practice.[97]

(7) Private ordering: evaluation

What can we make of the multi-factored private ordering scheme? We saw various instances in different contexts of the emerging literary field. Among the authors, literary norms of originality ruled; among the publishers, a partial system of commercial norms of publicly announcing forthcoming publications was used; the relationship between publishers and translators was based on contractual norms, supplemented with public shaming; the theatres' relationship with authors and translators was regulated by contracts and backed with a social enforcement mechanisms in the form of public shaming; the authors' relationship with publishers was similarly regulated by contractual norms supplemented with public shaming.

---

[95] Bialik, *Letters*, ibid, letters 407 (26 May 1924) at 5; 429 (15 September 1924), at 15; 431 (18 November 1925), at 26; 457 (24 June 1925), at 46; 473 (17 August 1925), at 59.
[96] S Z, 'Theft' (20 August 1926) *Ktuvim*, at 4 (Hebrew).
[97] 'In the Authors' Association' (20 August 1926) *Ktuvim*, at 5 (Hebrew).

The scheme excluded those already outside, like Beer-Hofmann in Vienna, or the Jewish newspapers in the United States.

The combination of literary norms, contractual commitments, commercial norms of public notices, and the practice of public shaming formed a de facto solution for the needs and problems of the Hebrew cultural field in the late 1920s. Scholars have documented various situations in which bottom-up social norms govern a certain area, rather than the formal law: a geographical area in the case of Robert Ellickson's famous study, or a business environment, such as the diamond industry.[98] Shaming is sometimes used by the state as a form of punishment,[99] but here the shaming was executed by individual members of the public as an enforcement tool.

Formal, state copyright law was absent from this picture, but this absence does not necessarily mean that the private ordering scheme was in conflict with the law. Each component had a distinct relationship with the law and a distinct function.

The literary norm among authors was not based on copyright law and it, in fact, exceeded it. The level of originality expected and maintained by the authors was higher than the (British) legal standard of originality at the time. The law's configuration of originality meant mostly that the author was the origin of the work.[100] The law did not require novelty. In contrast, the Hebrew authors were expected to do more. The authors had a deep sense of the high level of originality they were expected to show.

The commercial norms among the publishers can be viewed as a supplement to the law and perhaps it was possible only in the shadow of the law. A public announcement of forthcoming publications assumed a legal rule about ownership and exclusivity, and pre-empted a legal accident before it occurred. Indeed, when the notice regarding the translation of *Martin Eden* failed to achieve its goal, a lawsuit followed.[101]

The contractual norms between authors (and translators) and publishers assumed contract law but ignored copyright law rules about ownership. The social norm was identical to contract law: one's work should be rewarded, and a commitment should be honoured. Turning to social norms of public shaming for the purpose of enforcement was presumably easier and cheaper than suing in court. Given the often unequal power between the individual author and the publisher, shaming was an available tool. Another solution was for the authors to act together. The

---

[98] Ellickson's path-breaking work on norms among farmers, de facto replacing land law, is the beacon of such research. See Robert C Ellickson, *Order without Law: How Neighbors Settle Disputes* (Harvard University Press, 1991). For research on the role of social norms in the diamond industry, see Lisa Bernstein, 'Opting Out of the Legal System: Extralegal Contractual Relations in the Diamond Industry' (1992) 21 J Legal Stud 115.

[99] eg Eric A Posner, *Law and Social Norms* (Harvard University Press, 2000) 88.

[100] The leading case at the time was *University of London Press Ltd v University Tutorial Press Ltd* [1916] 2 Ch 601, ruling that 'the Act does not require that the expression must be in an original or novel form, but that the work must not be copied from another work—that it should originate from the author' (at 608–9).

[101] Above n 55.

HAA overcame the asymmetry of power. For example, in handling translators' rights in the mid 1940s.

The authors' use of *social norms* of public shaming against the theatres and publishers are probably the most intriguing, as they enforced the social norms, supplemented the law, and at least in some cases, it supplanted the law. Public shaming served several functions. First, it was meant to solve the immediate problem, the subject of the particular complaint. Second, in the case of the theatres, the shaming was meant to educate the theatres about the norms, thus, creating such norms. Copyright law could have achieved the same result. One lawsuit, we may guess, would have settled the issue once and for all. Third, as for publishers not paying authors, the shaming can be seen as an enforcement mechanism. Naturally, the publishers cared about their reputation for personal and commercial reasons. Fourth, as far as the moral right of attribution was concerned, the social norms served to reclaim the credit. In this case, the social norm filled a legal lacuna. Fifth, as for the foreigners, the shaming fulfilled the function of venting and perhaps an attempt to motivate the political field to act.

Was the public shaming an effective enforcement mechanism? I believe that at least for a while, during the second part of the 1920s, it was quite so. The authors kept returning to *Ktuvim*, the field's public billboard. Some of those shamed publicly replied. These are signs that the former considered the practice legitimate and useful, and that the latter cared about their reputation.

What made the tool of public shaming work? Several conditions are noted in the literature on social norms, in other cases.[102] First, there needs to be a place, physical or virtual, where all parties meet. *Ktuvim* provided such a billboard at the time. The meeting point reduced monitoring costs, and rendered the enforcement by public shaming effective. Second, participants should care about their reputation in the eyes of other participants. If someone has a particularly thick skin, they are unlikely to care much. Third, where the participants are repeat players, they are more likely to care about their reputation, as they intend to continue collaborating with the other participants in future projects. This was the case with almost all Hebrew authors and publishers. Fourth, none of the players on the accused side can be a monopoly. If they are the only player on their side of the field, they could mistreat all others. For example, the theatres' behaviour towards authors seems to have been a bit arrogant, either due to repeated mistakes, or a lack of understanding. We can assume that under conditions of real competition in the market, the theatres would have been more careful to respect the authors' rights. Finally, if the participants form a small enough community, which is close-knit, united by an

---

[102] See eg Bernstein, 'Opting Out', above n 98, at 140 (noting geographical concentration, ethnic homogeneity, and repeat dealing as necessary for the emergence of an extra-legal regime based on reputation. In the case of the Hebrew authors, all these factors were fulfilled); Judith van Erp, 'Reputational Sanctions in Private and Public Regulation' (2008) 1(5) Erasmus L Rev 145, 161 (identifying four characteristics of an effective reputational sanctions scheme: (1) activity that calls for high level of trust; (2) breaking agreements directly damages participants; (3) short relational distance between players; and (4) moral reasoning supports compliance).

ideology, public shaming seems to work better. This was clearly the case with the Hebrew authors in the 1920s.

This list describes the state of the Hebrew literary field in the 1920s. During the 1930s we see a decline in the non-formal, private ordering practices. In fact, *Moznayim*, the official literary journal of the HAA after it split from the *Ktuvim* faction, did not carry pubic shaming notices. It might have been the journal's policy that put an end to the practice—so there was no longer a central meeting point. It might be that the quick growth of the literary field in the 1930s, especially authors and publishers who fled from Germany to Palestine, was such that it was no longer a close-knit community. The diverse background of the authors and their personalities also may have contributed to the demise of the practice of public shaming. The group's cohesion decreased. Finally, the 1930s saw the gradual strengthening of the law in general, and the development of copyright law. The law became an available alternative to the private ordering.

Could public shaming be effective today in the cultural field? In recent years, copyright scholars identified several fields which have developed various non-legal norms, usually in cases where copyright law, does not provide sufficient protection, at least in the eyes of the participants in the particular field. These are a mix of social and industry norms. This is the case with fashion designs,[103] French chefs' recipes,[104] stand-up comedy in the United States,[105] and television formats.[106] Each of these markets/fields has developed various kinds of internal norms in the absence of a law. Importantly, these cases pose doctrinal difficulties, as it is not clear that utilitarian designs, factual recipes, or jokes enjoy copyright protection. The case of the Hebrew authors in the late 1920s in Palestine can join this list, with its own variation: there was an available law that could cover part of the issues, but was not used.

D. Conclusion

The law could be an important player in the construction of the Hebrew cultural field, but it was slow to join. This chapter argued that yet another central reason for delay in the application of copyright law was the state of the legal field. During the 1920s, as the Hebrew community in Palestine was busy constructing its cultural field, the legal field was somewhat lagging behind. It was in its early stages of development, but yet unready to handle a non-obvious legal field such as copyright

---

[103] Kal Raustiala and Christopher Sprigman, 'The Piracy Paradox: Innovation and Intellectual Property in Fashion Design' (2006) 92 Va L Rev 1687.

[104] Emmanuelle Fauchart and Eric von Hippel, 'Norms-Based Intellectual Property Systems: The Case of French Chefs' (2008) 19(2) Organization Science 187.

[105] Dotan Oliar and Christopher Sprigman, 'There's No Free Laugh (Anymore): The Emergence of Intellectual Property Norms and the Transformation of Stand-Up Comedy' (2008) 94 Va L Rev 1787.

[106] See Martin Kretschmer and Sukhpreet Singh, 'Strategic behaviour in the International Exploitation of TV Formats: A Case Study of the Idols Format' in Joost de Bruin and Koos Zwaan (eds), *Adapting Idols: Authenticity, Identity and Performance in a Global Television Format* (Ashgate, forthcoming 2012).

law. In the absence of a viable legal option and under circumstances of a close-knit community of repeat players, the authors and publishers developed bottom-up mechanisms of private ordering: contracts and industry norms, supplemented with social norms of public shaming to enforce the norms once infringed. This private ordering scheme fulfilled the various needs of the cultural community, in regulating important aspects of their internal relationships.

The next phase of colonial copyright takes us to the 1930s, to the sound of music, and to the activation of the law.

7

Setting the Law in Motion

> The issue of copyright is always in the tempo of andante morto, but all beginnings are difficult.
>
> Meir Kovalsky, PRS Agent in Palestine, 1933.[1]

A. Introduction

In 1930, copyright law was finally set in motion in Palestine. While the use of contractual norms backed by the law continued, the use of social norms decreased. Formal law filled in the vacuum. During the 1930s the local colonial courts dealt with at least twenty copyright cases. The law in the books was now routinely discussed and applied in the halls of justice. It was a dramatic change. Moreover, during this decade, copyright law started playing an active role in the backstage of daily cultural activity: it shaped the contents of contracts between publishers and authors; there was a gradual increase in the use of copyright notices in Hebrew books. The use of a copyright notice in Arab books caught on in the late 1930s, and was slower than the Hebrew books. Institutional users, namely cafes, cinemas, and the new radio station (1936) started paying royalties. Copyright became part of routine business.

This chapter closely traces this process of setting the law in motion. Framing the discussion within the model of *colonial copyright*, we should delve beyond the mere fact that the law was applied in courts. The process of the reception of the law is placed here under the magnifying glass. Archival findings draw a clear picture: foreign players, first the German performing rights society (GEMA) and then the British Performing Rights Society (PRS) were the ones responsible for activating the law, acting through a local (Jewish) energetic agent. In this sense, the law was in the spirit of the nineteenth century colonial copyright laws: it served foreigners rather than locals, and perhaps at the expense of the locals. The activation of the law soon resulted in a spill-over effect, as the local players in the cultural fields adopted similar patterns. A Hebrew performing rights society (ACUM) started operating informally in late 1934 and was incorporated in 1936. Local users were becoming accustomed to the idea of copyright law, and so were the lawyers. The local legal academia caught up a few years later, though, admittedly, in a minor fashion.

---

[1] Meir Kovalsky to Dr M Eliash (17 March 1933) CZA A417 (Eliash File).

This process, in which a foreign player is the first to activate colonial copyright has been documented in other colonies as well, though much more research is needed on this point. For example, this was the case in New Zealand, South Africa, and the Straits Settlements.

Activating copyright law in Palestine came hand in hand with new technologies. Whereas the 1920s were the decade of books, the 1930s were a decade of music and cinema. Recorded music surpassed live music as the dominant way to enjoy music; 'talkies' replaced silent movies, and the radio broadcasted its wondrous sounds all over. The result was that the debut of copyright law in Palestine started at an unusual point. Whereas modern copyright law originated in a world of print and developed its main principles around print, focusing on reproduction, Palestinian copyright law emerged in a world of then-cutting edge technologies, a world of sounds, where the focus was on performing music, rather than copying it.[2]

The discussion begins with a brief overview of the legal state of performing rights. We shall then meet Meir Kovalsky, the local entrepreneur who played a crucial role in the copyright scene. He was the pioneer of the field. The first copyright case to reach a local court will then be discussed and analysed: the Zion Theatre in Jerusalem played live music alongside a silent movie. We shall proceed to explore other music-related cases, the challenges that occurred, and the legal principles that were set. I shall then evaluate the role of copyright entrepreneurs in the reception of colonial copyright and its domestication, and argue that it provides a case of glocalization: the merger of the global (colonial) with the local.

B. Law, Sound, Action!

Copyright law was far from being at centre stage during the turbulent 1930s. Palestine was undergoing dramatic changes, with a substantial increase in the number of Jewish residents, new towns, cities, and infrastructure. Immigration and land law were controversial and at the centre of political attention. A fifth massive wave of Jewish immigration occurred, mostly of Jews escaping Germany.[3] Tension between Arabs and Jews intensified and turned violent. The Arab national movement strengthened, culminating in the Arab Revolt (1936–9). Europe sent chilling winds of racism and Anti-Semitism, and of a forthcoming war. Internal politics in the Hebrew Yishuv reached new levels of division.

Amidst all this drama the cultural fields stabilized. There was more cultural activity in all sectors of the population, it gained stronger institutional anchors, and became sustainable. New technologies of sound and vision replaced old ones. The legal field caught up. It matured and was quickly becoming anglicized. It was now ready to engage with new challenges. By 1930 the statutory framework of

---

[2] For the gradual extension of copyright law to music, see Michael W Carroll, 'The Struggle for Music Copyright' (2005) 57 Fla L Rev 907.

[3] Yoav Gelber, *New Homeland: Immigration and absorption of Central European Jews 1933–1948* (Yad Ben-Zvi, 1990) (Hebrew).

copyright was also in place. Performing rights were part of copyright law, in its international, imperial, and local incarnations.

(1) Performing rights

Today, we readily recognize that copyright is not a single legal right, but a bundle of rights, held exclusively by the owner for a limited time (subject to limitations and exceptions). But this was not always the case. Copyright began as a right to copy. In the United Kingdom, during the nineteenth century, this right gathered additional dimensions. The Dramatic Literary Property Act 1833 conferred authors of dramatic texts with the exclusive right to publicly perform them;[4] the Copyright Act 1842 extended the performing right to apply also to musical compositions.[5] Following what was conceived at the time as an abuse of the right, the Copyright (Musical Composition) Act 1882 subjected the right to a notice requirement: in the absence of a notice on the printed copies of the music sheets, there were no performing rights.[6] In 1902 and 1906 legislation was enacted to assist copyright owners in enforcing their rights. These two Acts also remained valid in the United Kingdom once the 1911 Act consolidated all previous copyright legislation.

On the international level, the Berne Convention of 1886 assured that musical works were protected and enjoyed the right of public performance (Articles 4 and 9 of the original text). The 1908 Berlin revision of the Convention confirmed this protection (Articles 2 and 11). Accordingly, the British Copyright Act 1911 included musical works in copyright's subject matter (section 1(1)), which included the right to perform the work in public (section 1(2)), backed with civil remedies (section 6(1)), and supported by evidentiary presumptions (section 6(3)). Public performance included acoustic representation and a performance by a mechanical representation (section 35). Thus, for example, singing on a public stage and playing a record both amounted to 'performance'. As a commentator at the time explained, the performance was a transitory use that did not consist of making a permanent record.[7] Copinger explained that the performing right was distinct from the reproduction right.[8] Thus, copyright became a bundle of rights.

The performing right gave rise to new enforcement challenges. First, the potential infringers were *users* of the works. Secondly, the idea of performing right was even less intuitive than the reproduction right. After all, the ephemeral use seemed to be the natural function of the work. Thirdly, those who wished to receive permission for intended use, had to search for the many copyright owners, negotiate, and pay them separately. This was costly and practically impossible. Finally, users who did not abide could easily avoid liability, as the transitory feature of the use of the musical works made it more difficult to detect. A small

---

[4] 3 & 4 Will IV, c 15.
[5] 5 & 6 Vict, c 45, s 20.
[6] Walter Arthur Copinger and J M Easton, *Copinger on Copyright* (5th edn, Stevens and Haynes, 1915) 12–18.
[7] E J Macgillivray, *A Treatise Upon the Law of Copyright* (John Murray, 1902) 16.
[8] *Copinger on Copyright*, above n 6, at 79.

portable recorder hidden in a pocket, ready to capture the performance as evidence, was not even science fiction.

The solution to all these challenges was the formation of collecting societies, which could serve as intermediaries between the composers, publishers, and users, and serve as a convenient meeting point for both sides as well as applying more efficient monitoring. The societies licensed their repertoire to institutional users such as theatres and cafes, collected the fees and then divided them among society members, who were authors, composers, and the music publishers. The first societies were formed on the Continent: in France (SACEM, 1851),[9] Austria (AKM, 1897),[10] and Germany (GDK-AFTA, 1903).[11] The model crossed the English Channel and in 1914, the Performing Rights Society (PRS) was established in London.[12] Initially, the members of the PRS retained their rights, and permitted the PRS to license their works on their behalf. Only in 1934, did the PRS insist that all its members transferred their rights, so that the PRS was the copyright owner of the performing rights.[13]

Case law in the United Kingdom followed. As from the late 1910, British courts dealt with issues such as the power of the PRS to sue in the name of the composers, the legality of the PRS itself, the 'public' element of the performing right, and the meaning of 'authorization' under section 2(3).[14] Later on, courts dealt with copyright in broadcasting.[15] This was the law that was applied in Palestine in 1924. Interestingly, the Ottoman Authors' Rights Act 1910 which was in place in Palestine until 1924 (subject to some amendments of the British 1920 Copyright Ordinance), included a public performance right which was limited to theatre plays and operas.[16]

---

[9] SACEM website, at http://www.sacem.fr/cms/site/en/home/about-sacem/history.
[10] AKM website, at http://www.akm.at.
[11] The GDK was established in 1898 as an authors and composers' union. In 1903 it transformed to the GDT, which established a collecting branch, AFTA. A second collecting society was formed in 1915: Genossenschaft zur Verwertung musikalischer Aufführungsrechte (GEMA). The two united in 1930, but survived until 1933, when the Nazi regime replaced it with a unified society. See GEMA website, at http://bit.ly/jvAuqq and Martin Kretschmer, 'The Failure of Property Rules in Collective Administration: Rethinking Copyright Societies as Regulatory Instruments' [2002] 24(3) EIPR 126, 128–30.
[12] For the official history of the PRS, see Cyril Ehrlich, *Harmonious Alliance: A History of the Performing Right Society* (Oxford University Press, 1989), and the earlier account, written by the General Manager of the PRS: Charles F James, *The Story of the Performing Rights Society* (PRS, 1951). See also a music publisher's point of view: in John Abbott, *The Story of Francis, Day & Hunter* (Francis, Day & Hunter, 1952) 74, and Gavin McFarlane, *Copyright: The Development and Exercise of the Performing Right* (John Offord Publications, 1980) 97 (arguing that the PRS was inspired by the French SACEM.)
[13] McFarlane, *Copyright*, ibid, at 98, 143.
[14] eg *Performing Right Society Ltd v The London Theatre of Varieties Ltd* [1922] 1 KB 539; *Performing Right Society v Cyril Theatrical Syndicate Ltd* [1924] 1 KB 1, and discussion in Walter Arthur Copinger, and F E Skone James, *Copinger on the Law of Copyright* (6th edn, Sweet & Maxwell, 1927) 66, 117–19, 149–50.
[15] Australian and American courts decided in 1925 in the affirmative, that copyright law applies to broadcasting. The authoritative British case was decided later on, in 1934.
[16] Authors' Rights Act 1910, ss 10, 32.

The PRS and its Continental sister societies grew alongside the music industry and followed the technological advancements step by step. In the early twentieth century, the main form of consumer music was through sheet music, singing or playing on musical instruments. Once the silent movie emerged, background music for films turned out to be a profitable use, resulting in substantial income to the PRS.[17] When talking movies replaced the silent ones, the music which was often incorporated in the films was subject to a fee. The emergence of the radio (the BBC was established in 1922) was yet another new frontier, soon to be covered by fees, initially calculated on the basis of the duration of the broadcast, and then on the basis of the number of users' licences.[18]

By the end of the 1920s, the model of a collecting society was live and active in Britain. In 1929 the PRS formed a cartel with the other European societies (the French, German, Italian, and Austrian): each was exclusively responsible for copyright in 'its' territories, with cross-representation and cooperation. The PRS was ready to follow the British flag to new musical territories. Palestine was an obvious destination.

(2) New tunes

Shortly after forming the cartel, the European societies sent John Woodhouse, the PRS's Consulting Director, to tour the Middle East.[19] His report to London did not include a detailed description of the cultural scene but he did quote figures (somewhat inaccurate) of twenty cinemas operating in Jerusalem, ten to fifteen restaurants, and four hotels, based on information provided to him by Meir Kovalsky, whom we shall meet shortly.[20]

Indeed, by the late 1920s, Palestine's cultural scene reached a new peak. Live music was popular in cafes and restaurants, serving as background music. Playing records was still uncommon. Cinema was highly popular as well. After a few years of occasional screenings in various places, permanent movie theatres popped up all over the country: in Tel-Aviv (1914), Jerusalem (1916), and during the 1920s, almost everywhere.[21] For Palestinians, going to the cinemas was a routine form of entertainment. Viewing a movie did not require literacy. The movies were from faraway places, perhaps allowing some escapism from daily hardships. No wonder, the public loved it. For their first fifteen years or so (beginning in 1914), the movies

---

[17] Ehrlich, *Harmonious Alliance*, above n 12, at 35.
[18] Ibid, at 47, 73. The per-licence basis of the fee began in 1929.
[19] Woodhouse was the Society's Controller from 1917–29 and then it's Consulting Director, a position which he held until his death in 1947. See James, *The Story*, above n 12, at 24, 58, 115. Woodhouse also initiated the PRS's activities in South Africa in 1925, see James, *The Story*, ibid, at 45.
[20] Woodhouse to PRS (December 1929) PRS-1. There were fewer cinemas and probably more restaurants. Hereafter I use PRS-1 to refer to Box A209, Palestine 1 in the PRS archive, and similarly to A209 [PRS-2], A326 [PRS-3], A326 [PRS-4], A293 [PRS-5], A293 [PRS-6], A293 [PRS-7] and to A319, Agranat Files 1 as PRS-A1.
[21] See Anat Helman, *Urban Culture in 1920s and 1930s Tel-Aviv* (Haifa University Press, 2007) 148–9 (Hebrew) (cinemas in Tel-Aviv); Kobi Cohen-Hatab, *Tour the Land: Tourism in Palestine during the British Mandate, 1917–1948* (Yad Ben-Zvi, 2006) 161–2 (Hebrew) (cinemas in Jerusalem).

were silent, and as in England, the practice was for live music accompanying the movies: usually a pianist or a violinist, and on occasion larger orchestras. The Zion Theatre hired musicians to play during the movie. The first contract with a musician dates back to 1922.[22] By 1928 it became a routine business practice.

Radio broadcasting had not yet surfaced. During 1929–30 the government issued only 278 wireless licences.[23] The radio sets were expensive, and were tuned to overseas broadcasts. Only in 1932 a first local radio broadcasted during the Levant Fair in Tel-Aviv for a few weeks and only in 1936 did the government establish the Palestine Broadcasting Service (PBS).[24]

Listening patterns followed patterns of immigration. The Jewish residents of Tel-Aviv, Haifa, and Jerusalem preferred classical music, composed mostly in Germany and Austria, or local tunes, often inspired by Russian tunes. Hebrew music and folk singing gradually became popular.[25] The Sephardi Jewish population either played its own music (especially the Yemenites), or listened to Arab music. Absent from this scene for some time was English music. There was a language barrier, and in any case, it was not highly appreciated compared to the central European music. In the 1930s, English became more popular. Many of the movies were American. The number of British soldiers in the country increased. The local scene responded.[26] Music played in cafes was increasingly in English, with the intention of meeting the musical preferences of British soldiers.

By the early 1930s the cultural field was vibrant, in the process of consolidation and ready for the next step. Technology offered new forms of listening to music. With the cultural field ripe, the legal framework of performing rights available for use, the maturation of the legal field, all was set for raising the curtains.

(3) Enter Meir Kovalsky

When John Woodhouse visited Palestine in December 1929, he found out that the French Society already had an agent in the region, Mr Levy of Beirut, who had an inactive agent in Tel-Aviv (Mr Hopincito).[27] Given that Beirut was under a French Mandate, it was clear to the PRS and to the newly formed European cartel that they needed an active local agent in Palestine. The choice was rather obvious: the German, Austrian, and Italian societies were already represented by Mr Meir Kovalsky of Tel-Aviv. He also had a lawyer, Kalman Friedenberg from Jerusalem.

---

[22] See contracts between Zion Theatre and musicians, JCA 472 File 80.
[23] See Government of Palestine, Report of the Committee on the Development of the Palestine Broadcasting Service, App A (1936) ISA M354/26 doc 1a.
[24] See Ch 8.
[25] Natan Shahar documented 4,456 folk songs, published and/or distributed in Hebrew, during 1882–1949. 16 per cent of which were composed by European composers; 31 per cent of the composers are yet unknown; and the remainder were composed by 195 Hebrew composers in Palestine. See Natan Shahar, 'The Eretz-Israeli Song, 1882–1948' in Zohar Shavit (ed), *The Construction of Hebrew Culture in Eretz Yisrael* (Bialik Institute, 1989) 495 (Hebrew), at 513, 515–16.
[26] See Cohen-Hatab, *Tour the Land*, above n 21.
[27] Until 1928 there was no related activity in Palestine. In that year, the PRS extended the mandate it gave the French society, to include also Palestine. James, *The Story*, above n 12, at 53, 62.

Woodhouse met both. He reported to London that Friedenberg was a barrister, educated in Russia and Germany but 'speaks English in a small piping voice (he is a little man)'. As for Kovalsky, Woodhouse was more impressed with his daughter. Kovalsky himself, Woodhouse reported, spoke no English, but the father and daughter were acting bona fides; they wanted to be pioneers in establishing performing rights in Palestine.[28] We can assume that the choice of the word, pioneer (*Halutz*), was no coincidence. Being a *Halutz* was the highest level to which a member of the Hebrew collective could aspire.

Meir Kovalsky was a well-known figure in the musical circles during the Mandate, though he has not yet deserved full recognition for his role. He was born in 1873 in Kherson, Ukraine, and immigrated to Palestine in 1904 (second wave of immigration).[29] After an unsuccessful rural settlement attempt, he returned to Jaffa, where he taught music. Later he moved to Jerusalem, taught music, and imported sheet music. In 1909 he established and managed the *Kinor Zion* (Hebrew: Violin of Zion) band. During World War I he was recruited to the Turkish (Ottoman) army and was the conductor and manager of one of its bands. In 1914 he opened a first shop for musical instruments in Jerusalem.[30] With the Mandate, pianos became more popular, and he expanded his business to Tel-Aviv (1923), and Haifa (1931). It was a family business: the shops were managed by his three daughters, son, and son-in-laws. Advertisements of the time, published in the newspapers indicate that his shops were a focal point for music events: one could buy tickets for concerts in 1930, register for musical classes in 1933, buy a violin or order a piano tuner at any time, or buy a radio set in 1936.

Kovalsky was clearly eager to represent the PRS and the cartel. He sensed the commercial opportunity, had the advantage of representing the other European societies, and he figured out the political situation in which the British were to stay for some time in Palestine. Perhaps he even sensed the changing mood in Germany and Austria. Within only a few years, music from Germany or music in German was (socially) banned from the local cultural scene. Kovalsky was keen to get the Cartel's agency. However, when the PRS Board met in October 1929, they had the information that GEMA was not that satisfied with Kovalsky, and that he had never initiated any lawsuit in court.[31] Friedenberg, the lawyer, wrote to the PRS in November, citing the 1911 Copyright Act and adding that 'not a single case under this Act was brought before the Court as yet and piracy continues unabated, the Act remaining a dead letter'.[32] But then, Kovalsky and Friedenberg proved that they were the right men for the job. Following their reports that nothing had been done until then, they quickly initiated a lawsuit, to be discussed shortly. When

---

[28] Woodhouse to PRS (21 December 1929) PRS-1.
[29] The biographical data was provided by Kovalsky's great-grandchild, Nitzan (Meir) Zeira, who is a musical producer and publisher. I am indebted to his kind assistance.
[30] Jehoash Hirshberg, *Music in the Jewish Community of Palestine 1880–1948: A Social History* (Oxford University Press, 1995) 113, 116.
[31] Minutes of the PRS Board (24 October 1929) PRS-1.
[32] Friedenberg to PRS (11 November 1929) PRS-1.

Woodhouse visited Palestine, he could report back home that the first case, handled by Friedenberg and Kovalsky as a test case, was already in process.[33]

Immediately after winning the case on behalf of GEMA, Kovalsky formally offered his services to the PRS.[34] Perhaps impressed by their action, perhaps no one else was suitable, or perhaps it was Kovalsky's daughter's charm that tilted the scales: a month later Woodhouse recommended that Kovalsky get the agency.[35] But the PRS took some time to decide. Kovalsky did not let go. He wrote to the French SACEM offering his services and more so, he wrote to the individual publishers—members of the European societies—asking that they recommend his appointment to their respective societies.[36] His efforts were worthwhile. In April 1930 the cartel transferred the Palestine business to the PRS, which then decided to appoint Kovalsky as its agent. While the details of the agency were discussed, the impatient Kovalsky announced his new business in flashy newspaper advertisements, informing the public that he was the PRS's agent.[37] The PRS frowned, writing that: 'This action on your part is somewhat premature, as the appointment is not yet actually effected until the agreement has been signed.'[38] Kovalsky replied in a language that the PRS could appreciate: 'The reason is that we feel very much annoyed seeing that the people is using property which does not belong to them and refuse to pay for it.'[39] The agency contract was signed in August 1930. It gave Kovalsky a commission of 50 per cent of all royalties he managed to collect. This was to cover all his expenses, legal costs included. This scheme assured that Kovalsky had a strong incentive to collect as much as possible, but also that he had an incentive to minimize his costs. This might be the key to explain some of his decisions in years to come, in forming the strategy of his business.

C. Mendelsohn, Beethoven, and Schumann in Zion

The first copyright lawsuit in Palestine was brought by Meir Kovalsky, represented by his lawyer, Kalman Friedenberg, on behalf of GEMA, the German performing rights society. The defendants were Israel Guth and Isaac Peretz, the owners of the Zion Theatre, represented by Daniel Auster, a Jewish lawyer from Jerusalem.[40] The judge was also Jewish, Dr Philip (Yeruham) Korngrün, who was appointed

---

[33] Woodhouse to PRS (21 December 1929) PRS-1.
[34] Kovalsky to PRS (9 January 1930) PRS-1.
[35] Woodhouse to PRS (12 February 1930) PRS-1.
[36] Kovalsky to SACEM (21 February 1930). The French asked Kovalsky to cease. Alpi Jean Bernard to Kovalsky (17 March 1930). Kovalsky apologized to the PRS. Kovalsky to PRS (27 March 1930) PRS-1.
[37] Kovalsky informed the PRS of his actions. See Kovalsky to PRS (3 July 1930) PRS-1.
[38] PRS to Kovalsky (11 July 1930) PRS-1.
[39] Kovalsky to PRS (24 July 1930) PRS-1.
[40] Auster was born in Poland and studied law in Vienna. He became a lawyer in Palestine in 1920. Later on he became the first Jewish Mayor of Jerusalem (1944). See David Tidhar, 'Daniel Auster' in 1 *Encyclopaedia of the Founders and Builders of Israel* (1947) 166 (Hebrew).

shortly beforehand.⁴¹ Kovalsky argued that the Theatre performed musical works alongside the silent movies. The works were then-modern adaptations of Mendelsohn, Beethoven, and Schumann, among others composers.

This is the first exposure of the case. It was not published or mentioned later on in the Palestinian case law. It had no formal legal precedential power, but it did set a practical precedent: performing rights were recognized and enforced. Theatre and cafe owners started paying royalties, albeit reluctantly.

(1) The lawyer's strategy

In contemporary copyright law terms, it is obvious that playing live music amounts to a public performance. But in Palestine in 1929, the core concept of copyright itself was as yet unfamiliar. The idea that a copyright owner had an exclusive right to control reproduction of a work had not yet resonated. The idea that a composer and music publisher could control the use of the music was even less intuitive: one might have wondered, what other purpose could the music have, other than play it?

Meir Kovalsky and Kalman Friedenberg brought the first lawsuit against the Zion Theatre in Jerusalem, in late 1929. Kovalsky was eager to impress the PRS. Friedenberg, as far as he was concerned, realized the business opportunity, and clearly fell in love with copyright law. Their choice as to whom to sue was an easy one. The Zion Theatre was the first cinema in Jerusalem, well established, and well known. It openly employed musicians. The copyright in this music was often owned by GEMA. The theatre published the movies to be screened in advance. It was a whole bucket of pennies under the spotlight, waiting to be taken. From a legal point, there had already been a British precedent, though it was unbeknown to Kovalsky and Friedenberg.⁴²

Perhaps it was Friedenberg's lack of experience in copyright law (there was no one else to learn from), or perhaps it was the interest in a quick result that could be a dowry for the PRS, that led him to choose a rather peculiar legal strategy. The first copyright case was undertaken as a criminal procedure rather than a civil action. The Magistrates' Courts (Jurisdiction) Ordinance 1924 allowed for such a private prosecution.⁴³

More peculiar was Friedenberg's choice of the specific criminal offence. The indictment itself was not found, and some details remain unclear. The court's judgment, discussed shortly, cites section 6(3) of the Copyright Ordinance 1924 as

---

⁴¹ Korngrün was born in 1883 and studied law in Lviv, then under Polish control (known in German as Lamberg; today in Ukraine). He earned his degree in 1906 and a doctorate in 1909. He immigrated in 1925, where he successfully passed the bar exam for foreign lawyers. He was appointed to be a judge in 1929. See David Tidhar, 'Dr Yeruham (Phillip) Korngrün' in 2 *Encyclopaedia of the Founders and Builders of Israel* (Hebrew) 659.

⁴² One of the first cases litigated by the PRS in Britain dealt with a pianist who played music alongside a silent movie. The PRS won. See *Performing Rights Society Ltd v Thompson* [1918] 34 Times LR 351, reprinted in E J MacGillivray (ed), *Copyright Cases 1917–1923* (1924) 38. The PRS considered this to be a remarkable judgment, described by its general manager as 'the Society's charter'—see James, *The Story*, above n 12, at 7.

⁴³ Section 9 allowed private prosecution, if the police declined to prosecute the case itself.

the basis for the conviction. But there was no such section in the Ordinance. After the decision was delivered, Friedenberg wrote the judge asking about this. The judge replied, or at least so Friedenberg reported to the PRS, that it was a clerical error and that it should have been section 3(6).[44] However, section 3(6) of the Ordinance dealt with something else: it instructed that the use of the criminal option does not prejudice the owner's right to bring about civil action.[45] It couldn't be the basis of the conviction in itself.

Based on Friedenberg's report about the judgment, the PRS was more than puzzled about Friedenberg's decision to pursue the criminal route.[46] His explanation was a lawyerly one: in civil proceedings, he wrote, one had to prove the local agent's right to sue on behalf of the copyright owner. There was no such proof. Hence he pursued the criminal avenue, in which it did not matter whose right was infringed, as long as the copyright was valid.[47] Indeed, in the following years proving ownership and producing the power of attorney consumed much energy and time. However, the PRS was still not impressed. It asked that in the future, Friedenberg sued under section 11 of the Copyright Act.[48]

This post-judgment exchange exposed yet other problems: on the PRS's side, it was evidently ignorant about copyright law in Palestine: section 11 of the 1911 Act did not apply in Palestine; its content was more or less duplicated in the Copyright Ordinance 1924. Far more serious was that it seems that Friedenberg was hardly familiar with the 1911 Copyright Act. In November 1929, just before the case was brought to court, Friedenberg wrote to the PRS and mentioned the 1911 Act, but asked for additional material.[49] After the case was decided, he asked the PRS to direct him to a text book on copyright law.[50] The PRS suggested the 6th edition of *Copinger on Copyright*.[51] This lack of familiarity might also explain the decision to opt for the criminal procedure rather than the civil one. Friedenberg partially learned the lesson. When he initiated the Palestine Telegraphic Agency (PTA) case, he brought both a civil lawsuit and criminal charges. Kovalsky himself was probably unaware of the Copyright Act itself until later in the day.[52]

---

[44] Friedenberg to PRS (8 May 1930) PRS-1.

[45] Friedenberg's enthusiastic letter in which he reported the case, also commented about other issues, including s 3(2) of the Ordinance, which dealt with unauthorized performance from an infringing copy. He believed he spotted a mistake, as the Ordinance mentioned a fine of LP5, whereas the English origin mentioned a fine of LP50. Friedenberg suggested that the PRS approach the Colonial Office and ask that this is amended. The PRS was confused. They thought that the judgment was based on s 3(2), something which clearly did not fit the case's circumstances. The proper section, they noted, was either s 1(2) of the Act (rather than the Ordinance), which deals with public performance, or s 2(3) of the Act, which imposes liability on a party that permits, for profit, another to publicly perform a musical work.

[46] PRS to Friedenberg (4 March 1930) PRS-1.
[47] Friedenberg to PRS (18 March 1930) PRS-1.
[48] PRS to Friedenberg (31 March 1930) PRS-1.
[49] Friedenberg to PRS (17 November 1929) PRS-1.
[50] Friedenberg to PRS (21 February 1930) PRS-1.
[51] PRS to Friedenberg (4 March 1930) PRS-1.
[52] See discussion at n 97.

(2) The judgment

Judge Korngrün's three page judgment discusses a few important legal points, about the source and validity of the Copyright Ordinance, about the performing right, about adaptations, and about the relationship between a civil suit and a criminal case. The judgment illustrates the peculiar start of copyright law in Palestine, beginning with public performance rather than with the right of reproduction. This could have happened only where the law originated from an outside donor, and transplanted in a different legal system in an artificial manner.

A first issue dealt with by the judgment was whether the law included a public performance right at all. The judge answered positively, explaining that the performing right is distinct from the reproduction right. He cited sections 1(2) and 35 of the Copyright Ordinance (the reference should have been to the Copyright Act), as well as section 2(3) about authorizing performance in one's entertainment venue.

A second issue decided, was that foreign copyright owners from members of the Berne Union (such as Germany), enjoyed protection in Palestine since it was a British Mandate, and as such, party to the Berne Convention. The judge commented that this would be so 'even were the Palestinian law silent about it'. This is an *obiter dictum* and in as much as it implied that the Berne Convention had direct effect in Palestine, it was erroneous.

Applying the law to the facts of the case, the judge found that: 'The accused had no right to employ in their cinema hall an orchestra, which as proved by witnesses and the admission of the defendants, played compositions belonging to various composers who enjoy the right of copyright of performance.' In other words, the factual issue was an easy one: the musical works were played without authorization. There was no question about ownership or Friedenberg's right to sue in the name of the Attorney General; neither was it disputed that the performance was 'public'.

The defendants raised two arguments in their defence. The first was that at least some of the compositions played were no longer protected by copyright, such as the works by Beethoven, Mendelsohn, and Schumann. The judge rejected this defence:

> It has been proven that the majority of those well known composers have written their compositions for symphonic orchestras and that for the purposes of cinema performances not the original works were used but adaptations arranged for small orchestras or for special instruments as violin, piano and the like. Such adaptations require from their authors special skill and every one adapts the music according to his own taste. Such intellectual creations belong to those modern composers who had adapted the works of the mentioned authors for purpose of use. They have a copyright in the work of adaptation as if it were an original composition.

Thus, the judge found that the public performance was of original adaptations. In this, the decision recognized that adaptations (derivative works), could enjoy copyright protection, independent of the underlying work, even if the latter was no longer protected. The test of originality applied was twofold: that the adaptation originated from the contemporary composer, and that the adaptor applied a special skill. Adapting music written for a symphony to be played by a small orchestra was sufficiently original in this sense. These principles were set almost in passing. They were crucial for rejecting the defence, and were part of the *ratio decidendi* of the case, but none of them was as self-evident and obvious as presented in the judgment.

A second defence was that the proper procedure was civil rather than criminal. The judge pointed to section 3(6) of the Ordinance and commented that 'by the wording of this section, the Government itself undertakes responsibility for the protection of intellectual creations and it is not necessary to bring at the same time a civil claim'. The plaintiffs can, the judge added, do so, and claim 'damages, injunction etc'. The comment about injunctions did not attract Kovalsky or Friedenberg's attention, as we shall see later on.

The finding was that defendants infringed copyright. As for the fine, the judge took into consideration the facts that defendants admitted the infringement; that in the meantime they entered into a contract with GEMA as to future performances, and finally 'the practice prevalent in this country up till now in regard to intellectual creations in Palestine'. The fine was one Palestine lira (LP) (equal to the British pound), a rather symbolic fine.

(3) The aftermath of the case

Kovalsky was delighted with the decision. The day the decision was delivered, 9 January 1930, was a busy day for him. He immediately offered the PRS his services. Friedenberg reported to the PRS that: 'Although the fine imposed was only nominal, this case, being the first prosecution in Palestine under the Copyright Ordinance, will serve as a precedent.'[53] The Hebrew *Haaretz* newspaper reported, more than can be found in the judgment, that the judge commented: 'This Act introduced Eretz-Israel to the union of civilised [cultural] countries, in which an author's work is not up for grabs.'[54] It is unclear whether the judge said so in the court, or whether this was a liberal reading of the judgment, perhaps building on the comments about the Berne Convention.

Despite Kovalsky's delight, the PRS was less impressed, especially with Friedenberg's strategy to take the criminal avenue. GEMA was unimpressed with the judgment itself: 'On examination of this Judgment, it does not appear to be well founded... It does not [seem] to be a satisfactory case on which to rely as a precedent in the event of any further actions being taken in Palestine for infringement of performing right.'[55]

The case did serve as a precedent for the Zion Theatre itself. On the same day the judgment was handed down, the theatre signed a contract with GEMA regarding its future performances of GEMA's works. The handwritten contract stipulated that the theatre received Kovalsky's permission to publicly perform the works of the societies he represented at the time (the German, Austrian, and Italian) for a year,

---

[53] Friedenberg to PRS (21 February 1930) PRS-1.
[54] 'Protection of Authors Rights in the Country' (16 January 1930) *Haaretz*, at 4 (Hebrew).
[55] GEMA to PRS (25 July 1930) PRS-1.

for LP3 per month.⁵⁶ The licence was non-transferable; the theatre's proprietors were to report on a monthly basis. No less important, Kovalsky was entitled to two free tickets for each show. The final clause instructed that: 'Unless this contract is not terminated by one of the parties, by a registered notice, at least one month before its end-date, then it will extend for another year.'

This final clause resulted in another round of litigation. The direct trigger was the new technology of sound. When Kovalsky decided to sue the Zion Theatre for the live performance it carried, it was the end of the life cycle of the silent movie. Overseas, there was already an exciting innovation and it reached Palestine shortly after the judgment was handed down. In fact, the Zion Theatre was the first in Palestine to introduce the talking movie, or 'talkie', as it was referred to at the time.⁵⁷ In June 1930 the Zion Theatre stopped screening silent movies and discontinued the orchestra's services. Thus, its proprietors figured, they no longer used the licensed musical repertoire; hence, their lawyer later argued 'the contract became annulled of itself'. Kovalsky and Friedenberg sued the Zion Theatre yet again.⁵⁸ Both parties raised the new legal issue: was a talking film protected by copyright law? But the judge refused to discuss the copyright issues and focused on the interpretation of the last clause of the licence, quoted above. The clause gave the Zion Theatre the option to terminate the contract only for the second year, but no such option existed for the first year. Kovalsky won LP21 and Friedenberg LP1 for advocates' fees. The Zion Theatre appealed to the district court, but lost.⁵⁹

Kovalsky learned important lessons: a successful judgment based on an old technology (the first case) might not help when a new technology appears, but a contract, achieved under circumstances when he was the stronger party, may yield a good outcome in the particular case (the second case). In the meantime, the first Zion case was highly beneficial for Kovalsky: he got the PRS agency. With this first legal victory, it was time for Kovalsky and Friedenberg to start working seriously on their new project. They knew that the local users were not acquainted with the idea of copyright. They also wanted to prove to the PRS that they were worthy of their trust. There was a lot of work to be done, and many important legal issues were waiting for resolution.

D. Enforcing Copyright

(1) A business plan

Having earned the agency of the PRS and being motivated by the success of the first case, Kovalsky and Friedenberg went straight to work. They gathered information

---

⁵⁶ Contract between Guth & Peretz and M Kovalsky & Son (9 January 1930) JCA 472 File 80.
⁵⁷ Cohen-Hatab, *Tour the Land*, above n 21, at 162.
⁵⁸ File 1442/31 *Kovalsky & Son v Gut & Peretz* (10 April 1931).
⁵⁹ CA 110/31 *Gut & Peretz v Kovalsky & Son* (9 June 1932). The judgment was one line: 'On consideration the Court sees no reason to interfere with the Magistrate's findings, dismisses the appeal and confirms the Magistrate's decision.'

about musical works performed in other cinemas, in cafes and other venues, such as the Hebrew Boy School in Jerusalem. They kept a close eye on their first counter-party, the Zion Theatre.[60] Kovalsky and Friedenberg also realized that they need to pursue the civil action option rather than the criminal one. They asked the PRS to provide letters of authorization to sue. They also contacted several cafe and cinema proprietors, demanding that they pay royalties.[61] By January 1931 they could report first licences with the King David Hotel and the Vienna Café in Jerusalem.[62] In the meantime, Kovalsky published notices in the newspapers and appointed agents in some places, which were also to serve as witnesses in court, if needed.

Both Kovalsky and Friedenberg reported to the PRS (separately), and quite intensively: the lawyer with legal issues about the power of attorney, and the agent with details about his progress. Kovalsky was determined to show the PRS that he is doing as much as possible to promote their interests, but at the same time, he kept lowering their expectations, perhaps so to justify the rather slow results and perhaps so that the PRS would appreciate his efforts. In October 1930 he wrote to the PRS that 'performing and copy Rights are sometimes very strange to any in this country, who never heard about it but practice will teach them'.[63] And again, a few months later when reporting the first licences: 'we have to do with people, most of whom never heard about Performing Rights'.[64]

Kovalsky and Friedenberg both came to the conclusion that lawsuits are an effective route. Friedenberg was optimistic about the power of litigation to bring about change:

> A series of actions will have to be started in the courts of the various towns of Palestine. The rights of the owners of copyright music are sufficiently protected by the law of Palestine, as they are in England, but the law must be set in motion and convictions obtained. Up till now the Copyright Ordinance, although in force for 6 years, has been a dead letter and is being disregarded in practice... After a few successful prosecutions during the first year of your activities, I trust that the persons concerned will prefer to obtain the necessary license instead of exposing themselves to an action in the Courts.[65]

This strategy, of using litigation as a means to educate users of performing rights was music to the ears of the PRS: they used litigation in the same way, mostly during the 1920s, to establish their rights.[66]

A few months later, Friedenberg was more cautious: 'I cannot express having an intelligent opinion as to the number of actions it may be necessary to bring so as to instil into the public in Palestine respect for the rights of composers and musical

---

[60] See eg notices Kovalsky sent to the Zion Theatre, regarding several movies: *As you Desire Me*—Kovalsky to Zion (14 December 1934); *Cynara*—Kovalsky to Zion (26 December 1934); *Dinner at Eight*—Kovalsky to Zion (4 January 1935), all at JCA 472 File 80; *David Copperfield*—Kovalsky to Zion (1 December 1935) JCA 471 File 20.
[61] See Kovalsky to PRS (18 September 1930, 25 September 1930, 11 December 1930) PRS-1.
[62] Kovalsky to PRS (29 January 1931) PRS-1.
[63] Kovalsky to PRS (29 October 1930) PRS-1.
[64] Kovalsky to PRS (29 January 1931) PRS-1.
[65] Friedenberg to Kovalsky (13 July 1930) PRS-1.
[66] James, *The Story*, above n 12, at 8.

publishers. It all depends upon psychological factors.'[67] The PRS urged the two to do more: 'This is indeed very slow progress over a period of several months. We trust, therefore, that the general conditions in Palestine will improve, and that you will shortly be able to report completion of a substantial number of contracts.'[68] As time passed with little more results, Kovalsky listed the difficulties: local unfamiliarity with copyright was a repeat theme, but now he added a new theme—he blamed the courts for being slow, and complained about the low fine set in the law, of LP5, compared to LP50 in English law.[69] The PRS had, again, to explain that the fine related to performing music from infringing copies, which was irrelevant to the cases Kovalsky handled.[70] Kovalsky now found an additional cause for the delays: Friedenberg, his lawyer, was too gentle for Kovalsky's taste.[71]

Thus, other than the second case against the Zion Theatre, Kovalsky focused on convincing users to buy licences for two years. Licensing—where successful—was easier, cheaper, and safer, and provided a steadily growing stream of income. Friedenberg assisted in writing the letters, but with no litigation.

The users were reluctant. An unusual client was Norman Bentwich, still the Attorney General, who was probably responsible for the early enactment of copyright law in Palestine back in 1920.[72] Bentwich was the chairman of the Jerusalem Musical Society, which gave public concerts. Kovalsky approached the Musical Society, demanding LP1 for concerts featuring local artists and LP3 for each concert featuring foreign performances. That was too high a fee, and Bentwich called the PRS directly, asking for a discount. He said the society could pay at most LP5 for the entire season (eight concerts). The PRS referred the matter to Kovalsky, but added that: 'In view of the important office which Mr Bentwich holds as Attorney General, we think it would be good policy to make some such concession to the Musical Society, and so to evince to him that the Society is willing to set in reasonable manner.'[73] Kovalsky obeyed.[74]

In the meantime, the relationship between the agent and his lawyer deteriorated. Kovalsky discontinued Friedenberg's retainer, and shifted him to a per-case payment—but there were hardly any cases. The lawyer complained to the PRS, which was quick to query this with Kovalsky, saying it was 'somewhat surprised', 'concerned', and 'anxious'.[75] But for another short while, the two managed to work together.

The PRS asked the Palestinian team to 'pursue these matters energetically', adding that: 'We feel that once you have obtained a favourable decision in the

---

[67] Friedenberg to PRS (3 November 1930) PRS-1.
[68] PRS to Kovalsky (6 February 1931) PRS-1.
[69] Kovalsky to PRS (13 May 1931) PRS-2.
[70] PRS to Kovalsky (21 May 1931) PRS-2.
[71] Kovalsky to PRS (13 May 1931) PRS-2.
[72] See Ch 4.
[73] PRS to Kovalsky (1 June 1931) PRS-2.
[74] Kovalsky to PRS (6 August 1931) PRS-2.
[75] Friedenberg to PRS (9 November 1931). Friedenberg also reported his successful lawsuit in the PTA case, discussed in Ch 9; PRS to Kovalsky (18 November 1931); Kovalsky to PRS (undated, 1931) PRS-2.

Palestine Courts, you will find it less difficulty to persuade other places of entertainment to take up licenses.'[76] The insistence from London was effective. Kovalsky now targeted the Grand Café. At first, the Café did not respond to his demands. He spotted several works that were performed without a licence (*Pretty Kitty Kelly*; *Shake and Let Us be Friends*; *Tap your Feet*; *When the Guards are on Parade*), and asked the PRS to send him a Power of Attorney.[77] He then reported that a licence was given to the Café, but later on, the Café refused to pay.[78] There was no choice but to take the Café to court: Kovalsky and Friedenberg won LP5.[79]

The PRS, its agent, and the lawyer had to accustom themselves to each other. This was not always easy. A lawsuit that Kovalsky brought against the Vienna Café in Jerusalem exposed some of the cultural gaps. During the hearing, the judge asked Kovalsky to contact the PRS and ask for their opinion on reducing the fees that the Café committed to pay. Kovalsky indeed communicated, but asked that the PRS sends him a letter saying that they could not reduce the fees. He asked that the letter be left undated, 'so that we may be able to pretend having received your letter at the time of the first trial'.[80] The stunned PRS refused, and disapproved the request which they conceived as deceiving the court.[81] The British judge now raised doubts about Kovalsky's power to sue in the name of the PRS. Kovalsky reported to the PRS and blamed them for not stating clearly in the Power of Attorney that he could sue on their behalf.[82] Fortunately for the relationship, the case was won.[83] The judge examined the agreement between the PRS and Kovalsky and found it adequate. Interestingly, the judge explained the role of the PRS as an intermediary that solved the problem of multiple individual contracts between users and composers. But the case itself was once again, like the second Zion Theatre case, decided on the basis of the contract between Kovalsky and the Café owners.

Finally, to add another note to the differences between London and Jerusalem, Friedenberg asked the PRS to write to the judge and commend him for the decision in this case and in the PTA case, which he also adjudicated. The PRS was clearly astonished by the idea. Friedenberg then explained, that 'it might be stimulating for a person working in a Colony to have his efforts and ability recognised and appreciated at home'. The PRS wrote a letter to Friedenberg, intended to be passed to the judge: 'We have read these judgments with considerable interest, particularly the former [the PTA case], and we should like to express our appreciation of the thorough grasp which they exhibit of such technical and complicated subject as the law of copyright.'[84]

---

[76] PRS to Kovalsky (13 August 1931) PRS-2.
[77] Kovalsky to PRS (23 August 1931, 11 September 1931) PRS-2.
[78] Kovalsky to PRS (6 November 1931, 4 January 1932) PRS-2.
[79] Kovalsky to PRS (22 February 1932) PRS-2.
[80] Ibid.
[81] PRS to Kovalsky (2 March 1932, 4 March 1932) PRS-2.
[82] Kovalsky to PRS (6 March 1932); the PRS rejected the accusations, PRS to Kovalsky (16 March 1932) PRS-2.
[83] *PRS v Klein & Hoiser* (15 March 1932) PRS-2.
[84] Friedenberg to PRS (7 April 1932, 28 April 1932); PRS to Friedenberg (6 May 1932) PRS-2.

Early 1933 saw an end to the Kovalsky–Friedenberg team. Kovalsky replaced the first copyright lawyer in Palestine with the leading law firm of Dr Mordechai Eliash, where he worked closely with two young lawyers, one was Yizhak Olshan in the Jerusalem office, and the other was Shimon Agranat, who soon moved to Haifa and opened his own practice. Both turned out to be eminent jurists. Olshan was the second Chief Justice of the Israeli Supreme Court (1954–65). Agranat replaced him as the third Chief Justice (1965–76).[85] Kovalsky himself also moved to Haifa in 1933.

The new lawyers quickly learnt the subject. Agranat, a graduate of Chicago Law School, received a copy of *Copinger on Copyright*, and corresponded in great detail with the PRS, which answered his legal questions as best as it could. It was a 'distance learning course' in copyright law.[86] Licensing now increased (by the end of 1934 there were over thirty paying users) and in the following years several lawsuits followed, raising new legal questions.

(2) Litigating copyright

(a) Copyright in talkies

Hiring a new lawyer meant going back to the courts. The burning issue was copyright in talkies. The issue had been raised in the second Zion Theatre case, but was not decided at the time. Kovalsky then reported the cinema owners' view: that when they hired a film, it included the licence to perform the musical works incorporated therein.[87] In contemporary legal words, the cinemas assumed that the hiring of the tangible object in which the work was fixed permitted them to perform not only the movie, but the music as well, or put differently, that the licence covered the synchronized music. The idea of synchronization rights was yet to be introduced.[88]

Olshan's first case was against the Eden Cinema in Jerusalem. At stake was the screening of a movie, based on Puccini's opera, *Madam Butterfly*. The judgment did not survive, but a report about it sheds some light on the arguments: the defendant argued that he hired the movie for screening, and that the distributor assured him that he could exhibit the movie. Olshan argued on behalf of the PRS that it had

---

[85] The major biographic work of Pnina Lahav reports that as a lawyer, Agranat dealt mostly with real property cases, and the collection of bills. See Pnina Lahav, *Judgment in Jerusalem: Chief Justice Shimon Agranat and the Zionist Century* (Am Oved, 1999) 94 (Hebrew). However, he served as the PRS's attorney for seven busy years (1933–40), and was involved in many copyright cases.

[86] eg Agranat to PRS (25 July 1933), asking about presumption of ownership; (15 August 1933), proof of first publication; amount of damages; proving identity in a case of pseudonym, PRS-A1; CZA A417.

[87] Kovalsky to PRS (13 May 1931) PRS-2.

[88] The practice of separating the performing rights in the movie from the performing rights in the synchronized music was not unique to Palestine. For an economic analysis of this practice in the United States, which ended in 1948 with antitrust litigation, see Ariel Katz, 'Copyright Collectives: Good Solution but for which Problem?' in Rochelle C Dreyfuss, Harry First, Diane L Zimmerman (eds), *Working within the Boundaries of Intellectual Property Law: Innovation Policy for the Knowledge Society* (Oxford University Press, 2010) 395.

explicitly excluded the performing right of the music from the licence given to the film producers. The court ordered the defendant to pay LP5.[89] There were two legal principles here. The first, was that the movie and the music which was incorporated in it, remained two separate works, each entitled to a separate performing right. The second, was that copyright law was a matter of strict liability: it did not matter whether the infringer knew about the copyright, or even if he was misled to believe he had the permission to use the work.

(b) Radio?

As the copyright owners and their representatives marked another victory, a new technology arrived: radio. The PRS learned that Mr Mendel Abramowitz established a radio station in Palestine.[90] Kovalsky downplayed the importance of the event, reporting that it was an amateur station which operated for a few weeks during the international Levant Fair in Tel-Aviv. He added that it 'mostly played Hebrew and Arabic gramophone records that are non copyright'.[91] One reading of Kovalsky's statement is that the Arab and Hebrew music were not in the PRS's portfolio. A less generous reading would see this as an orientalist, Eurocentric view of copyright law, excluding non-European music. The PRS did not let go. It insisted that broadcasting of copyrighted music is public performance.[92] When it learned that Abramowitz bought 2,000 records in the United States with the intention of setting up a radio station in Tel-Aviv, they wrote again. Kovalsky again downplayed the importance of this event. Abramowitz, whom he described as a poor radio supplier, had the idea of erecting a broadcasting station, but the government would not permit him to do so. Kovalsky assured the PRS that he would follow this, but it seems that he did not yet grasp the importance of radio on his business. The PRS was keen to follow the matter.[93] They also asked about a radio in Nazareth and kept an open eye and ear.[94] When Kovalsky finally reckoned that radio was the 'next big thing', it was too late for him. The PRS bypassed him and provided a licence directly to the PBS, established by the Mandate government. Kovalsky's repeated requests to receive his share of the lucrative deal were rejected.[95] Radio will be the subject of Chapter 8.

---

[89] *PRS v Eden Cinema (Mr Floyd)* (21 July 1933), reported in PR Gazette (October 1933) 196 (the Gazette was published by the PRS). See also Kovalsky's brief report to the PRS (25 July 1933) PRS-3.
[90] PRS to Kovalsky (16 September 1932) PRS-2.
[91] Kovalsky to PRS (14 February 1933) PRS-3.
[92] PRS to Kovalsky (24 February 1933); CZA A417.
[93] PRS to Kovalsky (20 October 1933); Kovalsky to PRS (25 October 1933); PRS to Kovalsky (24 February 1933) PRS-3.
[94] PRS to Kovalsky (27 September 1933) PRS-3.
[95] PRS to Kovalsky (1 February 1935) (informing Kovalsky that they are negotiating with the Postmaster General and asking that he does not interfere until instructed); Kovalsky to the PRS (11 October 1935) (inquiring, as the radio was soon to begin broadcasting); PRS to Kovalsky (22 October 1935) (replying that they are negotiating with the Postmaster General (PMG)); Kovalsky to PRS (30 January 1936) (asking for his share, after learning that the PRS reached an agreement with the PBS); PRS to Kovalsky, 12 February 1936 (denying his request); Kovalsky to PRS (23 February 1936) (Kovalsky disagreeing); PRS to Kovalsky (2 March 1936) (denying his second request explaining that

In the meantime, the PRS could probably not believe Kovalsky's request in 1934. He asked that they send him 'two copies of the Copyright Act 1911 (Great Britain), which serve as a means to acquaint the local judges with the Copy—and performing Right'.[96] Was it possible that Kovalsky did not have the Act (but only the Copyright Ordinance) at that late point, or was it just the copies that he sought?[97] Given that the Act was not formally published and its translation to Hebrew was to appear only in 1936, it is not unlikely that Kovalsky indeed held only the Ordinance.

(c) Applicable law

New legal challenges were raised in 1934: surprisingly, one of these was whether the Copyright Act applied at all in Palestine. At stake again was *Madam Butterfly*, this time played at a Haifa cinema. The defendant argued that the Act does not apply, as section 28 of the Copyright Act 1911 applied only to 'territories under his [Majesty's] protection'. The court interpreted the term broadly, to cover also a Mandate.[98] Moreover, it appeared, the judge wrote, that His Majesty also had the power to enact a copyright law by virtue of the Foreign Jurisdiction Act 1890. The question was raised once again in a 1937 case, and again the court found that the Act was properly extended to Palestine.[99]

The defendant further argued that the Act was not properly published, but the judge concluded, that the requirement of publication referred only to local Ordinances rather than Imperial Acts which were extended to Palestine.[100] The mechanisms of colonial law saved the Act.

The judge also ruled that foreign works (Italian, in that case) were protected in Palestine. Other cases reached the same conclusion regarding French and Dutch works,[101] and some cases took it for granted that British works were protected in Palestine. In Chapter 4 we saw the doubts about the legal protection of British works made before the Mandate commenced. There the court constructed a doubtful argument, interweaving the Ottoman Authors' Rights Act 1910 into the Copyright Ordinance 1920, so as to enable legal protection for such works.[102]

---

he was not involved in the negotiations); Kovalsky to PRS (12 March 1936) (bitterly complaining: 'it is not right from the moral and formal point of view'); PRS to Kovalsky (23 March 1936) (final denial of his request). All letters are available at PRS-4.

[96] Kovalsky to PRS (27 February 1934) PRS-3.
[97] PRS to Kovalsky (24 March 1934) CZA A417.
[98] The same question came up a decade earlier, during the legislative process. See HC to Secretary of State, Despatch 18 (5 January 1923) ISA M575/12.
[99] (Unnumbered case, probably Civil File 19/36) *Honegger v Homa et al* (18 February 1937) (ruling), (regarding the exhibition of *Les Miserables* in the Cinema Amphitheatre in Haifa), *affirmed* CA (Haifa) 86/37 *Homa v Honegger* (1 June 1937) PRS-5.
[100] (Haifa) *Ricordi & Co v Ein Dor Cinema, Haifa* (6 March 1934) (Preliminary Judgment) PRS-A1; *Honegger v Homa*, ibid.
[101] *Honegger v Homa*, ibid; File Civil 2056/35 *PRS v Wildhorn—Aviv Cinema* (27 October 1935) (Judge Korngrün) (regarding the screening of *Going Gay* at the Aviv Cinema, Haifa) PRS-A1.
[102] CC (Haifa) 20/36 *Francis, Day & Hunter, Ltd v Belozersky* (9 May 1937) PRS-A1.

Evidentiary presumptions were applied.[103] The presumption that a person whose name appears on the work was the copyright owner was applied in other cases as well,[104] though not always successfully. The PRS lost a case against the Arab owner of Café Paradise, as it produced only the deed of assignment of the music publisher to the PRS, but this was not proved in one of the ways set in the Proof of Foreign Documents Ordinance 1924.[105]

This was one of the few cases in which the PRS lost. Another such case reached the Supreme Court, the only PRS case to reach the highest court of the land (none reached the Privy Council). At stake was a performing licence that the licensee terminated by a personal service of a notice: it was handed to Kovalsky in person. However, the licence allowed termination only by way of a notice sent by registered post. We may assume that Kovalsky used the same language as in his licence with the Zion Theatre. The Supreme Court found that the licence did not exclude the personal service of the termination notice.[106]

Another defence that the cinema owners raised was that of the 'innocent infringer', per section 8 of the Act. In one case, the court found that the defendant had been warned,[107] thus sustaining Kovalsky's practice of continuous notifications. In another case, the court clarified that only a mistake as to the facts can give rise to the defence, but not a mistake about the legal situation.[108] Thus, the defence of innocent infringer was narrowed substantially.

The available remedies raised some doubts. As for damages, in *Ricordi v Ein Dor Cinema*, the court did not find any section in the Act that directly empowered it to order damages.[109] The judge then turned to the general local law that was still in power, namely the Ottoman Mejelle. It contained provisions for damages in property, but, based on dictionary definitions, the judge concluded that 'Copyright is more in the nature of a right appertaining to property'—but it was not 'property' in itself. The interim conclusion was that the 'Civil Law of Palestine gives no remedy for the infringement of a copyright'. This led the way to do what the British judges did best: applying the Common Law of England, according to section 46 of the Order in Council 1922. Damages were awarded. When a similar argument was raised in 1937 in another case, the judge commented that he did not quite understand the amount of argument devoted to the question of 'property', as the Act explicitly mentioned that the remedies apply to the infringements of rights and this term included copyright.[110]

---

[103] (Haifa) *R Ricordi & Co v Ein Dor Cinema, Haifa* (29 March 1934) (final judgment) PRS-A1.
[104] *PRS v Wildhorn*, above n 101.
[105] Civil No 38/36 *PRS v AIG Khayat* (19 May 1936) PRS-5.
[106] CA 81/36 *PRS v Café & Restaurant Vienna, Jerusalem* (27 May 1937), reproduced (18 June 1937) *Palestine Post*, at 2.
[107] *PRS v Wildhorn*, above n 101.
[108] *Honegger v Homa*, above n 99.
[109] *Ricordi & Co v Ein Dor Cinema*, above n 100. Section 6(1) of the Copyright Act 1911 instructed that the copyright owner is entitled to 'all such remedies...as are or may be conferred by law'. Presumably, the judge considered this insufficient, and searched for the procedural law which conferred the remedies.
[110] *Honegger v Homa*, above n 99.

Setting the Law in Motion 183

(d) Litigation strategy, injunctions, and disturbances

Kovalsky's usual business practice was to warn the cinemas and cafes, convincing them to get a licence, and if this did not work out, sue in court and then leverage the victory to sign a licence, on his terms. He never asked for an injunction. But in 1935 he concluded that the strategy was not working well enough. Kovalsky blamed the courts. He complained to the PRS about the 'deplorable state of procedure at the local courts', and explained that 'because of the Arab and Jewish Judges being so little acquainted with Copy Right Law we always prefer to bring our cases before English Magistrates who sit rather irregularly'. Furthermore, files were lost in the courts. 'All this,' he wrote, 'encouraged defendants to further disregard our claims.'[111]

This frustration led Kovalsky to devise a new strategy: 'The only way of pressing upon infringing parties is through frequent attacks, i.e.: action after action against the same infringing party (to a certain extent) without waiting for judgments of pending cases.'[112] In other words, a few years into running his business, Kovalsky became a true repeat player, using litigation as an instrument to advance his goals. As far as he was concerned, litigation itself was the means to gain power vis-à-vis the reluctant users. As for the content of the law—once he won a few cases, he was confident that the law was on his side. In 1936, Kovalsky again complained about the courts, and added that he would have to bring cases before 'Jewish Magistrates in order to hasten the procedure; although their knowledge in such matters is less than that of the English, it is more than that of the Arab Magistrates'.[113]

The PRS suggested another way: injunctions. It was discussed behind the scenes between Agranat, Kovalsky, and the PRS, but never materialized. Kovalsky (correctly) believed that the magistrate court cannot issue injunctions. But recall the court's comment in the first Zion Theatre case, about injunctions as an option. It was not tested.

The PRS suggested that cases are brought before the district court, which did have the power to issue injunctions, rather than the magistrate court.[114] Kovalsky explained that this was impossible, as the minimum damages sought in the district court was LP250.[115] The PRS was surprised to learn about the limited powers of the judicial system: if the magistrate court was not empowered to issue an injunction and given the high barrier of the district court, the result was that an injunction could not be sought in copyright cases.[116] Kovalsky answered that he would try to sue in a district court (he did not), but after some exchange, it occurred to him to ask what sort of an injunction the PRS had in mind: 'Are we to understand that it

---

[111] Kovalsky to PRS (12 December 1935) PRS-4.
[112] Ibid.
[113] Kovalsky to PRS (3 March 1936) PRS-4. Albeit, the judge in the first case—Korngrün—was Jewish.
[114] PRS to Kovalsky (12 March 1936) PRS-4.
[115] Kovalsky to PRS (27 April 1936) PRS-4.
[116] PRS to Kovalsky (5 May 1936) PRS-4. Their surprise was misplaced, as Agranat informed them of the legal situation re injunction back in 1933. See Agranat to PRS (24 January 1933) PRS-A1.

would be possible in such a case to restrict all performances at the infringer's (defendant's) establishment while the case is pending?'[117] The PRS explained that it did not intend a broad injunction, but added that perhaps it was worthwhile trying it.[118] Kovalsky then replied that he would try a different approach—ask the government for permission to sue in the district court for less than LP250.[119] There is no evidence that he attempted this option, but it illustrates his instrumental approach to the law: if it doesn't fit our needs, let's try and change it.

The performing rights business continued throughout the 1930s. The unstable political and economic situation in the country was bound to affect it. Shortly after the Arab Revolt erupted in April 1936, Kovalsky had to reconsider his strategy: most of the Tel-Aviv cafes dismissed their music bands; the curfew imposed in Jerusalem 'is further paralyzing all public musical life', and even if he could sue, many of the defendants went bankrupt.[120] The PRS deferred to Kovalsky's decision, but reminded him that the time of limitation in copyright cases was three years. It seems that the situation had somewhat calmed down in 1937, as the litigation efforts resumed.

(3) Hebrew music: ACUM

One important effect (a 'positive externality', economists would say) of the PRS's activities in Palestine was the establishment of a parallel Hebrew society: *Agudat Compositorim u'Mehabrim*—ACUM (in Hebrew, Composers and Authors Association), which still operates today. Its archives did not survive, but we do have its official story written by Pinhas Yorman in 1977, among other sources.[121]

The official story attributes the initiative to Ze'ev Markowitz, a Jewish immigrant from Poland who tried to engage in the small film industry, and to a young composer, Moshe Wilensky.[122] The two heard something about the Polish performing rights society and about Kovalsky's agency for the PRS. They tried to collect royalties for Hebrew works. A catalyst was a lawsuit, between Wilensky and *HaMatate* Theatre. Wilensky played the piano for the theatre on a regular basis. He privately composed some songs and recorded a record. The theatre claimed it owned the copyright (this probably referred to the compositions rather than the sound recording), rather than the composer. In other words, it was an ownership dispute. According to this report, Wilensky won.[123] Yorman also reports the 1940 bylaws of the new association, based on the PRS's bylaws—yet another

---

[117] Kovalsky to PRS (10 May 1936) PRS-4.
[118] PRS to Kovalsky (15 May 1936) PRS-4.
[119] Kovalsky to PRS (29 May 1936) PRS-4.
[120] Kovalsky to PRS (17 July 1936, 23 July 1936, 28 October 1936) PRS-5. For example, Kovalsky won the case against the Rotman House (CC (Jerusalem) 3588/36 *PRS v Rotman House* (1 December 1936) PRS-5), but reported that it was as good as bankrupt. He sued nevertheless, just to see what the new magistrate's attitude is toward copyright cases. PRS to Kovalsky (4 November 1936) PRS-5.
[121] Pinhas Yorman, *ACUM Story* (Publishers Association, 1977) (Hebrew).
[122] Yorman, *ACUM*, ibid, at 9–11. Markowitz published an op-ed in a daily newspaper explaining ACUM's mission: 'The Rights of Culture-Makers' (11 April 1938) *Davar*, at 4 (Hebrew).
[123] Yorman, *ACUM*, ibid, at 11. This is the only source about the case.

foreign influence on local copyright law.[124] During the late 1930s, ACUM managed to collect royalties from the PBS and in fact it was its main and almost only source of income for a while.[125] ACUM struggled with convincing cafe owners to pay royalties. It published occasional notices, but with little success.[126] It also struggled with the mechanisms to distribute the royalties among its members. The option of utilizing the law to promote its goals was mentioned every now and then, but there is no evidence of such lawsuits during the Mandate.[127]

ACUM's management and Kovalsky occasionally met, but to say the least, did not cooperate with each other. A first meeting took place in early 1935 without any conclusions;[128] Kovalsky watched the new association, but he was not bothered too much by it.[129] ACUM, on the other hand, was interested in establishing a 'national' performing rights society, which meant that it wanted to take over Kovalsky's business. The reference to the national interest was typical of the day. Hebrew national arguments trumped all other considerations, hence it was invoked wherever it could be effective.

Kovalsky refused, and in 1937 ACUM turned to attack him personally: it was Kovalsky, ACUM argued, that deliberately failed their petition to join the International Confederation of performing rights societies. ACUM informed the PRS that they regard Kovalsky as an opponent and 'Accordingly, we have no alternative but to attack him in exactly the same way as we should attack any other person standing in our way.' They threatened that they might also complain to the Jewish National Committee, which was the official executive organ of the Yishuv.[130] The PRS was apparently not impressed. Only after the State of Israel was established, did Kovalsky surrender his business to ACUM.

*

As the 1930s came to a close, the litigation activity decreased. In 1940, Agranat was appointed as a judge in Haifa. There were many licensees who routinely paid, and Kovalsky continued sending letters to other institutions, warning them. Perhaps he preferred the 50 per cent commission rather than the expensive litigation, or perhaps Kovalsky was getting a bit tired. He was in his late sixties by then. During World War all parties had other things on their mind, but the business continued. Kovalsky reduced the licence fee of the King David Hotel in Jerusalem, as the public performance was taking place in a smaller bar and the British forces occupied

---

[124] Yorman, *ACUM*, ibid, at 13. The original bylaws are available at ISA M361/61 doc 1a.
[125] Yorman, *ACUM*, ibid, at 18. ACUM had continuous discussions with the PBS. See Philip Joseph on behalf of ACUM to PMG (16 December 1937); PMG to CS (23 December 1937) ISA M361/15 docs 120, 120a; Director of Broadcasting to CS (2 June 1947); Solicitor General to CS (15 June 1947), and related correspondence at ISA M361/61; Dr H Goldberg, on behalf of ACUM to Broadcasting Department (20 January 1948); Director of Broadcasting to Dr Goldberg (11 February 1948), both at ISA M1879/26 docs 99a, 100. See also Ch 8, for ACUM's negotiations with the PBS.
[126] eg ACUM, Notice, October 1938, TCA Division 4, 1023, File C-1913. The notice explained that there is such a thing as performing right, protected by the English law that applied in Palestine. Those using music in such a manner were urged to contact ACUM. It mentioned also that the principle was approved by local courts.
[127] Yorman, *ACUM*, above n 121, at 21 (appointing a lawyer in 1943), 27 (threatening to sue).
[128] Kovalsky to PRS (13 February 1935) PRS-4.
[129] Kovalsky to PRS (6 November 1936) PRS-5.
[130] Markowitz to Kovalsky (7 September 1937) PRS-5.

most of the Hotel.[131] By November 1944, the number of licences reached a peak of 167.[132] ACUM represented Jewish musicians and authors. There was no collecting society of Arab musicians.

E. Copyright Glocalization

The PRS in London, and Kovalsky, Friedenberg, Olshan, and Agranat in Palestine, took copyright law out of the books and applied it in practice. Their incentives combined and formed a pioneering act, or perhaps put in contemporary terms, a start-up. The discussion thus far provided the micro-history of their dealings. These were the very first steps of the actual reception of colonial copyright in Mandate Palestine. We should now take a step back, and assess the overall meaning of these events. The criteria for such an assessment are a few questions: who, how, and what?

A first observation, already noted, is that foreigners were the ones who triggered the law. Kovalsky was a crucial player, but if it was not him, it would have been someone else. The reverse does not hold: Kovalsky could not sue without the copyright owners.

The foreign players (the local representatives included) had another important attribute: they were repeat players. This enabled them to correct mistakes: shifting from the criminal to the civil procedure, turning to licences where possible, making sure they can prove ownership and have the power to sue, and respond to defendants' arguments. Being repeat players also enabled them to meet several judges in more than one court over time. Moreover, they were able to leverage the judicial victories to the advancement of their licensing business. In fact, as we saw, they treated the law in a purely instrumental way: the litigation was meant to signal their counterparts: pay the fees or face the consequences. The law was deliberately sought as a means to achieve commercial change.

The identity of the defendants is also relevant to understand the activation of the law. The parties were not on equal standing. It was not an author–author or a publisher–publisher relationship of the kind we saw in Chapter 6. It also differed from the relationship between authors and publishers, where both parties were dependant on each other to conduct their business. An author could not publish without a publisher; a publisher could not do business without authors. The PRS had no such mutual dependency with the cafe and cinema owners. The parties were strangers. The initial state of the relationship between the copyright owners and the institutional users was of two separate parties: the cinemas could do without the copyright owners. The mission of the copyright owners was to shift this preliminary state into one in which the institutional users had to rely on them. The law created the dependency.

---

[131] Kovalsky to PRS (28 November 1943) PRS-6.   [132] PRS-7.

Kovalsky and his lawyers served as intermediaries. Scholars have noted the importance of various kinds of intermediaries in the process of legal transplants. Gregory Shaffer, for example, writes that: 'Intermediaries are the carriers, conduits, and points of entry for the circulation of transnational legal norms... They help to diagnose national situations, monitor national developments and responses, and translate, adapt and appropriate global norms for local contexts. Through their links with international institutions and transnational networks, they form part of transnational epistemic communities.'[133] Kovalsky and his lawyers fully fit this description.

A second observation is the way in which the local players learned about copyright law: it was not through formal legal education, nor did they learn only from the statute. The PRS and its local representatives created a small professional network in which they exchanged information. From London came information about British cases, relevant legal literature, and the practice elsewhere. From Palestine, the information was about local procedures, and about the everyday practices of the cultural, commercial, and legal fields.

This private network supplemented the formal legal transplant. It introduced the content into the statutory framework. The legal content was British, colonial, reinforcing the process of anglicization of the law in Palestine, but the local content that ran in the other direction was no less important: it provided the context and reasoning for the representatives' legal strategies. The combination of the judicial structure, Ottoman procedural rules that were still valid and the way the locals interacted with each other, created a unique outcome. Copyright law in Palestine was the British law, with a local spin. This is part of the broader picture of colonial law, which interacts in many ways with local law(s). Today we would call it glocalization: the meeting point of the global (represented by the colonial law), and the local.[134]

How did this process shape the content of the local law? It was constructed in an unusual manner: it started in the middle, skipping the beginning. Copyright law in the United Kingdom, France, Germany, and other places developed in a bottom-up process, gradually expanding. The first right recognized by the law was the reproduction right. Organic copyright laws developed fundamental—by definition—concepts of originality and principles such as the idea/expression dichotomy, the principle that copyright protects the creative work but not the tangible object in which it is embedded, and exceptions such as fair dealing. Other rights were born later as offspring of the copyright. These are, for example, the right to make derivative works, and the right to publicly perform musical works. The development of copyright law in Mandate Palestine started head on with the cutting-edge issues of the day: copyright in recorded music, in talking movies, and in broadcast matter. The result was that only later in the day did courts address

---

[133] Gregory Shaffer, 'Transnational Legal Process and State Change: Opportunities and Constraints' (2012) 37 Law & Soc Inq 229.
[134] For glocalization in the context of copyright law, see Michael D Birnhack, 'Global Copyright, Local Speech' (2006) 24 Cardozo Arts & Ent L J 491.

the basic concepts. Some of these principles were addressed in 1932, in the *PTA v Jaber* case, discussed in Chapter 9, but mostly, this task was carried out by the Israeli courts as late as the 1970s.[135] Even within the right of public performance, many questions remained for a later day, such as the meaning of 'public'.

Importantly, where the law developed from the middle, it is difficult to find any coherent theory that underlies the judicial outcomes. The courts applied the law rather literally, and when in doubt, opted for an expansive interpretation: the law applied in Palestine, it covered foreign works, it included performing rights in various media, and the innocent infringer's defence was interpreted rather narrowly. There were some hidden assumptions or principles taken for granted, such as the separation of the creative work and the physical object. But a theory of copyright law was yet to be developed.

Is such a development, 'from the middle', wrong? As a matter of positive law and doctrine, there is no inherent reason why the law should develop in one way rather than the other. The unique route taken might have been less tidy, and thus more difficult for lawyers and others to comprehend at the time. Neither do I claim that there is a normative necessity that the law develops from print to music, from copyrights to performing rights. The point is that the actual development of copyright law in Mandate Palestine diverged from its original British route. Colonial copyright took its own path.

F. Conclusion

By the end of the 1930s, copyright law in Palestine was no longer a dead letter. The PRS, Kovalsky, and his lawyers activated the law. Conceptualized in the framework of colonial copyright, despite some difficulties, the legal transplant imposed onto the colonized peoples did eventually catch up. The process was possible in a specific context, of a foreign party (acting through local representatives) which was a repeat player. The foreign player educated its representatives and through them, they educated other lawyers, judges, and the users of copyrighted works.

When Kovalsky visited London in 1947 he complained, as he always did, about the situation of copyright law in Palestine. He said that 'the greater part of the population being educationally backwards, their attitude towards copyright being opposing'.[136] But by then, the old piano merchant could look back and admit that he had taken copyright law out of the Mandatory law books and set it in motion. He fulfilled the promise he gave to John Woodhouse almost twenty years earlier: he was a copyright pioneer in Palestine. In early 1948, shortly before the British were to leave the country, Kovalsky sent his English partners a box of oranges. The clerks at the PRS were truly moved by the gesture and thanked him, but British as they were, they added a note, asking about the fate of the PRS after the Mandate

---

[135] The first case to reach the Supreme Court which dealt with originality was CA 136/71 *State of Israel v Achiman*, 26(2) PD 259 (1972) (Hebrew).

[136] Kovalsky (18 June 1947) PRS-7.

ends.¹³⁷ Kovalsky replied that he did not know. Three weeks after the State of Israel was established, he sent the last accounts.¹³⁸ A war broke out. The PRS queried copyright law under the new conditions.¹³⁹ In April 1949 the PRS informed Kovalsky that they would support ACUM's petition to join the International Federation of Authors Societies.¹⁴⁰ It was a sign for Kovalsky to retire. In October 1949 Kovalsky transferred his performing rights business to ACUM for 300 Israeli pounds.¹⁴¹ He died two years later. The PRS entered into a reciprocal contract of affiliation with ACUM.¹⁴²

[137] PRS to Kovalsky (4 February 1948) PRS-7.
[138] Kovalsky to PRS (3 May 1948) PRS-7.
[139] PRS to Kovalsky (22 September 1948) PRS-7.
[140] PRS to Kovalsky (22 April 1949) PRS-7.
[141] ACUM to PRS (11 June 1949), quoted in PRS to Kovalsky (13 September 1949) PRS-7.
[142] See James, *The Story*, above n 12, at 125.

8

Copyright on the Air

> I can imagine something of the confusion that is probably inseparable from starting anything in the East
>
> J B Clark, Director of the BBC Empire Service, 1935.[1]

A. Introduction

As the first copyright cases in Palestine made their way through the courts, dealing with music played alongside silent movies and with music publicly performed in cafes, a new technology arrived on the scene, revolutionizing the consumption of music: radio broadcasting. This exciting medium had been in operation in various places in the world since the 1920s. It reached Palestine only in the 1930s, and quickly swept through the country. The Palestine Broadcasting Service (PBS) went on air on 30 March 1936. The PBS was established, owned and run by the Mandate government for its entire duration, until it was split in 1948 into the Israeli and Jordanian radio stations. In its first few years, the PBS broadcasted for five hours a day, composed of one hour in English, one in Hebrew (*Kol Yerushalayim*—The Voice of Jerusalem), and one in Arabic (*Huna al-Kuds*— Here is Jerusalem). The remaining two hours included relays, namely re-broadcasting of the BBC, and music, mostly played from gramophone records. The radio revolutionized the consumption of music in Palestine.[2]

Copyright law was only a footnote to the story of the radio broadcasting in Palestine. The diligent plans written in Jerusalem did not take copyright into account until a foreign player drew attention to it: the BBC in London placed copyright on the table. None of those involved objected or even questioned the relevance of copyright law. Once they were aware of its relevance, their energy was channelled to the details, and especially to the costs. There were two main copyright issues: first, whether broadcasting music was 'public performance', and second, what was the legal implication of the governmental scheme of rural broadcasting, which involved the distribution of radio sets to large villages.

---

[1] Clark to Rendall (10 October 1935) BBC Written Archives Centre (BBC WAC) E1/1136/2 File 1b.

[2] Jehoash Hirshberg, *Music in the Jewish Community of Palestine 1880–1948: A Social History* (Oxford University Press, 1995) 141.

This chapter tells the story of copyright law in its governmental incarnation in Mandate Palestine. Copyright in radio broadcasting was dealt with behind the scenes without judicial involvement. Thus, its impact was less visible than the relentless litigation of the Performing Rights Society (PRS), discussed in the previous chapter, but it was no less substantial: while the copyright instances related to the PBS did not establish any legal principles, they did form an influential practice. Broadcasting turned out to be the single most important source of revenue for the copyright owners for many years to come, and thus, it was the engine of the emerging copyright practice. The copyright dealings in the PBS also familiarized the officers with this body of law: the few Arab citizens that raised formal legal copyright questions during the Mandate were PBS employees (discussed in Chapter 10).

Sources which have not hereto been consulted in the literature reveal that the level of the involvement of the BBC in establishing the PBS was greater than thus far acknowledged. The discussion begins with a background of the preparatory stages that took place behind the glass windows of the studio, before any microphone was switched on. We shall then turn to the place of copyright law in this story. The governmental dealing with broadcasting will draw our attention to the subtle play of identity politics in the operation of the Mandate government, a constant issue during the Mandate.[3] Identity played a role in forming the content of the broadcasts, divided into the three official languages. The story of copyright law exposes the differential attitudes of the government towards Arabs and Jews and reveals the Eurocentric character of copyright law.

B. The Road to the Radio

The early references to radio was wireless telegraphy, indicating that it was considered to be an extension of the one-to-one telegraph technology, but it was soon replaced with the more appropriate term of broadcasting, acknowledging its mass medium, one-to-many structure. Radio was an immediate medium, shortening the time between reporting and receiving, to zero. It rendered distance far less relevant, as it reached audiences in remote places at the same time it reached the ones closer to the broadcaster.[4] Listening to the radio did not require literacy. The only prerequisite was access to a radio set, privately owned, or at a friend's house, cafes, or public venues.

The first suggestion to establish a governmental radio station in Palestine was made in 1930, by a retired British colonial officer, who served in India. It took a while for the idea to resonate with the decision makers. The decision took place

---

[3] See Assaf Likhovski, *Law and Identity in Mandate Palestine* (University of North Carolina Press, 2006) 214.
[4] Joshua Meyrowitz, *No Sense of Place: The Impact of Electronic Media on Social Behavior* (Oxford University Press, 1985).

three years later, in mid 1933. It took three more years of planning until the first sounds were aired from Jerusalem, through a transmitter in Ramallah. There are only few scholarly discussions of broadcasting in Palestine.[5] Some of this literature tells the story from favourable Jewish/Hebrew or Arab perspectives;[6] the focus is mostly on the programming,[7] and none discuss copyright law. Our interest here is in the back-office consideration of copyright issues, which entered the picture only after the decision to establish the radio was made, and deserved a secondary place, at most, in the preparatory work.

(1) Initial thoughts and a growing demand (August 1930–May 1933)

During the 1920s, radio was making its first steps in the world. Radio stations popped up in Europe and elsewhere, though the Middle East lagged behind. It developed differently in different places. For example, the American radio developed in a commercial environment whereas the British equivalent developed as a public service.[8]

In the United Kingdom, organized broadcasting commenced in late 1922 with the establishment of the British Broadcasting Company, which a few years later was chartered as the British Broadcasting Corporation.[9] By the early 1930s, the BBC was already well established and respected. It considered itself a leader in the field of radio and was recognized as such by others, its reach extending far beyond the shores of the United Kingdom.[10] In the mid 1920s it assisted with the establishment of local radio stations in Durban, South Africa (1924), and in Ceylon (1926), and gave advice to other stations.[11] There was some competition in the global field.

---

[5] Zvi Gil, 'From the Voice of Jerusalem to the Voice of Israel' (1965) The Journalists' Ybk 295 (Hebrew); Andrea L Stanton, *A Little Radio is A Dangerous Thing: State Broadcasting in Mandate Palestine, 1936–1949* (PhD Dissertation, Graduate School of Arts and Sciences, University of Columbia, 2007). Other sources discuss specific cases: Eytan Almog, 'A Wireless Broadcasting Station in Palestine: The First Hebrew Radio Station in the World' (1996) 20 *Kesher* 66 (Hebrew) (discussing a radio operation by a Jewish citizen in 1932); Eytan Almog, 'The British Mandate Government in the Face of a Hostile Press in Palestine' (1994) 15 *Kesher* 85 (Hebrew) (discussing freedom of press); Tamar Liebes and Zohar Kampf, '"Hello! This is Jerusalem Calling": The Revival of Spoken Hebrew on the Mandatory Radio (1936–1948)' (2010) 29(2) J of Israeli History 137 (discussing the effect of the radio on the Hebrew language and community). For commentary in Arabic, see Abdallah Taya, *Educational Media in Radio and Television* (Ramallah, 2006) (Arabic) (brief summary of the PBS); Nasiry Al-Jawzi, *The History of the Palestinian Radio 'This is Jerusalem:' 1936–1948* (2010) (Arabic) (memoirs of a playwright whose works were played on the radio).

[6] Both Jewish and Arab authors argued that the broadcasting was used to subvert the British domination. See eg Gil, 'Voice of Jerusalem', ibid, as to the Hebrew Yishuv's perspective, and Al-Jawzi, *The History*, ibid, as to the Arab perspective.

[7] Stanton, *A Little Radio*, above n 5; Liebes and Kampf, 'Hello!', above n 5.

[8] Alice Goldfarb Marquis, 'Written in the Wind: The Impact of Radio during the 1930s' (1984) 19 J of Contemporary History 385.

[9] Asa Briggs, *The Birth of Broadcasting: 1896–1927* (Oxford University Press, 1995).

[10] See eg BBC to CO (12 April 1934) BBC WAC E1136/1 File 1a ('the B.B.C. is convinced of the desirability of the establishment of local broadcasting services in Colonies and other British territories where such do not at present exist').

[11] Briggs, *The Birth*, above n 9, at 295–6.

The French radio was also involved in foreign ventures.[12] In the late 1920s the BBC began discussing—internally and with the government—the option of imperial broadcasting.[13] Interestingly, copyright issues were raised during that process.[14] The efforts resulted in the inauguration of the Empire Services in December of 1932. To a large extent, the BBC became the voice of the Empire.

The quick emergence of radio needed some regulation on a regional level, as broadcasts from different stations used the same wavelengths, resulting in constant interferences. An International Union was established in the mid 1920s, which set several plans for allocating wavelengths: the Geneva Plan (1925); the Prague Plan (1929); and then the Lucerne Plan (1933), which was the one relevant to Palestine.[15]

In the Middle East, Turkey and Saudi Arabia discussed the idea of establishing radio stations. The Egyptian radio station commenced broadcasting in 1934, and was easily received in Palestine. Its broadcasting was popular, especially readings of the Koran.

The growing international excitement over the new technology backed by the British lead in the field reached Palestine with growing local interest.[16] A few shops started selling radio sets. In order to own a radio set in Palestine, one had to obtain an annual licence from the Post Office. Thus, we have a rather accurate picture of the diffusion of radio, based on the figures of the radio sets in use. The licences were available in any of the three official languages, thus serving as a reliable indication of the distribution among the different local communities. The first reference indicates 54 sets in 1924, with a continuous and substantial growth each year: during 1933 the numbers reached 2,313, and by the end of that year it reached 3,350. The numbers were increasing so fast that the Postmaster General asked for permission to delegate the authority to sign the licences.[17] Figure 8.1 represents the diffusion of sets, beginning with the first count up to the point when a decision to establish the radio was made.

The annual growth was between 40 per cent and 60 per cent per year until 1931; in 1932 the growth was 93 per cent, and in 1933—nearly 158 per cent. For a population of just over one million, the number was still small, but was growing fast. Listeners tuned in to foreign stations—and there more so available everyday: from France, Germany, Austria, Holland, Hungry, Poland, Czechoslovakia, and

---

[12] The first discussion of radio in the Hebrew Davar newspaper in 1925 was about the intentions of the Turkish government to establish a radio station with the assistance of the French. The report mentioned that France built seven radio stations outside France, and that half of the radio content used in the world was French. 'Here and There' (14 August 1925) *Davar*, at 2.

[13] See Briggs, *The Birth*, above n 9, at 294; Asa Briggs, *The Golden Age of Wireless* (Oxford University Press, 1965) 373–7.

[14] Briggs reports a conference at the Colonial Office in 1927, in which a participant commented that 'there are serious copyright difficulties.' Briggs, *The Golden Age*, ibid, at 371.

[15] For a technical report, see Clive McCarthy, *Development of the A.M. Transmitter Network, Ver. 4* (2004), available at the BBC Engineering website, http://bit.ly/qDFqcE.

[16] See eg newspaper reports, 'Here and There' (14 August 1925) *Davar*, at 2; 'Radio in Najd and Hijaz' (9 January 1931) *Davar*, at 6 (about a radio in Saudi Arabia).

[17] PMG to CS (11 March 1933) ISA M354/16 doc 1; HC Authorization (19 August 1933) ISA M354/16 doc 21a.

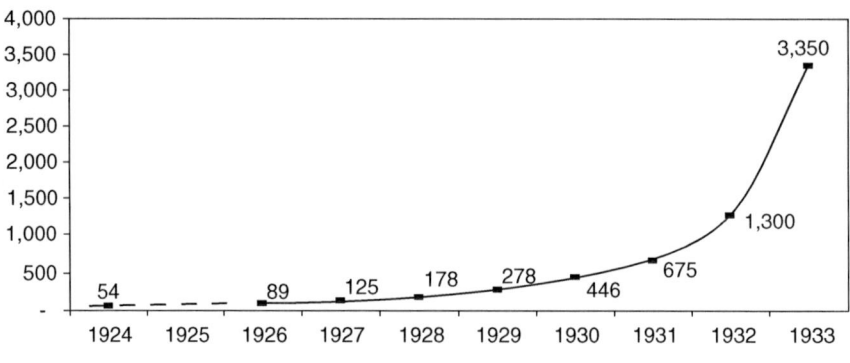

Fig. 8.1: Radio sets in Palestine, 1924–33[18]

Romania.[19] Interestingly, the first lists of available frequencies, published in local newspapers, did not include the BBC.

Broadcasting required a licence. Eytan Almog points that there were a few Jewish petitions in the late 1920s for such a licence, and that all were refused.[20] The first and only licence to broadcast was handed to a Jewish radio engineer and owner of a radio set shop, Mendel Abramowitz. Almog documented his temporary radio station in Tel-Aviv during the international Levant Fair in 1932.[21] The fair attracted 1,200 displays from different countries, and was a major event in the economic and cultural life of the *Yishuv*. Abramowitz broadcasted a few hours each day for the one month duration of the fair. The contents were live musical concerts, Hebrew music, and a few talks. Almog argues that Abramowitz turned the radio from entertainment and advertising to a Hebrew, Zionist platform, and that despite the technical problems, lack of organized programming, and controversial political balance (internal Yishuv politics) the broadcasting contributed much to the awareness of radio as a cultural, ideological, and political tool in Palestine.[22] After the fair, Abramowitz received a limited licence to broadcast from Tel-Aviv: the licence was revocable at any time, limited in its broadcasting power, limited to two hours per day, subject to pre-review, and limited in content with a prohibition of commercial advertisements.[23] Abramowitz portrayed his contribution to radio in Palestine in

---

[18] The data is based on ISA M354/26 doc 1a, Appendix A. For the interim figures of 1933, see ISA M354/1 doc 54a. The figures refer to the fiscal year which ended in March of the following year. No data is available for 1925.

[19] See listings of radio stations, their frequencies and programmes, published in (23 February 1933) *Palestine Post*, at 6; (9 March 1933), at 6.

[20] See eg Almog, 'The British Mandate', above n 5, at 85. The PMG wrote to the same effect: William Hudson, 'A Contribution to Happiness' (30 March 1936) *Palestine Post*, at 13 (writing that: 'None of the applications, alone, could be considered suitable for a concession of so comprehensive a character.').

[21] Almog, 'A Wireless', above n 5.

[22] Ibid, at 73.

[23] Ibid, at 75.

bright colours: 'I felt like a great innovator and pioneer of the first calibre.'[24] The choice of the adjective—pioneer—is no coincidence. Being a pioneer, a *Halutz*, was the highest possible status in the Hebrew society in those days. Abramowitz claimed it to himself. He presented his endeavour as motivated by Zionist ideology, rather than a commercial motivation.

The first concrete proposal to establish a broadcasting service in Palestine came earlier, in 1930, from Claude Francis Strickland, a retired colonial officer who spent a substantial time in the Indian Civil Service, where he served as the Registrar of Cooperative Societies, and specialized in credit systems of agricultural cooperatives. He suggested a scheme of rural broadcasting, sometimes referred to as vernacular broadcasting. The crux of the idea was to have broadcasting aimed to reach rural areas, and governmental distribution of radio sets, to be placed in central locations in the villages.

In 1930 Strickland was invited to Palestine to examine the economic position of the Arab villages, the *fellahin* (Arabic: peasants). The invitation was part of the governmental investigations in the aftermath of the 1929 Wailing Wall events— bloody clashes between Arabs and Jews that left hundreds of casualties. Strickland toured the country in July and August 1930, and wrote a long report about the financial aspects of the cooperative, as requested. However, the last paragraph of his report introduced an unexpected topic of rural broadcasting. He suggested a 'public utility company', under the partial control of the government, for broadcasting news in Arabic, addressed at the villagers. He explained:

I should like to see a receiving set and loud speaker owned or leased by the village as a whole, installed in the village meeting house and kept in order by the touring staff of the broadcasting company... The news supplied should of course not merely be Government statements or instructive material. General news which at present reaches the village in a distorted from could thus be supplied in a true form; there should also be amusing matter, music and other entertainment. The idea may be novel, but I am convinced that the great lack of rural life throughout the world is the lack of novelty and variety in interests.[25]

Although it is clear that Strickland wanted to promote the well-being of the potential listeners in the villages, he treated them in a paternalistic and orientalist manner. Andrea Stanton comments that Strickland saw Palestine through the lens of his experience in the Punjab.[26] Strickland actively campaigned for his proposal. Immediately upon concluding his visit to Palestine, he met with two senior BBC officials in London. The BBC was willing to assist from the very first day. Strickland tried to arrange a meeting between John Chancellor, the High Commissioner

---

[24] Mendel Aviv, 'Some Aspects of the Birth of Broadcasting in Israel' (1966) Technion Ybk 44 (Abramowitz changed his last name to Aviv). On the day of the inauguration of the PBS, Abramowitz published a lengthy advertisement (what we would today call an infomercial), publishing his radio shop. The title was 'Pioneering in Radio' (30 March 1936) *Palestine Post*, at 7.
[25] C F Strickland, *A Report on the Possibility of Introducing a System of Agricultural Cooperation in Palestine, submitted to the Government of Palestine* (1930).
[26] Stanton, *A Little Radio*, above n 5, at 99. Indeed, the report contains comments about the intelligence of the Arab farmer, and comparisons to Indian farmers.

of Palestine, and Sir John Reith, the BBC's Director General, but to no avail.[27] In the meantime, the BBC staff gathered some data, so to help 'certain enthusiastic officials'.[28] It composed a letter with unofficial and provisional notes to Strickland, addressing technological options for the kind of transmitter and its location, programming, and organization (responding to the Arab–Jewish structure of the Palestinian society).[29]

By the summer of 1933, Strickland had a more detailed proposal of his initial suggestion. He published a detailed article.[30] 'Palestine,' he stated, 'is one of the few countries under civilized administration which possess no system of wireless broadcasting.' This should be read as a direct reference to the civilizing mission of the British Empire. He repeated his views on the Arab villagers, and added his rationale for the establishment of rural broadcasting: 'Village life, moreover, is not merely backward and simple; it is also depressing and dull; and the boredom which prevails in the evenings, when work is over but artificial lighting is inadequate for intelligent amusements at home, is a contributory cause of both criminal and immoral behaviour. (It is not suggested that the Arab race as a whole is criminal or immoral.)'[31]

The updated proposal included Jewish villagers, though the emphasis was still on the Arab population. Strickland added another rationale: 'Private Arab or Jewish transmitting stations will create a very real danger, since no precautions taken by Government will prevent constant misuse or misinterpretation of a programme or statement issued on behalf of a single community.'[32] The concern was of partisan transmitters. The proposed governmental-run radio station would pre-empt local initiatives, and provide the government with control. The particular solution Strickland proposed, of the government distributing radio sets for communal listening in villages did not come out of thin air. The source and inspiration came from no less than Soviet Russia.[33] The article went into details of the expected costs, as well as the content of the broadcasts: official announcements and discussions of 'agriculture, education, co-operation and health'. He mentioned entertainment, which he considered an important component of broadcasting, though it was to serve as an instrumental role of allowing refreshment between lectures. Strickland revealed his differential treatment of Jews and Arabs: as for the latter, the source of entertainment can be Egypt (which 'has a larger supply of artists than Palestine'), whereas the former can provide their own content ('Jewish music in

---

[27] BBC Memorandum of Telephone Interview with Strickland (16 September 1930) BBC WAC E1/1142 File 1.

[28] Strickland continued advocating his scheme. See eg his talk at the Royal Central Asian Society in London, reported in 'Broadcasting in Asia: Wireless advocated to Combat Ignorance' (6 October 1933) *The Times*, at 6.

[29] BBC to Strickland (7 October 1930) BBC WAC E1/1142 File 1.

[30] C F Strickland, 'Broadcasting in Palestine' (1933) 20 J of the Royal Central Asian Society 410.

[31] Ibid, at 410.

[32] Ibid, at 411.

[33] Ibid, at 412. See also Joselyn Zivin, 'The Imagined Reign of the Iron Lecturer: Village Broadcasting in Colonial India' (1998) 32 Modern Asian Stud 717, 729, who notes that the British (Strickland included) were hardly concerned with the ideological aspects of the project.

Jerusalem is of good quality').[34] In the long run, Strickland's ideas were successful. The rural broadcasting scheme was implemented in Palestine, as well as in other places, most notably in India, according to his plan.[35]

Copyright was not mentioned even once during this initial phase. Did placing a radio set in a village, for communal—public—listening of music, amount to 'public performance'? The question had not yet been asked.

(2) Decision and planning (June 1933–April 1934)

By 1933, Palestine was ripe for its own broadcasting service. The technology was available; it was at the forefront of technological advancement, and associated with progress. Some of the new Jewish immigrants were exposed to radio in their countries of origin. The Arab population learned about radio in neighbouring countries. The number of local radio sets grew fast. The BBC had the knowledge and motivation to push for radio throughout the Empire, and there was a concrete plan on the table, promoted by Strickland. No doubt, the growing concerns that followed the rise of Nazi Germany, contributed to the interest and demand for immediate news. Viewed against this background, establishing broadcasting in Palestine was a no-brainer. The question thus is not why the British decided on a radio station in mid 1933, but why this did not happen earlier. The official explanation was a lack of local talent to provide sufficient content for the programmes.[36] Less favoured explanations would point to the government's hesitation and lack of vision.[37] It seems that the British were almost forced to establish broadcasting in Palestine, if they wanted to control it.

The decision to establish the Palestine Broadcasting Service, as soon as possible in the form of a government-run service was followed by intense planning, which took place from May 1933 to the end of 1934. It was to be a full scheme, broader than Strickland's focus on the peasant listeners.

On 16 May 1933, the High Commissioner, Sir Arthur Wauchope had a meeting at the Colonial Office in London, on the matter. Decisions were made: Wauchope would submit a proposal and the Colonial Office would consult the BBC.[38] At the

---

[34] Strickland, 'Broadcasting in Palestine', above n 30, at 413.

[35] Zivin, 'The Imagined Reign', above n 33. The community listening project in India lasted until the 1970s. PC Chatterji, *Broadcasting in India* (Sage Publications, revised and updated edn, 1991) 46. Chatterji mentions 150,000 sets distributed in the community listening project. The rural broadcasting scheme was implemented also in Turkey, as reported in the Lucerne Convention: PMG to HC (23 May 1933) ISA M354/1 doc 1b, and in Syria, in the early 1950s. See a comment in Edmund deS Brunner, 'Rural Communications Behavior and Attitudes in the Middle East' (1953) 18 Rural Sociology 149, 150.

[36] Hudson, 'A Contribution', above n 20.

[37] Stanton offers another explanation, pointing to the paradox: the radio creates a public space, but, '[a] public space is meant to serve the civil society of a self-governing people—but a colonial or mandate public space is divided, fractured by the incompatible needs of the governing authorities and those of the population.' A governmental radio solved this governmental dilemma. Stanton, *A Little Radio*, above n 5, at 8.

[38] Extracts from a Note of Discussion with Sir Arthur Wauchope at the CO (16 May 1933) ISA M354/1 doc 8.

same time, Palestine's Postmaster General, William Hudson, represented Palestine at the international conference of the Telecommunications Union in Lucerne. Palestine secured a wavelength.[39] On 1 June 1933 Wauchope circulated the first official proposal, entitled *Broadcasting*.[40] This document was the blueprint of the PBS. As promised, the Colonial Office approached the BBC, which replied promptly, addressing the issue of cost, and the conditions governing the relaying of BBC programmes. This reply contained a first reference to copyright law.[41] The following month saw the publication of Strickland's article, discussed above. Internal back-office work continued dealing with financial aspects and possible content.[42] Towards the end of the year, a committee of high ranking clerks was appointed to consider the scheme. It reported its proposals within eleven days.[43] In December the High Commissioner was able to submit an updated plan to the Colonial Office in London,[44] which again asked the BBC for its views. Copyright law was again raised by the BBC.[45] The Postmaster General accepted their views on this matter without challenging them. He amended the estimated cost for the annual programming, adding LP1,500 for payments to copyright owners, a sum which turned out to be higher than needed.[46]

The plan became more and more detailed. Two major issues were discussed: the budget and the technology. Intense discussions followed between those involved in Jerusalem, the Colonial Office, and the BBC.[47] Many of the differences were settled within a few days, during a successful visit of Palestine's Chief Engineer, William Kenneth Brasher, to London, in April.[48] On 24 April 1934, a confidential telegram arrived in Jerusalem. The Secretary of State informed the High

---

[39] The wavelength was to be shared with a radio station in Yorkshire. Hudson received advice from the BBC as to the wavelength, and then authorised the British delegation to require a wavelength on behalf of Palestine. Thereafter, he left the conference. See Hudson's memo (23 May 1933) ISA M354/1 doc 1b, and PMG to CS (26 March 1934) ISA M354/1 doc 71. Stanton's account, based on the documents from the Lucerne conference, indicates that Hudson excused his departure by saying that he was called to return to Palestine, when in fact it was he who realized that the Palestinian interests are better taken care of by the British delegation than by him. Stanton, *A Little Radio*, above n 5, at 11–13.
[40] ISA M354/1 doc 1a.
[41] ISA M354/1 docs 14, 14a; Graves (Director of BBC Empire Service) to CO (28 June 1933) BBC WAC E1/1136/1 File 1a.
[42] See the correspondence of the CS, the PMG, and the Treasurer, between June and December 1933, at ISA M354/1.
[43] ISA M354/1 doc 51 (appointment), and 52 (the Committee's report). The Committee's chair was the District Commissioner of Jerusalem, and its other members were the Director of Education, the PMG, and the Assistant Treasurer.
[44] HC to Secretary of State (23 December 1933) ISA M354/1 doc 59.
[45] The CO forwarded the BBC's report to the HC: Secretary of State to HC (13 March 1934) ISA M354/1 doc 67. See also CO to BBC (15 January 1934), and internal BBC comments (15 February 1934) BBC WAC E1/1136/1 File 1a.
[46] PMG to CS (26 March 1934) ISA M354/1 doc 71.
[47] See correspondence in ISA M354/1.
[48] Chief Engineer to PMG (5 May 1933) ISA M354/1 docs 82a, 82b. Brasher was a signals officer in World War I, he then worked for Marconi's Wireless Telegraphy Company, and later joined the colonial service. Upon his return to England he served as the Secretary of the British Institute of Electric Engineers till 1963. See 'The Council's farewell dinner to Mr W. K. Brasher' (1963) 9(102) J of the Institution of Electrical Engineers 265; Profile: 'WK Brasher: The Compass, not the Weathercock' (25 April 1957) The New Scientist 21–2.

Commissioner that: 'Expenditure of £32,000 on construction of Broadcasting Station and for services of technical staff in current year approved on the understanding that every effort will be made to render the service self-supporting.'[49] Thus, the decision was made: there was to be a broadcasting station in Palestine.

This intense sequence of events provides a rich ground to explore, especially the British motivations. A full discussion exceeds the scope of our current interest. In a nutshell, the motivations were a mix of British imperial interests: educating the local populations (which was a colonial civilizing mission); serving as a governmental means of communications in times of unrest (which was a security interest); and serving as a means to counter foreign propaganda (at the time the British thought of the Soviets, but the concern shifted to the Italians).[50] The governmental radio station was also to prevent local initiatives.[51]

From a structural perspective, the PBS was modelled after the BBC, with some important differences, required by the different languages and by the limited resources. Financial limits meant that the station would broadcast only five hours a day. Technology, namely the shared wavelength with a Yorkshire station, and the British assumptions as to prospective listening habits—that most would listen in the evening, after a day's work—dictated the timing of the broadcasting: 17:30–22:30.

Programming was discussed by the clerks in Jerusalem only after they were assured that the PBS would be financially viable. The Postmaster General submitted a proposal: one hour for each of the three official languages, and two hours for relaying foreign programmes, 'or to the use of gramophone records'.[52] From the outset it was clear that the broadcasting would have to be trilingual, in English, Arabic, and Hebrew. The British took great care to assure that the time allocated to the two local languages was equal. This was not a trivial decision: the Arab population outnumbered the Jewish population (which was on the rise, at 16.6 per cent in 1931 and 31.3 per cent in 1940), but at the same time, the Jews held far more radio sets (74.3 per cent of sets in 1933, compared to 13.4 per cent with the Arabs. These figures remained more or less steady. In 1944 the sets held by the

---

[49] Secretary of State to HC (24 April 1934) ISA M354/1 doc 80.

[50] In the late 1930s, the Italians turned against the British, especially through radio Bari, which broadcasted in Arabic. London considered using the PBS to counter the Italian propaganda, but realized that the Arabs were suspicious about it, because of its Hebrew broadcasting. The alternative was to establish a broadcasting station in Cyprus, but this could broadcast in medium length waves, while most Arabs had radio sets for shortwave broadcasting. Eventually, the result was the inauguration of the BBC's Arab Service in 1938. See Callum A MacDonald, 'Radio Bari: Italian Wireless Propaganda in the Middle East and British Countermeasures 1934–38' (1977) 13(2) Middle Eastern Studies 195; Peter Partner, *Arab Voices: The BBC Arabic Service 1938–1988* (BBC, 1988).

[51] Gil attributes the pre-emption argument solely to the British experience with the Levant Fair radio. See Gil, 'Voice of Jerusalem', above n 5, at 298. This view does not fit the fact that Abramowitz also received a licence to broadcast after the fair was over, during 1934 and 1935, however limited it was. The justification became relevant in the late 1930s and 1940s, when underground Jewish factions established illegal radio stations. See Douglas A Boyd, 'Hebrew-Language Clandestine Radio Broadcasting During the British Palestine Mandate' (1999) 6 J Radio Stud 101.

[52] PMG to CS (19 October 1933) ISA M354/1 doc 32.

Jews accounted for 77.5 per cent of the sets, with the Arabs holding 16.5 per cent. The rest were licences in English).[53]

The Broadcasting Committee appointed by the High Commissioner elaborated the general scheme.[54] It noted that relaying foreign programmes was 'now a matter of international practice and it is generally welcomed in the countries of origin'. It then proposed a detailed schedule, down to the minute. The Arabic hour was to include news, excerpts from Arabic newspapers on a topic of the day, Arabic music (relayed from Egypt or records), and a lecture or short talk. The Hebrew hour was to include similar elements, with the music originating from the studio or records, or relayed from Europe (opera or concert). The English hour was to begin with the time from the Big Ben, followed by the news, and then relaying programmes from the BBC. The remaining two hours were to be mostly of music.

To a contemporary copyright lawyer, the legal issues are clear: relaying foreign programmes today is not as welcome as it might have been at the time; playing music of all kinds is a matter of public performance; reading aloud newspapers and plays is also a matter of public performance; and playing records triggers also the mechanical rights in the sound recording. None of these was discussed by the committee, neither from the legal point nor from the financial point of view.

(3) Executing the plan (May 1934–March 1936)

Once the budget was approved and the financial details were settled, it was time to execute the plan. The equipment was ordered; a building committee was appointed, and selected a location for the transmitter near Ramallah.[55] Staff was recruited; the studio was built. One of the items on the 'to-do list' was the community listening project. The High Commissioner was interested in speeding up the broadcasting undertaking, and was now concerned with reaching out to the villagers.[56] In November 1934, he drew up the programme: there were 160 villages with a population of 1,000 and more. He ordered the purchase of 100 sets (instead of a previous suggestion of fifty). Eighty-five of these villages were to receive radio sets and loudspeakers, the remaining fifteen sets were for spares. One fifth would be for Jewish villages. The sets were to be free, but a maintenance fee should be charged. The sets should be pre-set with two alternate options: the PBS and the Cairo station.[57]

The scheme was executed. Sets were installed in various villages. At first, the criteria for receiving a free set were a bit unclear. The Jewish villages of *Kfar Azar*, with seventy-three families and *Kfar Hitim* with its 120 members, requested free

---

[53] For the number of sets in 1933, see ISA M354/1 doc 54a; for the 1944 figures, see D Gurevich (supervision), A Gertz (ed), A Zankar (assistant), *Statistical Handbook of Jewish Palestine* (Department of Statistics, The Jewish Agency for Palestine, Jerusalem, 1947).

[54] See ISA M354/1 doc 52.

[55] Stanton reports that the transmitter was in use by the Palestinian Broadcasting Corporation until 2001, when it was destroyed by the Israeli army. Stanton, *A Little Radio*, above n 5, at 228.

[56] HC Letter (30 October 1934) ISA M354/1 doc 125.

[57] HC, Wireless Station, Notes (November 1934) ISA M354/1 doc 127.

sets. Their requests were denied, as they were small villages. Israel Luxemburg of Tel-Aviv asked for a free set for himself—he was refused, as the sets were for the rural areas.[58] Later on there were some (British) concerns about the possibility of tuning the sets to receive the anti-British broadcasts from Bari, but apparently, altering the pre-set radios required technical skills and equipment. The Postmaster General opined that there were very few Arabs capable of doing that.[59] In the early 1940s more receivers were bought.[60] There are indications that the scheme continued throughout the remainder of the Mandate.[61]

Back to 1934: once the PBS's budget was approved by London, it was clear that a director was needed. The solution was found inside the BBC. R Anthony Rendall, the BBC's West Regional Programme Director, was selected to be the man to do the job, responsible for administration and programming.[62] The initial position was for six months, but it ended up being for one year. Rendall was to become the PBS's first Programme Director. He arrived in Jerusalem on 1 October 1935 and did not waste one moment. During the next year he sent several lengthy reports, but interestingly, the addressee was not the Colonial Office, which was now his employer through the Palestine government, but to the BBC. His first impression was rather dim. The only bright spot he found was the technological side. He found the time to look into the copyright issues:

Negotiations with the Performing Rights Society, the gramophone consortium, and Reuters are all in an unsatisfactory state. Clearly Palestine's reputation for Budget surplus and the knowledge that this is to be a Government concern have encouraged the various organizations to try and make a little extra money. The PRS would seem to be trying to play us off against the Egyptian State Broadcasting, who are at present negotiating for a new agreement.[63]

After several delays, the first broadcast approached, excitement grew. The local press published anticipating articles.[64] The BBC drafted a message of greeting to be published in the *Palestine Post*: 'It is the duty of those broadcasting organisations which are already firmly established to assist the development of all new ventures in this field.'[65] However, the Colonial Office advised against publication in the

---

[58] Kfar Azar to HC (January 1936) ISA M361/20 doc 1a; HaKotser (Kfar Hitim) (24 August 1937) ISA M361/20 docs 22, 23; Luxemburg to HC (April 1936) ISA M361/20 docs 9, 10.
[59] Quoted in a letter from CS (22 November 1938) ISA M361/20 doc 31.
[60] See list of villages that received such sets, in the letter of the District Commissioners of the Galilee and Lydia to CS (17 February 1940, 20 June 1940) ISA M361/20 docs 42, 50.
[61] See correspondence between the PMG, CS, and the Public Information Officer (November 1947) ISA M361/20 docs 109, 110.
[62] BBC Correspondence (26 July 1935) BBC WAC E1/1136/1.
[63] Ibid.
[64] See 'B.B.C. Officer for Palestine' (4 September 1935) *Palestine Post*, at 1 (reporting Rendall's appointment); 'Palestine's Broadcasting Station' (13 December 1935) *Palestine Post*, at 9 (reporting a visit to the transmitter's site); 'Jerusalem Calling on March 30' (15 March 1936) *Palestine Post*, at 1 (announcing the final date); 'Ten Days More to Initial Broadcast' (20 March 1936) *Palestine Post*, at 1 (providing details about the programmes).
[65] BBC Memo (18 November 1935) BBC WAC E1/1136/3.

Palestine Post, which was Jewish-owned, and instead suggested that the message be included in a letter to the High Commissioner.

30 March 1936 was the big day. Greetings from the BBC were received in Jerusalem. John Reith wrote: 'May it bring to all people of Palestine in full measure the benefits which the new science of broadcasting alone makes possible.'[66] The *Palestine Post* published an article by the Postmaster General, William Hudson. Whatever shortcomings might be, he wrote, the staff will do their best to make the PBS 'a means of contributing to the happiness of the population in this country'.[67] Adjunct to this article, the Post published a list of radio stations and their wavelengths. It included seventy-nine stations, ranging from Bombay to Rabat, from Pittsburgh to Moscow. Jerusalem was included in the list, in bold capital letters. The Post also paid tribute to Strickland, and reprinted his 1930 recommendation regarding broadcasting.[68]

The inauguration was ceremonial, with minor technical problems. The High Commissioner opened the broadcasting, and committed that: 'While the service would not be concerned with politics, it would be directed to advantage of all classes of all communities. The main object would be spread of knowledge and culture and claims of religion would not be neglected.'[69] Dr Katznelson, the Jewish member of the programme committee outlined the Hebrew programmes, and emphasized that the Hebrew broadcasting was 'the first and the only one the world over'. He concluded with hopes that the PBS would contribute to the happiness and peace of the country as a whole.[70] Amin Bey 'abd Al Hadi, the Arab programme manager, spoke of the role of the radio in promoting culture, and expressed his wonder at the technology's impact on shortening distances. The greatest advantage, he said, was that the radio spared women from going outside in their quest for pleasure and amusement. He then emphasized the importance of the radio on nationality, repeating it several times: 'It is a national task to utilise this service'; 'It is even a national duty that we should take part in the service and utilise it as a means to national useful service.'[71] Thus, the representatives of each sector spoke in one way or another about the nation, but each meant their own community. Three weeks later, the Arab Revolt, lasting for three years erupted.

Radio was a success. The number of listening licences kept rising throughout the Mandate, with a slowdown during World War II. Figure 8.2 is based on a compilation of sources.

The number of sets does not necessarily mean that all listeners were tuning in to the PBS—no doubt many in the Arab population listened to Arab stations broadcasting from Cairo as well as to Radio Bari from Italy; many of the Jews

---

[66] Reith to HC (30 March 1936) BBC WAC E1/1136/3 File 1a.
[67] Hudson, 'A Contribution', above n 20.
[68] 'Origin of Palestine Broadcasting: Mr Strickland's Idea' (30 March 1936) *Palestine Post*, at 13.
[69] Quoted in Rendall to BBC (30 March 1936) BBC WAC E1136/3 File 2a (suggesting a statement for the news).
[70] The speeches were printed in full. See A Katznelson, 'The Beginning of an Era' (1 April 1936) *Palestine Post*, at 5.
[71] Amin Bey 'abd Al Hadi, 'Messenger of Culture' (1 April 1936) *Palestine Post*, at 5.

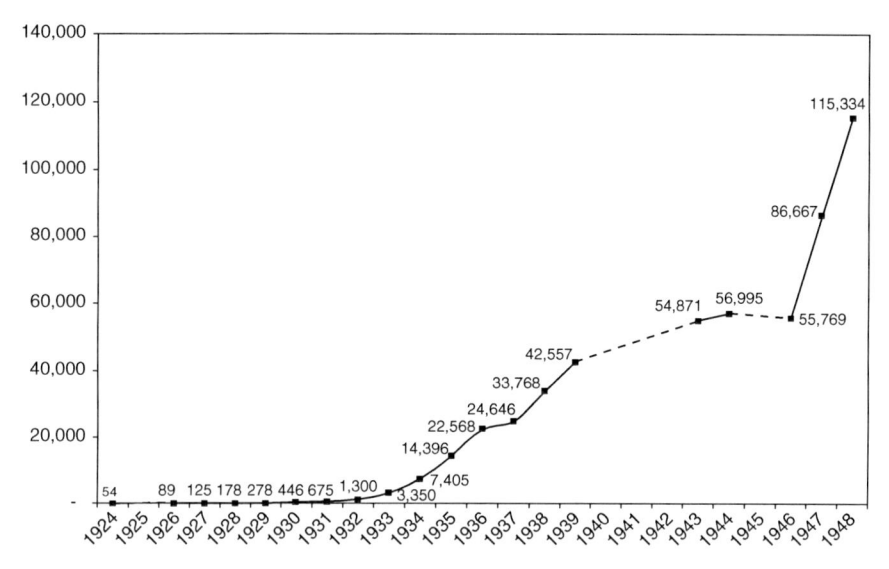

Fig. 8.2: Radio sets in Palestine, 1924–48[72]

listened to broadcasts from their European countries of origin. The radio became a powerful political and cultural tool, affecting the Hebrew language, Arab modernity, and much more.[73]

C. Copyright Issues

The institutional history of the PBS reveals that copyright law deserved rather little attention in the preparatory work towards its establishment. The different players involved were interested in the substance, in assuring that the PBS is financially self-supporting, and that everything worked as it should. They were not concerned with copyright per se. I have pointed to some copyright-related issues. There were two main copyright issues: the public performance of the PBS itself, in playing music and broadcasting other material, and the more complicated issues arising out of the communal listening project.

---

[72] The data for 1924–36 is based on ISA M354/26 doc 1a, Appendix A. For interim figures, see: 1932, 1933: ISA M354/1 doc 54a; 1934: ISA M354/1 docs 71, 129; 1935: ISA M361/14 doc 18. For later figures, see: 1937: ISA M361/14 doc 93; 1938–9: *Davar* (3 November 1938; 22 February 1939); 1939 and 1944: *Statistical Handbook of Jewish Palestine*, above n 53; 1943: ISA M354/16 doc 100; 1946: ISA M361/16 doc 31; 1947–8: ISA M361/39 docs 17, 26. No data is available for 1925, 1940–2, and 1945.

[73] Liebes and Kampf, 'Hello!', above n 5, argue that the Hebrew hour on the PBS created 'a virtual Hebrew space that served as a metonym for the Hebrew nation'. Gil, 'Voice of Jerusalem', above n 5, discusses the subversive use of the Hebrew hour to promote the Zionist cause. Stanton, *A Little Radio*, above n 5, discussed the cultural meaning of the PBS in the Arab society, arguing that the PBS brought an image of Arab modernity to the Palestinians.

(1) Copyright in broadcasting

Had it not been for the BBC, those involved would not have thought of the copyright aspects of broadcasting themselves. Copyright law was not yet integrated in the checklist of those dealing with cultural content. It is hard to blame them: copyright law was a relatively new matter, and broadcasting was even newer. Once again, as in the case of publicly performed music which we discussed in the previous chapter, foreign players were the ones that introduced copyright to the scene: the BBC directed, the Mandate government acted, the PRS insisted. Interestingly, no one in the Palestine government challenged the issue: once it became evident that copyright was omitted in the first plans, it was simply added to the calculations. No one questioned the relevance of copyright law or suggested that there was no problem at all. The matter was not referred to the Attorney General. No lawyers were involved in the process.

(a) Enter copyright

The first time copyright law was mentioned in connection with the establishment of the PBS was in the BBC's first comments, shortly after the High Commissioner distributed his blueprint plan in June 1933. Sir Cecil George Graves, the director of the newly established BBC Empire Service, drew the attention of the Colonial Office that 'the relayer is responsible for any copyright or other claims of third parties that may arise out of a rebroadcast in his country'.[74] The Colonial Office alerted the Chief Secretary in Jerusalem, and sent along the BBC's conditions for relaying its broadcasts.[75] The conditions clarified that different kinds of material had different legal statuses attached to them: original BBC material was freely available for relaying; the relayer was responsible for copyright claims of third parties, for example, when a relayed BBC broadcast included material by artists who set up claims in that respect; finally, the BBC clarified that it did not have copyright in the news bulletins it broadcast, which was retained by Reuters.

However, these first comments went unnoticed: the Mandate government in Jerusalem did not include copyright in its plans. By early 1934, the plans were more detailed. The five hour format with its division into the three languages had been decided. Neither the report of the broadcasting committee nor the High Commissioner's letter to the Secretary of State in December 1933 mentioned copyright. When the Colonial Office forwarded these documents to the BBC for comments, the BBC again pointed to the issue of copyright law, this time in an explicit and extended manner; copyright was now framed in financial terms:

> Although it is not known what copyright legislation obtains in Palestine, it is almost certain that, sooner or later, arrangements will have to be made either with the PRS or a similar body for ad hoc or annual payments to cover the use of copyright music and other material.

---

[74] Graves to CO (28 June 1933) BBC WAC E1/1136/1 File 1a.
[75] CO to CS (24 July 1933) ISA M354/1 doc 14.

For the confidential information of those concerned, it may be said that in Great Britain the B.B.C. pays annually to the P.R.S. approximately 5% of its net license revenues; and it is known that similar arrangements have been made in other parts of the Empire.[76]

Further comments were made regarding gramophone records, which required separate negotiations with the gramophone companies, and repeated the statement that the copyright in the news bulletins was held by Reuters. This time, the message registered, quite likely because it was framed in financial terms. The Postmaster General in Palestine acknowledged that 'in view of the suggested possibility of having to pay substantial sums to the Performing Rights Society and to gramophone companies it would, I think, be advisable to increase the amount [of programmes expenditure] to LP4,500'.[77] Thus, he allocated LP1,500 for copyright payments, a sum that exceeded the actual cost. Later on, after meeting Brasher, the BBC relaxed its estimate of copyright related costs, noting that:

Artistic talent, it appears, will be easily and cheaply acquired; the news service will not involve relatively high payments to agencies in view of the availability of official sources of news and other information; and if the programmes are to contain a considerable proportion of native music is should be possible to negotiate copyright payments on a lower scale than 5% of the net revenues tentatively suggested in the report of February 20th.[78]

Note the differentiation between native music and other kinds of music, namely European music. One hidden assumption underlying the above statement was correct, as the PRS handled only European music and did not handle local music. But there was yet another hidden assumption: that 'native music' was unprotected by copyright. The BBC did not ask whether there were any local performing rights societies or where the music came from. They assumed it was unprotected or that the copyright was unenforced. There was no legal or factual basis to hold such a view, since original works made in Palestine, were protected under the British copyright law. The exclusive attention to European music implied that the local music was unworthy of copyright protection.

In the following years the PBS played gramophone music but it also broadcasted live music, some of which was specially commissioned by it. In 1938 the PBS established its own orchestra.[79] Thus, it was able to save on the copyright expenses for local music, not because it was unworthy of legal protection, but because it was commissioned, and therefore presumably the PBS owned the copyright therein.

(b) Negotiations

It took several more months for the Postmaster General to approach the PRS in London. The initial inquiry was made in November 1934, followed by negoti-

---

[76] See BBC Memo (15 February 1934), attached to Secretary of States to HC (13 March 1934) ISA M354/1 docs 68, 68a.
[77] PMG to CS (26 March 1934) ISA M354/1 doc 71.
[78] BBC to CO (12 April 1936) ISA M354/1 docs 86b, 86c.
[79] See Hirshberg, *Music*, above n 2, at 141–3.

ations that lasted for over a year, up to the beginning of broadcasting. Meir Kovalsky, the PRS's agent in Palestine was left out of the negotiations; otherwise, he would have been entitled to a 50 per cent commission.[80] The Colonial Office closely followed the negotiations, as it considered it to be relevant for other colonies.[81]

In the course of the negotiations, the parties—the Postmaster General on behalf of the PBS, and the PRS—fleshed out the criteria for calculating the fees. The Postmaster already knew—the BBC informed him—that the basis for calculation was the net licence revenues.[82] Nevertheless, in his initial inquiry with the PRS, he mentioned the trilingual structure of the programmes, that the PBS was to be a non-profit station, that the bulk of the population was illiterate, that the cost of a receiving licence was ten shillings per set, and finally, the estimated number of licences.[83] The PRS was quick to clarify that the only relevant factors were the proportion of English music (as they did not control copyright in Hebrew or Arabic music), and the net licences revenue. The nature of the broadcasting and the illiteracy of the listeners were irrelevant factors as far as the PRS was concerned.[84] The PRS suggested an arbitrary sum of £250 for six months, to cover its entire repertoire.[85] The Postmaster General objected. His reasoning is telling:

> In suggesting a minimum payment of £250 for six months, your Society must, I think, have been under the impression that Palestine is essentially a country to the general population of which European programmes will make appeal. Such, however, is not the case. At least three fourths of the population are of Arab race; most of them are illiterate and the proportion who would prefer European music to local music is extremely small.[86]

This line echoes the BBC's comments that we saw earlier, namely the differential treatment of European music and native music. The PRS replied that it had no such impression: 'it is not practicable to base the payment on the extent to which the programmes may be listened to by various sections of the population—a factor which it would probably be impossible to ascertain—but that regard should be had rather to the probable extent of user (performance or relay) of Society's repertoire'.[87] Each side held to the arguments that were in its favour, as is often the case, but the two sides reflect deeper differences. The Palestinian government focused on the recipients' side: who received which kind of material, and how could they use it (with the not so implicit assumption that illiterate people could not enjoy European music). The PRS focused on the quantity of use, regardless of the use itself. This division echoes contemporary debates about copyright law. It is often the case that

---

[80] See Ch 7.
[81] Secretary of State to HC (29 October 1935) ISA M361/14 doc 4.
[82] In the UK, the BBC and the PRS used the number of receiving licences as the criterion for calculating royalties as of 1929, instead of the duration of the broadcast. See Cyril Ehrlich, *Harmonious Alliance: A History of the Performing Right Society* (Oxford University Press, 1989) 73.
[83] PMG to PRS (25 November 1934) ISA M361/14 doc 6a.
[84] PRS to PMG (7 December 1934) ISA M361/14 doc 6B.
[85] PRS to PMG (28 January 1935) ISA M361/14 doc 6D.
[86] PMG to PRS (12 September 1935) ISA M361/14 doc 6H.
[87] PRS to PMG (19 September 1935) ISA M361/14 doc 6J.

copyright owners emphasize the use of the property without regard to the way in which the works are used; users insist that not all uses require permission.

The exchange went on for a while, until the PRS eventually agreed that the arbitrary sum of £250 will be for a year, rather than six months.[88] The Secretary of State approved.[89] In years to come, the parties reached a formula for the calculation of the fees: an amount of 7d (pennies) per licensed listener, multiplied by the percentage of hours of foreign music out of the total broadcasting hours, multiplied by the number of licences.[90] In the meantime, the Colonial Office negotiated with the gramophone companies on behalf of Palestine.[91]

The PRS's success meant that in 1937, ACUM, the Hebrew performing rights society had an easier time to convince the government that it should be paid for the use of its growing Hebrew repertoire.[92] The PBS payments were ACUM's main source of revenue for many years.[93] However, ACUM was dissatisfied with cafe owners and the like who used radio sets for the pleasure of their patrons (replacing the gramophones). ACUM lacked the enforcement resources that the PRS had in Palestine. It approached the Postmaster General, demanding that the government enforces ACUM's rights vis-à-vis third parties.[94] The legal argument was that the listeners' licence (issued by the government) did not restrict public performance. The Postmaster General replied that the licence to hold a radio set did in fact include a clause stating that it did not authorize infringement of copyright,[95] and that the licence between the PBS and ACUM did not preclude the latter from suing third parties.[96] In other words, ACUM could sue the cafe owners directly, and the government need not intervene. It was the copyright owners' attempt to recruit the government to actively enforce their rights, one of many similar attempts from other copyright owners in future years. Importantly, there was no Arab performing rights society acting in Palestine. Arab music was left outside the loop.

Thus, at the same time that the mandatory courts were implementing copyright law in public performances against the often unwilling proprietors of cafes and cinemas, the government accepted the legal principle without challenging it: broadcasting was public performance. It set a de facto precedent, thus further

---

[88] PRS to PMG (18 October 1935) ISA M361/14 doc 6L.
[89] Secretary of State to HC (18 January 1936) ISA M361/14 doc 26.
[90] See eg Director of Broadcasting to CS (18 July 1946) ISA M361/16.
[91] The payment was of LP25 per 1,000 receiving licences. See Secretary of State to the Officer Administering the Government of Palestine (16 October 1935) ISA M361/14 doc 2; Secretary of State to HC (27 November 1935) ISA M361/14 doc 17. No direct record of this negotiation was found. The gramophone companies had just formed an association of their own, which is now IFPI. Unfortunately, IFPI does not hold documents from the relevant period.
[92] Dr Phillip Joseph, on behalf of ACUM to PMG (16 December 1937) ISA M361/15 doc 120a.
[93] See Pinhas Yorman, *ACUM Story* (Publishers Association, 1977) 18 (Hebrew).
[94] Joseph, on behalf of ACUM to PMG (16 December 1937) ISA M361/15 doc 120a.
[95] The trigger for the clause in the listening licences was the inauguration of the BBC World Service in late 1932. Anticipating the broadcasts, the Secretary of State for the Colonies circulated a dispatch to all colonies suggesting that the licence include the warning. See Secretary of State, Circular (10 February 1932) ISA M293/8 doc 56. The clause stated that: 'The license does not authorize the licensee to do any act which is an infringement of any copyright which may exist in the matter transmitted.' See in the PMG's letter (4 September 1935) ISA M354/16 doc 1.
[96] PMG to CS (23 December 1937) ISA M361/15 doc 120.

anchoring copyright law in Palestine, continuing the reception process of the legal transplant. The Eurocentric character of the law raised its head during this process, implying that not all kinds of music deserve the same treatment. Copyright owners of Arab music did not demand payment; the government did not seek them.

(2) The community listening project

Strickland's proposal to have rural broadcasting re-entered the planning in late 1934.[97] Now, that it was in government hands, the High Commissioner added his own notes about the distribution of the sets (one fifth to the Jewish settlements, the rest to the Arab villages),[98] which began in early 1936.[99] The copyright issues related to this scheme were more complicated and far less settled than those relating to direct broadcasting. However, by and large, the difficult legal questions were avoided. Recall that the scheme involved placing radio sets in public places, such as schools and cafes in large villages. Today the copyright issues of such a scheme are quite clear: operating a radio in a public, open, and accessible space, and broadcasting music or other copyrighted works, amounts to public performance, and hence requires the copyright owner's consent, otherwise it would infringe the performing rights. In the mid 1930s these questions were cutting edge not only in Palestine, but in many other countries.

Even though the first proposal of the scheme was aired in 1930, the particular copyright implications were raised only in July 1935. This time it was the Colonial Office. It directed the question to the BBC.[100] The trigger for the inquiry was a judicial decision—not a case from a Palestinian court—but one decided by the Court of Appeals in Britain: *Performing Rights Society Ltd v Hammond's Bradford Brewery Company, Ltd.*[101]

Hammond's was an important copyright law case, particularly for performing rights. The lawyers' arguments and the court's finding of the facts reflected the innovative use of radio and music in those days, in what became a prototype of performing rights cases: a hotel in Yorkshire installed a radio set and a loudspeaker so that guests could listen to the broadcasting. The BBC broadcasted a live performance of three musical works, performed at a cinema in Hammersmith. The PRS, which owned the public performance rights in those works, had licensed the BBC to broadcast its entire repertoire, for 'domestic and private use only'. It had not permitted the BBC to authorize a further transmission (the term used at the time was re-diffusion) by third parties. The PRS sued the hotel owner for infringing the public performance right. Thus, the legal question was, whether the owner of the hotel 'performed' the works in the legal meaning of performance.

---

[97] See Palestinian Government Memo (16 November 1934) ISA M354/1 doc 127.
[98] HC, Wireless Broadcasting, notes (November 1934) ISA M354/1 doc 129.
[99] See ISA M361/20 (Distribution of Radio Sets to Villages, January 1936–November 1947). The government signed a contract with the villages regarding the radio sets. See Stanton, *A Little Radio*, above n 5, at 130.
[100] CO to BBC (29 July 1935) BBC WAC E1/1142 File 1.
[101] [1934] Ch 121.

There was no dispute that it was 'public'. The lawyers and the court cited cases from the United States and Germany, alongside English cases. The defendant hotel argued that once the performers allowed the BBC to broadcast their performance, as they did, their rights were exhausted. The Court of Appeals rejected this argument: the owner of the hotel undertook 'further contrivances...for the purpose of rendering the sounds audible'.[102] The hotel's re-diffusion was public performance.

The BBC attended the issue a few weeks after the Colonial Office's inquiry; its legal conclusion was unequivocal: given that the Copyright Act 1911 applied in Palestine, the legal position in Palestine was analogous to that in Britain, and hence, *Hammond's* applied. There was no doubt that the use of loudspeakers in villages was 'public performance' in the legal meaning. Once the legal question was determined beyond any doubt, a practical suggestion followed, to include the re-diffusion in the PRS's licence to the PBS. The Colonial Office drew the attention of the Palestine government to the matter.[103] However, at that point in time, in early 1936, the PBS had already concluded its contract with the PRS, for the arbitrary annual sum of £250. The BBC urged the Colonial Office to achieve clarity, and to include the village scheme within the licence with the PRS explicitly.[104] The government, on the other hand, was concerned about the implications of reopening the negotiations with the PRS just a few weeks before the inauguration of the broadcasting.

The government could have tried the legal avenue, distinguishing *Hammond's*: unlike the hotel, which had no direct licence from the PRS, the PBS had such a licence, and it was the same body that broadcasted the copyrighted material and then re-diffused it by means of loudspeakers. This argument seems to be a plausible distinction of *Hammond's*, but it was not made. The PBS, and the Palestinian government chose not to pursue a legal avenue. Instead, they approached the PRS and asked that the already concluded licence also covered broadcasting in schools. The PRS partially agreed, emphasizing that it permitted public performances for educational purposes only, but refused to allow the public performance of music by installing radio sets.[105] The BBC's in-house lawyer, R Jardine Brown, tried to convince the Colonial Office (and indirectly, the Palestinian government) to cover all kinds of re-diffusion, even with paying a bit more.[106] However, the Colonial Office decided to let go and not to renegotiate the licence.[107] We can only speculate why the government preferred to do so: it might have assumed that the PRS would simply not know about other uses which might be infringing, or, a more generous speculation, that the government believed that it would be able to assure the PRS that the licence does cover other uses.

---

[102] Ibid, at 134.
[103] As the CO informed the BBC (6 February 1936) BBC WAC E1/1142 File 1.
[104] BBC to CO (12 February 1936) BBC WAC E1/1142 File 1.
[105] See summary of the negotiations in CO to BBC (22 April 1936) BBC WAC E1/1142 File 1.
[106] BBC Memo (27 April 1936) BBC WAC E1/1142 File 1.
[107] CO to BBC (22 May 1936) BBC WAC E1/1142 File 1.

In practice, the topic did not come up again between the PRS and the PBS. There is no record of cases in which the PRS sued for public performance conducted by way of operating a radio set in a public place. There was no *Hammond's* case tried in Palestine. The explanation is unlikely to be that no infringements took place. To the contrary, we can assume that infringements were widespread. The explanation is more likely to be found in the relationship between the PRS and its local agent, Meir Kovalsky. The latter was excluded from the PRS–PBS deal, to his explicit dismay; hence his motivation to support this scheme was minimal. Moreover, he concentrated on the more basic issues, of simple public performance cases. Embarking on a local version of *Hammond's* was too risky and expensive an avenue for him to undertake. The PRS did learn about some cases in which bands performed music, performances that were then broadcast on the radio, but they were after the band, not after any cafe owner that placed a radio set.[108]

D. Conclusion

The new technology of radio broadcasting finally reached Palestine during the 1930s. The institutional history of the establishment of the Palestine Broadcasting Service reflects the complex political situation in Palestine: a mixture of colonial–governmental interests on the British side, private British interests such as the PRS's, and the British representation of local interests, often painted in orientalist terms. One element of this story was copyright. The British handling of copyright issues did not affect the local legislation, nor did it reach local courts, but it did shape copyright practices.

Conceptualized in the framework of *colonial copyright*, and tracing the legal transplantation process, the story of copyright law and the PBS carries a few important lessons. First, foreign players were the ones that brought up copyright law. In the previous chapter we traced the role of the PRS; in the case of the radio, it was the BBC that triggered the law. Copyright was (again) applied from the outside in a top-down unorganic manner. Second, the legal discussion was conducted as if all parties (the Colonial Office, Jerusalem Government, BBC, and the PRS) were in Britain. But for a short reference to the Copyright Act 1911 that applied in Palestine, the discussion was framed entirely within the legal system of the colonizer. No attention was given to the local advancement of copyright law, the cases that had already been decided in the local courts, or any other local factor.[109] Third,

---

[108] See PRS to Kovalsky (17 June 1937) (pointing him to the PBS's programme, which reported a performance by the Moslem Orphanage Band); Kovalsky to PRS (2 July 1937) (replying that it was a one-time performance for the PBS in favour of the orphans and advising that he thought it unwise to sue the orphans); PRS to Kovalsky (13 July 1937) (agreeing that legal proceedings are not taken, but urging Kovalsky to follow the band). All documents are available at PRS-5.

[109] Yet another example of the first two points is the issue of ownership of works made by PBS employees. The institutional setting familiarized the employees with copyright law. When film and records companies approached the Arab music sub-director, seeking his permission to use his

the discussion reveals the orientalist approach of all British players towards 'native' music, which was a dismissive attitude, especially towards Arab music. The usually dormant Eurocentric character of copyright law became apparent. Fourth, legal questions were hardly asked. The substantial issues were rephrased in other terms, mostly financial ones: 'How much would it cost?' was the common question, rather than 'what is the scope of copyright law?'

This chapter focused on music, but we encountered some references to another kind of content—in news. The BBC kept reminding the other players that Reuters owned the copyright in news bulletins, and that the government should contact Reuters to negotiate the use of the latter's news. But was there copyright in news at all? Once again, a new technology raised new legal questions and challenges, which leads us to the next chapter.

---

compositions, the sub-director asked for the PMG's approval. The latter asked the government secretariat, and referred to the practices in the BBC. The secretariat relied, in its response, on the Copyright Act but nevertheless directed the question to the BBC, through the Colonial Office. See PMG to CS (24 May 1937); CS to PMG (15 June 1937); Officer Administering the Government to Secretary of State (3 July 1937); Secretary of State to the Officer Administering the Government (22 October 1937), all in ISA M354/27 docs 1, 5, 12, 16, respectively. The BBC's answer turned back to the Act. We will encounter another copyright incident of PBS employees, this time suing each other.

9

Telegraphic News

> The notorious fact that Mr Brown has a pink nose or that the Zionist Congress met in Basle for the 1931 session may not be subject to copyright, but the particular form of literary style in which this information is conveyed to a newspaper public is undoubtedly subject to copyright and entitled to protection.
>
> Judge Cressall, 1931.[1]

A. Introduction

In the never-a-dull-moment-Mandate-Palestine, newspapers provided a vibrant public sphere: they reported the events of the day, and played a crucial role in local politics. News was also a business. The late 1920s and early 1930s were a time of technological and commercial changes in the local news market. Telegraph (first landlines and then wireless) became the backbone of the business, carrying messages from news agencies to the newspapers. Readers could notice the bylines in the newspaper, attributing the source of the reports to the agencies, but much more was going on behind the scenes.

The developments culminated in a copyright case that brought everything together: a dispute about ownership of news. The suit was initiated by the Palestine Telegraphic Agency (PTA) joined by the *Palestine Bulletin*, both owned by a Jewish American entrepreneur, Jacob Landau. The defendant was a short-lived, Arab newspaper, *Al Hayat* (Arabic: Life), and its publisher, Adel Jaber. The plaintiffs argued that the newspaper copied telegraphic news which it claimed to own. The suit was brought to court in late 1931, and reached the Supreme Court in early 1933. By the time it ended, both the Bulletin and *Al Hayat* were no longer published; with the growing use of the telephone and the spread of radio, the telegraph was soon to become an obsolete means of transmitting news. Nevertheless, the case set some long lasting copyright principles. Its result was also a new *sui generis* legislation, protecting telegraphic news.

The question of ownership of news was not unique to Palestine. In fact, Palestine was one of the last to address the topic. The most famous case was *International News Service (INS) v Associated Press (AP)*, decided by the American Supreme Court

---

[1] *Palestine Telegraphic Agency v Jaber* (7 November 1931), available at ISA B28153/14 (Smoira Files).

in 1918.[2] The court ruled that news was not protected by copyright law, but it articulated a new doctrine of misappropriation of hot news. In the meantime, other places, many British colonies included, addressed the matter by enacting *sui generis* laws, of the kind enacted in Palestine in 1932, protecting telegraphic news. Importantly, no such law was enacted in the United Kingdom.

The story of telegraphic news, told through the copyright litigation in *PTA v Jaber*, provides another example of the patterns of *colonial copyright*: this time it was not a top-down imposition of the law, but rather a local interpretation of a law (though turning to the imperial law for guidance) and local legislation. Contextualizing the case on the background of the local business, technological, and national interests crystallizes the colonial situation: the regulation of the technology and its related market were subject to the direct interests of the colonial government, in this case, the interest in controlling the flow of information.

We begin with the field of news in Palestine in the early 1930s: the players, their interactions, and the technologies they used. We next encounter the problem of news ownership and the responses elsewhere. This background will enable us to closely examine the *PTA v Jaber* case and its impact.

B. News in Palestine

Like many other aspects of life during the Mandate, the local press was undergoing extensive changes. The number of readers increased in all sectors of the population. Print, cinema, and then radio enabled different channels of disseminating news, each requiring different kinds of preconditions (literacy, access). Following national and language divides, the Jewish and Arab sectors had separate media, but there were some interesting interactions. The telegraph provided such a meeting point, and it turned out to be a conflicting one.

(1) Local press

The Arab press was smaller than its Hebrew parallel, even though the Arab population was much larger than the Jewish one. Literacy rates among Arabs were rather low, although they did increase substantially during the Mandate.[3] The Ottoman censorship (somewhat eased after the 1908 Young Turks Revolution) and the larger Arab cultural centres in Cairo and Damascus, meant that that the Arab Palestinian print industry developed slower than in neighbouring countries. Under the Mandate, beginning in the 1920s there was a substantial growth of the journalistic activity.

Ami Ayalon, who studied the written culture of the Arab population in Palestine, describes some of the features of the local Arab press: newspapers were cheap to

---

[2] 248 US 215 (1918).
[3] Adnan Abu-Ghazaleh, 'Arab Cultural Nationalism in Palestine during the British Mandate' (1972) 1(3) Journal of Palestinian Studies 37.

produce (compared to books), they were printed at small local printers, and most did not last for long.[4] Reading was often a social event rather than the individual reading to which we are accustomed today. Newspapers were read aloud in cafes, which had become a social and cultural centre in towns and villages—at least for men.[5] Later on, when radio emerged, sets were often placed in these cafes.

Journalism was often associated with the cultural and political elite.[6] There were some local journalists and publicists. Another source for the news was other news outlets: copying news was a common practice,[7] which did not go unnoticed. In one of the British government's internal communications discussed below, the Postmaster General commented that 'newspapers published in Egypt reach Palestine the next day and are therefore available for quotation by the local press'.[8]

The British attitude towards the Arab press was quite dismissive. In 1931 the Postmaster General commented that: 'The Average Arab newspaper in this country is not so much a newspaper, as a political pamphlet.'[9] Later on, a British journalist who worked in Palestine was even blunter: 'From a strictly journalistic viewpoint, there is little that can be said in favour of the Arab press. Its main aim seems to have been to incite, rather than to inform. Its strongly worded editorials, however, were widely read and discussed. If Arab editors were no journalists, they certainly were excellent propagandists.'[10]

The 1929 Wailing Wall violent clashes between Arabs and Jews created political waves throughout the region; some of which had cultural implications. One of these was a growing interest in current events, which manifested itself inter alia in an expansion of the Arab press.[11] In 1931, there were two daily newspapers: *Filastin* (Arabic: Palestine), published in Jaffa, and *Al Jami'a al-Islamiya* (Arabic: The Islamist Society), each with several thousand readers.[12]

---

[4] Ami Ayalon, *Reading Palestine: Printing and Literacy, 1900–1948* (University of Texas Press, 2004) 60–1.
[5] A British journalist who worked in Palestine wrote in 1949 that: 'Since only about 40 per cent of the Arabs are literate, it is customary in Arab villages for the men to gather around some literate person in the local coffee house and to listen to the paper being read and expounded.' Leslie John Martin, 'Press and Radio in Palestine under British Mandate' (1949) 26 Journalism Q 186, 187. For the role of the cafe in the cultural lives of the Arabs in Palestine, see Baruch Kimmerling and Joel S Migdal, *Palestinians: The Making of a People* (Harvard University Press, 1993) 48; Ayalon, *Reading Palestine*, ibid, at 103–8; Salim Tamari, 'The Short Life of Private Ihsan' (2007) 30 Jerusalem Q 31, who describes the rise of the cafe culture as a post-World War I phenomenon.
[6] Bayan Nuweihid Al-Hout, 'The Palestine Political Elite during the Mandate Period' (1979) 9(1) Journal of Palestine Studies 85, 103.
[7] Ayalon, *Reading Palestine*, above n 4, at 60.
[8] PMG to CS (3 May 1929) ISA M353/3 doc 12.
[9] PMG to CS (2 April 1931) ISA M353/3 doc 92.
[10] Martin, 'Press and Radio', above n 5, at 187.
[11] Yuval Arnon-Ohanna, *The Internal Struggle within the Palestinian Movement, 1929–1939* (Shiloah Center for Middle East and African Studies, 1981) 197.
[12] Arnon-Ohanna, ibid, at 199. For an overview of Arab press during the Mandate, see Adnan A Musallam, 'Palestinian Arab Press Developments under British Rule with A Case Study of Bethlehem's Sawt al-Shab 1922–1939' available at http://admusallam.bethlehem.edu/bethlehem/Sawt_Al-Shab.htm. For later developments in the Arab press, see Abu-Ghazaleh, 'Arab Cultural Nationalism', above n 3.

This was the background for the appearance of a new daily newspaper, *Al Hayat*, in 1930. It did not last for long, but it was to contribute, unwillingly, to the development of copyright law in Palestine and the local field of news. Its founding publisher was Adel Jaber (1889–1953). He was a member of the local elite: an educator, teaching at the Supreme Muslim Council, where he later became a librarian. After his publishing adventure, he worked for the government as a member of the Central Censorship Board, and then on the board of the Archaeological Advisory Board. In 1939 he was appointed as a council member in Jerusalem's municipality.[13]

Al Hayat was a mid-sized newspaper. At its peak, it reached a circulation of about 1,500, about half the circulation of *Filastin*, the largest Arab newspaper.[14] For the duration of its short existence, it struggled with financial difficulties. *Al Hayat* was not just another newspaper. It was the voice of a new, younger generation with a clear political line, one which was more nationalist than the other newspapers. Until the early 1930s the Arab press was critical of the Jewish immigration and settlement, but usually did not go farther. During 1931, *Al Hayat* became the leading platform of a more critical line: it criticized not only the Zionist project, but also the British Mandate, and harshly so. It offered a pan-Arab vision which was also critical of the mainstream Arab politics, exemplified by the Arab Executive.[15] This nationalist position was a prelude to the Arab Revolt of 1936–9.

Akram Zu'atyir of Nablus and Kheir al-Din al-Zarkali from Syria were active in a new political party, *Istiqlal* (Arabic: Independence). They joined *Al Hayat*. Weldon Matthews concluded that the two managed to control the newspaper in the spring of 1931. Jaber, the publisher, was far more moderate in his politics: he worked for the British government both before and after his publishing venture.[16] Matthews points out that the nationalist political line of *Al Hayat* drew the attention of the British government, which was soon to enhance its censorship.[17] The political line of the newspaper explains its intense interest in Zionist affairs.

Al Hayat ceased to publish in September 1931, following the arrest of Zu'atyir. This timing coincided with *Al Hayat*'s publications about the Zionist Congress,

---

[13] The biographic data was reported with Jaber's 1939 appointment: 'Adel Jaber New JLM. Councillor' (27 July 1939) *Palestine Post*, at 2. Kabha provides some more details: Jaber was born in Jaffa, studied political science and economics in Istanbul and Geneva, and worked for the British Education Department (1918–21). After the 1948 War he resided in Jordan, where he became a member of parliament in 1951. He died in 1953. See Mustafa Kabha, *Journalism in the Eye of the Storm: The Palestinian Press Shapes Public Opinion 1929–1939* (Yad Ben-Zvi, 2004) 22 (Hebrew). Tamari provides some details about Jaber during World War I, describing him as a lawyer and journalist who took a pro-Ottoman position. See Tamari, 'The Short Life', above n 5, at 40, 45.

[14] For the figures, see Kabha, *Journalism*, ibid, at 29; Arnon-Ohanna, *The Internal Struggle*, above n 11, at 200.

[15] See Weldon C Matthews, *Confronting an Empire, Constructing a Nation: Arab Nationalists and Popular Politics in Mandate Palestine* (I B Tauris, 2006) 84–101; Kabha, *Journalism*, above n 13, at 22; Arnon-Ohanna, *The Internal Struggle*, above n 11, at 161–79. For the Istiqlal Party, see also Kimmerling and Migdal, *Palestinians*, above n 5, at 98–101.

[16] Later on, the Istiqlal Party criticized Jaber for his pro-British positions. For example, he participated in the inauguration of the YMCA building in Jerusalem in April 1933, despite Istiqlal's non-cooperation programme. See Matthews, *Confronting an Empire*, ibid, at 182.

[17] Matthews, *Confronting an Empire*, ibid, at 99.

which were at the heart of the copyright case that would follow. The case should be read also on the background of this political context: a Jewish-owned business based on a new technology sued a nationalistic Arab newspaper. The British government had no reason to interfere in such a dispute; it was probably all too happy to see that its interests in silencing the Arab national views were fulfilled by others, through the seemingly innocent tool of copyright law.

The local Hebrew press in the early 1930s was divided along political lines: *Do'ar HaYom* (Hebrew: Daily Mail) was a tabloid, affiliated with the right, Revisionist movement, especially in the late 1920s.[18] *Haaretz* (Hebrew: The Land), was a politically independent paper, with a liberal editorial line.[19] *Davar* (established in 1925) was affiliated with the *Histadrut*—the powerful union and with the leading political party in the Yishuv, *Mapai* (the Labour Party).[20] All three newspapers were Zionist and interested in local events as well as important foreign affairs, especially those relating to Jewish affairs. The Hebrew newspapers were passive bystanders in the current story.

The Hebrew newspapers employed few reporters; official notices were another source of news, as well as foreign newspapers. The Arab press had similar sources, but as of the mid 1920s to the 1930s, the Hebrew press turned to telegraphic news agencies, first the PTA in Palestine, which as of 1929 also distributed Reuters' news, and as of 1934, also PalCor (Palestine Correspondence) run by the Jewish Agency.[21] Foreign news came mostly from Reuters and United Press International.[22]

In the course of the 1930s, foreign radio stations became another important source for news, a matter which was of some concern to the government. The BBC commenced its Empire Service in late 1932, but it did not have its own news production for quite a while, and relied on Reuters. In fact, the BBC's charter explicitly prohibited it from having its own news, so as to protect the financial

---

[18] It was established in 1919 by Eliezer Ben-Yehuda, the reviver of Hebrew, modelled after the English *Daily Mail*. Its circulation saw ups and downs, reaching a peak of 7,000 copies in 1928, and being the most read newspaper for a while. See 'Do'ar HaYom' in *An Encyclopaedic Lexicon for Media and Journalism* (2008) (Hebrew), available at http://www.the7eye.org.il/Lexicon/Pages/Doar_Hayom.aspx; Aharon Even Chen, 'Itamar Ben Avi and "Doar Ha-Yom"' (1987) 1 Qesher 55 (Hebrew).

[19] It was established in 1919, under the name *Hadshot HaAretz* (News of the Land). It suffered frequent economic difficulties, until it was bought in 1937 by Salman Schocken, whom we shall meet again in Ch 10. See Benny Morris, 'Response of the Jewish Daily Press in Palestine to the Accession of Hitler, 1933' (1999) 27 Yad-Vashem Studies 363, 364.

[20] Davar was edited by Berl Katznelson, one of the celebrated ideologists of the Hebrew Labour movement and then the Labour Party. See Historical Jewish Press, 'Davar', available at http://jpress.org.il/publications/davar-he.asp (Hebrew).

[21] Interestingly, there was one predecessor for the practice of receiving news via the telegraph, in Ottoman days. Ouzi Elyada notes that Jerusalem was connected to a telegraph line as early as 1865, but at the time, the cost was too high for daily use, until *HaZvi*, edited by Eliezer Ben-Yehuda, managed to cross this barrier in 1898, and received telegrams from a Turkish news agency. However, when the prices went up, the paper turned to local news. See Ouzi Elyada, 'The Sensational Journalism in Eretz-Israel at the Early Twentieth Century' (1992) 11 Kesher 70 (Hebrew).

[22] Morris, 'Response', above n 19, at 366 (Morris did not mention the official notices). News from Palestine outwards was delivered by the PTA. In 1946, a group of Jewish foreign correspondents established the Central Press News Agency, providing services to Jewish newspapers in Australia, UK, and Canada. See their petition to operate, submitted to the government in January 1946. See ISA M367/4.

interests of news agencies.²³ Towards the inauguration of the service, the Colonial Office circulated a despatch, reminding the colonies of copyright. It recommended, 'as a precaution against unauthorized rebroadcast and reproduction' that listeners' licences include a notice explaining that the licence does not authorize infringements.²⁴ The Palestine Broadcasting Service (PBS) did not have its own news bulletins.

(2) Telegraph and news agencies

The telegraph served a central backbone of Palestine's growing news market. The first lines were built during Ottoman times in the nineteenth century, but they did not survive World War I. The British built new lines, first between Haifa and Jerusalem, and later between Jaffa and Jerusalem. The lines required technical maintenance of the infrastructure. Operating the telegraph required trained staff. An operator had to send the telegram on behalf of the sender, and another operator at the other end of the line had to receive the messages and decipher them. In other words, one could not use the telegraph independently; its technological architecture was a mediated one-to-one technology. In the case of Palestine, the intermediary was the government. Put in economic terms, there were high fixed costs of building the telegraph network and operating it. The users of the service were those that could afford it: the government, repeat players such as Reuters and other businesses, and occasionally individuals.

The introduction of wireless telegraphy challenged the governmental control of the infrastructure, and hence, its control over the content. The government's solution was legal control. The Wireless Telegraphy Ordinance 1924 required a licence in order to operate a wireless station. The licence was to be issued by the High Commissioner, who had full discretion as to the form of the licence, its duration, restrictions, and conditions.²⁵

News agencies were established in Europe and the United States in the nineteenth century. By the time the telegraph was utilized to convey news in Palestine, Associated Press was the leader in the United States, and Reuters was well established in Britain.²⁶ Reuters, the French agency (Havas), and the German agency (Wolff) divided the world into regions of operation. Reuters had the Empire.

---

²³ See Asa Briggs, *The Birth of Broadcasting, 1896–1927* (Oxford University Press, 1995) 130–3. Briggs reports the government's policy, which was that 'no news should be broadcast which had not previously been published in the press', the reason being stated explicitly by the Postmaster General, to prevent competition with news agencies 'as considerable capital is invested in those undertakings and a large amount of Post Office revenue is derived from them' (at 130, quoting the Postmaster General in 1922). The result was that the BBC paid the agencies for the news, which was broadcast only after 7:00 pm, accompanied with a message about the agencies' copyright. Only in 1927 was the BBC allowed to have early news bulletins (at 265).

²⁴ Secretary of State to HC (10 February 1932) ISA M293/8 doc 56.

²⁵ Wireless Telegraphy Ordinance 1924, 2 Laws of Palestine 1543 (Drayton). In at least one reported incident the government applied the Ordinance to close a German telegraphic agency in Jerusalem, in the early 1930s. See Gershon Agron, *The Loyal Rebel* (M Newman Publishing House, 1964) 84 (Hebrew).

²⁶ Graham Storey, *Reuters' Century, 1851–1951* (Parrish, 1951).

Donald Read explains that: 'Within that huge part of the world, Reuter alone had the right to collect and to sell news for the allowed agencies.'[27] The Empire and Reuters had close links. The agency supplied world news throughout the Empire, and conveyed messages from London to its colonies. Read concludes that 'Reuter was ready to employ its news service (sometimes covertly) to assist official policy'.[28] The close relationship served both parties. The Empire had a powerful tool of dissemination of information, and Reuters could trust the government to protect its business interests.

This pattern of relationship was transposed to Palestine. The Mandate government protected Reuters' interests more than once. In 1929 the government agreed to waive the local terminal charges (6.25 centimes per word) for Reuters' use of the lines. That was a substantial subsidy, making it difficult for newcomers to enter the market. Reuters published the government's telegrams, and the government received a few free copies of the news bulletin.[29] Thus, Reuters had a substantial financial advantage over any other potential competitor.

(3) The market of telegraphic news

On top of this physical infrastructure, a complex business superstructure developed.

(a) The Jewish Telegraphic Agency

Jacob Landau had many business endeavours in the market for news. Landau was born in Austria in 1892, and grew up in the United States. He was a sharp entrepreneur, always with an open eye for new business opportunities. During World War I he identified the need for news about the Jewish people in Europe. Jews were spread all over Europe, the United States, South America, Palestine, and elsewhere.[30] Landau figured out that a news agency tailored to Jewish affairs would have a sufficiently viable global market. He embarked on a long career as a journalist mogul with a Jewish mission. The Jewish Telegraphic Agency (JTA) explains today that Landau realized that the 'Jewish People needed its own reliable source of information'.[31]

In 1917, at the age of 25, Landau and a few others established the Jewish Correspondence Bureau in The Hague. It took some years for the agency to

---

[27] Donald Read, 'Reuters: News Agency of the British Empire' (1994) 8(2) Contemporary Record 195–6.

[28] Read, ibid, at 196.

[29] PMG to CS (26 January 1929) ISA M353/3 doc 1; CS to Reuters, Cairo (26 February 1929) ISA M353/3 doc 5.

[30] Between 1904 and 1914, over 1.2 million Jews emigrated from Eastern Europe to other countries, in this order: United States, England, Argentina, France, Canada, South Africa, and Palestine. See Gur Alroey, *Immigrants: Jewish Immigration to Palestine in the Early Twentieth Century* (Yad Ben-Zvi, 2004) 13 (Hebrew).

[31] JTA, 'History', available at http://www.jta.org/about/history.

stabilize, and in 1923 it was renamed the JTA, which still operates to this day.[32] Landau was right: there was a demand for news about Jewish affairs. By the end of the 1920s the JTA had 146 correspondents. An observer at the time noted that it served all Jews, regardless of their attitude towards Zionism or their religious movement or views.[33] By 1933 the JTA provided news to thirty-eight Jewish daily newspapers around the world, and to ninety-one Jewish weeklies, in various languages; through arrangements with other agencies, it claimed to reach more than 4,000 newspapers.[34] It had offices in New York, London, Paris, Berlin, Warsaw, and Jerusalem, and later on also in Prague. As the Nazis came into power the offices shut down: in Berlin (1933), Prague (1938), Warsaw (1939), and Paris (1940).[35]

(b) The Palestine Telegraphic Agency, the Bulletin, and the Post

The JTA's office in Palestine was the Palestinian Telegraphic Agency (PTA). It registered in Palestine in 1923, and began its actual operation in 1925. The PTA was an independent legal entity, though for all practical matters, Landau treated it as a branch of the JTA.[36]

The JTA was proud to announce that 'Palestine is to have its own news agency'. The PTA's coverage was geographic—Palestine—rather than the Jewish criteria of the JTA. The JTA's announcement explained that the PTA was 'to provide a general news gathering service for the Holy Land'.[37] The PTA provided its news to the JTA, which then distributed it to its members. In this sense, as a 1930 commentator explained, 'incidentally, the service [the PTA] was to interpret current events in mediation between the East and the West and thus to help shape the relations between the Jews and the peoples among whom they live'.[38]

In each of the countries in which the JTA operated, it published a local bulletin. The Palestinian version was the *Palestine Bulletin*, which first appeared in January

---

[32] For the history of the JTA, see Verena Dohrn, 'Diplomacy in the Diaspora: The Jewish Telegraphic Agency in Berlin (1922–1933)' (2009) 54(1) Leo Baeck Institute Yearbook 219. For a later personal account of an American Jew who worked with Landau in the 1940s, see Allen Lesser, *Israel's Impact, 1950–1: A Personal Record* (University Press of America, 1984) 123–37.

[33] Victor Rosewater, *History of Cooperative News-gathering in the United States* (D Appleton & Co, 1930) 368.

[34] The figures appear in the JTA's own infomercial, see JTA, 'The Jewish Telegraphic Agency at Work' (16 March 1933) JTA Archive, available at http://archive.jta.org/article/1933/03/16/2798376.

[35] See Dohrn, 'Diplomacy', above n 32, at 241.

[36] The lines between the entities were often blurred to the outside world as well. Landau often used the JTA's letterhead for PTA correspondence and occasionally also vice versa. A scholar, who was a journalist in *Haaretz* during the late Mandate, wrote that the PTA's headquarters was in New York; this probably referred to the headquarters of the JTA. See Haviv Knaan, 'The Hebrew Press in Palestine during the British Government' in Dan Caspi and Yechiel Limor (eds), *Mass Media in Israel: A Reader* (Open University, 1998) 146 (Hebrew).

[37] JTA, 'Palestine News Agency Launched' (9 July 1923) JTA Archive, available at http://archive.jta.org/article/1923/07/09/2755425. See also Alfred McClung Lee, *The Daily Newspaper in America: The Evolution of a Social Instrument* (Routledge/Thoemmes Press, 2000) 542 (describing the general purpose scope of the PTA).

[38] Rosewater, *History of Cooperative Newsgathering*, above n 33, at 369.

1925.[39] It was owned by the PTA. The Bulletin was initially a four-page publication (later six pages) of dense text, published in English and Hebrew.[40] For the first two months, the Bulletin stated that it was 'Published Daily By The Palestine Telegraphic Agency Ltd'. The byline also stated: 'copyright', indicating that the Bulletin—and Landau—were aware of the legal aspects at an early stage. During the Bulletin's first five years, the format remained more or less the same: the first two pages contained foreign telegraphic news, attributed to the PTA. The third page carried local news, without attributing the source. The fourth page was for advertisements.

The Bulletin employed local editors: they decided what would go into the paper and in which order; they edited the telegrams, often combining separate stories into one coherent report. At a later stage, editing turned out to be a crucial point in the litigation. One of the editors was an English barrister who immigrated to Palestine, Edward David Goitein (1900–61). He was with the Bulletin from 1929 to 1931; in 1932 he passed the foreign advocates examination so as to practice law in Palestine.[41] He then quit the press, and joined the law firm of Abacarius Bey, a prominent Arab lawyer, in what was the only Arab–Jewish law firm in Palestine.[42] Bey and Goitein represented the defendant in the PTA's lawsuit. Goitein knew first-hand what the (plaintiff) editors' tasks were.

Another editor was Gershon Agronsky (later: Agron).[43] He was born in Ukraine, and raised in the United States until immigrating to Palestine. Agronsky was involved in several journalistic publications, as an editor for the JTA in New York, as an editor for the *Palestine Weekly*, and as the head of the Press Department of the World Zionist Organization. He joined the Palestine Bulletin as its chief editor.[44]

In March 1932 Landau and Agronsky fell out; Landau instructed that Agronsky cease writing the Bulletin's editorial opinion. Agronsky decided to quit the Bulletin and establish a new English paper. One of his friends commented that Agronsky was determined to ruin the Bulletin.[45] The timing was bad. The news from Germany was daunting. Soon, Hitler became the German Chancellor, and Landau had to close the Berlin office. In the end, Landau and Agronsky worked out their different opinions, and decided to transform the Bulletin into a new newspaper, which they jointly owned. Agronsky was the chief editor. The Bulletin's last edition

---

[39] The JTA's report about its own operation mentioned the Palestine Bulletin, although when it was circulated in March 1933, it was no longer true, as the Bulletin ceased publication three and a half months earlier, and transformed to the *Palestine Post*. See 'The Jewish Telegraphic Agency at Work', above n 34.

[40] The Bulletin is available at the National Library, Jerusalem.

[41] See the *Palestine Bulletin's* report (15 April 1932), at 4.

[42] Gabriel Strassman, *Wearing the Robes: A History of the Legal Profession until 1962* (Israeli Bar Association Press, 1984) 32–3 (Hebrew). Goitein later became the Israeli ambassador in South Africa, and a Justice of the Israeli Supreme Court (1953–61) (at 281–2).

[43] After his long journalistic carrier, he became the mayor of Jerusalem (1955–9).

[44] See his memoires, Agron, *The Loyal Rebel*, above n 25, at 65–6.

[45] The friend was Haim Arlozoroff, a rising star on the Zionist political map, who was assassinated the following year. Arlozoroff's comments are quoted in Agron, *The Loyal Rebel*, above n 25, at 78.

appeared on 30 November 1932 and the *Palestine Post* published its first edition on the following day.[46] The British considered the Post to represent the Yishuv's voice.[47] The Post maintained the close affiliation with the PTA. It published a notice stating that: 'The Palestine Telegraphic Agency is exclusively entitled to all news originating with the Palestine Post.'[48] After the establishment of Israel it changed its name to the *Jerusalem Post*, and runs to this day.

(c) The PTA's business

In 1929, Landau, who was busy expanding his global network, devoted some attention to his activities in Palestine. He wanted to strengthen the PTA's position, and increase revenues. He proceeded in two strategies: concluding a deal with Reuters, and approaching the government for various concessions and preferential treatment.

Reuters had an office in Jerusalem, but without local journalistic activity; the nearest journalistic office was the important Cairo office.[49] The PTA reached an agreement with Reuters: the PTA received the exclusive right to redistribute Reuters' news telegrams in Palestine to local newspapers.[50] Reuters' daily telegram, composed of 125 words, was delivered six days a week. Reuters' caption was to appear on the telegrams. An important condition was that the distribution was to be universal: the PTA had to supply Reuters' telegrams 'without priority, to all newspapers in Palestine at a uniform rate of subscription for daily and weekly newspapers'. To complete the deal, the PTA provided Reuters with news from Palestine.[51]

The agreement was for five years (1929–34), and was then extended for three more years,[52] but in early 1936 the contract was discontinued and was transformed into a covenant not to compete.[53] We can only assume the reason for the discontinuation of the contract: the PBS was about to commence broadcasting, which included news bulletins, based on Reuters' news.

As for the second, governmental strategy, Landau met and corresponded with the Secretary of State in London, and then with the Mandate government's officials. The British realized the importance of the PTA: the Secretary commented about Landau that 'his organisation is of some importance, and in so far as it disseminates news about our good work both in this country and in the United States can be of real help'. But the British were still a bit suspicious about the

---

[46] See Agron, *The Loyal Rebel*, above n 25, at 79.
[47] See Knaan, 'The Hebrew Press', above n 36, at 144.
[48] (4 December 1932), *Palestine Post*.
[49] The Cairo office opened in 1867. See Jack Henry, *Reuters in the Middle East* (A survey of Reuters, Reuter Archive 8412904, 1988).
[50] PTA–Reuters Agreement (20 March 1929) Reuters Archive LN229 1/8712614.
[51] JTA, 'Palestine Telegraphic Agency Concludes Agreement with Reuters" (18 April 1929) JTA Archive available at http://archive.jta.org/article/1929/04/18/2776861. A similar report under the same heading was published in the *Palestine Bulletin* (21 April 1929) ISA M353/3 doc 6.
[52] PTA–Reuters Agreement (6 March 1934) Reuters Archive LN229 1/8712612.
[53] Landau to Reuters (16 March 1936; 17 March 1936) Reuters Archive LN242 1/8714730.

American entrepreneur, as the PTA's reports in Palestine 'have not infrequently sent a good deal of unconfirmed rumour'.[54]

Landau had concrete requests. He first suggested that the government distribute Reuters' news to its administrative districts, using his services. This suggestion was rejected outright: the government refused to allow the repetition of Reuters' news and continued circulating it by post. A second request was that the PTA would enjoy priority in distributing the government's announcements. The government refused to engage in a discriminatory practice.[55]

Landau then offered his services to the government for LP150 per year; reported his recent agreement with Reuters, and wrote that he intended to invest LP2,500 in the *Palestine Bulletin*.[56] He further asked for 'the same facilities as granted to Reuter', namely, the free delivery of telegraphs over the governmental wires. Landau explained: 'I have the most earnest wish to place our service on a high level of efficiency, accuracy and objectivity.' There was yet another bold request, for a *sui generis* legal protection:

May I also submit a request that the Government protect our news service from reprint by newspapers which have no arrangement with us by enacting regulations customary in other countries by which the property right of news is recognized and its republication for a period of 48 hours is prohibited. May I suggest that this period be extended in Palestine to four or five days. In any one language country 48 hours would suffice to render the news valueless, but it is different in Palestine where the population is divided in three different linguistic groups; where cables in a Hebrew of English daily reprinted by an Arab weekly would still be of news value to its readers.

The government contemplated the requests seriously. As for the legislative proposal, the initial (internal) comment was by the Postmaster General, who did not object but for the duration of the protection: 'I can see little reason for extending the period beyond 48 hours. It must be remembered that newspapers published in Egypt reach Palestine the next day and are therefore available for quotation by the local press.'[57] The matter was referred to the Attorney General, who at that time was still Norman Bentwich. He confirmed that there was no legal basis for the protection of news in Palestine, and mentioned that the issue was discussed in a conference of the League of Nations in Geneva in 1927. He drafted an Ordinance according to the conference's recommendations, but placed the draft in his draw. Bentwich decided that the enactment should only be considered if there was a 'considerable demand'.[58] Landau's demand, apparently, was inadequate. The Chief Secretary informed Landau that 'Government are not prepared at present to make regulations for the protection of Press news'.[59] He did not disclose the fact that a draft had been prepared. The draft would remain in the draw for three more years.

---

[54] Secretary of State to HC (12 March 1929) ISA M353/3 doc 8.
[55] PMG to CS (4 April 1929) ISA M353/3 doc 7.
[56] Landau to CS (29 April 1929) ISA M353/3 doc 10.
[57] PMG to CS (3 May 1929) ISA M353/3 doc 12.
[58] A-G to CS (7 June 1929) ISA M353/3 doc 28.
[59] CS to Landau (13 June 1929) ISA M353/3 doc 35.

Telegraphic News 223

Landau's financial requests occupied the government for a while. The Postmaster General suggested that if the government supports the PTA, it should be in the form of payment rather than remission of charges (the charges reached the Post Office, whereas direct payments to the PTA would be made from another department). The Chief Secretary was willing to subsidize Landau's ventures up to the amount of LP100 and waive the terminal charges, subject to the same conditions as applied to Reuters.[60] Landau updated, that he had already undertaken steps to improve his business: he reported that he had hired Goitein to edit the Bulletin, that he had appointed Agronsky to be in charge of the news delivered from Palestine to other places, and that he planned to develop yet another service, the Mid-Eastern News Agency.[61]

There was one problem, though. Jerusalem's response to Landau noted that the Secretary of State should approve the agreement. But the Secretary declined.[62] Landau was furious. 'The communication,' he wrote, 'means a blow to our Agency and even a menace to the continuation of its work.' He further wrote that he relied on the agreement with the government, and entered in an agreement with Reuters.[63] A request for reconsideration was denied.[64] Landau did not give up. The PTA was acting in the name of Reuters, he now explained, and hence it was not asking for a new concession *like* Reuters', it was asking for the *very same* concession that the government had awarded to Reuters.[65] He was again dissatisfied with the negative replies.[66] The PTA then argued that on the basis of the alleged agreement, it concluded agreements with the newspapers. The government was sceptical, and asked to see the contracts with the newspapers.[67]

Correspondence continued, to the growing impatience of the officials. In early 1930 there was a new concern: that without governmental support, the PTA would discontinue its agreement with Reuters to distribute Reuters' news to local newspapers. In such a case, the Chief Secretary warned, the Jewish press might turn to central European news services.[68] In other words, the government had an interest

---

[60] CS to Landau (8 May 1929) ISA M353/3 doc 17.
[61] Landau to CS (10 May 1929) ISA M353/3 doc 19.
[62] Secretary of State to HC (26 July 1929) ISA M353/3 doc 38 ('I do not consider it desirable, on general grounds, to grant special privileges of the kind proposed to a particular agency, and I do not, therefore, see my way to approving the proposals contained in the above-mentioned despatch.').
[63] PTA to CS (22 August 1929) ISA M353/3 doc 45a.
[64] PMG to PTA (11 September 1929) ISA M353/3 doc 47a.
[65] Landau to HC (19 September 1929) ISA M353/3 doc 50.
[66] Landau turned to another strategy: publicly embarrassing the government. *Haaretz* newspaper (not under Landau's control) reported that the government cancelled its concession to the PTA and commented that 'it would appear that the Government of Palestine intends to take charge of the control of the incoming and outgoing news of Palestine'. Quoted in PMG to CS (29 November 1929) ISA 353/3 doc 64a.
[67] See Landau to HC (19 September 1929) ISA M353/3 doc 50; PMG to Acting CS (17 December 1929) ISA M353/3 doc 69. Upon reviewing the contracts, the government was not impressed with the alleged losses. See PMG to CS (10 January 1930) ISA M353/3 doc 75.
[68] CS to PMG (29 January 1930) ISA M353/3 doc 83.

that Reuters continued to be the de facto exclusive foreign news provider for Palestine. The government trusted Reuters and could control it.[69]

Discussions continued during 1931 through 1933. In the meantime, the PTA switched to wireless telegraphy, which was cheaper; newspapers increasingly used the telephone to gather news;[70] soon they would discover yet another source—foreign broadcasting.

(d) Power and control

The discussion thus far introduced us to the players and their interests:

The government had several interests: promoting the progress of the country was a colonial and Mandatory mission, and the introduction of new technologies fitted this mission. But the government's chief interest was to maintain control over the means of communication so as to control the flow of information. It achieved control by its ownership of the telegraph infrastructure, and by the law requiring a licence for wireless telegraphy; it further achieved control by relying on the long-standing close relationship between the Empire and Reuters. Ownership of the technological infrastructure and the friendly partner enabled the government to control the flow of news into the country. To maintain the control, it had to protect Reuters and to assure that all newspapers were treated equally, so to receive the same sources of information.

The governmental interest explains its caution in dealing with Landau. The government had less control over the PTA. It was an American business, newer than Reuters, and it was Jewish. The PTA's agreement with Reuters aligned the two together, and assured that the main source of news in Palestine remained Reuters.

Reuters had substantial power in the local media field, as it had the exclusive and free use of the telegraph lines which it successfully leveraged to the contract with the PTA. As in other places in the Empire, the government's interests converged with Reuters'. Reuters also had exclusivity over news on the radio, extending its British power over the BBC to the PBS (in 1936).

The PTA and Landau had commercial interests. As we saw, Landau tried everything he could to increase his power: seeking governmental concessions (unsuccessful), exclusivity with the government (unsuccessful), exclusivity from Reuters (successful), and self-interested protective legislative proposals (materialized only later on). Nevertheless, he had quite a powerful position: the PTA received news from Reuters and the JTA, and provided news about Palestine through these

---

[69] Later on, the PTA (on a JTA letterhead) asked Reuters to discontinue the service, citing the Mandate government's position. JTA to Reuters (6 March 1931) ISA M353/3 doc 90a. Reuters was quick to write to the HC (12 March 1931) ISA M353/3 doc 90. However, the PMG was not impressed: he considered it to be the same request for concession in a new guise. PMG to CS (2 April 1931) ISA M353/3 doc 92.

[70] PMG to CS (11 August 1932) ISA M353/3 doc 138; HC to Secretary of State (22 September 1932) ISA M353/3 doc 152. Agron reported the use of the telephone in the *Palestine Post*, eg in reporting riots in Syria. Agron, *The Loyal Rebel*, above n 25, at 83. In 1934 journalists petitioned the government to provide them with telephone lines, emphasising the importance of the telephone to their work. ISA M354/3.

channels; he owned the *Palestine Bulletin*, the only daily newspaper in English in Palestine, and then co-owned the *Palestine Post*.

One player was absent from this picture: the local population. Not only wasn't the impact of the regulation of the news market on free speech considered, the motivation of the parties was to increase their control of the technological infrastructure and the channels of dissemination so as to control the content. The Mandate government was not a democratic one. The ideas of free press and free speech were yet to enter the local discourse.

C. News in the Courts

The expanding local market of news, the introduction of wireless telegraphy, broadcast, telephone, and the mix of interests of all those involved, meant that each party tried to shape the field using whichever tools it had at its disposal. The government had legislative and executive powers; Reuters and the BBC relied on their British affiliation; the PTA lobbied. Each made commercial, political, and at times proprietary arguments. It was time for a new avenue, copyright litigation. The issue was ownership of news.

(1) Owning news

The legal debates about the protection of news contributed much to shaping modern copyright law around the world. Here is the crux of the legal problem: news is composed of facts about current events. Bare facts are not the independent original creation of any person or entity, but gathering the facts, editing them, presenting the news report, and distributing it, requires the investment of labour and costs. Thus, the case of news presents a challenge for copyright law, of defining the contours of its subject matter: what does it take for the news to become a proper subject matter of copyright law? Is the investment of labour sufficient? What is the original contribution of the journalist (or the editor or the newspaper) that turns unprotected bare facts into a copyrightable expression?

In the United States, during the nineteenth century, it became a common practice for newspapers to copy from one another.[71] The practice was indirectly supported by the government, which subsidized the postal distribution of newspapers.[72] Robert Brauneis explains that the practice enabled newspapers to have a broader pool of sources. The newspapers were not in competition with one another, as all had local readership. A newspaper in New York did not compete with a newspaper in San Francisco. Even if there was such competition, perhaps between newspapers in closer cities, it was minimized by the lead time: a newspaper could copy from another only after the first had already published the news, and

---

[71] Robert Brauneis, 'The Transformation of Originality in the Progressive-Era Debate over Copyright in News' (2009) 27 Cardozo Arts & Ent L J 321, 323.
[72] Brauneis, ibid.

after the physical copy of the first newspaper reached the second.⁷³ Another explanation is that a property right, had there been one, would have been difficult to enforce.⁷⁴

The arrival of the telegraph and its commercial use in the mid-nineteenth century shortened both the distance and the lead time. The technology eliminated the physical barriers: those who had previously cooperated with one another now became competitors. A new business model emerged: news agencies, building on the new, nationwide gathering and distribution channels. AP was established in 1848. Those who invested the time and money in gathering the news had a clear interest in controlling their news. Otherwise, their entire business model would be undermined: if a non-subscribing newspaper could copy the news from a subscribing paper (without authorization), no one would subscribe and the service would not be able to recoup its costs.

The legal challenge was how to enable a viable market while not limiting the diffusion of news. It soon became clear that copyright law would not protect news as such. The facts about the events of the day were not original, in the copyright sense of the term. The first attempt to solve the problem was by amending the legislation. An 1884 bill, backed by AP, drew much attention and raised a public discussion, but it did not become law.⁷⁵ A second attempt was through litigation. A series of cases followed—but failed. For example, in 1902 the Court of Appeals for the seventh Circuit found that: 'It is inconceivable that the copyright grant of the constitution, and the statutes in pursuance thereof, were meant to give a monopoly of narrative to him, who, putting the bare recital of events in print, went through the routine formulae of the copyright statutes.'⁷⁶

The judicial engagement with property in news culminated in the famous *INS v AP* case, decided by the US Supreme Court in 1918. The facts of the case are well known: INS copied news from newspapers which were AP's subscribers. INS then transmitted the news to its own subscribers. In some cases, such as transmitting the news from the east to the west coast, INS eliminated the lead time of the subscribing newspapers. This standard understanding of the case, as an unauthorized taking between two competing news agencies,⁷⁷ has recently been challenged. Douglas Baird argued that it is better understood as a case about the regulation of a natural monopoly: the high fixed costs of building a network of (physical) telegraph lines

---

⁷³ Ibid, at 339–40.
⁷⁴ Ibid, at 339.
⁷⁵ Ibid, at 351–9.
⁷⁶ *National Telegraph News Co v Western Union Telegraph Co* 119 F 294, 297 (7th Cir 1902). At stake was a subscriber of a telegraph news service, who received the messages through a ticker machine, and redistributed them. The court concluded that it was a service rather than authorship (at 299). Nevertheless, the court articulated a self-defined precedential equitable remedy, and affirmed the injunction against the redistribution of the news.
⁷⁷ The Supreme Court noted that: 'The parties are in the keenest competition between themselves in the distribution of news throughout the United States', *INS v AP*, 248 US, at 230.

rendered the landline telegraph such a monopoly. The legal rivalry, he argues, was concocted.[78]

The Supreme Court took it for granted that: 'Complainant's news matter is not copyrighted.'[79] The majority, however, proceeded to create a new common law tort: misappropriation of hot news. The tort was framed as a matter of unfair competition: 'What we are concerned with is the business of making [news] known to the world, in which both parties to the present suit are engaged.'[80] It was not a property rule that operated against the world at large: it was applied only between the rival parties 'as between them, it [the news] must be regarded as quasi property'.[81] Thus, it was a liability-based tort.

In years to come, *INS v AP* was much criticized for its dubious foundations and for its limitation of free speech.[82] The powerful dissent of Justice Louis Brandeis, stated that: 'The general rule of law is, that the noblest of human productions—knowledge, truths ascertained, conceptions, and ideas—become, after voluntary communication to others, free as the air to common use.'[83] Recently, there has been a fresh argument, explaining the misappropriation tort in a brighter light. Shyamkrishna Balganesh explains that misappropriation is the result of the meeting point of the law of unjust enrichment and the common law doctrine of unfair competition.[84] Balganesh emphasizes the high costs of gathering news. Under such circumstances, free riding would be an obstacle to the collective model of news gathering by news agencies. Thus, he presents the misappropriation doctrine as a tailored, proportional measure that was meant to obliterate free riding, and that was meant to encourage cooperative models.

In the United Kingdom, *sui generis* legislation also failed.[85] The issue of copyright in news reached the courts. A first precedent was set in 1892, in the case of *Walter v Steinkopff*, later also cited by the Palestinian Supreme Court.[86] At stake was *St James' Gazette's* copying of two-fifths of an article by Rudyard Kipling, published in *The Times* on that same day, and twenty-two other articles, though the dispute was narrowed to fewer articles, due to lack of sufficient copyright formalities. The court stated that whereas there might be no copyright in news, there may be copyright in the particular mode of expression. The court further rejected the

---

[78] Douglas G Baird, 'The Story of INS v. AP: Property, Natural Monopoly, and the Uneasy Legacy of a Concocted Controversy' in Jane C Ginsburg and Rochelle Cooper Dreyfuss (eds), *Intellectual Property Stories* (Foundation Press, 2006) 9.

[79] *INS v AP*, 248 US, at 233.

[80] Ibid, at 235.

[81] Ibid, at 236.

[82] Yochai Benkler, 'Free As the Air to Common Use: First Amendment Constraints on Enclosure of the Public Domain' (1999) 74 NYU L Rev 354.

[83] 248 US, at 250 (Brandeis J, dissenting).

[84] Shyamkrishna Balganesh, '"Hot News": The Enduring Myth of Property in News' (2011) 111 Colum L Rev 419.

[85] Lionel Bently, 'Copyright and the Victorian Internet: Telegraphic Property Laws in Colonial Australia' (2004) 38 Loy LA L Rev 71, 169–70.

[86] [1892] 3 CD 489.

defendants' reliance on a custom of copying amongst newspapers.[87] Unlike the United States, courts did not construct a common law tort.

The challenges raised by the new technologies also troubled other jurisdictions. In the Empire, the first to address these challenges were the Australian colonies. Following petitions of large local newspapers, a series of laws was enacted beginning in the 1870s in some of these colonies (but not all).[88] The laws, though criminal rather than civil, provided the first newspaper to print news which originated from a telegraphic message, with the power to prohibit others from publishing the same news, for a limited time. Thus, the initial lead time that was eliminated by the telegraph, was recreated by the laws. The Australian laws served as a model for at least ten other colonies over the years. As we shall see later, Palestine was second to last in this line, enacting a Telegraphic Press Message Ordinance in 1932, followed only by Kenya, in 1934.

Yet other countries had specific references to news, either excluding it from protection, or subjecting it to specific conditions. Interestingly, the Ottoman Authors' Rights Act 1910 (no longer valid in Palestine, but still valid in neighbouring Trans-Jordan), allowed copyright in news articles, as long as they were accompanied with a copyright notice.[89]

Thus, by the time the issue of ownership of news reached Palestine, there were at least three legal models to address it: no protection for the facts but only for the original expression thereof (United Kingdom); *sui generis* laws (the Australian model), or a common law tort (United States).

(2) Litigation strategy

In the meantime, in 1931, Jacob Landau spotted a weak link in his Palestinian business: the local Arab newspapers. They did not subscribe to his PTA–Reuters service. The governmental refusal to subsidize his business meant that he could not afford to turn a blind eye to those who avoided licensing. Landau now turned to litigation. He learnt that the Arab newspapers copied news from the *Palestine Bulletin*, news which originated from the PTA. He hired a lawyer, Kalman Friedenberg, whom we met as the first lawyer of the foreign performing rights societies (Chapter 7).

We do not know who came up with the idea to go to court:[90] Landau was surely familiar with the idea of property in news from his business elsewhere. Friedenberg had already had some copyright experience. He already knew that litigation was an efficient tool to convince reluctant users to join the licensing scheme.

Their first litigation decision was to choose the PTA to be the plaintiff: that was where Landau's commercial interests were. He was interested in expanding the

---

[87] Ibid, at 499–500.
[88] Bently, 'The Victorian Internet', above n 85, at 75.
[89] Authors' Rights Act 1910, s 4. See Ch 4 for discussion of the Act.
[90] Friedenberg's files were not kept; Landau's office in New York was destroyed by fire, see Dohrn, 'Diplomacy', above n 32; the *Palestine Post's* offices were destroyed by a bomb in 1948.

number of licensees to the telegraphic news service. But shortly into the litigation, it was clear that the Palestine Bulletin, the newspaper that edited and printed the telegraphic news, was a better plaintiff. Landau considered both to be one commercial entity, but legally, they were separate. With the judge's permission, the Bulletin was added as a second plaintiff.

A second decision was to choose the defendant. *Al Hayat* was an easy target. It was a new newspaper, not yet well established; due to its nationalist editorial line, it did not enjoy the government's support, which otherwise might have interfered, for example by not allowing a private criminal procedure. Finally, there was clear evidence of copying. *Al Hayat* published stories about the Zionist Congress that convened in Basle in July 1931. Given the available sources of the local newspapers, such a story could be obtained only from the PTA, probably through the JTA. The stories were translated into Arabic without authorization.

The defendants were Jaber, the publisher, and two other editors, Khaleed Douzdar and Kahir Eddir el-Zarkali.[91] They were represented by the law firm of Abacarius Bey, who litigated the case in the magistrate phase and the first appeal to the district court. In the second appeal, to the Supreme Court, David Goitein, appeared on behalf of the defendants.

A third pre-litigation decision was the procedure. In his first copyright litigation, *GEMA v Zion Theatre*, Friedenberg opted for the criminal avenue. He explained that it enabled him to bypass the tricky issue of proving ownership in the musical works that were publicly performed by the theatre. In the PTA case, ownership turned to be a decisive one. Nevertheless, perhaps a bit traumatized by the critical comments of GEMA and the PRS on his first case, Friedenberg decided not to take chances. He brought both criminal charges and a civil action.

(3) Judgments

(a) *The magistrate court*

The case landed with Judge Cressall, the British magistrate in Jerusalem. We do not have the courts' documents, other than the decisions in the case gathered from different archives.[92] Based upon the defendants' consent, the judge tried the criminal and civil cases together. Later on, the Court of Appeals was not impressed with this joint procedure and quashed the criminal conviction.

Abacarius Bey had a preliminary argument: that the Copyright Act was invalid, as it was not duly published in an official publication. Recall that the copyright

---

[91] This was the spelling in the court's decision. It is quite likely misspelled. Zarkali is probably Kheir al-Din al-Zarkali.

[92] See the two Magistrate's decisions: *Palestine Telegraphic Agency v Jaber* (9 October 1931), published in the Palestine Bulletin (11 October 1931) (hereafter: PTA-1), and the final judgment of 7 November 1931, published in part in the *Palestine Bulletin* (9 November 1931), with the additional sections that were edited out of the Bulletin's publication, available at ISA B28153/14 (Smoira Files) (hereafter: PTA-2); the district court's decision: CA 236/31 *Palestine Telegraphic Agency v Jaber* (not dated) CZA JAS/1 (hereafter: PTA-3); the Supreme Court's decision: CA 66/32 *Palestine Telegraphic Agency v Jaber* [1933] 1 PLR 780 (hereafter: PTA-4).

legislation in Palestine was composed of two pieces of legislation. The first was the 1911 Imperial Copyright Act, which was extended to Palestine in 1924 by the King's Order in Council. The extending Order was published in Palestine's Official Journal and promulgated by the High Commissioner, but the extended Act itself, the 1911 Act, was not published. The second piece of legislation was the Copyright Ordinance 1924. It was a local enactment by the High Commissioner. It dealt with customs and with the criminal aspects of copyright. The Ordinance was published in the Official Journal.

The judge handed down a separate ruling on the validity of the Act.[93] He discussed at length the different kinds of legislation, and concluded that the 1911 Act conferred on the King the power to extend the Act to countries under British protection; the extending orders were Orders in Council, which had the force of an Act of Parliament. These, did not require promulgation to become effective, and they applied as of the date of royal assent, or as of the date mentioned in the Order itself. The road was paved to discuss the substantive issue.

According to one news report, the judge heard some witnesses: the head of the PTA's office in Jerusalem, and one of the Bulletin's employees.[94] The following month, the judge delivered the judgment on the merits of the case. A first factual finding was straightforward: that in some cases, *Al Hayat* translated the stories that appeared in the Bulletin or published colourable imitations thereof. A second factual finding was crucial: the Bulletin did not print the PTA's telegrams in their original form. Rather, the Bulletin edited the telegrams, applying judgment and skill, and produced the stories in a form fit for publication. The editing included printing a 'definite literary style, divided into paragraphs'. The judge further found that *Al Hayat* copied the latter, namely from the Bulletin, to which it had access, rather than the original PTA telegrams.

Legal analysis followed, based on the definitions of the 1911 Act and on English case law: copyright subsists in every original work (section 1); the author of the work is the first owner thereof (section 5); copyright means the right of preventing all others from copying a published literary work.[95] The term 'copyright' means, the judge summarized, 'the statutory right of preventing the appropriation of the labours of an author by another'. Applying the doctrine to the case, the legal conclusion was that the PTA did not establish the infringement of its own copyright, as the defendant did not copy its telegrams, but rather the defendant copied the Bulletin's reports. The news was utilized, the judge found, only after it had been '"dressed" and put into the language and literary style of the Palestine Bulletin'.

But did the PTA have rights in the news, in their bare form? The judge replied in the negative: 'news, as such, may not be the subject of copyright, protection is given to, and can be demanded for, the particular form of language or modes of

---

[93] PTA-1.
[94] 'Law Suit of Jewish PTA against *Al Hayat*' (24 October 1931) *Filastin* (Arabic).
[95] The English cases cited were *Jeffrey v Boosey* [1854] 4 HLC 920; *Walter v Steinkopff*, 69 LT 87 (1892); *Walter v Lane* [1900] AC 550.

expression by which information is conveyed to the public'. He illustrated and elaborated:

> The notorious fact that Mr Brown has a pink nose or that the Zionist Congress met in Basle for the 1931 session may not be subject to copyright, but the particular form of literary style in which this information is conveyed to a newspaper public is undoubtedly subject to copyright and entitled to protection. This is based on the principle that where independent labour has been exercised in producing literature which, although derived from facts common to all is the result of mental exertion, such composition is regarded as 'original', and is entitled to the protection of the Act.

The application of the legal principles to the facts meant that *Al Hayat* engaged in 'literary larceny', but the Bulletin was the author and owner of the original literary works, rather than the PTA. The judge went on to explain the legal rules that applied to the journalistic field: the use of articles for the purpose of review or criticism is allowed, but the unauthorized copying from another newspaper is illegal; a universal custom of copying, often asserted by newspapers, does not justify taking something one is not entitled to.

The defence further argued that the damages sought were not sufficiently specified. The lawyer pointed to the Ottoman procedural law that was still valid, and applied to the Mandate's judicial proceedings. But the judge concluded that the Mejelle (the Ottoman civil code) related to contract. Copyright, he stated, was a matter of tort.

Taking into account that *Al Hayat* did not directly compete with the Bulletin, due to the language differences and the delay in publication—the copied stories appeared a day after the Bulletin's publication—the judge ordered damages of LP10. The judge refused to issue an injunction: the law did not authorize him to do so; only the district court had the power to issue an injunction. Finally, Jaber was convicted in the criminal charges, and fined by the sum of 100 mils (LP1 had 1000 mils). The two editors were acquitted, as they did not have sufficient knowledge of copying.

(b) The district court

Both Jaber and the PTA appealed to the district court in Jerusalem in late 1931. The appeals were heard in January 1932.[96] Jaber's appeal was against both the civil judgment and the criminal conviction. The PTA appealed against losing its copyright. Importantly, the Bulletin did not appeal—it had nothing to appeal against. The panel was a mixed one, with a British judge residing (de Freitas), a Jewish judge (Valero), and an Arab judge (Majid).

The civil appeal focused on two legal points: the validity of the 1911 Act in Palestine and the unspecified damages. As for the first argument, Bey relied on the Palestine Order-in-Council 1922 and on Ottoman law. The court dismissed the

---

[96] See PTA-3, and a news report about the hearing indicates that it took place in January 1932. See 'Appeal in the Copyright Case' (20 January 1932) *Haartez* (Hebrew).

Ottoman source, as it was no longer in force in Palestine. The Order-in-Council required publications of local ordinances, not of British enactments. The extending Order in Council 1924, which applied the Imperial Copyright Act to Palestine was published and proclaimed by the High Commissioner, as required. However, the court did recommend that the government publish the 1911 Act. As we saw in Chapter 4, such publication took another two years to materialize. The issue of specification of damages was more difficult. The Magistrates' Court Jurisdiction Act limited the jurisdiction of those courts to cases in which the damages claimed did not exceed LP100. However, the Copyright Act allowed plaintiffs to obtain an account of profits. The district court sided with the magistrate court, without elaborating. Jaber's criminal conviction was quashed, due to the wrong tying of the civil and criminal proceedings.

The PTA's appeal was dismissed. The judges did not elaborate, but they did quote from the Empire Dijest (sic), the headnote about a copyright case in New Zealand (without further details): a newspaper copied a news agency's telegrams, first published in another newspaper. The summary of the New Zealand case was that 'as the property had merely a prospective existence there could be no copyright in it'. The judges added nothing more to explain how this applied to the PTA case.

Thus, the decision in the appeal was mostly formalistic, discussing the procedural issues, and not delving at all into the copyright questions.

(c) The Supreme Court

The President of the district court allowed an appeal to the Supreme Court regarding three questions of law: ownership of the copyright in news published by licence of a telegraphic agency in a newspaper, standing to sue, and the question of injunction.[97] Thus, the issues of the validity of the law, the joining of the civil and criminal procedures, and the specification of damages were no longer disputed. The Supreme Court heard the case in January 1933, and announced its decision on that same day.[98] The panel was once again a mixed one, with the British Chief Justice (McDonnell) residing, along the Jewish (Frumkin), and Arab (Khayat) justices.

Only the PTA appealed, arguing that it owned the copyright rather than the Bulletin. Jaber did not dispute his civil liability (he had no leave to do so). He was the respondent in the case, but once the permission to appeal was limited to the above questions, Jaber was for all matters, a neutral bystander; neither did the Bulletin appeal (it was not even listed as a respondent).

To an outsider, it might seem like a battle between the PTA and the Bulletin, but both were under the same ownership. So what was going on there? Why was it important for the PTA to insist that it was the owner of the news, rather than its sister company that owned the Bulletin? By the time the appeal was discussed, the

---

[97] PTA-4.
[98] PTA-4. That the decision was given on the same day is inferred from a report in *Haaretz*, *The PTA's Appeal in the Copyright Case* (5 January 1933) *Haaretz*.

Bulletin no longer existed; it was transformed into the *Palestine Post*. The PTA was not after the LP10 that the Bulletin won—in any case the damages reached the same pocket. The PTA sought a legal principle: that a news agency owns copyright in the news, rather than the newspapers that received and edited the bare facts.

It was a peculiar setting. Imagine the courtroom: Jaber's lawyer in the appeal was Goitein. He had little to say on behalf of his client at that point, but he himself was there. Goitein was an editor at the Bulletin prior to joining the law office of Abacarius Bey. He was with the Bulletin in 1931, at the time of the publications at stake. It is not unlikely that he himself edited some of the stories that his client, Jaber, copied. The PTA argued, nevertheless, that it, rather than the Bulletin, owned the copyright.

The judges delivered a one paragraph decision. They relied on the lower courts' factual findings, that the Bulletin edited the news it received from the PTA. The judges quoted the English 1892 case of *Walter v Steinkopff*: 'There is or may be copyright in the particular forms of language or modes of expression by which information is conveyed, and not the less so because the information may be with respect to the current events of the day.'[99] The result was that the Bulletin was the owner of the copyright at stake. The court, having answered the first two questions of the appeal, declined to address the third question about injunctions.

Thus, the PTA case articulated several fundamental legal principles. First and foremost, was the fact/expression dichotomy: copyright law provides protection only to original expressions but not to bare facts. Second, the courts indicated their understanding of the requirement of originality. The magistrate court said the most about this point. The investment of independent labour in editing and styling the facts, gave rise to the copyright in the published reports. We do not know what exactly the editors at the Bulletin did with the raw material. The magistrate judge wrote that they 'dressed' the facts, but we do not know how much labour or creativity they invested. These were difficult questions at the time and remain so today: the meaning of originality in copyright law is still much debated in Israel and elsewhere.[100]

Unlike the US Supreme Court in *INS v AP*, none of the courts searched for non-statutory sources of protection. Constructing common law principles such as the misappropriation doctrine was completely out of question. The Palestinian courts were British in their jurisprudence. The courts understood the law as a closed set of rules, and their judicial role as a limited one—to interpret statutory law. A judicial creation of a non-statutory tort would simply be implausible at the time.

The procedural legal conclusion about the lack of power to issue an injunction, left undecided by the Supreme Court, was an important one. It endured well into the future: for decades Palestinian, and then Israeli plaintiffs in intellectual property cases, had either to sue in the district court and petition for an injunction, or split

---

[99] PTA-4, quoting *Walter v Steinkopff* [1892] 3 CD 489, 495. The judges omitted the beginning of the paragraph, which stated: 'It is said that there is no copyright in news. But there is...'.
[100] See eg Michael Birnhack, 'Originality in Copyright Law and Cultural Control' (2002) 1 Aley Mishpat 347 (Hebrew).

their cases and sue for damages in the magistrate court, and for an injunction in the district court.[101]

It is also interesting to compare the kind of discourse applied in the case: we do not know how Friedenberg phrased his arguments, but we did see the arguments of Abacarius Bey: he placed much emphasis on procedural issues and relied more than once on Ottoman law. The court, however, replied in substantive rather than procedural statements, and with citing English rather than Ottoman authorities. The law was shifting more and more towards the English colonial system, away from the previous legal system. The process of receiving the legal transplant of *colonial copyright* advanced one step further.

To complete the picture, we should note that perhaps naturally, the local press, in all languages, reported the case.[102] The reports were informative, and in some cases included large sections of the judgments. No legal or other commentary on the case was found.

D. The Impact of the Case

By the time the Supreme Court delivered its opinion, *Al Hayat* had already closed down, and the *Palestine Bulletin* was replaced with the *Palestine Post*. A new law was enacted, protecting telegraphic news. Arab newspapers now subscribed to the PTA's services. There are no reports of further copyright litigation regarding news, but nevertheless, unauthorized copying continued. In 1938 the Secretary of State circulated a confidential despatch among the colonies, asking about the dissemination of British news.[103] The High Commissioner replied that: 'Only three of the Jewish and none of the Arab daily newspapers take and pay for [Reuters'] service, though certain organs are suspected of making piratical use of Reuters news, from both British and Palestine Broadcasting Services.'[104] The

---

[101] Only in 2003 did the Knesset, the Israeli Parliament, amend the law so to authorize the district court to adjudicate intellectual property cases even if the damages sought are within the lower court's jurisdiction, thus allowing a unified damages and injunction case. Courts Act [Consolidated Version] 1984, s 40(4).

[102] See eg 'Appeal in the Copyright Case' (20 January 1932) *Haartez* (Hebrew); 'Ownership of Copyright' (5 January 1933) *Palestine Post*. The JTA also reported the case: 'Copyright Act in Palestine: Palestine Telegraphic Agency Wins Important Case against Arab Paper' (31 October 1931) JTA Archive, available at http://archive.jta.org/article/1931/10/31/2792191. *Al Hayat* did not live to report its own case, but other Arab newspapers reported it, *Filastin* being the most popular one. See 'Delay in the Law Suit of the PTA against Al Hayat' (10 October 1931) *Filastin*, at 5 (Arabic); 'The Royal Act is Valid, Al Hayat Litigation' (13 October 1931) *Filastin*, at 6 (Arabic); 'The Law Suite of the Jewish PTA against Al Hayat' (24 October 1931) *Filastin*, at 7 (Arabic); 'The PTA and Al Hayat' (31 October 1931) *Filastin*, at 6 (Arabic).

[103] The first question was about Reuters' news. The entire confidential file reached Reuters at the time, leaving us with the safe conclusion that Reuters was behind the survey.

[104] HC to Secretary of State (21 March 1938) Reuters Archive LN733 1/970123, 5312/B/38 doc 21. Of the other colonies that responded and mentioned copyright, Gibraltar and Mauritius mentioned that Reuters' news was reproduced by the press without authorization (see docs 36, 43 respectively).

response indicates that the field has once more changed following the introduction of a new technology: broadcast.

(1) Statutory protection for telegraphic news

In November 1932, while the PTA's appeal in the Supreme Court was still pending, the government published a draft of the Telegraphic Press Message Ordinance. It became law on 28 December 1932, a week before the Supreme Court decided the appeal.[105] The Supreme Court did not mention the Ordinance, but we can assume that it saved the judges the need to contemplate a local common law doctrine.

The Ordinance protected telegraphic news originating from news agencies for seventy-two hours after their first publication in a local newspaper. Although it was a criminal law, the Ordinance deposited the power to allow a second publication in the hands of the newspaper that received the message lawfully from the news agency. The Ordinance allowed the publication of similar news messages that were received in a lawful manner (section 3(b)); the protection was accorded only if the first published message included a heading about the telegraphic source (section 3(c)); transmitting the telegraphic message for the purpose of publication was also was prohibited (section 4); there were evidentiary presumptions (section 5), and finally, penalties (up to LP20 fine for the first conviction; LP50 for subsequent convictions) (section 6).

No evidence regarding back office legislative procedures were found. There was no legislature in Palestine; all work was done by the government, occasionally after consulting an advisory board. Unlike Australia or America, there was no public debate about the bill.[106] The draft was published, and a month later it became law. We have some external indications about the process: Landau's 1929 petition, indicating the private initiative; the government's 1929 internal discussions, and Bentwich's draft of an Ordinance, indicating familiarity with the topic. The JTA reported that: 'The new law has been issued after consultation with the Jewish Telegraphic Agency here, and the Palestine Hebrew and Arab Press.' The report also summarized the PTA case, indicating the connection between the two.[107]

There was no law that could be extended from the motherland to Palestine. The informal colonial network was at work: the *sui generis* telegraphic news laws that began in the Australian colonies in the 1870s spread throughout the Empire in a horizontal manner, copied by colonies from one another rather than imposed by London. Palestine was the sixteenth territory to have a telegraphic news law.[108]

---

[105] 2 Laws of Palestine 1404 (Drayton).

[106] See in Australia: Bently, 'The Victorian Internet', above n 85, at 108–25; in the United States: Brauneis, 'The Transformation', above n 71, at 352–9.

[107] 'Copyright in Palestine; Important News Protection Law Promulgated' (2 December 1932) JTA Archive, available at http://archive.jta.org/article/1932/12/02/2796834.

[108] For this feature of the telegraphic press laws, see Bently, 'The Victorian Internet', above n 85, at 167–8; Lionel Bently, 'The "Extraordinary Multiplicity" of Intellectual Property Laws in the British Colonies in the Nineteenth Century' (2011) 12 Theoretical Inq L 179–81. Kenya was the last country

In its contents, the Ordinance was similar to the colonial laws, with minor changes: it included telegrams transmitted from within Palestine, and excluded broadcast.[109]

One element of the Ordinance turned out to be particularly important. The Ordinance protected telegraphic news 'other than a message which is broadcast for general public reception' (section 2). In other words, the Ordinance was technology-based.[110] This technology specificity was soon to render the Ordinance obsolete, as newspapers copied broadcast matter rather than telegraphic messages. The Ordinance was subject to judicial interpretation only once, in Israeli courts in the early 1980s.[111] It is still valid law in Israel, though a dead letter it is.

(2) Broadcast vs telegraph

The problem just mentioned, of the Ordinance protecting the telegraphic news agencies in a technology-based manner, was noticed at the time of its enactment. As the new law was set in place, a newer technology arrived, once again shuffling the cards in the field of news gathering: radio. By 1933, those who owned or had access to one of the 1,300 radio sets in Palestine,[112] could tune in to the BBC Empire Service, where they could listen to Reuters' news, or they could also tune in to other radio stations, including those from less friendly countries such as the Soviet Union, Germany, and later Italy. This was no minor development. It reflected a trend which is as relevant for the twenty-first century: globalization. The technology of broadcasting defied national borders. It was less controllable than the telegraph. The government did require users to have a licence for their radio set, but it was unable to control what they did with the set, other than the pre-tuned sets which the government itself distributed to the villages.

The shift from the local telegraphy to the global radio meant that the business models of some of those involved were threatened. Let us return to Agronsky in early 1933, shortly after he established the *Palestine Post*. He tried to bypass the PTA–Reuters monopoly by using the BBC's news, only to find out that Reuters

known to have such a law. Unlike the Palestinian Ordinance, the Kenyan Act did not exclude broadcast; the protection there lasted for eighty-four hours. See Telegraphic Press Messages Act 1934, 14 Laws of Kenya, C 512.

[109] Bently listed eight characteristics of the Australian telegraphic news legislations, see Bently, 'The Victorian Internet', above n 85, at 72–3.

[110] See Bently's discussion regarding the Australian telegraphic news legislations, Bently, 'The Victorian Internet', above n 85, at 175.

[111] CA 361/80 *ITIM v Nathan* 38(2) PD 154 (1983). ITIM, an Israeli news agency, sued Avraham (Abie) Nathan, a well-known peace activist who founded and managed the Voice of Peace, a radio station that broadcast from an offshore boat. The Voice of Peace transmitted the news broadcasts of the Voice of Israel. ITIM argued that the VoI's news bulletins included its own news, hence the retransmission violated the Ordinance. The Israeli Supreme Court interpreted the Ordinance narrowly, to refer only to messages transmitted through telegraph, and aimed to print newspapers.

[112] ISA M354/1 doc 54a Appendix A. The figure related to the end of the fiscal year of 1932, ie March 1933. By the end of the 1933 there were already 2,313 sets. See figures in Ch 8.

controlled it as well.[113] Agronsky now pulled another card: he complained to the government that local press used radio broadcasting from Continental stations as a source for news.[114] This was shortly after Hitler was appointed to be Chancellor in Germany. The government then received a similar complaint from Reuters and the PTA, specifically addressed at the Hebrew *Haaretz*: they complained that *Haaretz* reproduced news from Continental stations. Unlike Agronsky, Reuters' representative did not frame his complaint as a British concern, but as Reuters' interest. He knew that the government considered Reuters' interest as its own, and there was no need for a pretext.[115] The government was indeed concerned, but the officials realized that there was little they could do, but to draw the newspapers' attention to the radio set licence. They wrote to the Colonial Office in London, emphasizing their concerns, in this order: protection of the BBC's copyright; protection of telegraphic agencies, the government's interests in loss of telegraph revenue, and lastly, the danger of undesirable Soviet and other propaganda.[116] Eventually, the government's press officer sent the newspapers a short and rather hollow warning letter.[117]

The business interests of some newspapers in hindering competition, the news agencies' interest in assuring their monopoly, and the government's political and fiscal interests, all converged. Copyright was resorted to as a possible tool to assure control of the news, but it was too weak to serve the purpose. Indeed, the government increasingly used direct censorship. In 1933 it enacted the Press Ordinance, which required a licence to publish a newspaper, and authorized the government to shut down a newspaper.[118]

E. Conclusion

PTA v Jaber declared fundamental legal principles of the non-copyrightability of news, the fact/expression dichotomy, and originality. The local courts turned to English law as the legal source, thus further anchoring the reception of the foreign legal transplant. But copyright law did not develop out of the blue: it was constructed within technological, commercial, legal, and political contexts. The decision to turn to copyright law was the initiative of a foreign player, in this case Jacob Landau. We have already seen this pattern, where interested foreigners activate the local law. They are often assisted by local intermediaries, in this case it was a lawyer.

---

[113] See Agronsky to CS (26 December 1932) ISA M293/8 doc 79; Officer Administering the Government to Secretary of State (11 January 1933) ISA M293/8 doc 83; Secretary of State to HC (16 February 1933) ISA M293/8 doc 86; CS to the *Palestine Post* (28 February 1933) ISA M293/8 doc 90.
[114] PMG to CS (8 March 1933) ISA 293/8 doc 92 (reporting Agronsky's comments).
[115] Internal memo, ISA 293/8 comment on doc 97 (date unclear, 1933) (reporting Reuter's complaint).
[116] Ibid.
[117] See Press Officer to *Palestine Post* (21 April 1933) ISA 293/8 doc 102, and similar letters to Hebrew and Arab newspapers (docs 102a, 102b).
[118] Press Ordinance 1933, 2 Laws of Palestine 1214 (Drayton).

Each territory had its unique context. In Australia, as noted by Bently, the law protecting telegraphic messages was initiated by leading newspapers. The laws were a tool to raise the barriers for their competitors. In the United States, as argued by Baird, the idea to turn to courts and seek a common law protection for news was a concocted strategy to regulate a natural monopoly—the costly telegraph network.

In Palestine, the market structure was different. The problem of natural monopoly was solved by the government which built the network; the costs of gathering news were not a local problem, as the news at stake were foreign, and gathered by Reuters'. The relevant cost was of accessing and using Reuters' news. Unlike the free markets in the United States, or the self-governing dominion of Australia, the Mandatory government had its own interests in controlling the flow of information. Its ownership of the infrastructure and the extension of Reuters' preferred status enabled it to do so. As long as these combined interests were maintained, the government did not care much about the battles between the newspapers and the news agencies. Thus, within this space, the PTA could pursue its goals, of strengthening its own monopoly in the market of delivering news.

Hence, a news agency, rather than the local newspapers, was the one to seek legal protection for news. In fact, the newspapers at stake, the *Palestine Post* and *Al Hayat*, were not in competition with each other. Each appealed to a different audience, along national and language divides, with very little spillovers. Returning to the framework of *colonial copyright*, the copyright principles that emerged from this complex setting further turned the foreign transplant into a local reality.

10
Arab Copyright

A. Introduction

The multifaceted process of transplanting copyright law in Mandate Palestine provides yet another illustration of the complex interaction of law and identity in the region.[1] This chapter focuses on the place of *colonial copyright* law in Palestine's Arab society. It teaches us, once again, that the process of legal transplantation is not a unilateral, one-way act, but a dialectic, interactive process, that takes place between the foreign source and the local legal culture. In the case of colonial copyright, the law at stake is a law about culture.

There were several interactions between the colonizer and the colonized, and between the groups that composed the latter, that deserve attention. The first copyright identity-based legal–cultural friction was between the British and the local populations. Copyright law was a top-down imposition, not a response to a local (Jewish or Arab) demand. As such, it also carried its European cultural baggage: various assumptions about creativity, about the makings of culture, and about cultural consumption. Although copyright was made available to local players, namely authors, publishers, and the newer content industries such as music companies and cinema producers, it was first picked up and used by foreign players who spotted the opportunities made possible by the new legal situation (eg The Performing Rights Society (PRS), discussed in Chapter 7).

A second copyright identity-based interaction that we encountered, was the government's (both the Mandate government in Jerusalem and the Colonial Office in London) differential treatment of the different populations in Palestine: the Arab majority and the growing minority of Jews. We saw one such incident in the case of the translation of the law (in Chapter 4), and another in the government's dealing with the copyright issues related to the establishment of the governmental radio station, the Palestine Broadcasting Service (PBS, discussed in Chapter 8).

A third copyright identity-based interaction occurred between the different segments of the population. This was a rare situation: the cultural fields of the Jewish and the Arab populations developed mostly parallel to one another, with little interference. There were some mutual cultural influences: the figure of the Arab inspired some Jewish artists for a short while in the 1920s with some

---

[1] See Assaf Likhovski, *Law and Identity in Mandate Palestine* (University of North Carolina Press, 2006).

musical influences (mostly of Arab on Hebrew music),[2] but these were the exceptions. In the main, cultural activities were separate, due to language barriers and political tensions. But it was not only the content that was apart. The backstage of the two cultural fields was separate: ownerships of cinemas and concert halls, publishing houses, and newspapers, movie and music production to the extent they existed, were all separate; professional unions were separate, instruction and training was separate, and the reading, listening, and viewing audiences hardly mixed.[3] Thus, the few situations in which the two cultural fields met were in areas of conflict. The case of telegraphic news—in which a Jewish-owned telegraphic agency sued an Arab-owned newspaper (Chapter 9)—illustrated this tension.

Before we delve into the transplantation process of copyright into the Arab community in Mandate Palestine, two preliminary comments are in place. First, the timeline of this exploration ends in 1948. In late 1947 the United Nations recommended the partition of Palestine into two states, Jewish and Arab. A civil war followed, and after the establishment of the state of Israel in May 1948, a regional war broke out. By the end of the war (which for Israel was the War of Independence), the Arab Palestinian society broke down. Hundreds of thousands of Arabs were deported or fled (either to other parts of Israel, to what became to be known as the West Bank and the Gaza Strip, or to neighbouring Arab countries). They could not return to their homes in the now-Israeli territory. In the Arab collective memory, the 1948 breakdown is known as *A-Naqba*, meaning the catastrophe. The events of 1947–8 have had long lasting ramifications, and are much-disputed to this day. The discussion in this chapter is narrower. I am interested in the reception of the foreign copyright law in a society that ceased to exist as such in the British territory in 1948. Interestingly, British copyright law survived until the present day in the West Bank and Gaza, at least in the books: first, under Jordanian rule (in the West Bank) and Egyptian rule (in Gaza), and then, following the occupation of these territories by Israel in 1967, British copyright law continued to be the law of the land, and still continues to be the law under the Palestinian Authority.[4] In fact, the Palestinian territories which are governed by the Palestinian Authority are the last stronghold of the British 1911 Copyright Act.

---

[2] Hirshberg argues that Arabic music was also played on the PBS's Hebrew hour, by two Jewish musicians, Ezra Aharon and Rahamim Amar. They were both immigrants from Arab countries. See Jehoash Hirshberg, *Music in the Jewish Community of Palestine 1880–1948: A Social History* (Oxford University Press, 1995) 144.

[3] The Hebrew and Palestinian economies had various interactions, but were mostly separate. See Jacob Metzer, *The Divided Economy of Mandatory Palestine* (Cambridge University Press, 1998). For discussion of cases in which there was cooperation between Arabs and Jews, see Ilan Pappe (ed), *Jewish–Arab Relations in Mandatory Palestine: A New Approach to the Historical Research* (Institute for Peace Research, 1995).

[4] For the continuity of the British copyright law in the West Bank and Gaza throughout the Jordanian, Egyptian, and Israeli rule, see Ihab G Samaan, *A Historical View of Intellectual Property Rights in the Palestinian Territories* (LLM Thesis, University of Georgia, 2003) 11–12, 14, 36. Samaan mentions Palestinian bills to amend the law, but these have not yet been enacted. See also Elad Lapidot, 'Damaging the Interests of Creators and Israeli Companies in the West Bank' (2000) 14 Law & Army 289, 292 (Hebrew).

Second, the archival resources available are limited. Many written resources have not survived the political changes and the military conflicts in the region. Other sources which might have survived are not accessible to an Israeli researcher. Thus, the discussion here is based on some primary sources: British governmental documents and a few court cases, alongside secondary sources. I do not provide an overall discussion of Arab Palestinian culture during the Mandate—but do search for the features that are relevant to copyright law. The purpose is to explore the process of the transplanting/reception of copyright law. This limited purpose leaves many gaps for further research. For example, there might have been copyright-related disputes that were dealt with by internal Arab institutions and legal tribunals. There are some indications regarding the social norms of creative content and it's (re)use, but this too, deserves a separate study.

We begin with a broad-brush outline of the state of Arab Palestinian culture during the Mandate, continue with the British attitude towards the Arab culture, which was a dismissive one, recap Jewish–Arab copyright interactions, and end with the only copyright case that reached the colonial (Mandatory) courts, in which both parties were Arabs. The argument here is that the British copyright law was irrelevant to the local Arab community, even more so than to the emerging Hebrew culture.

B. The Arab Cultural and Legal Fields

The Arab Palestinian population in Mandate Palestine constituted the majority in the region under the British administration, but Jewish immigration kept increasing. In 1922 there were 668,000 Muslim and Christian residents in Palestine (89 per cent of the population); in 1931—858,000 (83 per cent), and in 1941—1,111,000 (69 per cent).[5] The Arab community followed the progress of the Zionist project with growing concern and anxiety. Issues of land acquisition and ownership, and Jewish immigration, were burning items on the political agenda throughout the period. The tensions between Jews and Arabs intensified, with violent clashes in 1921 and 1929. In the 1930s, the objection to Zionism gradually changed into a political objection to the British government. In 1936–9 the objection turned into, first, a civil strike and political protest, and then into violent clashes with the Jews and with the British, a period known as the Arab Revolt.

Thus, it is not surprising that the literature on the Arab society in Mandate Palestine is focused on political events. In recent years there is a growing body of literature that addresses other aspects of the Arab society in Mandate Palestine. As far as culture is concerned, the literature focuses more on the content and somewhat less on the institutional structure. The Arab culture, not surprisingly, was imbued with political issues and the developing sense of nationalism: the cultural was political and national, not unlike the Hebrew community. The

---

[5] D Gurevich (supervision), A Gertz (ed), A Zankar (assistant), *Statistical Handbook of Jewish Palestine* (Department of Statistics, The Jewish Agency for Palestine, Jerusalem, 1947) 37.

discussion that follows is instrumental: I first search for elements in the cultural field that are relevant to copyright law, and then outline the Arab legal field in Mandate Palestine.

(1) The cultural field

Cultural activities took place alongside dramatic political events and within particular economic, religious, and ethnic circumstances. The culture was highly political. Adnan Abu Ghazaleh writes that Palestinian cultural leaders of the time 'saw a consciousness of Arab history and culture as the necessary basis for a consciousness of Arab nationalism'.[6]

During the Mandate, the majority of the Arab population lived in villages, with agriculture as its main source of income. Amos Nadan provides the figures: in 1922, 65 per cent of the Arab population was employed in agriculture.[7] The figure declined to 55 per cent in 1945 towards the end of the Mandate, but agriculture remained the first and foremost source of income, generating up to 25 per cent of the Arab output.[8] The figure was higher for the Muslim majority as compared to the Christian population, the latter being the smaller of the two segments of the Arab population in Palestine, and which was more prevalent in the cities than in the villages.

Literacy among the Arabs in Palestine was substantially lower than that of the Jewish population, but increased during the Mandate. The British government devoted attention to the elementary educational system, leaving secondary and higher education to local initiatives. Based on figures provided by Abu Ghazaleh: in 1911, under Turkish rule, 23 per cent of school age children attended school; by 1946 the number reached 34 per cent.[9] But, Abu Ghazaleh points out that enrolment in the cities was much higher than in the villages, with far more boys than girls. The rate of attendance among city boys was as high as 85 per cent.[10] Accordingly, the rates of literacy were rather low. Ami Ayalon provides the figures, based on the 1931 British census, and later sources: in 1931, 14 per cent of the Muslims and 58 per cent of Christians were literate. In 1947 the figures were 21 per cent and 75 per cent, respectively.[11] There were several private academic institutions, namely colleges, Arab and foreign, but no Arab university.[12] Those who wanted to study and could afford it, travelled to neighbouring countries, to the

---

[6] Adnan Mohammed Abu-Ghazaleh, *Arab Cultural Nationalism in Palestine during the British Mandate* (Institute for Palestine Studies, 1973) 38.
[7] Amos Nadan, *The Palestinian Peasant Economy under the Mandate: A Story of Colonial Bungling* (Harvard Center for Middle Eastern Studies, 2006) 125–6.
[8] Ibid.
[9] Abu-Ghazaleh, *Arab Cultural Nationalism*, above n 6, at 89. See also Khalil Totach, 'Education in Palestine' (1932) *The Annals of the American Academy of Political and Social Science* 155.
[10] Ibid, at 90.
[11] Ami Ayalon, *Reading Palestine: Printing and Literacy, 1900–1948* (University of Texas Press, 2004) 16–17.
[12] Abu-Ghazaleh, *Arab Cultural Nationalism*, above n 6, at 93–4.

American University in Beirut, *el-Azhar* University in Cairo, or later, to British Universities.[13]

Printed matter is often considered as a measure for evaluating cultural activity, but should be analysed with caution: print is easier to trace than oral cultural output. Thus, in tracing print, there is an inherent Western cultural bias that appreciates some forms of culture (those fixed in a tangible form) over other forms (such as oral culture). Note that this is the same Eurocentric bias that underlies copyright law, which focuses on the non-oral forms of culture.[14] With this caveat in mind, we can turn to the available figures. Ayalon studied various sources about the publishing of books in Arabic in Mandate Palestine. The figures were low: according to one source he documents, between 1923 and 1931, only ninety-six publications were printed, fifty-seven of which were pamphlets. According to another source, between 1919 and 1944 the number of Arabic books printed in Palestine was 209.[15] The breakdown of the books indicates that the 1930s were an especially productive period.[16] Textbooks for teaching were a prominent item in the relatively short list. Only a few dozen books were translated into Arabic during the entire period.[17] The printed output of the Jewish community in Palestine was manifold higher. As for the content of the printed matter, other than non-fiction, the local output included novels, short stories, and poetry, that dealt mostly with national issues.[18]

Newspapers were a more popular printed matter.[19] Following the 1908 Young Turk Revolution in Turkey, the Ottoman control was somewhat eased, resulting in a proliferation of printers and then newspapers. There were quite a few of these, periodicals as well as a few daily newspapers. We have met one of them—*Al Hayat*—in Chapter 9, though it was not the leading Arab newspaper. This spot belonged to *Filastin* (established in 1911, which became a daily newspaper in 1929), alongside *al-Jami'a al-Islamiya* (The Islamist Society; established in 1931), and later also *al-Difa* (Defence; established in 1934).[20]

The low literacy rates meant that for printed matter, especially newspapers, to reach illiterates, intermediaries were needed. Reading the newspapers aloud in local cafes in villages became a popular way of consuming the news; a practice that was later on replaced with radio.[21] The Arab intellectual elite created intellectual

---

[13] Albert M Hyamson, *Palestine under the Mandate 1920–1948* (Methuen & Co, 1950) 188.
[14] See Ch 2.
[15] Ayalon, *Reading Palestine*, above n 11, at 66–9. See also Baruch Kimmerling and Joel S Migdal, *Palestinians: The Making of a People* (Harvard University Press, 1993) 55, who note that between 1919 and 1932, fifty-four books were published, and in the following decade, 1933–4, the number almost tripled.
[16] See list in Ishaq Musa al-Husayni, *The Return of the Boat* (Al Muquades, 1946) 38 (Arabic).
[17] Abu-Ghazaleh, *Arab Cultural Nationalism*, above n 6, at 68–9.
[18] Abu-Ghazaleh, *Arab Cultural Nationalism*, above n 6, at 58–69.
[19] See Mustafa Kabha, *Journalism in the Eye of the Storm: The Palestinian Press Shapes Public Opinion 1929–1939* (Yad Ben-Zvi, 2004) (Hebrew).
[20] Abu-Ghazaleh, *Arab Cultural Nationalism*, above n 6, at 50–1; Ayalon, *Reading Palestine*, above n 11, at 60–5.
[21] Leslie John Martin, 'Press and Radio in Palestine under British Mandate' (1949) 26 Journalism Q 186, 187; Kimmerling and Migdal, *Palestinians*, above n 15, at 48.

environments. Abu Ghazaleh reports about thirty cultural clubs that operated during the Mandate. These were formed as literary societies. Typically, a club held public lectures, literary and political discussions, supported students, and maintained a library.[22]

The low literacy rates and the relatively low levels of local printed matter should not imply that cultural activity was minimal. Palestine imported books and other cultural productions from neighbouring Arab countries, especially Egypt in the south, and Lebanon and Syria in the north.[23] Ami Ayalon concluded that Palestine was 'a literary satellite in the Egyptian and Lebanese orbits'.[24] Moreover, other forms of cultural activities were not recorded: live music, folk dancing, oral poetry, musical-drama performances, and storytelling. Note again the asymmetry of copyright law in this matter: an original music score or dance movement performed but not transcribed or recorded in any way, was unlikely to enjoy copyright law's protection (to the extent that there was a requirement of fixation), but if one publicly performed someone else's music, it was an infringement, however difficult it might have been to obtain evidence.

Local theatre was rather successful, with one source pointing to a total of forty-three drama groups and seventy plays between 1929 and 1948.[25] Gertz and Khleifi describe the emergence of Palestinian theatre in the educational environment, namely schools. They attribute the theatre's success to the political contents of the plays.

Performing arts were quite popular, with the scene occupied by both local and foreign performers coming from Egypt, Syria, and Lebanon. The locals offered mostly live performances that included poetry and live music, and were often based on improvisation.[26] In any event, they were not pre-recorded, nor was there simultaneous recording alongside the performance. Technology has not yet reached that level. Recording music was made possible by the PBS. Playing recorded music was reserved for cafes, as the cost of gramophones was too high for the average person.[27]

In the field of photography, there were Arab photographers operating in Palestine as of the late nineteenth century; they had small studios and offered photography services.[28] Other creative fields were less institutionalized, and operated on a smaller scale. There were only few film producers, and they too started working

---

[22] Abu-Ghazaleh, *Arab Cultural Nationalism*, above n 6, at 96–8.
[23] For the Egyptian influence on Palestine after World War I, see eg Salim Tamari, 'The Short Life of Private Ihsan' (2007) 30 Jerusalem Q 26, 41.
[24] Ayalon, *Reading Palestine*, above n 11, at 51.
[25] Nurith Gertz and George Khleifi, *Palestinian Cinema: Landscape, Trauma and Memory* (Indiana University Press, 2008) 17–18, citing Muhammad Al Batrawi, 'The Pre-Naqba Theatre' (2002) Azzawia Q (Arabic).
[26] A comprehensive research of Arab music in Israel in the 1960s indicates a similar pattern, with performers often modifying both the text and the music. See Dalia Cohen and Ruth Katz, *Palestinian Arab Music: A Maqam Tradition in Palestine* (University of Chicago Press, 2006) 33–4, 237.
[27] See Ayalon, *Reading Palestine*, above n 11, at 9.
[28] See eg discussion in Issam Nassar, 'Early Local Photography in Palestine: The Legacy of Karimeh Abbud' (2007) 46 Jerusalem Q 23, 24.

rather late in the day (that is—long after equivalent Jewish activity). The first Arab film produced in Palestine dates to 1935: a twenty minute silent documentary about a visit of a Saudi prince to Palestine. A Palestinian film production and studio were established only in 1945.[29] There were Arab-owned cinemas, but the movies screened were foreign—mostly from Egypt.[30]

Taken together, and viewed through a copyright lens, we can draw some intermediate conclusions: while there was much cultural activity going on, most of it was not formally institutionalized. Some of the cultural fields had only few players (eg cinema production), or relied entirely on foreign content (eg recorded music). There were no collective bodies (such as a performing rights society) that could initiate or handle copyright-related demands. The content industries were either small and unstable (eg printing houses), or simply non-existent until later in the day (film production, music companies). The state of technology was such that the vast majority of consumers (today we would call them users) of cultural content, lacked the means to reproduce—to copy—others' works. Only publishers and those who had access to such publishers could technically copy, as well as authors, that could—technologically speaking—copy from one another. Moreover, much of the cultural production was not fixed in a tangible medium: live music, improvised poetry and performances, and folk dancing. To the extent that these works fell under the definition of 'dramatic work', as per section 35 of the 1911 Copyright Act, they did not qualify for copyright protection, as the Act required fixation for this kind of works. The works that did qualify for copyright protection, especially literary works, were small in numbers. Social norms seem to have allowed copying of some works, especially news reports, as we saw in Chapter 9. The overall meaning of this picture was that the colonial law was hardly relevant to most local Arab cultural fields for most of the Mandate period.

(2) The legal field

Political developments under the British Mandate also affected the legal system. After the end of World War I, the British established a judicial system.[31] They soon realized that there were only a few lawyers in the country, most of whom were educated under Ottoman law, which was becoming less relevant under the Mandate government. Thus, the government established Law Classes in Jerusalem, open to all creeds. However, on the Jewish side, a legal field—rather than just individuals who practiced law—formed rather quickly. The first Jewish bar association was established in 1922, and then on a national level in 1928; several legal journals and books were published during the period.[32]

---

[29] The producer was Ibrahim Hassan Sirhan. See Gertz and Khleifi, *Palestinian Cinema*, above n 25, at 13–14.
[30] Gertz and Khleifi, *Palestinian Cinema*, above n 25, at 18.
[31] Nathan Brun, *Judges and Lawyers in Eretz Yisrael* (Magnes, 2008) (Hebrew).
[32] See Likhovski, *Law and Identity*, above n 1, at 26.

On the Arab side, however, the pace was different. Assaf Likhovski gathered the numbers: in 1922 there were 123 registered lawyers, of which 85 were not Jewish (69 per cent). By 1937 there were 358 registered lawyers, including only 112 (31 per cent) Arab lawyers. The Hebrew University of Jerusalem (which required Hebrew as its teaching language, thus creating a high entry barrier for Arab students) did not have a law faculty until later on, although it did offer some legal classes; in 1935, a Law and Economics school was established in Tel-Aviv. There was no equivalent on the Arab side.[33] An Arab Bar Association was established only in 1945.[34] Likhovski studied the one Arab legal journal, *al-Huquq* (The Laws) that was published in Palestine during the Mandate, between 1923 and 1928. It provided various legal news much of which was from foreign countries.[35] Interestingly for our purpose, Likhovski points out that many of the stories in *al-Huquq* were copied from Egyptian sources.[36] We can only assume that no permission was sought. The journal had a political-legal line: it objected to the anglicization of the law in Palestine.[37]

The state of the Arab legal field further explains why no copyright lawsuits were initiated. In previous chapters we saw the important role played by a few individuals who realized the law's potential for their needs (Friedenberg, Olshan, and Agranat.) There were no lawyers who identified a need for copyright law among the Arab population. When an Arab newspaper was sued for copyright infringement, its Arab lawyer made procedural argument, based on Ottoman law. His Jewish partner appeared in the appeal in the Supreme Court, but had little to argue at that point.

One possible explanation is the state of the Arab legal field, which lagged behind the Jewish one. Copyright law was not taught in the Law Classes until much later in the day. A second explanation looks not at the lawyers, but at the law. As we saw in the previous section, foreign copyright law was simply irrelevant to the Arab cultural fields.

Considering the state of the Arab cultural field in Palestine during the Mandate, its features, and the state of the Arab legal field, it is not surprising that we hardly see any Arab engagement with the British copyright law during the Mandate. The archives of the British government include evidence of various local interactions in copyright matters, but hardly any from the Arab community.

---

[33] Law faculties were established in an-Najah University only in 1995, and in Bir-Zeit University in 2004.
[34] Likhovski, *Law and Identity*, above n 1, at 173.
[35] Ibid, at 175–91.
[36] Ibid, at 179.
[37] Ibid, at 187. The Jewish colleagues did not think very much of the Arab journal. Dr Yizhak Nofech, a Russian born Jewish jurist, who studied law both in Russia and in Istanbul, and was a judge in Jaffa and then in Tel-Aviv, published in 1926 a harsh review in a Hebrew law journal. He singled out one article which he praised, and then commented on all the rest: 'primitive, childish and immature are the original articles in [*al-Huquq*], addressed to the undeveloped reader, who tasted only a few bits of modern culture, and by their way of explanation, they are better suited to secondary school pupils in Europe, and most will be boring for them'. See Yizhak Nofech, 'The Legal Arab Journal, al-Huquq' (1926) 1 HaMishpat HaIvri 169, 171 (Hebrew).

C. The British Attitude

In previous chapters we encountered several cases in which the British explicitly referred to the local residents of Palestine, in the context of copyright law. I shall not discuss these cases here in full, but will rather highlight the British attitude to the Arab population. In a nutshell: the British government either ignored the cultural needs of the Arab community, or dismissed their culture as unworthy of copyright protection. The government used only one pair of glasses to consider the regulation of the Arab cultural field: its own, British, foreign, colonial perspective.

(1) The Copyright Act

A first case was the official publication and translation of the Copyright Act 1911, the main copyright legislation in the country (this episode is discussed in detail in Chapter 4). Recall that the British extended the Act to Palestine by the King's Order in Council 1924. The extending Order was published in the Official Journal, alongside a supplementary Copyright Ordinance issued by the High Commissioner. But the underlying Act—the 1911 Act that was extended—the very foundation of the entire body of law was left unpublished. The lack of publication was raised in court, in the suit brought by the Palestine Telegraphic Agency (PTA) against the Arab *Al Hayat* newspaper (discussed in Chapter 9). Abacarius Bey, *Al Hayat*'s Arab lawyer argued that in the absences of an official publication, the 1911 Act was not valid in Palestine. The courts (magistrate and district) rejected the argument, explaining that there was no legal duty to publish Orders in Council in Palestine.

Despite winning the case on this point, the plaintiffs' lawyer was concerned, and he urged the British government to publish the law in the official publication. The attempt failed. The government's top Intellectual Property official in Palestine, the Registrar of Patents and Designs, advocated that the law be published. He explained that copyright law was unique and that 'it is hardly possible to point out that with the large Jewish population in Palestine the position is somewhat different from that of other British Colonies'.[38] The Arab population was excluded from this reasoning. The High Commissioner declined to accept the suggestion, and decided not to publish the Act. His reasoning had a dismissive tone: 'no practical necessity for doing so, and publication would involve translating the Act into Arabic and Hebrew... the subject is not one with which the average member of the public is closely concerned', whereas lawyers would be able to find the Act.[39] This time, the dismissive tone was directed at both the Jewish and Arab populations. The 1911 Act was finally published in English in 1934 with a translation into the local languages in 1936.

---

[38] Director of the Department of Customs, Excises & Trade to Chief Secretary (CS) (21 June 1932) ISA M32/2 doc 57.
[39] High Commissioner (HC) to Secretary of State (9 July 1932) ISA M32/2 doc 67.

(2) The radio

The British handling of the establishment of the PBS—the governmental radio station—was a second incident that revealed the condescending British attitude toward Arab culture. In Chapter 8 we discussed the institutional history of the PBS. It commenced its broadcasting in 1936, in three languages: English, Arabic, and Hebrew. During the administrative preparatory work, the BBC raised the issue of copyright, and the government realized that broadcasting of music amounted to public performance, under copyright law. Accordingly, permission of the copyright owner was required. As a result, the government held long negotiations with the PRS in London. The PRS's repertoire included British music as well as German, Austrian, Italian, and French works. The government did not dispute the copyright or the need to pay. The negotiations were about the cost. In this context, the government made repeated statements about the illiteracy of the local populations, as an argument to reduce the royalties. The Postmaster General wrote to the PRS that: 'At least three fourths of the population are of Arab race; most of them are illiterate and the proportion who would prefer European music to local music is extremely small.'[40] The PRS was not impressed.[41] The calculations took into account the total time of European music and the number of listeners' licences. The number of radio sets among Arabs was substantially lower than those held by the Jewish population.

The dismissive British attitude to the local Arab cultural production was apparent also in the design of the programming. The Director of Programmes, Anthony Rendall, seconded from the BBC, commented that: 'It is evident that the Arab section of the community here is backward compared to Egypt; moreover the lack of large centres of population here implies a lack of musical activity which is the product of years of urban civilization.'[42] When calculating the budget of the PBS, the BBC and the Mandate government's officials agreed that: 'Artistic talent, it appears, will be easily and cheaply acquired... and if the programmes are to contain a considerable proportion of native music is should be possible to negotiate copyright payments on a lower scale.'[43] The 'payments' in this statement referred only to European music, which was included in the PRS's repertoire.

When the Hebrew Performing Rights Society, ACUM (established in the mid 1930s), applied to receive its share for the performance of Hebrew music, the government paid. But there was no equivalent Arab performing rights society. The British government did not actively search for one, nor did it reach out for the musicians themselves, or reserve funds for future payments. The Arab musicians were simply ignored. There was one exception: some of the PBS's employees composed works that were aired. They received a salary, not royalties.

---

[40] Postmaster General (PMG) to PRS (12 September 1935) ISA M361/14 doc 6H.
[41] PRS to PMG (19 September 1935) ISA M361/14 doc 6J.
[42] Rendall to BBC (24 October 1935) BBC Written Archives Centre (WAC) E1/1136/2 File 1b.
[43] BBC to Colonial Office (CO) (12 April 1936) ISA M354/1 docs 86b, 86c.

A related case that reveals the dismissive governmental attitude to Arab culture in the copyright context was another prong of the establishment of broadcasting in Palestine. The PBS's rural broadcasting project was aimed mostly at the Arab population. The idea, the brainchild of C F Strickland, a retired colonial officer in India, materialized.[44] The idea was to reach out to the villagers: programmes aimed specifically for them were one element of this scheme—educational programmes about agriculture; another element was the placement of governmental radio sets at central locations in large villages: schools and cafes. Once again, the issue of copyright came up. The Colonial Office asked the BBC for its advice on the matter. The reply was clear: the placement and use of the radio sets amounted to public performance under copyright law and required permission.[45] To the extent that the broadcasts included original content, produced by the PBS, there was no legal problem. The PBS initiated and broadcasted many original musical works, but playing records was a different issue. The PBS settled the matter with the PRS as far as British and European music was concerned. But as for Arab music—no equivalent step was taken.

*

These incidents accumulate to indicate that the governmental implementation of copyright law was handled regardless of the local needs. It reinforces one of the explanations I offered in Chapter 4, for the British motivation for enacting copyright law in Palestine to begin with: it was an item on the colonial checklist rather than a response to local demand. As such, the government was agnostic to the local culture(s) and its needs. At most, we can say that the introduction of copyright law in Palestine was intended for the use of the Jewish community. First, the League of Nations' Mandate for Palestine stated its purpose towards the building of a national home for the Jews in Palestine. The Mandate also included general instructions about enacting copyright law.[46] Second, to the extent that the Palestinian Attorney General, Norman Bentwich, was involved in the enactment of copyright law in Palestine—he had also a Zionist motivation.[47] The Arabs were not taken into account in the first place, were ignored later on, and at most, treated as a passive audience (for example, as an audience to which broadcasting is aimed to educate), but not as potential creators.

---

[44] See Ch 8.
[45] BBC Memo (7 August 1935) and BBC to CO (9 August 1935) BBC WAC E1/1142 File 1.
[46] Art 19 of the Mandate for Palestine 1922 instructed the Mandatory government to adhere on behalf of Palestine to international conventions, including in 'literary, artistic or industrial property'.
[47] Likhovski points to Bentwich's Zionist motivation in the legislative project in general. Likhovski, *Law and Identity*, above n 1, at 57. In his writings on Palestine, Bentwich was clearly impressed with the Jewish culture, discussing education, music, drama, and even plastic arts, but had very little to say on the Arab culture, other than that: 'The Palestine Government, on its side, aims at fostering traditional arts and crafts among the Arab population which have survived in many villages.' See Norman Bentwich, *Palestine* (Benn, 1934) 255. A similar attitude is found in an official British report, prepared for the Anglo-American Committee of Inquiry. It listed at length Jewish cultural institutions (the Hebrew University, the press, opera, bands, theatre, literature, and much more), but in its discussion of the Arab community, no equivalent was found. See *A Survey of Palestine, prepared in December 1945 and January 1946 for the information of the Anglo-American Committee of Inquiry*, Vol II.

D. First Steps towards Active Usage of Copyright

The players in the Arab cultural field had little copyright-related interaction with the government, as just seen. Neither did they encounter many other formal copyright law issues.

The PRS's operations in Palestine illustrate the passive role allocated to local Arab culture. The PRS's Jewish agent in Palestine, Meir Kovalsky, rarely enforced its rights in the Arab sector. In one such rare case, Kovalsky lost, as he failed to meet the evidentiary requirement to prove the deed of assignment of the copyright.[48]

It might be that he assumed that the British-European music was not played there, or he might have had other reasons. The PRS followed from London, and alerted Kovalsky to public events that seemed to involve their works. In the summer of 1937 the PRS saw an advertisement about a performance of a Muslim Orphanage Band, and referred the matter to Kovalsky. He replied that the band had only one performance on PBS radio, and that action was 'not advisable'. He did not elaborate. Recall that this was at the height of the Arab Revolt. The PRS accepted his decision, but asked him to keep an open eye.[49] As for a cafe in Jerusalem, the PRS noted that it performed only oriental music,[50] meaning that the music was not in the PRS's repertoire. When it noticed that the Band and Pipes of the Arab Legion of Trans-Jordan played its music, the PRS again asked Kovalsky to act.[51] Thus, some Arab users have met copyright law, but on the user's, defensive side.

The second issue which brought copyright law to the attention of broader circles among the Arab population was the PTA's lawsuit against an Arab newspaper. In short, the Jewish PTA and its Bulletin sued the Arab *Al Hayat* for copying its telegraphic news. The case raised some important questions, such as the official publication of the Act mentioned above, procedural and substantive issues. In the previous chapter I argued that the case was initiated in the first place so as to encourage the Arab newspapers to subscribe to the PTA's services. The goal was achieved for a short while, through a *sui generis* legislation, but by then, telegraph was hardly used as a means of gathering and delivering news.[52] However, the unique circumstances of the case, the fact that the defendant was an Arab newspaper, and that the case was discussed in all three judicial instances, resulted in several news reports in Arabic newspapers. It is hard to assess the case's impact in raising awareness to copyright law among the Arab authors and users. No direct evidence of its impact was found, but there are some indications that copyright law was slowly becoming less of a foreign concept.

One such indication is the growing use of copyright notices in books. Fifty-one books published in Arabic in Palestine during the Mandate were examined. This

---

[48] Civil No 38/36 *PRS v AIG Khayat* (19 May 1936).
[49] PRS to Kovalsky (17 June 1937); Kovalsky to PRS (2 July 1937); PRS to Kovalsky (13 July 1937) PRS-5 A239.
[50] PRS to Kovalsky (9 March 1938) PRS-6 A-293.
[51] PRS to Kovalsky (28 March 1938) PRS-6 A-293.
[52] See Ch 9.

is approximately quarter of the books published in Palestine, in Arabic during the Mandate.[53] The books are stored at the Tel-Aviv University library, and all are non-fiction. Thus, the sample might not be a representative one. Recall that the law did not require a copyright notice: as per the Berne Convention, revised in Berlin in 1908, original books were protected without any formal requirement. The first copyright notice was found in a 1924 book published by a Monk of the Franciscan Order. The notice was that the rights were reserved for the publisher. A second notice appeared in a 1925 legal book, which was an annotated translation of Ottoman law. The notice indicated that the printing and redistribution rights were reserved for the translator. But these were the exceptions, at least for a while. Eight other books published until 1932 carried no notice. In 1933 we see a change: at least one publisher, *Beit el-Maqdes* (The Temple) in Jerusalem started carrying a copyright notice in its publications, stating that the printing and translation rights were reserved by the author. Other publishers followed later on: in 1937 we find notices by the *Maktabat el-Andalus* publisher (all rights reserved by the authors), and by the French Publishers (printing rights are reserved). Of the thirty-five books that were published between 1937 and 1947, surveyed here, twenty-two carried some form of copyright notice. It might be that the publishers saw similar notices in foreign or perhaps even Hebrew books, or simply copied one another, but the trend was clear: as of the early 1930s, there was an increase of copyright notices in books. The PTA case might have contributed to this trend.

While the British government did not actively consider the Arab community in its copyright dealings, it was not hostile either. When a question from the PBS came up about the copyright of the Arab music sub-director, it was treated on merit. Aside from his administrative tasks, the sub-director, Yahia Lababidi, was also a composer.[54] He was approached by Baidaphone, a Lebanese record company. The producers asked for permission to use some of Lababidi's compositions, which he had prepared for the PBS.[55] The question was discussed in Jerusalem and London. The government consulted section 5 of the Copyright Act, the work made for hire doctrine, and concluded that musical works that were composed in the course of employment at the PBS and written for the PBS, were owned by the government.[56] But the government did not settle for the law in the books, it was interested in the practice. Not surprisingly, it looked at the BBC, where the practice was, that upon application, the BBC released their rights to the employee for a specific work. The employee could then receive payments from outside sources. The BBC added that it did not normally condition the release on receipt of some of the payment.[57] Accordingly, the Palestinian government allowed Lababidi to

---

[53] See figures of publications of Arabic books, above n 15–18.
[54] Lababidi was born in Beirut (1900), and died in 1943. For his biography, see Nasiry Al-Jawzi, *The History of the Palestinian Radio 'This is Jerusalem': 1936–1948* (Syrian General Organization of the Book, 2010) 151–2 (Arabic).
[55] PMG to CS (24 May 1937) ISA M354/27 doc 1.
[56] Officer Administering the Government to Secretary of State (3 July 1937) ISA M354/27 doc 12.
[57] Secretary of State to Officer Administering the Government (22 October 1937) ISA M354/27 doc 16.

license his works, emphasizing that it was an act of grace for that specific occasion, rather than a legal right.[58] When Lababidi was again approached, this time by the Egyptian State Broadcasting which asked that he compose five songs for them, the PBS suggested a detailed scheme to allow such use, as long as it had a first option to use the works.[59]

That copyright law came up in the context of the PBS is not surprising: it was a British governmental institution that had already acquired some experience in dealing with copyright law. Lababidi was probably exposed to copyright during his work for the PBS. Turning to the BBC for advice was a regular approach for the PBS. The BBC's experience was considered more worthy than the black letter rule. Once again, copyright law was shaped by a foreign player. There was no real attempt to evaluate the local law.

In the 1940s we find a few further indications for the active usage of copyright law among the Arab population. In 1943 an Arab lawyer, Hanna Atalla, sent a cease and desist letter on behalf of his client, an Arab photographer, Boulos 'Afif.[60] The letter was addressed to a Jewish photographer, named Kovatch, who owned a photography shop in Jerusalem. A copy of the letter was found in the Israeli State Archive, suggesting that it was also sent at the time to the Mandate government. 'Afif learned, wrote his lawyer, that Kovatch had copied a series of fourteen photographs taken by 'Afif, entitled *Via Dolorosa*. The letter included direct references to copyright law. There is no record of a response, or of a lawsuit.

Thus, there were few copyright incidents indicating that there was a very slow change: growing familiarity with copyright law. The next stage was a copyright lawsuit between two Arabs.

E. El-Amiri v Katul

At the heart of the dispute were three school textbooks about health: one, authored by the plaintiff, Mohammad Adib el-Amiri: *Mabadi Hifz el Sihhah* (Principles for Keeping of Health), and two textbooks authored by the defendant, Selim Katul: *Ilm Hifz el Sihha* (Knowledge about Preserving Health), and *Al-Ulum al-Haditheh* (The Modern Sciences). The first edition of all three books was published in 1937 and strangely enough, by the same publisher: *Beit el-Maqdes*. El-Amiri's book was composed of two volumes; it carried a copyright notice, mentioning the author as the copyright owner.[61] Katul's books also carried copyright notices, referring potential users to the Arab College, Katul's employer, and to the publisher. His *Al-Ulum al-Haditheh* was an especially successful book, composed of five volumes, with six editions published between 1937 and 1946. By the fourth edition, the book included a warning—'any copy that does not carry the author's signature will

---

[58] Acting CS to PMG (15 November 1937) ISA M354/27 doc 17.
[59] PMG to CS (25 May 1939) ISA M354/27 doc 26.
[60] Atalla to Kovatch (23 March 1943) ISA P233/28.
[61] Some of the editions of the relevant books are available at the National Library, Jerusalem.

be presumed stolen and its holder will be liable in court'. His other book, *Ilm Hifz el Sihha,* was published in two editions: the first by the same publisher, and the second by another publisher.

The lawsuit was brought in 1945. It was the first and only copyright case in which both parties were Arab, that was litigated in the colonial courts. The timing and the context are not surprising: by 1945 the number of local Arabic books was increasing; textbooks were a rather popular genre as the demand for such books increased with the continuous increase in school attendance. The books at stake were popular, and in great demand. By then, copyright law was no longer a strange legal field to the Arab population, though it was far from being a routine matter.

The identity of the parties further explains the rare occasion. El-Amiri, born in 1907 in Jaffa, was an assistant to the Director of the Arabic section at the PBS. He was a science teacher and educator, and later also studied law, but did not practice it.[62] One of his roles was to select plays for the radio. A playwright reports that el-Amiri realized that many of the proposals submitted for his review were non-original infringements of other works. He rejected them.[63] He was thus sensitive to copyright issues. Once again, we see that the corridors of the PBS were an incubator for copyright issues, spreading beyond the radio. The PBS fulfilled the informal role of an intermediary, introducing copyright to the Arab community. The defendant, Katul, ten years older than el-Amiri, also worked for the government, in the education department. He was also a lecturer at the Arab college, which instructed teachers.[64]

The allegation was rather straightforward: el-Amiri argued that Katul copied parts of his book, and reproduced them in his two books without permission. El-Amiri's lawyer, Georges Elia, asked for an injunction, and compensation of LP1,000—an unusually high sum.[65] The suit was brought to the District Court of Jerusalem as a court of first instance. In Chapter 7 we saw the legal doubts and difficulties related to the division of jurisdiction between the magistrate and district courts in copyright cases: only the latter could issue a restraining order, but it had jurisdiction only in suits claiming high damages. One way to avoid splitting a lawsuit into two separate litigations, one for a restraining order and the other for damages, was to sue for a higher sum. This might explain the damages cited in the suit.

Katul's lawyer, Henry Cattan, submitted a statement of defence.[66] He argued that el-Amiri's book was not an original literary work; that el-Amiri was in fact

---

[62] After 1948, el-Amiri became the General Director of the Jordanian radio station and later served in several ministerial positions. In 1967 he was in the Jordanian foreign affairs ministry. He died in 1978. About el-Amiri, see Jawzi, *This is Jerusalem,* above n 54, at 29–31.

[63] Jawzi, *This is Jerusalem,* ibid.

[64] Katul was born in 1897; he worked for the Ministry of Education as of 1921, and in 1932 was promoted to be a lecturer at the Government Arab College. See *Government of Palestine, Palestine Junior Service Staff List* (1931); Government of Palestine, *Civil Service List* (1938) 148.

[65] Civil Case 42/45 (District Court of Jerusalem) *el-Amiri v Katul*: Statement of Claim. The case is found in the Archive of the Supreme Court. Access to the files was permitted by Judge Geula Levin, Supreme Court Registrar (December 2009).

[66] Statement of Defence (submitted to the court on 2 May 1945).

a student of Katul, and that el-Amiri's book was the result of substantial assistance and collaboration with Katul. The statement did not detail the legal argument, but it is clear that it was a direct attack on the originality of the allegedly infringed book, and possibly an argument about joint authorship. Cattan added a procedural argument—that the action should be denied due to limitation. The latter argument seems to have some merits: the first edition of Katul's book was published in 1937; the lawsuit was brought in 1945.

However, the substantial arguments were never litigated. The defendant's lawyers (now Mr Merguerian took the lead) submitted a motion to the court: the defence insisted that the plaintiff give particulars of the alleged infringement of copyright. In other words, the defendant wanted to know exactly which parts of the plaintiff's book he was accused of copying.[67] Plaintiff objected, relying on English law sources. Judge Ali bey Hasns, an Arab judge, agreed with the defendant. He ordered the plaintiff to file another statement of claim, one that would be 'better, more clear and with more details explaining what was mentioned in [his original claim] in that he should refer to the paragraphs which he alleges to be copied from his book'.[68]

El-Amiri's lawyers asked for leave to appeal, which the district court refused, hence they turned to the Supreme Court for such permission. The grounds were stated generally: 'In cases of infringement of copyright no particulars or details of the infringement need to be specified by the plaintiff.'[69] They then submitted another intriguing motion, that the case be heard by a 'British Court only'.[70] In other words, the plaintiff did not want the Jewish or Arab justices to take part in deciding the case. There was no explanation for this request.

The Mandate's Supreme Court, in what turned out to be its last engagement with copyright law, relied on procedural law. It ruled that particulars need not be stated in a statement of claim, but when required, details should be given. The leave to appeal was refused.[71] There is no record of what happened thereafter. The case was not reported in the newspapers. It might be that el-Amiri abandoned his suit, or that it was heard in the district court, but the court did not keep the files.

Thus, by the end of the Mandate, the foreign copyright law—colonial copyright—was finally also applied within the Arab community.

F. Conclusion

The reception of the foreign legal transplant of copyright law in the Arab community in Mandate Palestine was slow and partial, compared to the reception of the law in the Jewish community. The British government hardly paid attention to

---

[67] Motion 222/45 *Katul v el-Amiri* (6 June 1945).
[68] Motion 222/45 *Katul v el-Amiri*, Order of the Court (30 June 1945).
[69] CA 320/45 *el-Amiri v Katul*, Motion under Rule 317 (nd).
[70] CA 320/45 *el-Amiri v Katul*, Application for a British Court (nd).
[71] CA 320/45 *el-Amiri v Katul* [1946] PLR 189.

the Arab cultural–copyright needs, and dismissed it as unworthy of legal protection. Few Arabs found themselves on the defending side. Copyright became a more familiar legal concept among a small minority of intellectuals and Arab lawyers, culminating with the only copyright lawsuit to be brought by one Arab against another in the colonial courts, in 1945. The PBS played an informal (and unintentional) role here, as an intermediary that spread knowledge about copyright law.

The explanations for this slow reception of copyright law turn to all parties. The British were interested in checking a box on the colonial checklist: copyright law was not conceived as a legal tool meant for the local population, especially not the Arab population. The Jewish population was better organized than the Arab population, and it was keen to organize sustainable cultural structures. It had active intermediaries that promoted copyright law: the PRS's agent, local industries, and knowledgeable lawyers. The Arab population had a less fortunate starting point, with lower literacy and education rates, greater reliance on importing cultural content from neighbouring Arab countries, and a legal field that did not develop as fast as the Jewish one.

But there was yet another explanation: the Arab cultural activity in Palestine developed separate cultural patterns, distinct from the cultural patterns that underlie the foreign, European, colonial copyright. While the law conditioned the legal protection of dramatic works upon fixation in a tangible form, namely recording the work in one way or another, local performances (theatre, poetry, playing music) were oral, often with improvisations. They did not meet the technical prerequisite for the law's protection. Only works that were produced or recorded by the radio met the fixation requirement, but then they were owned by the British government rather than by the authors. As in the case of the Hebrew authors in the 1920s (Chapter 6), social norms seem to have filled the gap. Ethnomusicologist research on Arab Palestinian music in post-Mandate times teaches us that there were such norms: performers were expected to apply musical specific genres (a genre would not deserve copyright protection), and perform musical works (the music and text were protected by copyright, at least *de jure*), but they were also expected to modify both the music and the text during the performance.[72] This practice began earlier. The role of social norms in substituting for copyright law, in determining what could be done and what was out of line, has yet to be studied.

Thus, *colonial copyright* played differently in different local communities. It was not a smooth transplantation, and to a large extent, it was simply an irrelevant body of law.

---

[72] See Cohen and Katz, *Palestinian Arab Music*, above n 26; David A McDonald, 'Performing Palestine: Resisting the Occupation and Reviving Jerusalem's Social and Cultural Identity through Music and the Arts' (2006) 25 Jerusalem Q 5, 7.

11
At a Crossroad

> Be strong and courageous in this battle of literary envy.
> Yom-Tov Lewinsky, Dvir Press to Meir Benayahu, 1946.[1]

A. Introduction

By the mid 1930s and until the end of the Mandate in May 1948, copyright law was slowly becoming more familiar and a bit less of an enigma in Palestine: creators, publishers, and lawyers were increasingly turning to the law, though with much confusion. Newspapers reported local and foreign cases. Publishers increasingly used copyright notices, and addressed copyright issues in contracts with authors. Musicians, some film producers, and photographers learnt more about copyright, and some have asserted these rights in dealing with the related industries. The Hebrew musicians established ACUM, the Hebrew performing rights society. The social norms among the Hebrew authors, regarding creative works, waned. Local copyright owners initiated a few lawsuits, and courts handled their cases better. More lawyers engaged in copyright issues. The 1911 Act was finally published (in 1934, and translations to Hebrew and Arabic in 1936). The government gained knowledge of copyright, especially through its preparatory work towards the establishment of the Palestine Broadcasting Service (PBS). There were even early buds of scholarly engagement with copyright. The continuous growth and maturation of the legal and the cultural fields contributed much to this progress.

The first phase in the process of legal transplantation included the enactment of the foreign law (Chapter 4), and setting it in motion (Chapter 7). By the mid 1930s, we can identify a second phase: the absorption of the transplant and its integration into the recipient's body. But yet, the reception of the foreign transplant was still far from complete. In fact, the full integration of the *colonial copyright*— what can be considered as a third phase of the transplantation process took place only much later, under the State of Israel.

This chapter traces the second phase. First, we shall see three copyright cases that took place within the Hebrew community, two of which addressed the writings of the most important Zionist thinkers: Theodor Herzl and Asher Ginzberg, better

---
[1] (25 June 1946) Benayahu Private Archive.

known by his penname, Ahad Ha'am (Hebrew: one of the people). The third case dealt with a popular and prestigious book: a biblical concordance. All cases had common legal features: they dealt with books first published in Europe, under different legal regimes. The alleged infringements (in one case, the potentially future infringement) took place in Palestine. The result was that the law that was applied was an amalgam of the (local) British law, alongside local Ottoman rules of procedure that have survived, with the addition of the foreign law: Austrian, German, Russian, and Polish. Thus, the law followed patterns of immigration and reflected the melting pot.

The discussion of the concordance will lead us to yet another community in Palestine, the orthodox Jewish community, and a copyright case that stirred a small group of scholars of ancient texts. Jewish law does address issues that fall under contemporary copyright law, but the case at stake was litigated in a colonial rather than in a rabbinical tribunal. Studying the way in which this community handled the copyright dispute, provides us with yet another meeting point of the foreign law with the local communities.

The remainder of this chapter will briefly relate some other copyright stories of the last few years of the Mandate, ranging from rights to a tombstone, rights to one's image, to Winston Churchill's urgent query in the midst of the War. Overall, the last phase of the Mandate was still a transitional period for colonial copyright.

B. Herzl, Ahad Ha'am, and the Biblical Concordance

The three cases that we shall encounter here share a common factual basis, and raise similar legal questions: which law should apply to works made outside the jurisdiction under a foreign copyright law, but that were allegedly infringed in Palestine? Another similarity among the three cases is the parties: the plaintiffs were the heirs of the authors in two of the cases, and in the third case, an editor that claimed to have copyright. All three sued publishers. This is an important difference compared to the cases we discussed in previous chapters, in which a foreign, repeat-player sued institutional users (the English Performing Rights Society and cafe owners, Chapter 7); a governmental colonial body engaged with copyright (the PBS, Chapter 8); a content industry who sued a rival (the telegraphic news agency's suit against a newspaper, Chapter 9). The identities of the parties in the cases we discuss here fall into a different category: local, private people, and at least in one case, a romantic author, were now suing the industry. Each case had its unique peculiarities. Due to the proximity of two of the cases, the discussion that follows is not in chronological order.

(1) Herzl's writings

Benjamin Ze'ev Theodor Herzl (1860–1904) is considered the founder of modern Zionism and the Visionary of the Jewish State. Herzl was a prolific writer: he authored two influential books: *Judenstaat* (German: The Jewish State), published in 1896, and *Altneuland* (German: Old, New Land), published in 1902. He was also a playwright and journalist. He died at the age of 44, when Zionism was already a popular political movement, gaining supporters among Jews in Europe, but still a long way before the vision became a reality. There was a continuous interest in Herzl's writings, resulting in publishers' interest in issuing new editions, and in two copyright disputes. The first dispute took place in Palestine in 1936, and was settled by an arbitrator. The second took place in the early 1950s, and was litigated in an Israeli court. The latter dispute sheds light on the earlier events.

A first contract was probably made by Herzl's heirs and a publisher in 1905. The publisher was the *Jüdischer Verlag* (JV) (German: Jewish Press), which operated in Berlin. It was established in 1902, following a decision by the Zionist Congress. As its name indicates, it specialized in printing Jewish (and Zionist) books. The contract was not found, and its very existence and scope were later disputed.[2] It is also unclear whether it was a full transfer of copyright of some of the writings (*The Jewish State*, and a collection of essays known as the *Zionist Writings*), or referred only to the publication in the original language—German, in Germany.

A second contract was signed on 8 December 1933 by Herzl's only surviving daughter, Trude (Margaret) Neumann, and the JV.[3] The daughter was hospitalized in a sanatorium in Vienna. Dr Siegmund Katznelson, who owned the JV,[4] signed the contract on behalf of the publisher. The contract referred to a five-volume edition, covering some of Herzl's Zionist writings that had already been published by the JV in the past, some new, yet unpublished writings, Herzl's diary, which was also previously published by the JV, and *Altneuland*, which had previously been published by other publishers. The contract was made under German law. It permitted the JV to publish the edition, and for the daughter to receive a lump sum for the publication of those writings that had already been published, and royalties for the first publication of the yet unpublished material.

The timing of the contract was not a coincidence. According to both the German and Austrian copyright laws that were in effect when Herzl died, the copyright term was for thirty years after the author's death. Thus, the copyright was about to expire at the end of 1934. However, a week after the contract was signed, the Austrian law was amended and the copyright term extended to fifty years posthumously. Austrian law applied to the works first published in Austria. Did the publisher anticipate the extension? Did the hospitalized daughter know about the amendment? A year later, and just a fortnight before the copyright was about to expire in Germany, the German copyright law was also amended in a similar way. The extension meant twenty more years of revenue. But who was to enjoy it?

Importantly, the 1933 contract was entitled as a publishing contract. At the time, German and Austrian laws regulated copyright and publishing rights in two separate laws: the Copyright Act (*Urheberrecht*), and the Publishing Rights

---

[2] See statement of the defendants in CC 139/50 (Jerusalem, District Court) *Hotza'ah Ivrith v World Zionist Organization* (5 February 1951).
[3] A Hebrew translation is available at CZA S41/35.
[4] See Katznelson's testimony in the later litigation, CC 139/50 (16 March 1953).

Act (*Verlagsrecht*). The title and contents of the contract clarify that it dealt only with publishing rights, rather than a transfer of copyright. The daughter remained the copyright owner of her late father's writings, including the translation rights.[5]

In late 1934, in Palestine, the *Mitzpe Press* published a twelve volume edition of Herzl's writings in Hebrew. It included two biographical volumes, *Altneuland*, a selection of stories, the *Zionist Writings*, a few plays, and Herzl's diaries. The daughter filed a suit in Palestine, using the services of the JV's lawyer in Palestine.[6] The Jewish Agency suggested an arbitrator, Yosef Aharonovitch, who was a Zionist journalist, publisher, and involved in the local Hebrew field.[7] The suit emphasized that the Mitzpe edition was published during 1934, when the copyright was still valid in Austria, the place of first publication (and where Herzl lived and died, and where his daughter lived at the time).[8] Herzl-Neumann stressed that she did not ask for an injunction but rather for a payment of 10 per cent of the sales of the various writings. As for the diaries, apparently, her late brother, Hans (who died in 1930), had sold the translation rights to another publisher. Yet, she argued that under the extension of the copyright term in Austria, the rights had reverted to the heirs. For the translations, she asked for 4 per cent of the sales, the lawyer commenting that this would be considered as an appropriate payment.

The legal framework is telling. The suit was framed within the British Copyright Act that applied in Palestine, ie the 1911 Copyright Act. The Act also protected foreign works, ie works first published in countries that adhered to the Berne Convention as revised in Rome in 1928. Austria was such a country. The protection of foreign works in Palestine was subject to the 'shorter term rule', namely that if the foreign country provided a shorter term of protection than Palestine, the shorter term was to apply. Thus, the British colonial law served as a vessel to import Austrian and German law.

The arbitrator's judgment did not provide any reasoning. He ordered *Mitzpe Press* to pay Herzl-Neumann LP125 as compensation for the unauthorized translation, and that the translation rights were to be permanently transferred to the press.[9]

The suit and the arbitration referred only to the translation rights. The 1933 contract between Herzl's daughter and the JV referred to publishing Herzl's writings in German only. The dual structure of German law—the Copyright Act and the Publishers' Act—provided the heirs with a smooth and easy way to split the copyright, authorizing the publication in Germany and yet retaining copyright.

Katznelson, the JV's owner, immigrated to Palestine in 1937 where he established a new press, *Hotza'ah Ivrith* (Hebrew Press). He then assigned all the JV's

---

[5] Publishing Rights Act (*Verlagsrecht*) 1901, s 2(2).
[6] Later on, Katznelson (of the JV) admitted that he acted behind the scenes and it had initiated the suit brought on behalf of Herzl's daughter. CC 139/50 Katznelson testimony (13 April 1953).
[7] Aharonovitch was also one of the founders and the chief executive of Bank HaPoalim. See David Tidhar, 'Yosef Aharonovitch' 2 *Encyclopaedia of the Founders and Builders of Israel* (1947) 886 (Hebrew).
[8] *Neumann v Mitzpe Publishing Co* (12 January 1936) CZA S5/11321.
[9] *Neumann v Mitzpe Publishing Co*, Judgment (5 May 1936) CZA S5/11321.

assets, namely the copyright it held, and its debts—the JV's obligations to himself—to the new press.[10] The JV was shut down by the Nazis in 1939; Trude Herzl-Neumann died in a Nazi concentration camp in 1943. However, the copyright disputes were not yet over. Herzl's writing reached the courts once again, in 1950, by then under Israeli law.[11]

(2) Ahad Ha'am

Asher Ginzberg (1856–1927) was one of the most influential Zionist thinkers and writers, better known as *Ahad Ha'am*. His essays, advocating *Cultural Zionism*, served as a catalyst for the national movement. The most important of these essays were gathered in his book, *Al Parashat Derachim* (*At the Crossroads*). This important book, initially composed of four volumes, was at the heart of a copyright dispute. Some of the features of this case were similar to the case of Herzl's writing: the work was authored and first published in Europe; the Jüdischer Verlag in Berlin made a contract with Ahad Ha'am; the JV's Palestinian reincarnation, *Hotza'ah Ivrith*, was the defendant in the lawsuit that followed. Unlike Herzl's case, it was litigated in a colonial court, rather than in a private arbitration; the law that was discussed, was the foreign (not the colonial) law, but eventually it was British procedural law, rather than the very complex substantive law that was decisive.

Ahad Ha'am was born in Russia in the mid-nineteenth century; his essays were first published in Russia and in Poland, but he then moved to England (1908). The contract with the JV was signed on 30 August 1920 in Berlin. He immigrated to Palestine in 1922, and died in 1927. The multiple locations are crucial: which law should apply? The answer mattered, as Russia was not a member of the Berne Union.

The 1920 Berlin contract was a publishing contract, made under the 1901 German Publishing Rights Act (*Verlagsrechet*). The contract explicitly referred to translation rights (unlike Herzl's daughter's contract with the JV). There was another important clause, which provided, that if the publisher wished to transfer the rights to another publisher, the author's consent was required.[12] Indeed, in 1939, two years after Katznelson's immigration to Palestine and after the Nazis shut down the JV, its rights were transferred to the newly established press in Palestine, *Hotza'ah Ivrith*.

---

[10] Jüdischer Verlag to Hotza'ah Ivrith (15 December 1938) (the date appears as 1930, but this is clearly an error) CZA S41/35.

[11] CC 139/50 (Jerusalem, District Court) *Hotza'ah Ivrith v World Zionist Organization*. Most of the case's documents are available at CZA S41/35 (statement of defence); S512455 (the hearings and related documents).

[12] The second paragraph of s 1, read: 'In case of the publishing house being dissolved or passing by sale into other hands and not continuing its publishing activities, it shall be bound to obtain the author's consent previous to a transfer to another publishing house of the contractual rights. The rights revert to the author if there should be no such transfer.' The contract is available in the case documents, available at the Supreme Court Archive. Access to the files was permitted by Judge Geula Levin, Supreme Court Registrar (December 2009).

By the early 1940s, *Al Parashat Derachim* was standard reading in Hebrew schools in Palestine. Ahad Ha'am's heirs, two of his children who were still alive, were anxious that a new edition would be published. But no publisher was willing to undertake such an endeavour, as *Hotza'ah Ivrith* publicly disputed the heirs' rights and claimed that it owned the rights of the book. In January 1943, the heirs turned to the district court. The dominant figures were first, Ahad Ha'am's daughter, Rachel Ginzberg-Ossorguine, who was a lawyer herself.[13] She is the first female copyright actor in Mandate Palestine to act on her own. The second figure was the heirs' lawyer, the highly esteemed Moshe Smoira (later the first Chief Justice of the Israeli Supreme Court). They sought a declaratory judgment: that the respondent, *Hotza'ah Ivrith*, was not entitled to interfere with their rights to print the works of Ahad Ha'am, or to publish a translation thereof.

There were many complex issues at stake: what was the applicable law? There were some factual disputes as to the nationality of Ahad Ha'am when his writings were published, since by that time, he had fled Russia, and arguably was no longer a Russian citizen. There was an additional dispute about the place of first publication of the book: was it in Russia, or in Poland—in a region then under Russian rule? Given the transfer of rights from the JV to *Hotza'ah Ivrith*, was the author's consent (or his heirs) required, under the 1920 contract, as interpreted under German law?

The district court heard the case. A first issue was procedural, and was initially set aside, but it turned out to be a decisive point later on. The defendant press argued that the declaratory procedure was inappropriate, as no infringement had as yet taken place. The press argued that the court lacked jurisdiction in such a case. The President of the court, Judge Paget Bourke dismissed the argument, noting that there was a real question and a real interest at stake. The press made it clear that it was indeed interested in publishing the book, thus, the judge concluded that: 'At this stage, I am unable to discern anything improper in seeking a declaratory relief.'[14] The press asked and received permission to appeal to the Supreme Court, but did not submit such an appeal. The case was now on track for a full hearing.

Professor Leon Roth, the Rector of the Hebrew University in Jerusalem who held the Ahad Ha'am chair of philosophy, testified about the importance of the book to Zionism and to Hebrew literature. Roth compared Ahad Ha'am to John Stuart Mill and Herbert Spenser in their influence. He emphasized the need for a one-volume edition instead of the four-volume edition that was available.[15]

Dr Salli Hirsch testified as the applicants' expert on German law. Hirsch practiced law in Berlin from 1912 to 1935, and had also counselled the JV for a while.[16] He explained the dual structure of German law on the matter: the

---

[13] Rachel Ossorguine was born in 1885 in Kiev, and moved with her parents to London in 1908. She studied law in Rome, practiced there and later in Moscow. She immigrated to Palestine in 1933. Her marriage to a non-Jew resulted in her father distancing himself from his daughter. See 'Rachel Ginzberg- Ossorguine' in Eyal Katvan, Ruth Halperin-Kaddari, Tamar Trau-Zitnitski (eds), *First Women Lawyers in Pre-State Israel (1930–1948)* (2009) 37 (Hebrew).
[14] Motion 190/43 *Ossorguine & Ginzberg v Hotza'ah Ivrith Ltd*, Ruling (19 May 1943).
[15] Roth testimony (2 July 1943).
[16] Hirsch testimony (2 July 1943; 15 September 1943).

Copyright Act and the Publishing Rights Act, and classified the 1920 contract as a typical publishing contract. The applicable German Act allowed the assignability of the contracted rights, unless the parties agreed otherwise. The contract at stake, he opined, included such a stipulation, requiring the author's consent to any transfer of the rights. The respondent tried to argue otherwise, that the contract was a copyright transfer, not just a publishing right. The judge commented that: 'I find the greatest difficulty in comprehending Mr Katzenstein's [respondent's lawyer] explanation—but the object may become more apparent later. I will allow him much latitude in a difficult matter like this of ascertaining what is the German Law and its bearing.'[17]

The publisher further argued that the book was subject to Russian law and given that Russia did not join the Berne Convention and its Rome Revision, the book was not protected in Palestine. A librarian at the Hebrew University testified as to the place of first publication of each of the four volumes: the first volume was published in Odessa (in 1895); the other three volumes were published in Warsaw (1903–13), but printed in Berlin. Later editions were published in Poland and Germany.

Rachel Ginzberg-Ossorguine testified about the heirs' relationship with the JV and its owner, Katznelson, who by then owned *Hotza'ah Ivrith*.[18] She explained the interest in having a new edition of the book: the heirs were not interested in the royalties; rather, they wanted the books to be available for educational purposes.

The court now again raised the procedural issue, on which it had ruled earlier. The trigger for re-examining the appropriateness of the procedure was an English case that was brought to the court's attention: *Odham Press Ltd v London & Provincial Sporting News Agency*, decided in 1936.[19] The court explained why its previous ruling was not wrong, but now, in light of *Odham Press*, it reversed, and dismissed the case: no infringement had yet taken place. The judge explained: 'It might properly be said to the applicants here: "Wait until you can prove the copyright you claim has been infringed before you seek a declaration from the Court."'[20] The complex legal questions about the applicable law or the interpretation of the 1920 contract were avoided.

The heirs' appeal to the Supreme Court was dismissed. The justices commented that Smoira's argument on behalf of the heirs, was 'extremely plausible', but that 'the applicants are not seeking a declaration as to their right to the sole copyright but a declaration that the Respondents are not entitled to interfere'. Again, relying on the British case of *Odham Press*, the Supreme Court found that without an infringement, an order cannot be made. 'Had the motion been differently framed,' the Court concluded, 'it is possible that the applicants might have succeeded.'[21] This formalistic reasoning met a critical scholarly comment by Dr Ludwig Bendix.

---

[17] Court hearing (15 September 1943).
[18] Ossorguine testimony (16, 17 September 1943).
[19] [1936] 1 All ER 217.
[20] Motion 190/43 *Ossorguine v Hotza'ah Ivrith Ltd*—Judgment (1943) Selected Cases of the District Courts 148.
[21] CA 332/43 *Ossorguine v Hotza'ah Ivrit Ltd* (1944) PLR 419.

The critique could easily fit within the much later Critical Legal Studies' school; it was also the single such comment in copyright law scholarship in Palestine throughout the Mandate.[22] Bendix argued that the transfer of the rights from the JV to the Hebrew press in Palestine amounted to an infringement, and that in any case, the court should have applied judicial discretion rather than a formalistic interpretation.

What does the case teach us about the reception process of colonial copyright? It indicates the level of anglicization of the local law: the British copyright law provided the legal basis for the discussion, in that it protected foreign works. Colonial copyright carried with it the global legal framework. The court was willing to interject other foreign laws into the British framework, under the relevant international treaties. The result could have been a complex legal transplant, in which one transplant (British, colonial law), serves as a conduit for another foreign law. But British procedural laws trumped all other options. Moreover, the way the case developed teaches us about the level of legal sophistication, and about the lawyers' familiarity with both local and foreign copyright law. Finally, once again we realize the importance of key players in the copyright field. *Hotza'ah Ivrith* played such a role in the development of the law, first due to its important position in its previous incarnation as the JV in Berlin, and then due to its commercial strategies.

A year after the Supreme Court ruled, the parties finally reached an agreement for the publication of a new edition of the book by *Hotza'ah Ivrith* and *Dvir Press*.[23]

(3) The concordance

Another dispute lasted for almost two decades, beginning in Germany and ending in Palestine, with subsequent events in Israel. The case dealt with a work first published in Germany but allegedly infringed in Palestine. The pattern was similar to the previous two cases: a person claiming to be the copyright owner—an editor in the current case—sued a local publisher. The book at stake was a biblical concordance: a lengthy index of all words mentioned in the Bible.

The story begins in 1896 with the publication of the concordance, *Heichal HaKodesh* (Hall of Sanctity), by Shlomo Mandelkern, in Leipzig, Germany. Mandelkern died in 1902. Thus, under the German 1901 Copyright Act, the copyright was to last until the end of 1932.

The central figure in the story entered the stage in 1913: Faivel Margolin was a Lithuanian Jew, a publisher of two Hebrew journals in Vilna. In 1913 he bought the rights for the concordance from a German publisher. Margolin then spent the next twelve years proofreading the book, correcting mistakes, and adding original

---

[22] L Bendix, 'Early Protection of the Author's Right' (1945) 2 HaPraklit 216 (Hebrew). Bendix (1877–1952) was a Jewish lawyer who immigrated to Palestine from Germany, but in 1947 emigrated to the US. See his son's biography: Reinhard Bendix, *From Berlin to Berkeley: German-Jewish Identities* (Transaction Publications, 1986).

[23] Contract between Ossorguine and Ginzberg, and Hotza'ah Ivrith and Dvir Press (10 December 1945) CZA S41/35 doc 39 (Herzl writings file).

text: a table of contents, a list of the Bible's books, an introduction to the new edition, ten pages of missing material, and six pages of a table of corrections. The result was a second edition, published in 1925. It was a 1568 page book, half-leather bound, offered for sale for 130 marks.[24] The costs of production were high. In 1927 Margolin borrowed 12,000 marks from a German company, which was affiliated with the many businesses of Salman Schocken.

Schocken was the second central figure in this story. He was a Jew born in Poland who first moved to Germany, and later to Palestine. He was a self-made businessman. He owned a chain of department stores in Germany, but was also engaged in cultural activities, such as a lifelong patronage of Shmuel Yosef Agnon, later a Nobel Laureate. Schocken established the Schocken Verlag in Berlin, in 1931.[25]

The book served as Margolin's pledge for the loan. He failed to repay the loan, resulting in seizure of the copies of the books. This is where the story became complicated: it was unclear whether Schocken Verlag gained control only of the physical books, or also the rights therein, and to the extent that it was the latter, which rights: the publishing rights under the Verlagsrecht Act, or the copyright?

Margolin embarked on a long legal battle to regain control of the book. A first stop was the German courts. These proceedings are reported in the subsequent events. In 1929, he asked a German court to compel Schocken to enter into arbitration, presumably to settle the ownership of copyright in the book. He lost.[26]

Eight years passed by. Margolin immigrated to Palestine. In late 1935, he sued Salman Schocken again, this time in the Ashkenazi Rabbinical Court in Jerusalem. It was the internal tribunal of the ultra-orthodox, anti-Zionist community, rather than the court which operated under the Chief Rabbinate. The choice of the tribunal remains peculiar: Margolin was not a member of that community, let alone Schocken. Margolin argued that Schocken violated a contract—probably referring to the loan.[27] Schocken replied in writing. He denied the allegations, and informed the court that he had no intention of appearing there. He explained that upon Margolin's failure to repay the loan and other debts, his assets were seized and confiscated.[28] The court issued a *Ktav Seruv* (Hebrew: refusal notice). The notice had a dual meaning. First, it indicated that Margolin obeyed the rule to sue in a Jewish court, and was now permitted to sue in external courts. Secondly, a refusal notice could be a condemnation of the refusing party. This was utterly irrelevant to Schocken.[29]

---

[24] See Margolin's brochure, announcing the 1925 edition, Gnazim 512/25280.

[25] For Schocken's biography, see Anthony David, *The Patron* (Schocken Publishing House, 2006) (Hebrew).

[26] See Schocken's account, in his reply to the rabbinical court in Jerusalem (10 December 1935) Gnazim 512/2078714, and Margolin's account, in Appendix B of the draft of his appeal, submitted to the A-G in November 1937, Gnazim 512/25277-B.

[27] Invitation to Salman Schocken, Ashkenazi Rabbinical Court, Jerusalem (21 November 1935) Gnazim 512/2078714.

[28] Schocken's office to Ashkenazi Rabbinical Court, Jerusalem (10 December 1935), ibid.

[29] For the meaning of *Ktav Seruv*, see Ya'akov Shapira, 'Law and Judgment: The Separation of Religion and State: An Old Dispute Revisited: The Limits of Judicial Authority under Jewish Law and in Rabbinical Courts' (2004) 8 Sha'arey Mishpat 425, 449–59 (Hebrew).

In 1937 Margolin learnt that the concordance was offered for sale in Germany and in Palestine, by the Schocken Verlag, then, still based in Berlin (a year later it was banned by the Nazis, relocated to Palestine, and reincarnated as the Schocken Publishing House). The price was 30 marks in Germany (compared to 130 marks that Margolin charged in 1925), or LP2.400 in Palestine.[30] Margolin complained that the Schocken edition was copied in its entirety from his edition, including the original material he had added. His name had been omitted from the cover and first pages, and had been replaced with Schocken Verlag.

In hindsight, it seems that the core of the dispute was whether the Schocken Verlag possessed the copyright of the concordance as a result of Margolin's failure to repay the loan, or (only) the physical object: the unbound copies of the book which the Schocken Verlag bought in a public auction in Leipzig.[31] The press rebound them with its own binding, which carried the title of the Schocken Verlag. Thus, the Schocken edition was not a third edition, but rather the very same second edition, albeit with a new binding. The new cover did not include Margolin's name, but only that of Schocken. If Schocken possessed the copyright, there was no infringement; if he possessed only the physical object—then there was no reprinting of the book, and hence no copyright infringement. In the latter case, the relevant legal framework was not that of copyright, but the separate regulation of publishing rights, under the German Verlagsrecht Act, to the extent that it would be applied in Palestine.

Margolin's next stop was the court of public opinion. He published a lengthy advertisement in *Haaretz*—now owned by Schocken himself. Margolin announced Schocken's refusal to litigate the case in the Ashkenazi Rabbinical Court, and warned booksellers, especially Rubin Mass of Jerusalem, not to sell the Schocken edition.[32] The Schocken Verlag in Berlin then replied, explaining that the ownership had lawfully been passed to it. The press did not specify whether it meant the copyright or the ownership of the books.[33]

The next stop was the magistrate court in Tel-Aviv, in 1937, where Margolin brought criminal charges against Schocken and against the distributors of the book. This time, the charges were based on the Copyright Ordinance 1924, that prohibited commercial transactions of infringing copies. This was the first copyright case between Jews in Palestine to be litigated in a colonial court.

At this point, Schocken took the matter more seriously. His top-of-the-league lawyers, Felix Rosenblüth (later known as Pinhas Rosen, the first Israeli Minister of Justice), and Moshe Smoira, petitioned the Attorney General in Jerusalem, asking that the Attorney General stay the proceedings.[34] They rehearsed their arguments, and added that the copyright of the first author of the book, Mandelkern, had

---

[30] See advertisements announcing the book, printed in *Haaretz* (5 March 1937, 1 April 1937).
[31] This is evident in correspondence between Schocken Publishing House Ltd and the Hebrew Authors' Association, sometime after the litigation was over. See G Schocken to David Shimonovitz (14 September 1943) Schocken Publishing House Archive.
[32] *Haaretz* (18 March 1937), copy available at Gnazim 512/207814.
[33] Ibid.
[34] Rosenblüth to A-G (2 July 1937) ISA M698/13 doc 6.

already expired in 1932. The 1934 German extension of the copyright term did not apply to works that were already out of copyright. As far as the second edition (1925) was concerned, it was the British Copyright Act that should be applied, as that was the law in Palestine. Relying on *Copinger on Copyright* (6th edn, 1927), and an expert opinion on German law, they argued that the second edition should not be considered a new work. Other than the impressive legal arguments, the lawyers had yet another original argument: 'The Schocken publishers', they wrote, 'enjoy a high reputation.' They added: '[Margolin] knows that it would be most inconvenient for Mr Salman Schocken who is the Chairman of the Executive Council of the Hebrew University and a prominent figure in contemporary Jewry, to appear in the dock of a Court and to be exposed to a sensational criminal charge.'[35] The Attorney General denied the request in an apologetic tone. There were issues of fact and law to be decided, he explained, and 'if I were to decide the issue between you, I would be usurping the functions of a court'.[36]

The magistrate court acquitted the accused.[37] The judge concluded that there was doubt whether Margolin still held the copyright, given the circumstances of the unpaid loan. Furthermore, Margolin did not prove that Salman Schocken was the owner of the Schocken Verlag. Last but not least, the court found that Margolin had failed to prove the accused's *mens rea*—their knowledge of the criminal act.

Margolin did not give up. He wrote to the Attorney General asking him to appeal the decision, or to allow him such an appeal.[38] The request was denied. He then tried again. He prepared lengthy documents for the purpose of the appeal, but these were not submitted.[39] The infringement that he referred to in the draft of the appeal was more expansive than the original charges. He claimed that his rights were infringed both as a publisher of the 1925 edition and as the author. He added yet another cause of action: that the attribution to the publisher (himself) was omitted, and that changes were made to the original text he had written. This claim had no legal merits under local law, as copyright law in Palestine did not include moral rights.

Margolin's relentless campaign did not end. In 1938 he approached the League for Rights of Man in Tel-Aviv, affiliated to the National Council for Civil Liberties in London.[40] Margolin's frustration is evident in the letters. His language escalated: theft, fraud, cheating, and extensive use of 'scandal'. The League attempted to set arbitration, but met with a refusal of Schocken and the other defendants, who referred to the acquitting decision.[41] Another three years passed by and Margolin invited Schocken to arbitration, threatening that if he refused, he would commence

---

[35] Ibid, at para 13 of the letter.
[36] A-G to Smoira (7 July 1937) ISA M698/13 doc 7.
[37] Criminal Case 5756/37 *Margolin v Schocken et al* (M Kanterovich, J, 16 September 1937) Gnazim 512/20787/4.
[38] Margolin to A-G (23 September 1937) Gnazim 512/20787.
[39] See draft of Criminal Appeal (15 October 1937) Gnazim 512/20787/4 and appendixes, Gnazim 512/25277/A-B-C.
[40] Margolin to League for Rights of Man (11 July 1938) Gnazim 512/20787/4.
[41] League for Rights of Man to Margolin (19 September 1938; 20 October 1938) Gnazim 512/5120/A, B.

a civil action.⁴² The story did not end here. After Margolin died (in 1942), Schocken offered his widow a compromise, via the Hebrew Authors' Association.⁴³ The offer was met with a refusal: the widow demanded 'Justice, not mercy'.⁴⁴ Three more years passed by, and in 1946 a settlement was finally reached.⁴⁵

The long crusade of the frustrated editor once again reflected the complexities of life in Mandate Palestine. Cultural activities were carried on from Europe to Palestine, but the law travelled less smoothly. The legal system injected one foreign law (British) into a new country, whereas the particular copyright-related needs of the local Hebrew population were based on another legal system, German law in this case. Placing one legal system on top of another resulted in numerous legal mistakes: Margolin did not know all the relevant facts, he did not use a copyright specialist, and he focused on issues which were not applicable in Palestine, such as the right of attribution. His choice of procedure—criminal rather than civil litigation—was yet another mistake. On the other hand, Smoira's law office familiarized itself with copyright law and the complex legal questions.

C. Jewish Copyright Law and Old Texts

The discussion in this book has thus far focused on three main segments of Mandate Palestine: the British government, the Hebrew community, and the Arab community. Within the latter two groups, there were further sub-communities. One of them deserves special attention: the Jewish orthodox community. The few copyright incidents that were found relating to this community provide yet another social–cultural space where the foreign legal transplant of colonial copyright met a different, local context. In this case, the interface of the foreign law was with a different body of law: Jewish law, known as the *Halakha*.

The Orthodox Jewish community in Palestine was composed of several groups. One such group was the members of the Old Yishuv, namely, the Jews that lived in the region before the Zionist waves of immigration in the late nineteenth century, and their descendants. This group was further fragmented according to ethnic origin, with the main division being between Sephardi Jews—those who came to Palestine from Spain (Sepharad, in Hebrew) after the expulsion of Jews from Spain in 1492, and the Ashkenazi Jews, originating from central Europe. A second group within the Orthodox community was the non-Zionist ultra-orthodox Jews who immigrated to Palestine, mostly from Poland and Lithuania. Some of them—the *Haredi* community—were anti-Zionists.

---

⁴² Margolin to Schocken (7 October 1941) Gnazim 512/20787/4.
⁴³ G Schocken to Shimonovitz (14 September 1943) Schocken Publishing House Archive.
⁴⁴ H Margolin to Shimonovitz (26 October 1943) Schocken Publishing House Archive.
⁴⁵ Agreement between Schocken Publishing House, Ltd and the heirs of F Margolin (30 December 1946) Schocken Publishing House Archive. In 1955 the Schocken Publishing House published a new edition of the concordance and reached a new agreement with Margolin's widow. Margolin's heirs received royalties until 1979, when they donated the royalties to charity.

As was the case in all segments of the population, the ultra-orthodox community was undergoing dramatic transformation as it grew in numbers and worldviews. Members of the orthodox group were more religious than the Zionist immigrants, only some were Zionists, and few were anti-Zionist.[46] For our purposes, the orthodox did not carry with them European notions of copyright law. Their creative output was mostly textual, mostly avoiding artistic and dramatic works, and creativity based on modern technologies such as photography, film-making, and recorded music. The writings were all religious texts; exclusively written by male authors.

In case of legal disputes, the natural inclination of a member of this group was to turn to Jewish law, rather than to foreign laws or secular ones. The tribunals were divided. Some of the Orthodox factions had their own internal courts, such as the one that Margolin applied to in his pursuit of Schocken, discussed above. The main Rabbinical court operated under the Chief Rabbinate, a position established by the government. It was limited in its powers and scope. Under Ottoman law, non-Muslim communities, including the Jewish, enjoyed some autonomy in operating their own religious–legal affairs, namely issues of personal status. This principle was carried on into the British Mandate, and was explicitly enumerated in the 1922 Order in Council, Palestine's Constitutional document.[47] Each congregation received the power to adjudicate issues of personal status according to its religion. But, only one judicial system was recognized per congregation. Thus, to the extent that they were interested in the state's approval, the various groups within the Jewish community had to cooperate in this matter. The forced cooperation soon led to internal divisions, and enhanced the fragmentation.[48]

As Elimelech Westreich discusses, other legal issues were largely left outside the ambit of the (official) rabbinical courts.[49] Thus, it is not surprising to find that there were hardly any copyright incidents within the rabbinical system. The unofficial internal courts might have dealt with copyright matters, but no direct evidence of such litigations was found. Margolin's suit against Schocken in the Ashkenazi, *Haredi* court was an unusual one. Absent Schocken's consent, the court had no power. Given that Schocken or the other defendants were not members of the Orthodox community, there was no effective social pressure that could force them to consent.

---

[46] For the relationship between the Old Yishuv and the New, Zionist Yishuv, see Yehoshua Kaniel, *Continuation and Change: The Old Yishuv and the New Yishuv during the First and Second Aliyah* (Yad Ben-Zvi, 1982) (Hebrew).

[47] Palestine Order in Council 1922, art 51. Matters of 'personal status' included marriage, divorce, alimony, maintenance, guardianship, legitimation and adoption of minors, property of incompetent persons, successions, wills, and the administration of property of absent people. See also arts 52–4, which detail further powers of the religious courts.

[48] See Menachem Friedman, *Society and Religion: The Non-Zionist Orthodox in Eretz-Israel, 1918–1936* (Yad Ben-Zvi, Jerusalem, 1977) (Hebrew).

[49] See Elimelech Westreich, 'The Legal Activities of the Chief Rabbis during the Period of the British Mandate: A Response to the Zionist Challenge' in Avi Sagi and Dov Schwartz (eds), *A Hundred Years of Religious Zionism* (Bar-Ilan University Press, 2003) 83, 85, 127.

(1) Jewish copyright law

Jewish law, *Halakha*, is the body of rules developed over two millennia, composed of biblical commandments and rules, Talmudic interpretations, later rabbinical opinions (Responsa), formal and informal judicial decisions, customs, and traditions. It was applied and used by Jewish communities in Europe, North Africa, and the Middle East, sometimes enjoying the local sovereign's recognition, allowing some judicial autonomy in internal matters. It is still applied today in orthodox communities. This extensive body of law deals with civil matters such as personal status, and private disputes, such as torts.

Within this body of law, various rules address rights of authors and publishers. Contemporary scholars, notably the pioneering work of Nahum Rakover, and the recent work of Neil Netanel and David Nimmer—whom I follow in referring to the overall body of law as Jewish copyright law—have gathered and traced these rules, and analyse their development and implications.[50]

Copyright was not considered a distinct legal concept and was often integrated with other fields, such as—to use contemporary terms—unfair competition or property law.[51] The rules were drawn from several sources: economic/commercial reasoning, philosophical concepts, other doctrines in Jewish law, and religious and community interests. For example, in the late eighteenth century, a question was raised, referring to two editions of the same book: which should the buyers buy?[52] The book at stake (*Mishne Torah* by Maimonides) had long since been in the public domain. One view was that buyers should purchase the first edition, even if it was more expensive, so as not to deprive the first publisher of income. The opposite view relied first on religious reasons, that new editions of religious texts increase the diffusion of the Torah, and hence they should be encouraged, and second, on community reasons that took into account the geographical diffusion of the Jewish communities.[53]

A 1985 decision by Rabbi Ezra Bazri in the Israeli Rabbinical Court provides a valuable overview.[54] The issue of copyright is new, Bazri confided, and was hardly discussed in the rabbinical literature. The concrete rules, he found, should be deduced from the Torah's laws.

Contemporary scholars have expanded on Jewish copyright law, and readers can find there a detailed account and (especially in Netanel's and Nimmer's treatment)

---

[50] See Nahum Rakover, *Copyright in Jewish Sources* (Jewish Legal Heritage Society, 1991) (Hebrew); Neil W Netanel and David Nimmer, *From Maimonides to Microsoft: Jewish Copyright Law Since the Birth of Print* (Oxford University Press, forthcoming 2012). For discussion of moral rights in Jewish copyright law, see Roberta Rosenthal Kwall, *The Soul of Creativity: Forging a Moral Rights Law for the United States* (Stanford Law Books, 2010) 138–40.

[51] The meaning of these categories is not necessarily identical to contemporary classifications. See Neil W Netanel and David Nimmer, 'Is Copyright Property? The Debate in Jewish Law' (2011) 12 Theoretical Inq L 241.

[52] See Shilo Raphael, 'The Protection of Author's Rights' (1985) 26 Torah She-be-Al-Pe 68 (Hebrew).

[53] Ibid.

[54] Reprinted in Ezra Bazri, 'Authors' Right' (1985) 6 Tehumin 169 (Hebrew).

a critical analysis. One central feature deserves attention here: that of the social–religious construct of the *haskama* (Hebrew: consent; plural form—*haskamot*). The *haskama* is a rabbinical approbation, containing praise for the author and the book, perhaps an early version of the Western blurb or contemporary introductions of the kind often found in non-fiction works. A typical *haskama* also mentioned the labour and expenses undertaken by the author, perhaps an intuitive reference to a 'sweat of the brow' theory.[55] This kind of *haskama* had a social role: it was a stamp of approval of the quality and the contents of the book. The practice of such *haskamot* began in the late fifteenth century, and spread to all other Jewish communities, following, step by step, the diffusion of the new invention of movable type.[56] Upon a petition by the author or the publisher, and after reviewing the book, the local rabbis in each community would write a *haskama*, which was then printed therein.

Some of the *haskamot* contained more than approbation: they banned other publishers from reprinting the book without the first publisher's permission. The practice for this second kind of *haskamot* began in the early sixteenth century.[57] Such a *haskama* accorded the publisher with exclusivity for several years, typically for ten years.[58] It was backed by the extremely powerful, ultimate threat of excommunication.[59] For a member of the Jewish community to turn to non-Jewish courts against another Jew was prohibited, and out of the question.[60]

The explanations for the rise of the *haskamot* are telling. One explanation is political: Italian rabbis were concerned that books written by Jews would be damaging to the entire community. Indeed, the widespread burning of the Talmud in 1553, according to a Papal Order, was the aftermath of a copyright dispute between a Jewish and a Christian printer.[61] Thus, the *haskamot* were born as an internal community censorship tool. A second explanation is legal: a proprietary view of the authored text inspired the rabbinical recognition thereof. Some language to this effect is found in the first documented *haskamot* of the early sixteenth century. However, Netanel explains that the property phrasing is closer to contemporary concept of unfair competition law, rather than to contemporary proprietary

---

[55] Rakover, *Copyright*, above n 50.
[56] Rakover, *Copyright*, above n 50, at 125, dates the first *haskama* of this kind to 1490, in Naples.
[57] Netanel and Nimmer discuss the case of Eliyahu Bakhur and the *haskama* he received in 1518, which they argue was the first which included a restriction on reprinting.
[58] Ze'ev Markon, 'The People and the Book: Material on the History of Author's Rights' (1927) 2 HaMishpat 192, 195 (Hebrew) (emphasizing that the *haskama* was given to the publisher, rather than the author).
[59] Bazri explains that there was a dispute as to the nature of the *haskama*: one view was that the set duration of exclusivity was to limit the protection, and allow the copying after the set time, whereas the second view was that the set term was the source of the prohibition to copy the book. Above n 54, at para D2. In other words, the first view considered the author's right as initially perpetual and thus limited by the rabbis so to ensure it would fall into the public domain, whereas the second view considered the *haskama* as the creation of the legal right. These two views of course echo modern views of copyright.
[60] This legal and social norm developed by the rabbinic sages in the first century (the Tanna'im), see Shapira, 'Law and Judgment', above n 29, at 436–41.
[61] Neil Netanel, 'Maharam of Padua v. Giustinian: The Sixteenth-Century Origins of the Jewish Law of Copyright' (2007) 44 Houston L Rev 822.

views.⁶² Rakover provides yet a third explanation: that the *haskamot* were meant to provide incentives to authors and publishers.⁶³ This is clearly a modern phrasing of the economic analysis of copyright law, but it was coupled with particular community goals: to further the spread of the Torah,⁶⁴ or to rephrase in English copyright terms, the *haskamot* were to encourage the learning of a specific body of religious knowledge. Additional explanations turn to commercial norms among publishers and to general, state law.⁶⁵ Netanel and Nimmer compare the *haskamot* to state privileges, the pre-modern European form of copyright law. They conclude that the rabbis borrowed heavily from the early privileges, omitting the enlightenment rhetoric of secular copyright.⁶⁶

By the end of the sixteenth century, the *haskamot* were widely used. The continuous practice crystalized a general rule of a limited legal protection accorded to publishers and authors. Thus, in the case discussed by Bazri in 1985 in Israel, he could conclude that books whose authors are alive or heirs are known, should not be copied without permission, even in the absence of a *haskama*.⁶⁷

Back to Palestine. A sample of thirty Jewish Halakhic books that were published in Palestine during the Mandate, in Hebrew, was examined.⁶⁸ Eleven books carried some form of a copyright notice.⁶⁹ Recall that a notice was not required by the colonial law.⁷⁰ Only five books included a *haskama*.⁷¹ However, none of the latter mentioned any term of protection: they contained only praise for the authors and the books, and served as a stamp of approval, and perhaps promotion for the book. Interestingly, there is not a single overlap between the two groups. The remaining fourteen books carried neither a copyright notice nor a *haskama*. One might conclude that this sample indicates a transition from a community-based norm to state law, but this is likely to be too quick a conclusion. The community norm of Jewish copyright law applied for those interested in it, also in the absence of a *haskama*, and state law did not require a notice as a prerequisite for protection.

Rakover's, and Netanel's and Nimmer's discussions of Jewish copyright law do not provide examples from the Orthodox community in Mandate Palestine. This is not an omission. Rather, it reflects the reality of very little happening in this field in

---

⁶² Netanel, ibid, at 849–53.
⁶³ Rakover, *Copyright*, above n 50, at 199. See also Ze'ev Falk, *The Intellectual Property in Israel Law: Sources and Inquiries on Authors' and Inventors' Rights* (1947) 20–1 (Hebrew), who emphasizes the need for such protection for books that were unlikely to enjoy wide distribution, but were, nevertheless, highly important.
⁶⁴ Rakover, *Copyright*, above n 50, at 201; Netanel, 'Maharam of Padua', above n 61, at 860.
⁶⁵ Bazri, above n 54, at para D.5.
⁶⁶ Netanel and Nimmer, *From Maimonides to Microsoft*, above n 50.
⁶⁷ Bazri, above n 54, at paras E, F.
⁶⁸ The books range from 1921 to 1947, were examined in the Jewish Books Section at the Sourasky Central Library, Tel-Aviv University.
⁶⁹ In 1924, 1929, 1933, 1940, 1941 (two books), 1943, 1944 (two books), 1947 (two books).
⁷⁰ For example, Avraham Zvi Broudno, *Sefer Kizur Tania* (Jerusalem, 1924) (Hebrew) includes the author's notice, stating that 'It is known the author of a new book has a right, according to Din Torah [Torah law] and according to the government's laws, that he is not trespassed. And I am sure that a tort shall not be conducted, and this book will not be printed without my permission, not in this country nor in another country.'
⁷¹ In 1934, 1935, 1937, 1939, 1941.

Palestine. Jewish copyright law developed mostly before the Mandate. Interestingly, two of the academic works about copyright law published in Hebrew, in Palestine, were in fact about Jewish copyright law. The first was an article by a Russian Jew, Ze'ev Markon (1927),[72] and the second was a booklet by Ze'ev Falk (1947).[73] None of the examples they provide dealt with cases in Palestine.

We have seen one reason for the lack of copyright dealings among Jewish Orthodox: the (official) rabbinical courts' narrow authority. The other, internal rabbinical courts, might have dealt with such issues, but that could happen only when both parties consented to the court's authority. Other possible explanations are the kind of works produced: mostly religious texts, where the rules were relatively settled within the community, as a result of several centuries of development of Jewish copyright law. Add the small size of the community and its character as relatively close-knit, and obedient to the authority of rabbis, and the position of the Palestine Orthodox vis-à-vis other Jewish communities in the world: it was not the most important scholarly centre at the time. The Halakhic centres were still in Europe—until their devastation during the Holocaust, and increasingly, in the United States. Taken together, it is quite clear that whatever copyright-related problems might have been, they were either avoided or solved informally, without leaving a record. The single case that diverges is that of the dispute over copyright in old texts.

(2) Old texts

The dispute erupted in 1946.[74] It shocked the small group of autodidact scholars in Jerusalem engaged in the study of Jewish communities in the Middle East (applying a Eurocentric point of view, the field is often referred to as Eastern Studies). The two main figures involved, the plaintiff, Menachem Azuz, and the accused, Meir Benayahu, were both Sephardi.

Little is known about Azuz. In the legal proceedings that followed, he described himself as unemployed, living in Jerusalem. A news report on the case described him as a retired 'traditional slaughterer', who follows Jewish law, a *Shochet*. He was interested in ancient texts from Jewish communities, and possessed some original documents. It seems that he was more of a collector than a scholar. He published only one article, which he was zealous to protect.[75]

At the time of the events, Meir Benayahu was only twenty years old. He was the son of Rabbi Yizhak Nissim, an Iraqi-born Jew who immigrated to Palestine in 1925. Rabbi Nissim immediately became part of the local elite of the Sephardi community in Jerusalem, composed of members of the Old Yishuv, and new

---

[72] Markon, 'The People and the Book', above n 58.
[73] Falk, *The Intellectual Property in Israel Law*, above n 63.
[74] The story I tell here is reconstructed from documents found in Benayahu's personal archive, and supported by a few external references, thus some parts are missing. I am indebted to Hanan Benayahu, who opened his father's studio, and assisted in deciphering the texts.
[75] Menachem Azuz, 'On the History of the Jews in Adrianopolis' in Avraham Elmaliach (ed), *Hemdat Israel* (Misgav Ladach Hospital Press, 1946) 157 (Hebrew).

immigrants. Later on, he served as the Chief Sephardi Rabbi of Israel (1955–72). His son, Meir, born in 1926, was a scholar from a very young age. He published his first article when he was only seventeen years old. At the time of the dispute, he was a student at the Hebrew University. Later on he became an eminent scholar. He died in 2009.

The contrast between the characters was sharp: on the one hand, an old, poor person, with no formal scholarly background, a bit of an outsider in the small community of scholars in the then emerging academic field of Jewish Eastern communities, and a young, rising star scholar, from a well-to-do and well-connected elite family.

Azuz possessed several original documents, handwritten by members of the Jewish community of Adrianopolis (today: Edrine), in North West Turkey, written in the late eighteenth and the beginning of the nineteenth centuries. Azuz was writing an article based on the original texts.[76] He might have shared the original documents with others, perhaps even showed them to Benayahu himself, or, as we shall see shortly, it was not unlikely, that there were several copies of the same documents. At some point, Azuz learnt that Benayahu had access to original texts from Adrianopolis, of the same period, and that he was writing his own article on the same subject.

Another figure enters the story, Rabbi Yizhak Badhab (born in 1859). He was an elder member of the Sephardi community of Jerusalem, and an avid collector of ancient Jewish texts.[77] He was the one who introduced the study of old texts from Eastern Jewish communities to young Benayahu.[78] At the time of the Azuz-Benayahu dispute, in 1946, Badhab was 87 years old. He died the following year. Badhab wrote a letter to the Chief Sephardi Rabbi, Ben-Zion Meir Hai Uziel. Badhab, explicitly referring to Azuz's claims against Benayahu, denied that he had accused Benayahu of stealing manuscripts from him. He added, that in case he had done so and forgot, he apologized wholeheartedly.[79] The rabbis who received the letter (not the Chief Rabbi himself) approved the apology.[80] It is unlikely that Badhab accused Benayahu of stealing texts. Perhaps the letter was written to discredit Azuz's claims. It is not unlikely that Badhab's letter was a result of young Benayahu pulling the strings, pre-empting any possible accusations or rumours.

Three weeks later, Azuz brought criminal charges to the Jerusalem Magistrate Court.[81] The handwritten indictment carries a short notice of the police station in the *Mahane Yehuda* market in Jerusalem, stating that the police refused to deal with the complaint but permitted Azuz to proceed in court. Thus, under section 17

---

[76] Azuz, 'On the History', ibid.
[77] See 'Yizhak Badhab' in Ya'akov Shavit, Ya'akov Goldstein, Haim Be'er (eds), *Leksikon HaIshim shel Eretz-Israel 1799–1948* (Am Oved, 1983) (Hebrew).
[78] Correspondence (December 2009) with Hanan Benayahu, recalling his late father's experience.
[79] Badhab to Uziel (12 May 1946) Benayahu Private Archive.
[80] Signed by rabbis Avraham Ezriel and Mordechai Meyuhas (12 May 1946) Benayahu Private Archive.
[81] Crim Case 6899/46 (Magistrate Court, Jerusalem) *Azuz v Benayahu* (submitted 6 June 1946) Benayahu Private Archive.

of the Magistrates' Jurisdiction Ordinance 1939, Azuz could initiate the criminal proceedings himself. This in itself was not unusual: we have encountered the use of criminal charges several times by now, by the Performing Rights Society (Chapter 7), by the Palestine Telegraphic Agency (Chapter 9), and by Margolin (this chapter). Azuz succinctly argued that without his permission, Benayahu copied several original manuscripts that belonged to him, with the intention to print, publish, and sell them. He cited Benayahu's newly published article, about the destructive fires in Izmir (1772) and Adrianopolis (1801). Azuz cited the Copyright Ordinance 1924, section 3, which set a criminal offence for knowingly making an infringing copy for sale. Indeed, Benayahu's article quoted long passages from various original texts, which he explicitly described as letters he possessed, and that were published for the first time.[82]

Azuz, it seems, has read at least the Copyright Ordinance (but he might not have read the Copyright Act), and clearly got it wrong. The original texts, written in Turkey, were no longer protected by copyright. Copying the original documents could not be a copyright infringement, and hence, even if Benayahu had copied the text from the tangible objects owned by Azuz, it was not an infringing copy. In other words, Azuz failed to distinguish between the physical object in which the text was fixed, and the text itself. Either he was unaware that the manuscripts were not protected by copyright law, or that he believed that his ownership of the object enabled control the content.

Benayahu did not try to refute the accusations on their merits. Instead, he pulled all the strings he could. Badhab's pre-trial letter seems to be a first effort in this direction. Another attempt was to activate the Chief Rabbinate. The Rabbinate issued a letter to Azuz: 'According to the law of the Torah, you are not entitled to submit a suit in [foreign] Courts without the [Rabbinical] Court's approval, and you should cancel your suit in Court, otherwise you shall be considered as one who refused.'[83] In other words, the rabbinical court warned Azuz that he breached the Jewish law rule, that suits between Jews should be litigated only in rabbinical courts. Without the rabbinical court's prior approval, Azuz would be deemed as an outcast. We do not know if Azuz responded.

Benayahu, in any case, continued to gather support. One letter was from the editor of the book in which he published his article.[84] The editor stated that Benayahu submitted his draft a year earlier, thus indicating that he could not have copied Azuz's letters. The editor concluded, encouraging Benayahu, with a reference to a famous Talmudic saying, that the jealousy of scholars increases wisdom.[85] Another source of support was a letter from a colleague, addressed 'to whom it may concern'. The colleague was a prominent Zionist figure, Yizhak Ben-Zvi, later to become the second President of the State of Israel. Ben-Zvi was

---

[82] Meir Benayahu, 'The Big Fires in Izmir and Adrianopolis' 2 Rashumot (Dvir Press, 1946) 144 (Hebrew).
[83] Chief Rabbinate of Palestine-Eretz-Israel to Azuz (19 June 1946) Benayahu Private Archive.
[84] Yom-Tov Lewinsky to Benayahu (25 June 1946) Benayahu Private Archive.
[85] Above n 1, echoing *Baba Bathra* (Last Gate) chapter 2, Mishna III.

a renowned scholar of Jewish communities. He attested to the multiple copies of the same original documents, and to the norms among the small group of scholars:[86]

> I hereby testify that there are notebooks and manuscripts that are 'all inclusive', and contain rhymes, letters, letters of messengers, sermons, historical memos, etc., and are hand-copied by amateurs and people of the Torah, and are used by them as an example for the style, content and writing. I have seen myself such files in Aram Tzova [Aleppo (Halab), Syria], in Izmir [Turkey] and in Jerusalem, and I also possess such. The existence of a few copies of the same negated, I believe, their copyright value as to their publication. And it is a fact, for example, that such letters are simultaneously published in different anthologies and from different sources, without any limitation.

Ben-Zvi's letter might explain that Azuz's concerns were misguided, and that Benayahu did in fact gain access to different copies of the same or similar texts.[87] Ben-Zvi's comment on copyright law carries an implicit understanding of the concept of originality. Ben-Zvi studied law in Istanbul some thirty years earlier, though it is doubted that he studied copyright law there.[88]

In the meantime, the magistrate court dismissed the charges altogether. The reason was purely technical. In an appeal he submitted to the district court, Azuz argued that the trial was set for 10:30 am, but the judge dismissed the case at 09:15, before the prosecutor and his witnesses arrived in court.[89] The proceedings or decision in the appeal were not found, but the sequence of other documents suggests that the case was remanded to the magistrate court.[90] The *Palestine Post* then reported that the case was dismissed, citing a less-technical reasoning: that the charge sheet did not disclose sufficient particulars.[91] While the report does not elaborate more, and the judgment itself was not found, the court's language rings a bell: a year earlier, the Supreme Court dismissed the civil copyright suit of *el-Amiri v Katul* (Chapter 10), with a similar reasoning.[92] Accordingly, a plaintiff should specify which parts of the protected work were allegedly copied. A failure to do so resulted in dismissing the civil suit. Carrying this logic to the criminal field was an easy step.

---

[86] Ben-Zvi (16 July 1946) Benayahu Private Archive.
[87] Benayahu's and Azuz's articles do not cite or quote the same sources, but it might be that Azuz omitted material that had already been published by Benayahu.
[88] Benayahu and Ben-Zvi collaborated in their academic interests and co-founded a research institute, later to be renamed as Yad Yizhak Ben-Zvi. After Ben-Zvi's death, Benayahu edited a volume in his memory, and authored a chapter discussing Ben-Zvi's scholarship of ancient texts.
[89] Crim Appeal 18/47 (District Court, Jerusalem) *A-G v Benayahu* (submitted 2 February 1947) Benayahu Private Archive. According to the Appeal, the magistrate court decided the case on 21 January 1947.
[90] The magistrate's decision is of 21 January 1947; the appeal was submitted on 2 February 1947. A news report about the case, referring to the magistrate court is of 30 June 1947, and a note from Benayahu's lawyer to Azuz's lawyer, demanding that Azuz pays Benayahu's fees, indicates that Benayahu indeed won the case.
[91] 'Rights to Use of Ancient Letters' (30 June 1947) *Palestine Post*, at 3.
[92] CA 320/45 el-*Amiri v Katul* [1946] PLR 189.

The case in itself is a unique event, and as such, it would be a mistake to draw any broad conclusions. The dispute was entirely local in nature, limited to the time, place, and context. But it does tell us that copyright was not a strange idea in the Sephardi orthodox community in Jerusalem, despite Azuz's legal mistakes. Nevertheless, copyright was a background rule. Both Jewish copyright law and colonial copyright were only the decoration. The dispute is best understood as a sour relationship between rival scholars. It was a human relationship throughout, rather than legal, with jealousy, distrust, anger, and poor communication. On a more general level, the case teaches us, once again, that social norms work well within small, close-knit communities, but are not effective regarding an outcast.[93] At the end of the day, the young Benayahu, terrified as much as he was by the accusation, was better equipped to respond, even before reaching the merits of the case, which in any case, it is quite likely that he would easily have won.

D. Copyright becomes Routine

Palestine was turbulent, as always. The Arab Revolt of 1936–39 intensified all communities' relationship with each other, and with the British government. The end of the Arab Revolt met with the beginning of World War II. Jews continued to immigrate to Palestine, legally and illegally. The Hebrew community now routinely clashed with the British as to internal affairs, but supported it in the War effort. The relationship between Jews and Arabs continued to deteriorate. In the meantime, by the mid 1930s, the anglicization of the local law was a fact. The legal field continued to grow and stabilize, as did the local cultural fields, in all communities. Amidst these dramatic events, copyright law was no longer a completely foreign body of law.

As far as legislation was concerned, there were no major developments. A special Emergency Act was enacted in 1939.[94] It empowered the Registrar of Trademarks, Patents and Designs to grant licences of the enemy's intellectual property. In the meantime, more countries were subject to the Imperial 1911 Copyright Act,[95] or entered into copyright relationship with Britain and Palestine.[96] But there were no other changes to the local law.

Courts continued to deal with the PRS cases (Chapter 7), and a few sporadic cases, about the copyright dispute between two Arab authors (Chapter 10), and those discussed earlier in this chapter. I found only two additional copyright cases that were litigated in courts. One was framed in copyright law terms, though today

---

[93] For the discussion of copyright law and social norms, see Ch 6.
[94] Patents, Designs, Copyright and Trade Marks (Emergency) Ordinance 1939, 973 Palestine Gazette, 171. The main importance of the emergency measures was for patents.
[95] See eg ISA M32/2 docs 125–35 (North Borneo, enacting the 1911 Act); ISA M32/2 docs 136–40 (Sarawak, same).
[96] See eg Copyright (Rome Convention) (Morocco (Spanish Zone)) Order 1935, 511 Official Gazette 423; Copyright (Rome Convention) (Vatican City) Order 1935, 598 Official Gazette 367; Copyright (Rome Convention) (Latvia) Order 1937, 721 Official Gazette 855.

we would conceptualize it as a case about the right of publicity. Pessach Steinberg, a graduate of an Air Pilots' Training School, sued Dubek, a large cigarette manufacturer firm, for the unauthorized use of his photograph on cigarette packets, posters, and advertisements. The judge had no patience, and stopped the trial as he found there was no case to answer (even though this was a civil case). He concluded that the photographs were commissioned by the training school, and were not owned by the pilot.[97]

A second case was a bit peculiar in its subject matter, but not from a legal point. Moshe Ziffer (born in Poland in 1902, immigrated to Palestine in 1919, was first a road builder, and in 1924 turned to sculpture) designed a tombstone in 1936 for the grave of Rabbi Meir Aharonson. A contract between Aharonson's daughter, Genia Butlitsky, and Carmel (the constructor) stipulated that the latter should construct the stone according to Ziffer's instructions.[98] Two years later, upon the death of the rabbi's wife, Carmel constructed an identical tombstone on her grave. Ziffer brought criminal charges for the alleged copyright infringement. After hearing experts, the magistrate judge found that the tombstone was an original architectural work, and ruled in Ziffer's favour.[99]

Copyright was also discussed outside the courts, in the government. The Solicitor General's office was an address for complaints and queries. It handled specific issues, such as the ownership of governmental officers in scholarly articles they published;[100] conditions for using governmental maps;[101] and the Palestine Archaeological Museum's query, whether it could sell or give copies of illustrations and photographs contained in books that the museum held to the public, for the purpose of study, lectures, or publication. The reply to the latter inquiry was that if the copyright had not elapsed, the selling or giving the public copies of such material would not be in accordance with the Act.[102]

Eric Mendelsohn, the celebrated German Jewish architect who designed many important public and private buildings (including Schocken's department stores

---

[97] CC 344/40 (Tel-Aviv, District Court) *Steinberg v Dubek Ltd* (1941) Reports of the District Court of Tel-Aviv 25.

[98] Contract, dated September 1936; Ziffer Archive, Tel-Aviv University.

[99] The opinion in the case was not found, but newspaper reports and other sources fill in the details. The decision was handed on 21 February 1941. See 'Copyright on a Tomb' (20 February 1941) *Davar*, at 3 (Hebrew); 'A Special Case' (19 February 1941) *Haaretz* (Hebrew); 'Copyright of a Tombstone' (undated) *Palestine Post*. The graves are located in the Trumpeldor cemetery in Tel-Aviv. According to the writing on the tombstones, Meir Aharonson died on 23 October 1935. The above mentioned contract required that the tombstone is ready by 6 October 1936, which is just before the first anniversary. The wife, Dvora Aharonson, died on 10 February 1938. See photographs of the tombs here: http://bit.ly/jEjjns.

[100] The Department of Antiquities asked how to handle a request by George Horsefiled, the Director of the Antiquities Department in the Trans-Jordan government and the author of a book about Petra, who was interested in entering an agreement with the department, towards publication in the Quarterly of the Department. ISA M698/13 docs 1–2 (January 1936).

[101] The regulation was prompted by an inquiry of a resident of Rishon LeZion. See correspondence in ISA M698/13 doc 3 (29 January 1937), the notice itself (20 February 1937) CZA A192/618, and the reply to the inquirer, Commission of Surveys to Idelovitch (10 May 1937).

[102] Department of Antiquities to A-G (30 April 1937) ISA M698/13 doc 4; Solicitor General to Department of Antiquities (28 May 1937) ISA M698/13 doc 5.

in Germany), was commissioned to plan a governmental hospital in Haifa (*Rambam* hospital) in 1936.[103] It was, in his words, 'on the shore of the Mediterranean, follow[ing] the sweep of the blue bay and the tender contour of Mount Carmel—the real one—in the background'.[104] When Mendelsohn left Palestine, he handed the original drawings and plans, but offered to sell the copyright therein to the government. Without such a transfer of rights, he warned, 'the client is not entitled to complete any building unit or to build any extension, whether following the architect's drawing or not—nor entitled to copy or re-erect the whole building or parts of it or to publish any plans or photographs or to show the plans to another architect, without the express permission of the architect'.[105] While some of these claims are dubious, given that Mendelsohn was commissioned to do the work and that moral rights of the integrity of the work did not apply in Palestine, the Solicitor General agreed. Mendelsohn received LP62.400, a large sum in those days.[106]

An unusual inquiry arrived in September of 1941. On the eve of the Jewish New Year, the Secretary of State in London sent a confidential telegram to the High Commissioner. His attention was drawn, he wrote, to the publication of a new book in Hebrew, in Tel-Aviv, about the Prime Minister. The book, *Winston Churchill, War Leader*, contained letters and speeches by the Prime Minister. The Secretary wrote: 'Company has not obtained Prime Minister's permission to publish extracts from his letter(s) and speech(es). Please consider whether there has been infringement of copyright and telegraph your comments.'[107] A prompt investigation in Palestine found that the publisher had obtained the rights through a chain of licences.[108]

Another case that was dealt by the government was about a geographical atlas for schools, published by the Department of Education. Dr Braver, the editor of the Hebrew edition, complained that a publisher in Tel-Aviv reproduced fourteen maps, without permission. Braver admitted that he did not own the 'commercial right', but only 'the moral right to my spiritual contribution', but his concern was that a 'spoilt plagiarism should not find its way to schools'.[109] The unauthorized reproduction reduced the maps but not the accompanying scale. The copyright

---

[103] Mendelsohn had a close friendship with the High Commissioner (HC), Sir Arthur Wauchope. It was argued that the HC personally secured the commission of the Haifa Hospital for Mendelsohn. See Ita Heinze-Greenberg, 'Architecture in Palestine 1934–1941' in *Erich Mendelsohn: Dynamics and Function: Realized Visions of a Cosmopolitan Architect* (Hatje Cantz Publishers, 1999) 204, 232. Mendelsohn himself reported that the HC offered him the job, on the condition that he spent enough time in Palestine to devote himself to the job. See Oskar Bayer (ed), Geoffrey Strachan (trans), *Eric Mendelsohn, Letters of an Architect* (Abelard-Schuman, 1967) 147. For an evaluation of his work, see Ziva Sternhell, 'Eric Mendelsohn: From Berlin to Jerusalem' (2008) 32 Alpayim 177 (Hebrew).

[104] Mendelsohn, *Letters*, ibid, at 170.

[105] Director of Public Works Department to A-G (1 April 1941) ISA M698/13 doc 9.

[106] Solicitor General to Director of Public Works Department (10 April 1941) ISA M698/13 doc 10, and the contract between the department and Mendelsohn (not dated) ISA M698/13 doc 11.

[107] Secretary of State to HC (23 September 1941) ISA M698/13 doc 13a.

[108] Public Information Officer to A-G (3 October 1941) ISA M698/13 doc 13; Solicitor General to Public Information Officer (7 October 1941) ISA M698/13 doc 14; HC to Secretary of State (10 October 1941) ISA M698/13 doc 15.

[109] Braver to Department of Education (18 May 1944) ISA M698/13 doc 29a.

owners were a British publisher (Phillip & Son), and a local publisher (*Omanut*). The Attorney General's office concluded that it was likely a case of copyright infringement, but that in light of the small penalty, a criminal prosecution will not be undertaken. The copyright owners were directed to a civil action.[110] There is no evidence of such an action taken.

Thus, awareness within the government and among those in the content industries enhanced, as were cases of infringement, and as the atlas case illustrates, also first cases of piracy, ie mass reproductions for commercial purposes.

E. Conclusion

By the last decade of the Mandate, copyright issues were not as strange as they were twenty years earlier. The content industries and other repeat players were still the leading players in the field: the PBS, PRS, and publishers. But the cases discussed in this chapter signal a change: the plaintiffs were the one-shot players, those who do not routinely engage with copyright law. Such were the cases of Herzl's and Ahad Ha'am's heirs, Margolin's endless campaign, and even Azuz's battle, misguided as it was. Courts faced complex legal questions, though they did not always delve into the doctrine let alone its underlying theories. More lawyers engaged with copyright law. The government internalized the concept of copyright law, and addressed various questions. No one questioned the legitimacy, reasoning, or need for copyright law. Of course, it was still far from being a widespread legal field. Copyright law was still a new, exciting, and cutting edge field, but the colonial transplant had passed the first stages of legal reception: it was no longer ignored, as it was in the 1920s, nor was it rejected. Yet, much more was needed for copyright law to become fully integrated within the local legal system and its culture.

---

[110] Crown Counsel to Solicitor General (13 June 1944); Solicitor General to Director of Education (20 June 1944) ISA M698/13 docs 30, 31.

Conclusion

> The following Orders made under these Acts can be revoked although the Board are advised that on the termination of the Mandate such Orders would lose all force and effect.
> Board of Trade to Undersecretary of State, Colonial Office, 1948.[1]

Colonial copyright was made so to serve imperial interests, but it had taken a life of its own in each of the colonies in which it was applied. When the sun finally set on the British Empire, colonial copyright—along many other laws—persisted. What is the legacy of colonial copyright in a postcolonial era? No one answer fits all former colonies (dominions, mandates, and protectorates included). For some newly independent countries, the foreign law remained in the books for decades, with little if any local use. Later on, in the 1990s, such countries could tick the box in the checklist of the new global intellectual property order: they already had copyright laws in place that required only some relatively minor amendments. The actual practice of the law and its enforcement might be a different story. At the same time, in other former colonies, the colonial law was fully absorbed within the local legal, economic, and cultural systems. Thus, some transplants were more successful than others. However, unlike the hardly implicit message of the transplant metaphor, none of the transplants was a life-saving procedure for the recipient jurisdictions. It was a transplant meant to help the donor rather than the recipient.

Christopher Tomlins writes that: 'To *colonize* means, fundamentally to appropriate, to take possession...Colonization is a matter of intellectual as well as material possessing that, in the act of taking, reinvents what it appropriated for its own purposes.'[2] What did the British appropriate from the colonized, in their act of imposing their copyright law in the colonies? It was an act they conveniently described in the seemingly neutral term of 'extending' (their law to the colonies). Did the extension deprive the colonies of material or intellectual possessions? On a general level, the British deprived the colonized peoples of the power to make their own decisions for themselves. This is a political taking. More specifically, the

---

[1] (6 January 1948) NA CO 323/1893/11.
[2] Christopher Tomlins, 'Law's Empire: Chartering English Colonies on the American Mainland in the Seventeenth Century' in Diane Kirkby and Catherine Coleborne (eds), *Law, History, Colonialism: The Reach of the Empire* (Manchester University Press, 2001) 26, 27.

colonizers made decisions for the colonized about the best course of development of their local cultures, by subjecting them to their own, British, Western, European notions of culture, creativity, and cultural development.

One reason for imposing the British view of creativity, was pure self-interest: the British believed that the unification of copyright law throughout the Empire would enhance the power of British authors and publishers to control their works. Paul Saint-Amour has expressed this view bluntly, saying that the 'imbalance in intellectual property' has been 'one of imperialism's most durable legacies'.[3] Another reason was the colonizer's genuine belief that it was performing a civilizing mission, in educating the colonized peoples. Multiculturalism was an idea still far from being formed. Copyright law, conceived in London as a tool to advance learning, was an obvious civilizing mechanism to apply. However, in the process of executing this benevolent motivation, local notions of culture in the colonized territory were marginalized, ignored, and eventually suppressed. Other modes of creative production were left unacknowledged by the Eurocentric law: oral works or works made by a group of people over time rather than by an identified author, did not meet the legal prerequisites of fixation and originality, and did not deserve protection. Different perceptions of learning were ignored. For example, colonial copyright, by protecting works in a property-like manner, enabled owners to exclude others until the very long (and increasingly longer) term of protection expired. This approach allowed only a much-delayed free access to works of authorship. It excluded a different view, one that preferred the promotion of learning through immediate sharing of cutting-edge knowledge in an uncommodified manner, and a keen interest in current, unfettered access to contemporary scholarship.

British colonial copyright carried with it also a capitalist worldview. By recognizing protectable property interests in intangible creative works it commodified these works and subjected them to the logic of the market. This market-based worldview replaced, in some cases, other views of creative works, for example, that a work reflects—and perhaps constitutes—the personality of its author. British colonial copyright did not include moral rights that could have protected this aspect. It opted for an instrumentalist view of copyright, what we today call the incentive theory: that copyright law is an incentive to authors to make original works so that in the long run, the public can benefit from these works. The British view had an additional element, that of just rewards for the investment of labour. This is not the place to measure these theories against each other or decide which is right or wrong or better than the other. The point is that colonial copyright carried with it a particular underlying theory of copyright law, which displaced other possible theories, not by winning a philosophical debate, but by the power of the Empire.

Colonial copyright was closely affiliated with the notion of the rule of law, another of the foundational tenets of British imperialism. In the case of copyright law, it was not a law that replaced brute use of power, but a law that was to replace benign systems of social norms. The law was not just another option, it was a

---

[3] Paul K Saint-Amour, 'Introduction: Modernism and the Lives of Copyright' in Paul Saint-Amour (ed), *Modernism and Copyright* (Oxford University Press, 2011) 1, 30.

preferable one. Although colonial copyright did not outlaw the use of social norms in the daily regulation of culture, it did, by providing an alternative system, backed by the state's power, lessen the power of local communities to address their own affairs. The state-sponsored system also offered a formal avenue to address disputes among people from different communities, which might have not shared the same social norms or the same social institutions to solve such disputes.

The great extent of the British Empire meant that imposing/extending the same unified law to all colonies and dominions (with minor deviations in only a handful of territories) was an effective way to install copyright law on a global scale. In this sense, colonial copyright was an early form of globalization. Today, intellectual property is at the forefront of globalization efforts. Patent, copyright, and trademark laws are probably one of the most globally unified fields of law today. The means of achieving this global status have been studied elsewhere.[4] The methods involved sophisticated diplomacy, such as bundling different issues together, forum shifting, tying of multilateral, bilateral, and unilateral tools to ratchet-up the level of legal protection, along economic and political pressures. In imperial times, all of this was much easier: a few bureaucratic decisions in London and the local offices of the British government in the colonies, a few dispatches, and only very little opposition (mostly from Canada).[5]

Thus, colonial copyright was anchored in a particular theory of copyright, it carried with it a capitalist spirit, and it nicely fitted the Empire's self-proclaimed civilizing mission. It was applied on a wide scale, paving the way for late twentieth century globalization. It was also a Eurocentric body of law, reflecting European notions of authorship, creativity, and progress. Accordingly, colonial copyright was an ideological device to extend not only technical rules, but a worldview, one that had not always matched the local practices and views.

*

This book offered a general model of analysis, to study the mechanisms of colonial copyright. I suggested that we locate copyright law (or in fact, any other field of law that we study) at the centre of the interaction of three conceptual frameworks: legal transplants, colonial law, and the particular legal field with its unique characteristics. For copyright, these characteristics were identified as the idea of progress, the Eurocentric view of the authorship and the creative process, and the intangibility of the subject matter, that meant that cross-border transfers of works deserved special attention. This general model should then be localized, by examining how the

---

[4] See especially, Peter Drahos with John Braithwaite, *Information Feudalism: Who Owns the Knowledge Economy?* (New Press, 2002); Laurence R Helfer, 'Regime Shifting: The TRIPS Agreement and New Dynamics of International Intellectual Property Lawmaking' (2004) 29 Yale J International L 1; Peter K Yu, 'The First Ten Years of the TRIPS Agreement: TRIPS and Its Discontents' (2006) 10 Marq Intell Prop L Rev 369; Neil Netanel (ed), *The Development Agenda: Global Intellectual Property and Developing Countries* (Oxford University Press, 2008).

[5] For the Canadian resistance, see Pierre-Emanuel Moyse, 'Colonial Copyright Redux: 1709 v. 1832' in Lionel Bently, Uma Suthersanen and Paul Torremans (eds), *Global Copyright: Three Hundred Years since the Statute of Anne, from 1709 to Cyberspace* (Edward Elgar, 2010) 144; Catherine Seville, *Literary Copyright Reform in Early Victorian England: The Framing of The 1842 Copyright Act* (Cambridge University Press, 1999) 78.

political, economic, social, technological, and legal circumstances in each jurisdiction affected the process of reception of the colonial transplant.

Mandate Palestine (1917–48) provided the main case study for tracing the details of the process of legal transplant. We began the journey with the British motivation to apply the law to Palestine, continuing with the first steps of so doing and the initial indifference of the local communities to the law, which, at least for a while, preferred to continue using local systems and social norms. This was the case with Hebrew authors in the 1920s, and with Arab musicians and performers throughout the Mandate. The law was then activated, in the sense that it was no longer ignored, that it was applied by publishers and other content industries, and first lawsuits made their way to courts. Those who activated the law were not local users, but rather foreign players: interested parties and the government itself. This is no surprise. After all, this was the purpose of colonial copyright to begin with. A similar pattern was identified in other colonies. Only later, in tandem with other processes such as the growth and transformation of the local legal and cultural fields, did copyright law gain wider familiarity and acceptance. First were the institutional players, namely publishers, who used the law (not necessarily in court, but, for example, by an increasing use of copyright notices or by referring to copyright in contracts). Later on, individual, one-shot players joined the legal game of copyright law, argued for their copyright (such as the photographers working with the Jewish institutions), and even initiated few lawsuits.

By the end of the Mandate, copyright law was no longer a strange concept in Palestine. It was still reserved mostly to those in the business: institutional players (the government included), local and foreign content industries, and authors. It would take another fifty years, for the digital revolution to shift copyright law into an issue that is relevant to all so-called end-users, or in a less functional language, all of us.

As the British were hastily wrapping up their business in Palestine towards the formal termination of the Mandate and the establishment of the state of Israel in May 1948, they also found the time to consider the fate of copyright law. From the British side, Palestinian Ordinances were to lose their power, pertinent to the Parliament's Palestine Act 1948, that revoked the 1922 Palestine Order in Council—the legal basis of the local Ordinances.[6] The Orders in Council, made in London, each required attention. Our interest here is in the 1924 Order that extended the 1911 Act to Palestine. The initial thought in London was that the Orders should be revoked, a language that was then changed to 'can' be revoked, but finally, the officials in the Colonial Office and the Board of Trade concluded that the Order 'will continue in force as part of the law of Palestine until it is altered by the successor authorities', and that the Order should not be revoked.[7] The reason was not technical, but rather one of substance: to maintain existing obligations under international conventions. In other words, the British were

---

[6] Palestine Act 1948, 11 & 12 Geo 6 c 27.
[7] Board of Trade (BoT) to Colonial Office (CO) (17 December 1947, 6 January 1948); CO to BoT (16 April 1948) NA CO 323/1893/11.

interested in the continuing protection of their own works that were first published in Palestine and in maintaining the fabric of international copyright law. As for the local copyright issues—these were left to the successor governments.

The events of 1947–8 changed the map in the Middle East. The civil war between the Jews and the Arabs, followed by the departure of the British and the end of the Mandate, and then the war in 1948 (referred to as The Independence War by Israelis and *A-Naqba*—the catastrophe—by the Palestinians). The result was that most of the territory was now under Israeli rule, with the exclusion of the Gaza Strip, then still under Egyptian control, and the West Bank, then under Jordanian rule (until 1967). The Palestinian Arab society collapsed. Hundreds of thousands were either forced to leave their homes or left but were not allowed to return. They became refugees in Gaza, the West Bank, in neighbouring countries, or within Israel, but away from their homes.

Copyright law did not play any role in these events. The new state retained all British legislation as its own, with obvious constitutional changes and subject to subsequent legislation.[8] Thus, the Copyright Act 1911 and the Copyright Ordinance 1924 remained intact. The first time that Israel addressed copyright law was in 1953.[9] The British law was amended: the title of the Act was changed. It was no longer 'copyright' (written in Hebrew, in a phonetic way), but *Zchut Yotsrim*, Hebrew for Authors' Right. The 1911 Act was also amended so to meet the requirements of the 1948 Brussels revision of the Berne Convention, especially in setting the term of protection to fifty years posthumously. Thus, the colonial law has won the stamp of approval of the new sovereign: the substance remained the same; the dual structure of the 1911 Act alongside the Copyright Ordinance 1924 remained intact, and the principle of following international treaties was maintained. The change of the title was symbolic. It reflected the domination of the Hebrew language rather than a shift towards a Continental, *droit d'auteur* view of the law.

Subsequent amendments followed throughout the years.[10] The legal protection of copyright was expanded, by extending the duration to seventy years (in 1971), by enhancing enforcement measures (in 1988, and again in 2002), and covering new forms of subject matter, such as software (in 1988). As time passed, the distance between the British origins of the law and the local, Israeli version had both diverged and converged. It diverged in that Israel added new elements to its law that did not fully fit the (British) instrumentalist view of copyright law. A first deviation was in 1981, when moral rights were added.[11] But while this step deviated from the British sources, it followed the Berne Convention. British law lagged behind, but followed the same international sources, by adding moral rights

---

[8] Administration and Justice Ordinance 1948.
[9] Copyright Act (Amendment) 1953, LSI 38.
[10] For an overview of these developments, see Michael Birnhack, 'Mandatory Copyright: From Pre-Palestine to Israel, 1910–2007' in Ysolde Gendreau and Uma Suthersanen (eds), *A Shifting Empire: 100 Years of the Copyright Act 1911* (Edward Elgar, forthcoming 2012).
[11] Copyright Ordinance (Amendment No 4) 1981, LSI 300.

in its Copyright, Designs, and Patents Act 1988. Thus, the previous source of the law and its recipient have converged by both adhering to a third source.

The imprimatur of colonial copyright was, nevertheless, long lasting. Israeli courts followed British precedents for several decades, often turning to *Copinger on Copyright* as an authoritative source. In 2003 the Israeli Supreme Court stated that: 'In Anglo-American law, the basic justification of these laws [copyright] is perceived as the wish to provide an author with incentives, so to achieve the public's maximal access to the work. The tradition of Israeli copyright law is this same tradition.'[12] In the meantime, the legal field continued to expand. Specialized scholarly works were published; law schools started offering intellectual property courses; ACUM—the Composers and Authors Association extended its reach, and new collecting societies followed, protecting producers of sound recordings, performers, and later on also television and film directors.

The reliance on British law waned in the 1980s and more so in the 1990s. Israeli law had slowly but continuously distanced itself from British roots by turning more and more to American law. Copyright was part of this general trend. For example, the 1981 Amendment followed US copyright law by introducing statutory damages.[13] Courts increasingly turned to American precedents for inspiration. The 1916 British case of the *University of London Press*, a leading case on the meaning of originality, was replaced with the American 1991 *Feist* case.[14] The famous four factors of the American fair use defence were read into the fairness element of the British fair dealing defence.[15] The shift was completed in 2007, with a new Copyright Act, a rich mix-and-match of many sources: American (completing the shift to fair use), Australian (subjecting moral rights to a defence of reasonability), international sources (adopting a right to make a work available to the public, inspired by the WIPO Copyright Treaty of 1996), as well as a series of bilateral commitments, and of course the TRIPs Agreement.[16] Israeli law was able to detach itself from one global system, the colonial copyright, only to be replaced with another global system.

As for the people and institutions we met along the way, many left the stage with the end of the Mandate. The British officers returned home. Upon his retirement from the British government (after an assassination attack that left him wounded) Norman Bentwich became a professor of international law at the Hebrew University in Jerusalem. He retired in 1951 and returned to London. Most of the Hebrew authors that were at the centre of the 1920s informal system of social norms died. The close-knit character of that community is evident today in the old Trumpeldor

---

[12] CA 326/00 *City of Holon v NMC Music Ltd*, 57(3) PD 658 (2003), at para 15.
[13] Copyright Ordinance (Amendment No 4) 1981, LSI 300, following 17 USC § 504.
[14] See respectively, *University of London Press, Ltd v University Tutorial Press, Ltd* [1916] 2 Ch 601, 608; *Feist Publications, Inc v Rural Telephone Service Company, Inc*, 499 US 340, 345 (1991).
[15] CA 2687/92 *Geva v Walt Disney Co*, 48(1) PD 251 (1993).
[16] Copyright Act 2007, LSI 34. English translation available at http://www.tau.ac.il/law/members/birnhack/IsraeliCopyrightAct2007.pdf. For current Israeli copyright law, see Michael D Birnhack, 'Israel' in Paul Edward Geller (ed), 2 *International Copyright Law and Practice* (Matthew Bender, 2012) Isr-1.

cemetery, at the heart of Tel-Aviv: a small and crowded plot of authors, poets, editors, and others in the content industry. The younger generation, the modernist authors, have come to dominate the literary scene.

Meir Kovalsky, the energetic local agent of the Performing Rights Society (PRS) died in 1951, leaving his heirs shops of musical instruments and the love of music. His great grandson, named after him, is an Israeli musician and music publisher. Kovalsky's first lawyer, Kalman Friedenberg died in 1953. The other lawyers of the PRS, Yizhak Olshan and Shimon Agranat, became justices of the Israeli Supreme Court, and then Chief Justices. After his retirement, Olshan was an arbitrator in at least one copyright dispute. Agranat authored important copyright decisions about copyright in architectural works, and about the interpretation of contracts to transfer ownership.[17] The PRS transferred its activities to the Israeli society, ACUM. The Palestinian Broadcasting Station split into the Israeli Broadcasting Authority and the Jordanian Radio station. The transmitter in Ramallah later served the Palestinian Authority, until it was destroyed by the Israeli army in 2001. The Palestine Telegraphic Agency (PTA) was absorbed in the Jewish Telegraphic Agency; the *Palestine Post* transformed into the *Jerusalem Post*. Its editor, Gershon Agronsky, now Agron, became mayor of Jerusalem. Adel Jaber, the publisher of *Al-Hayat*, left to Jordan in 1948, where he became a member of the Jordanian Parliament. He died in 1953. David Goitein, another figure in the PTA case, served as Israel's diplomatic representative in South Africa and in Washington, and then appointed to the Supreme Court.

Mohammad Adib el-Amiri became a Jordanian statesman. Trude Herzl-Neumann died in a Nazi concentration camp in 1943; Faivel Margolin died in 1942, without regaining control of his life project. Salman Schocken remained a powerful figure in Israel until his death in 1959. Schocken's grandchildren own and run the Schocken Press and the influential *Haaretz* newspaper. Rachel Ginzberg-Ossorguine died in 1957. She could have seen two more editions of her late father's *Al Parashat Derachim*, published in 1947 and 1957. Many more editions were printed in the following decades. The book is still taught at schools.

The stories of these people, each a pioneer in his activity, whether willingly or unwillingly, shaped the course of copyright law in Mandate Palestine and left its impact for years to come. Their contribution was in different points of the implementation of the foreign law and its reception in Palestine. They acted step by step, with many trials and many more errors. They were not just pawns in a larger, imperial plan. They added their own backgrounds to the mix: they injected intuitive notions about creativity (the Hebrew authors' intuitions, resulting in social norms; Margolin's agony over his moral rights), their practices carried from Eastern Europe (the publisher's practice of pre-empting competitors by announcing their forthcoming publications), their legal knowledge of central European law (the distinction between publishing rights and copyright, found in German law). They also injected their passion to be pioneers (Kovalsky and Friedenberg), and

---

[17] CA 448/60 *Lev v HaMashbir HaMerkazi*, 16 PD 2688 (1962) (architectural works); CA 464/65 *Unger v Paris-Israel Movies Ltd*, 20(3) PD 6 (1966) (interpretation of contract).

many of them added their national character, whether Jewish or Arab. Most of the authors, publishers, and even lawyers in Palestine acted not only with their own interests at mind, but with strong awareness of their role in a larger, national scheme.

Much remains to study and explore, regarding Palestine and elsewhere. We need more studies of the processes of colonial copyright, both in the British Empire and in other empires.[18] Most current literature focuses on the British point of view, without asking enough about the fate of the law in the colonies, other than its feedback impact on the Empire. The colonized peoples' perception of the transplant process is still vastly missing. Along the discussion, I pointed to several broader themes and similar patterns of reception in different colonies, such as the initial activation of the law by foreigners. This and other patterns require further study. For example, an interesting avenue to explore is whether a dominant content industry shaped the development of the law in each jurisdiction.[19] The parallels between the condition of colonial copyright and contemporary globalization is yet another area for further research, so to better understand how the earlier form of globalization by colonization has affected the latter phase.

The interest in the interaction of copyright law and social norms is now catching up, with few important works on specific issues, such as the norms amongst American stand-up comedians, French chefs, or fashion designers.[20] This formal–informal law interaction needs to be studied also in a historical perspective. In this book, we saw two main such occasions, with the Hebrew authors and Arab musicians, but we need to learn more about the meeting place of the social and the legal, at the time that the latter purported to replace the former.

Another conclusion that emerges from the discussion draws our attention to the author as a national character. Much work has been done in the past two decades on understanding the role of the author, or more accurately, the image of the author, in the development of copyright law.[21] The literature pointed to the figure of the romantic author and occasionally to some other attributes, such as gender. The national identity of the author—the self-image of the author as acting as part of a broader group, based on a national identity—also requires closer attention and more case studies from different cultures.

---

[18] For a study of colonial copyright in the Spanish Empire, see Jose Bellido, 'Latin American and Spanish Copyright Relations (1880–1904)' (2009) 17 J of World IP 1.

[19] See eg Shubha Ghosh, 'A Roadmap for TRIPS: Copyright and Film in Colonial and Independent India' (2011) 1(2) Queen Mary J of IP 146, who focused on the role of the film industry in the development of Indian copyright law.

[20] See Dotan Oliar and Christopher Sprigman, 'There's No Free Laugh (Anymore): The Emergence of Intellectual Property Norms and the Transformation of Stand-Up Comedy' (2008) 94 Va L Rev 1787; Emmanuelle Fauchart and Eric von Hippel, 'Norms-Based Intellectual Property Systems: The Case of French Chefs' (2008) 19(2) Organization Science 187; Kal Raustiala and Christopher Sprigman, 'The Piracy Paradox: Innovation and Intellectual Property in Fashion Design' (2006) 92 Va L Rev 1687.

[21] See Martha Woodmansee and Peter Jaszi (eds), *The Construction of Authorship: Textual Appropriation in Law and Literature* (Duke University Press, 1994); Mario Biagioli, Peter Jaszi, Martha Woodmansee (eds), *Making and Unmaking Intellectual Property: Creative Production in Legal and Cultural Perspective* (University of Chicago Press, 2011).

The research here pointed to some specific gaps in the literature that merit attention. The almost unnoticed story of the Ottoman Authors' Rights Act is such a case. The Ottoman law was amended in Palestine in 1920 and repealed in 1924; it was repealed in Turkey in 1951. Its last holding was Jordan, where it lasted until 1992. The sources, development, and impact of this law carry the potential to reveal an alternative copyright course, one that did not prevail in the long run. The development of copyright law in the West Bank, now partially occupied by Israel, is yet another place to look at. The Palestinian Authority seems to be the last jurisdiction where the 1911 Copyright Act still governs.[22] The history of the neighbouring fields of patent law and trademark law also require attention.

At the end of the day, the British left, but their legal tradition, copyright included, persisted. With the end of the Mandate, the Board of Trade opined that the copyright laws can be revoked, though it later modified its views that the international commitments need to be maintained. The Copyright Act lapsed, the Copyright Ordinance was terminated, but they were immediately reaffirmed by the new government of the land. Copyright law was dead, long live copyright law.

---

[22] See Ihab G Samaan, *A Historical View of Intellectual Property Rights in the Palestinian Territories* (LLM Thesis, University of Georgia, 2003); Palestinian Legal and Judicial System Al-Muqtafi, Institute of Law, Bir-Zeit University, available at http://muqtafi.birzeit.edu/en/.

Bibliography

ARCHIVES

BBC Written Archives Centre, Reading (Boxes: E1/1136, 42)
Benayahu Private Archive, Jerusalem
Central Zionist Archive, Jerusalem (Files: L2, A192, A417, 525/5504, KKL2, KKL5, S5/11321, S512455, S41/35)
Hebrew Authors Association—Gnazim, Tel-Aviv (Boxes: 84840, 84850–2, 512)
Israel State Archive, Jerusalem (Boxes: B28153, M32/2, M32/3, M293/8, M353/3, M354/1, M354/3, M354/16, M354/26, M354/27, M361/14, M361/15, M361/16, M361/20, M361/39, M361/61, M575/12, M698/13, M1879, P233)
Jerusalem City Archive, Jerusalem (Boxes: 471, 472, 473, 477)
National Archives, London (Boxes: CO 123/281, CO 137/726, CO 295/516, CO 321/276, CO 321/279, CO 321/299, CO 323/646, CO 323/655, CO 323/692, CO 323/764, CO 323/920, CO 323/1098, CO 323/1747, CO 323/1893, CO 733/22, CO 733/41, CO 733/170, CO 794/1, CO 814/6, CO 886/8, T 1/11521)
Performing Rights Society, London (Boxes: A209, A293, A319, A326)
Reuter Archive, London (Files: LN229, LN242, LN733, 8412904)
Rubin Mass Ltd, Jerusalem (contracts from the years: 1936–43, 1945, 1947)
Schocken Publishing House Archive, Tel-Aviv (Margolin files)
Supreme Court Archive, Jerusalem
Tel-Aviv City Archive, Tel-Aviv (Boxes: 566, 1023)
Tel-Aviv University, Tel-Aviv (Files: 19, 20)
Ziffer Archive, Tel-Aviv University, Tel-Aviv

NEWSPAPERS & PERIODICALS

Davar (Hebrew) (1925, 1927, 1929, 1931, 1935, 1938–39, 1941, 1946)
Filastin (Arabic) (1931)
Haaretz (Hebrew) (1921, 1926–28, 1930, 1932–33, 1935, 1937, 1941)
Ktuvim (Hebrew) (1926–30)
Moznayim (Hebrew) (1929–31)
Palestine Bulletin (English) (1931–32)
Palestine Post (English) (1932–33, 1935–36, 1939, 1941, 1943, 1947)
The Times (London)

GOVERNMENTAL PUBLICATIONS

Canada

Cavoukian, Ann, *Privacy by Design* (Information and Privacy Commissioner, Ontario, 2009).

MANDATE PALESTINE

An Interim Report, Civil Administration of Palestine, During the Period 1st July, 1920–30th June, 1921
Government of Palestine, *Palestine Junior Service Staff List* (1931)
Government of Palestine, *Civil Service List* (1938)
Statistical Abstract for Palestine (Office of Statistics, Jerusalem, 1936)

UNITED KINGDOM

Report from the Selected Committee of the House of Lords on the Copyright Bill, 1899 Session
Strickland, C F, *A Report on the Possibility of Introducing a System of Agricultural Cooperation in Palestine, submitted to the Government of Palestine* (1930)

UNITED STATES

Library of Congress, *Report of the Delegate of the United States to the International Conference for the Revision of the Berne Copyright Convention, Held at Berlin, Germany, October 14 to November 14, 1908*, Copyright Office Bulletin, No 13 (Washington, 1908)

OTHER SOURCES

Bently, Lionel, and Martin Kretschmer (eds), Primary Sources on Copyright (1450–1900), http://www.copyrighthistory.org
Gurevich, D (supervision), Gertz, A (ed), Zankar, A (assistant), *Statistical Handbook of Jewish Palestine* (Department of Statistics, The Jewish Agency for Palestine, Jerusalem, 1947)
McCarthy, Clive, 'Development of the A.M. Transmitter Network, Ver 4' (2004)
Tidhar, David, *Encyclopaedia of the Founders and Builders of Israel* (1947)

BOOKS

Abbott, John, *The Story of Francis, Day & Hunter* (Francis, Day & Hunter, London, 1952)
Agnon, Shmuel Yosef, *My Dear Esterline, Letters, 1924–1931* (Schocken, Jerusalem, 1983) (Hebrew)
Agron, Gershon, *The Loyal Rebel* (M Newman Publishing House, Jerusalem, 1964) (Hebrew)
Akavia, A A (ed), *The Memories of the Publisher Shlomo Sherbrek* (Sherbrek, Tel-Aviv, 1955) (Hebrew)
Al-Husayni, Ishaq Musa, *The Return of the Boat* (Al Muquades, Jerusalem, 1946) (Arabic)
Al-Jawzi, Nasiry, *The History of the Palestinian Radio 'This is Jerusalem': 1936–1948* (Syrian General Organization of the Book, Damascus, 2010)
Alexander, Isabella, *Copyright Law and the Public Interest in the Nineteenth Century* (Hart, Oxford, 2010)
Alroey, Gur, *Immigrants: Jewish Immigration to Palestine in the Early Twentieth Century* (Yad Ben-Zvi, Jerusalem, 2004) (Hebrew)
Amegatcher, Andrew Ofoe, *Ghanaian Law of Copyright* (Omega, Accra, 1993)
Amichay-Michlin, Dania, *The Love of AJ Stybel* (Bialik Institute, Jerusalem, 2000) (Hebrew)
Arnon-Ohanna, Yuval, *The Internal Struggle within the Palestinian Movement, 1929–1939* (Shiloah Center for Middle East and African Studies, Tel-Aviv, 1981)

Ashcroft, Bill, Gareth Griffiths, and Helen Tiffin, *The Empire Writes Back: Theory and Practice in Post-Colonial Literatures* (2nd edn, Routledge, London, 2002)
Atkinson, Benedict, *True History of Copyright: The Australian Experience 1905–2005* (Sydney University Press, Sydney, 2007)
Ayalon, Ami, *Reading Palestine: Printing and Literacy, 1900–1948* (University of Texas Press, Austin, 2004)
Barthes, Roland, *Image, Music, Text* (Hill and Wang, New York, 1978)
Battiste, Marie and James Youngblood Henderson, *Protecting Indigenous Knowledge and Heritage: A Global Challenge* (Purich Pub, Saskatoon, 2000)
Bayer, Oskar (ed), Geoffrey Strachan (trans), *Eric Mendelsohn, Letters of an Architect* (Abelard-Schuman, London, 1967)
Be'er, Haim, *Their Love and Their Hate: H.N. Bialik, Y.H. Brenner, S.Y. Agnon Relations* (Am Oved, Tel-Aviv, 1992) (Hebrew)
Ben-Zvi, Izhak, *Eretz-Israel under Ottoman Rule: Four Centuries of History* (Yad Ben-Zvi, Jerusalem, 1969) (Hebrew)
Bendix, Reinhard, *From Berlin to Berkeley: German-Jewish Identities* (Transaction Publications, New Brunswick, 1986)
Benjamin, Walter, *The Work of Art in the Age of its Technological Reproducibility and other Writings on Media* (Harvard University Press, Cambridge, 2008 (1936))
Benkler, Yochai, *The Wealth of Networks: How Social Production Transforms Markets and Freedom* (Yale University Press, New Haven, 2006)
Bentwich, Margery and Norman Bentwich, *Herbert Bentwich: The Pilgrim Father* (Hotza'ah Ivrith, Jerusalem, 1940)
Bentwich, Norman, *England in Palestine* (Kegan Paul, Trench, Trübner & Co, London, 1932)
Bentwich, Norman, *Palestine* (Benn, London, 1934)
Bentwich, Norman, *Fulfilment in the Promised Land, 1917–1937* (Soncino Press, London, 1938)
Bentwich, Norman, *Wanderer between Two Worlds* (Kegan Paul, Trench, Trübner & Co, London, 1941)
Berlovitz, Yaffa, *Inventing a Land, Inventing a People* (HaKibbutz HaMeuchad, Tel-Aviv, 1996) (Hebrew)
Bernstein, Deborah S, *Constructing Boundaries: Jewish and Arab Workers in Mandatory Palestine* (State University of New York, Albany, 2000)
Bernstein-Cohen, Miriam, *A Drop in the Sea* (Massada, Ramat-Gan, 1971) (Hebrew)
Bhabha, Homi, *The Location of Culture* (Routledge, London, 1994, 2010)
Biagioli, Mario, Peter Jaszi, and Martha Woodmansee (eds), *Making and Unmaking Intellectual Property: Creative Production in Legal and Cultural Perspective* (University of Chicago Press, Chicago, 2011)
Biger, Gideon, *Crown Colony or National Homeland? British Influence upon Palestine, 1917–1930, A Geo-Historical Analysis* (Yad Ben-Zvi, Jerusalem, 1983) (Hebrew)
Birrell, Augustine, *Seven Lectures on The Law and History of Copyright in Books* (Cassell and Co Ltd, London, 1899)
Blagden, Cyprian, *The Stationers' Company: A History 1403–1959* (Stanford University Press, Stanford, 1960)
Bourdieu, Pierre, *The Field of Cultural Production: Essays on Art and Literature* (Cambridge University Press, New York, 1993)
Boyle, James, *Shamans, Software, and Spleens: Law and the Construction of the Information Society* (Harvard University Press, Cambridge, 1996)

Briggs, Asa, *The Golden Age of Wireless* (Oxford University Press, New York, 1965)
Briggs, Asa, *The Birth of Broadcasting: 1896–1927* (Oxford University Press, London, 1995)
Briggs, William, *The Law of International Copyright* (Stevens and Haynes, London, 1906)
Brun, Nathan, *Judges and Lawyers in Eretz Yisrael* (Magnes, Jerusalem, 2008) (Hebrew)
Bugbee, Bruce W, *Genesis of American Patent and Copyright Law* (Public Affairs Press, Washington, 1967)
Campos, Michelle U, *Ottoman Brothers: Muslims, Christians and Jews in Early Twentieth Century Palestine* (Stanford University Press, Stanford, 2011)
Chatterji, P C, *Broadcasting in India* (Sage Publications, New Delhi, revised and updated edn, 1991)
Chege, John Waruingi, *Copyright Law and Publishing in Kenya* (Kenya Literature Bureau, Nairobi, 1978)
Cohen, Dalia and Ruth Katz, *Palestinian Arab Music: A Maqam Tradition in Palestine* (University of Chicago Press, Chicago, 2006)
Cohen-Hatab, Kobi, *Tour the Land: Tourism in Palestine during the British Mandate, 1917–1948* (Yad Ben-Zvi, Jerusalem, 2006)
Cole, J S R and W N Denison, *Tanganyika: The Development of its Laws and Constitution* (Stevens, London, 1964)
Colles, William Morris and Harold Hardy, *Playright and Copyright in All Countries* (Macmillan, London, 1906)
Copeling, A J C, *Copyright Law in South Africa* (Butterworths, Durban, 1969)
Copinger, Walter Arthur, *The Law of Copyright in Works of Literature and Art* (Stevens and Haynes, London, 1870)
Copinger, Walter Arthur and J M Easton *The Law of Copyright in Works of Literature, Art, Architecture, Photography, Music and the Drama* (5th edn, Stevens and Haynes, London, 1915)
Copinger, Walter Arthur and F E Skone James, *Copinger on the Law of Copyright in Works of Literature, Art, Agriculture, Photography, Music and the Drama* (6th edn, Sweet & Maxwell, London, 1927)
Daldy, Frederic R (ed), *The Colonial Copyright Acts* (Longmans & Co, London, 1889)
David, Anthony, *The Patron* (Schocken Publishing House, Jerusalem, 2006) (Hebrew)
Davison, Roderic H, *Reforms in the Ottoman Empire 1856–1876* (Gordian Press, Princeton, 1973)
Daykan (Dikshtein), Paltiel, *The History of the Hebrew Law of Peace: Trends, Activities and Achievements* (Yavne Press, Tel-Aviv, 1964) (Hebrew)
Deazley, Ronan, *On the Origin of the Right to Copy: Charting the Movement of Copyright Law in Eighteenth-Century Britain (1695–1775)* (Hart Publishing, Oxford, 2004)
Deazley, Ronan, *Rethinking Copyright: History, Theory, Language* (Edward Elgar, Cheltenham, 2006)
Drahos, Peter with John Braithwaite, *Information Feudalism: Who Owns the Knowledge Economy?* (New Press, New York, 2002)
Drahos, Peter and Ruth Mayne (eds), *Global Intellectual Property Rights: Knowledge, Access and Development* (Palgrave Macmillan, Basingstoke, 2002)
Dupont, Jerry, *The Common Law Abroad: Constitutional and Legal Legacy of the British Empire* (Fred B Rothman Publications, Littleton, 2001)
Edmunds, Lewis and Herbert Bentwich, *The Law of Copyright in Designs* (2nd edn, Sweet & Maxwell, London, 1908)
Egerton, Hugh Edward, *British Colonial Policy in the XXth Century* (Methuen, London, 1922)

Ehrlich, Cyril, *Harmonious Alliance: A History of the Performing Right Society* (Oxford University Press, Oxford, 1989)
El Said, Mohammed, *The Development of Intellectual Property Protection in the Arab World* (Edwin Mellen Press, Lewiston, 2008)
Elias, T Olawale, *British Colonial Law: A Comparative Study of the Interaction between English and Local Laws in British Dependencies* (Stevens & Sons, London, 1962)
Ellickson, Robert C, *Order without Law: How Neighbors Settle Disputes* (Harvard University Press, Cambridge, 1991)
Falk, Ze'ev, *The Intellectual Property in Israel Law: Sources and Inquiries on Authors' and Inventors' Rights* (1947) (Hebrew)
Feather, John, *Publishing, Piracy and Politics: An Historical Study of Copyright in Britain* (Mansell, New York, 1994)
Feldstein, Ariel L, *Pioneer, Toil, Camera: Cinema in Service of the Zionist Ideology, 1917–1939* (Am Oved, Tel-Aviv, 2009) (Hebrew)
Fortna, Benjamin C, *Learning to Read in the Late Ottoman Empire and the Early Turkish Republic* (Palgrave Macmillan, Basingstoke, 2011)
Friedman, Batya (ed), *Human Values and the Design of Computer Technology* (Stanford University Press, Stanford, 1997)
Friedman, Menachem, *Society and Religion: The Non-Zionist Orthodox in Eretz-Israel, 1918–1936* (Yad Ben-Zvi, Jerusalem, 1977) (Hebrew)
Gamzu, Haim, *Painting and Sculpture in Israel: The Plastic Arts from Bezalel Period to the Present Day* (Eshkol, Tel-Aviv, 1951)
Geertz, Clifford, *The Interpretation of Cultures* (Basic Books, New York, 1973)
Gelber, Yoav, *New Homeland: Immigration and Absorption of Central European Jews 1933–1948* (Yad Ben-Zvi, Jerusalem, 1990) (Hebrew)
Gertz, Nurith and George Khleifi, *Palestinian Cinema: Landscape, Trauma and Memory* (Indiana University Press, Bloomington, 2008)
Giladi, Dan, *The Yishuv during the Fourth Wave of Immigration (1924–1929): An Economic and Political Discussion* (Am Oved, Tel-Aviv, 1973) (Hebrew)
Gluzman, Michael, *The Politics of Canonicity: Lines of Resistance in Modernist Hebrew Poetry* (Stanford University Press, Stanford, 2003)
Gnessin, Menachem, *My Way with the Hebrew Theatre* (HaKibbutz HaMeuchad, Tel-Aviv, 1946) (Hebrew)
Goadby, Frederic M, *Introduction to the Study of Law: a Handbook for the Use of Law Students in Egypt and Palestine* (3rd edn, Butterworth, London, 1921)
Goadby, Frederic M, *International and Inter-religious Private Law in Palestine* (Hamadpis Press, Jerusalem, 1926)
Gross, Nathan and Jacob, *The Hebrew Movie: Chapters in the History of the Silent and Talking Movie in Israel* (Nathan and Jacob Gross, Jerusalem, 1991) (Hebrew)
Halachmi, Joseph, *Fresh Wind: The First Zionist Film in Palestine 1899–1902* (Carmel, Jerusalem, 2009) (Hebrew)
HaLevy, Shoshana, *First Issues in the Yishuv's History* (Jerusalem, 1989) (Hebrew)
Hanioğlu, M Şükrü, *A Brief History of the Late Ottoman Empire* (Princeton University Press, Princeton, 2008)
Harris, Ron, Alexandre (Sandy) Kedar, Pnina Lahav, and Assaf Likhovski (eds), *The History of Law in a Multi-Cultural Society: Israel 1917–1967* (Ashgate Publishing, Aldershot, 2002)
Hasian, Marouf A, *Colonial Legacies in Postcolonial Contexts: A Critical Rhetorical Examination of Legal Histories* (Peter Lang publishing, New York, 2002)

Helman, Anat, *Urban Culture in 1920s and 1930s Tel-Aviv* (Haifa University Press, Haifa, 2007) (Hebrew)
Hirschberg, A S, *The Way of the New Yishuv in Eretz Yisrael* (photocopy of the Vilna Edition), 1901 (Yad Ben-Zvi, Jerusalem, 1979) (Hebrew)
Hirshberg, Jehoash, *Music in the Jewish Community of Palestine 1880–1948: A Social History* (Oxford University Press, Oxford, 1995)
Hooper, Charles A, *The Civil Law of Palestine and Trans-Jordan* (Sweet & Maxwell, London, 1936)
Hyamson, Albert M, *Palestine under the Mandate 1920–1948* (Methuen & Co, London, 1950)
Inbari, Assaf, *Home* (Yediot Ahronot—Hemed, Tel-Aviv, 2009) (Hebrew)
James, Charles F, *The Story of the Performing Rights Society* (PRS, London, 1951)
Jeffries, Charles Joseph, *The Colonial Office* (Allen and Unwin, London, 1956)
Kabha, Mustafa, *Journalism in the Eye of the Storm: The Palestinian Press Shapes Public Opinion 1929–1939* (Yad Ben-Zvi, Jerusalem, 2004) (Hebrew)
Kaniel, Yehoshua, *Continuation and Change: The Old Yishuv and the New Yishuv during the First and Second Aliyah* (Yad Ben-Zvi, Jerusalem, 1982) (Hebrew)
Karpat, Kemal H with Robert W Zens, (eds), *Ottoman Borderlands: Issues, Personalities and Political Changes* (University of Wisconsin Press, Madison, 2003)
Kasaba, Reşat, *The Ottoman Empire and the World Economy: The Nineteenth Century* (State University of New York Press, Albany, 1988)
Keith, Arthur Berriedale, *The Governments of the British Empire* (Macmillan & Co, New York, 1935)
Kelly, Kevin, *What Technology Wants* (Viking, New York, 2010)
Kimmerling, Baruch and Joel S Migdal, *Palestinians: The Making of a People* (Harvard University Press, Cambridge, 1993)
Kirkby, Diane and Catherine Coleborne (eds), *Law, History, Colonialism: The Reach of the Empire* (Manchester University Press, Manchester, 2001)
Krikorian, Gaëlle and Amy Kapczynski (eds), *Access to Knowledge in the Intellectual Property Age* (Zone Books, New York, 2010)
Kohansky, Mendel, *The Hebrew Theatre: Its First Fifty Years* (Israel Universities Press, Jerusalem, 1969) (Hebrew)
Kushner, David (ed), *Palestine in the Late Ottoman Period: Political, Social and Economic Transformation* (Yad Ben-Zvi, Jerusalem, 1986)
Lachover, P (ed), *Letters of Haim Nachman Bialik* (Dvir, Tel-Aviv, 1938) (Hebrew)
Ladwig-Winters, Simone, *Anwalt ohne Recht: das Schicksal jüdischer Rechtsanwälte in Berlin nach 1933* (Be.bra, Berlin, 2007) (German)
Lahav, Pnina, *Judgment in Jerusalem: Chief Justice Shimon Agranat and the Zionist Century* (Am Oved, Tel-Aviv, 1999) (Hebrew)
Lake Tee, Khaw, *Copyright Law in Malaysia* (Lexis Law Pub, Singapore, 1994)
Lesser, Allen, *Israel's Impact, 1950–1: A Personal Record* (University Press of America, Lanham, 1984)
Lessig, Lawrence, *Code: Version 2.0* (Basic Books, New York, 2006)
Levitsky, Serge L, *Introduction to Soviet Copyright Law* (Sythoff, Leyden, 1962)
Likhovski, Assaf, *Law and Identity in Mandate Palestine* (University of North Carolina Press, Chapel Hill, 2006)
Loomba, Ania, *Colonialism/Postcolonialism* (2nd edn, Routledge, London, 2005)
Loon, Ng-Loy Wee, *Law of Intellectual Property of Singapore* (Thomson Sweet & Maxwell Asia, Singapore, 2008)

Lugard, Frederick D, *The Dual Mandate in British Tropical Africa* (5th edn, Frank Cass, London, 1965)
Macgillivray, E J, *A Treatise Upon the Law of Copyright* (John Murray, London, 1902)
Makover, Rachela, *Government and Administration of Palestine, 1917–1925* (Yad Ben-Zvi, Jerusalem, 1988) (Hebrew)
Malchi, Eliezer, *The History of Law in Eretz Yisrael: A Historical Introduction to the Law in Israel* (2nd edn, Dinim, Tel-Aviv, 1953) (Hebrew)
Manor, Dalia, *Art in Zion: The Genesis of Modern National Art in Jewish Palestine* (Routledge, London, 2005)
Mathiopoulos, Margarita, *History and Progress: In Search of the European and American Mind* (Praeger Publishers, New York, 1989)
Mattei, Ugo and Laura Nader, *Plunder: When the Rule of Law is Illegal* (Blackwell, Oxford, 2008)
Matthews, Weldon C, *Confronting an Empire, Constructing a Nation: Arab Nationalists and Popular Politics in Mandate Palestine* (I B Tauris, London, 2006)
Mautner, Menachem, *Law and the Culture of Israel* (Oxford University Press, Oxford, 2011)
McCarthy, Justin, *The Population of Palestine: Population History and Statistics of the Late Ottoman Period and the Mandate* (Columbia University Press, New York, 1990)
McClung Lee, Alfred, *The Daily Newspaper in America: The Evolution of a Social Instrument* (Routledge/Thoemmes Press, London, 2000)
McFarlane, Gavin, *Copyright: The Development and Exercise of the Performing Right* (John Offord Publications, Eastbourne, 1980)
Merton, Robert K, *On the Shoulders of Giants: A Shandean Postscript* (University of Chicago Press, Chicago, 1993)
Metzer, Jacob, *The Divided Economy of Mandatory Palestine* (Cambridge University Press, Cambridge, 1998)
Meyrowitz, Joshua, *No Sense of Place: The Impact of Electronic Media on Social Behavior* (Oxford University Press, New York, 1985)
Milstein, Uri (ed), *Rachel* (Smoira-Bittan, Tel-Aviv, 1985) (Hebrew)
Nadan, Amos, *The Palestinian Peasant Economy under the Mandate: A Story of Colonial Bungling* (Harvard Center for Middle Eastern Studies, Cambridge, 2006)
Negroponte, Nicholas, *Being Digital* (Vintage, New York, 1996)
Netanel, Neil (ed), *The Development Agenda: Global Intellectual Property and Developing Countries* (Oxford University Press, Oxford, 2008)
Netanel, Neil W and David Nimmer, *From Maimonides to Microsoft: Jewish Copyright Law Since the Birth of Print* (Oxford University Press, Oxford, forthcoming 2012)
Neumann, Boaz, *Land and Desire in Early Zionism* (Am Oved, Tel-Aviv, 2009) (Hebrew)
Nisbet, Robert A, *The History of The Idea of Progress* (Transaction Publishers, New Brunswick, 1994)
Nowell-Smith, Simon, *International Copyright Law and the Publisher in the Reign of Queen Victoria* (Oxford University Press, Oxford, 1968)
Ocheme, Peter, *The Law and Practice of Copyright in Nigeria* (Ahmadu Bello University Press, Zaria, 2000)
Palmer, Alan, *The Decline and Fall of the Ottoman Empire* (J Murray, London, 1992)
Pappe, Ilan (ed), *Jewish-Arab Relations in Mandatory Palestine: A New Approach to the Historical Research* (Institute for Peace Research, Giva't Haviva, 1995) (Hebrew)
Parkinson, Charles O H, *Bills of Rights and Decolonization: The Emergence of Domestic Human Rights Instruments in Britain's Overseas Territories* (Oxford University Press, Oxford, 2008)

Partner, Peter, *Arab Voices: The BBC Arabic Service 1938–1988* (BBC, London, 1988)

Patterson, Lyman Ray, *Copyright in Historical Perspective* (Vanderbilt University Press, Nashville, 1968)

Patterson, L Ray and Stanley W Lindberg, *The Nature of Copyright: A Law of Users' Rights* (University of Georgia Press, Athens, 1991)

Pokorovski, I A, *The Fundamental Problems of Civil Law* (A Litai (trans), Y Yonovich (ed), Poalim Press, Jerusalem, 1923) (1917) (Hebrew)

Pollard, Sidney, *The Idea of Progress: History and Society* (Penguin, Harmondsworth, 1968)

Posner, Eric A, *Law and Social Norms* (Harvard University Press, Cambridge, 2000)

Quataert, Donald, *The Ottoman Empire, 1700–1922* (Cambridge University Press, New York, 2000)

Rakover, Nahum, *Copyright in Jewish Sources* (Jewish Legal Heritage Society, Jerusalem, 1991) (Hebrew)

Ransom, Harry, *The First Copyright Statute: An Essay on an Act for the Encouragement of Learning, 1710* (University of Texas, Austin, 1956)

Raymond, André, *Arab Cities in the Ottoman Period* (Ashgate, Aldershot, 2002)

Reuveny, Jacob, *The Administration of Palestine under the British Mandate 1920–1948: An Institutional Analysis* (Bar-Ilan University Press, Ramat-Gan, 1993) (Hebrew)

Ricketson, Sam, *The Berne Convention for the Protection of Literary and Artistic Works: 1886–1986* (Kluwer, London, 1987)

Robinson Divine, Donna, *Politics and Society in Ottoman Palestine: The Arab Struggle for Survival and Power* (Lynne Rienner Pub, Boulder, 1993)

Rose, Mark, *Authors and Owners: The Invention of Copyright* (Harvard University Press, Cambridge, 1993)

Rosenthal Kwall, Roberta, *The Soul of Creativity: Forging a Moral Rights Law for the United States* (Stanford Law Books, Stanford, 2010)

Rosewater, Victor, *History of Cooperative News-gathering in the United States* (D Appleton & Co, New York, 1930)

Rozin, Orit, *Duty and Love: Individualism and Collectivism in 1950s Israel* (Tel-Aviv University Press, Tel-Aviv, 2008) (Hebrew)

Rubin, Avi, *Ottoman Nizamiye Courts: Law and Modernity* (Palgrave Macmillan, New York, 2011)

Saint-Amour, Paul (ed), *Modernism and Copyright* (Oxford University Press, Oxford, 2011)

Saposnik, Arieh Bruce, *Becoming Hebrew: The Creation of a Jewish National Culture in Ottoman Palestine* (Oxford University Press, Oxford, 2008)

Segal, Yerushalayim, *Memoirs: Yerusahalayim in Tel-Aviv* (Moledet, Tel-Aviv, 1993) (Hebrew)

Sela, Rona, *Photography in Palestine in the 1930s–1940s* (HaKibbutz Hameuchad, Herzlyia, 2000) (Hebrew)

Seville, Catherine, *Literary Copyright Reform in Early Victorian England: The Framing of The 1842 Copyright Act* (Cambridge University Press, Cambridge, 1999)

Seville, Catherine, *The Internationalisation of Copyright Law: Books, Buccaneers and the Black Flag in the Nineteenth Century* (Cambridge University Press, Cambridge, 2006)

Shalit, David, *Projecting Power: The Cinema Houses, the Movies and the Israelis* (Resling Publishing, Tel-Aviv, 2006) (Hebrew)

Shapira, Anita, *New Jews, Old Jews* (Am Oved, Tel-Aviv, 1997) (Hebrew)

Shavit, Zohar, *The Literary Life in Eretz Yisrael 1910–1933* (HaKibbutz HaMeuchad, Tel-Aviv, 1982) (Hebrew)

Shavit, Zohar (ed), *The Construction of Hebrew Culture in Eretz Yisrael* (Bialik Institute, Jerusalem, 1989) (Hebrew)
Sherman, A J, *Mandate Days: British Lives in Palestine, 1918–1948* (Thames and Hudson, London, 1997)
Sherman, Brad and Lionel Bently, *The Making of Modern Intellectual Property Law: The British Experience, 1760–1911* (Cambridge University Press, Cambridge, 1999)
Sherman, Brad and Alain Strowel (eds), *Of Authors and Origins: Essays on Copyright Law* (Oxford University Press, Oxford, 1994)
Skouteris, Thomas, *The Notion of Progress in International Law Discourse* (TMC Asser Press, The Hague, 2010)
Slaughter, Anne-Marie, *A New World Order* (Princeton University Press, Princeton, 2005)
Smith, Adam, *An Inquiry into the Nature and Causes of the Wealth of Nations* (Edwin Cannan (ed), Random House, New York, 1994) (1776)
Smith, Barbara J, *The Roots of Separatism in Palestine: British Economic Policy, 1920-1929* (I N Tauris and Co, Ltd, London 1983)
Spadafora, David, *The Idea of Progress in Eighteenth Century Britain* (Yale University Press, New Haven, 1990)
Sterling, J A L, *World Copyright Law* (2nd edn, Thomson Professional Pub, London, 2003)
Storey, Graham, *Reuters' Century, 1851–1951* (Parrish, London, 1951)
Storrs, Ronald, *Orientations* (Nicholson & Watson, London, 1937)
Strassman, Gabriel, *Wearing the Robes: A History of the Legal Profession until 1962* (Israeli Bar Association Press, Tel-Aviv, 1984) (Hebrew)
Taya, Abdallah, *Educational Media in Radio and Television* (Dar el-Majid, Ramallah, 2006) (Arabic)
Trajtenberg, Graciela, *Between Nationalism and Art* (Magnes, Jerusalem, 2005) (Hebrew)
Trollope, Anthony, *Autobiography of Anthony Trollope* (Serenity Publishers, Rockville, 2009) (originally published posthumously by Henry Trollope, 1883)
Twopeny, R E N, *Town Life in Australia* (Elliot Stock, London, 1883)
Vertheimer, Abraham Y M (ed), *Rabbi Yisha'ya DeTrani, The Responsa of Hary"d* (Rubin Mass, Jerusalem, 1975) (Hebrew)
Walterscheid, Edward C, *The Nature of the Intellectual Property Clause: A Study in Historical Perspective* (W S Hein & Co, Buffalo, 2002)
Wasserstein, Bernard, *The British in Palestine: The Mandatory Government and the Arab-Jewish Conflict 1917–1929* (2nd edn, Blackwell, Cambridge, 1991)
Watson, Alan, *Legal Transplants: An Approach to Comparative Law* (2nd edn, University of Georgia Press, Athens, 1993 (1974))
Wei, George, *The Law of Copyright in Singapore* (Singapore National Printers, Singapore, 1989)
Woodmansee, Martha and Peter Jaszi (eds), *The Construction of Authorship: Textual Appropriation in Law and Literature* (Duke University Press Books, Durham, 1994)
Yorman, Pinhas, *ACUM Story* (Publishers Association, Tel-Aviv, 1977) (Hebrew)
Ziff, Bruce H and Pratima V Rao (eds), *Borrowed Power: Essays on Cultural Appropriation* (Rutgers University Press, New Brunswick, 1997)
Zimmerman, Moshe, *Signs of Cinema: the History of Israeli Cinema, 1896–1948* (Dionon, Tel-Aviv, 2001) (Hebrew)

ARTICLES

Abrams, Norman, 'Interpreting the Criminal Code Ordinance, 1936: The Untapped Well' (1972) 7 Isr L Rev 25

Abu-Ghazaleh, Adnan, 'Arab Cultural Nationalism in Palestine during the British Mandate' (1972) 1(3) Journal of Palestinian Studies 37

Agmon, Iris, 'Late-Ottoman Legal Reforms and the Sharia Courts: A Few Comments on Women, Gender, and Family' in Eyal Katvan, Margalit Shilo, Ruth Halperin-Kadari (eds), *One Law for Man and Woman: Woman, Rights and Law in Mandatory Palestine* (Bar-Ilan University Press, Ramat-Gan, 2010) 117 (Hebrew)

Almog, Eytan 'The British Mandate Government in the Face of a Hostile Press in Palestine' (1994) 15 Kesher 85 (Hebrew)

Almog, Eytan 'A Wireless Broadcasting Station in Palestine: The First Hebrew Radio Station in the World' (1996) 20 Kesher 66 (Hebrew)

Aviv, Mendel, 'Some Aspects of the Birth of Broadcasting in Israel' (1966) Technion Yearbook 44 (Hebrew)

Azuz, Menachem, 'On the History of the Jews in Adrianopolis' in Avraham Elmaliach (ed), *Hemdat Israel* (Misgav Ladach Hospital Press, Jerusalem, 1946) 157 (Hebrew)

Baird, Douglas G, 'The Story of INS v. AP: Property, Natural Monopoly, and the Uneasy Legacy of a Concocted Controversy' in Jane C Ginsburg, Rochelle Cooper Dreyfuss (eds*), Intellectual Property Stories* (Foundation Press, New York, 2006) 9

Balganesh, Shyamkrishna, '"Hot News": The Enduring Myth of Property in News' (2011) 111 Colum L Rev 419

Bar-Shira, Israel, 'About the Substance of the Comrades' Law' (1930) 4 HaMishpat 103 (Hebrew)

Bazri, Ezra, 'Authors' Right' (1985) 6 Tehumin 169 (Hebrew)

Be'eri, L, 'Movies and Silent Movie Cinemas' in A B Yaffe (ed), *Literature and Art in Small Tel-Aviv, 1909–1929* (HaKibbutz HaMeuchad, Tel-Aviv, 1980) 272 (Hebrew)

Bellido, Jose, 'Latin American and Spanish Copyright Relations (1880–1904)' (2009) 17 J World IP 1

Bellido, Jose, 'Colonial Copyright Extensions: Spain at the Berne Convention (1883–1899)' (2011) 58 J Copyright Soc'y of the USA 243

Benayahu, Meir, 'The Big Fires in Izmir and Adrianopolis' in 2 *Rashumot* (Dvir Press, Tel-Aviv, 1946) 144 (Hebrew)

Bendix, L, 'Early Protection of the Author's Right' (1945) 2 HaPraklit 216 (Hebrew)

Benkler, Yochai, 'Free As the Air to Common Use: First Amendment Constraints on Enclosure of the Public Domain' (1999) 74 NYU L Rev 354

Bently, Lionel, 'Copyright and the Victorian Internet: Telegraphic Property Laws in Colonial Australia' (2004) 38 Loy LA L Rev 71

Bently, Lionel, 'Copyright, Translations, and Relations between Britain and India in the Nineteenth and Early Twentieth Centuries' (2007) 82 Chi Kent L Rev 1181

Bently, Lionel, 'R v The Author: From Death Penalty to Community Service' (2008) 32 Colum J L & The Arts 1

Bently, Lionel, 'The "Extraordinary Multiplicity" of Intellectual Property Laws in the British Colonies in the Nineteenth Century' (2011) 12 Theoretical Inq L 161

Bentwich, Norman, 'The Legislation of Palestine 1918–1925' (1926a) 8 J Comp Legis & Int'l L 9

Bentwich, Norman, 'Palestine' (1918) 2 J Comp Legis & Int'l L 168

Bentwich, Norman, 'Palestine' (1922) 4 J Comp Legis & Int'l L 177

Bentwich, Norman, 'Palestine' (1926b) 8 J Comp Legis & Int'l L 228
Berkeley Tech L J, 'The Law & Technology of Digital Rights Managements: Symposium Issue' (2003) 18(2) Berkeley Tech L J 487
Berkowitz, Daniel, Katharina Pistor, Jean-Francois Richard, 'The Transplant Effect' (2003) 51 AJCL 163
Bernstein, Lisa, 'Opting Out of the Legal System: Extralegal Contractual Relations in the Diamond Industry' (1992) 21 J Legal Stud 115
Birnhack, Michael D, 'The Idea of Progress in Copyright Law' (2001) 1 Buff IP L J 3
Birnhack, Michael D, 'Originality in Copyright Law and Cultural Control' (2002) 1 Aley Mishpat 347 (Hebrew)
Birnhack, Michael D, 'Global Copyright, Local Speech' (2006) 24 Cardozo Arts & Ent L J 491
Birnhack, Michael D, 'Trading Copyright: Global Pressure on Local Culture' in Neil Weinstock Netanel (ed), *The Development Agenda: Global Intellectual Property and Developing Countries* (Oxford University Press, Oxford, 2008) 365
Birnhack, Michael D, 'Israel' in Paul Edward Geller (ed), 2 *International Copyright Law and Practice* (Matthew Bender, New York, 2012) Isr-1
Birnhack, Michael D, 'Mandatory Copyright: From Pre-Palestine to Israel, 1910–2007' in Ysolde Gendreau and Uma Suthersanen (eds), *A Shifting Empire: 100 Years of the Copyright Act* 1911 (Edward Elgar, forthcoming, 2012)
Bowrey, Kathy and Natalie Fowell, 'Digging Up Fragments and Building IP Franchises' (2009) 31 Sydney L Rev 185
Boyd, Douglas A, 'Hebrew-Language Clandestine Radio Broadcasting During the British Palestine Mandate' (1999) 6 J Radio Stud 101
Bracha, Oren, 'The Ideology of Authorship Revisited: Authors, Markets and Liberal Virtues in Early American Copyright' (2008) 118 Yale L J 186
Bracha, Oren, 'The Statute of Anne: An American Mythology' (2010) 47 Hous L Rev 877
Brauneis, Robert, 'The Transformation of Originality in the Progressive-Era Debate over Copyright in News' (2009) 27 Cardozo Arts & Ent L J 321
Burrell, Robert, 'Copyright Reform in the Early Twentieth Century: the View from Australia' (2006) 27 J Leg Hist 239
Burroughs, Peter, 'Imperial Institutions and the Government of Empire' in Andrew Porter (ed), 3 *The Oxford History of The British Empire: The Nineteenth Century* (Oxford University Press, Oxford, 1999) 170
Çakmak, Diren, 'Concerning the Ottoman Copyright Legislation' (2007) 21 Selçuk U Turcology Study J 191 (Turkish)
Carroll, Michael W, 'The Struggle for Music Copyright' (2005) 57 Fla L Rev 907
Chander, Anupam, and Madhavi Sunder, 'The Romance of the Public Domain' (2004) 92 Cal L Rev 1331
Charny, David, 'Nonlegal Sanctions in Commercial Relations' (1990) 104 Harv L Rev 373
Chon, Margaret, 'Postmodern "Progress:" Reconsidering the Copyright and Patent Power' (1993) 43 DePaul L Rev 97
Cohen, Julie E, 'The Place of the User in Copyright Law' (2005) 74 Fordham L Rev 347
Cohn, Margit, 'Legal Transplant Chronicles: The Evolution of Unreasonableness and Proportionality Review of the Administration in the United Kingdom' (2010) 58 AJCL 583
Daniels, Ronald J, Michael J Trebilcock, and Lindsey D Carson, 'The Legacy of Empire: The Common Law Inheritance and Commitments to Legality in Former British Colonies' (2011) 59 AJCL 111

De Vries, David, 'The Making of Labour Zionism as a Moral Community: Workers' Tribunals in 1920s Palestine' (2000) 65 Lab Hist Rev 139

Deazley, Ronan, 'Breaking the Mould? The Radical Nature of the Fine Arts Copyright Bill 1862' in Ronan Deazley, Martin Kretschmer, Lionel Bently (eds), *Privilege and Property: Essays on the History of Copyright* (Open Book Publishers, Cambridge, 2010) 289

Deazley, Ronan, 'What's New about the Statute of Anne? Or Six Observations in Search of an Act' in Lionel Bently, Uma Suthersanen, Paul Torremans (eds), *Global Copyright: Three Hundred Years since the Statute of Anne, from 1709 to Cyberspace* (Edward Elgar, Cheltenham, 2010) 26

Delmage, Rutherford E, 'The American Idea of Progress, 1750–1800' (1947) 91 Proceedings of American Philosophical Society 307

de S Brunner, Edmund, 'Rural Communications Behavior and Attitudes in the Middle East' (1953) 18 Rural Sociology 149

Dikshtein, Paltiel, 'On the Expansion of the Function of the Hebrew Law of Peace' (1927) 1 HaMishpat 154 (Hebrew)

Dohrn, Verena, 'Diplomacy in the Diaspora: The Jewish Telegraphic Agency in Berlin (1922–1933)' (2009) 54(1) Leo Baeck Institute Yearbook 219

Eisenman, Robert, 'The Young Turk Legislation, 1913–17 and its Application in Palestine/Israel' in David Kushner (ed), *Palestine in the Late Ottoman Period: Political, Social and Economic Transformation* (Yad Ben-Zvi, Jerusalem, 1986) 59

Elyada, Ouzi, 'The Sensational Journalism in Eretz-Israel at the Early Twentieth Century' (1992) 11 Kesher 70 (Hebrew)

Engle Merry, Sally, 'Law and Colonialism' (1991) 25 L & Soc Rev 869

Epstein-HaLevy, Eliahu, 'Hebrew Law of Peace, Its Direction and Needed Changes' (1927) 2 HaMishpat 120 (Hebrew)

Erp, Judith van-, 'Reputational Sanctions in Private and Public Regulation' (2008) 1(5) Erasmus L Rev 145

Even Chen, Aharon, 'Itamar Ben Avi and "Doar Ha-Yom"' (1987) 1 Qeshar 55 (Hebrew)

Even-Zohar, Itamar, 'The Rise and Consolidation of a Local, Indigenous, Hebrew Culture in the Land of Israel, 1882–1948' (1980) 16 Katedra 165 (Hebrew)

Fauchart, Emmanuelle, and Eric von Hippel, 'Norms-Based Intellectual Property Systems: The Case of French Chefs' (2008) 19(2) Organization Science 187

Feuchtwanger, Naomi, 'Barukh (Boris) Schatz' in Ze'ev Tzahor (ed), *The Second Aliyah: Biographies* (Yad Ben-Zvi, Jerusalem, 1997) 392 (Hebrew)

Finn, Jeremy, 'Particularism versus Uniformity: Factors Shaping the Development of Australasian Intellectual Property Law in the Nineteenth Century' (2000) 6 Aust J Legal Hist 113

Fitzpatrick, Peter, 'Custom, Law and Resistance' in Peter Sack, Elizabeth Minchin (eds), *Legal Pluralism* (Proceeding of the Canberra Law Workshop VII, 1986) 63

Fitzpatrick, Peter, 'Terminal Legality: Imperialism and the (de)composition of Law' in Diane Kirkby, Catherine Coleborne (eds), *Law, History, Colonialism: The Reach of the Empire* (Manchester University Press, Manchester, 2001) 9

Foucault, Michel, 'What Is an Author?' in Paul Rabinow (ed), *The Foucault Reader* (Pantheon, New York, 1979) 101

Friedman, Lawrence, 'Some Comments on Cotterrell and Legal Transplants' in David Nelken, Johannes Fees (eds), *Adapting Legal Cultures* (Hart Publishing, Oxford, 2001) 93

Friedmann, Daniel, 'Infusion of the Common Law into the Legal System of Israel' (1975) 10 Isr L Rev 324

Geiger, Christophe, 'The Influence (Past and Present) of the Statute of Anne in France' in Lionel Bently, Uma Suthersanen, Paul Torremans (eds), *Global Copyright: Three Hundred Years since the Statute of Anne, from 1709 to Cyberspace* (Edward Elgar, Cheltenham, 2010) 122

Geller, Paul Edward, 'Legal Transplants in International Copyright: Some Problems with Method' (1994) 13 UCLA Pac Basin L J 199

Gervais, Daniel, 'The 1909 Copyright Act in International Context' (2010) 26 Santa Clara Comp & High-Tech L J 185

Getzler, Joshua, 'Transplantation and Mutation in Anglo-American Trust Law' (2009) 10 Theoretical Inq L 355

Ghosh, Shubha, 'A Roadmap for TRIPS: Copyright and Film in Colonial and Independent India' (2011) 1(2) Queen Mary J IP 146

Gil, Zvi, 'From the Voice of Jerusalem to the Voice of Israel' (1965) The Journalists' Yearbook 295 (Hebrew)

Ginsburg, Jane C, 'A Tale of Two Copyrights: Literary Property in Revolutionary France and America' in Brad Sherman, Alain Strowel (eds), *Of Authors and Origins: Essays on Copyright Law* (Oxford University Press, Oxford, 1994) 131

Ginsburg, Jane C, and John M Kernochan, 'One Hundred and Two Years Later: The United States Joins the Berne Convention' (1988) 13 Colum VLA J L & the Arts 1

Glover, Graham, 'Maybe the Courts are not Such a "Bleak House" After All? Or "Please, Sir, I Want Some More Copyright"' (2002) 119 S African L J 63

Goldfarb Marquis, Alice, 'Written in the Wind: The Impact of Radio during the 1930s' (1984) 19 J of Contemporary History 385

Graziadei, Michele, 'Comparative Law as the Study of Transplants and Receptions' in Mathias Reimann, Reinhard Zimmerman (eds), *The Oxford Handbook of Comparative Law* (Oxford University Press, Oxford, 2006) 441

Graziadei, Michele, 'Legal Transplants and the Frontiers of Legal Knowledge' (2009) 10 Theoretical Inq L 723

Haramati, Shlomo, 'Zerubbabel: The First Play in Eretz-Israel' (2002) 5 Hed HaHinuch 28 (Hebrew)

Harris, Ron, and Michael Crystal, 'Some Reflections on the Transplantation of British Company Law in Post-Ottoman Palestine' (2009) 10 Theoretical Inq L 561

Harvard Law Review Board, 'A Treatise Upon the Law of Copyright in the United Kingdom and the Dominions of the Crown and in the United States of America, Containing a Full Appendix of All Acts of Parliament, International Conventions, Orders in Council, Treasury Minutes, and Acts of Congress Now in Force' (1903) 16 Harv L Rev 234

Heinze-Greenberg, Ita, 'Architecture in Palestine 1934–1941' in *Erich Mendelsohn: Dynamics and Function: Realized Visions of a Cosmopolitan Architect* (Hatje Cantz Publishers, Germany, 1999) 204

Helfer, Laurence R, 'Regime Shifting: The TRIPS Agreement and New Dynamics of International Intellectual Property Lawmaking' (2004) 29 Yale J Int'l L 1

Hesse, Carla, 'Enlightenment Epistemology and the Laws of Authorship in Revolutionary France, 1777–1793' (1990) 30 Representations 109

Hettinger, Edwin C, 'Justifying Intellectual Property' (1989) 18 Phil & Pub Aff 31

Hirshberg, Jehoash, 'Western Music in Mandatory Jerusalem' in Yehoshua Ben-Arieh (ed), *Jerusalem and the British Mandate: Interaction and Legacy* (Yad Ben-Zvi, Jerusalem, 2003) 433

Hughes, Justin, 'The Philosophy of Intellectual Property' (1988) 77 Geo L J 287

Jaszi, Peter, 'Toward a Theory of Copyright: The Metamorphosis of "Authorship"' (1991) 41 Duke L J 455

Kahn-Freund, Otto, 'On Uses and Misuses of Comparative Law' (1974) 37 MLR 1

Katz, Ariel, 'Copyright Collectives: Good Solution but for which Problem?' in Rochelle C Dreyfuss, Harry First, Diane L Zimmerman (eds), *Working within the Boundaries of Intellectual Property Law: Innovation Policy for the Knowledge Society* (Oxford University Press, Oxford, 2010) 395

Knaan, Haviv, 'The Hebrew Press in Palestine during the British Government' in Dan Caspi, Yechiel Limor (eds), *Mass Media in Israel: A Reader* (Open University, Tel-Aviv, 1998) 146 (Hebrew)

Kretschmer, Martin, 'The Failure of Property Rules in Collective Administration: Rethinking Copyright Societies as Regulatory Instruments' [2002] 24(3) EIPR 126

Kretschmer, Martin, and Sukhpreet Singh, 'Strategic behaviour in the International Exploitation of TV Formats: A Case Study of the Idols Format' in Joost de Bruin and Koos Zwaan (eds), *Adapting Idols: Authenticity, Identity and Performance in a Global Television Format* (Ashgate, Farnham, forthcoming 2012)

Lapidot, Elad, 'Damaging the Interests of Creators and Israeli Companies in the West Bank' (2000) 14 Law & Army 289 (Hebrew)

Legrand, Pierre, 'What "Legal Transplant"?' in David Nelken, Johannes Fees (eds), *Adapting Legal Cultures* (Hart Publishing, Oxford, 2001) 55

Liebes, Tamar, and Zohar Kampf, '"Hello! This is Jerusalem calling": The Revival of Spoken Hebrew on the Mandatory Radio (1936–1948)' (2010) 29(2) J of Israeli History 137

Likhovski, Assaf, 'Is Tax Law Culturally Specific? Lessons from the History of Income Tax Law in Mandatory Palestine' (2010) 11 Theoretical Inq L 725

Lin, Li-Wen, 'Legal Transplants through Private Contracting: Codes of Vendor Conduct in Global Supply Chains as an Example' (2009) 57 AJCL 711

Lissak, Moshe, 'Images of Society and Status in the Yishuv and Israeli Society: Patterns of Change in the Ideology and Class Structure' in Eisenstadt, Adler, Bar-Yossef, and Kahana (eds), *The Social Structure of Israel* (Academon, Jerusalem, 1965) 203 (Hebrew)

MacDonald, Callum A, 'Radio Bari: Italian Wireless Propaganda in the Middle East and British Countermeasures 1934–38' (1977) 13(2) Middle Eastern Studies 195

Markon, Ze'ev, 'The People and the Book: Material on the History of Author's Rights' (1927) 2 HaMishpat 192 (Hebrew)

Martin, Leslie John, 'Press and Radio in Palestine under British Mandate' (1949) 26 Journalism Q 186

McDonald, David A, 'Performing Palestine: Resisting the Occupation and Reviving Jerusalem's Social and Cultural Identity through Music and the Arts' (2006) 25 Jerusalem Q 5

McLaren, John, 'Reflections on the Rule of Law: The Georgian Colonies of New South Wales and Upper Canada, 1788–1837' in Diane Kirkby, Catherine Coleborne (eds), *Law, History, Colonialism: The Reach of the Empire* (Manchester University Press, Manchester, 2001) 46

McLay, Geoff, 'New Zealand and the Imperial Copyright Tradition' in Ysolde Gendreau, Uma Suthersanen (eds), *A Shifting Empire: 100 Years of the Copyright Act 1911* (Edward Elgar, forthcoming 2012)

Michaels, Ralf, 'Comparative Law by Numbers? Legal Origins Thesis, Doing Business Reports and the Silence of Traditional Comparative Law' (2009) 57 AJCL 765

Miller, Jonathan M, 'A Typology of Legal Transplants: Using Sociology, Legal History and Argentine Examples to Explain the Transplant Process' (2003) 51 AJCL 839

Morris, Benny, 'Response of the Jewish Daily Press in Palestine to the Accession of Hitler, 1933' (1999) 27 Yad-Vashem Studies 363

Moyse, Pierre-Emanuel, 'Canadian Colonial Copyright: The Colony Strikes Back' in Ysolde Gendreau (ed), *An Emerging Intellectual Property Paradigm* (Edward Elgar, 2008) 107

Moyse, Pierre-Emanuel, 'Colonial Copyright Redux: 1709 v. 1832' in Lionel Bently, Uma Suthersanen, Paul Torremans (eds), *Global Copyright: Three Hundred Years since the Statute of Anne, from 1709 to Cyberspace* (Edward Elgar, Cheltenham, 2010) 144

Musallam, Adnan A, 'Palestinian Arab Press Developments under British Rule with A Case Study of Bethlehem's Sawt al-Shab 1922–1939', http://admusallam.bethlehem.edu/bethlehem/Sawt_Al-Shab.htm

Nassar, Issam, 'Early Local Photography in Palestine: The Legacy of Karimeh Abbud' (2007) 46 Jerusalem Q 23

Nelken, David, 'Towards a Sociology of Legal Adaptation' in David Nelken, Johannes Fees (eds), *Adapting Legal Cultures* (Hart Publishing, Oxford, 2001) 16

Netanel, Neil, 'Maharam of Padua v. Giustinian: The Sixteenth-Century Origins of the Jewish Law of Copyright' (2007) 44 Houston L Rev 822

Netanel, Neil W and David Nimmer, 'Is Copyright Property? The Debate in Jewish Law' (2011) 12 Theoretical Inq L 241

Nofech, Yizhak, 'The Legal Arab Journal, al-Huquq' (1926) 1 HaMishpat HaIvri 169 (Hebrew)

Nuweihid Al-Hout, Bayan, 'The Palestine Political Elite during the Mandate Period' (1979) 9(1) Journal of Palestine Studies 85

Ojwang, Jackton, 'Legal Transplantations: Rethinking the Role and Significance of Western Law in Africa' in Peter Sack, Elizabeth Minchin (eds), *Legal Pluralism* (Proceeding of the Canberra Law Workshop VII, 1986) 99

Oliar, Dotan, 'The (Constitutional) Convention on IP: A New Reading' (2009) 57 UCLA L Rev 421

Oliar, Dotan, and Christopher Sprigman, 'There's No Free Laugh (Anymore): The Emergence of Intellectual Property Norms and the Transformation of Stand-Up Comedy' (2008) 94 Va L Rev 1787

Örücü, Esin, 'Turkey: Change under Pressure' in Esin Örücü, Elspeth Attwooll, Sean Coyle (eds), *Studies in Legal Systems: Mixed and Mixing* (Kluwer Law International, The Hague, 1996) 89

Örücü, Esin, 'Law as Transposition' (2002) 51 ICLQ 205

Ouma, Marisella, 'Copyright and the Music Industry in Africa' (2004) 7 J World IP 919

Oz-Salzberger, Fania, and Eli M Salzberger, 'The Hidden German Sources of the Israeli Supreme Court' (2000) 15 Tel-Aviv U Stud L 79

Özsunay, Ergun, 'Turkey' (2001) 7 International Encyclopaedia of Laws: Intellectual Property 32

Pfister, Laurent, 'Author and Work in the French Print Privileges System: Some Milestones' in Ronan Deazley, Martin Kretschmer, Lionel Bently (eds), *Privilege and Property: Essays on the History of Copyright* (Open Book Publishers, Cambridge, 2010) 115

Pollack, Malla, 'What is Congress Supposed to Promote?: Defining "Progress" in Article I, Section 8, Clause 8 of the United States Constitution, or Introducing The Progress Clause' (2002) 80 Neb L Rev 754

Raphael, Shilo, 'The Protection of Author's Rights' (1985) 26 Torah She-be-Al-Pe 68 (Hebrew)

Raustiala, Kal, and Christopher Sprigman, 'The Piracy Paradox: Innovation and Intellectual Property in Fashion Design' (2006) 92 Va L Rev 1687

Read, Donald, 'Reuters: News Agency of the British Empire' (1994) 8(2) Contemporary Record 195

Reidenberg, Joel R, 'Lex Informatica: The Formulation of Information Policy Rules through Technology' (1997–8) 76 Texas L Rev 553

Rubin, Avi, 'Legal Borrowing and its Impact on Ottoman Legal Culture in the Late Nineteenth Century' (2007) 22(2) Continuity and Change 279

Rubin, Avi, 'Ottoman Judicial Change in the Age of Modernity: A Reappraisal' (2009) 7(1) History Compass 119

Rubinshtein, Elyakim, 'The Jewish Institutes and the Yishuv's Institutions' in Binyamin Eliav (ed), *The Jewish National Home: From the Balfour Declaration to Independence* (Keter, Jerusalem, 1976) 136 (Hebrew)

Samuelson, Pamela, 'The Copyright Grab' (1996) Wired 4.01, http://www.wired.com/wired/archive/4.01/white.paper.html

Sela-Sheffy, Rakefet, 'The Jekes in the Legal Field and Bourgeois Culture in Pre-Israel British Palestine' (2003) 13 Iyunim BiTkumat Israel 295 (Hebrew)

Shachar, Yoram, 'The Sources of the Criminal Code Ordinance, 1936' (1979) 7 Tel-Aviv U L Rev 75 (Hebrew)

Shaffer, Gregory, 'Transnational Legal Process and State Change: Opportunities and Constraints' (2012) 37 Law & Soc Inq 229

Shamir, Ronen, 'Lex Moriendi: On the Death of Israeli Law' in Menachem Mautner, Avi Sagi, Ronen Shamir (eds), *Multiculturalism in a Democratic and Jewish State: The Ariel Rosen-Zvi Memorial Book* (Ramot, Tel-Aviv, 1998) 589 (Hebrew)

Shamir, Ronen, 'The Comrades Law of Hebrew Workers in Palestine: A Study in Socialist Justice' (2002) 20 Law & Hist Rev 279

Shapira, Ya'akov, 'Law and Judgment: The Separation of Religion and State: An Old Dispute Revisited: The Limits of Judicial Authority under Jewish Law and in Rabbinical Courts' (2004) 8 Sha'arey Mishpat 425 (Hebrew)

Sherman, Brad, 'What is a Copyright Work?' (2011) 12 Theoretical Inq L 99

Shva, Shlomo, 'The Eretz-Israeli Photojournalism' (1989) 5 Kesher 110 (Hebrew)

Sternhell, Ziva, 'Eric Mendelsohn: From Berlin to Jerusalem' (2008) 32 Alpayim 177 (Hebrew)

Strickland, C F, 'Broadcasting in Palestine' (1933) 20 J of the Royal Central Asian Society 410

Tamari, Salim, 'The Short Life of Private Ihsan' (2007) 30 Jerusalem Q 26

Tawfik, Myra J, 'History in Balance: Copyright and Access to Knowledge' in Michael Geist (ed), *From Radical Extremism to Balanced Copyright* (Irwin Law, Toronto, 2010) 69

Teubner, Gunther, 'Legal Irritants: Good Faith in British Law or How Unifying Law Ends Up in New Divergences' (1998) 61 MLR 11

Tomlins, Christopher, 'Law's Empire: Chartering English Colonies on the American Mainland in the Seventeenth Century' in Diane Kirkby and Catherine Coleborne (eds), *Law, History, Colonialism: The Reach of the Empire* (Manchester University Press, Manchester, 2001) 26

Totach, Khalil, 'Education in Palestine' (1932) The Annals of the American Academy of Political and Social Science 155

Twining, William, 'Diffusion of Law: A Global Perspective' (2004) 49 J Legal Pluralism 1

Uvieghara, Egerton, 'Copyright Protection in Nigeria: New Trends and Prospects' in Bankole Sodipo, Bunmi Fagbemi (eds), *Nigeria's Foreign Investment Laws and*

Intellectual Property Rights (Centre of Commercial Law Studies, Queen Mary University, London, 1994) 158

Westreich, Elimelech, 'The Legal Activities of the Chief Rabbis during the Period of the British Mandate: A Response to the Zionist Challenge' in Avi Sagi and Dov Schwartz (eds), *A Hundred Years of Religious Zionism* (Bar-Ilan University Press, Ramat-Gan, 2003) 83 (Hebrew)

Whitman, James Q, 'Western Legal Imperialism: Thinking about the Deep Historical Roots' (2009) 10 Theoretical Inq L 308

Wilf, Steven, 'Copyright and Social Movements in Late Nineteenth-Century America' (2011) 12 Theoretical Inq L 123

Woodmansee, Martha, 'The Genius and the Copyright: Economic and Legal Conditions of the Emergence of the Author' (1984) 17 Eighteenth-Century Studies 425

Yadin, Uri, 'Reception and Rejection of English Law in Israel' (1962) 11 ICLQ 59

Yakubu, Musa, 'Origins and Practice of Legal Pluralism in Nigeria' in Peter Sack, Elizabeth Minchin (eds), *Legal Pluralism* (Proceeding of the Canberra Law Workshop VII, 1986) 83

Yu, Peter K, 'The First Ten Years of the TRIPS Agreement: TRIPS and Its Discontents' (2006) 10 Marq IP L Rev 369

Zer-Zion, Shelly, 'The Eretz-Israel Theatre: Moving between Cultural Peripheries' (2007) 99 Zmanim 16 (Hebrew)

Zivin, Joselyn, 'The Imagined Reign of the Iron Lecturer: Village Broadcasting in Colonial India' (1998) 32 Modern Asian Stud 717

DOCTORAL DISSERTATIONS AND MASTER THESES

Alexander, David, *Ha'Kumkum: The First Satirical Theatre in Israel (1926–1929)* (MA Thesis, Faculty of Arts, Theatre Arts Department, Tel-Aviv University, 1975) (Hebrew)

Dean, Owen H, *The Application of the Copyright Act 1978 to Works Made Prior to 1979* (Doctoral Dissertation, University of Stellenbosch, South Africa, 1988)

Eisenman, Robert H, *Islamic Law in Mandate Palestine and Modern Israel: A Study of the Survival and Repeal of Ottoman Legislative Reform* (PhD, Columbia University, 1977)

Leshem, Sara, *T.A.I.* (MA Thesis, Faculty of Fine Arts, Department of Theatre, TAU, 1990)

Martin, Edwin Thomas, *Thomas Jefferson and the Idea of Progress* (PhD dissertation, University of Wisconsin, 1941)

Mun, Seung-Hwan, *Culture-Related Aspects of Intellectual Property Rights: A Cross-Cultural Analysis of Copyright* (PhD dissertation, University of Texas, Austin, 2008)

Paz, Omri, *Crime, Criminals and the Ottoman State: Anatolia between the late 1830s and the late 1860s* (PhD Dissertation, Tel-Aviv University, 2010)

Samaan, Ihab G, *A Historical View of Intellectual Property Rights in the Palestinian Territories* (LLM Thesis, University of Georgia, 2003)

Stanton, Andrea L, *A Little Radio is A Dangerous Thing: State Broadcasting in Mandate Palestine, 1936–1949* (PhD Dissertation, Graduate School of Arts and Sciences, University of Columbia, 2007)

Index

Abbady, Izhak 107
Abramowitz (Aviv), Mendel 133 n 115, 180, 194–5, 199 n 51
Abrams, Norman 56
Abu Ghazaleh, Adnan 242, 244
ACUM 285
    establishment 19, 113, 155, 163, 184–6, 256
    and Kovalsky 185, 189
    and Palestine Broadcasting Service 207, 248
    and Performing Rights Society (PRS) 189, 207, 286
Agadati, Baruch 118, 124, 147, 155
Agnon, Shmuel Yosef 89, 119, 122, 129, 152, 264
    and Richard Beer-Hofmann 152
    and Salman Schocken 119, 264
Agranat, Shimon 179, 185–6, 246, 286
    and Ottoman Authors' Rights Act 87
    and Performing Rights Society 87, 142–3, 179, 183
Agronsky (Agron), Gershon 220–1, 223, 236–7, 286
Ahad Ha'am (Asher Ginzberg) 20, 131, 260–3
    Al Parashat Derachim 260–3, 286
    Ossorguine v Hotza'ah Ivrith Ltd 144, 157, 257, 260–3, 279
Al Hayat 106, 212, 215–16, 229–34, 238, 243, 247, 250, 286
Al-Huquq 246
aliyah, *see* immigration
Amichay-Michlin, Dania 154
Arab Community in Palestine 2, 13–16, 19, 49, 80, 94, 106, 107, 109, 120–1, 140, 190–1, 195, 239–55
    A-Naqba 240, 284
    author 120, 146, 250, 252–3, 276, 287
    cultural field 19, 86, 88–9, 90, 126–7, 182, 186, 207–8, 211, 241–55, 283
    demographics, *see* Palestine—demographics
    education 89, 126, 196, 242, 244, 246, 249, 252–3, 255
    fellahin (peasants) 195, 197
    and Jewish culture 113, 120–1, 124, 168, 239–40
    judges 140, 183, 231–2, 254
    lawyers, *see also* Bey, Abacarius; Cattan, Henry 90, 107 n 138, 141, 220, 246, 247, 252–5
    literacy 62, 80, 82, 89, 120, 126, 206, 213, 242–4, 255
    music 49, 168, 186, 207–8, 211, 248–9, 251, 283, 287
    nationalism 16, 19, 164, 214–16, 229, 241–2
    photography 244, 252

    press 106, 120–1, 142, 212–16, 222, 228–9, 234–5, 240, 243, 247, 250
        Al Hayat, see *Al Hayat*
        Al Jami'a al-Islamiya 214, 243
        Filastin 214–15, 243
    print 163, 241–4, 250–1, 253
    and radio 190–1, 195–7, 200–3, 206, 248–9, 251, 253
    (Arab) Revolt 1936–9 16, 19, 164, 184, 202, 215, 241, 250, 276
    villages 19, 190, 195–7, 200, 208–9, 214, 236, 242–3, 249
architecture, *see* copyright—in architecture
art exhibitions 111, 126
Ashkenazi Jews 114, 123–4, 131, 264–5, 267–8
Ashkenazi Rabbinical Court 264–5, 268
attribution, right of 47, 115, 131, 154–8, 160, 266–7
Australia 1, 11, 29, 31 n 43, 51, 56, 60, 65–6, 73–4, 228, 235, 238, 285
    1905 Copyright Act 72
    telegraph 11, 38, 228, 235, 238
authorship 3–4, 12–14, 46–9, 52, 55, 84, 128–9, 134–6, 254, 282
    Arab, *see* Arab Community in Palestine—author
    critique 13, 48, 134
    Hebrew, *see* Hebrew—author/s
    national author 13, 134–5, 137, 287
    project 3, 9, 12–14, 46–9, 128–9, 134–6
    romantic author 12–14, 46–8, 110, 118, 128–31, 133–7, 153, 155, 257, 287
Ayalon, Ami 89, 213, 242–4
Azuz, Menachem 272–6, 279
Azuz v Benayahu 272–6

Badhab, Yizhak 273–4
Balfour Declaration 15, 78
Balganesh, Shyamkrishna 227
Bazri, Ezra 269, 270 n 59, 271
BBC 19, 167, 190–202, 204–6, 208–11, 216, 217 n 23, 225, 236, 248–9, 251–2
    and copyright 190, 198, 204–6, 208–11, 237, 248
    Empire Services 190, 193, 197, 204, 216, 236
    global position 19, 192–3
    and Palestine Broadcasting Service 190–1, 195–202, 204–6, 208–9, 248–9
    Reith, John 196, 202
Be'er, Haim 152
Beer-Hofmann, Richard 152, 159
Ben-Dov, Jacob 116

308

Index

Ben-Yehuda, Eliezer 125, 216 nn 18, 21
Ben-Zvi, Yizhak 274–5
Benayahu, Meir, see also *Azuz v Benayahu* 256, 272–6
Bendix, Ludwig 144, 262–3
Bently, Lionel 11, 17, 38, 42, 61, 68, 238
Bentwich, Herbert 99
Bentwich, Norman 93–4, 96, 98–9, 108, 126, 177, 222, 249, 285
   family, see also Bentwich, Herbert; Yellin, Thelma 98–9, 126
   legislation 94, 96, 98–9, 108, 222, 235
   and Performing Rights Society 99 n 97, 177
   telegraphic news 222, 235
   Zionist motivation 98, 249
Berne Convention 53–4, 61–2, 68, 70–3, 75, 77, 80, 84, 90–2, 96–7, 100, 103, 137, 145, 147, 165, 173–4, 251, 259–60, 262, 284
   Berlin Revision 62, 71–3, 75, 80, 92, 96, 137, 165, 251
Bernstein-Cohen, Miriam 114, 151 n 62
Bey, Abacarius 220, 229, 233–4, 247
Bezalel School of Arts and Crafts 89, 111
Bhabha, Homi 40, 44
Bialik, Haim Nahman 118–19, 130, 133–4, 152, 158
   Authors Association 119, 130, 133–4
   and Beer-Hofmann 152
   transactions 158
Birrell, Augustine 40, 65 n 21
Board of Trade 76, 100, 102, 104, 280, 283, 288
Brandeis, Louise 5, 227
Brasher, William Kenneth 198, 205
Brauneis, Robert 225
Brenner, Yosef Haim 15, 89, 118, 129
British Empire 1, 11, 17, 19, 22, 27–32, 36–7, 50–2, 55–8, 61–4, 68–9, 72–8, 80–1, 92, 97, 100, 142, 193, 196, 218, 224, 228, 235, 280–2, 287
   condominium territories 28–9
   criminal law 46, 50, 56–7, 73, 75–6, 97, 140
   Crown colonies 2, 28–9, 31, 64, 66, 73–6, 80, 103
   legislative process 30–2
   Mandate, see Mandate
   protectorates 22, 28–9, 56, 104–5, 142, 280
   self-governing dominions 1, 29–31, 33, 38, 51–2, 54–5, 57, 60, 65–6, 68, 71–8, 95, 238

café 18, 113, 163, 166, 171, 178, 182–6, 191, 207, 210, 214, 243, 249
   in the Arab community 182, 208, 214, 243, 249
   and music 113, 167–8, 171, 176, 178, 182–6, 190, 207, 210, 244, 250

Canada 1, 11, 29, 49, 51, 53, 57, 60, 65, 73–4, 100, 282
   and colonial copyright 49, 57, 60, 65, 100, 282
   Copyright Act 1921 74, 100
Cattan, Henry 253–4
Churchill, Winston 92 n 58, 97–8, 100, 257
   and copyright legislation 97–8, 100
   Winston Churchill, War Leader 278
cinema, see movies
'Code is law', see Lessig, Lawrence 8
Cohen, Ellie 104, 142
collectivism 13, 18, 48–9, 110, 114, 128–36, 146, 156
Colonial Office 17, 19, 31, 33, 37, 39, 57, 72, 75–6, 78, 94–5, 97, 100, 104, 197–8, 201, 204, 206–10, 217, 237, 239, 249, 283
colonialism 10, 17, 22–3, 26–8, 32–6, 44–5, 52, 54–5, 57–9, 67, 78, 281
   and the law 10, 17, 22–3, 33–5, 39–41, 54–5, 58–9, 66, 78
   rule of law 27–8, 32, 35, 39, 61, 79, 281
company law 56–7, 95
concordance 20, 157, 257, 263–7
Copinger on Copyright 69, 87, 143, 165, 172, 179, 266, 285
copyright
   in architecture 3, 277–8, 286
   in broadcasting 166, 180, 187, 190–1, 203–5, 207, 209–10, 217, 236, 249
   criminal aspects 73, 75–6, 85, 87, 92, 94, 97, 101, 142–3, 171–4, 176, 186, 228–32, 235, 265–7, 273–5, 277, 279
   culture 1, 3–6, 9, 12, 36
   Eurocentric perspective 13, 20, 28, 41, 48–9, 51, 123, 180, 191, 208, 211, 243, 272, 281–2
   formalities 70–1, 73, 80, 84–7, 91, 97, 137, 163, 165, 227–8
   history 2–3, 11, 21, 38, 60, 129
   intangibility 17, 41, 50–4, 55, 62, 78, 143, 281–2
   international dimension 11–12, 16–18, 20, 22, 40–1, 51, 53–5, 58, 60–3, 68–71, 72, 75, 77–8, 80, 94, 96–8, 100, 103, 107, 128, 137, 157–8, 165, 263, 283–5, 288
   moral rights, see moral rights
   in news 204–5, 211, 212–13, 222, 225–8, 230–8, 250
   notice 19, 71, 80, 84–6, 91, 97, 163, 165, 228, 250–2, 256, 271, 283
   ownership 4, 47, 50–1, 73, 78, 96, 101, 110, 112, 116, 136, 140, 152–3, 159, 166, 171–3, 182, 184, 186, 208, 210 n 109, 212, 225, 229, 232, 252, 264, 274, 277, 286
   performing right, see performing right

progress, *see* progress, the idea of
technology 3–4, 6–9, 17, 19, 48, 51, 73, 77, 96, 102, 164, 175, 180, 190, 211, 228, 235, 237
  in a tombstone 112, 257, 277
  regime 4–5, 9, 14, 72, 105, 109, 137
Copyright Act 1911 73
  contents 47, 50, 73, 101, 136, 165, 245
  criminal aspects 73, 76, 172
  customs 73–6
  diffusion in the Empire 61, 73–5, 102, 240, 259, 276
  Imperial Conference 33, 72, 78
  in Israel 107 n 142, 234 n 101, 284, 288
  injunctions 101, 174, 183–4
  innocent infringer 182, 188
  Palestine
    extension to 100–2, 181, 209–10, 232, 283
    publication 79, 105–7, 145, 181, 230–2, 247, 256
    translation 107
Copyright Ordinance 1920 18, 92–8, 100, 166, 181
  legislative process 80, 96–9
Copyright Ordinance 1924 76, 100–1, 109, 120, 122, 127, 166, 171–2, 174, 230, 247, 265, 274, 284, 288
  legislative process 100–1
creativity 5–7, 36, 43, 45–9, 55, 57–8, 127, 137, 233, 239, 268, 281–2, 286
Crystal, Michael 56, 95
culture 1
  and copyright 4–6, 9, 12, 36, 51, 282
  cultural balance 41, 51–5, 70, 80
  cultural field 45, 47, 82, 87–90, 101, 105, 110–11, 113–14, 118, 120, 122, 125, 127–8, 135–6, 139, 145–7, 152, 159, 161, 163–4, 168, 239–41, 242–7, 250, 256, 276, 283

Deazley, Ronan 21
Dickens, Charles 37, 64
Dizengoff, Meir 118
Donaldson v Becket 42

Eden Theatre, *see* movies
el-Amiri, Mohammad Adib 253, 286
el-Amiri v Katul 146, 252–4, 275
Elisheva 129, 131
Ellickson, Robert 159

Falk, Ze'ev 144, 272
fellahin, *see* Arab Community in Palestine
fine arts
  Hebrew 110–12, 121
  legal protection 63, 70–1, 73
  Tel-Aviv Museum 112
Fitzpatrick, Peter 28

Foreign Jurisdiction Act 1890 100, 181
Foreign Reprint Act 1847 10, 64, 66, 68
Foucault, Michel 12, 46
Friedenberg, Kalman 106, 142, 246, 286
  and Kovalsky 168–71, 175, 177, 179
  Palestine Telegraphic Agency v Jaber, *see also* Palestine Telegraphic Agency 106, 228–9, 234
  and Performing Rights Society 143, 168–78, 186
  Zion Theatre case, *see also* Zion Theatre 170–2, 174

Geller, Paul Edward 54
GEMA 18, 163, 166 n 11, 169–71, 174
Germany 12, 16, 46, 70, 112, 124, 130, 134, 141, 157, 161, 164, 166, 168–9, 173, 187, 193, 197, 209, 220, 236–7, 258–9, 263–5, 278
  copyright law 187, 258–63, 265–7, 286
Ghana 52, 67
Ginzberg, Asher, *see* Ahad Ha'am
Ginzberg-Ossorguine, Rachel 261–2, 286
global copyright, *see also* globalization; TRIPs 12, 105
globalization 2, 12, 23, 54, 58, 236, 282, 287
glocalization 58, 164, 186–8
Gluzman, Michael 136
Gnessin, Menachem 109, 114, 134, 150–2
Goitein, Edward David 107 n 138, 220, 223, 229, 233, 286
Gutman, Nachum 155

Haaretz 133, 155, 174, 216, 237, 265, 286
HaBima 114
Hagada 104–5, 142
Halutzim, *see also* immigration 15, 122–3, 132–3, 136, 169, 195
HaMeiri, Avigdor 117, 155
Harris, Ron 56, 95
Hebrew
  author/s 13, 15, 18, 49, 90, 108–10, 120, 123, 128–37, 139, 146, 152, 157, 159–61, 255–6, 283, 285–7
  culture 15, 88, 109, 124–5, 128, 134, 137, 241
  journalism 89 n 45, 119, 130, 134, 216, 220
  language 88, 90–1, 114, 119–20, 124–5, 246, 248, 284
  translations 90, 125
Hebrew Authors Association 118–19, 130, 133–4, 141, 144–6, 158–61, 267
  arbitration 141, 267
  establishment 118–19
  internal disputes 119, 130, 133–4, 161
  translations 119, 141, 159–60
Hebrew Law of Peace 116, 140
Hebrew University 111, 126, 142 n 17, 143, 273, 285

Herzl, Theodor
  copyright cases 20, 141, 157, 256–60, 279
  family 258, 260, 286
  writings 257–8
Hesse, Carla 129
Hirshberg, Jehoash 113
Histadrut 131, 140, 216
Hotza'ah Ivrith 259–63
Hudson, William 198, 202

immigration 14–16, 80, 88, 91–3, 98, 109–10, 113–14, 119, 121, 123–4, 141, 156, 164, 168, 215, 241, 257, 259, 267, 272, 276
  image of immigrants 121–3, 129, 131–2
  waves of 14–15, 88, 92, 110, 112, 121–2
    first wave 14–15, 88, 123, 132
    second wave 14–15, 88, 114, 132, 135–6, 169
    third wave 15, 109–10, 114, 132, 135–6, 141
    fourth wave 15, 109–10, 113, 118, 122–3, 129, 132, 136, 141
    fifth wave 112, 164
  Yemenite immigration 123–4
International News Service (INS) v Associated Press (AP) 19, 212, 226–7, 233
Israeli copyright law 3, 107 n 142, 123 n 74, 149 n 51, 188 n 135, 256, 258, 260
  amendments 3, 20 1, 101, 102 n 100, 234 n 101, 284
  American influence 20, 285
  creativity 5
  moral rights 101
  reception (of British law) 20, 283–5
Italy 16, 70, 130, 167–8, 174, 181, 199, 202, 236, 248, 270
  Abyssinian war 16
  Radio Bari, *see* radio—Bari

Jaber, Adel 19, 106, 212–15, 229, 231–3, 286
Jaffa 15, 83, 89, 113, 115, 120, 169, 214, 217, 253
Jaszi, Peter 47, 129
Jerusalem 16, 83, 88–9, 93, 99, 111, 113, 115, 117, 121–2, 126, 129, 164, 167–8, 170–1, 176, 178–9, 184–5, 192, 202, 215, 217, 221, 250, 252, 272–3, 276
Jerusalem Music Society 99, 126, 177
Jewish Agency 90, 105, 216, 259
Jewish copyright law 144, 267, 269–72, 276
  haskama 270–1
Jewish National Fund 112, 141
Jewish Telegraphic Agency 19, 218–20, 224, 229, 235, 286
Jordan 14, 86, 190, 228, 240, 250, 284, 286, 288
Jüdischer Verlag 258–63

Kahn-Freund, Otto 25

Katznelson, Siegmund 258–60, 262
Katul, Selim, see also *el-Amiri v Katul* 252–4
Kenya 67, 74 n 65, 228, 235 n 108
kibbutz 122, 132, 135
Korngrün, Philip (Yeruham) 170–1, 173
Kovalsky, Meir 163–4, 186–9
  and ACUM 185, 189
  and Arab music 184, 250
  biography 113, 169, 179, 189, 286
  and GEMA 169–71, 174–5
  legal strategy 171–2, 174–9, 183–4
  and Performing Rights Society 117, 163, 168–82, 184–5, 250
  and radio 180, 206, 210
  and Woodhouse 167–70
Ktav Seruv 264–5, 270

Lababidi, Yahia 251–2
Landau, Jacob 212, 218–24, 228–9, 235, 237
Latin America 39
law classes 141–4, 245–6
League of Nations 14, 29, 44, 80, 94, 98, 126, 222, 249
  and Mandates 29, 44
  and Palestine 14, 80, 94, 126, 249
  and progress 44, 126
legal transplants, *see* transplants
Legrand, Pierre 24
Lessig, Lawrence 8
Levant Fair 168, 180, 194
Likhovski, Assaf 14, 32, 36, 95–6, 98, 246
Liphshitz, Nahum 104–5
Lissak, Moshe 131
literary journals 119, 139, 145–6, 152, 154, 161
  Hedim 119, 152
  Ktuvim 119, 130, 133, 148–1, 153, 155, 158, 160–1
  Moznayim 119, 145, 149, 161
London, Jack 148, 159

Malay colonies 49, 67, 103 n 113
Mandate, *see also* Tanganyika
  classes 29, 80, 101
  of Palestine, *see* Palestine
Mandelkern, Shlomo 263, 265
Manor, Dalia 124
Manor, Giora 123
Markon, Ze'ev 144, 272
Margolin, Faivel 263–8, 274, 279, 286
Margolin v Schocken 263–7
Matthews, Weldon 215
Mendelsohn, Eric 277–8
Mitzpe Press 148–9, 259
moral rights, *see also* attribution 47, 73, 85, 101, 137, 154–6, 158, 160, 266, 278, 281, 284–6

Index   311

movies 7, 113, 115–18, 123, 125, 127, 147, 167–8, 245
  in Arab Community 115, 240, 244–5
  Eden Theatre 115
  Liberated Judea 116
  Polish-Palestine Chamber of Commerce inquiry 117
  silent movies 7, 113, 115–18, 164, 167–8, 171, 175, 190, 245
  talkies 7, 113, 115, 164, 167, 175, 179–80, 187
  theatres in Palestine 111, 115–17, 167, 245
  This is the Land [*Zot Hi Haaretz*] 118, 147, 155
  Wandering Oded [*Oded HaNoded*] 117
Moyse, Pierre-Emmanuel 57
music, *see also* performing right 7, 9, 17–18, 48, 51, 53, 70, 84, 87, 89, 96, 101, 110–13, 121–2, 155, 164–9, 171, 173, 175–7, 179–80, 182, 184–8, 190, 196–7, 200, 203–8, 229, 239, 248, 255–6, 286–7
  in Arab Community 49, 168, 180, 182, 200, 205–8, 211, 240, 244–5, 248–51, 255, 283, 287
  English music 168, 205–16, 249–50
  Jerusalem Music Society 99, 126, 177
  live music 19, 113, 115, 118, 164, 167–8, 171, 194, 205, 210, 244–5
  in the Yishuv 89, 110–11, 112–13, 122, 124, 167–8, 184–6, 194, 287

Nadan, Amos 242
Napster 8
National Home 14–16, 78, 80, 126, 132, 249
Nelken, David 23
Netanel, Neil 269–71
New Zealand 1, 29, 37, 51, 65–6, 68 n 36, 73–4, 164, 232
news agencies 19, 212, 216–19, 223, 226–7, 232–3, 235–8, 257, 262
Nigeria 11, 32–3, 48, 56, 67
Nimmer, David 269, 271
1921 Jaffa Events, *see also* Brenner 15
Nisbet, Robert 42–3

Odham Press Ltd v London & Provincial Sporting News Agency 262
Old Jew 14, 121, 124, 132, 134
Olshan, Yizhak 179, 186, 246, 286
originality 44, 107 n 142, 146–7, 158–9, 173, 187, 233, 237, 254, 275, 281, 285
Örücü, Esin 24
Ottoman Empire 14, 27, 33, 80, 127
  administration 27, 81, 83
  French influence 81, 82 n 14, 84, 87, 95–7, 100
  legal system 81–2, 95, 187, 245, 257
  literacy 82
  Mejelle 82, 84, 182, 231
  Nizamiye court system 81, 86
  press 213, 217, 243

  Tanzimat 81–2, 84
  Young Turks Revolution 82, 84, 89, 127, 213, 243
Ottoman copyright law
  Authors' Rights Act 1910 2, 17, 20, 80–1, 83–92, 96–7, 100–1, 105, 142, 147, 166, 181, 228, 288
  contents 84–5, 90–1, 97
  formalities 84–5, 96–7
  international relations 70, 84, 91, 100
  in news 84–5

Palestine
  anglicization 34, 95–6, 164, 187, 246, 263, 273
  British administration 14, 33, 80, 92–3, 98, 111, 127, 241
  copyright law, *see* Copyright Act 1911—Palestine; Copyright Ordinance 1920; Copyright Ordinance 1924; United States—copyright relations with Palestine
  demographics 15, 88 n 39, 193, 199, 241–2, 248
  law libraries 140, 143
  lawyers, *see also* Agranat, Bey, Cattan, Cohen, Friedenberg, Goitein, Olshan 81, 90, 104, 107, 139, 141–3, 145, 163, 170, 179, 187–8, 204, 208–9, 220, 228, 237, 245–7, 252–3, 255–6, 261, 263, 265–6, 279, 286–7
  legal education, *see also* law classes, School of Law and Economics 141–3, 187, 245–6
  legal system 32, 81, 86, 140–1, 183, 245, 267–8, 279
  legislative process 80, 93–6, 99, 108
  Mandate 14, 21, 29, 44, 80
  Order in Council for Palestine 1922 33 n 51, 66 n 26, 94–5, 97, 100–1, 106, 182, 231–2, 268, 283
  period 3, 21, 86, 95
  territory 14, 83
Palestine Act 1948 283
Palestine Archaeological Museum 277
Palestine Bulletin, see also *Palestine Telegraphic Agency v Jaber* 106, 212, 219–20, 222–3, 225, 228–34, 250
Palestine Broadcasting Service (PBS), *see also* radio; Strickland
  and ACUM 185, 207
  and Arab music 19, 49, 205, 207, 248–9
  and BBC 19, 190–1, 195–201, 204–6, 208–9, 248–9, 251–2
  copyright 19, 190–1, 198–201, 204–10, 252, 256–7, 279
  employees 191, 201, 210 n 109, 248, 251–3, 255
  establishment 19, 126, 168, 190–1, 197–202, 239, 256

Palestine Broadcasting Service (PBS), (cont.)
   initiative 191–3, 195–7
   listening licences 193–4, 202–3
   news 200, 204, 211, 217, 221, 224, 234
   programming 199–200, 250
   and PRS 19, 180, 201, 205–10
   rural broadcasting 19, 190, 195–7, 200–1, 208–10, 249
Palestine Post 1–2, 221, 225, 233–4, 236, 238, 275, 286
Palestine Telegraphic Agency 219–24
   and Jewish Telegraphic Agency 219–20, 286
   Palestine Telegraphic Agency v Jaber 19, 106, 142, 172, 178, 188, 212–13, 228–37, 247, 250–1, 286
   and Reuters 221–4 , 228, 236–7
Palestinian Authority, *see also* West Bank 102 n 108, 240, 286, 288
performing right 97, 150, 164–9, 171, 173–4, 176–7, 180–1, 184, 185 n 126, 188, 205, 208
Performing Rights Societies, *see* ACUM; GEMA; Performing Rights Society
Performing Rights Society (PRS)
   and ACUM 163, 185, 189, 207, 286
   and the Ottoman Authors' Rights Act 87
   and the Palestine Broadcasting Service 180–1, 204–10, 248–9
   representation in Palestine, *see also* Kovalsky 117, 163, 167–70, 176–8, 206, 210, 250, 255, 286
Performing Rights Society Ltd v Hammond's Bradford Brewery Company Ltd 208–10
photographs, photography 50, 63, 71, 73, 84, 96, 101, 110, 112, 116, 128, 141, 244, 252, 256, 268, 277–8, 283
Pokorovski, I A 143
progress, the idea of 1, 17, 27–8, 36, 40, 41–5, 55, 57, 62, 77, 80, 82, 84, 98, 100, 135, 197, 282
publicity right 276–7
publishers, see also *Hotza'ah Ivrith*; *Jüdischer Verlag*; *Mitzpe Press*; *Rubin Mass Press*; Schocken—Schocken Verlag; Stybel 10, 37, 42, 51, 53, 62, 64–5, 85, 89–91, 102, 105, 110, 118, 122, 128–9, 145, 147–62, 239, 251–3, 256–63, 266, 269–71, 278–9, 283, 286–7
   and authors 110, 118–20, 136, 141, 147–8, 152–62, 186, 269
   in Nazi Germany 157, 260, 265
   publishing market 53, 119–20, 147–62, 186
Pukhachewsky, Nehama 130

Quataert, Donald 82

Raab, Esther 130
Rachel (Bluwstein) 129, 131, 135–6
radio, *see also* BBC; Palestine Broadcasting Service 3, 7, 9, 19, 113, 120, 124, 127–8, 163–4, 167–9, 180–1, 190–203, 208–10, 212–14, 216, 224, 236–7, 239, 243, 248–9, 253, 255, 286
   Bari, Italy 199 n 50, 201
   diffusion 193–4, 199–200, 202–3, 212
   Egypt 193, 196, 200–1, 248, 252
   rural broadcasting 19, 190, 195–7, 200–1, 208–10, 249
Rakover, Nahum 269, 271
Reidenberg, Joel 8
Rendall, R Anthony 201, 248
Reuters 201, 204–5, 211, 215–18, 221–5, 228, 234, 236–8
Reuveny, Jacob 95
Rishon LeZion 103 n 118, 112–13, 122
Rose, Mark 129
Routledge v Low 63
Rubin, Avi 81–2
Rubin Mass Press 153–4, 265
rule of law 27–8, 32, 35, 39, 61, 79, 227, 281
Ruppin, Shulamit 113

Samborsky, Daniel 155
Saposnik, Arieh Bruce 89, 110
Schocken, Salman 119, 264–8, 277, 286
   Margolin v Schocken, see *Margolin v Schocken*
   Schocken Publishing House 265
   Schocken Verlag 264–6
School of Law and Economics 142, 246
Sela, Rona 112
self-governing dominions, *see also* Australia; British Empire; Canada; New Zealand; South Africa 1, 29–31, 33, 38, 51–2, 54–5, 57, 60, 65–6, 68, 71–8, 95, 238
Sephardi Jews 113–14, 123–4, 131, 168, 267, 272–3, 276
Seville, Catherine 11, 17, 51, 57, 60
Shachar, Yoram 56
Shaffer, Gregory 187
shaming 18, 125, 139, 150, 152–6, 158–62
Shavit, Zohar 118–19, 126
Sherbrek, Shlomo 91
Shergorodska, Fania 156
Shlonsky, Avraham 130
Silman, Kadish 133 n 116, 151
Skouteris, Thomas 28
Smoira, Moshe 261–2, 265, 267
social norms, *see also* shaming 2, 18–20, 49, 127, 139, 146–7, 150–2, 154, 159–60, 162, 163, 241, 245, 255–6, 276, 281–3, 285–7
South Africa 1, 11, 29, 37, 51, 63–5, 67, 68 n 36, 73–4, 164, 192, 286
Spadafora, David 43
Straits Settlements 67, 68 n 36, 164
Strickland, Claude Francis 195–8, 202, 208, 249
Stybel, Avraham 148, 149 n 52, 150, 153 n 69, 154

Tanganyika 11, 29, 74, 76, 101, 104
Tchernichovsky, Saul 150–1, 154–5

Technion 111, 125
technology
  and copyright 6–9, 48, 63, 77, 245
  determinism 8
  and law 3, 9, 213, 236
Tel-Aviv 15, 109, 111–15, 117–18, 122, 125, 142, 167–8, 180, 184, 194, 246, 278, 286
Telecommunications Union 198
telegraph, see also *International News Service v AP*; Palestine Telegraphic Agency; Reuters 3, 7, 9, 11, 17, 19, 38, 50, 94, 103, 106, 191, 212–13, 216–22, 224–9, 232, 234–8, 240, 250, 257, 286
  news agencies, see news agencies
  Telegraphic Press Message Ordinance 103, 228, 235
Teubner, Gunther 24
theatre, see also Bernstein-Cohen; Gnessin 53, 82–4, 89, 109, 111, 114–15, 121–2, 126, 148, 150–6, 158, 160, 166, 184, 244
  in Arab Community 244, 255
  Eretz-Israel Theatre 109, 114, 134, 148, 150, 152
  HaBima 114
  HaKumkum 114, 155
  HaMatate 114, 184
  HaOhel 114
  Hebrew Theatre 114, 148, 151
  Zerubbabel 114
Tolstoy, Leo 91
Tomlins, Christopher 280
Trajtenberg, Graciela 130
translations
  in the Berne Convention 70–1, 90, 137
  in the Copyright Act 1911 73–4, 101, 147
  and the Hebrew Authors Association 141, 160, 259
  Jewish Agency Project 90–1, 148
  and the Ottoman Authors' Rights Act 84–5, 90–2, 147
  and publishers 147–50, 152, 154
transplants 17, 23–6
  colonialism 10, 22, 25, 27, 34–6, 39, 45, 56, 80, 173, 188, 282, 287
  copyright 1–2, 16, 22, 40–1, 54–5, 59, 76, 81, 109, 137, 210, 234, 237, 239–41, 254–5, 267, 279
  critical view of 24–6, 35, 39, 187
  metaphors 23–4, 36, 55, 280
trade marks law 50–1, 93, 103, 142–3, 276, 288

TRIPs 12, 54, 285
Trollope, Anthony 135

United States 5, 8, 10–2, 20, 43, 53, 62, 72, 119, 128, 134, 145, 157–9, 161, 168, 192, 209, 212, 217–18, 225, 228, 235, 238, 272, 285, 287
  and Berne Convention 53, 70, 75, 77, 102–3
  and British works 53, 57, 50, 62, 65, 69, 103–5, 142
  Constitution 43
  copyright relations with Palestine 18, 102–5, 142, 158

Wailing Wall Riots 1929 16, 195, 214
Walter v Steinkopff 227, 233
Watson, Alan 23–6
Wauchope, Arthur 79, 197–8, 278 n 103
West Bank 14, 83, 102 n 108, 240, 284, 288
Westreich, Elimelech 268
Wilensky, Moshe 184
Woodhouse, John 167–70, 188
Woodmansee, Martha 46, 129
World Intellectual Property Organisation (WIPO) 12, 71, 285
  Copyright Treaty (WCT) 12, 285
World Trade Organisation (WTO) 12
World War I 14–15, 29, 44, 80, 88, 90, 111, 141, 169, 217–18, 245
World War II 16, 103, 126, 202, 276
  emergency legislation 103, 276

Yellin, Thelma 99, 126
Yemenite Jews 123–4, 168
Yiddish 91, 114–15, 124–5, 157–8
Yishuv 17–18, 88, 109, 111, 114–15, 120–1, 126–7, 131–2, 140, 164, 185, 194, 216, 221
  Old Yishuv 17, 88, 114, 121, 123–4, 267, 272

Zadek, Walter 112 n 14
Zarkali, Kheir al-Din al- 215, 229
Zefira, Bracha 124
Ziffer, Moshe 277
Zion Theatre 115, 117, 164, 168, 170–9
  contracts with musicians 113 n 21, 168
  lawsuits 170–9, 183, 229
Zionism 13–14, 18, 20, 88, 90, 109–11, 112, 118, 124–5, 127, 130, 132, 137, 219, 241, 257–8, 260–1, 268
  and authors 13, 18, 110, 132
  immigration, see immigration
Zu'atyir, Akram 215